William Morris

a reference guide

A
Reference
Guide
to
Literature

Marilyn Gaull
Editor

William Morris
a reference guide

GARY L. AHO

G.K.HALL &CO.
70 LINCOLN STREET, BOSTON, MASS.

Library of Congress Cataloging in Publication Data

Aho, Gary L.
  William Morris, a reference guide.

  (A Reference guide to literature)
  Includes indexes
  1. Morris, William, 1834-1896—Bibliography.
I. Title. II. Series.
Z8595.A37 1985   [PR5083]   016.821'8   85-17708
ISBN 0-8161-8449-6

This publication is printed on permanent/durable acid-free paper
MANUFACTURED IN THE UNITED STATES OF AMERICA

Contents

The Author

Gary L. Aho is a Professor in the English Department at the University of Massachusetts in Amherst. He received his Ph.D. from the University of Oregon, writing a dissertation on religious themes in Old English and Old Icelandic. He has published articles and reviews on Old Icelandic literature, on Arthurian literature, on Victorian Medievalism, on William Morris, and on J.R.R. Tolkien. He is chairman of the Governing Board of the William Morris Society in America and edits its Newsletter.

Chronology

1834 March 24, WM born at Elm House, in Walthamstow.

1848-51 Attends Marlborough College.

1853-55 Attends Oxford.

1856 Oxford and Cambridge Magaazine: Conducted by Members of the Two Universities (includes "The Story of The Unknown Church," "A Dream," "Frank's Sealed Letter," "Gertha's Lovers," "Svend and His Brethren," "Lindenborg Pool," "The Hollow Land," "Golden Wings," "The Churches of North France," "'Death the Avenger' and 'Death the Friend,'" and a review of Browning's Men and Women). Employed in architectural offices of G.E. Street.

1857 Oxford Union murals and decorations.

1858 The Defence of Guenevere, and Other Poems.

1859 April 26, marries Jane Burden.

1860-65 The years at Red House.

1861 Jenny Morris born. Formation of Morris, Marshall, Faulkner, and Co.

1862 May Morris born.

1866 The Firm wins commission to decorate rooms at St. James Palace.

1867 The Life and Death of Jason.

1868-70 The Earthly Paradise.

1869 The Story of Grettir the Strong (with Magnusson).

1870 Volsunga Saga: The Story of the Volsungs and the Niblungs (with Magnusson). A Book of Verse (several of these lyrics were published in Poems by the Way; a facsimile of the entire decorated book was not published until 1980.48).

1871   Leases Kelmscott Manor (with Rossetti). First journey to Iceland. Translates The Story of Kormak (with Magnusson; not published until 1970.5).

1872   Love Is Enough, or The Freeing of Pharamond. The Novel on Blue Paper (not published until 1982.15).

1873   Second journey to Iceland.

1875   The Aeneids of Virgil. Three Northern Love Stories, and Other Tales (with Magnusson). Includes translations that had appeared earlier in magazines: Gunnlaug's Saga, 1869, and Frithiof the Bold, 1871; the third is Viglund the Fair. The tales (Icelandic "thaettir") are "Hogni and Hethinn," "Roi the Fool," and "Thorstein Staff-Smitten." Takes full control of the Firm, thereafter Morris and Co.

1876   The Story of Sigurd the Volsung and the Fall of the Niblungs. "England and the Turks" (first political letter). Becomes treasurer of the Eastern Question Association.

1877   "The Principles of the Society for the Protection of Ancient Buildings." Founds SPAB. Offered the Chair of Poetry at Oxford; he declines. "The Decorative Arts" (first public lecture).

1878   "Wake, London Lads." Moves to Kelmscott House, Hammersmith.

1881   Shifts the Firm's works to Merton Abbey.

1882   Hopes and Fears for Art (includes "The Lesser Arts of Life" [formerly "The Decorative Arts"], "The Art of the People," "The Beauty of Life," "Making the Best of It," and "Architecture and Civilization"). Raises funds for the Iceland Famine Relief Association.

1883   Joins Democratic Federation, renamed in August, 1884 the Social-Democratic Federation (SDF).

1884   Summary of the Principles of Socialism (with Hyndman). "A Factory as it Might Be." Contributes to Justice.

1885 Chants for Socialists. "Manifesto of the Socialist
     League." "Socialists at Play." Leaves SDF; helps found
     the Socialist League. Arrested at Dod Street
     demonstrations for freedom of speech.

1885-90 Contributes to Commonweal.

1886 Pilgrims of Hope (serialized in Commonweal, 1885-86). A
     Short Account of The Commune of Paris (with Bax and
     Dave).

1887 The Odyssey of Homer. Socialist Diaries (not published
     until 1981.8). The Tables Turned, or Nupkins Awakened.
     "Alfred Linnell: A Death Song." Attacked by police at
     Trafalgar Square demonstrations on November 13, "Bloody
     Sunday."

1888 A Dream of John Ball (serialized in Commonweal, 1886-87).
     The House of the Wolfings. A King's Lesson (first
     appeared in Commonweal, in 1886, as "An Old Story
     Retold"). Signs of Change (includes "How We Live and How
     We Might Live," "Useful Work vs. Useless Toil," "The
     Aims of Art," "Whigs, Democrats, and Socialists," "Feudal
     England," "The Hopes of Civilization," and "The Dawn of a
     New Epoch").

1889 The Roots of the Mountains.

1890 Founds Kelmscott Press. Leaves the Socialist League;
     founds the Hammersmith Socialist Society.

1891 Poems by the Way. News from Nowhere (serialized in
     Commonweal, 1889-90). The Story of the Glittering Plain
     (first appeared in 1890, in English Illustrated
     Magazine). The Saga Library, vol. 1 (with Magnusson).
     Includes The Story of Howard the Halt, The Story of the
     Banded Men, and The Story of Hen Thorir.

1892 The Saga Library, vol. 2 (with Magnusson). Includes The
     Story of the Ere-Dwellers and The Story of the Heath
     Slayings. Sounded out about becoming the Poet Laureate;
     he declines.

1893 Socialism, its Growth and Outcome (with Bax). Gothic
     Architecture (originally a lecture given in 1889 for the
     Arts and Crafts Exhibition Society). The Tale of King
     Florus and the Fair Jehane.

1893-95	The Saga Library, vols. 3-5 (with Magnusson). Includes Heimskringla: The Story of the Kings of Norway Called The Round World.
1894	The Wood Beyond the World. Of the Friendship of Amis and Amile. The Tale of King Coustans the Emperor. The History of Over Sea.
1895	The Tale of Beowulf, Sometime King of the Folk of the Weder Geats (with Wyatt). Child Christopher and Goldilind the Fair.
1896	The Well at the World's End. Old French Romances (includes The Tale of King Coustans the Emperor, Of the Friendship of Amis and Amile, The Tale of King Florus and the Fair Jehane, and The History of Over Sea). October 3, WM dies at Kelmscott House, in Hammersmith; buried three days later in the church yard at Kelmscott, in Oxfordshire.
1897	The Water of the Wonderous Isles. The Sundering Flood.
1898	A Note by WM on his Aims in Founding the Kelmscott Press.
1899	The Life of WM, by Mackail (1899.10, the authorized biography).
1902	Architecture, Industry and Wealth (includes "The History of Pattern Designing," "The Lesser Arts of Life," "Art, Wealth, and Riches," "Art and Socialism," "Textile Fabrics," "Art Under Plutocracy," "The Revival of Architecture," "The Revival of Handicraft," "Art and Industry in the Fourteenth Century," "The Influence of Building Materials Upon Architecture," and "On the External Coverings of Roofs").
1906	The Saga Library, vol. 6 (with Magnusson). Includes notes and indexes, most of them by Magnusson; his obituary of WM also appears here.
1910-15	The Collected Works of WM, 24 vols., edited by May Morris (1910.9).
1936	WM: Artist, Writer, Socialist,, 2 vols., edited by May Morris (1936.9). The second volume includes Shaw's memoir, "WM as I Knew Him" (1936.12).
1950	The Letters of WM to his Family and Friends, edited by

Philip Henderson (1950.8).

1969   The Unpublished Lectures of WM, edited by E.D. LeMire.
Includes "Art: A Serious Thing," "The Gothic Revival I,"
"The Gothic Revival II," "Art and Labour," "The
Depression of Trade," "Of the Origins of Ornamental Art,"
"Early England," "The Early Literature of the
North--Iceland," "The Present Outlook in Politics," and
"What Socialists Want" (1969.18).

1983   The Juvenilia of WM, edited by Florence Boos.

1984   The Collected Letters of WM, edited by Norman Kelvin.

Preface

In this Reference Guide, I have attempted to list and annotate every book and article about WM, as well as those studies that have significant commentary upon his life, achievements, and influence, written between 1897, the year after his death, and 1982.

Dozens of citations were omitted, notably those appearing in handbooks, encyclopedias, general histories, and the like, which contained standard, or predictable, biographical sketches and summaries of WM's significance within a particular area. Handbooks on interior design, on calligraphy, on the art of collecting fine books; encyclopedias of design or sci-fi fantasy; treatises on textiles or translation; histories of socialism, of printing, of architecture, or of literature; studies of the Bauhaus, the Arts and Crafts Movement, the Pre-Raphaelites (many coffee-table books here), the Small Press--all these, and many more, devote a paragraph or a page to WM, and obviously I could not include them all. A few such citations remain, either as representative types, or because their exposition was unusually informative, perhaps unique in some way.

Anyone familiar with the Victorian age knows how many memoirs, diaries, letters, and autobiographies have survived. Because WM was a well-known public figure for decades, first as a poet of international stature, then as a successful businessman, decorater, and designer, finally as a prominent agitator for social change, he is referred to in many of these primary sources. I have, however, included here only a small proportion of such references, these the most substantial, from associates and friends like Allingham, Blunt, Shaw, and Yeats. Seemingly inconsequential references or recollections have sometimes been retained if penned by personages like Veblen or Kipling. Many others, such as Kegan Paul's memory of WM swearing in church, have been omitted. But enough remain to give a firm sense of the strong and lasting impression WM made on a wide range of Victorian luminaries.

Significant commentary also occurs frequently in studies and biographies of contemporaries like Burne-Jones and Rossetti. The few biographies of the former, WM's lifelong friend, have of course been included, as have several of the many biographies of Rossetti, WM's one-time mentor and his wife's lover, one whose talents and personality exerted an influence on WM's life and work still not fully understood. Biographies of Yeats and Shaw, younger men who were influenced by WM, whose memories of him during the years of the Hammersmith Socialist Society remained powerful, appear here, and so do biographies of associates like Philip Webb and Eleanor Marx, of acquaintances like York-Powell and De Morgan. Every biography of Ruskin is likely to mention WM, as a "disciple," or the most important admirer of "The Nature of Gothic," or the like. Such references are predictable, and they are therefore not included. Some of my inclusions might seem arbitrary, and I have no doubt missed some biographies with significant commentary, but I have tried to include here those books with both representative and important references to ways that WM impinged upon the life and achievements of others.

There are scores of editions of WM's writings, and again many of these had to be omitted. I have included the most important, the twenty-four volumes which make up the Collected Works, edited by May Morris and published between 1910 and 1915 (1910.9), and the two-volume supplement, Artist, Writer, which came out two years after the centenary (1936.9). Also included are influential editions, like Cole's Nonesuch (1934.20), and Asa Briggs's (1962.4), the one marking the centenary with previously unpublished political prose, the other published in conjunction with an important exhibition, "The Work of WM" (1962.42), and intended to introduce a large audience to WM's achievements. I have included recent editions of works never before published, such as WM's Socialist Diaries (1981.8), and the so-called Novel on Blue Paper (1982.15). Omitted are the numerous fine press editions of single poems, lectures, or prose romances, editions of the sort Thomas Mosher produced in Maine at the turn of the century. Even though such books sometimes have interesting and useful introductions, there are simply too many of them; a glance at the bibliography which Susan O. Thompson included in 1977.38 will give some indication of their range and number; they are, moreover, often difficult to locate. I have also excluded recent Ballantyne editions of the late prose romances, most of the "re-tellings," for youthful audiences, of Sigurd and selected poems from Paradise, pamphlets containing socialist lectures, and most of the foreign editions of Nowhere, which has been translated into forty-three languages.

Likewise excluded here are references within transactions and newsletters, though these are often lively and informative, of the WM Society, whether from the parent stock in Britain, or its American and Canadian branches. WM, or a character obviously meant to represent him, appears in a few novels, and he is the subject of several poems and of a few recent films. Many of his poems have been set to music: (1979.13); "Rapunzel" has been made into an opera. I have made no systematic attempt to locate and include such

works. Nor have I included book reviews. I have also been
constrained to exclude various limited runs of pamphlets or
"keep-sakes" from the dozens of small presses that have in this way
attempted to signal their debt to WM and his achievement at the
Kelmscott Press. Such publications should not be considered
ephemera; their number, their inaccessibility, made it impractical
to add them to my lists.

I have included doctoral dissertations (seventy of them) if WM
and his works are apparently their central concern, and over thirty
exhibition catalogues. The latter appear at the end of the
alphabetized lists for a particular year, and under their title
rather than the location of the exhibition. Auction catalogues,
except for 1898.25, have not been included; the most important are
listed in Fredeman (1965.7). I have attempted to be as
comprehensive as possible with regard to books and articles on WM
and upon any one of his many interests, achievements, and types of
influence. I have used all previous special and periodical
bibliographies, incorporating their lists, and this Reference Guide
therefore should supersede them all. I have read all but some fifty
titles of the nearly 1,900 (150 in fourteen foreign languages)
included here. Items I was unable to examine are designated with an
asterisk preceding the entry number. The interlibrary loan staff at
the University of Massachusetts has been very helpful in finding
dozens of studies. Edla Holm turned up titles I had given up on;
her patience, her good sense and good cheer were remarkable. To her
assistants, Ute Bargmann and Marion Grader, I am likewise indebted.
I wish also to express my gratitude to librarians and staff at
Amherst College, the Boston Public Library, Columbia, Harvard, the
Library of Congress, the New York Public Library, Mount Holyoke,
Smith, and Yale. I must also thank the English Department staff at
the University of Massachusetts for help with typing, especially
Mary Coty and Joanna Paddock.

Among my colleagues in the English Department here at the
University of Massachusetts I wish to thank, first, Michael Wolff
for encouraging me, over a decade ago, to prepare a paper on
"William Morris and Iceland." He thereby introduced me to the
versatile Victorian whose works have provided me so much joyful
labor over the past several years. Everett Emerson first suggested
this bibliography to me, and he encouraged me at the outset. For
similar encouragement, for needed help at various stages, I must
also thank Vince DiMarco. Other colleagues who gave me titles and
advice, are George Carey, David Clark, Dan Collins, Jim Freeman,
Roberts French, Richard Haven, Sid Kaplan, Bob Keefe, Alex Page,
David Paroissien, Meredith Raymond, Paul Saagpakk, and Jack Weston.
Joe Donohue shared with me his wide knowledge of both
nineteenth-century British literature and of computer programming.
It is due to him and to two of our recent PhD's in English, Ruth

Berggren and Elisa Campbell--both of whom have become computer genuises, both of whom have cheerfully dealt with my obstinate ignorance of machine technology--that all the material in this Reference Guide, as well as supplementary data for nearly every entry, is stored on computer discs. Information about this data and the availability of the discs will be supplied upon request. Dr. Conrad Wogrin, director of the University of Massachusetts Computing Center, has generously supported my work at every stage of its progress.

For translating for me articles in Japanese and in the Slavic languages I am indebted to Yasuho Fukumi, Robert Rothstein, and to my friend and colleague Tamas Aczel.

This Reference Guide is fuller and more accurate because all of the following people answered my requests for precise data on certain entries, and for references to WM in books otherwise obscure to me. Many thanks to M. Baber, Mac E. Barrick, John Bidwell, Carey S. Bliss, Florence Boos, Victor H. Borsodi, Guido Bulla, Noel Carrington, Carolyn Collette, Eleanor Cooper, James Crouch, Bernard Darcy, Glen Dawson, L. Sprague De Camp, Willi Erzgraber, A.A. Evans, Peter Faulkner, B.F. Fisher, Mary S. Flaherty, Ian Fletcher, William S. Fox, W.E. Fredeman, P.A. Gallner, Kristine Ottesen Garrigan, H.E. Gerber, Henry Glassie, Margaret Goostray, Wayne C. Hammond, Lou Harrison, Betty Isseman, Reamy Jansen, Frederick Kirchhoff, Mark Samuels Lasner, Raymond Lister, Margaret W. Marshall, Richard Mathews, Charles Mitchell, Jocelyn W.F. Morton, Sandra Muir, Jon Nilson, David Alan Novak, Paul H. Oehser, Patrick Parrinder, Eileen C. Piazzi, Tony Pizzo, Chris Purcell, Aleksis Rannit, Ward Ritchie, Louise Ritenour, Gabriele A. Rolle, Melinda Rozenweig, Aeta C. Salba, Morris U. Schappes, Carole Silver, Reyton Skipworth, Richard C. Smith, Joanne Soroka, Maynard Solomon, David Staines, Michael P. Sternberg, Susan O. Thompson, Joan Toshima, John C. Van Horne, Andrew Von Hendy, Gay Walker, Jack Walsdorf, and Susan Woodruff. Joseph R. Dunlap belongs among this group for his courteous and helpful replies to several letters, but he also stands apart for allowing me to use his huge collection of WM materials, for fetching me pamphlets, offprints, and catalogues, and for offering me tea and friendly advice on two successive days last summer. A special note of gratitude to him. He was also one of a small group of dedicated Morrisians who agreed, at a late stage in the book's progress, to read the introduction and check the annotations. He and the six others (Florence Boos, W.E. Fredeman, Peter Faulkner, Frederick Kirchhoff, Richard Mathews, and Carole Silver) noted many errors and stylistic problems, all of which I have attempted to correct. Along with all users of this Reference Guide, I am in their debt.

I shall end these acknowledgments in a time-honored way; my wife has provided advice when I most needed it, prodded me when I fell into lethargy, and displayed remarkable forbearance and good spirits in the face of my complaints about obtuse critics and computer glitches. She has, moreover, become an aficinado of WM, excited about his pattern designs if not his translations from the Icelandic. Thank you, Pat.

Introduction

In her comprehensive introduction to WM's socialist diaries
(1982.7) Florence Boos has remarked that WM's "achievements
routinely exhaust the enumerative abilities of his biographers." I
would never challenge this statement, but I think it may be helpful,
especially for those readers unfamiliar with any of the thirty
existing biographies, to place some of WM's achievements within a
short biographical sketch. If used with the chronology, this sketch
may make clearer and more useful my subsequent remarks on changes
WM's reputation has undergone, as socialist, as man of letters, and
as designer.

WM was born in 1834 in Walthamstow, just east of London, and he
enjoyed a privileged and happy childhood within a prosperous
middle-class family. His father, a London broker, purchased in 1840
a large estate bordering Epping Forest. Here, under the indulgent
eyes of older sisters and a loving mother, WM romped across fields
now covered by London suburbs and rode a pony through green glades
now cut by motorways. Here WM chalked up his first achievement, one
remarked upon by most of his biographers: he apparently read all the
Waverly novels by the age of seven.

In 1848, a year after his father died (leaving a considerable
fortune), WM attended Marlborough College, a recently opened private
school, where his studies did not interfere with long walks in the
Wiltshire countryside, and where he explored old churches and
learned the names and habits of birds and all manner of plants. He
read omniverously, especially in history, mythology, and romance.
He became an expert at old-fashioned sports like single-stick and
gained a reputation for his strength, independent ways, and
retentive memory. And perhaps he took part in a student rebellion,
which a recent biographer (1975.36) has seen as a harbinger of WM's
radical politics in the 1880s.

In 1853 he went on to Exeter College, Oxford, learning less
from the dons than he did from a talented set of close friends,
among whom was Burne-Jones. Such friends, and the entire ambience
of Oxford, nourished WM's interests in things medieval: in
Froissart, Chaucer, Malory; in illuminated manuscripts and Gothic
architecture; in writers who anchored their polemics, their novels

and treatises, in medieval models or chivalric idealism--writers like Carlyle and Ruskin, Yonge and Digby. WM and Burne-Jones contemplated starting a monastic brotherhood that would engage in a "crusade and holy warfare against the age." This plan was abandoned, but later, in practical situations, WM would test ideals based on cooperation, first at Morris, Marshall, Faulkner and Co. (which became Morris and Co. in 1875), later in the Socialist League and the Hammersmith Socialist Society. Though many of his achievements were won through solitary labors, he always returned to the theme of fellowship, which he came to regard as life itself.

In 1855 WM took his degree but did not leave Oxford. He entered the architectural offices of G.E. Street, where he learned of Neo-Gothic fashions and restoration schemes at first hand; no achievement remains from this one period (less than a year) when he was in someone else's employ. But it was at Street's that he met Philip Webb, who became a fast friend, the one who would design for him Red House, who would become a pillar for the Firm (offering sound advice and sending round rich clients for interior decorations), and who would design the gravestone under which all the Morrises now rest in the small churchyard at Kelmscott.

It was in Oxford, in 1856, that WM and several equally enthusiastic and idealistic friends launched the Oxford and Cambridge Magazine. In ten of its monthly issues, WM published several "Gothick" tales, a handful of lyric poems, a few articles, and at least one review. An essay on churches in northern France, charged with appreciative detail, anticipates his committed work during the last twenty years of his life for the Society for the Protection (not Preservation) of Ancient Buildings (SPAB), which he founded in 1877 and which still exists. The magazine folded in December of 1856, and WM did not regard it, nor his contributions to it, as of any real worth (modern critics have disagreed; see 1982.32), but his tasks for it as editor, principal writer, and financial backer prefigure those he was to assume for a vastly more important periodical, Commonweal, in 1885.

And it was in 1856, while visiting Burne-Jones in London, that WM met Rossetti who admired the younger man's poetry, professing astonishment at the ease with which he wrote it. Rossetti encouraged WM to take up painting. He tried, becoming part of the boisterous crew Rossetti assembled during the summer of 1857 to paint murals, based on scenes from Malory, in the great debating hall at the Oxford Union. The new surfaces were not properly treated, and the figures quickly faded, though the tales of the happy artists, of the "chaff" directed at WM, have tended to grow richer with each retelling; the Oxford Union murals have become part of the lore of the Pre-Raphaelites, and some account of his attempt to render a scene from Tristram appears in every WM biography. And

that same summer Rossetti and WM met Jane Burden, whom WM was to
marry two years later; she became the model for his one surviving
oil painting, La Belle Iseult. In this painting there is an
angularity and awkwardness about the figure that has disturbed most
viewers; there are similarly confusing and opaque qualities in his
verbal portraits of medieval characters in Defence, his first book,
which was published in 1858 and dedicated to Rossetti. The poems in
this volume reveal WM's passions for Malory and Froissart, as well
as his taste for the shocking and dramatic sides of medieval life.
Unfortunately, the book did not sell well, but on a few of its
poems, like "A Haystack in the Floods," WM's modern reputation as a
poet has rested. The other more leisurely narratives, which won him
international fame while he was still in his thirties, have only
recently been seriously reconsidered. And before WM took pen in
hand to write them, Jason and Paradise, he was busy with other
matters, ones that led to significant new achievements in the realm
of the decorative arts.

WM and Jane Burden were married in 1859, and the following year
they moved into a red brick home which Webb designed for them.
Known as Red House, this structure still stands in a remnant of
apple orchard in a suburb of London. Some have hailed it, with some
exaggeration, as the first "modern" home, an adumbration of Bauhaus
principles of integrity of materials and function, and the like. It
is certainly true that Red House was important for WM; here he
enjoyed the happiest years of his marriage, here the two daughters
were born, and here began the ideas for a business, for what became,
in 1861, the decorating firm of Morris, Marshall, Faulkner and Co.
Because, in that "age of shoddy," the newlyweds could not purchase
beautiful or useful furnishings, they made their own (some wonderful
embroideries that WM and Janey worked on together survive). Their
friends joined in and themselves became members of the Firm, the
reputations enjoyed by Rossetti and Burne-Jones brought some early
commissions, and the enterprise soon made its mark, especially with
stained glass. WM designed his first wallpaper before the Firm was
a year old, and he was deeply involved with all aspects of its work,
searching into the nature of materials and learning how earlier
artisans had worked with them to achieve such brilliant results in
their colored glass, in their dyes for tapestries, and in the
richness and durability of their decorations for a wide variety of
everyday wares. WM thus laid the basis for his later critiques of
nineteenth-century industry and art; the former sacrificed materials
and techniques for profits, and art lost fiber and authenticity as
it separated itself from the lives of common people. In 1875 WM
assumed full control of the Firm; its products earned him a good
living and a solid reputation as a designer and producer of many
artifacts, but particularly of wallpapers and chintzes, of
tapestries and carpets. He was almost as widely known for the Firm,
which had offices on Oxford Street until 1940, as he was for his

poetry, and he is said to have appreciated the appelation "poetic upholsterer." Some now think him the greatest flat pattern designer who ever lived.

Plans to add another wing to Red House, for Burne-Jones and his family, fell through and in 1865 the Morrises moved back to the city. WM began writing poems again, copying some of them out in his own fine hand and placing them within decorated borders that are astonishingly fine, nearly as beautiful as the medieval manuscripts that were his chief inspiration. A Book of Verse, made for Georgie Burne-Jones in 1870, has recently been published in a facsimile edition (1980.48) that demonstrates WM's great talents as a calligrapher and decorator of books. During this period he somehow found the time to copy out over 1,500 pages, adding marginal designs and elaborate initials, of various favorite texts, ranging from Horace to Icelandic sagas, and to write Jason and the twenty-four narratives that make up Paradise, and also to continue his design work at the Firm.

In 1868 WM met Eirikr Magnusson who taught him Icelandic and with whom he began translating, almost immediately, Icelandic sagas. Among the first of the dozen or so they rendered into WM's own distinctive English was Volsunga Saga, a tale of heroic passions and tragic love, parts of which WM thought absolutely inspired. It formed the basis for his Sigurd, the longest epic poem written in English in the nineteenth century, one which was much beloved of Yeats and Shaw, and of all his works WM's favorite.

Magnusson was WM's guide on his first journey, in 1871, to Iceland. They visited saga sites and rode sturdy Icelandic horses on treks across the interior and to the northern coasts, through lava wastes and over mountain ranges. WM enjoyed the rough life on this excursion and returned in the summer of 1873. His Icelandic Journals, not published during his lifetime, are among the best travelers' accounts we have of Iceland. The landscape provided WM insights into the plots of the sagas and the minds of their heroes, and his descriptions of those savage and weird vistas evoke the unique beauty of Iceland and provoke new readings of many scenes in the sagas. These journals do not, however, reveal the personal anxieties WM was undergoing during these years. A few letters from Iceland suggest how disturbed he was, and so too does Love Is Enough, a kind of formal masque he labored over in 1871 and 1872. These anxieties arose from the attentions his former mentor continued to pay to his wife. Rossetti had stayed with Janey and the two daughters at Kelmscott Manor during both of those summers when WM was in Iceland, and their affair has received a good deal of critical attention, especially since the release of their correspondence (described in 1964.6 and published in 1976.4). Some have speculated on ways the affair influenced WM's achievements, pushing him always into new endeavors, causing him to return in his own tales to themes of thwarted love and despondent husbands. What emerges from these revelations, and the more recent ones regarding Janey and Blunt (described in 1981.19), at least for me, is increased respect for WM, for the decent, sane, and patient ways he dealt with those closest to him.

In 1876 WM joined the forces of reason who were trying, through their efforts in the Eastern Question Association, to keep Britain from war with Russia; and in the following year he founded SPAB. His work for these organizations, the speeches he gave, and the brilliant letters he wrote led him ever deeper into public life and finally into prominence as a key figure in the SDF, which he joined in 1883. He wrote several articles for its journal, Justice, and became a valued colleague of its leader, H.M. Hyndman. But it was Hyndman's arrogant policies which caused WM, along with Eleanor Marx and others, to leave the SDF and in 1885 become a founder of the Socialist League. WM thereby began another string of achievements as impressive as those he had already recorded as a man of letters and a pioneering designer. His activities in both of those spheres, one must note, continued apace. So even as he preached socialism up and down Britain, lecturing and organizing, writing editorials and polemical reviews, attending meetings and rallies, he was translating Icelandic sagas and Homer; he was, moreover, overseeing the dyeing and printing of fabrics at Merton Abbey, making sure that Morris and Co. carpets and wallpapers were properly installed in clients' homes, designing new patterns, and maintaining his successful business.

In 1885, WM founded Commonweal, a journal whose one professed aim was the "propagation of Socialism." In its pages appeared articles and reviews by Engels, Eleanor Marx, Aveling, Shaw, and a host of other prominent political thinkers and writers; here appeared for the first time, in serial form, Pilgrims, John Ball, and Nowhere, the socialist narratives into which WM poured his dreams of fellowship and his convictions that a revolution could and would set aside the iniquities of industrial capitalism and allow all humans to find joy in work, in each other, and in the wonders of a natural world scrubbed clean of grime. For Commonweal WM also wrote articles, editorials, reviews, notes--a huge body of polemical and sometimes brilliant prose that for years was regarded, if at all, as mere journalism, barely touched upon by his biographers and excluded from the Collected Works. Scholars like E.P. Thompson (1955.15) have resurrected this prose, using themes from it and the socialist lectures as evidence that WM was a political and social theorist whose stature must be recognized, and whose reputation and relevance should be second only to that of Marx.

WM left the Socialist League, and <u>Commonweal</u>, in 1890, because of disagreements with anarchists within the League, but he did not withdraw from public life, as some of his biographers have maintained. He still lectured widely, and he worked strenuously for the Hammersmith Socialist Society, hawking penny pamphlets on streetcorners, presiding over the famed Sunday evening lectures in a long shed next to Kelmscott House. Political emigres from Europe, leftist intellectuals from all over Britain, curious workers, all rubbed elbows in audiences that might at one time have included Kropotkin, Shaw, Yeats, Eleanor Marx, and both Walter and Stephen Crane. WM's achievements and reputation attracted a wide circle of diverse and talented people. Yet there is evidence, especially in the nostalgic and erotic prose romances he wrote during the last six years of his life, that he was lonely, unfulfilled in significant ways. But these same romances do offer bright portraits of heroic individuals and models of social happiness.

It was also at this time that he embarked on his "adventure" at the Kelmscott Press, giving new impetus to the making of fine books and the revival of the art of printing. The care and intelligence lavished upon the fifty-three works (in sixty-six volumes) printed between 1891 and 1898 have made them unique, a continuing inspiration to book lovers and to the dozens of private presses that have attempted to emulate this final achievement of a remarkable Victorian polymath.

WM's energies and interests seemed boundless, leading him into activities and work that he almost invariably finished: hence the wide-ranging achievements enumerated above and also the continuing attention he has received from scholars and critics. Shifts in this attention are reflected in the numbers of yearly entries in this Reference Guide. For the year 1897, for instance, there are thirty-two entries; in 1902 there are sixteen, and then six in 1915, seven in 1916 and in 1917, six in 1918. Other low years are 1919 (nine), 1941 (six), 1942 (six), 1943 (five), 1945 (six), 1946 (seven), 1949 (six). For 1934, the centenary year, there are eighty-eight entries, and for every year since 1960 the numbers are consistently high, ranging from twenty-two in 1964 to sixty-seven in 1978. Such quantifying is mildly interesting, suggesting the effects of wars and depression. But one must beware mere numbers. Three of those six entries for 1918, for instance, are of substantial importance. Clutton-Brock's thoughtful essay on war and socialism (1918.4); Bax's irascible memoirs (1918.1) and Herford's balanced scholarship on the use of Norse themes in WM's poetry (1918.5)--any one of these entries is worth a score, or more, of the centenary essays.

A central point is that WM's many and diverse achievements have caused him never to fall entirely from public notice. Historians of printing or of socialism, literary scholars, and commentators on the arts and crafts, among others, have written on WM. This same diversity has made it difficult for any single writer to appreciate (or communicate) the importance of every aspect of WM's many achievements. This fact will become apparent in what follows, a discussion and review of shifts in WM's reputation as a socialist, as a poet and man of letters, and as a designer.

Mackail (1899.10), the official biographer, was a classicist and he was therefore capable of suggesting that translating Homer was a more "normal" activity for WM than preaching socialism. Mackail was not as apolitical or conservative, however, as many of the biographers who followed him. Cary, for instance, asserted, in 1902.2, that the socialist lectures raised "havoc" with WM's aesthetic principles, and Noyes (1908.9) claimed that socialism substituted "death for life." A majority of the shorter studies, mirroring puzzled attitudes that obtained while WM was alive, ignored WM's political writings entirely or expressed regret that the great poet and pioneering designer had wasted so much time writing them and agitating on drafty streetcorners and in smoke-filled rooms; some have suggested he thereby shortened his life.

But the one book that did the most damage to WM's reputation as a socialist was written, ironically, by one of his disciples, J. Bruce Glasier (1921.3). The clouded recollections and Christian reconstructions in these memoirs served to turn WM into a good-hearted reformer, one who did not really understand Marx. Good Englishmen therefore had no reason to associate WM with radicals or with what had recently happened in Russia. Such recollections allowed politicians, especially during the centenary year, to lay claim to WM's political heritage. Both Stanley Baldwin and Clement Attlee did just that, and thus Arnot was moved to fury, and he fired the opening salvos, in 1934.2 and 1934.3, in a committed campaign to rescue WM the radical socialist from establishment politicians. E.P. Thompson's massive political biography (1955.15) completed the rescue mission. Using many new sources, notably WM's writings for <u>Justice</u> and <u>Commonweal</u>, Thompson demonstrated WM's brilliance as a political thinker and proved that he was an advocate of revolution, not reform. He also demonstrated how Glasier used half-truths to create his own comfortable portrait of WM.

The foregoing might suggest that no one before Arnot dealt fairly with WM's socialism, but that is not the case. The chapter on WM's socialism in Aymer Vallance's biography (1897.21; this is the revised, unglossy second edition) is thorough and balanced, and it deserves to be better known. So does a study by John Spargo

(1906.19), whose claim that WM's corpus "contains nothing finer than the best of the socialist writings," is grounded in extensive research into primary sources. But this monograph was published by a small press in Westwood, Massachusetts, and has never been reissued.

Anna Phelan's 1908 dissertation was also based on careful research and pointed out exactly why WM was against parliamentary palliation; of course, few would have had a chance to read it. It was, however, published by a university press (1927.7) and has been reprinted four times since 1974, by houses like Folcroft and Norwood, publishers of unaltered reprints. It seems unfortunate that serious works by scholars like Spargo and Phelan were not available in Britain earlier. Had they been, perhaps the "Morris myth" that Arnot railed against would not have been so powerful. But because of the polemics of Arnot and the scholarship of E.P. Thompson such bourgeois myths regarding WM's politics are unlikely to arise again. I do not mean to undervalue writers like Cole (1931.4) and Murry (1932.13) who had appreciated the importance of WM's socialist work even before Arnot, but they were definitely in the minority.

All of the following writers, many of them influenced by E.P. Thompson, take WM's socialism seriously. Williams (1958.14) argues that WM was a pivotal figure between nineteenth-century radicalism and twentieth-century socialism, and he regrets that so few readers know his socialist lectures. The audience for those lectures has been increased by the publication of LeMire (1969.18) and Morton (1973.25), and Morton has also edited the three socialist narratives that originally appeared in Commonweal, making in an inexpensive paperback edition (1968.27) Pilgrims available to a wide audience for the first time. (These Lawrence and Wishart paperbacks seem always to remain in print and make ideal texts for undergraduate courses in literature or political science.)

Paul Meier has pursued to vast lengths that "vindication" begun by Arnot, arguing throughout his two-volume study (1972.19) not only that WM was a committed and conscious Marxist, but that in Nowhere he borrowed directly from Marx's early writings. Goode (1971.10) uses neo-Marxist categories to offer new readings of Sigurd and Wolfings, and Pierson (1973.31) sheds new light on WM as a pioneer socialist thinker, linking him to twentieth-century Marxist intellectuals like Silone. In the postscript (1976.50) to the second edition of 1955.15, E.P. Thompson remarks favorably upon these efforts by Meier, Goode, and Pierson, but finds in other commentaries only a "disappointing harvest," going on to underline WM's immense significance as a prescient diagnostician of the alienations capitalism has fostered. Perry Anderson (1980.3) has faulted E.P. Thompson for overlooking WM's significance as the first

writer to undertake a "frontal engagement with reformism in the
history of Marxism." Faulkner's introductory biography (1980.17)
stresses WM's political relevance to our times; the ills he preached
against in his age have become epidemics in ours, in communist as
well as capitalist societies. Boos (1982.7) argues for WM's
importance as a socialist agitator in his own time, and as an
educator and theorist for ours. Some of the most exciting and
pertinent recent work on WM concerns his socialism, and it seems
unlikely that there will be a return to those views that so enraged
Arnot.

Though Jason and the narrative poems in Paradise had won for WM
early fame, which lasted throughout his lifetime, his reputation as
a poet declined through the opening decades of the twentieth
century. Drinkwater, a poet himself, made discerning comments, in
1912.3, on WM's poetry, and essays by Lubbock (1911.9) and Lucas
(1930.8) are graced by trenchant and convincing appreciations, but
few such positive evaluations were made between the wars.
Justifying the greater weight he gave the prose in his Nonesuch
centenary edition of WM's writings (1934.20), G.D.H. Cole claimed
that WM's poetry had fallen out of fashion because its soft,
"picture-making" qualities did not appeal to audiences accustomed to
the "angularity" of modern poetry. Other centenary celebrants made
similar points. Evans (1934.25) lamented that few read WM's poetry,
and that many thought of him as a Beerbohm caricature, if at all.
Tinker (1934.69) after praising a few poems from Defence, suggested
that WM's "career as a poet reveals a progressive impoverishment."
West (1934.76) claimed that both WM's prose and poetry are "quite
out-dated," and Zabel (1934.80) contrasted WM's reputation as poet
and prose-writer to that enjoyed by Hopkins and Butler, whose large
reputations rest on only one book apiece; and so Zabel (here
striking a note often heard in WM criticism) conjectures that
perhaps WM attempted to do too much, and that therefore his
reputation as a writer had necessarily diminished. A nadir is
reached in Bush's condescending remarks about the lack of appeal
WM's poetry must naturally have for "mature" readers (1937.2).

Such a rough sketch suggests a steady and absolute decline in
WM's poetic reputation, but this was not exactly the case. During
the late thirties, Litzenberg wrote a series of articles on WM's
inspired use of Icelandic themes and literary structures, and
Margaret Grennan's full, intelligent, sensitive analysis of the ways
medieval ideas influenced WM's works appeared in 1945. If there was
no steady decline in WM's literary fortunes, few critics were
concerned with his poetry in the 1940s and into the 1950s. But many
studies have appeared since the 1960s, these ranging in length and
importance from notes on an image to an ambitious three-volume
survey and critical analysis of WM's poetic corpus by a French
scholar, Baissus (1980.6). Since 1970, moreover, several new

editions of WM's literary works have appeared; a few, like the
translation of Kormak's Saga (1970.5) and the edition of WM's
aborted novel (1982.15), had not been published before. Others,
like Redmond's edition of Nowhere (1970.31) and Lourie's of Defence
(1981.34) have undoubtedly increased the audience for these works.
These scores of critical studies and these new editions suggest that
the acclaim WM's literary works received a century ago has begun to
return.

Carole Silver (1982.34) accounts for this "resuscitation" of
WM's literary reputation by recalling for us the advent of new
criticism, and the parsing techniques developed by dozens of critics
in the 1950s and 1960s, techniques that almost demanded the striking
and incongruous images and meters, the themes everywhere partaking
of Jungian archetypes, not to mention the delightful layers of
ambiguity, found in the Defence poems. Hence dissertations of the
sort written by Silver herself (1967.23) and in the same year by
Stallman (1967.25), dissertations which provided the seeds for
several intriguing articles by both of them. Silver also pointed
out that the popularity of Tolkien in the 1960s generated interest
in WM's prose romances (which Tolkien knew well: 1981.57), both by
commercial publishers and by serious critics like Mathews (1973.24).
Finally, Silver mentioned the increased attention given in the 1970s
to the Pre-Raphaelites; WM's early tales and poems, with their stark
and painterly images, have become required reading for anyone
interested in literary Pre-Raphaelitism. Though Silver does not
single out the work of any one critic, her own writings on WM, from
the aforementioned dissertation to her recent book (1982.35), which
breaks new ground in every chapter, have helped to breathe new life
into WM's literary works and to expose them to a new generation of
readers.

Another critic whose works have been influential in redirecting
attention to WM's literary output is Jessie Kocmanova. She argued,
in 1964.17, that now that writers like E.P. Thompson have rescued WM
the socialist from "revisionist Labour leaders," it is time to
reevaluate his poetry, to show how it too, from Paradise onwards,
can help us to perceive WM as a realist coming to grips with history
and art, rather than that "idle dreamer" passed on to posterity by a
dwindling number of academics. Her readings of each of the Paradise
narratives, of Love Is Enough, and of Sigurd demonstrate how this
reevaluation might proceed. Her commentary on the later lyrics
reveals their ideological themes which, she claims, must have had a
direct influence on Commonweal readers. In another article
(1967.12) Kocmanova's notions about the role of human labor within
history combine with her exacting analyses of WM's socialist
lectures to support fresh and provocative conclusions about the
development of WM's aesthetic. In these and several other studies,
Kocmanova has contributed a great deal to that reevaluation of WM

she had insisted, back in 1960, was long overdue.

These studies by Silver and Kocmanova represent divergent but
equally productive approaches to WM's literary works; they have
joined many others in checking, and then reversing, the decline in
WM's literary reputation. Philip Henderson's biography (1967.11)
reflects his earlier work upon the WM letters (1950.8), which
accounts for the particularly rich details buttressing descriptions
of WM's family and associates. Henderson was the first biographer
able to utilize the letters Janey and Rossetti exchanged (1976.4),
and he could therefore present new readings of the lyric poetry WM
wrote during that troubled period of the relationship, or affair,
between his wife and erstwhile mentor. Mackail had hinted at the
autobiographical portent of this poetry, but (as the son-in-law of
Georgie Burne-Jones, to whom WM had turned for consolation), he
could do no more. Henderson felt no such restraint, nor did
Lindsay, whose biography (1975.36) often follows Henderson's closely
(and without proper acknowledgment). Lindsay speculates boldly upon
assignations in the moon light and tearful partings, finding proof
in specific lyrics, thus redirecting critical attention to them.
Throughout the book, Lindsay focuses on WM's happy childhood
memories which provided him images of leaf and bird for the poems,
themes of fellowship and security for the prose tales, and
inevitable tensions in every depiction of lovers, these tensions
arising from the "close bond" WM had with his sister, Emma, until
she "ruptured" it by her marriage to the Reverend Joseph Oldham in
1850. This adolescent love, and disappointment, lies behind the
rich characterization of females, Lindsay claims, in most of WM's
narratives. Despite his unacknowledged dependence on Henderson and
Mackail, and also--for Freudian notions--upon Le Bourgeois
(1971.14), Lindsay provides many new insights into WM's literary
works, as well as into the truly radical nature of his socialism.

Also important for advancing WM's reputation as a literary
artist, as well as for indicating that an audience for the poetry
and prose narratives exists, are book-length studies by Calhoun
(1975.11), Oberg (1978.42), Kirchhoff (1979.24), Faulkner (1980.17),
and Silver (1982.35). Faulkner's discussions of the poetry, from
Defence to Sigurd, include fresh analyses of specific passages and a
wealth of contemporary critical reaction, the latter serving to
remind us that he was the editor of the Critical Heritage volume
(1973.11). Faulkner's commentary on Nowhere, his claim that it
"remains relevant and suggestive in our time," is compelling and
convincing. This canny introduction to all of WM's achievements is
complemented by Silver's presentation of WM as one who "perceived
the self and the world with the eyes of a latter-day romantic.
Through the genre of romance, he strove to create them both anew."
Silver applies romance motifs to WM's quests into the past, to his
use of dreams, and to his attempts to mold himself into a hero who

could slay contemporary dragons. She also explicates with skill and authority all of WM's literary works.

The WM Society, begun in 1955, has contributed effectively to the renaissance of WM the literary artist; its founders pointed out that "the very breadth and diversity of WM's work and interests has hindered the comprehensive appreciation of his outlook as a whole and of his contribution to art, crafts, literature, and social and political thought." From the outset, the WM Society has encouraged new ideas about WM as a writer. Lindsay's 1958 lecture, published in 1961.22, argued that the increasing attention paid to WM the designer and WM the socialist must not obscure the fact that there are "elements of greatness in his writing, above all in his earlier poems, in Nowhere, in many of his later lectures and essays." Other experts the Society has encouraged are Arnot on WM and Shaw (1957.1); Jordan on WM and medievalism (1960.18); Swanell on WM and Old Norse (1961.33); and Purkis on WM's Icelandic "jaunt" and the journals in which he recorded events and impressions (1962.28). Purkis argued that the Icelandic Journals are of more "value than many of WM's more widely known writings. They show him grappling with facts instead of turning away from experience, and using his own instead of a borrowed style. If Morris had written more often like this, the rescue operation of the past ten years would not have been necessary." Happily, a few years later, these important journals were reissued (1969.22), and many new readers have been able to appreciate WM's responses to that ultimate island, cradle of the sagas which he loved.

The WM Society has also published monographs by G.D.H. Cole on WM and socialism (1960.8); by Faulkner on WM and Yeats (1962.13); by Joseph R. Dunlap on WM and Caxton (1964.9); by E.P. Thompson on WM and communism (1965.22); and two further studies by Faulkner, one comparing WM to another rebellious artisan, Eric Gill (1975.16), and the second discussing the peculiar relationships Wilfrid Scawen Blunt had with the Morrises (1981.19). Given the diversity of WM's achievements and the radiating circles of his influence, such monographs on single topics are more likely to contribute fresh substance to the biographical record than a full-fledged biography of the Eshleman/Grey stripe (1940.8 and 1949.4), or of the eccentric sort which stresses WM's "mandalic" experiences (1979.33). It is a pleasure to note that the Society continues to sponsor lectures and to find the means to publish them in well-printed, sturdy, and inexpensive editions.

Another important contribution of the Society is its journal; since its first number in 1961 and up through 1982, seventy-nine articles and notes on WM have appeared (all of them are annotated herein); one quarter of these are on WM the literary artist. So the JWMS has had an significant role in the rehabilitation of WM the man of letters. Its indefatigable first editor (also honorary secretary of the Society), R.C.H. Briggs, hoped that the JWMS would become "a bridge by which members, who are to be found in many different parts of the world, may communicate with one another" (1961.5). It has provided such a bridge, and conversations between British and American Morrisians have continued over the past twenty years, thanks not only to the JWMS and to the monograph publications, but also to the labors of the secretary of the American branch. Joseph R. Dunlap published News from Anywhere, singlehandedly, for years; it preceded the JWMS, and he has also helped edit three pioneering collections of critical essays on WM's literary works, originally papers given at special sessions of the Modern Language Association: papers on the late romances (1976.46), on Sigurd (1978.24), and on WM and Pre-Raphaelitism (1982.32). The eighteen essays (all annotated herein) in these collections are by some of the most lively and learned critics of Victorian literature presently at work in America.

So now, more than eight decades into the twentieth century, thanks to writers like Arnot and E.P. Thompson, there is wide agreement that WM was, and remains, an important radical socialist. And thanks to the work of many critics and biographers, only a few of whom are mentioned above, the reputation of WM the man of letters has gained strength in the last generation. The prose, early and late, romantic and socialist, and all of the poetry, from lyrics in Defence to skaldic verses imbedded in the saga translations, continues to receive sustained attention.

It remains to speak of WM the designer. Again, the diversity of his achievements and the surpassing grace and simple ease he demonstrated in mastering so many crafts and types of design work have made critiques difficult, and have encouraged a kind of "Morrisolatry" that even his most devout admirers in the fields of politics and literature do not engage in. Let me attempt to be more specific, beginning with the work that filled his final years with such joy and yielded the dozens of fine volumes produced at the Kelmscott Press. Of all his design work, though his wallpapers and the so-called Morris chair are also well known, the books he designed and saw through each stage of production at the Press he founded near his Hammersmith home have attracted the most attention. Articles, remarks in memoirs, chapters in histories of the book, are commonly laced with superlatives when this final achievement of WM is described. He is called "the greatest figure since Gutenberg" (1934.27), a Kelmscott Press volume is said to be the "typographic consummation of author, decorator, and painter" (1934.64), and his influence on the growth of private presses in England, America, and Germany is generally regarded as nothing short of phenomenal. WM and the Kelmscott Press have been memorialized in special issues of magazines (1934.82) and celebrated in many exhibitions. Although a

few of those writing during the centenary year raised a few
questions on, say, the nature and extent of WM's influence on
American printing (1934.11) or about his typography (1934.37), one
even asserting that Kelmscott Press books were illegible (1934.32),
such comments were inundated in the kinds of praise these unusual
books have elicited from the beginning. Vallance's lavishly
illustrated chapter on the wonders of the Press (1897.22), and
Cockerell's loving descriptions of the care WM took in choosing
materials and in decorating margins (1898.3), set the tone; no
discordant notes were struck in the first book-length treatment of
the Press (1924.6) by Halliday Sparling. As WM's son-in-law and
secretary of the Press, he was in a position to offer fresh and
precise details about WM's attention to the casting of types, the
manufacturing of paper, the carving of wood blocks, and the like.
It is therefore a valuable addition to our understanding of the
operations of the Press, and of WM's specific contributions.

The inevitable exaggerations in such a book (that WM changed
forever the art of printing) have been modified by several recent
exhibitions and book-length studies.

"The Typographical Adventure of WM" (the first exhibition
organized by the WM Society) opened in London in 1957 and traveled
to many cities in Britain and on the Continent. Many thousands saw
and pondered the 168 items shown (fewer than twenty Kelmscott Press
volumes), arranged so that both WM's early interests in calligraphy
and the book arts and also his wide influence on twentieth century
fine presses were brought into prominence. R.C.H. Briggs wrote the
useful and detailed catalogue (1957.12) for this exhibition, and it
is unfortunate that only 1,250 copies were originally printed. It
is now difficult to locate even among the collections of large
research libraries. I wish that those aforementioned publishers of
unaltered reprints, the ones who flourished a few years ago in
Pennsylvania, had paid attention to such catalogues instead of those
dessicated biographies, unimportant even in their first printing.

Another exhibition sponsored by the WM Society (1962.42)
included only a few Kelmscott Press items, but its information about
the Press reached a large audience, because the exhibition was
staged to mark the publication of a long overdue anthology of
selections from both WM's writings and his designs. This Penguin
paperback (1962.4) was edited by Asa Briggs, and it has been
reprinted four times, thus reaching thousands of readers.

Of the many other modern exhibitions featuring or touching upon
the Kelmscott Press, the most important have been "In Fine Print: WM
as Book Designer" (1976.58) and "WM and the Art of the Book"
(1976.38). The former reflected the variety and richness of the
holdings at the WM Gallery, in Walthamstow, and the items it

purchased in 1954 and 1956 from the Mackail and Cockerell estates. The second exhibition was more important because the Pierpont Morgan Library had purchased, early in this century, many manuscripts and rare books once part of WM's own library, and it put them on display in this large exhibit. Its catalogue includes essays by John Dreyfus (1976.13), Joseph R. Dunlap (1976.15), and Paul Needham (1976.39) which discuss, respectively, WM as typographer, calligrapher, and collector. Needham selected the items to be exhibited and wrote the catalogue proper, a handsome and informative contribution to our understanding of WM and his lifelong concern with the appearance and construction of books.

A few other such contributions must be mentioned before I move on to a brief discussion of the scholarship on other aspects of WM's design work.

Grace Calder's handsome edition (another noteworthy publication of the WM Society) of WM's translation of The Story of Kormak (1970.5) includes not only her own helpful introduction--in which she traces links between the saga's plot and WM's marital problems--to this previously unpublished work, but also a dozen fine plates that demonstrate WM's great skills as a calligrapher and decorator of literary texts he admired. Fairbank's essay (1970.11) discusses these plates and WM's love for "painted books," both those he collected and those he made, and concludes with an "Annotated List of the Manuscript Work of WM," a list with eighteen books on it.

Other important contributions to our understanding of WM and the book arts were generated by an elaborate illustrated edition of Paradise that he and Burne-Jones started but never finished. Why this book "never was" is explained in detail by Dunlap (1971.6); his patient work with the extant illustrations and engravings provides a sense of how the illustrated Paradise would have looked. In this regard, we are also indebted to A.R. Dufty's work on the same abandoned project, more particularly upon the only Paradise poem ("Cupid and Psyche") whose illustrations were substantially completed. Dufty's two-volume edition (1974.7) repeats and adds to many of Dunlap's conclusions; moreover, he brings together for the first time the complete text of the poem--here set in Troy type--and all of the illustrations. One hundred boxed sets of proofs of illustrations and engravings were offered as an optional accompaniment to these elegant twin volumes. The whole package is obviously intended for well-heeled collectors, which seems a pity, for the prohibitive cost will necessarily limit the audience for this edition. Such fancy editions of WM's works, often with significant commentary enshrined within, have appeared frequently in the past eighty years.

The books by Calder, Dunlap, and Dufty have elucidated for us WM's pre-Kelmscott Press experiments and achievements in the book arts. Susan O. Thompson has now clarified for us the post-Kelmscott Press effects WM and his "adventure" had on American book design, bringing order into a tangle of assertions about WM's influence on American printers and designers like Updike, Rogers, Goudy, Bradley, Cleland, Dwiggins, Ransom, Nash, and Rollins. In her important study (1977.38) she discusses the presses such men established and the books they produced, sorting out and defining clearly--and this had not been done before--differences between "Arts and Crafts" and "Aesthetic" book styles, and showing why a term like "Art Nouveau" should be used to describe characteristic ornamentation for books rather than to label yet another distinctive style. This book, with its more than one hundred illustrations, its extensive bibliography, and its appendix, "Morris's Statements on Book Design," is a valuable and comprehensive reappraisal of WM's varied influence on American book design; and, as such, it complements Schmidt-Kunsemuller's detailed chapter on WM's influence on German presses (1955.12) and Vervliet's article on WM's influence on Dutch printers (1958.13), and it joins many other recent studies that have brought WM and the book arts into much clearer focus.

Many of these studies, like Robinson's guide to the Kelmscott Chaucer (1975.42) and Peterson's anthology of WM's statements on the arts of the book (1982.29), deserve more than passing mention, but I must proceed to commentary upon WM's other achievements as a designer.

Though Thorsten Veblen (1899.17) found it easy to sneer at WM's design ethics and to characterize him as someone who exalted even "the defective," so long as it was both hand-crafted and expensive, intelligent praise for WM's design work is much more typical, and we find such praise from the very outset, in both Vallance (1897.21) and Mackail (1899.10), as well as in a lavishly illustrated essay by Day (1899.4), and in several scattered articles, some of the more perceptive by European writers like Sondheim (1898.16), van de Velde (1898.22), and Syukiewicz (1900.13). Morris and Co., its products and its influence, received encomiums from the beginning, again often in foreign works. Muthesius on the British house (1904.11) is important, and so is a biographical article by von Schleinitz (1907.13).

Not all American reactions were like Veblen's; some of WM's most ardent admirers and imitators, men like Elbert Hubbard and Gustav Stickley, flourished on this side of the Atlantic. The former established his Roycrofters' community of artisans at East Aurora, New York, before the turn of the century and wrote frequently on WM; in his own lusty, huckstering, inimitable style (inimitable until Sinclair Lewis created Babbitt), Hubbard

celebrated WM's life and works; and he flattered Morris and Co.
artifacts and Kelmscott Press books with his limp imitations.
Gustav Stickley also established an artisans' community, at
Eastwood, New York, and through its reputation and in an elegant
journal he published, the Craftsman, he became a leading spokesman
for arts and crafts ideals in America. The first issue of the
journal was devoted to a "criticism and study upon the life and
work" of WM (1901.21). Subsequent issues often referred to WM and
his design work, and to the social importance of the decorative
arts. And Stickley's massive oaken furniture--in the so-called
"Mission" style--probably attracted more attention than similar
Roycrofters' products.

Both Hubbard and Stickley, through artifacts made at their
workshop communities and through the journals that publicized these
artifacts while preaching the Arts and Crafts gospel, acquainted
thousands of Americans with WM and his ideas about design, about joy
in work, and about crafts and a healthy society. They must have
influenced men like Triggs (1902.14), a charter member of the
Chicago group that started a Morris Society (1903.10) and published
its own bulletin for a few years. Lecture tours by Oscar Wilde,
Walter Crane, and C.R. Ashbee--who visited Chicago three times and
traveled all the way to Stanford to lecture--also served to make
WM's name known in America. But other attitudes about design began
to prevail, and their force is suggested in a lecture Frank Lloyd
Wright gave at the Chicago Arts and Crafts Society in 1901
(1960.31). He called WM a great socialist and a great designer, but
he insisted that the machine with its new techniques and material
must and would take precedence over the "lesser arts" that WM
valued. Such attitudes won out, and even before Stickley went
bankrupt in 1913, and Hubbard went down with the Lusitania in 1915,
interest in WM and his design work seems to have waned, both in
America and abroad.

An essay by Crane (1911.4) on WM, design, and education and a
detailed monograph by Marillier (1911.10) on the "Morris Movement"
are both important, but after 1905 WM the socialist and WM the
literary artist attracted more attention than WM the designer (I am
here excluding references to book design and the Kelmscott Press).
This situation remained much the same for decades, right up into the
1950s, with only a few exceptions. These include many lively and
informative vignettes within the introductions May Morris wrote for
the Collected Works (1910.9). She tells stories of Red House
decorating projects, and mines letters from her father and from
co-workers like Webb and Faulkner, to present fresh descriptions of
cartoons and commissions for stained glass, of designs for chintzes
and wallpapers, and the like. These are interspersed, often with
interesting effects, among discussions of poems WM was working on
concurrently. From bright early memories we are provided pictures

of May and Jenny Morris watching, fascinated, as their father
applied gold leaf to a decorated initial or cut a figure into a wood
block propped up on its leather cushion. From descriptions of
Kelmscott House interiors, we get a firm sense of what household
objects WM thought to be beautiful or useful, and why Shaw's remarks
(1936.12) on the furnishings of these rooms are so apt. There are
also interesting comments upon the Hammersmith rugs manufactured in
the next-door shed (a few years later the site of the famed Sunday
evening socialist lectures), and upon WM's successful efforts to
teach himself, at a bedside loom, how to weave tapestries. Even
though May Morris's main concerns in these twenty-four introductions
are with her father's literary works, anyone interested in WM's
design work or in the problems and satisfactions (indeed the
livelihood) Morris and Co. brought him over the years, should read
them. They have recently been reissued (1973.9) in a two-volume
edition which includes the many illustrations and photographs that
graced the original twenty-four volumes.

The spate of articles and celebratory notices that appeared
during the centenary year include only one significant work on WM
the designer. This is a monograph (1934.21) by Crow, of particular
value for its many plates and full-page illustrations. Though the
Morris and Co. show-rooms remained open on Oxford Street until 1940,
there seemed by 1934 a general sense that WM designs had given way
to starker tastes (1934.25) and that his decorative arts belonged in
a museum rather than in a home (1934.76).

This relative lack of interest in WM the designer (at least on
the part of writers; Morris and Co. designs were often pirated by
makers of wallpapers and fabrics) obtained for the next fifteen
years. Lethaby's biography of Webb (1935.2) does have some fresh
points on WM as designer, and May Morris's introduction to the first
volume of Artist, Writer (1936.9), drawing upon published letters
and diaries and upon memories of her father inspired by the recent
centenary, adds new details about WM's design work. Nikolaus
Pevsner published an article (1936.10) that claimed that WM was the
most significant artist of the nineteenth century because he had
asked, "What business have we with art unless all can share it?"
And Pevsner predicted that 1861, the year the Firm opened, would
become an epoch-making date. Similarly strong statements about WM
as "pioneer" and "prophet," the shaper and harbinger of the modern
movement, do occur in the next several years, but mainly in the
writings of Pevsner (1940.14 and 1943.3).

The prevailing attitude during these years, as Cole pointed out
in a sensible and informed essay (1938.1), seems to have been that
WM's designs were too ornamental for the modern world. There were
few references to WM and design in the next decade. Writers like
Mumford (1944.7) and Read (1945.4) dropped his name into discussions

of the plight of modern industrial societies, and Charles Mitchell reported upon the striking, even revolutionary, influence the Firm had on "official decorative taste" (1947.11) because of the commissions it won to decorate rooms at St. James Palace in the 1860s and 1880s. But even though Morris and Co. fabrics still adorned the Council Chamber in 1947, they reflected earlier tastes; their time of influence had certainly passed. A writer in TLS, wondering why WM's influence on British design had not been greater (1950.15), surmised that a Scandinavian "ease of touch" was lacking. The following year--a year when the Festival of Britain exhibitions and celebrations must have made many people more conscious of British design traditions--Norman Prouting wrote an article lamenting that "WM's work as an artist, particularly in the decorative sphere, still awaits rediscovery," and that the "Victoria and Albert opens his famous refreshment room no longer, and can show but one example of his furniture." He concluded that the time was perhaps "ripe for a revival of Morris taste" (1951.13). Apparently it was--if not for a revival, then certainly for a renewal of interest.

This renewal was marked by a significant exhibition staged by Peter Floud, in 1952, one celebrating the centenary of the Victoria and Albert Museum. When it was still the South Kensington Museum, the Firm had decorated its Green Dining Room (the "famous refreshment room"), and the importance of the museum's collections to WM has long been known (1975.37), so it was both understandable and proper that this centenary exhibition should have a section devoted to "WM and His Associates" (1953.10). Under this rubric appeared eighty-four items, ranging from furniture to wallpapers (the book arts were excluded from the entire exhibition), which were described along with the works of other artisans and then precisely located within nineteenth-century traditions of applied design and decorative art. Because WM's actual contributions to design, both in theory and practice, were here clarified and separated from vague half-truths and glowing assertions about his unique significance, informed interest was awakened regarding WM's real importance and influence as a designer.

Soon afterward, in two talks which he prepared for the B.B.C. (1954.9 and 1954.10), Floud made known the results of some of the research he had undertaken for the aforementioned exhibition. Using previously untapped evidence from the records of design patents, Floud was able to place, for the first time, WM's wallpaper and chintz designs in precise chronological order, and he found that certain patterns, especially those done after 1876, "were much more directly inspired by historic examples than had hitherto been supposed." Floud punctured claims about the revolutionary and unique nature of WM's pattern designs, and his assistant at the Victoria and Albert, Barbara Morris, has made similar contributions through her research into WM's designs for woven textiles (1961.26), for carpets and tapestries (1961.27), and for embroidery (1962.26). Because her focus is narrow, her conclusions about WM's achievements in design are specific, weighty, and informative--a far cry from what Paul Thompson in his survey of WM's work (1967.29) has called "aesthetic hagiography." The work of scholars like Floud and Morris has engendered still more good research, of the type Ray Watkinson exemplifies in his detailed and useful book on WM and design (1967.35). WM's reputation as a designer now seems secure indeed.

Numerous exhibitions have drawn attention to WM the designer, to his achievements at Morris and Co. In 1961, the Victoria and Albert celebrated the centenary of the Firm with an exhibition (1961.40) whose ninety-two items revealed the broad range of the Firm's products. An exhibition at Stanford, based on a large private collection, revealed still more about Morris and Co. (1975.58) and WM's astonishing activities at both design and execution over a period of more than thirty years. The extensive activities of the Firm in Cambridge furnished the themes for an interesting exhibition (1980.38). Some WM patterns for both textiles and wallpapers have been exhibited by Sanderson's (1971.31), where it is also possible to purchase replicas. Recently Morris and Co. textiles were displayed at the largest exhibition on that subject ever organized (1981.17). The catalogues for these exhibitions are important contributions to WM scholarship, with detailed tables, and with articles and analyses by experts. The catalogue that accompanied an exhibition on WM's associations with Kelmscott and Kelmscott Manor (1981.65) describes the many treasures and artifacts displayed, and it also includes sixteen essays (all annotated herein), a few of which go well beyond mere introductions.

Another scholar whose narrow focus has led to significant new understanding of WM and Morris and Co. designs, this time with stained glass, is A.C. Sewter, whose series of articles on Morris and Co. windows preceded his massive and thorough two-volume study (1974.25) of the stained glass produced at Morris and Co. from its beginnings up until the Firm closed in 1940. This work has multiple appendixes, over 600 illustrations, and sixteen splendid full-color plates.

Other studies which have focused, to good effect, on one aspect of WM and his achievements, or influence, in design must at least be mentioned here. These include Madsen on WM and art nouveau (1956.10 and 1967.14), Boe on WM and design theory (1957.2), Aslin on Morris and Co. furniture (1962.1), Creese on WM and the Garden City Movement (1966.2), Goldzamt on WM and Polish architecture and design (1967.8), Aslin on WM and the Aesthetic Movement (1969.2), Naylor on WM and the Arts and Crafts Movement (1971.24), Barnard on WM and decorative tiles (1972.1), MacCarthy on WM and British design

(1972.15; revised 1979.30), Clark on WM wallpapers and chintzes
(1973.7), Cromey-Hawke on WM and painted furniture (1976.10), Mashek
on WM and the "carpet paradigm" (1976.34), Morris on WM and table
glass (1978.40), Naslas on WM and town planning (1979.38), Davey on
WM and architecture (1980.14), Harrison on WM and stained glass
(1980.22), Lambourne on WM and the Arts and Crafts Movement
(1980.27), Thompson on WM and tapestries (1980.45), Myers on WM and
tiles (1982.26), and Oman and Hamilton on WM and wallpapers
(1982.28).

    I have made this list rather long for a number of reasons.
First, it demonstrates again just how diverse WM's interests and
achievements in design actually were. That the list might have been
made still longer underscores a point I borrowed from Florence Boos
to open this introduction: "Morris's achievements routinely exhaust
the enumerative abilities of his biographers." While I am not his
biographer, as a compiler of works about WM, I have become familiar
with the astonishing array of his achievements, and with the
astonishing array of critical and scholarly reactions to those
achievements over the past eighty-five years. I have in the
preceding pages attempted to trace fluctuations and trends, patterns
of response to WM's achievements in politics, in literature, in
design. The concluding list of specific studies, most of them
written by experts on design, could of course be replicated with
similar lists of informed studies on WM the political activist and
on WM the man of letters. Stopford Brooke is reported (by May
Morris) to have said of WM that the world did not know "how great he
was, nor will realize for many years to come how much he has done,
and how great an originator he was" (1936.9). Recent studies have
made it possible for us to realize how great a man he was, and how
much his life and achievements have relevance for our times.

Abbreviations

Artist, Writer	WM: Artist, Writer, Socialist, 1936
Beowulf	The Tale of Beowulf, Sometime King of the Folk of the Weder Geats, 1895
Chants	Chants for Socialists, 1885
Collected Works	The Collected Works of WM, 1910-15
Commonweal	Commonweal: The Official Organ of the Socialist League
Defence	The Defence of Guenevere and Other Poems, 1858
ELH	English Literary History
Flood	The Sundering Flood, 1897
Grettir	The Story of Grettir the Strong, 1869
"Gudrun"	"The Lovers of Gudrun," 1870
Hopes	Hopes and Fears for Art, 1882
Icelandic Journals	Journals of Travel In Iceland, 1871, 1873
Jason	The Life and Death of Jason, 1867
John Ball	A Dream of John Ball, 1888
JPRS	Journal of Pre-Raphaelite Studies
Justice	Justice: The Organ of Social Democracy
JWMS	Journal of the WM Society

Kelmscott Chaucer	The Works of Geoffrey Chaucer, 1896
Laxdoela	Laxdoela Saga
Looking Backward	Bellamy's Looking Backward, 2000-1887, 1888
Love Is Enough	Love Is Enough, or The Freeing of Pharamond, 1872
MLN	Modern Language Notes
MP	Modern Philology
Nowhere	News from Nowhere, 1890
N and Q	Notes and Queries
Oxford and Cambridge Magazine	The Oxford and Cambridge Magazine: Conducted by Members of the Two Universities, 1856
Paradise	The Earthly Paradise, 1868-1870
Pilgrims	The Pilgrims of Hope, 1886
Plain	The Story of The Glittering Plain, 1891
PMLA	Publications of Modern Language Association
"Pool"	"Lindenborg Pool," 1856
PQ	Philological Quarterly
RIBA	Journal of The Royal Institute of British Architects
Roots	The Roots of the Mountains, 1889
SEL	Studies in English Literature
SDF	Social-Democratic Federation
Signs	The Signs of Change, 1888
Sigurd	The Story of Sigurd the Volsung, 1876
SP	Studies in Philology
SS	Scandinavian Studies

Abbreviations

SPAB	Society for the Protection of Ancient Buildings
"Svend"	"Svend and His Brethren," 1856
TLS	Times Literary Supplement
VIJ	Victorian Institute Journal
Volsunga	Volsunga Saga: The Story of the Volsungs and the Niblungs, 1870
VP	Victorian Poetry
VS	Victorian Studies
Water	The Water of The Wondrous Isles, 1897
Well	The Well at The World's End, 1896
Wolfings	The House of The Wolfings, 1888
Wood	The Wood Beyond The World, 1893

Writings about William Morris, 1897-1982

<u>1897</u>

1   BETTS, CRAVEN LANGSTROTH. "WM." <u>A Wreath of Sonnets</u>. New
    York: James T.White, n.p.
        This sonnet, one of twenty dedicated to diverse literary
figures, marks WM as the "burly radical of dreamy rhyme."

*2 CAZALIS, HENRI [Lahour, Jean]. "WM et le mouvement nouveau de
    l'art decoratif." Dissertation, University of Geneva.
        Cited in 1936.3.

3   COCKERELL, S.C. Foreword to <u>Some German Woodcuts of the</u>
    <u>Fifteenth Century</u>. London: Kelmscott Press, 36 pp.
        Discusses the catalogue of his library WM was planning before
his death; the fifteenth-century books are described in detail and
twenty-nine woodcuts from them are here reproduced.

4   COCKERELL, S.C. "The Printing of WM." <u>Book Buyer</u> 14, no. 2
    (February):168-69.
        Letter corrects point made by De Vinne in earlier article on
the extent of Burne-Jones's design work for Kelmscott Press: 1897.8.

5   COLEBROOK, FRANK. <u>WM: Master Printer</u>. Tunbridge Wells: Lewis
    Hepworth, 39 pp.
        Describes WM's many achievements as a printer and formulates
his "Ten Commandments for Printers," pointing out then the ways that
Kelmscott Chaucer exemplifies the commandments.

6   CRANE, WALTER. "Note on the Work and Life of WM." <u>Magazine of</u>
    <u>Art</u> 20:89-91.
        Praises WM's poetry and his work for social change, pointing
out how his socialism arose from his concerns for art. Comments
upon Morris and Co. and the importance of Rossetti to the growth of
the Firm. Discusses WM's achievements at Kelmscott Press.

7   CRANE, WALTER. "WM." Scribner's Magazine 22, no. 1
     (July):88-99.
         Discusses the works of Morris and Co., ways their sound
materials and workmanship soon created a vogue from which grew both
cheap imitations and the beginnings of the Aesthetic Movement.
Describes WM at the Firm as "an artist working with assistants," not
a manufacturer directing a business. Comments also on WM's
exquisite calligraphy, on the high art of Kelmscott Press volumes,
on how and why WM's socialism grew out of his concern for art and
his sense of history.

8   DE VINNE, THEODORE LOW. "The Printing of WM." Book Buyer 13,
     no. 12 (January):920-23.
         Praises WM's attempts to reform typography, recounting
principles regarding type that he gleaned from WM at an 1893
interview.

9   FORMAN, HENRY BUXTON. The Books of WM Described, with some
     Account of His Doings in Literature and in the Allied Crafts.
     Chicago: Way and Williams; London: Frank Hollings, 224 pp.
     Reprint. New York: B. Franklin, 1969. London: Holland Press,
     1976.
         Suggests that a "true presentment" of WM might be the result
of "setting forth in a connected narrative the public appearances of
Morris in literature" from his earliest, his articles and tales for
the Oxford and Cambridge Magazine, to his latest, the volumes he
published at the Kelmscott Press. This amounts to a useful
annotated bibliography, one which includes the forged pamphlets
attributed to T.J. Wise (1934.17) as well as those done up by
Forman himself (1972.3). Appendixes include lists of articles WM
wrote for Justice, Commonweal, and other newspapers and periodicals,
as well as a summary list of the Kelmscott Press volumes.

10   FRANTZ, HENRI. "Un renovateur de L'art industriell: WM."
     Gazette des beaux-arts, 3d ser., 18 (May):503-9.
         Comments upon the remarkable range and influence of WM's work
in the applied arts. Biographical survey stresses Morris and Co.
and Kelmscott Press.

11   HANNIGAN, D.F. "WM: Poet and Revolutionist." Westminster
     Review 147, no. 2 (February):117-19.
         Celebrates WM's achievements as an Englishman who worshipped
"the Beautiful" and not Mammon, quoting from Paradise and Pilgrims
to demonstrate the "immense chasm" that separates WM the dreamer
from WM the revolutionary.

12 HILL, GEORGE BIRKBECK, ed. Letters of Dante Gabriel Rossetti to William Allingham: 1854-1870. London: Unwin; New York: Frederick Stokes, pp. 176-78.
Among the best and most detailed letters Rossetti wrote, several have oft-quoted comments and anecdotes about the youthful WM, about his "facility at poeticizing," and the "intensely medieval" furniture he and Burne-Jones designed for their Red Lion Square digs.

13 J.J.C. "WM--The Poet." Book Buyer 13, no. 12 (January):917-18.
Celebrates WM, the "many-sided man," but draws particular attention to Paradise: "a shaft of sunlight breaking the clouds of serious thought with which the Victorian poets had overcast the sky of poetry" and to Sigurd: "an attempt to draw the epic sword out of the great tree of English literature."

14 KENWORTHY, JOHN C. "WM: A Memory, Personal and Otherwise." New Century Review 1:77-82, 124-32.
Demonstrates the unity of WM's art and socialism through personal reminiscences and detailed discussion of WM's growth as a socialist, offering reasons why he could be neither anarchist nor Fabian, suggesting fresh approaches to works like John Ball.

15 RICKETTS, CHARLES, and PISSARRO, LUCIEN. De la Typographie et de' l'harmonie de la page imprimee: WM et son influence sur les arts et metiers. London: Vale Press, 31 pp.
WM's love for the Middle Ages was reflected in his attitudes toward work and art in the nineteenth century, attitudes given concrete form in his achievements at Kelmscott Press, which are here discussed. Translated: 1952.7.

16 SCOTT, TEMPLE. A Bibliography of the Works of WM. London: G. Bell and Sons, 127 pp. Reprint. Ann Arbor, Mich.: Gryphon Books. London: Carl Slienger, 1977.
A bibliography of WM's published works with items listed under the following sections: Poems, Romances, Art, Socialist Writings, Translations, and Contributions to Periodicals; the last includes twenty-eight articles for Justice, ninety-two for Commonweal. Also cites letters he wrote to newspapers, and reviews written of his books. Concludes with a list of Kelmscott Press volumes and a useful chronological survey of all of WM's writings.

17 SMITH, NOWELL. "The Poetry of WM." Fortnightly Review 62, no.
    377 (1 December):937-47.
        A general survey of WM's poetry offers a few reasons why he
    is unlikely to become an "immortal," and concludes that WM judged
    himself and his poetry correctly in the six modest stanzas (in the
    "Apology") that introduce Paradise.

18 STATHAM, H.H. "WM, Poet and Craftsman." Edinburgh Review 185
    (January):63-83.
        Surveys WM's poetry, commenting upon the Pre-Raphaelite
    qualities of Defence, upon his "Homeric gifts for visualizing a
    scene." In most of the verse that followed, however, there is a
    "ravaging monotony of style." Asserts that WM's influence on design
    and on public taste in household effects will be more lasting than
    on literature. Comments also on the inappropriateness of
    Burne-Jones's illustrations for the Kelmscott Chaucer. Reprinted.
    1973.11.

19 STUART, G.B. "To WM, A Poem." Argosy (London), 63:136.
        Five stanzas of thanks, evoking themes from WM's poetry.

20 TYNAN, KATHERINE. "Some Memories of WM." Book Buyer 13, no. 12
    (January):925-26.
        Recalls seeing WM at Oxford and at Kelmscott House Sunday
    evenings, wondering that such a sensitive artist would have chosen
    to become a socialist.

21 VALLANCE, AYMER. WM, His Art, His Writing, and His Public
    Life. London: G. Bell and Sons, 462 pp. Reprint. 1898, 1909.
    Kennebunkport, Me.: Milford House, 1971. Boston: Longwood
    Press, 1977.
        A revised and expanded version of the elaborate, deluxe
    edition published six months earlier. Among the seven new chapters
    is one on socialism; given its sensible and sensitive treatment of
    WM's efforts to change society, it is surprising that this chapter
    has been ignored by nearly all subsequent critics and biographers.
    A chapter on Iceland has a useful review of all of WM's associations
    with that country and its literature, and there are discussions of
    the Eastern Question Association and SPAB, of WM's list of "Best
    Books," of his attitudes toward museums generally, the South
    Kensington in particular. Includes a "Chronological List of Printed
    Works of WM," this based on the Scott bibliography appended to the
    earlier edition (1897.22).

22 VALLANCE, AYMER. The Art of WM. London: G. Bell and Sons, 205
    pp.
        A deluxe edition with lavish illustrations, one that promises
to stress WM's art rather than his life. Discusses the early
commissions of Morris, Marshall, Faulkner Co., why their stained
glass and tapestries were of particular excellence. Each volume
printed at Kelmscott Press is discussed in detail, and so are WM's
calligraphy and his designs for his own book covers. Since Vallance
had WM's permission to use Morris and Co. files, Kelmscott Press
records, and the illustrated manuscripts owned by Georgie
Burne-Jones, this is an important study. Concludes with the
thirty-page bibliography published by Scott (1897.16). Revised and
expanded: (1897.21).

23 WATTS, THEODORE. Review of Water. Athenaeum, no. 3658 (21
    November):777-79.
        Judges the late prose romances to be the "most original
compositions in the imaginative literature of our time," accounting
for their unique qualities by pointing out that WM detested both
realistic prose fiction and blank verse and hence created these new
"prose-poems." Reprinted. 1973.11.

24 WINSLOW, HENRY. "WM, the Artist." New England Magazine, n.s.,
    16, no. 2 (April):161-77.
        Surveys WM's life and achievements, stressing that his
socialism grew out of his convictions that art could never prosper
in a sick society. Comments on the image of the skeletons aboard
the ship of state, borrowed from Poe, which WM and Bax neatly
employed in Socialism: Its Growth and Outcome.

25 [Kisses in Water]. Academy 52 (18 December):549.
        Reports on a curious analysis, previously cited in The
Chapbook, of the 105 kisses Birdalone receives in Water.

26 "A Note on WM's Poetry." Scribner's Magazine 21, no. 4
    (April):519-20.
        Comments upon the theme of death in WM's poetry, suggesting
that it is peculiar to him alone.

27 "Kelmscott Press." Athenaeum, no. 3657 (27 November):751.
        Warns that particular attention must be paid to the colophons
of the final books printed at Kelmscott Press, since WM was not able
to finish all the decorations he intended.

28   "Originality in Printing."   Inland Printer 18:413-14.
        Response to a French writer's judgment that British printing,
because of WM and Kelmscott Press, is the best in the world, while
American printing "fails in originality." Arguments for American
originality, for everyday "vigor of design," display not only
chauvinism, but also a frank appreciation of WM's success at
Kelmscott Press.

29   "Recollections of WM."   Artist (London) 20:61-63.
        Recollects moments at Kelmscott Manor when WM was "chaffing"
his guests about fishing or taking them on tours of local sites;
comments on the recently established WM Church at Leek, also written
about by Abbott (1898.1).

30   Review of Flood.   Academy 53 (19 March):304-5.
        States that the setting is an unlikely combination of
medieval England and the "wild territory of dream," that the
language is "uninspired," and that the characters are flat and
unchanging, "at the end what they were at the beginning."
Reprinted: 1973.11.

31   "WM."   Scribner's Magazine 21, no. 1 (January):130.
        Muses upon WM's reputation, the claims and counterclaims
recently made about his poetry and his design, concluding that
perhaps the most wonderous aspect of WM was that he usually finished
what he set out to do.

32   "WM and the Reviewers."   Citizen of Philadelphia 2, no. 1
        (January):362-64.
        Collates, and comments upon, several obituary notices,
quoting Watts-Dunton and Shaw at length; the latter praised WM's
acting abilities.

                                  1898

1   ABBOTT, LEONARD.   "The WM Labour Church at Leek."   Book Buyer
        16:31-33.
        Describes the Labour Church Movement and its founder, John
Trevor. This church at Leek, a Staffordshire market-town, was the
first in England to raise a memorial, in the form of portraits and
some of his tapestries, to WM.

2   BLOCK, LOUIS J.   "WM's Last Romances."   Dial 24 (16 May):320-22.
     Discusses WM's progress as a writer, suggesting that the late
prose romances were a natural culmination.   Paraphrases Water and
Flood.

3   COCKERELL, S.C.   "A Short History and Description of Kelmscott
     Press."   In A Note by WM on His Aims in Founding Kelmscott
     Press: Together with a Short Description of the Press by
     Cockerell and an Annotated List of the Books Printed Thereat.
     London: Kelmscott Press, pp. 7-20.
     Carefully composed by WM's executor and secretary to the
Press, it is appropriate that this factual history appeared in its
final volume.   Now-familiar details about the care WM took with
materials, his collaboration with Walker, and the like, appeared
here for the first time.   Includes a list of ephemera published at
the Press and illustrations of typefaces and initials.   Reprinted in
1924.6, 1934.82, and 1982.29.

4   COTTON, ALBERT LOUIS.   "Kelmscott Press and the New Printing."
     Contemporary Review 74 (August):221-31.
     Reviews WM achievements at Kelmscott Press, discusses the
work of various illustrators (Burne-Jones is contrasted with Crane,
whose illustrations for Plain are deemed inappropriate), and speaks
of the salutary influence Kelmscott Press had, for example, on
Chiswick and Vale presses, on the printing of Daniel at Oxford.

5   ELLIS, F.S.   "The Life Work of WM."   Architect and Contract
     Reporter 59 (10 June):369-72, 386-88.
     Reprinted from 1898.6.

6   ELLIS, F.S.   "The Life Work of WM."   Journal of the Society of
     Arts 46, no. 2375 (27 May):618-28.
     Ellis, a friend and disciple of WM for thirty years, lauds
his achievements, placing detailed discussions of them within a
useful biographical sketch.   Counters some claims made by Vallance
(1897.21) regarding WM's high regard for his own early stories (WM
actually hoped everyone would forget them).   But it was perhaps this
lecture which initiated a story that has often been repeated by his
biographers, because picked up by Mackail (1899.10), about a
sacrifice WM made for socialism: "He was not overburdened with ready
money at the time, and even sold his cherished books to provide
funds."   No such sale occurred.   Concludes with several responses,
mini-memoirs, from other WM intimates who were in the audience.
Originally a paper read before the Applied Art Section of the
Society of Arts.   Reprinted: 1898.5.

7   FORMAN, HENRY BUXTON. "Kelmscott Books on Vellum." Athenaeum,
    no. 3665 (22 January):120.
         Explains the chronological scheme he used in his book on WM's
    publications (1897.9), attempting to clarify points raised in a
    recent review. Appended to this are letters from Ellis and
    Cockerell that add further clarification.

8   GWYNN, STEPHEN. "WM." Macmillan's Magazine 78 (June):153-60.
         Vallance's study (1897.21) provided the occasion for this
    review of WM's achievements, one that praises Jason and Paradise,
    that judges the Defence poems to be "spasmodic" and "constricted,"
    obviously written under the influence of Rossetti, and that claims
    Sigurd to be WM's greatest poem. But WM's importance as a designer
    and decorative artist is stressed; Morris and Co. tapestries and
    stained glass are judged to be more significant than the poetry and
    certainly than the socialist prose, which is "too personal to
    last."

*9 HOLST, H.R. "WM als letterkundige." De nieuwe tijd 2, no. 7
    (January).
         In Dutch. Cited in New York City Public Library Catalogues.

10 JESSEN, PETER. "WM." Museum: Eine Anleitung zum Genuss der
    Werke bildender Kunst 3:29-32.
         A general appreciation of WM's life and works, one that
    stresses his achievements in the decorative arts and concludes that
    he was "ein ganzer Mann."

11 LOUBIER, JEAN. "Bibliographien von WM's Schriften."
    Zeitschrift fur Bucherfreunde 2, no. 5-6
    (August-September):256-57.
         Discusses bibliographies of WM's works recently published in
    England: Forman (1897.9), Scott (1897.16), and Cockerell (1898.3).

12 NEVINSON, HENRY. "The New Printing: The Mantle of WM." Academy
    54 (6 August):127-28; (13 August):157.
         Offers names and examples of printers and artists who
    followed WM, whose work suggests a "revolution in bookmaking."
    Based in part on 1898.3.

13 RICHMOND, WILLIAM BLAKE. <u>Leighton, Millais, and WM: A Lecture</u>
    <u>Delivered to the Students of the Royal Academy</u>. London and New
    York: Macmillan, 32 pp.
         Lecture strains to find connections between these two artists
    and WM, other than the fact they all died within the same two-year
    period. Judges that in WM "England has lost one who has done more
    than any other artist to elevate the taste of the classes of
    England."

14 SCUDDER, VIDA. <u>Social Ideals in English Letters</u>. Boston:
    Houghton Mifflin. Revised ed., 1923. Reprint. New York and
    Boston: Johnson, 1969, pp. 289-93, passim.
         Praises WM, calling him the "one notable and delightful
    figure" of an entire generation, but she sneers at his socialist
    work, asserting that no one would ever call him a serious thinker,
    that <u>Nowhere</u> has only a "monotonous charm." Includes, however,
    useful comments on <u>John Ball</u> and on its last chapter with its
    "profoundly stirring and troubling passages of social idealism."

15 SEDDON, JOHN. "WM, Poet and Designer, Messrs. Morris,
    Marshall, Faulkner and Co., Decoration Firm." In <u>King Rene's</u>
    <u>Honeymoon Cabinet</u>. London: Batsford, pp. 4-5.
         Discusses a commission the Firm received from Seddon to cover
    ten panels on a large cabinet with depictions of the Fine Arts. WM
    was responsible for the designs that connected the paintings to the
    crude framework of the cabinet. Includes several illustrations.

16 SONDHEIM, MORIZ. "WM." <u>Zeitschrift fur Bucherfreunde</u> 2, no. 1
    (April):12-20.
         A survey of WM's life and achievements, one that stresses
    Kelmscott Press and brushes by the socialist activities.

17 SONDHEIM, MORIZ. "WM und die moderne Stil." <u>Freies deutsches</u>
    <u>Hochstift</u> (Frankfurt) 14:124-32.
         Opens with comments about style being dictated in earlier
    times by king and court, but in the nineteenth century by money;
    therefore WM's success with Morris and Co. in initiating new
    attitudes about interior design was remarkable. Mentions Voysey,
    the importance of the monthly, <u>Studio</u>, the ideas of the Frenchman,
    Laborde, relating all these to WM's innovations.

18 STURGIS, RUSSELL. "The Art of WM." Nation 66, no. 1702 (10
    February):111-12.
        Uses appearance of Vallance's sumptuous book (1897.21) to
criticize Kelmscott Press books: "is there one page which satisfies
the eye of the book-lover as does one page of even an inferior Book
of Hours? Is there one border which is really well designed for its
place? Is there one initial letter which the skilled designer could
not improve?" Also comments upon WM's inability to draw figures.

19 STURGIS, RUSSELL. "The Art of WM." Architectural Record 7, no.
    4 (April-June):441-61.
        Opens with appreciative remarks about the "incredible" amount
of work WM accomplished, blaming hostile reviews some of his
writings received on prejudices inspired by his "revolutionary
socialism." A useful and detailed biographical sketch lingers over
Kelmscott Press volumes and the "Woodpecker Tapestry," which he
finds "clever and spirited," not marred by the excessive medievalism
he perceives in other designs and artifacts.

20 SWARZENSKI, GEORG. "WM und die Entwicklung des modernen
    dekorativen Stils in England." Deutsche Rundschau 9:198-210.
        Accounts for widespread British influence on the decorative
arts on the Continent by tracing various ideas and artifacts back to
WM and the correspondence he insisted upon between beauty and
function. Goes into some detail about Morris and Co. products,
especially the tapestries and the furniture, and also discusses
Kelmscott Press and its extraordinairy influence.

21 TWOSE, GEORGE M.R. "WM: His Work and His Life." Dial 25 (16
    November):343-46.
        A review-essay inspired by Vallance (1897.21), one which
castigates both modern industrialists who make cheap and sell dear,
and modern critics who slight WM as a mere medievalist, observing
that they might as well call him a mere Persian, since he borrowed
designs and a certain spirit from that sector also. Discusses, in
tones that WM would admire, the ways that British colonial policy in
India caused the decline of popular arts there.

22 VAN DE VELDE, HENRY. "WM, artisan et socialiste." Avenir
    social 3:35-48, 65-77.
        WM'S life and work had an immense significance, for in both
theory and practice he carried forward the romantic critique of
industrial capitalism, building upon the ideas of Ruskin in
illuminating ways, stressing always the connections between work,
art, and life. Biographical details support sensible
generalizations about the development of WM's socialist politics.

23 WYZEWA, TEODORE DE. "Un roman posthume de WM: Flood." Revue
    des deux mondes 146 (15 April):935-45.
        A favorable review of Flood, consisting mainly of paraphrase
    and long passages from the romance; concludes that in style and
    content, Flood is quite similar to the other prose romances.

24 "The Arras Tapestries of the San Graal at Stanmore Hall."
    International Studio 6, no. 22 (December):98-104.
        Discusses the Grail story, explaining the significance of
    scenes in the different panels of this magnificent tapestry, one of
    the singular achievements of Morris and Co. Points out that this is
    the "only example of a complete set of arras tapestries designed and
    wrought for a given room; it stands alone and memorable." Includes
    five illustrations.

25 Catalogue of a Portion of the Valuable Collection of MSS, Early
    Printed Books, etc., of the Late WM. London: Sotheby, Wilkinson
    and Hodge, 50 pp.
        At this auction, which lasted over a period of six days, were
    sold the medieval manuscripts and incunabula which WM had purchased
    during his last decade, often "in connection with his art and
    typographical work." The range and quality of the 1,125 lots here
    described are impressive.

1899

1   ABBOTT, LEONARD. "WM's Commonweal." New England Magazine,
    n.s., 20, no. 4 (June):428-33.
        Asserts that the "records of English journalism can show
    nothing more remarkable or interesting--certainly nothing with more
    romantic associations--than the story of WM's Commonweal," which ran
    as a monthly for one year beginning in February 1885, and then as a
    weekly until November 1890, when WM resigned as editor. Surveys the
    great variety of writers and artists who appeared in Commonweal
    during those years, the amazing number of notes, poems, satirical
    dialogues, articles, songs, translations, etc., that its editor
    contributed, suggesting that his stalwart work for Commonweal
    "throws into relief the personality of WM," a man who was "greatest
    of all when he ceased merely dreaming of an earthly paradise and
    began to work for one."

2   BATE, PERCY. The English Pre-Raphaelite Painters: Their
     Associates and Successors. London: G. Bell and Sons. 2d ed.,
     1901. Reprint. New York: AMS Press, 1972, pp. 79-80.
          Refers to WM's only oil painting, judging it to be "akin to,
     but distinct from, the note that makes the early pictures of
     Rossetti." Calls it Queen Guenevere rather than La Belle Iseult.

3   CRANE, WALTER. "Note on the Late President of the Society,
     WM." Arts and Crafts Exhibition Society. Catalogue of Sixth
     Exhibition of the Arts and Crafts Exhibition Society. London:
     Arts and Crafts Exhibition Society, pp. 11-15.
          Commends the work of WM, who tapped the Middle Ages "as an
     artist, not an archaelogist." Mentions the WM items set aside in
     the South Gallery at the exhibition, which included some drawings
     and designs not shown previously, as well as the oil painting of
     Iseult; these WM items are described on pages 96-111 of the
     catalogue.

4   DAY, LEWIS FORMAN. "WM and His Art." Art Journal, n.s., 51
     (April):1-32.
          Suggests that WM was "born at just the right moment," because
     Ruskin, and others, had gotten people thinking about art. Points
     out that WM's reputation as a poet helped his career in marketing
     the decorative arts, and offers specific descriptions of tapestries,
     embroideries, calligraphy, the book arts, descriptions that are
     enhanced by many illustrations and plates. Reprinted: 1900.5.

5   DE VINNE, THEODORE LOW. "The Diary of a Literary Wanderer: WM
     and Prince Kropotkin." New Century Review 28 (April):261-68.
          Recalls the times he heard WM and Kropotkin lecture at the
     International Club in Manchester and recounts interesting anecdotes
     (WM's angry answer when asked about personal charity), some of which
     are marred by a tendency to exploit Jewish stereotypes.

6   GILDER, J.L. "WM." Critic 35 (July):620-27.
          Recollections, triggered by the publication of Mackail
     (1899.10), of a pleasant visit to Kelmscott Manor in 1894.

7   HUBBARD, ELBERT. "WM." Philistine: A Periodical of Protest
     9:97-106.
          A sketch that leans toward overstatement, and even over into
     error: WM is said to have been a blacksmith, and "a musical composer
     of no mean ability."

8   KENYON, JAMES B. "WM--Poet, Socialist, and Master of Many
     Crafts." Methodist Review 81 (May):386-400.
         A chronological survey of the main events and influences in
WM's life, interspersed with selections from letters and reviews,
with more attention given to the poetry and a few of the crafts,
especially weaving, than to the romances. Points out that WM's
socialism grew out of his perception of the "terrible contrast
presented by the life of the workman of the past and the life of the
workman of today." Reprinted: 1901.11.

9   KROPOTKIN, PETER. Memoirs of a Revolutionist. London: Swan
     Sonnenschein, p. 93.
         Comments upon WM's "hatred of machines," suggesting that his
inability to conceive of their "power and gracefulness" was one of
his few limitations.

10   MACKAIL, J.W. The Life of WM. London and New York: Longmans, 2
     vols., 760 pp. Reprint. 1901, 1907, 1911, 1912. World Classics
     Series. London and New York, 1950. New York: Benjamin Blom,
     1968.
         Judicious and thoughtful, learned, humane, wholly sympathetic
to its subject, this book, the official biography, has set a high
standard for all subsequent WM biographers. With access to personal
letters, diaries, journals, through conversations with relatives and
friends, including of course the Burne-Joneses (his in-laws) Mackail
employs well-chosen details and moves with measured pace and steady
eloquence from descriptions of WM's parents and boyhood through
somber evocations of the mood at WM's simple funeral, which he had
attended. Extensive quotations from previously unpublished
materials, like the Icelandic Journals and the socialist diaries, as
well as from dozens of letters, have made this book, like Georgie
Burne-Jones's biography of her husband (1904.3), an important source
for later biographers, most of whom have used it freely. Here occur
for the first time the now hackneyed points about WM having read the
Waverly novels by the age of seven, of his great energy (restless
fingers making netting) and strength (formidable opponent at
single-stick) and temper (beating his head with his fists) and
knowledge (of the habits of birds and the names of medieval
artifacts), and so forth. Stories about the "set" at Oxford, the
beginnings of the friendship of WM and Burne-Jones, the journeys to
France, the bohemian days at Red Lion Square, the decorating and
partying at Red House, the boating trips up the Thames, stories that
have become part of the lore about WM, appear here for the first
time, and they are related with skill and calm authority. Other
stories were left untold, but certain hints ("In the verses that
frame the stories of Paradise, there is an autobiography so delicate
and so outspoken that it must needs be left to speak for itself")
have been noted by later biographers, have indeed been spoken about:
Henderson, 1967.11. Furthermore, WM's commitment to radical
socialism is sometimes blurred (but not as completely or

                                 13

474366

systematically as recent leftist critics have charged), especially
when Mackail suggests that translating the Odyssey and writing
romances were for WM more "normal" endeavors than preaching
revolution. Discussions of the poetry, of the translations
(especially of Homer and "Scenes from the Fall of Troy"); of the
1871 journey to Iceland; of the works at Merton Abbey and fruits of
Kelmscott Press; of WM's love for his daughters, his mother, a few
intimates; of ways that WM and Dr. Johnson were similar--these are
some of the high points of this exemplary biography. The World
Classics edition has an important introduction by Cockerell: 1950.3.

11 MARILLIER, H.C. Rossetti: An Illustrated Memorial of His Art
    and Life. London: G. Bell and Sons. 3d ed., pp. 34-57, passim.
        Detailed descriptions of the Rossetti watercolors done in
1857, which WM bought; he "used their romantic and sweet-sounding
titles as themes to base his two poems on; and this has led to a
confused idea that the pictures illustrate the poems. In reality,
they have nothing in common but their names, and for these the
painter, not the poet, was responsible." Since Rossetti's name did
bring business to the Firm, it is suggested that he should have
received more compensation from WM than he did when the Firm was
reorganized.

12 N.N. "WM and the Arts and Crafts in London." Nation 69, no.
    1791 (26 October):313-15.
        Discusses a recent Arts and Crafts Society Exhibition,
commenting upon WM's influence on the decorative arts, conjecturing
about "make-believe medievalism."

13 SHAW, GEORGE BERNARD. "WM." Daily Chronicle, 20 April.
        Asserts that Mackail (1899.10) depicted WM's socialist
endeavors unfairly, treating street-corner rallies and the like as
"vulgar follies" that had shortened his life; Shaw suggests that
such venues were healthier than interminable meetings in
smoke-filled rooms. Points out that WM took over leadership of the
Socialist League with the same "practicality that distinguished him
as an artist, though with much less natural aptitude." Includes
shrewd comments on the difficulties Mackail faced in attempting to
write with tact about the closest friend of his in-laws. Reprinted:
1932.17.

14 STEELE, ROBERT, and LETHABY, W.R. "WM, Poet and Artist."
    Quarterly Review 190, no. 380 (October):487-512.
        While generally applauding Mackail's graceful erudition and
thoroughness (1899.10), finds fault with his coverage of "art
methods," with his literary criticism, with fact that many of WM's
"life-long friends are not so much as named." Concludes with plea
that a comprehensive collection be immediately begun of all of WM's
design work with all that he had written about each work. (Such a
collection plus commentary still needs doing.)

15 STREETER, A. "WM and Pre-Raphaelism." Month 94
    (December):595-608.
        Asserts that WM applied Pre-Raphaelite ideals to daily life,
thus achieving a "diffusion of culture among the masses," but few
specific examples are brought forward as proof.

16 TURNER, THACKERAY. Society for the Protection of Ancient
    Buildings: A Chapter of its Early History. London: Society for
    the Protection of Ancient Buildings, 31 pp.
        Surveys the rationale behind the many restorations undertaken
between 1840 and 1877 until the teachings of Ruskin took root and
caused WM to ask "a few like-minded men, archaeologists, painters,
architects, to meet in Queen Square to consider with him what ought
to be done." Only ten came to the first meeting, but by the end of
the year "all the most respectable names in literature and in the
arts" had joined. Quotes WM on the evils of restoration, discussing
his continuing efforts to sustain SPAB.

17 VEBLEN, THORSTEIN. The Theory of the Leisure Class. New York:
    Macmillan. 2d ed., 1912. Reprint. New York: Viking, pp.
    115-16.
        Speaks of both Ruskin and WM as "eager spokesmen of that
exaltation of the defective," no matter what, so long as it is both
hand-crafted and expensive, and asserts that Kelmscott Press volumes
are examples of conspicuous consumption.

18 WHIBLEY, CHARLES. "WM." Blackwood's Edinburgh Magazine 156,
    no. 1005 (July):16-26.
        Accuses Mackail (1899.10) of offering too "timid" a portrait
of WM, but of exaggerating the importance of his writings and of his
design work. Suggests that WM was a nineteenth-century Dr.
Johnson, concluding that his work as a socialist only proves that he
was a "living paradox."

19 WHITE, GREENOUGH. "A Study in Biography." <u>Conservative Review</u>
    2, no. 2 (November):347-63.
        A biographical sketch of WM is followed by a discussion of
Mackail (1899.10), concluding with a "summary of the most
conspicuous limitations of our hero and his biographer." Points out
that all that WM hated, from railroads to Milton, suggests "pitiful
weaknesses in a grown man." Doubts that another biography of WM
will ever be needed and wishes that Mackail had said less about
Iceland and socialism, more about WM's heredity, his home-life, his
religion.

20 "WM's Great Achievement." <u>Critic</u> 35 (October):910-19.
        Discusses WM's aims and methods at Kelmscott Press, adding
details of current prices of the fifty-two volumes, which have
enjoyed an "astounding appreciation in money value." Comments upon
the quality of the books and manuscripts WM bought after 1889, ways
he used them as models for Kelmscott Press volumes.

<u>1900</u>

1   ARONSTEIN, PHILIP. "WM." <u>Zukunft</u> 31:490-95.
        An essay on WM's life and achievements, one occasioned by
Mackail (1899.10), one that concludes with high praise for WM, "the
prophet of beauty."

2   BALMFORTH, RAMSDEN. "WM: Poet and Socialist." In <u>Some Social</u>
    <u>and Political Pioneers of the Nineteenth Century</u>. London: Swan
    Sonnenschein, pp. 179-86.
        Sketches in the range and quality of WM's works, asserting
that "by the death of WM, England lost a personality which stood to
our modern social life in somewhat the same relation as the Hebrew
prophets and psalmists stood to the age in which they lived."

3   C.C.B. "WM as a Man of Business." <u>N and Q</u>, 9th ser., 6 (24
    November):406.
        Concerns a suggestion made by Mackail (1899.10) that WM's
"neglect of detail" served him well in business, wondering if it
might also account for the monotony of <u>Paradise</u>.

4   CHESTERTON, GILBERT K. "The Literary Portraits of G.F. Watts,
    R.N." <u>Bookman</u> 19 (December):80-83.
        Finds the green and silver decorations within Watts's portrait
of WM to be exquisitely appropriate and chortles over the ironies of
his portrait hanging, in the National Gallery, next to that of John
Stuart Mill, the "monk of science."

5   DAY, LEWIS FORMAN. "WM and His Art." In The Art Annuals: Great
     Masters of Decorative Art. London: H. Virtue, pp. 1-32.
         Reprint of 1899.4.

6   DE VINNE, THEODORE LOW. "Kelmscott Typography." In The
     Practice of Typography: A Treatise on Title Pages. New York:
     Century Co. Reprint. Haskell House, 1972, pp. 387-401, passim.
         Describes the designs and types used on the title pages of
     Kelmscott Press volumes, pointing out that the Gothic capitals were
     often overpowering, lamenting that some of these bad practices of WM
     found imitators.

7   DE VINNE, THEODORE LOW. The Practice of Typography: Plain
     Printing Types. New York: Century Co., pp. 206-8, passim.
         Detailed descriptions of the differences between the three
     types WM designed for Kelmscott Press.

8   HUBBARD, ELBERT. "WM." In Little Journeys to the Homes of the
     Great. Vol. 5. East Aurora, New York: Roycrofters, pp. 9-36.
         Reports upon a visit to WM at Kelmscott House, one supposedly
     made in 1894 or 1895; WM is called a famous blacksmith, and he is
     reported to have had 3,000 workers at Morris and Co.

9   KASSNER, RUDOLF. "WM und Burne-Jones: Die Burde der Spiegel."
     In Die Mystik, die Kunstler, und das Leben. Leipzig: Eugen
     Diederichs, pp. 193-219.
         Claims that WM and Burne-Jones shared spiritual and
     intellectual affinities with other artists and thinkers, from Plato
     to Knut Hamsen. Includes useful comments upon the Burne-Jones
     illustrations for Kelmscott Chaucer, characterized as "eine Octave
     zu tief."

10   LEATHAM, JAMES. WM: Master of Many Crafts. London: New Century
     Press, 129 pp. 2d ed., Peterhead: Sentinel, 1903.
         Has useful comments on WM's enlightened views on sex and
     marriage, on the connections that WM posited between pleasure in
     work, the decay of art, and the need for socialism. Uses lively
     anecdotes to defend WM against accusations regarding his parsimony
     and his godlessness.

11 MAC DONALD, FREDERIC. "The Oxford and Cambridge Magazine." In
    In a Nook with a Book. New York: Eaton and Mains, pp. 207-21.
         Discusses, often rapturously, the effects the Oxford and
Cambridge Magazine had upon himself as a young, idealistic reader.
Comments upon the serious outlook of all of the magazine's
contributors.

12 PITE, BERESFORD. "A Review of the Tendencies of the Modern
    School of Architecture." RIBA Journal, 3d ser., 8, no. 4 (22
    December):84-85.
         WM is here highly praised for the ways he stressed the
"practical alliance of artists with craftsmen," an idea which
influenced many young architects.

13 SYUKIEWICZ, WOJCIECH. "Apostol piekna" [Apostle of beauty].
    Biblioteka Warszawsks 2:136-66.
         In Polish. A discussion of the Victorian critique of
industrialism which WM carried forward from Carlyle and Ruskin
precedes a full biographical sketch, one which stresses the ways
that WM tried to bring pattern and order to all aspects of his life
and work.

14 TAYLOR, UNA A. "WM and Rossetti." Edinburgh Review 191
    (April):356-79.
         A review-essay inspired by Mackail (1899.10) and studies of
the Pre-Raphaelites. Discusses the ways that boyhood experiences
colored the poetry of both WM and Rossetti, how images of the Essex
countryside prevail in the former, of London streets in the latter.
Comments also upon medieval interests that linked Rossetti and WM,
as reflected in poems from Defence, and that linked Burne-Jones and
WM, as reflected in Paradise. Concludes that these three men started
a revolution in art.

15 TIFFANY, FRANCIS. "WM, Craftsman and Socialist." New World 9,
    no. 33 (March):103-14.
         This essay was inspired by Mackail (1899.10), and it
therefore repeats, and paraphrases, many of its observations, but
the tone is more adulatory: "Morris stands in such marked contrast
to the poets and artists of his day, as to suggest an altogether
different breed." Has substantial and specific points to make about
WM and architecture, concluding that his "rapt pursuit" of socialism
caused his early death.

16 TRIGGS, O.L. WM: Craftsman, Writer and Social Reformer.
    Chicago: Triggs Publishing Co., 46 pp.
        An enthusiastic biographical sketch by one of the founders of
    the Chicago WM Society, one that claims that only Tolstoy approached
    the "universal genius" of WM. Has useful comments on the ways that
    SPAB led WM toward other social concerns, but anticipates Glasier
    (1921.3) when he says that WM's socialism was poetic rather than
    practical. A five-page appendix, "Travel Notes in the Morris
    Country," is interesting for an American's impressions of Edwardian
    England.

17 VALLANCE, AYMER. "The Decorative Art of Burne-Jones." In Great
    Masters of Decorative Art. London: H. Virtue, pp. 1-32.
        Reprint of 1900.18.

18 VALLANCE, AYMER. "The Decorative Art of Burne-Jones." Art
    Journal, n.s., 52 (April):1-32.
        Continually stresses lifelong influence of WM on Burne-Jones,
    pointing out also that WM was responsible for bringing into the
    decorative arts "the talents of the greatest painter the world has
    known since the fifteenth century." Many Burne-Jones stained glass
    cartoons and illustrations for Kelmscott Press books are here
    reproduced, accompanied by concise commentary. Reprinted: 1900.17.

19 WARDLE, GEORGE. "WM as a Man of Business." N and Q, 9th ser.,
    6 (22 December):495-96.
        Answers the charge, made in 1900.3, that WM was a neglectful
    businessman and poet, asserting that he paid attention to the
    details that mattered, like all great workers.

*20 WYZEWA, TEODORE DE. "WM." In Le roman contemporain a
    L'etranger. Paris: Perrin, pp. 87-107.
        Cited in 1936.3.

21 "Kelmscott Press." Scottish Review 36 (July):19-35.
        WM'S early interests in calligraphy and medieval books
    underlie Kelmscott Press works, which "form one of the most
    remarkable contributions, not alone to the printing, but to the
    craftsmanship in general of the nineteenth century." As proof of
    WM's attention to detail, the author discusses the eighty-one
    individual designs which form the Golden Type, the careful
    measurements of every margin, the choice of Hanover ink, fine
    vellum, specially woven silk ties. A table gives full particulars
    for each Kelmscott Press volume: type used, number of copies
    printed, issue price, etc. Finds that the "aggregate original cost
    of Kelmscott Press volumes was 145 pounds, and in March 1900 the
    same volumes would cost 561 pounds, concluding "whether these books

will enjoy a still further advance there is, of course, a difference
of opinion."

22 "The Arts and Crafts Movement at Home and Abroad." Brush and
    Pencil 6, no. 1 (April):110-21.
        Asserts that WM "did for arts and crafts what George
Washington did for America--he founded it." But also mentions some
specific influences on individuals like Miss Foote of the Nordhoff
Bindery, Louise Anderson, and Louis C. Tiffany.

23 "WM and Kelmscott Press Volumes." Critic 36 (April):305.
        Records some of the prices fetched for Kelmscott Press books
from the library of the late Carl Edelheim of Philadelphia. A
Kelmscott Chaucer sold for 485 dollars.

                             1901

1   ASHBEE, CHARLES. An Endeavour Towards the Teaching of Ruskin
    and WM. London: Edward Arnold, 52 pp. Reprint. Folcroft, Pa.:
    Folcroft Library Editions, 1973. Norwood, Pa.: Norwood
    Editions, 1977. Philadelphia: R. West, 1978.
        Short history of Guild House, tracing its beginnings from a
small class of Ruskin's students in 1886 through conflicts with the
Educational Board and success with many students and workers in the
Industrial Arts up until 1895. Final pages deal with Ruskin and WM,
offering reasons why the teaching of the former and the example of
the latter should receive wider and fuller application; both British
industry and life would improve. Printed at Essex House Press, this
book is a fine example of Kelmscott Press influence.

2   BEERS, HENRY A. A History of English Romanticism in the
    Nineteenth Century. New York: Henry Holt, pp. 314-40, passim.
        Makes detailed points about connections between Rossetti's
watercolors and WM poems in Defence. Suggests that Rossetti's
"reincarnations" of the Middle Ages are "Florentine" while WM's are
"Norman." WM was, in fact, "twice a Norman, in his love for the
Romances and Gothic builders of northern France; and in his
enthusiasms for the Icelandic sagas." Discusses medieval motifs and
themes in Paradise, Jason, and Sigurd, comparing WM's position in
the second half of the century to Scott's in the first; both
popularized the Middle Ages, but in different ways, for WM was not
interested in pomp and regalia, in "other such rubbish" to the
degree that Scott was. Comments also upon WM's translations and
prose romances.

                              20

3 BLATCHFORD, ROBERT. "WM: Song-Smith, and John Ball." In My
Favorite Books. London: Clarion Press, pp. 90-115.
Argues that Defence is better than all WM's prose, with the
exception of John Ball, a tale full of bright pictures of "brave
soldiers and clever bowmen." These literary reflections are marked
by good sense and interesting insights.

4 BROADHURST, HENRY. Henry Broadhurst, MP: The Story of his Life,
from a Stonemason's Bench to the Treasury Bench, Told by
Himself. London: Hutchinson and Co., pp. 79-84.
Records the circumstances that spawned the first large public
meeting on the Eastern Question, how he urged WM to "write an
inspiriting song to be rendered as a prelude to the Chairman's
address." The result was "Wake, London Lads" whose "burning words
were thundered forth by the vast assembly."

5 C.C.B. "WM as a Man of Business." N and Q, 9th ser., 7 (19
January):54.
Reply to Wardle's reply (1900.19), reminding him that details
can always matter and of what was lost for want of a nail. (This
minor exchange stops here; the index is in error: WM is not
mentioned on pages 118, 172, 296, 431.)

6 CARY, ELISABETH L. "WM and some of his Books." Book Buyer
22:309-13.
Describes Kelmscott Press books collected by Philadelphian,
Harold Pierce. Traces high points of WM's career, commenting on his
philosophy of work and creativity, calling him "The Last of the
Vikings."

7 COCKERELL, S.C. "Kelmscott Press." Athenaeum, no. 3826 (23
February):244.
Points out that Kelmscott Press type will "never be in the
market," and that wood-blocks for ornaments had been left to the
British Museum.

8 CROWDY, WALLACE L. "WM." Literature 9, no. 204 (14
September):243-48.
A general survey of WM's life and works, one that politely
sneers at WM's socialism: "Morris seemed to think that to spread
discontent was the readiest way to provoke remedies." But
sympathetic and accurate in descriptions of the work of SPAB, of
WM's efforts to save a face of St Mark's basilica, as well as the
essential structures of many British buildings.

9   FREY, EUGEN. WM: Eine Studie. Beilage zum Programm des
    Gymnasiums und der Industrieschule Winterthur. Winterthur:
    Geschwister Ziegler, 139 pp.
         This school text opens with a reliable biographical sketch,
which is followed by brief discussions of Defence, Jason, all the
tales of Paradise, Love Is Enough, and Sigurd. The sections on
Sigurd, stressing sources used, are the fullest, the romances and
the socialist writings receiving less attention.

10 HOLME, CHARLES, ed. Modern British Domestic Architecture and
    Decoration. London: Studio, p. 84.
         Photographs of hallway in house designed by J. Crouch and E.
Butler, in Warwickshire, that has a frieze of WM's John Ball and
glass windows depicting John Ball and Wat Tyler.

11 KENYON, JAMES B. "WM--Poet, Socialist, and Master of Many
    Crafts." Loiterings in Old Fields: Literary Sketches.   New
    York: Eaton and Mains, pp. 51-81.
         Reprint of 1899.8.

12 LETHABY, WILLIAM. WM as Work Master. London: John Hogg;
    Birmingham: Cornish Brothers, 23 pp.
         A lecture given in Birmingham in October 1901 that outlines
WM's "art-teaching and life," touching upon and quoting from several
of the lectures on the arts and crafts.

13 MACKAIL, J.W. "Morris, William. 1834-1896." DNB Supplement.
    Edited by Sidney Lee. Oxford: Oxford University Press.
    Reprint. 1922, 1938, 1950, 1960, 1964, 1968.
         Biographical summary includes all the significant dates,
persons, achievements, presented with the sure touch one expects
from Mackail, the authorized biographer (1899.10) and son-in-law of
Burne-Jones. Four of the article's twelve columns are devoted to
WM's socialist writings and activities.

14 MACKAIL, J.W. WM. London: National Home Reading Union, 24 pp.
    Reprint. London: Hammersmith Publishing, 1902. Portland, Me.:
    Thomas Mosher, 1902. Folcroft, Pa.: Folcroft Library Editions,
    1974. Norwood, Pa.: Norwood Editions, 1976. Philadelphia: R.
    West, 1977.
         A lecture first given in 1900 to the Hammersmith Socialist
Society, repeated on 15 January 1901 for the London Branch of the
International Labour Party. Sets forth the basic facts of WM's
life, adding "a few words as to what I conceived to be the central
lesson for Socialists which these facts involve." Even though WM
knew by 1887 that a revolution was not imminent, he continued to
preach socialism, to make converts, and Mackail exhorts his

audiences not to despair, to remember that "He that shall endure shall be saved."

15 MORTON, JAMES. WM: An Appreciation. London: Chiswick Press, 47
     pp.
        A lecture given before the XL Club in Glasgow in March 1901,
     with the usual details borrowed from Mackail (1899.10); it stresses
     WM's importance for Morton's own career in textiles and for the
     growth of proper attitudes toward work and art.

16 NORDBY, CONRAD HJALMAR. "By the Hand of the Master." In The
     Influence of Old Norse Literature upon English Literature.
     Columbia University Germanic Studies. New York: Columbia
     University Press, pp. 37-73.
        Briefly discusses the first British writers to borrow from
     Old Norse literature, from Thomas Gray through Scott and Carlyle,
     all this in preparation for the section on WM, who "contributed
     almost as much material to the English treasury of Northern gold as
     did all the writers we have so far considered. Were it not for WM,
     the examination that we are making would not be worthwhile." The
     translations, lyrics in Poems by the Way on Icelandic themes,
     receive much less attention than "Gudrun" and Sigurd, which are
     paraphrased, quoted, highly praised. "After WM the northern strain
     that we have been listening for in the English poets seems feeble."

17 SARGENT, IRENE. "Morris and Company: Decorators." Craftsman 1,
     no. 1 (October):25-32.
        Suggests that Morris and Co. was a success because some of
     that Oxford vision of a brotherhood "against the age" became
     instilled in the Firm, in its workshops. Discusses the wide range
     of the Firm's work, takes WM's side on the controversy which led to
     its reorganization.

18 SARGENT, IRENE. "WM: His Socialist Career." Craftsman 1, no. 1
     (October):15-24.
        Traces the development of WM's socialism from the early work
     with the Eastern Question Association through his editorship of
     Commonweal, suggesting nonetheless that his socialism was of the
     heart rather than the head.

19 SARGENT, IRENE. "WM: Some Thoughts Upon His Life, Work, and
    Influence." Craftsman 1, no. 1 (October):1-14.
        Comments upon WM's significance in literature, in art, in
socialist thought. Biographical sketch dwells on the importance of
Morris and Co. and discusses WM's skills with textiles as colorist
and print designer. Like "Chaucer's Parson, 'first he wrought, and
afterward he taught.'" One point of his teaching was that art and
socialism are indivisible.

20 SARGENT, IRENE. "WM and Burne-Jones." Craftsman 1, no. 1
    (October):39-45.
        Argues that "any record of the life of WM would indeed be
incomplete" without some account of Burne-Jones, and she thus offers
a biographical sketch, pointing out how different his Birmingham
backgrounds were from WM's in a London suburb. Describes the range
and importance of Burne-Jones's art, suggesting that by capturing
him for the decorative arts, WM was able to spread his gifts
democratically.

21 STICKLEY, GUSTAV. Foreword to Craftsman 1, no. 1
    (October):i-ii.
        Introduces premiere issue of Craftsman, organ for the United
Crafts of Eastwood, N.Y., a new association that "has had but one
parallel in modern times," that being Morris and Co. This American
association promises "to promote and to extend the principles
established by Morris, in both the artistic and socialistic sense,"
and this first issue is thus a "criticism and study upon the life
and work of WM."

22 "WM." Library, 2d ser., 2, no. 6 (April):113-19.
        WM was a real expert on medieval manuscripts and incunabula,
and it therefore took him only seven or eight years to amass a
significant collection, in fact one of the best in Britain.
Castigates certain ministers for not acquiring the collection for
the nation; it is now split, one half sold to individuals, the other
half to a Manchester tycoon who would have had it all, except that
he did not like books over thirteen inches in height.

23 "WM, Printer and Collector: Kelmscott Books and Editiones
    Principes by Morris at Auction." Literature 9, no. 204 (14
    September):249.
        Presents a chart which shows that, with the exception of the
Kelmscott Chaucer, Kelmscott Press volumes seem to have diminished
in value between 1899 and 1901. Includes current prices for other
editions of WM's works.

1902

1   CARY, ELISABETH L. "WM in the Making." Critic 41, no. 3
     (September):195-208.
        A detailed biographical sketch attempts to demonstrate the
     truth of the following: WM was a "man of one preoccupation amounting
     to an obsession--the reconstruction of social and industrial life
     according to an ideal based upon the more poetic aspects of the
     Middle Ages." Stresses the significance early on of Rossetti's
     influence on WM.

2   CARY, ELISABETH L. WM: Poet, Craftsman, Socialist. New York
     and London: G.P. Putnam's Sons, 305 pp. Reprint. Folcroft, Pa.:
     Folcroft Library Editions, 1974. Norwood, Pa.: Norwood
     Editions, 1977. Philadelphia: R. West, 1978.
        Since Mackail did the "personal life," this biographer would
     reveal "the man and his work as they appeared to the outer public."
     She does not do this as well as Vallance had done (1897.21).
     Presents some new material from Rossetti letters, but she sees
     Rossetti as a "saving influence" on WM. Has interesting discussions
     of Pilgrims, of WM's work for SPAB, but she says that he had trouble
     with socialism because "he had not a reasoning mind," and moreover
     that the socialist lectures "bear sad witness to the havoc made in
     the aesthetic life of their author." Includes Cockerell's annotated
     list, with "certain slight additions," of Kelmscott Press volumes,
     as well as many illustrations.

3   CHESTERTON, GILBERT K. "WM and His School." In Twelve Types.
     London: Humphreys, pp. 15-26.
        Graceful generalities about WM's significance are undermined
     by questions about his medieval preferences and his writing, which
     is compared to his wallpaper. "His characters, his stories, his
     religion and political views, had, in the most emphatic sense,
     length and breadth without thickness." Reprinted: 1903.2.

4   CORRINGTON, FITZROY, ed. Introduction to The Doom of King
     Acrisius by WM. New York: R.H. Russell, pp. 9-16.
        Recounts the plans for the illustrated edition of Paradise,
     the "book that never was" (Dunlap, 1971.6), and discusses the
     Burne-Jones illustrations completed for this April tale, ways that
     they sometimes follow the classical original rather than WM's
     version. Twelve photographs of the Burne-Jones illustrations are
     reproduced in this handsome edition.

5   DE VINNE, THEODORE LOW. "The Kelmscott Style." <u>Bibliographer</u>
    1, no. 1 (January):1-10.
        Surveys WM's achievements at Kelmscott Press, going into some
    detail regarding typefaces and formats, the effects of spacing,
    abbreviations, page decorations. Concludes that the "great merit of
    the Kelmscott book is in its perfect press-work." Has six
    illustrations.

6   FLETCHER, WILLIAM YOUNGER. "WM, 1834-1896." In <u>English</u> <u>Book</u>
    <u>Collectors</u>. London: Kegan, Paul, pp. 423-27.
        Biographical sketch includes specific information about the
    fine library of incunabula and medieval manuscripts WM acquired
    during the Kelmscott Press years, how that library was purchased by
    a Manchester collector, for 20,000 pounds, who kept only one half
    the manuscripts, one third of the books; the remainder was sold in
    December 1898 by Sothebys for 10,992 pounds. Prices for many of the
    items given.

7   GRAUTOFF, OTTO. "WM." <u>Borsenblatt</u> <u>fur</u> <u>den</u> <u>deutschen</u> <u>Buchhandel</u>
    22 (28 January):849-50.
        Surveys the backgrounds of Morris and Co. and Kelmscott
    Press, and discusses their influence on German design.

8   HAKE, THOMAS. "Aylwin." <u>N</u> <u>and</u> <u>Q</u>, 9th ser., 9 (7 June):450-52.
        Identifies Kelmscott Manor scenes and rooms as transmogrified
    by Watts-Dunton in his <u>Aylwin</u> into Hurstcote. The character,
    Wilderspin, is not modeled on WM, but a certain enthusiastic angler
    is.

9   POMEROY, ELTWEED. "A Visit to the Shop of WM." <u>Craftsman</u> 1,
    no. 5 (August):43-48.
        Recounts a visit to Morris and Co. showrooms on Oxford
    Street, and describes the interior: a few sample goods tastefully
    laid about, chintzes in a rack along the wall, a set of Kelmscott
    Press volumes in a bookcase, rugs and embroideries on the second
    floor.

10 RAE, FRANK B. <u>Those</u> <u>Who</u> <u>Followed:</u> <u>Being</u> <u>a</u> <u>Few</u> <u>Words</u> <u>Upon</u> <u>the</u>
    <u>Recent</u> <u>Renaissance</u> <u>of</u> <u>the</u> <u>Work</u> <u>of</u> <u>Handicrafts</u>. Ridgewood, N.J.:
    Alwil Shop, 7 pp.
        An essay celebrating a new interest in American crafts hails
    WM's influence: "Some dozens of years ago came a man born late, a
    relic of the Middle Ages; a jousting knight let loose in a city of
    pettifoggers; a handicraftsman brought to face the shibboleth
    'labor-saving,' an honest soul in an epoch of thievery." This
    fine-print pamphlet is a reprinting of an essay in a March 1902
    <u>Impressions</u> <u>Quarterly</u>.

11 RIGBY, J. SCARRATT. "Remarks on WM Work and its Influence on
    British Decorative Arts of Today." Art Workers Quarterly 1:2-5,
    61-64.
        Suggests reasons any discussion of decorative arts is
    inevitably tied to WM's name, tracing the growth of his reputation
    and influence from the 1860s down to the end of the century.
    Arguing that his pattern designs have had the greatest influence,
    the author presents detailed descriptions of several of them and
    also comments on stained glass, carpets, and other work of Morris
    and Co.

12 RINDER, FRANK. "Kelmscott Press." Connoisseur 1
    (September-December):258-67, 270.
        Discusses the founding of Kelmscott Press, going into some
    detail about the size of type and the width of margin, judging then
    that such a review is "particularly fitting," since Sothebys had
    just sold eighty-one Kelmscott Press lots from the estate of F.S
    Ellis, WM's publisher and friend for thirty years. Includes a table
    with specific details regarding publishers, numbers of copies, and
    differences between issue price and present price for all Kelmscott
    Press volumes. Most had risen in value.

13 SARGENT, IRENE. "Beautiful Books." Craftsman 2, no. 1
    (April):1-20.
        Conclusion of an essay on beautiful books lauds the
    achievements of WM at Kelmscott Press, the undivided attention he
    gave to every detail of a book's production. Judges the Kelmscott
    Chaucer to be "the noblest book ever printed."

14 TRIGGS, OSCAR L. "WM and His Plea for an Industrial
    Commonwealth." Chapters in the History of the Arts and Crafts
    Movement. Chicago: Bohemia Press, pp. 59-141, passim. Reprint.
    New York: Benjamin Blom, 1971. New York: Arno Press, 1979.
        Stresses how social concerns became wedded to WM's attitudes
    about the arts and crafts, how both Ruskin and WM had contributed to
    the Arts and Crafts Exhibition Society in 1888. Offers details
    about how events turned WM toward socialism, quoting key excerpts
    from letters and lectures.

15 VON SCHLEINITZ, OTTO. "Verkauf der 'WM Bibliothek' an Mr.
    Pierpont Morgan." Zentralblatt fur Bibliothekwesen 19, nos.
    9-10 (September-October):471-74.
        Raises questions about what European libraries should do in
    the face of such American buyers, when "Priese gar keine Rolle
    spielt." Morgan is said to have spent over five million marks for
    these manuscripts and incunabula, some of which are here briefly
    described.

16 YEATS, W.B. Preface to Cuchulaine of Muirthemne. Translated by
    Lady Gregory. London: J. Murray. 4th ed., 1911, pp. xii-xiv.
        Claims that in these translations, "Lady Gregory has
    discovered a speech as beautiful as that of Morris" in the prose
    romances. Recalls a WM visit to Dublin when they spoke of the Irish
    tales; WM contrasted the Norse and Irish accounts of the Battle of
    Clontarf: "the Norsemen had the dramatic temper, and the Irishman
    the lyrical." Reprinted: 1962.36.

1903

1   BELL, MALCOLM. Sir Edward Burne-Jones. London: G. Bell and
    Sons, pp. 74-83, passim.
        Surveys Burne-Jones's friendship and his associations with
    WM; discusses the designs Burne-Jones made for Morris and Co.
    stained glass and textiles. An appendix lists cartoons and
    locations of extant windows designed by Burne-Jones.

2   CHESTERTON, GILBERT K. "WM and His School." In Varied Types.
    New York: Dodd, Mead, pp. 15-26.
        Reprint of 1902.3.

3   DAY, LEWIS FORMAN. "WM and His Decorative Art." Contemporary
    Review 83 (June):787-96.
        WM inherited the mantle of Pugin and Ruskin, but he put his
    own individual stamp on their use of medieval art to critique
    Victorian society, for he personally mastered a number of medieval
    crafts and understood why they could not flourish under modern
    conditions. Surveys WM's successes with designs and dyes drawn from
    nature, with ancient techniques for weaving and embroidery, and
    suggests that his influence shall increase. His Kelmscott Press
    books "attract the artist, but do not invite the reader," and so his
    influence on the book-arts has been indirect.

4   MACKAIL, J.W. The Parting of the Ways: An Address. London:
    Hammersmith Publishing Company, 34 pp.
        Address given in WM Labour Church in Leek, a town where WM
    often visited Thomas Wardle in the 1870s, to learn from him dyeing
    techniques. Mackail quotes from letters WM wrote to London at that
    time, thus leading into his topic which is politics; he makes
    interesting distinctions between liberals and socialists (Greeks and
    Zionists), suggesting that political choice should involve a
    "parting of the ways," advising his audience to "choose
    righteousness," reminding them that WM thought socialism was "a
    belief involving the very noblest ideals of human life and duty."

28

5   PUDOR, HEINRICH. "WM, Kaufman." Gegenwart (Berlin) 64:156-57.
      Contrasts medieval times, when men produced their own goods,
to modern times, when they buy ready-made shoddy. Celebrates WM as
merchant-reformer and suggests that his theories and his work at
Morris and Co. point to alternative strategies for modern craftsmen
and consumers.

6   SHAW, GEORGE BERNARD. "Editor's Note." In Communism by WM.
      Fabian Tract, no. 113. London: Fabian Society, pp. 3-5.
      Discusses the backgrounds of both the SDF and the Socialist
League, asserting that WM had gained so much knowledge of socialism
by 1893 because he had come into conflict with every section of the
movement. Suggests that Fabians were able to make more progress
because they were "more acceptable to a timidly conservative
nation."

7   STRINGER, ARTHUR. "WM as I Remember Him." Craftsman 4, no. 2
      (May):126-32.
      Recalls WM, the man, rather than WM, the artist, poet, and
socialist. Reports that he had once asked WM, at a time when he was
disheartened at the lumpishness of British workers, if he ever
wished he had undertaken social change in America, a "land of new
ideas and new ideals. To this he always shook his head."

8   WILEY, EDWIN. "WM, Master-Craftsman." In The Old and the New
      Renaissance: A Group of Studies in Arts and Letters. Nashville,
      Tenn.: M.E. Church, pp. 169-221.
      A biographical sketch precedes general appreciation of WM's
social aims, but these are presented so as to suggest that WM was a
latent Christian. Repeats errors that appear in Elbert Hubbard's
sketch (1900.8).

9   YEATS, W.B. "The Happiest of Poets." Fortnightly Review 79,
      no. 435 (1 March):535-41.
      Asserts that WM was "the one perfectly happy and fortunate
poet of modern times," for he understood and wrote of well and tree
as "images of the one thing." Says of WM's depiction of scene and
character in the romances, "it is as though Nature spoke through him
at all times in the mood that is upon her when she is opening the
apple blossom," and of his socialism that, "books of economics vexed
and wearied him." WM instead, "knew as Shelley knew, by an act of
faith, that the economists should take their measurements not from
life as it is, but from the vision of men like him." Reprinted:
1912.18, 1968.46.

10 "Notes" [organization of the Morris Society in Chicago].
    Craftsman 4, no. 5 (August):393-94.
        The first meeting of "The Morris Society" was held on 7 May
    1903 in Chicago; it was convened by professors Moulton and Triggs
    and Mr. Twyman. A general program, here reprinted, was adopted at
    the second meeting a week later. Declares that its aim is
    educational, and that it shall maintain club rooms, cafe, library,
    museum.

11 "The Pre-Raphaelite WM." Academy 65 (1 August):111-13.
        WM'S reputation rests on Paradise, and he "stands for
    somewhat dreamy and immeasurably diffuse narrative poetry," but a
    completely different WM is suggested by the poems in Defence, and
    this WM deserves to be better known. To this end, the author
    presents passages from several Defence poems and comments upon their
    vivid imagery and dramatic qualities, and upon their Pre-Raphaelite
    features.

1904

1   BEERBOHM, MAX. The Poet's Corner. London: Heinemann. Reprint.
    London and New York: Penguin Books, 1943, p. 15.
        Briefly commenting on the only two caricatures he drew of WM,
    the artist explains that he had made WM a blond in the earlier
    drawing because he associated him with Viking stock, and upon
    learning the truth, he "wished the error to stand, as an awful
    warning against guess-work by the young." Both drawings appear
    here, in plates 2 and 23.

2   BENSON, ARTHUR C. Rossetti. London: Macmillan, pp. 36-41,
    passim.
        Includes anecdotes about Rossetti's "unscrupulous" sense of
    humor, and also perceptive comments on his strength of will and
    personality first attracting and then repelling WM.

3   BURNE-JONES, GEORGIANA. Memorials of Burne-Jones. London:
    Macmillan, 2 vols., passim.
        Henderson (1967.11) suggested that the actual hero of this
    biography was WM rather than Burne-Jones; it is certainly true that,
    along with Mackail (1899.10) and May Morris's introductions (1910.9)
    to the Collected Works, it is among the essential sources. In 1851,
    Burne-Jones and WM became fast friends as Oxford undergraduates, and
    for forty-five years Burne-Jones's "great pleasure was in the
    society of one with whom no hours were wasted in dispute" since they
    shared so many attitudes about art and life, about work and society,
    about everything except Iceland and the efficacy of direct political
    agitation. Georgie had access to her husband's letters and papers,
    to the diaries of his studio assistant, Thomas Rooke (1981.30), and

to many who knew Burne-Jones and WM well. Her own memories of WM
extended back to 1855; for the period just before she asks, "how can
a woman hope to describe the life of men at college?" But her
descriptions make the Oxford years come to life, and the same is
true for the Red House years; about the aborted plans for the
Burne-Jones family to move into an extension of Red House, she
writes, "it is curious to think how differently all our lives would
have gone if this scheme had been carried out." She does not
elaborate; such hints of marital difficulties in the 1870s have
excited some critics more than other aspects of these gracious and
detailed memoirs of her husband, whose life was truly his work,
whose collaborator on significant projects, from stained glass for
Morris and Co. to the Kelmscott Chaucer, was his greatest friend,
WM.

4   COLWELL, PERCY R., ed.   Introduction to The Poems of WM.   New
     York: Thomas Y. Crowell, pp. xi-xxxiv.
       Many of the facts and anecdotes in the introduction to this
selection of WM's poems, sixty-five in all, are drawn from Mackail
(1899.10), but it is also maintained here that Teutonic legend was a
"dominant force" in WM's life and that his "idea of social reform
was a restoration of the ancient Icelandic folk-rule." Colwell is
likewise wrong in saying there was a third journey to Iceland.
Includes a four-page bibliography, notes, and index.

5   DE LISLE, FORTUNEE.   Burne-Jones.   New York: Dodge Publishing,
     passim.
       Since she recognizes that the biography will "shortly be
forthcoming from the one better qualified than anyone else to write
it" (1904.3), she elaborates only upon the paintings and designs,
and since these often involved collaboration between Burne-Jones and
WM, there are many significant references to the latter.

6   DUNN, HENRY T.   Recollections of Rossetti and His Circle.
     London: Elkins Matthews, pp. 22, 32, passim.
       Includes references to WM as model for figures Rossetti used
in stained-glass cartoons.

7   HEALY, CHRIS.   "WM and Prince Kropotkin."   In Confessions of a
     Journalist.   London: Chatto and Windus, pp. 1-18.
       Recalls seeing WM on a socialist platform in Manchester, of
going with him for "long walks through the slums of Ancoates and
Salford," of WM's eloquent silence. He wrote to WM suggesting that
John Ball might be redone as drama, and WM responded, "You do it."
He admitted to no interest in the tale as drama, only as socialist
doctrine.

8   MEIER-GRAEFE, JULIUS. "WM and His Circle." In <u>Modern Art, Being a Contribution to a New System of Ethics</u>. Stuttgart: J. Hoffmann, 3 vols. Translated by F. Simmonds and G.W. Chrystal. London: Heinemann; New York: G.P. Putnam's Sons, 1908, 2:235-46, passim.

       A biographical sketch that stresses WM's originality, the ways he enriched what he borrowed from the past. Points out that Red House was not so important an influence on architecture as it was on design, since it led to the formation of the Firm, whose work is here discussed in some detail. British artisans and artists had the support of bourgeois wealth to an extent unknown on the Continent, and the development of all the arts was thus more "vigorous" in Britain.

9   MORRIS, MAY. "Decorative Art: 1800-1895." In <u>Social England</u>. Edited by H.D. Trail and J.S. Mann. Vol. 6. London: Cassell and Co., pp. 636-37.

       Comments on the "marked success" of Morris and Co., concluding that its arras tapestries shall probably become the most "enduring decorative works of the century."

*10   MOULTON, RICHARD GREEN. <u>The Poetry and Fiction of WM, A Syllabus of Private Study</u>. Chicago: University of Chicago Press, 33 pp.

       Cited in 1936.3.

11   MUTHESIUS, HERMANN. "Der Innenraum im neunzehnten Jahrhundert: WM, die Entwicklung durch Ihn und neben Ihm." In <u>Das englische Haus</u>. Berlin: Ernst Wasmuth. 2d ed., 1908-11, 3:79- 88, 102-7, passim.

       Discusses the founding of Morris, Marshall, Faulkner Co. and its development and influence on British decoration. Why and how the well-known artists who were part of the original group were significant in the Firm's growth is discussed in some detail, as are the Firm's products, from wallpapers and tapestries to chairs and cabinets. Has many illustrations. Translated: 1979.37.

12   PRINSEP, VAL C. "A Chapter from a Painter's Reminiscences. The Oxford Circle: Rossetti, Burne-Jones, and WM." <u>Magazine of Art</u> 27, n.s. 2:167-72

       Despite Prinsep's professed inability to paint, Rossetti insisted that he take on one of the Arthurian murals being done on the high walls and ceiling of the Oxford Union; here he recalls how he gained confidence about his own painting when he saw WM's: his "details were monstrous," with Tristram and Iseult kissing and Palomides "squatting in one corner looking on." Other anecdotes from those happy days are recounted, and these--like WM with the armour--have often reappeared in subsequent biographies of WM and histories of the Pre-Raphaelites.

13 RADFORD, ERNEST. "Kelmscott Press: The Beginnings of a Great
    Undertaking." Academy 66 (6 February):150-51.
       The writer received from WM one of the first pages pulled
    from the Press; this page, from Plain, is here reproduced, and it
    provides the basis for comments upon WM's painstaking care, his
    "architectural" sensitivity, with regard to producing books.

14 SIEPER, ERNST. "WM, sein kunstlerisches Glaubensbekenntnis.
    Morris' Eigenart als Dichter." In Das Evangelium der Schonheit
    in der englischen Literatur und Kunst des xix. Jahrhunderts.
    Dortmund: F.W. Ruhfus, pp. 339-63.
       Two of thirty lectures given in Munich in 1902-03; the first
    stresses Ruskin's influence on WM's attitudes toward art and
    architecture, and the second discusses correspondences between the
    poetry of Keats and WM.

15 SYMONS, ARTHUR. "WM's Prose." In Studies in Prose and Verse.
    London: J.M. Dent, pp. 91-96.
       Generalizes, gracefully, upon the particular charms of the
    prose romances, upon the "elaborately simple language" of Water; in
    these tales, it is apparent that WM "loved all visible beauty
    indifferently, as a child does." Essay was originally written in
    1897.

16 TWYMAN, JOSEPH. "The Art and Influence of WM." Inland
    Architect and News Record 42, no. 6 (January):43-45.
       Describes a meeting with WM, in 1883, at Merton Abbey, and
    celebrates that place as well as WM's ideas about medieval crafts,
    work, art, and socialism, pointing out that proper political systems
    will not promise freedom from labor, but freedom through labor.
    Originally a lecture given in Chicago in December 1903.

                                  1905

1   COBDEN-SANDERSON, T.J. The Arts and Crafts Movement. London:
    Hammersmith Publishing, pp. 8-14, passim.
       Claims the "honour of being the real author of Kelmscott
    Press," since he had invited Walker to give the famed lantern slide
    lecture which set the imagination and energy of WM free to make
    books. Comments also on a lecture WM gave on textiles, how he
    stressed there, as always, that workers never forget the nature and
    characteristics of their material, that its limitations should be a
    pleasure, not a hindrance, and that they also never forget the
    function of the artifact.

2   CRANE, WALTER. "Of the Arts and Crafts Movement: Its General
     Tendency and Possible Outcome." In Ideals in Art. London: G.
     Bell and Sons, pp. 15, 20, 24.
        Points out that neither WM nor Burne-Jones were among the
original members of the Arts and Crafts Exhibition Society, that
when WM became its president, exhibitions were scheduled every three
years rather than annually. This was originally an address to the
Society.

3   DAY, LEWIS FORMAN. "A Disciple of WM." Art Journal, n.s., 57
     (January):84-89.
        Reports on a visit to Merton Abbey, where WM's influence
abides and where the works continue: "if Morris were to come back
tomorrow, he would find everything practically as he left it," this
largely due to the presence of Mr. Dearle, whose designs are
mentioned here. Includes several illustrations.

4   HUNT, WILLIAM HOLMAN. Pre-Rapaelitism and the Pre-Raphaelite
     Brotherhood. Vol. 2. London: Macmillan, pp. 224, 387, 406. 2d
     ed., 1913.
        Discusses WM as one of a group of "undergraduates" attracted
to Rossetti in the 1850s, enthusiasts impelled by an "archaic spirit
of Gothic times." He is positive about WM's energy and ability as a
designer, and he affirms that Morris and Co. did improve British
tastes in design, but he suggests that the young men at Morris and
Co. had only acted upon ideas that he and Millais had promulgated as
early as 1848.

5   JAMES, GEORGE WHARTON. "WM, the Man." Craftsman 7, no. 4
     (January):412-20.
        Attempts to approach WM from the "human side," and includes
quotes from socialist lectures and Sigurd within a general
biographical sketch.

6   LANG, ANDREW. "Mr. WM's Poems." In Adventures Among Books.
     London: Longmans, pp. 99-117.
        Prefers early romances like "Hollow Land" to socialist works
like Nowhere, the saga translations to the "paraphrastic paraphrase"
of Sigurd. Asserts that the poetic style of Defence was unique and
suggests that it was unfortunate that WM never returned to it.

7   MENZIES, W.G. "The Present Value of the Publications of
     Kelmscott Press." Connoisseur 12 (May-August):42-44.
        Between 1900 and 1903, the prices for Kelmscott Press volumes
     decreased by half, an aggregate set bringing 500 pounds in 1900, 255
     in 1903; even the vellum volumes brought reduced prices. Concludes
     with a table which has a complete record of values for each volume
     from 1892 through March 1895; several of them fell even below their
     issue price.

8   NEVINSON, HENRY. "The Last of Romances." In Books and
     Personalities. London: Lane. Reprint. Freeport, N.Y.: Books
     for Libraries Press, 1968, pp. 66-72.
        General appreciation of WM's last prose romance; after making
     a few useful points, showing that Malory's influence is more
     apparent here than earlier, he attempts to make another point about
     WM's style by spoofing it: "though not by any means the noblest
     piece of the master's work, there is nothing really unked or
     kenspeckle about it."

9   ROWLEY, CHARLES. "WM." In A Workshⴰ   ⴰⴰ ⴰe and Other
     Papers. London: Sherrat and Hughes, ⴰⴰ. ⴰ. ⴰ8.
        Memoir avers that WM "was above all a rare, a gifted, and a
     jolly comrade," one whom the author had gotten to know well because
     WM often lectured at Anscoats; the author also helped to heal the
     breach between WM and Brown, when the latter was doing the murals at
     the Manchester Town Hall.

*10 SCHUTZE, MARTIN, et al. WM Society Bulletin. Chicago: WM
     Society, 71 pp.
        Cited in New York City Public Library Catalogues.

                              1906

1   BARTELS, HEINRICH. WM, "The Story of Sigurd and the Fall of the
     Niblungs"; eine studie uber das verhaltnis der epos zu dem
     quellen. Munster: Buchdruckerei Robert Noske, 86 pp.
        Scholarly discussion of editions of the Eddas and sagas that
     were available to WM followed by tentative evaluations of ways that
     he used these sources, and to what effect, in Sigurd.

2   BENN, ALFRED W. The History of English Rationalism in the
     Nineteenth Century. London: Longmans. Reprint. New York:
     Russell and Russell, 1962. 2:289-93.
          Defines WM's religion as "a simple worship of earth,"
     pointing out that both he and Rossetti separated their medieval
     interests from religion, and thus contributed to a victory for
     rationalism. WM excised "theological accretions" from his medieval
     themes and created a new kind of joyful romantic poetry.

3   BRAUN, LILY. "Eine Traum von WM." Neue Gesellschaft 2, no. 34
     (22 August):405-8.
          Describes conditions for workers at Cadbury's chocolate
     factory, suggesting that WM's dream for all, in Nowhere, is being
     realized for some at this model Birmingham factory complex.

4   BRIGHT, NORMA. "Social Intercourse Among the Pre-Raphaelites."
     Book News Monthly 24, no. 286 (June):691-95.
          In a general discussion of Pre-Raphaelites, of problems the
     young painters had in securing models, the author comments upon the
     "wonderful chance that two of the chief men of the group should come
     to possess as wives women of rarest beauty and charm." Other
     aspects of the "constant coming and going between the homes" of
     Rossetti, Burne-Jones, and WM are discussed.

5   CARY, ELISABETH L. "The Handicraft of the Pre-Raphaelites."
     Book News Monthly 24, no. 286 (June):699-700.
          Mentions furniture at Red Lion Square, how Red House
     decorating led to opening of Morris, Marshall, Faulkner Co. Points
     out how limited were Rossetti's interests in applied design as
     compared to those of WM, whose "reputation as the leader of the
     modern movement in household art was won by magnificent personal
     effort."

6   CLUTTON-BROCK, A. "A Literary Causerie: The Later Poems of
     WM." Academy 71, no. 1792 (8 September):228-29.
          Though many admirers of WM's poetry believe that he, like
     Milton, wasted his talents "upon the bitterness of controversy,"
     they do not realize that a "few poems of Morris' later life are of a
     different order of greatness from anything he wrote while he was
     still content to be only a poet and artist." Quotes from some of
     these later poems, from "Message of the March Wind" and "Mother and
     Son." Reprinted: 1906.7.

7   CLUTTON-BROCK, A. "The Later Poems of WM." Living Age 251, no.
     3251 (27 October):241-45.
         Reprint of 1906.6.

8   DAWSON, WILLIAM J. "WM." In The Makers of English Poetry. New
     York: Revell, 2d ed., pp. 368-79.
         WM called the "third great name," behind Rossetti and
     Swinburne, associated with the revival of romanticism in
     nineteenth-century poetry. Comments upon several of the poems from
     Defence, as "original and powerful," mentions the themes of
     Paradise, and skirts the later poetry entirely.

9   DICKINSON, THOMAS. "WM and Esthetic Socialism." Arena (Boston)
     36, no. 205 (December):613-17.
         Because Ruskin, Tolstoy, and WM were born into wealth, their
     political ideals became linked to art and beauty rather than to
     economic equality; they perceived that people could not appreciate
     beauty because a "system of life in which all endeavor is bent to
     material accumulation has perverted the springs of joy," the
     possibilities for finding joy in the creative and sensible work
     another system might provide. Contrasts Wilde's desires to protect
     art from the people to WM's efforts to create a society where the
     people could enjoy its liberating possibilities.

10   DOUGLAS, JAMES. Theodore Watts-Dunton. New York: Lane, pp.
     170-82.
         Quotes from some of the many reviews Watts-Dunton wrote of
     WM's poetry, from his recollections of WM's indifference to
     criticism. Recalls WM's passion for angling, and suggests that
     between WM and Watts-Dutton there was "an intimacy of the closest
     kind."

11   EDGAR, MADALEN, ed. Introduction to Stories from "Paradise,"
     Retold from WM. London: Harrap, pp. 9-16.
         A general introduction to WM and Paradise precedes prose
     paraphrases of fourteen of the tales. Reprinted 1907, 1908, 1910,
     1912, 1916, 1917, 1919, 1923, 1933.

12   ELTON, OLIVER. Frederick York Powell: A Life. Oxford:
     Clarendon Press. 1:234-37, passim.
         York Powell thought "Gudrun" sentimental, Jason a major
     achievement. Anecdotes are also reported of his visits with WM at
     Merton Abbey, at Hammersmith, the last time just after WM's return
     from Norway in 1896. Recalls then the gathering at Paddington that
     saw the body off to Kelmscott. Quotes from an 1893 letter to W.P.
     Ker on WM's efforts to stop restoration of the spire at St. Mary's
     in Oxford.

13 HUNT, WILLIAM HOLMAN. The Story of the Paintings at the Oxford
    Union Society. Oxford: Oxford University Press, 15 pp.
        Essay has biographical sketches of all the artists and
    descriptions of their paintings; WM's rendition of a scene from the
    Tristram tales was "striking for its bold and decorative
    originality. On its completion he undertook the ornamentation of
    the roof with a novel device, which established at once that in such
    design lay his real strength." Includes large photographs of each
    of the paintings.

14 MAC CLELLAND, NANCY VINCENT. "The Ideal Home of WM." Book News
    Monthly 24, no. 286 (June):701-3.
        Impressions of a visit to Red House, of why it is that "from
    the weather vane on top of the house, formed of Morris's initials
    and the date 1859, everything down to the ground expresses the
    personality of the man for whom it was built." Describes the
    interior also, mentioning items from furniture to frescoes.

15 MACKAIL, J.W. "The Genius of WM." Independent Review 11, no.
    37:51-57.
        To understand WM's genius, we must realize that his central
    purpose was to reintegrate art and life; separated since medieval
    times, "both had gone desperately wrong. Without art life ceased to
    be of value, because it lost the two qualities that make it
    valuable, beauty and happiness. Removed from life, art became
    dead." Argues that WM sought, and created, patterns within
    literature, the arts, society, life itself.

16 MARCH-PHILLIPS, L. "Pre-Rapaelitism and the Present."
    Contemporary Review 89 (May):704-13.
        Recounts aspirations and achievements of members of
    Pre-Raphaelite Brotherhood, in both its phases, concluding that WM
    was the one "who consistently and to the end," through his vigorous
    work in all the crafts, through his teaching about the relationships
    between art, work, and social well-being, maintained the ideal of
    "the living power of art."

17 POLLARD, ALFRED W. Preface to Catalogue of Manuscripts and
    Early Printed Books from the Libraries of WM, Richard Bennett,
    Bertram, 4th Earl of Ashburnham and other Sources, Now Forming
    Portions of the Library of J. Pierpont Morgan. Vol. 1. London:
    Chiswick Press, pp. 7-12.
        Most of the fifteenth-century German books in this collection
    were brought together by WM, and his tastes as a collector are here
    discussed. Some of the descriptions of individual items in this
    sumptuous four-volume catalogue are very full and detailed.

18 ROSSETTI, WILLIAM. <u>Some</u> <u>Reminiscences</u>. New York: Scribners, 2
    vols., pp. 214-18, passim.
        Regards WM "as about the most remarkable man all around--the
most uncommon man--whom I have known." Tells anecdotes about a
brusque WM who delighted in the "chaff" his companions, especially
Rossetti, gave him, and repeats with equanimity a story about
himself which he first encountered in Mackail (1899.10), about WM's
grumbling that he had to put on a "company grin" and go to a wedding
of two people he did not like; William Rossetti was the groom, and
here he remarks, "that WM did not care for either of us (he gave us
as a wedding present a Nuremberg chronicle of 1493) cannot now be
helped." On the controversy surrounding the break-up of Morris,
Marshall, Faulkner and Co., the author has to side with his wife,
Brown's daughter, but he seems reluctant to do so.

19 SPARGO, JOHN. <u>The</u> <u>Socialism</u> <u>of</u> <u>WM</u>. Westood, Mass.: Ariel
    Press, 52 pp.
        Claims that not one of WM's biographers has given proper
attention to his socialist writings, which include his best work.
Discusses the range of WM's contributions to both <u>Justice</u> and
<u>Commonweal</u> and presents facts about Hyndman, the Socialist League,
and the like, drawn from interviews with WM associates like Bax.
Anticipates points made in Arnot (1934.3) and E.P. Thompson
(1955.15).

20 WEYGANDT, CORNELIUS. "Two Pre-Raphaelite Poets: WM and
    Rossetti." <u>Book</u> <u>News</u> <u>Monthly</u> 24, no. 286 (June):687-90.
        Points to similar ways Rossetti and WM used medieval themes
in their poetry. Asserts that <u>Defence</u> poems are of "far finer
stuff" than the narrative poems which WM was to write later.

21 YEATS, W.B. "Literature and the Living Voice." <u>Contemporary</u>
    <u>Review</u> 90, (October):472-82.
        Judges that WM created a new type "because he studied the
earliest printing, the formats of type that were made when men saw
their craft with eyes that were still new, that were without the
restraints of commerce and custom." Makes an interesting point
regarding the supposed influence of Chaucer on WM, especially on
<u>Paradise</u>: if WM had read aloud his poetry to the audiences of
average men to whom he later taught socialism, then "he would have
been forced to Chaucer's variety." Reprinted: 1962.37.

22 "Pre-Raphaelitism in Outline: WM, the Mechanical Genius of the
   Movement." Book News Monthly 24, no. 286 (June):696-98.
      Includes biographical sketches of major Pre-Raphaelite
figures, and of WM; why WM is called a "mechanical genius" remains
unclear.

1907

1   AGRESTI, ANTONIO. "Artisti e decoratori: WM e Crane." Nuova
    antologia, 5th ser., 137 (16 December):621-35.
       Biographical sketch lingers over the associations WM had with
Crane, the illustrations the latter did for Socialist pamphlets and
also for Kelmscott Press. Publication of the Kelmscott Chaucer
discussed in some detail.

2   ALLINGHAM, WILLIAM. A Diary. Edited by H. Allingham and D.
    Redford. London: Macmillan, pp. 140-43, passim. Reprint.
    Carbondale: Southern Illinois University Press, 1967.
       Recalls overnight visits to Red House, the elaborate plans WM
and Burne-Jones had for "Cupid and Psyche." Judges that their work
in general "might perhaps be called a New Renaissance." Fewer
references to WM in later years, though Tennyson's assertion upon
hearing of WM's socialism, that "he has gone crazy," is here
reported.

*3 BIEBER, ARTHUR. "Studien zu WM's Prose Romances."
    Dissertation, University of Greifswald.
       Cited in 1968.25.

4   CRANE, WALTER. An Artist's Reminiscences. New York: Macmillan,
    pp. 249-74, 325-28, passim.
       Suggests that modern urban squalor, contrasts between the
wealthy and the poor, drove WM to adopt socialist causes, that his
clearheaded convictions allowed him to convert many to the cause,
among them Crane himself. Includes interesting anecdotes,
respectful references to WM's positions on art, politics, and
education.

5   HUBBARD, ELBERT. WM Book. East Aurora, N.Y.: Roycrofters, 67
    pp.
       Duplicates, except for a few omissions, the same curious and
erroneous assertions and anecdotes found in 1900.8. But here there
are also appended seven letters that WM had sent to an American,
Robert Thompson, about his essential beliefs in socialism and
reasons for his dissatisfaction with politicos like Hyndman.

6   JAMES, M.R. Preface to Manuscripts and Early Printed Books from
    the Libraries of WM, Richard Bennett, Bertram, 4th Earl of
    Ashburnham and Other Sources, Now Forming Portions of the
    Library of J. Pierpont Morgan. Vol. 3. London: Chiswick Press,
    pp. 9-11.
        Discusses the manuscripts cataloged in this volume, pointing
out that "almost all of the very best examples were at one time in
the possession of WM."

7   MACKAIL, J.W. WM and His Circle. Oxford: Clarendon Press, 22
    pp. Reprint. Folcroft, Pa.: Folcroft Press, 1969. New York:
    Haskell House, 1971. Folcroft, Pa.: Folcroft Library Editions,
    1973. Norwood, Pa.: Norwood Editions, 1977.
        Invites an Oxford audience to imagine how Oxford appeared to
WM and Burne-Jones when they first arrived, in 1853, as
undergraduates. Discusses the probable influences of that
essentially medieval Oxford on WM's later achievements, especially
at Morris and Co. Talks of WM's poetry in terms of hope and
courage, of the fellowship needed to nourish both art and society.
A lecture given at Oxford Examination Schools, 6 April 1907.

8   MAYNADIER, G.H. The Arthur of the English Poets. Cambridge,
    Mass.: Harvard University Press, pp. 356-63. Reprint. New
    York: Haskell House, 1966.
        Discusses title poem of Defence, pointing out how faithful
its themes are to those in Malory, except that Guenevere has lost
her queenly composure and Gawain has become her accuser. Suggests
that this depiction of Gawain influenced Tennyson's. Comments on
the other three Arthurian poems in Defence, concluding with praise
for WM's vivid medieval portraits.

9   MELLOR, WILLIAM. "A Pilgrimage to Kelmscott." Bookbinding
    Trades Journal, nos. 15-16:231-32, 243-45
        Recollects hearing WM lecture in Manchester to
"half-incredulous work folk," and surmises that such outdoor
activities shortened his life. Recalls a visit, made in 1905, to
Kelmscott and decribes the village, the church, the manor itself,
borrowing passages from WM's own writings to do so.

10 NOYES, ALFRED. Introduction to The Early Romances of WM in
    Prose and Verse. London: J.M. Dent; New York: E.P. Dutton, pp.
    xi-xx.
        Recounts the usual biographical facts, stressing the
importance for his romantic imagination of WM's childhood
experiences, saying that "he turned to the Middle Ages not as a mere
aesthete seeking an anodyne, but as a child turns to fairyland."
Edition includes the Defence poems as well as the Oxford and
Cambridge Magazine prose tales, which "represent something new and

bold in English literature." Reprinted in 1910, 1913, 1920, 1925.
Noyes's introduction and the prose tales make up 1976.36.

11 PAYNE, WILLIAM MORTON. "WM." In Greater English Poets of the
    Nineteenth Century. New York: Henry Holt, pp. 316-47.
        Celebrates the "mastery" achieved by WM in poetry and in the
arts and crafts, commenting upon the "sincere reproduction of the
manner" of the Middle Ages in Defence, upon the "cast of melancholy"
that hovers over the Paradise tales, upon the importance of Iceland
and its ancient stories to "Gudrun" and Sigurd and also to the
development of WM's attitudes about self and society. Discusses the
Eastern Question Association and SPAB in terms of the growth of WM's
socialism.

12 SMITH, ARNOLD. "Neo-Romanticism: WM." In The Main Tendencies
    of Victorian Poetry: Studies in the Thought and Art of the
    Greater Poets. London: Simpkin, Marshall, Hamilton and Kent;
    Birmingham: St. George, pp. 196-208.
        Compares WM to Chaucer, pointing out why he lacked his
master's powers, especially of characterization. Claims that WM's
best poetry is in Defence, because of its specific and convincing
pictures of medieval life, that all the other poetic narratives are
too drawn-out and vague. Concludes that WM will therefore be
remembered as a prose writer rather than as a poet.

13 VON SCHLEINITZ, OTTO. "WM: Sein Leben und Wirken." Zeitschrift
    fur Bucherfreunde 11, nos. 1-4 (April-July):27-44, 59-78,
    107-24, 146-65.
        Lavishly illustrated biographical article, one with the usual
details and anecdotes borrowed from Mackail (1899.10), but with an
emphasis given to WM the artist and his associations with other
artists; there are thus very full accounts of the early painted
furniture, of Rossetti's influence, of Morris and Co. designs by
Burne-Jones for tapestries and stained glass, and of Crane's
socialist cartoons. Given the audience of bibliophiles, relatively
little on Kelmscott Press.

14 "WM." In A Child's Socialist Reader. London: Twentieth Century
    Press, pp. 41-45.
        A biographical sketch, aimed at an audience of children,
stresses WM's love of beautiful things and his consequent desire for
a different society, where "it would be possible for the people to
live a beautiful life." Includes quotations from the socialist
lectures and illustrations by Crane.

1908

1   ASHBEE, CHARLES. Craftsmanship in Competitive Industry.
    London: Essex House Press, pp. 5, 194, passim.
        This record of over twenty years of the experiences of the
    Guild House workshops often refers to WM, to points from his
    lectures, and to his "titanic energy," which always served as an
    inspiration to Ashbee and his followers.

2   BENSON, ARTHUR C. "Kelmscott and WM." In At Large. New York
    and London: G.P. Putnam's Sons, pp. 240-63.
        A rapturous description of an April visit, probably in 1907,
    to Kelmscott Manor, in which Benson tries to bring village and manor
    into line with preconceptions drawn from Rossetti's letters. A
    grumpy gardener bars entry to the manor, so Benson quotes several
    passages from Nowhere and then blames WM's untimely death on all
    those outdoor speeches he gave in inclement weather.

3   BIRKEDAL, UFFE. WM og han Betydning, en Levnetsskildring [WM
    and his significance: A biographical description]. Copenhagen:
    S. Bernsteen, 29 pp.
        In Danish. Biographical sketch hits all the high points of
    WM's life and achievements, stressing how and why socialism was
    knitted into his art. Includes a short bibliography and several
    woodcuts of WM's various homes.

4   BROOKE, STOPFORD A. "WM." In Four Victorian Poets. London:
    Duckworth; New York: Pitman, pp. 205-99. Reprint. New York:
    Russell and Russell, 1964.
        Compares WM to Keats: poets who worshipped Nature, who
    rejected the present, who wrote "pure romantic poetry." Discusses
    several of the Defence poems, where WM proved himself a "young eagle
    flushing his wings." Discursive comments, sprawling huzzahs, on
    Paradise, Sigurd, and the prose romances, which are seen as WM's
    solace from the sordid streets where he preached socialism, are
    often interesting. Claims that Icelandic sagas "suited his autumn
    character," that "living in these stories nursed the modern
    revolutionist in Morris."

5   DURRANT, WILLIAM SCOTT. "The Influence of WM." Westminster
    Review 169, no. 5 (May):542-49.
        Detects a general change in popular attitudes to "beauty and
    grace as educative and ennobling forces," and suggests this change
    due in part to WM, who "infused new life and soul into handicraft,"
    who also "gloried in the assertion of public right over any form of
    private greed; he felt that every museum, garden, or simple public
    pleasure helped to bridge the gap between rich and poor."

6   JACKSON, HOLBROOK. WM: Craftsman, Socialist. Vol. 3 in Social
    Reformers Series. London: Fifield, 59 pp. Reprint. Folcroft,
    Pa.: Folcroft Library Editions, 1974. Norwood, Pa.: Norwood
    Editions, 1976, 1979. Philadelphia: R. West, 1977.
        This short study, the third volume of the Social Reformers'
Series, stresses the connections between WM's craftsmanship and his
politics. The early chapters make the customary points, many drawn
from Mackail (1899.10), but the later chapters have useful
definitions of socialism, discussions of ways WM molded ideology to
earlier convictions about medieval art, guilds, the ideas of Ruskin.
Why WM was against both anarchists and Fabians is neatly stated
here, and John Ball is called the "great parable of English
Socialism." This book anticipates both Arnot (1934.3) and E.P.
Thompson (1955.15). Revised: 1926.6.

7   LATOUCHE, PETER. "WM: Artist, Poet, and Anarchist." In
    Anarchy!: An Authentic Exposition of the Methods of Anarchists
    and the Aims of Anarchism. London: Everett and Co., pp. 187-90.
        WM'S socialist ideals made to fit within what purports to be
an impartial investigation of anarchism, and Nowhere said to be the
"sanest, fullest, most comprehensive and most courageous exposition
of Anarchism in this or any other language."

8   MARKS, JEANETTE. "The Beautiful for the People." South
    Atlantic Quarterly 7, no. 2 (April):143-54.
        A celebration of WM's commitment to socialism; no matter what
one thinks of his poetry, of his wallpaper, romances, or political
economy, "as one watches him fighting for the right, for the
beautiful, for peace, one's admiration for the man becomes
unbounded." She laments that there still remains "a system which
brings to operatives food, clothing, poorish lodgings, and a little
leisure, and to capitalists enormous riches," but she goes on to
suggest that merely preaching about art and beauty will bring about
politcal change.

9   NOYES, ALFRED. WM. English Men of Letters Series. London:
    Macmillan, 164 pp. Reprint. 1914, 1921, 1926. New York:
    Benjamin Blom, 1971. Freeport, N.Y.: Books for Libraries Press,
    1972.
        Accuses Mackail (1899.10) of including too many "niggling
details" and useless anecdotes. He promises to stress only the
"essential factor" of WM's career, which is, he insists,
"undoubtedly, the poetic spirit in him." Compares WM's poetry to
that of Keats and Tennyson, in ways unflattering to WM; offers other
comparisons which are sometimes bizarre: "Gudrun" is like King Lear,
and Sigurd is a greater epic than Paradise Lost. Noyes is critical
of WM's politics, calling socialism a "system which, literally,
means the substitution of death for life." This bias is reflected
in the fact that he devotes less than a paragraph to John Ball,

thirty pages to Jason; of Nowhere, he says "there is no more
hopelessly illogical book in the language," that its characters are
"limply organized creatures who moon along through the story in a
sensuous mist of complete selfishness."

10 PENNELL, E.R., and PENNELL, J. The Life of James McNeill
    Whistler. London: Heinemann. 5th ed., 1911, pp. 85, passim.
         Avers that Whistler's insistence that walls be merely painted
    with flat color had "the virtue of utility and cheapness which
    Morris forever preached but never practiced." Quotes an unfavorable
    contemporary reaction to Whistler's Nocturnes, one that compares
    them to WM's wallpapers.

11 PHELAN, ANNA AUGUSTA VON HELMHOLTZ. "The Social Ideals of WM."
    Dissertation, University of Wisconsin.
        Revised for publication: 1927.7.

12 VALLANCE, AYMER. Some Examples of Merton Abbey Tapestries.
    London: Morris and Co., 25 pp.
         With useful details about techniques, about specific
    tapestries--many of which are here reproduced in both black and
    white and color illustrations--the author introduces a sampling of
    Merton Abbey tapestries, concluding that in the twelve years since
    WM's death, "there has been not only no falling away, but no
    departure from the founder's tradition."

                                1909

1   ASHBEE, CHARLES. The Private Press: A Study in Idealism.
    Chipping Camden: Essex House Press, pp. 4-5.
         Discusses the origins of Kelmscott Press, stressing the links
    between it and Essex House Press, their common cencerns for fine
    craftmanship.

2   BAYNE, THOMAS. "WM and a Scotch Verger." N and Q, 10th ser.,
    11 (20 February):144.
         Points out why an anecdote about a Scots verger in the Noyes
    biography (1908.9) must be in error.

3   BINZ, GUSTAV. "WM als Buchdrucker." Gutenberg
    Gesellschaft-Jahresbericht 8:51-70.
        Sketches in biographical backgrounds; offers detailed
comments about Kelmscott Press typefaces, the books which used each
of them. Discusses decorations employed in initials and on borders
and the ways these affect readability. Comments also upon Kelmscott
Press influence on several German presses.

4   CAINE, HALL. My Story. New York: D. Appleton and Co., pp.
    50-51, passim.
        Asserts that Janey was the "purest" of influences on
Rossetti. Includes fresh anecdotes of WM declaiming verses from
Paradise to an empty garden at Rossetti's Cheyne Walk residence.

5   DODDS, T.L. "WM: Handicraftsman, Socialist, Poet, and
    Novelist." Proceedings of the Liverpool Philomathic Society
    55:52-80.
        Parades through the usual biographical anecdotes, many of
them drawn from Mackail (1899.10), but there are several mistakes,
and he is misleading about WM's socialism. Provides paraphrases of
the narrative poems and of the prose romances, asserts that WM's
"robust and anti-morbid" writings offer "a corrective to the
introspective sentimentality of much present-day literature."

6   GUYOT, EDOUARD. L'idee socialiste chez WM. Paris: Arthur
    Rousseau, 129 pp.
        Briefly surveys the state of socialism in England in 1882,
the reasons WM joined the SDF and then left it, and the nature of
his later socialist work. Points out that WM mediated between the
heart of Ruskin and the reason of Marx, that Anatole France admired
Nowhere, and that all modern generations must be thankful WM had
such aspirations to improve society.

7   MAGNUS, LAURIE. "WM, 1834-1896." In English Literature in the
    Nineteenth Century: An Essay in Criticism. London: Melrose; New
    York: G.P. Putnam's Sons, pp. 321-25.
        Has useful, general comments about Rossetti's influence on
WM, which waned when the latter became a "propagandist."

8   MORE, P.E. "WM." Nation 88, no. 2280 (11 March):243-46.
        Uses Noyes's English Men of Letters biography (1908.9) to
reflect upon WM's life and achievements, offering the usual survey
but also pondering upon other matters, like the youths who wrote for
the Oxford and Cambridge Magazine, lamenting "the absence of those
little societies in our American universities. How utterly lonely
and unhelped is the path of many college men." Makes rather
disparaging comments about Paradise and Sigurd and of WM's "sense

for moral values," called "rudimentary." Reprinted, with some minor
additions: 1910.8.

9   MUIR, M.M. PATTISON.   "The Prose Romances of WM." Oxford and
    Cambridge Review 7 (Midsummer Term):37-60.
        Discourses upon WM's prose romances, paraphrasing them and
quoting at great length those passages which deal with universal
themes of love and joy, of sorrow and righteous battle, and the
like. Praises WM's narrative skills, characterizing his prose as a
"delicate robe of many colours." More appreciation here than
analysis.

10 WATTS-DUNTON, THEODORE.   "Rossettiana: A Glimpse of Rossetti and
    WM at Kelmscott." English Review 1 (January):323-32.
        Recalls visiting Rossetti at Kelmscott Manor and listening to
him speak about WM's mannerisms and appearance: his eyes are "very
little--blue-grey--but they see everything."

11 "Anarchistische Portraits: WM." Der Anarchist 1:14-16.
        Biographical sketch, misleading when it celebrates WM's
anarchistic tendencies without mentioning his distaste for actual
anarchists.

12 "The Vision of WM." Current Opinion 46, no. 5 (May):515-18.
        Asserts that in the thirteen years since WM's death, "his
name and fame have gone to the ends of the earth. Two pretentious
biographies and a small library of lesser studies have been devoted
to his career." Discusses the high points of three of these lesser
works: books by Noyes (1908.9), Jackson (1908.6), and Spargo
(1906.19), concluding that "socialism undoubtedly betrayed Morris
into a good deal of slip-shod journalism," but it did not mar his
poetry.

                              1910

1   ASHBEE, CHARLES.   "Man and the Machine: The Pre-Raphaelites, and
    Their Influence upon Life." House Beautiful 27
    (February):75-77; (March):101-4, 112.
        Argues that the Pre-Raphaelites, though a small group of men,
"powerfully irradiated English life" and that their influence was
due largely to Morris and Co. products.

2   BUCHHORN, WILHELM. WM's Odyssee Ubersetzung. Konigsberg: Karg
     and Monneck, 66 pp.
         Tests Mackail's suggestion (1899.10) that WM's translation of
the Odyssey is good enough to become the standard English version by
examining carefully the diction, especially the repetitions and the
epithets. Reviews problems of turning Greek meter into Germanic,
presents lists of WM's formulas, and discusses his artistry; WM's
version is preferred to both Chapman's and Pope's.

3   CHAPMAN, EDWARD MORTIMER. "The Doubters and the Mystics." In
     English Literature in Account with Religion, 1800-1900. Boston
     and New York: Houghton Mifflin, pp. 450-54.
         WM is placed within this study of Christian influences in
literature because "his overmastering zeal as a champion of the
oppressed, a reformer of bad industrial conditions, and a social
revolutionist brought him into vital touch with essential
religion." Asserts that "The Message of the March Wind" echoes the
teachings of Christ.

4   DE BOM, EMMANUEL. WM en zijn invloed op het boek [WM and his
     work with the book]. Amsterdam: Ipenbuur and van Seldam, 55 pp.
         In Dutch. A biographical sketch and a discussion of WM and
the book arts, one that includes the standard facts and anecdotes
about the establishment of Kelmscott Press, the three typefaces cut
by Prince, the quality of the influence the Press exerted on private
presses in Britain and America and on the Continent. Includes ten
plates.

5   HUEFFER, FORD MADOX. "An Old Circle." Harper's Monthly
     Magazine 120 (February):364-72.
         Anecdotes about WM's boisterous ways and frank language are
used to exemplify the point that among the inner circle of those who
"fathered and sponsored the Aesthetic Movement there was absolutely
nothing of the languishing. They were to a man rather burly,
passionate creatures, extraordinarily romantic and most impressively
quarrelsome." Reprinted, with additions: 1911.6.

6   LLOYD, HENRY DEMAREST. "A Day With WM." In Mazzini and Other
     Essays. London and New York: G.P. Putnam's Sons, pp. 42-70.
         Generalizes about revolutionaries who also managed to make
money in the mercantile world, quoting rather haphazardly from Shaw
and others, suggesting that WM was a disciple not only of Ruskin but
also of Wordsworth, Byron, Mazzinni, Wagner, and Millet. The
original version was a lecture to the Chicago Literary Club, 7
December 1896.

7   MACKAIL, J.W. <u>WM</u>. London: Longmans, 29 pp. Reprint. Folcroft,
     Pa.: Folcroft Library Editions, 1974. Norwood, Pa.: Norwood
     Editions, 1976. Philadelphia, Pa.: R. West, 1977.
          Twisting in anecdotes gracefully, Mackail speaks of the many
     links WM had with Birmingham, where this lecture was originally
     given. Discusses WM's growth as a poet, pointing out that <u>Sigurd</u> is
     among "the noblest of English poems," for themes of courage and hope
     therein show the way "toward fellowship." Reprinted: 1926.9.

8   MORE, P.E. "WM." In <u>Shelburne</u> <u>Essays</u>. New York and London:
     G.P. Putnam's Sons, pp. 95-118.
          Reprint of 1909.8. Adds passages from Noyes (1908.9) and
     Pater and a two page conclusion that comments upon WM's prose and
     socialist activities as aspects of his work not to be taken "quite
     seriously." Judges <u>Nowhere</u> to be "merely funny, if it were not
     tiresome" and Rossetti to be more generous, more noble than WM.

9   MORRIS, MAY, ed. Introductions to <u>Collected</u> <u>Works</u>. London:
     Longmans, 24 vols. Reprint. New York: Russell and Russell,
     1966.
          These introductions are much richer than those that usually
     grace literary editions, since May Morris worked closely with her
     father on many of his projects and shared the same wide circle of
     friends and acquaintances. She did embroidery for Morris and Co.,
     she was active in the Hammersmith Socialist Society, and after his
     death she was protective of his reputation and of the causes he had
     been identified with. She of course also speaks with unique
     authority about the family, and these introductions are particularly
     valuable for personal contexts woven around each work, as May Morris
     recalls her father speaking about a given poem, or working up a
     certain lecture, or putting aside one job to take up another.
     Quotes extensively from previously unpublished letters, from early
     drafts of manuscripts, and the like. Each volume has a useful
     "Bibliographical Note," which lists the publishing history of works
     within that volume. These twenty-four volumes were supplemented by
     1936.9, and the introductions have been reprinted and published
     separately in two volumes: 1973.9.

10   SAINTSBURY, GEORGE. "The Pre-Raphaelite School: WM." In <u>A</u>
     <u>History</u> <u>of</u> <u>English</u> <u>Prosody</u>. London: Macmillan, 3:316-34.
          Suggests that the great popularity of <u>Jason</u> and <u>Paradise</u>
     tended to lower WM's reputation as a serious poet, and that this is
     extremely unfortunate, since "for variety and idiosyncracy of
     important meters, and for management of that variety, WM was quite
     exceptionally noteworthy." Surveys corpus of WM's poetry, giving
     special attention to "The Wind" and "The Blue Closet," to the meters
     of <u>Paradise</u> and <u>Sigurd</u>. Concludes that WM's prosody has both
     "extreme beauty intrinsically" and real historical interest, and he
     therefore hopes that terms like "Wardour-Street English" will soon

be discarded, that WM's poetry will again receive the serious attention it deserves.

11 SINCLAIR, WILLIAM. "Socialism According to WM." Fortnightly
     Review 90 (October):723-35.
         Attempts to define WM's brand of socialism by reviewing the important events and achievements in his life, from the days of the Brotherhood at Oxford to the disappointment of Bloody Sunday, an event that turned WM into a "passive socialist." Concludes that WM remained the "greatest man the Socialist movement has yet claimed."

*12 SWINBURNE, ALGERNON CHARLES. Letters on WM, Omar Khayyam and
     Other Subjects of Interest. London: Privately printed, 31 pp.
         Cited in 1936.3.

13 TAYLOR, G.R.S. "WM." In Leaders of Socialism, Past and
     Present. New York: Duffield, pp. 110-18.
         Biographical sketch, with high praise for WM's work as a socialist: "his teaching carried the theories of the movement to a further point of thought than any other of the Master-Socialists had reached." That point involves work, the idea that it yield pleasure rather than more and cheaper products.

14 THOMPSON, TOLLEF B. "Beitrage zur Entstehungsgeschicte des
     Paradise." Germanisch-Romanische Monatsschrift 2, no. 4:505-9.
         Discusses possible sources and parallels for Paradise tales; tries to locate what parts of Europe both tales and tellers might have come from.

15 THOMPSON, TOLLEF B. Skandinavischer Einfluss auf WM in den
     ersten Stadien, "Paradise". Berlin: G. Schade, 106 pp.
         A detailed discussion of the Scandinavian tales and analogues that WM might have known and used for the Paradise poems, "The Land East of the Sun and West of the Moon" and "The Fostering of Aslaug." Similar scrutiny given to Laxdaela Saga, the source for "Gudrun."

16 VILLIERS, BROUGHAM. The Socialist Movement in England. London:
     T. Fisher Unwin, pp. 108-12, 260.
         Suggests that because the "whole doctrinairre side of current socialism was totally alien to him," because he brought aesthetic criteria to bear, "WM was the greatest personality that has ever been connected with Socialism in England, and perhaps in the Modern World."

17 WM: Some Books and Periodicals in the Cleveland Public Library.
    Cleveland: Cleveland Public Library, 16 pp.
        Lists dozens of titles of both primary and secondary works,
including articles, held by the Cleveland Public Library. The
fourth category, "Critical Estimates," has six subcategories and
includes over one hundred items, all of which are included in the
present book.

                                1911

1   BARTON, J.E. "The WM Note." Saturday Review 111, no. 2902 (10
    June):708-10.
        Praises WM's poetic gifts, calling him a "skillful and rapid
craftsman." Questions his optimism about social change and his
turning to the past for standards of beauty.

2   BURDON, CHARLES. "Kelmscott Press Type." N and Q, 11th ser., 4
    (28 October):345, (25 November):435-36.
        Points out that required registration of typefaces offers
only limited protection, that several British and American firms
have copied WM types, and that a leading American foundry has also
produced WM borders and initials. Includes a description of a
technique for copying type from a "grown" matrice.

3   BURGESS, JOSEPH. John Burns: The Rise and Progress of a Right
    Honourable. Glasgow: Reformers' Bookstall, pp. 15, 102.
        WM seen selling Justice at curbsides, standing bail for
socialist colleagues, and speaking at the funeral of Linnell.
Includes fresh details about police tactics at Trafalgar Square
Riot.

4   CRANE, WALTER. "WM and His Work." In WM to Whistler, Papers
    and Addresses on Art and Craft and the Commonweal. London: G.
    Bell and Sons, pp. 3-46, passim.
        A general appreciation of WM's ideas about Art, why it must
be made available to all, for both the good of art and the body
politic. Crane's attitudes about education, making it manual and
applied instead of ceremonial, are close to those of WM. Sardonic
attacks on Bellamy accompany accolades for Nowhere.

5   HENDERSON, ARCHIBALD. George Bernard Shaw: His Life and Works,
     A Critical Biography. London: Hurst and Blackett; Cincinnati:
     Stewart and Kidd, pp. 205-12, passim.
          Comments upon Shaw's pleasure when he found out that WM
     admired An Unsocial Socialist and the essay on Nordau. Even though
     Shaw and WM ended up at opposite ends of the socialist movement,
     they remained good friends; Shaw often spoke at the Hammersmith
     Socialist Society, and WM even checked his disdain for all dramatic
     productions just long enough to attend one of Shaw's plays. The
     same material, with some additions, appears in Henderson's
     subsequent books on Shaw (1932.8 and 1956.5).

6   HUEFFER, FORD MADOX. Ancient Lights and Certain New
     Reflections. London: Chapman and Hall, pp. 119-21, passim.
     Published in America as Memories and Impressions: A Study in
     Atmospheres. New York: Harpers, 1911.
          An irreverent, and unreliable, account of many Pre-Raphaelite
     personalities, one which consistently sneers at WM's socialism but
     which also has memorable lines: WM "dragged across the way of
     Aestheticism the red herring of socialism." Includes a sensible
     account of the dissolution of the Firm; first appeared in 1910.5.

7   HYNDMAN, H.M. "WM." The Record of an Adventurous Life. London
     and New York: Macmillan, pp. 319-36, passim.
          Recalls his surprise when WM, a man of such "remarkable
     capacities," obviously not the usual type recruited by the SDF,
     decided to leave his "library and studio and workshop for the
     crowded meeting and the rough and tumble gathering at the street
     corner." Has fresh anecdotes about WM's strong memory for
     geographical details and historical dates, discusses his own chagrin
     when WM left the SDF, causing a lasting split that set socialism
     back twenty years, which he calls a "national disaster." Disclaims
     any responsibility for that split, indicating he has correspondence
     that would demolish WM's "contentions both personal and political."
     But such correspondence was never released.

8   JACKSON, HOLBROOK. "The Ideas of WM." Bookman 39
     (February):226-29.
          Insists that to understand WM we must comprehend how his
     activities as artist, poet, and craftsman merge in "Morris the
     socialist," and how design is a key concept: the design of life
     itself.

9 LUBBOCK, PERCY. "The Poetry of WM." Quarterly Review 215, no. 429 (October):482-504.

Praises May Morris's introductions (1910.9) to the Collected Works, especially for the new insights that they provide into WM's poetry and decorative arts. Comments upon the raw dramatic power in several of the Defence poems, a quality not present in the later work; our literature "might have lost a great dramatist." Contrasts WM to Chaucer in a discussion of the pilgrims who tell their tales in Paradise, and insists that "Gudrun" marks a significant transition in the series of tales; Iceland's influence has asserted itself, and the "honey-tongued story-teller" has disappeared, because WM has now moved from romance to epic. Briefer comments on Sigurd and Love Is Enough conclude this useful and detailed survey.

10 MARILLIER, H.C. A Brief Sketch of the Morris Movement and of the Firm Founded by WM to Carry Out His Designs and the Industries Revived. London: Privately Printed, 64 pp.

A concise introduction to all aspects of decorative arts undertaken by Morris and Co., still going strong when this sketch was written. Suggests that the "Morris Movement" actually began in 1853 when WM met Burne-Jones at Oxford, and offers the usual details about Red House and the beginnings of the Firm, but there are fresh points made about techniques used at Merton Abbey.

11 ROWLEY, CHARLES. "WM." In Fifty Years of Work without Wages. New York and London: Hodder and Stoughton, pp. 129-39.

Judges WM to have been the "most all-round gifted man of the nineteenth century" and recalls lectures he gave in Manchester and his reconciliation there with Brown, when the latter was painting the murals at the Town Hall. Includes other anecdotes about WM at Kelmscott Manor and diatribes he heard WM deliver about the restoration of ancient buildings.

12 SHINN, CHARLES HOWARD. "The Ideals of WM." Public 14 (14 April):355-56.

Laments that many of WM's books, mainly the prose romances, are out of print, finding this sad because these tales of struggle and fellowship could now inspire those who must fight for social reconstruction.

13 STEELE, ROBERT. "The Revival of Printing: Kelmscott Press." Academy 81 (18 November):639-41.

Mentions the ways commercial considerations led to inferior printing in the nineteenth century. Discusses the appeal Chiswick Press typefaces had for WM, and the background of the founding of Kelmscott Press. Goes into detail about sources for WM's decorative motifs for Kelmscott Press books, especially the Kelmscott Chaucer.

Argues that "in all essentials and in many particulars" Kelmscott
Press books were unique in their time.

14   THOMAS, EDWARD. "WM." Bookman 39 (February):219-26.
         Reflects upon the first four volumes of the Collected Works
     and also upon the oft-used comparison of WM to Chaucer, saying that
     they are actually quite different since Chaucer merges with his age
     and WM--like many modern poets--stands in isolation. Morris the
     man, "himself a poem," shall outlive his poetry.

15   VIDALENC, GEORGES. "Les idees de WM." Mercure de France
     92:5-21.
         Discusses WM's credo about art arising from pleasure in work
     and traces it back to Keats and Ruskin. Extensive commentary upon
     Morris and Co. origins, philosophy, and products concludes with
     comments upon the Firm's influence in France and with the point that
     WM made precise and practical what was vague and theoretical in
     Ruskin.

16   "Modern Developments in Ballad Art." Edinburgh Review 213
     (January):158-79.
         Discusses the imagery in several poems from Defence, linking
     their "unison of tone" to that found in ballads.

17   "The Influence of Kelmscott Press." TLS, no. 507 (28
     September):345-46.
         Sets forth the principles of fine printing espoused by WM,
     how he typically discovered them by going "at once to the root of
     his craft." Uses recently published books as examples of those
     principles, discussing, among others, books from Doves, Ashendene,
     Clarendon, and Florence presses.

                              1912

1   BYRON, MAY C. [Gillington]. A Day with WM. London: Hodder and
     Stoughton, 38 pp.
         Follows WM through a typical June day in 1879; he works for
     three hours at his loom, goes downstairs to write out the lines he
     had composed while weaving, has a hearty breakfast, and then to the
     Queens Square dye works. But such minor mistakes do not mar this
     presentation for children, which includes quotations from Defence
     and Paradise and five color illustrations.

2   DIXON, W. MAC NEILE. English Epic and Heroic Poetry. London:
    J.M. Dent; New York: E.P. Dutton, pp. 315-25.
        Suggests that no other nineteenth-century poet, not even
Keats, had "so loved the outer and inner life of the Middle Ages,"
and this is apparent in WM's narrative poems. Has high praise for
Jason, but misgivings about Paradise and Sigurd, especially the
latter, which is "too long and languid."

3   DRINKWATER, JOHN. WM: A Critical Study. New York: M.
    Kennerley; London: Martin Secker, 202 pp. Reprint. Folcroft,
    Pa.: Folcroft Press, 1969. Norwood, Pa.: Norwood Editions,
    1975. Folcroft, Pa.: Folcroft Library Editions, 1975.
    Philadelphia, R. West, 1977.
        Acknowledges his debt to Mackail (1899.10), but makes new
points about WM's writings, especially the poetry, for "Morris is
for me among the supremely important poets." Perceives immaturity
and "a certain vagueness of outline" in Defence poems, but argues
that WM is "perfectly lucid" in the narrative poems, that Jason and
Sigurd are magnificent. Claims that characters in Nowhere are
esentially English, but "stripped of the excrescences of an effete
and degraded society." Finds unities within WM's literary output in
a "high regard for naked life, the insistence of labor being joyful
if it was not to be abominable, the fierce worship of beauty and the
courageous acceptance of its passing." Concludes that for WM "art
was gospel, and all his social teaching and activity were but an
effort to bring his gospel to pass upon earth."

4   GREEN, A. ROMNEY. "WM: The Craftsman as Poet." Poetry Review
    1, no. 7 (July):300-311.
        Suggests that healthy interests in craftsmanship changed WM
from a morbid and silly poet in Defence into an "incomparably saner
man" in Jason and Paradise. In much of his poetry and in his
socialist lectures, WM "shows just that sanity which Socrates has
taught us to expect from the artificer rather than the politician."
Sympathetic on WM's attempts to link a revival of the arts to social
revolutuion.

5   GREVILLE, FRANCIS EVELYN, COUNTESS OF WARWICK. WM, His Homes
    and Haunts. London: Jack; New York: Dodge, 68 pp. Reprint.
    Folcroft, Pa.: Folcroft Library Editions, 1974. Philadelphia:
    R. West, 1978.
        Admits to relying heavily on Mackail (1899.10). Discusses
all the important achievements, citing all the customary influences,
friendships, and associations. Attempts to account for WM's
peculiar aptitudes and interests by stressing the freedoms he
enjoyed in childhood and the lack of financial cares later.
Journeys to Iceland are treated sensibly and the importance of the
Eastern Question Association as the means for WM's political
awakening is discussed in detail; his subsequent socialism is linked

to his achievements in decoration as well as to his theories about
art and work.

6   HYNDMAN, H.M. Further Reminiscences. London: Macmillan, pp.
     354-57, 367-68.
          Recalls that in 1882, "Morris himself joined in the great
     fight, and certainly no more valuable recruit ever came to us
     thereafter than when Crane too enlisted in the Socialist army in
     1894," going on then to offer other specific points of comparison
     between WM and Crane.

7   JACKSON, HOLBROOK. "WM." In All Manner of Folk:
     Interpretations and Studies. London: Grant Richards, pp.
     159-66.
          Asserts that Ruskin was an important influence on WM, but he
     remained a medievalist, while WM became a modernist, one who would
     go back "only to pick up the lost tradition of good workmanship."
     Has general appreciation of Nowhere, "that perfect piece of English
     prose."

8   KERMODE, H. SYBIL. "The Classical Sources of WM's Jason." In
     Primitiae: Essays in English Literature by the Students of the
     University of Liverpool. Liverpool: University Press. London:
     Constable, pp. 158-82.
          Discusses Jason as a "latter-day pseudo-classical romance,
     lineally descended from Chaucer's Troilus and Cressida," but more
     importantly as a poem that betrays WM's careful reading of classical
     sources like Pindar and Apollonius Rhodius. Compares several
     passages from these sources to scenes in Jason, concluding that WM's
     "instinctive sympathy with Greek melancholy is startling."

9   MOORHOUSE, E. HALLAM. "Aspects of WM." Fortnightly Review 92
     (September):464-76.
          Praises WM's many achievements, suggesting that "Bigness" was
     at the heart of everything WM attempted and accomplished. Comments
     favorably on poems like "Message of the March Wind," but suggests
     that WM shortened his life because of his efforts in the socialist
     cause.

10   PENNELL, E.R., and PENNELL, J. "Whistler as Decorator, with an
     Incidental Comparison of the Influence of Whistler and that of
     WM." Century Illustrated Monthly Magazine 83, no. 4
     (February):500-513.
          Claims that Whistler had no sympathy for what is here called
     WM's attempts "to resurrect the past and to live in it," and then
     goes on to contrast WM's ornateness to Whistler's simplicity, both
     in interior decoration and in the book arts, concluding that

Whistler's influence shall certainly outlast WM's.

11 RHYS, ERNEST, ed. Introduction to <u>Jason</u>. London: J.M. Dent;
    New York: E.P. Dutton, pp. vii-x.
      Indicates why <u>Jason</u> is a "craftsman's poem, devised by one
who cared for every human and beautiful detail."

12 ROGERS, BRUCE. "Progress of Modern Printing in the United
    States." <u>Times</u>, 10 September, p. 18.
      Notes that "for a period of ten years the work of WM at
Kelmscott Press had an enormous influence upon American
printing--and not, on the whole, a beneficial one except in its
insistence on sound craftsmanship." Briefly discusses Kelmscott
Press, its influence on Updike at the Merrymount Press and on Goudy
at the Village Press. Reprinted: 1953.5.

13 SAINTSBURY, GEORGE. <u>A History of English Prose Rythym</u>. London:
    Macmillan. Reprint. London and Bloomington: Indiana University
    Press, 1965, 1967, pp. 435-37.
      Discusses several examples of WM's use of archaic diction in
the prose romances, pointing out ways such diction fits the themes
of the tales, comparing WM to Malory who also used unconventional
diction to shape chivalric themes.

14 SCOTT, W. DIXON. "The First WM." In <u>Primitiae: Essays in
    English Literature by Students of the University of Liverpool</u>.
    Liverpool: University Press; London: Constable, pp. 183-236.
      Contrasts <u>Defence</u> poems, which are "unsparingly optical,"
that cause readers to be "dizzied by this ceaseless play upon one
nerve," to <u>Jason</u>, "a soothing nepenthe," and "one of the longest
sleeping-draughts in the language." Asserts that <u>Defence</u> "is a
victory for forces he was later to subdue" and offers as proof some
tame revisions which WM did seventeen years later, revisions never
published but which WM actually thought better than the "feverish"
originals. Contrasts WM's prosody in <u>Defence</u>, "all jerks and
emphasis," to smoother prosody of Rossetti, and also judges Rossetti
to be a better storyteller, linking WM's inability to tell a story
to his "naive theories of society."

15 STILLWELL, MARGARET BINGHAM. <u>The Influence of WM and Kelmscott
    Press</u>. Providence, R.I.: E.A. Johnson, 16 pp.
      Reports upon the 1911 Brown University Exhibition of WM and
Kelmscott Press and its influence, insisting that WM was primarily a
medievalist. Reprinted from a Brown University alumni magazine,
March 1912.

16 TOWNSHEND, EMILY. WM and the Communist Ideal. Fabian Tract,
    no. 167. London: The Fabian Society, 23 pp. 5th printing, 1934.
    Reprint. Folcroft, Pa.: Folcroft Library Editions, 1974.
        A biographical sketch, divided into short sections that move
from "Boyhood" through "Poetry," precedes a much fuller discussion
of WM's years of active socialist work, with useful analyses of the
importance of the Eastern Question Association and SPAB in the
development of ideas in the socialist lectures and in Commonweal
(here highly praised and said to contain some of WM's best work).
Claims that state socialism angered WM, "though one does not deny
that toward the end of his life he was brought in a chastened spirit
to bow his neck to the Fabian yoke." Suggests that to use WM "for
organizing meetings and speaking at street corners was to dig with a
damascened sword blade." Reprinted: 1976.52.

17 VIDALENC, GEORGES. "La derniere oevre de WM: L'Imprimerie de
    Kelmscott." Mercure de France 99:768-76.
        Discusses ways that Kelmscott Press works fulfilled WM's
hopes about work and pleasure, his claims that the two combined
could yield art.

18 YEATS, W.B. "The Happiest of Poets." Bibelot 18:112-28.
    Reprint of 1903.9.

19 "WM in the Present." TLS, no. 552 (8 August):312.
        An editorial response to Drinkwater (1912.3), which insists
that WM's poetic reputation is undergoing a revaluation, since "the
young are beginning to think of him as if he were a new writer."

                                    1913

1   CHESTERTON, GILBERT K. The Victorian Age in Literature. Home
    University Library. New York: Henry Holt; London: Williams and
    Norgate, pp. 196-200, 232. Reprint. 1914, 1918, 1919, 1920,
    1923, 1925, 1927, 1928, 1931, 1936, 1938, 1944, 1946.
        Asserts that WM was more virile than either Swinburne or
Rossetti because he was a craftsman: "at last an aesthete had
appeared who could make something." Though he does seem to
appreciate the poetry, about WM's politics the humour barely
disguises animosity: "he was not a socialist; he was a sort of
Dickensian anarchist," and Nowhere is dismissed as "irresponsible."

2   COLE, G.D.H. "WM." Blue Book 1, no. 5:353-66.
        Discusses the scope of WM's writings, using the volumes of
the Collected Works already published as his exemplar: "Those who
judge WM only by what he wrote will always judge him partially and
amiss." Useful comments about WM's designs, their pertinence to his
socialist beliefs.

3   COMPTON-RICKETT, ARTHUR. WM: A Study in Personality. London:
        Herbert Jenkins; New York: E.P. Dutton, 325 pp. Reprint.
        Folcroft, Pa.: Folcroft Press, 1969. Port Washington, N.Y.:
        Kennikat Press, 1972. Norwood, Pa.: Norwood Editions, 1976.
        Philadelphia: R. West, 1977.
        Aims to "deal particularly with the personal equation," and
so for this "study in personality and temperament" he "sought the
firsthand impressions of as many, as possible, of Morris's intimates
and acquaintances." He thus includes fresh anecdotes about WM's
gestures and prejudices as well as insights into the motivations of
a man who perhaps preferred crafts over people, who enjoyed the
complexities of design and avoided those of personality.
Sympathetic to WM's socialism but calls him an "aesthetic
reformer." Includes an "analytical biography," a useful
chronological table of events, as well as a sympathetic introduction
by R.B. Cunninghame-Graham.

4   COURMONT, ANDRE. "Guthrun Osvifursdottir og WM." Skirnir 87,
        no. 3:193-205.
        In Icelandic. Biographical sketch and description of frame
of Paradise precede a discussion of WM's handling of the tragic love
tale in Laxdoela Saga, the tale he turned into his "Gudrun," which
is here paraphrased and lauded as a loftier, purer tale ·than its
Icelandic source. A lecture given before a student audience in
Iceland on 6 April 1913; it was evidently assumed that everyone in
the audience had previous knowledge of WM.

5   FEGAN, ETHEL S. "Modern Fine Printing Since Kelmscott Press."
        Library Association Record 15 (16 June):301-27.
        A detailed discussion of the fine presses influenced by
Kelmscott Press, one that compares specific types used at the
following Presses: Vale, Eragny, Ashendene, Essex House, Caradoc,
Doves, Cuala, and Pitt in England; the Merrymount in America; and
the Ernest Ludwig in Germany. Concludes with comments on fine
printing in Italy and France.

6   FULLER, EDWARD. "The Work of WM." Bookman (New York) 37
     (July):577-81.
         Speculates upon reasons for the decline of WM's fame, blaming
it finally upon the variety of his accomplishments, concluding that
his "gift of poetry was the supremest."

7   GLOVER, W.J. Tales from "Paradise" by WM. London: Adam and
     Charles Black, 280 pp.
         A selection of twelve of the Paradise tales, turned into
prose, "rendered for children, largely in Morris's own words."

8   GUYOT, EDOUARD. "Le socialisme de WM." In Le socialisme et
     l'evolution de l'Angleterre contemporaire. Paris: Alcan, pp.
     379-424.
         The development of WM's socialism is here discussed with
ample reference to intellectual influences, like Ruskin's writings,
and to political and social pressures that turned WM into both a
social theorist and an activist for revolution. Includes a full
discussion of John Ball, the socialist lectures, and Nowhere.

9   JACKSON, HOLBROOK. "Art and Life." In The Eighteen-Nineties:
     Art and Life at the Close of the Century. London: Grant
     Richards; New York: Mitchell Kennerly. Reprinted, with a new
     preface, 1927; Harmondsworth: Penguin, 1939; Sussex: Harvester
     Press, 1976; Atlantic Highlands, N.J.: Humanities Press, 1976,
     pp. 244-54.
         Discusses ways that WM "gave a fresh turn to the teaching of
Ruskin," how his work and lectures caused a passion for good
craftsmanship that nearly became a "national movement." Ironically,
the success of the Arts and Crafts Movement, which WM did not
initiate, led to to "artistic" shoddy and kitsch.

10   JACKSON, HOLBROOK. "The Revival of Printing." The
     Eighteen-Nineties: Art and Life at the Close of the Century.
     London: Grant Richards; New York: Mitchell Kennerly. Reprinted,
     winew Preface, 1927; Harmondsworth: Penguin, 1939; Sussex:
     Harvester Press, 1976; Atlantic Highlands, N.J.: Humanities
     Press, 1976, pp. 255-56.
         A printing revival began "when Messrs. Charles Whittingham
revived Caslon's famous founts on the Chiswick Press in 1844," and
it reached a Golden Age in the 1890s with the Vale, Kelmscott,
Eragny, Essex House, and Doves presses, for these printers turned
back to the old masters who understood the "due relation of letters
to pictures or other ornaments." Recounts the beginnings of the
Press, describing the three founts, listing Kelmscott Press titles
and mentioning the influence Kelmscott books had on subsequent
presses.

11 JACKSON, HOLBROOK. "WM: Super-Craftsman." T.P.'s Weekly
    22:709.
        Celebrates WM's "psychological gift, his ability to live in
    the form of design," as it lauds the new insights available in a new
    study of WM, one by Compton-Ricketts (1913:3).

12 LEIBLEIN, EMIL. Prinzipium und Anwendung des Stabreims in WM's
    "Sigurd". Amorbach: Gottlob Volkhard, Druckerei, 102 pp.
        Exhaustively quantitative with every possible vowel and
    consonant head-rhyme tabulated, speculated upon. A final chapter
    compares alliteration in Sigurd to that in the WM and Magnusson
    translations of poems from the Elder Edda.

13 LEVETUS, A.S. "WM und die Wiederbelebung der dekorativen Kunst
    in England." Mitteilungen des Erzherzog Ranier-Museum in Brunn
    9:129-36.
        Drawn from a museum lecture, this article argues that WM was
    a genius whose achievements in the decorative arts had a broad and
    continuing influence in England, and on the Continent. Biographical
    anecdotes are interspersed with comments about cultural life in
    England and Germany, sometimes in interesting ways.

14 MARILLIER, H.C. A Note on the Morris Stained Glass Work.
    London: Privately printed for Morris and Co., 37 pp.
        Claims that the best account to date of Morris and Co.
    stained glass is by Vallance (1897.21), offering here only a brief
    history of the Firm's work with glass, from early experiments to the
    many commissions completed for Bodley-designed churches. Includes
    details concerning windows designed by Rossetti and Burne-Jones,
    giving their present locations. A list of churches and public
    buildings with Morris and Co. windows done between 1862 and 1912 has
    over 300 names.

15 RAWSON, GRAHAM STANHOPE. "WM's Political Romance: Nowhere."
    Dissertation, University of Jena.
        Revised for publication: 1914.8.

                              1914

*1 BART, CAROL S. "The Influence of Medieval French Literature
    Upon WM's Defence." Dissertation, University of Chicago.
        Cited in 1936.3.

2   CLUTTON-BROCK, A. WM: His Work and Influence. Home University
     Library of Modern Knowledge. London: Butterworth; New York:
     Holt. 5th printing, 1931, 256 pp.
          Judges WM to be "the chief representative of that aesthetic
     discontent which is peculiar to our time," and has useful comments
     upon the ways that WM's socialism grew out of his discontent with
     both modern society as well as modern art, why solutions must
     involve changing attitudes toward and conditions surrounding work,
     which WM regarded as sacred. Embellishments upon Mackail (1899.10)
     ("WM understood Gothic art as the child Mozart understood music")
     are sometimes obtrusive, and so are some mistakes (WM did not start
     learning Icelandic in 1860, but in 1868), but this study is
     generally reliable and it does fulfill its aim of introducing new
     readers to the "greatness" of WM. There are, moreover, fresh
     insights in every chapter; the discussion of why WM preferred
     Iceland to Italy is one example.

3   DYCE, ALAN. "WM." Sewanee Review 22, no. 3 (July):257-75.
          Mentions spate of recent studies of WM, suggesting that
     Noyes's enthusiastic but "hopelessly ill-balanced" book (1908.9)
     seems to have broken an eight-year silence concerning WM who "must
     be counted among the giants of his century," especially if all his
     work is considered, which this article attempts. Celebrates Defence
     and John Ball and asserts that Nowhere is the best of all modern
     Utopias and the late romances trivial; brushes by WM's socialism,
     but waxes enthusiastic about WM and the decorative arts: his many
     achievements here have led to a true revolution in British taste.
     Concludes by equating WM with Darwin, who "gave us a new world," but
     WM "gave us a new art."

4   FRANCILLON, R.E. "The 'Decemviri.'" Mid-Victorian Memories.
     London: Hodder and Stoughton, p. 172.
          Judges that WM did not have the figure or demeanor of a poet,
     and recalls a dinner party in the 1860s when Rossetti's attentions
     to Janey seemed excessive.

5   HOLIDAY, HENRY. Reminiscences of My Life. London: Heineman,
     pp. 152-53, 291.
          The author's sister embroidered large designs for WM, who
     evidently appreciated her skills immensely. Comments upon WM's
     influence as a designer, and recalls attending a few of his
     lectures, chatting with him afterwards about why he would not mind
     being a cook.

6   KAHN, GUSTAVE. "L'exposition anglaise des arts et metiers."
    Mercure de France 110 (16 July):403-6.
      Appreciative comments about WM's correct perceptions as to
the role of popular arts occur in this review-article of an arts and
crafts exhibition.

7   MORRIS, MAY. "Sonnets by WM." Athenaeum, no. 4541 (7
    November):480.
      Answers inquiry in a previous issue, 1914.10, about two
sonnets signed only "WM," asserting that they were indeed written by
her father.

8   RAWSON, GRAHAM STANHOPE. WM's Political Romance: "Nowhere."
    Its Sources and Its Relationship to "John Ball" and "Looking
    Backward". Leipzig: Buchdruckerei R. Noska, 99 pp.
      Discusses both John Ball and Looking Backward as important
sources for Nowhere. A useful appendix compares chapters from
Nowhere as they appeared in Commonweal and in the first separately
published editions, where interpolations were made. Revision of
1913.15.

9   VAUGHAN, CHARLES E. Bibliographies of Swinburne, WM and
    Rossetti. English Association Pamphlet, no. 29. Oxford:
    Clarendon Press, pp. 7-10. Reprint. Folcroft, Pa.: Folcroft
    Press, 1969. Folcroft, Pa.: Folcroft Library Editions, 1977.
    Norwood, Pa.: Norwood Editions, 1978.
      Short bibliography has both primary and secondary sources.
Supplements 1897.16; all the secondary materials are included in the
present book.

10 WADDINGTON, SAMUEL. "Sonnets by WM." Athenaeum, no. 4539 (24
    October):430.
      Recalls that in 1880 he received a letter from WM that
admitted to only one sonnet: a prefatory poem to the 1869
translation of Grettir's Saga, but in a recent issue of the Atlantic
Monthly two sonnets signed "WM" appeared. Inquires whether anyone
knows if they were actually by WM. They were indeed: 1914.7.

11 WOOD, ESTHER. "WM, the Man: An Intimate Memory of a Prophet and
    Song-Smith." Book Monthly 11:231-35.
      Pleasant reminiscences which include some fresh anecdotes
about WM's sense of humor and his antipathy to socialist locals that
were antidrink. Asserts also that WM was not prejudiced against
science so much as "experts," and discusses his admiration for
Oriental art.

12 "The Prose Romances of WM." TLS, no. 625 (8 January):9-10.
       Offers useful analysis of the sorts of realism present in the
late prose romances, contrasting WM's characters and settings to
those of Scott, who was interested in the "mere trappings" of
medievalism, while WM created romances "full of passion and trouble
and delight and sin," medieval tales in which "he was able to
express his own sense of reality most clearly." Points made about
the reality of a passage in Well, one on the practicality of owning
slave-maidens, remind one of the early Lukacs.

                                1915

1   BELL, A.F. "Rossetti, WM and Swinburne." In Leaders of English
       Literature. London: G. Bell and Sons. Reprint. 1920, 1926,
       1934, pp. 215-23, 228.
       Comments usefully on Defence, on the "strange wistfulness"
that characterizes many of the poems in that volume. Stresses WM's
"great debt" to Rossetti; and, noting the diffuseness of WM's later
verse, says he "would have done well had he followed the example of
his early master more closely in his habit of careful revision."
Concludes that these "three poets together started a minor Romantic
revival, a revolt against convention and meaningless classicism."

2   BROOKS, VAN WYCK. America's Coming of Age. New York: B.W.
       Huebsch, pp. 175-77.
       Celebrates the "contagious personality of WM which opposed
the ideal of craftsmanship to the ideal of cheapest work and largest
money," suggesting that he was one who must have had an effect on
the "average artisan." Reprinted: 1934.13.

3   COCKERELL, T.D.A. "WM and the World Today." Dial 59 (9
       December):545-48.
       Opens with lines from WM letter to Georgie Burne-Jones
expressing pain: "I am older and the year is evil," in order to
comment upon a dreary American scene, where the "sloth" of
moviegoers suggests a general "levelling downward," and concludes
with hope that Americans might become alarmed enough to learn from
WM's example and change their lives.

4   DE SELINCOURT, ERNEST. English Poets and the National Ideal:
       Four Lectures. London: Oxford University Press, pp. 117-19.
       Judges that WM "strove less to reveal the life and soul of
the people than to raise the song of battle for their deliverance."
Has high praise for Pilgrims, especially for its lyric, "Mother and
Son," asserting that it is better than anything in Paradise.

5   EVANS, C.S. Introduction to Stories from "Paradise" by WM. New
    York: Longmans; London: Edward Arnold, pp. 1-6.
        A biographical sketch and commentary upon the structure of
Paradise; the twelve tales are retold in archaic prose that utilizes
some of the imagery from the original poems.

6   MASSE, H.J.L.J. "WM as Craftsman." Architect and Contract
    Reporter 93 (19 February):172-74.
        Summarizes a lecture given to architects and contracters that
reviewed biographical facts and commented upon WM's large influence
on the decorative arts in Britain and Germany.

1916

1   ALDRED, GUY A. "The Socialism of WM." Spur 2, no. 8
    (January):70-72.
        A biographical sketch is followed by reminders of WM's
relevance to modern socialists; remarks upon parallels between
political situations in 1915 and 1876, when WM spoke out against
British militarism, class hatreds, and the like.

2   CARPENTER, EDWARD. My Days and Dreams. London: Allen and
    Unwin, pp. 216-18.
        Recalls WM staying at Millthorpe for a few days, reading
aloud from Jeffries's recently published After London; "he read page
after page of it to us with glee, since he hated modern
civilization, and London as its representative, with a fierce
hatred--its shams, its hypocricies, its stuffy indoor life, its
cheapjack style, its mean and mongrel ideals." Judges that WM
"certainly was no drawing room sort of man" and that Nowhere
incorporates both a scientific forecast and an ideal of a free
brotherhood.

3   H.K., ST. J.S. "WM's Sigurd." N and Q, 12th ser., 11 (2
    December):448.
        Points out that in book 3 of Sigurd, "there is one line
lacking its fellow," line 1365, and suggests that this omission must
be due to a printer's error.

4   HEARN, LAFCADIO. "WM." In Appreciations of Poetry. New York:
    Dodd, Mead, pp. 239-79.
        Reprinted from notes for lectures given in Tokyo at the turn
of the century, this chapter on WM's poetry is full of graceful but
misleading generalizations. Claims, for instance, that WM is "the
most prolific poet of the century; and he was in all respects the
nearest in his talent and sentiment to Sir Walter Scott." Points
out parallels between Chaucer's Canterbury Tales and Paradise,

suggesting that WM's narrative cycle is better only because it is complete. Patient explication, and paraphrase, of several of poems from Defence, and of Sigurd, are useful. Reprinted: 1922.7.

5   MAC IVER, GRANT. "WM Issue." Spur 2, no. 8 (January):57-69.
        Brings together selections from WM's lectures and essays to demonstrate the nature of his "anti-war sentiments," and also the ways his attitudes toward imperialism contrasted with those of Hyndman.

6   STILLWELL, MARGARET BINGHAM. "The Heritage of the Modern
     Printer." Bulletin of the New York Public Library 20, no. 10
     (October):737-50.
        Ties a revival of printing to Kelmscott Press, discussing briefly the earlier commercial interests that had put the book arts in jeopardy. Has a biographical sketch of WM, a description of Kelmscott Press volumes, and comments on Vale, Essex House and Doves presses. Invites friends of the New York Public Library to think of donating fine press volumes to the Library's collections.

7   WATTS-DUNTON, THEODORE. "WM, 1834-1896." In Old Familiar
     Faces. London: Herbert Jenkins, pp. 240-76.
        Memoirs, which originally appeared as obituary and reviews, contain quotations and anecdotes often used by WM biographers. In 1896, WM told Watts-Dunton, "I have enjoyed my life--few men more so--and death in any case is sure." And here we have WM being scornful of Watts-Dunton for not paying full attention to his fishing line. In an unsigned introduction Watts-Dunton is quoted as saying that Janey was "superior to Morris intellectually."

1917

1   ATKINS, WILLIAM. WM: Artist, Painter, and Man of Business.
     London: Saint Bride School, 16 pp.
        Since this was a lecture given to a London Printers' Association, one would expect that Kelmscott Press matters would be stressed, but there is a wealth of biographical detail, most of it borrowed from Mackail (1899.10) and turned into near hagiography. Sketches in backgrounds of Kelmscott Press and includes a list of books published there.

2 DRINKWATER, JOHN. "WM and the State." In Prose Papers.
London: Mathews. Reprint. Freeport, N.Y.: Books for Libraries
Press, 1969, pp. 138-46.
        Praises the socialist essays and lectures, claiming that they
all have one basic theme: "Capitalism destroys the delight in labor,
which is the greatest privilege of man and the secret of all
communal health." Suggests that World War I might not have engulfed
Europe if more leaders had had deeper interests in the arts;
conjectures about WM's intense dislike of Milton; perhaps he could
not sympathize with Milton's "capacity for investing compromise with
moral dignity."

3 GOSSE, EDMUND. The Life of Swinburne. London and New York:
Macmillan, pp. 42-43, passim.
        Asserts that the relationship between WM and Swinburne was
close at Oxford where the latter was like a "devoted younger
brother," and at Red House where he was always welcome. Comments
upon references Swinburne makes to WM in "A Channel Passage" and
"Astrophel."

4 LOANE, GEORGE. "A Mannerism of WM." TLS, no. 798 (3 May):214;
no. 799 (10 May):226; no. 801 (24 May):250; no. 804 (14
June):285.
        An exchange of letters that begins with Mr. Loane's
observation that a certain poetic "mannerism" seems peculiar to WM,
one that "places a substantive after the first of two epithets
connected by 'and'" ("a gentle sea and kind"). He has found
twenty-six such examples in Jason and wonders if anyone else has
noted this "mannerism." Promptly answered by Shipman whose wife
recalls WM in a lecture using "a faithful servant and kind." Rogers
responds with the observation that the phrase occurs in the prose
romances: "a tall man and a proper." Loane caps the whole exchange,
concluding that the letters received suggest that WM "uses this
arrangement with a frequency quite unparalleled among English
writers."

5 THOMAS, EDWARD. "WM." In A Literary Pilgrim in England.
London: Dodd, Mead. Reprint. Freeport, N.Y.: Books for
Libraries Press, 1969, pp. 82-88.
        Speaks briefly of Oxfordshire countryside WM loved, judging
that Nowhere is "saved, if at all, by what comes straight from
Morris's experience of the Thames, and of Thames-side houses at
Kelmscott and Hammersmith." Praises "earth-feeling" in "Message of
the March Wind," ignoring entirely its socialism.

6   WILKES, J.A. "Memories of Kelmscott House." Socialist Review
    14:325-31.
        Recalls Sunday evening lectures at the Hammersmith Socialist
    Society, when personalities like Annie Besant, Keir Hardie,
    Carpenter, and the Russians Kropotkin and Stepniak spoke to
    enthusiastic audiences. Concludes that "those were great days, for
    out of such beginnings has sprung the movement which even in these
    dark times fills one with hope for the future."

7   WROOT, HERBERT E. "Pre-Raphaelite Windows at Bradford."
    International Studio 63, no. 249 (November):69-73.
        In 1862, a Bradford merchant commissioned WM to do thirteen
    window-panels for his music room. This was the Firm's first job for
    windows at a private residence, and the love of Tristan and Isolde
    was chosen for a theme; four of the windows were designed by WM.
    Includes eleven monochrome illustrations.

                              1918

1   BAX, E. BELFORT. Reminiscences and Reflections of a Mid and
    Late Victorian. London: G. Allen and Unwin, pp. 75-76, 79-88,
    117-22, passim. Reprint. New York: Kelley, 1967.
        Irascible and unpredictable, given to outbursts against
    capitalist stupidities, Bax was a delight to WM. Many details here
    about problems with the SDF are familiar, but other descriptions are
    fresh: of H.H. Champion, of Bax's surprise when WM said he would
    prefer being reincarnated an Athenian rather than a Goth. Concludes
    with high praise for WM: "We shall not look upon his like again."

2   BELL, CLIVE. "WM." In Pot-Boilers. London: Chatto and Windus,
    pp. 146-55.
        An essay inspired by Clutton-Brock's biography (1914.2)
    suggests that he overrated WM, who "as an artist was cursed with two
    of the three modern English vices: that he was provincial and
    amateurish." Asserts also that WM was "neither a great artist nor a
    great thinker, but he was a great man."

3   BROOKS, VAN WYCK. Letters and Leadership. New York: B.W.
    Huebsch, pp. 103-9.
        Contrasts WM and Whitman; the former's ideas about joy in
    labor "released the creative energies of men," thus impelling them
    to change their world. Whitman only "universalized the miraculous
    animality that summed up his own experience." WM's ideas about the
    importance of work served to nudge Britain forward, while America
    remained under the sway of a Henry Ford who caused people "to seek
    reality in anything else than their work." Reprinted: 1934.14.

4   CLUTTON-BROCK, A. "Waste or Creation." TLS, no. 842 (7
    March):109-10.
        Points out that the social catastrophe WM often predicted has
arrived, that this great war has caused many now to realize more
important truths WM taught, namely that labor must not be wasted
making useless or trivial things. WM saw such waste as "one of the
chief causes of poverty in time of peace, whereas we see it as a
hindrance to victory in time of war. We have for war purposes
acquired the conscience that he wished us to acquire for all
purposes. The question is whether we shall keep it when the war is
over." This essay raises other interesting points about the war
creating socialist behavior.

5   HERFORD, CHARLES HAROLD. "Norse Myth in English Poetry."
    Bulletin of the John Rylands Library 5:75-100.
        Asserts that WM, more than any other English poet, felt the
"power of Norse myth; none has done so much to restore its terrible
beauty." Offers proof by surveying poetry with Norse themes written
by Gray, Arnold, and a few others; discusses and paraphrases Sigurd,
claiming that it is the only great epic poem of the nineteenth
century.

6   JACKSON, HOLBROOK. "The Revival of Printing." Ars Typographica
    1, no. 1 (Spring):3-22.
        Reprint of 1913.10.

                              1919

1   BLUNT, WILFRID SCAWEN. My Diaries: Being a Personal Narrative
    of Events, 1888-1914. London: Martin Secker; New York: Knopf,
    1921. One-volume edition, London: Martin Secker, 1932, pp.
    227-38, passim. Reprint. New York: Octagon, 1980.
        What this one-time diplomat, world traveler, and critic of
British colonialism had to say about WM is always interesting. He
first met WM in 1884; he spent some time with him in 1889, when both
were becoming less engaged in political work: "my talks with him
that summer confirmed me in my resolution politically to retire into
my shell, and I think my resolution had a corresponding influence on
him." Anecdotes about fishing for gudgeon during Kelmscott Manor
afternoons and discussing politics during the evenings are detailed
and lively. Blunt's friendship with WM is, however, now being
reappraised: 1981.18-19.

2   CLUTTON-BROCK, A. "Waste or Creation?" In Essays on Art.
    London: Methuen. Reprint. Freeport, N.Y.: Books for Libraries
    Press, 1968, pp. 132-44.
        Reprint of 1918.4.

3   COLE, G.D.H. Labour in the Commonwealth. London: Headley
    Bros., pp. 220-23.
        Concludes this "study for the younger generation" with
    comments on WM: "I share to the full WM's happy conviction that joy
    in life, and art as the expression of that joy, are fundamental,
    and, if you will, natural, to free men and women." A good life for
    all can only occur within a political system where all are involved
    in "good making and doing."

4   GLASIER, J. BRUCE. Socialism in Song: An Appreciation of WM's
    "Chants". Manchester: National Labour Press, 42 pp.
        An introductory section insists that "political movements
    have derived whatever idealism or spiritual vehemence" they have
    from poetry, and that this has been true for socialism. Cites
    several examples and then says, "it is to WM that the movement owes
    its richest dower of song." Eleven of these, from "The Day Is
    Coming" to "Mine and Thine" are here briefly discussed.

5   GLASIER, J. BRUCE. The Meaning of Socialism. Manchester and
    London: National Labour Press, 1919, pp. 95-99, passim.
        Quotes WM's "How We Live and How We Might Live," on the ways
    a socialist system shall allow everyone to do varied and pleasant
    work, thus "giving fullness to life and enriching the
    commonwealth."

6   KENT, CHARLES. "Kunsten og jordens skjonhet" [Art and earth's
    beauty]. In Dagdrommen [Daydreams], Kristiana: H. Aschehoug,
    pp. 51-99.
        In Norwegian. Discusses all the usual biographical facts,
    paraphrasing the longer narrative poems, and celebrating WM's
    anti-industrial stance. One of five essays on similar thinkers,
    including Ruskin.

7   MORRIS, MAY. "WM." TLS, no. 905 (22 May):280.
        Desires to correct impression of coldness in Blunt's recently
    published statement (1919.1) that WM "had no thought for anything or
    person, including himself, but only for the work he had in hand."
    May Morris rightly feared that this might develop into a "legend,"
    and so she points out that while her father could shut out the world
    when he was engrossed, "he also had the talent of giving himself to
    his friends in holiday time, and indeed to some few in work time
    also." Despite this statement, and corroboration from A.W. Pollard

the following week (29 May, p. 296), May Morris's fears have been
realized; Blunt's observation has been used by many subsequent
biographers.

8   YEATS, W.B. "If I were Four and Twenty." Irish Statesman 1,
     nos. 9-10 (August):212-13, 236-37.
        Recalls WM coming to Dublin "to preach us into Socialism,"
and how he was mocked: "they condemned Morris's doctrine without
examination. Now for the most part, they applaud it without
examination." Says also that "Morris was and is my chief of men,"
but that his disbelief in numinous powers, his belief that "man
needed no spur of necessity," that "all men would do all necessary
work with no compulsion but a little argument," these attitudes
puzzled Yeats, and caused WM, and Shaw as well, "to delight the
Garden City Mind." Reprinted: 1962.38

9   "The Modernity of WM." Arts and Decoration 12, no. 1 (15
     November):61.
        Quotes WM on the importance of the decorative arts, asserting
that herein is much to value while lamenting that his artistic sense
was "weakened only by an excessive socialistic trend of thought."

                              1920

1   BLORE, G.H. "WM: Craftsman and Social Reformer." In Victorian
     Worthies: Sixteen Biographies. London: Oxford University Press,
     pp. 302-22.
        Recounts the usual biographical details, drawing largely from
Mackail (1899.10), but with some sympathetic comments on WM's
socialism, to which "he gave of his best with the same thoroughness
as in all his crafts."

2   BLUEHER, RUDOLF. Moderne Utopien: Ein Beitrag zur Geschicte des
     Sozialismus. Bonn: K. Schrieder, pp. 59-71, 89-103, passim.
        Discusses the society of Nowhere under headings like
"Organization and Production," "Art and Science," and "Family and
Society." Also makes useful points about ways the society of
Nowhere differs from the one Bellamy created in Looking Backward.

3   BURNS, C. DELISLE. "WM and Industry." In The Principles of
     Revolution: A Study in Ideals. London: Allen and Unwin, pp.
     67-88.
        Begins by stressing, as WM had, the need for revolution
rather than mere reform, pointing out that "no man has ever said
more clearly than Morris that what is wrong with our world is not
simply the suffering of those who suffer, but the incompetence of
those who do not." WM could see because of his study of history and

love of art that we need a "distribution of vitality" rather than of
wealth, and that such a distribution might occur if attention were
paid to people's occupations, to people as joyful producers rather
than mere consumers.

4   CLUTTON-BROCK, A. "The Prose Romances of WM." In Essays on
    Books. New York: E.P. Dutton. Reprint. Freeport, N.Y.: Books
    for Libraries Press, 1968, pp. 27-38.
        Laments that the prose romances, "except those two which have
    a political purpose," are so seldom read. General comments about
    their appeal, about that "world of wonder and beauty and terror,"
    follow.

5   GLASIER, J. BRUCE. "A Proletarian Epic." Socialist Review
    (London and Manchester) 17:322-25.
        Regrets that so few socialists know Pilgrims, since it is the
    "only poetical narrative of modern proletarian revolt which we
    possess." Offers a paraphrase and many generalities about WM's
    ability to apprehend "human passion" and the "deeper moral
    vicissitudes of modern human existence."

6   HUIZINGA, JOHAN. "The Problem of the Renaissance." In Man and
    Ideas. Translated by J. Holmes and H. Van Marle. New York:
    Meridian Books, p. 278.
        Comments on WM's "fruitful conviction" that there were real
    spiritual and communal benefits to life in the Middle Ages, then
    argues that any collectivist or synthetic view of the Middle Ages is
    not tenable.

7   HUTCHINSON, HORACE GORDON. "WM." In Portraits of the
    Eighties. London: Allen and Unwin. Reprint. Freeport, N.Y.:
    Books for Libraries Press, 1970, pp. 174-87.
        Though he confesses to a dislike for WM's "type of socialism"
    and for Kelmscott Press volumes, he celebrates the "boisterous"
    force whereby WM won through to most of his goals. Exaggerates the
    importance of Iceland to WM's personal and social philosophy.

8   LYND, ROBERT. "The Personality of WM." In The Art of Letters.
    London: T. Fisher Unwin; New York: Scribner's, pp. 150-55.
        This essay is full of warm appreciation for the achievements
    of WM, if not for those of Compton-Rickett (1913.3), which inspired
    the essay originally. Stresses the childlike absorption in work
    which was at the center of WM's personality, adding that "he is a
    figure of whom we cannot be too constantly and vividly reminded."

9   PENNELL, E.R.   "Some Memories of WM."   <u>American</u> <u>Magazine</u> <u>of</u> <u>Art</u>
    11, no. 1 (November):124-27.
        Recalls hearing WM speak on socialist issues both in Hyde
    Park and at Hammersmith, and those recollections are favorable, but
    others are not; she wonders, for instance, why only a few of that
    communal audience at Sunday lectures stayed for dinner, what
    possible role WM the Oxford Street shopkeeper might have in Utopia,
    and the like.

10 PENNELL, JOSEPH.   <u>The</u> <u>Graphic</u> <u>Arts:</u> <u>Modern</u> <u>Men</u> <u>and</u> <u>Modern</u>
    <u>Methods</u>.   Chicago: University of Chicago Press, pp. 88-91.
        Applauds WM's "decorated books which have never been
    surpassed in modern times and probably never will be equalled
    again." Has more specific comments about the beauties of the
    Kelmscott Chaucer and also about the influences Kelmscott Press
    books have had upon other designers.

11 VIDALENC, GEORGES.   <u>La</u> <u>transformation</u> <u>des</u> <u>arts</u> <u>decoratifs</u> <u>au</u>
    <u>19ieme</u> <u>siecle:</u> <u>WM,</u> <u>son</u> <u>oevre</u> <u>et</u> <u>son</u> <u>influence</u>.   Paris: Alcan, 166
    pp.
        Discusses the nature of various influences on WM's attitudes
    toward art. Explores the importance of his achievements at Morris
    and Co. and at Kelmscott Press, charting their influence in Britain,
    in America, and on the Continent. Comments upon ways that WM and
    his ideas and examples colored important exhibitions, their artists
    and wares, before World War I.

12 WILLIAMSON, CLAUDE C.H.   "WM: Aesthete and Socialist."   In
    <u>Writers</u> <u>of</u> <u>Three</u> <u>Centuries:</u> <u>1789-1914</u>.   London: Grant Richards,
    pp. 276-83.
        Graceful appreciation of the medieval themes and diction in
    WM's poetry, one that laments that fewer and fewer readers seem to
    be taking that poetry seriously.

                            <u>1921</u>

1   BEER, MAX.   <u>A</u> <u>History</u> <u>of</u> <u>British</u> <u>Socialism</u>.   London: G. Bell and
    Sons.   1:259-58, passim.
        Discusses reasons for split within the SDF, the subsequent
    development of the Socialist League, and WM's arguments against
    parliamentary reform. Claims, however, that he was "infinitely more
    of an artist and humanitarian than socialist and statesman."
    Includes other details of WM's work with the Socialist League and
    <u>Commonweal</u>, saying "no paper has ever been directed by a man of
    greater genius."

2   BERNSTEIN, EDUARD. My Years of Exile; Reminiscenses of a
     Socialist. Translated by B. Miall. London: Leonard Parsons;
     New York: Harcourt, Brace, pp. 171, 206-7, 255.
         Claims that the "magnificent" WM never became an intimate of
Engels because "Morris was the central star of a circle of his
own." Argues that WM was by no means a socialist aesthete; he was
at the very core of the movement, working, agitating, lecturing; he
spoke most effectively to small groups, because "rhetoric, properly
speaking, was not natural to him. His whole nature was
anti-rhetorical."

3   GLASIER, J. BRUCE. WM and the Early Days of the Socialist
     Movement. London: Longmans, 217 pp. Reprint. Folcroft, Pa.:
     Folcroft Press, 1969.
         May Morris in a short preface has high praise for Glasier,
both as a socialist and as a loyal friend to her father. In this
book, however, the loyalty often surfaces, thirty years after events
recalled, as hero-worship: WM is compared, for instance, to the
Venerable Bede and to Baldur the Beautiful. Many of the anecdotes
are fresh, and those about Glasier's visits to London, WM's to
Scotland; of in-fighting with the anarchists within the Socialist
League, are full of colorful incident, but Glasier's insistence that
WM did not understand Marx, nor want to, has undermined WM's modern
reputation as a socialist thinker, as Arnot (1934.3) and E.P.
Thompson (1955.15) have pointed out. A final chapter tries to
square socialism with Glasier's own deepening Christianity and
perhaps contains clues to his misleading portrayal of WM's radical
politics. An appendix includes twenty-four letters from WM to
Glasier, and these are full of detail and incident, offering a rich
sense of Socialist League work and problems, especially in Scotland.

4   HAMILTON, MARY ALICE. "WM and Bruce Glasier." Socialist Review
     (London and Manchester) 18:245-49.
         Asserts that socialists have not appreciated WM the artist,
nor artists WM the socialist, but that Glasier appreciated both.
Essay inspired by 1921.3, and it is not a review so much as a
reverie, one that celebrates Glasier more than WM.

5   POLLARD, ALFRED W. Introduction to The Library of William
     Andrews Clark, Jr. Part One: Kelmscott Press. Edited by R.E.
     Cowan et al. San Francisco: J.H. Nash, pp. xi-xxxviii.
         Describes the formation of Kelmscott Press, stressing the
importance of Walker and an article he wrote in 1888, as well as the
famed lantern-slide lecture he gave. Has useful details about the
books WM chose to print: "twenty-two were written or translated by
Morris himself," and all of the fifty-three titles were books he
liked, "readable" books. Discusses borders and initials, the ways
the three typefaces were utilized, many of the small presses
influenced by WM's high standards of craftmanship and his insistence

upon quality ink, paper, etc. This detailed introduction precedes a
reprinting of "Note by WM on His Aims in Founding Kelmscott Press"
and a sixty-four-page descriptive list of the Kelmscott Press
volumes in the Clark Library.

6   SALT, HENRY S. Seventy Years Among the Savages. London: Allen
    and Unwin; New York: Thomas Selzer, pp. 79-80, passim.
        Recalls WM at socialist meetings speaking "bluntly," being
impatient with "trappings" of socialism, like vegetarianism, and
with colleagues who were teetotalers.

7   YEATS, W.B. "Four Years, 1887-1891." London Mercury 4, nos.
    21-22 (July-August):259-70, 364-77.
        Recalls debates and dinners at Hammersmith, some of the
personalities who congregated for the Sunday evening socialist
sessions; tells several anecdotes about WM, his "chief of men."
Comments on some of his writings, saying of the prose romances that
"they were the only books I was ever to read slowly that I might not
come too quickly to the end." Admits that he "turned socialist
because of Morris's lectures and pamphlets," but thought it
"unlikely that Morris himself could read economics." After a great
outburst when he insisted that a change of heart must precede a
socialist revolution, Yeats quit attending the Hammersmith Sundays.
Reprinted: 1938.12.

8   "New Reminiscences of Oscar Wilde and WM." Current Opinion 71,
    no. 2 (August):226-29.
        Discusses Yeats's association with WM and Wilde, men who had
little in common except their attraction to socialism. For Wilde,
socialism was a "flower to set in his buttonhole, while for Morris
it was a faith calling for unending sacrifice." Quotes also some of
Yeats's descriptions of Kelmscott House interiors and of WM's
creative life.

                                1922

1   APGAR, GENEVIEVE. "WM's 'The Lady of the Land.'" Poet-Lore 33
    (Summer):274-85.
        Asserts that "The Lady of the Land," the shortest of the
Paradise narratives, deserves more critical attention. She
therefore discusses its imagery, argues that its theme (fear is
destructive) is less important than the poem's sensuousness.

2   BATHO, EDITH C., and DOBREE, BONAMY. "The Pre-Raphaelites and
     After: WM." In The Victorians and After: 1834-1914.
     Introductions to English Literature. Vol. 4. London: Cresset
     Press. 3d ed., 1962, pp. 224-25, passim.
          Introductory sketch, one that has high praise for the
     socialist lectures, precedes a basic bibliography of WM's writings.
     A few secondary sources also listed.

3   BULLEN, HENRY LEWIS. "WM, Regenerator of the Typographic Art."
     Inland Printer 69 (June):369-74.
          A biographical sketch precedes a detailed discussion of the
     "respectable mediocrity" of nineteenth-century printing; this
     provides a useful backdrop to aid us in judging the extent and
     significance of WM's contribution to the printing arts in the
     twentieth century. Mentions Phinney's 1895 printing of WM's
     Kelmscott Press types, a "specimen" that influenced American
     printers, and also discusses WM's influence on German printers.

4   CARPENTER, NILES. Guild Socialism: An Historical and Critical
     Analysis. London and New York: D. Appleton and Co., pp. 45-50.
          Discusses the ways that WM's example, his designs and his
     writings, inspired and influenced advocates of Guild Socialism.

5   CARR, J. COMYNS. Some Eminent Victorians: Personal
     Recollections in the World of Art and Letters. London:
     Duckworth and Co., pp. 78, 208-10.
          Carr, a good friend to Burne-Jones, saw WM frequently: he was
     "not easy to know well. There was a certain rough shyness in his
     manner." But suggests that WM must "have had deeply lovable
     qualities to have become so endeared, as he was, to Burne-Jones,"
     who is here reported as saying, "I think Morris's friendship began
     everything for me, everything that I afterwards cared for."
     Contrasts WM's passionate treatment of Arthurian story to Tennyson's
     "ethical teaching."

6   GOLDING, LOUIS. "Evolution and WM." Saturday Review 133, no.
     3463 (11 March):253.
          Essayist evidently assumes that theories of evolution apply
     to literature and art and can therefore accuse WM of turning to the
     past to tell "tales of dead lands in a dead tongue."

7   HEARN, LAFCADIO. "WM." In Pre-Raphaelite and other Poets:
     Lectures. Edited by John Erskine. New York: Dodd, Mead.
     Reprint. 1930, pp. 262-310.
          Reprinted from 1916.4.

8   JACOBI, CHARLES T. "Kelmscott Press, 1891-1898." Penrose
     Annual 24:17-22.
          Recalls when he superintended the printing of Wolfings and
     Roots in 1890, the Gunnlaugs Saga in 1891, at the Chiswick Press.
     Discusses Kelmscott Press typefaces and illustrations, concluding it
     seems a pity (the founts being available) "that some scheme could
     not be arranged to carry on as far as possible the traditions of the
     press to which Morris devoted so much of his valuable time and
     energy."

9   MUMFORD, LEWIS. "How WM and W.H. Hudson Renew the Classic
     Tradition of Utopias." In The Story of Utopias. New York: Boni
     and Liveright, pp. 171-89.
          Discusses Nowhere as one of three "utopias of escape" (The
     others: Hudson's A Crystal Age and Wells's A Modern Utopia).
     Suggests that "with five million people in England, and perhaps half
     a million in the Thames Valley, the thing would not be impossible."

10   NEWDIGATE, B.H. "Mr. Pennell and Kelmscott Chaucer." London
     Mercury 6, no. 33 (July):299; 6, no. 36 (October):641-42.
          Argues against the observation, by Pennell (1920.10), that
     Burne-Jones had not done the drawings for the Kelmscott Chaucer, by
     printing a letter from May Morris that sets the record straight:
     Burne-Jones executed the drawings, which were then "translated" by
     Catterson-Smith and photographed onto blocks and engraved by W.H.
     Hooper. Concludes with a response from Pennell that asserts that
     the May Morris letter supported his initial contention.

11   NOYES, ALFRED. "WM." In Modern English Essays. Edited by E.
     Rhys. London and Toronto: J.M. Dent; New York: E.P. Dutton,
     5:150-63.
          Argues that the key to understanding WM's work, its
     coherence, is located at Woodford Hall, his boyhood home. "Like
     most great men, Morris retained his childhood to an exceptional
     degree." That childhood, thanks to the medieval customs at Woodford
     Hall, was linked to the Middle Ages, a continuing influence and
     inspiration.

12   OGILVY, THOMAS.   "Evolution and WM."   Saturday Review 133, no.
       3464 (18 March):285.
           Disagrees with essay (1922.6) that had relegated WM to the
     rank of "minor" poet.

13   ORAGE, ALFRED.   "Norse in English."   In Readers and Writers.
       London: Allen and Unwin, pp. 167-68.
           Comments upon C.H. Herford's judgment (1918.5) that WM
     restored to the modern world the power and beauty of Norse myth and
     then asks, "Who reads Morris's poetry today? Has he a home in our
     hearts? Are his Norse enthusiasms really anything to us?"

14   PETERSON, G.   "The Saga on the Stage: WM's Comment."   TLS, no.
       1080 (28 September):616.
           Quotes letter WM wrote on 12 September 1894 to a Scottish
     professor who had inquired about staging Volsunga; WM traces in some
     detail the ways that Volsunga is a redaction of earlier tales and
     poems, containing "huge and vague figures of the earlier times,"
     concluding that "such a subject is impossible for the stage, even
     when helped by the music of a great master."

15   PRANCE, C.R.   "The Collected Edition of WM."   TLS, no. 1058 (27
       April):276.
           Anticipating Dunlap (1973.9) by half a century, this writer
     extends a "plea for a reprint of the Introductions" to the Collected
     Works, since they are "full of literary matter of the highest
     interest." He also argues that there should be cheap editions
     available of WM's own works.

*16 PUNDT, HERBERT.   "Rossetti's Einfluss auf die Gedichte des
       jungen WM."   Dissertation, University of Breslau.
               Cited in 1960.1.

17   ROBERTSON, LIONEL.   "Reviving the Spirit of WM."   House and
       Garden 41, no. 4 (April):43, 126, 128.
           Generalizes about WM's pattern designs, referring to
     illustrations of "Pomegranite" and "Daisy" and commenting on a
     medieval arras and mille-fleurs used in a recent decorating scheme
     at the Chicago University Club.

18 SANDOR, IZSAK, trans. "A gyari munka" [On factory work].   In
    Szocializmus. New York: Hungarian Socialist Society, 39 pp.
        In Hungarian. Translation of "A Factory as it Might Be" is
appended to a 1905 lecture by T.J. Holmes on the history of
socialist thought and WM's role in shaping it.

19 STIRLING, A.M.W. William DeMorgan and His Wife. New York:
    Henry Holt, pp. 74-78, passim.
        Discusses the DeMorgan designs for tiles and pottery used by
Morris and Co. Has fresh anecdotes about Red Lion Square days and
the famed narratives of the Thames trips between Kelmscott House and
Kelmscott Manor.

20 UPDIKE, DANIEL BERKELEY. Printing Types: Their History, Forms,
    and Use: A Study in Survivals. Cambridge, Mass.: Harvard,
    2:203-10.
        Stresses that Kelmscott Press influence was greater in
America and Germany than in England. Offers some technical
descriptions of the three Kelmscott Press types, and asserts that a
Kelmscott Press page revealed "how imposing and even magnificent,
masses of strong type, closely set and well inked, combined with
fine decorations, may be."

21 WALKER, HAROLD E. "WM on Fascismo." Nation and the Athenaeum
    32, no. 6 (11 November):233.
        Points out that descriptions in Nowhere of "The Friends of
Order" offer uncanny parallels, even concerning the defense of
factories, to Fascist organizations and tactics in Italy in 1921,
when paramilitary, middle-class groups turned out to combat
communism.

1923

1   ACKERMAN, PHYLLIS. Wallpaper: Its History, Design and Use. New
    York: Frederick Stokes, pp. 61-64, passim.
        Briefly discusses WM's wallpaper designs, the great care of
his supervision "from the moment the original drawing left his hands
until the finished rolls were ready to market." Comments on WM's
ideas about the proper "underlying structure" for a wallpaper
design, and upon the advice he had for other colorists and
designers.

*2   BASCHIERE, KARL. "WM." Dissertation, University of Vienna.
       Cited in 1960.1.

3   BROERS, BERNARDA CONRADINA. "WM." In Mysticism in the
       Neo-Romanticists. Amsterdam: University Press. Reprint. New
       York: Haskell House, 1966, pp. 103-22.
           WM said to be a follower of Keats, except more "realistic."
   Discusses the images and effects of several poems from Defence,
   among them "The Blue Closet," "Rapunzel," and "The Wind," concluding
   that because of the intensity of his attitudes toward both art and
   love WM may be classified as a mystic poet.

4   BUCHAN, JOHN. Introduction to WM. Edited by Henry Newbolt.
       London and Edinburgh: Thomas Nelson and Sons, pp. vii-xii.
           Introduction has useful information on WM's early poetry and
   prose, and it also asserts that Defence "inaugurated an epoch, as
   much as did Wordsworth's Lyrical Ballads." The anthology includes
   several Defence poems, several books from Jason, three Paradise
   tales, and two of the early prose romances: "Unknown Church" and
   "Hollow Land."

5   CRAWFORD, NELSON, ed. Introduction to Poems of WM. no. 492 in
       the Little Blue Book Series, edited by E. Haldeman-Julius.
       Girard, Kans.: Haldeman-Julius Co., pp. 5-37.
           A full introduction with both basic biographical facts and
   useful discussions of the literary works. The anthology includes
   several poems from Defence, a selection from Sigurd, and some poems
   first published in Commonweal, like "Mother and Son."

6   DRINKWATER, JOHN. Victorian Poetry. London: Hodder and
       Stoughton. Reprint. New York: George H. Doran, 1924; Port
       Washinton, N.Y.: Kennikat Press, 1966, pp. 128-34, passim.
           Even though WM used the same medieval sources that Tennyson
   had, and even borrowed some of his "florid" diction, he did
   something unique: "he made an archaic idiom a living, personal and
   original thing. The complaint about Wardour Street diction is
   stupid and indefensible." Implies that WM was only slightly
   inferior to Chaucer as a narrative poet.

7   DURYEA, MINGA POPE. "Cobden-Sanderson's Garden at Hammersmith,
       with Glimpses of the Gardens of WM and Rossetti." Scribner's
       Magazine 74, no. 1 (July):25-34.
           Descriptions of a few Kelmscott House rooms and of garden,
   with an elegant fountain, as they appeared in 1923, but supposedly
   unchanged since WM's death.

8   FINGER, CHARLES J. "WM (1834-1896): An Introduction." In
    Thirteenth Century Prose Tales by WM. no. 352 in the Ten Cent
    Pocket Series, edited by E. Haldeman-Julius. Girard, Kans.:
    Haldeman-Julius, pp. 3-10.
        Lusty huzzahs for fellowship and hard work grace this
particularly American introduction to WM's life and achievements,
one which also notes parallels between WM's socialism and Gandhi's
ideas about the politics of hand-spinning. This "pocket edition"
includes "Unknown Church," "Pool," and "A Dream."

9   HUBBARD, ELBERT, ed. Elbert Hubbard's Scrapbook. New York:
    W.H. Wise, pp. 37, passim.
        Several snippets from WM's poetry and prose are here
reprinted in a collection of aphorisms, a typically American guide
to gracious living.

10 JOCHUMSON, MATTHIAS. "Vilhjalmur Morris, 1834-1896."
    Eimreithin 29, nos. 5-6:261-89.
        In Icelandic. A biographical sketch includes skaldic verses
in praise of heroic poets, inclusions which imply correspondences
between WM and Egill Skallagrimssonar (WM would have appreciated,
and chuckled over, these parallels). Discusses the two Icelandic
journeys and recalls his own visit to WM at Hammersmith in 1885.

11 MAC DOWELL, GEORGE TREMAINE. "The Treatment of the Volsung Saga
    by WM." SS 7, no. 6 (February):151-68.
        Touches upon WM's collaborations on matters Icelandic with
Magnusson and upon the two journeys to Iceland, before going on to
compare their translation of Volsunga to WM's retelling of it in
Sigurd, noting even slight alterations. Characterizes the frequent
elaborations in descriptions of setting or character as "romantic
embroidery," suggesting that Sigurd is "over-stressed as
peace-bringer" and that "Gudrun" is unduly "sentimentalized."
Concludes that as an original nineteenth-century Victorian epic,
Sigurd is of high rank, but as a re-creation of heroic Northern epic
"decidedly imperfect."

12 MANN, TOM. Tom Mann's Memoirs. London: Labour Publishing.
    Reprint. London: Macgibbon and Kee, 1967, pp. 29-33.
        Quotes "Manifesto" issued by the majority faction, led by WM,
that split from the SDF in 1884. Recalls the scene, and topic, of a
WM lecture delivered in Victoria Park.

13 MAVOR, JAMES. "WM." In My Windows on the Streets of the
    World. New York: E.P. Dutton, pp. 193-202.
        Discusses WM's work with the Glasgow branch of the Socialist
League, telling anecdotes that illustrate his great abilities, his
influence on Geddes, his love for Mark Twain, and his "chronic
pugnacity."

14 MORISON, STANLEY, and JACKSON, HOLBROOK. A Brief Survey of
    Printing History and Practice. New York: Knopf, pp. 18-23.
        Comments on WM's "virile genius" and the ways it found outlet
at Kelmscott Press as well as on its influence; some imitators, both
those who made "shameless pieces of charlatanry" and the others,
like Ricketts and Pissarro, are discussed.

15 MORRAH, HERBERT ARTHUR. "Art at the Union: Rossetti, WM,
    Burne-Jones and the Pre-Raphaelite Movement: A Tragic Comedy
    still Ripening." In The Oxford Union: 1823-1923. London:
    Cassell, pp. 161-91.
        How the "broad belt of wall" within the newly constructed
Oxford Union Hall attracted the attention of Rossetti, and how he
enlisted WM, Burne-Jones, and others to cover that wall with
Arthurian murals, how and why their work, carried on from Summer
1857 to Spring 1858, became legendary--all is fastidiously set forth
in this detailed chapter, a kind of wry interlude in the serious
history of a century of the great debating society. WM'S rendition
of a scene from the Tristram story is described in some detail, as
are the other decorations he made. Reviews contemporary reactions
to the ill-fated paintings, various suggestions regarding their
possible restoration, concluding that this still might occur since
many photographs, with that end in mind, were taken in 1906; these
were published in 1906.13.

16 OLIVERA, FEDERICO. "Sull' Paradise di WM." Rivista d' Italia
    26:321-29.
        A short biographical sketch celebrates the diversity and
depth of WM's achievements, and then various tales from Paradise are
discussed, with long quotations offered and with wide-ranging
comparisons made to other European narrative traditions and to other
British poets, like Keats and Browning. The decorations on
Kelmscott Press borders and the illustrations of Burne-Jones are
said to convey passions as bland as those in the tales.

17 SCHEU, ANDREAS. "WM." In <u>Umsturzkeime: Erlebnisse eines</u>
    <u>Kampfers</u>. Vienna: Weiner Volksbuchhandlung, pp. 65-103.
        Scheu was an intimate of WM throughout the years of his most
active socialist work, and his reports on, for instance, the
intrigues of Hyndman that caused WM and others, Scheu among them, to
leave the SDF to set up the Socialist League, are marked by details
and bolstered by extensive quotations from letters which WM had sent
to him. Includes fresh anecdotes about WM as host at Kelmscott
House, as a street-corner agitator, and as a warm friend and
colleague.

18 "Eton Memorial Tapestries." <u>Times</u>, no. 43,516 (5 December):15.
        Article on the Eton Memorial Tapestries, just completed at
Merton Abbey, comments upon the looms and weavers there, the
"craftsmen who carry on the Morris tradition."

19 "WM and His Wallpaper Designs." <u>Arts</u> <u>and</u> <u>Decoration</u> 19, no. 5
    (September):57.
        Discusses commercial interests in wallpaper which provoked WM
into designing the Trellis, in 1862, and continuing to make
wallpapers a staple of the Firm. Other WM patterns are mentioned,
and so is his influence on continental designers and on Kate
Greenaway, whose drawings found their way onto nursery wallpapers.

                            <u>1924</u>

1   BENSON, ARTHUR C. <u>Memories</u> <u>and</u> <u>Friends</u>. London: John Murray,
    pp. 239, 245-46.
        Comments upon relations between WM and Murray, between WM and
Rossetti, and how he grew to resent Rossetti's presence at Kelmscott
Manor.

2   IONIDES, LUKE. "Memories: WM and Richard Wagner."
    <u>Transatlantic</u> <u>Review</u> 1, no. 2 (February):36-40.
        The author's memories of WM extended back to 1865, and these
contain fresh anecdotes about WM and money, about his use of prosaic
language, and his disdain for Wagner's wife.

3   JACKSON, HOLBROOK. "The Nonage of Nineteenth Century
    Printing." <u>Fleuron: A Journal of Typography</u>, no. 2:87-97.
        Stresses that "readability" must be the most important
quality in any book: "one bows before the beauty of Kelmscott
Chaucer, but one reads the Father of English Poetry in small pica
and octavo." WM seen as important for throwing printing "back into
the primitive," thus providing a new start, "but neither he nor his
followers have produced typography which you can do more than admire
and respect." Reprinted. 1939.4.

4   LYTTON, NEVILLE. "A Discussion about WM." Nation and Athenaeum
     34, no. 23 (8 March):793-94.
         Recalls a conversation with Walker, who said that future
generations would find it "as difficult to think that the world will
produce another Morris as another Shakespeare." In discussing WM's
medievalism, he points out that when the hounds had lost the scent,
WM was able to bring them back to the spot where they had first took
up the cry, so that they could begin anew.

5   MORISON, STANLEY. Introduction to Four Centuries of Fine
     Printing. London: Ernest Benn. 4th rev. ed., 1960, pp. 42-44,
     passim.
         Comments on WM and Kelmscott Press within a detailed
historical introduction that precedes 192 facsimile pages from
presses established between 1465 and 1924. Praises WM's work,
pointing out that its influence "was enormous, but it is infinitely
to be regretted that his enthusiasm for the Middle Ages led him to
go behind the Roman letter," since his Golden type is "coarse and
heavy."

6   SPARLING, H. HALLIDAY. The Kelmscott Press and WM,
     Master-Craftsman. London: Macmillan, 185 pp. Reprint.
     Folkstone: Dawsons, 1975.
         As son-in-law, assistant editor of Commonweal, and secretary
of Kelmscott Press, the author had several years of "intimate
contact" with WM, and this study thus has significant details and
important insights into WM's achievements at the Kelmscott
Press--and also some exaggerations: as "science must reckon with
Darwin, so must art with Morris." Early chapters chart WM's
continuing interest in the book arts, and discuss the history of
printing, especially in the nineteenth century when speed and
economy became controlling criteria rather than design and clarity
and beauty. Reviews attention WM gave to the design of Wolfings and
Roots, and then--after the famed Walker lecture--to the shapes and
casting of type, to the manufacture of paper, to problems with
carving wood blocks, to every facet of the work of the Press.
Details support the contention that WM became "The Master Printer"
whose achievement with the Kelmscott Press changed the art of
printing. Four appendixes include WM's note on his aims in founding
the Press, Cockerell's description (1898.3) of the Press, an
annotated list of the books published there, and a list of various
ephemera printed at the Press.

7   SYMONS, ARTHUR. "The Decay of Craftsmanship in England." In
     Studies in Seven Arts. London: Martin Secker, pp. 121-29.
     Reprint. New York: AMS Press, 1973.
          Though "for fifteen years the Society of Arts and Crafts has
     done its best to foster and reward the making of beautiful things
     for everyday use" it has, generally, failed; "what is called the
     movement of Morris was literally Morris's vivid, personal movement;
     it began, and all but ended, in himself." Implies that WM attempted
     to create a revolution in art rather than society. First written in
     1903.

8   SYMONS, ARTHUR. "WM." In Studies in Two Literatures. London:
     Martin Secker, pp. 3-11.
          Celebrates WM's diversity of talent, his refusal to channel
     his energies into only one art or craft, for wherever it led, "he
     followed beauty." His poetry, in its "clear designs," is compared
     to his tapestries, and in Defence he "invented a new movement, doing
     easily, with a certain appropriate quaintness, what Tennyson all his
     life had been trying to do."

9   WILSON, STELLA P. "WM and France." South Atlantic Quarterly
     23, no. 3 (July):242-55.
          Recalls WM's early estimation of French cathedrals as "the
     noblest work of human invention," quoting other paeans he sang to
     the trees and fields of Northern France. Discusses then the ways
     that cathedrals figure in the early romances, why French scenery is
     almost as important as Froissart to Defence poems. It appears also
     in Jason and in the prologue to Paradise, four of whose tales are
     based on French sources. In his design work WM turned to medieval
     French books for information on dyes and embroidery techniques, late
     in life he translated medieval French romances and published them at
     Kelmscott Press, and during his last illness he was comforted by
     viewing medieval French manuscripts.

10   WOLFF, LUCIEN. "Le sentiment medieval en Angleterre au XIXe
     siecle, et la premiere poesie de WM." Revue anglo-americaine 1,
     no. 6 (August):491-504; 2, no. 1 (October):29-38.
          Biographical sketch stresses WM's early interests and
     expertise in matters medieval; detailed and helpful discussions of
     several of the poems from Defence follow, with attention paid to the
     ways WM used Froissart.

11 "The WM Works at Merton Abbey." <u>Bookman's Journal</u> 9
    (January):152.
        Notes that work on tapestries, chintzes, and stained glass,
continues at Merton Abbey, "in a spirit and manner worthy of its
founder."

                            <u>1925</u>

1   BURDETT, OSBERT. <u>The Beardsley Period: An Essay in</u>
    <u>Perspective</u>. New York: Boni and Liveright; London: Bodley Head,
    passim.
        Asserts that WM's decorations caused such a "revolution in
domestic interiors" that everyone appreciated the point of Gilbert's
caricature in <u>Patience</u>. Suggests that Beardsley's book designs,
because not so fecund, were better than WM's. Repeats the false
story about Wilde's visits to WM during his final illness; Wilde was
actually in jail at the time.

2   EVANS, B. IFOR. <u>WM and His Poetry</u>. London: Harrap, 156 pp.
    Reprint. Folcroft, Pa.: Folcroft Press, 1969. New York: AMS
    Press, 1971, 1972. Folcroft, Pa.: Folcroft Library Editions,
    1974. Norwood, Pa.: Norwood Editions, 1976. Philadelphia: R.
    West, 1977.
        Opens with the September 1885 court scene when WM made a
"just estimate of himself" as "well-known throughout Europe." The
poetry that brought him that reputation is here discussed in general
terms, accompanied by paraphrase and liberal quotation, but fresh
and useful points often occur; for instance, the terza rima of "The
Defence of Guenevere" is judged as "one of the few successful uses
of that metre in English." Comments upon Poe's influence in
<u>Defence</u>, upon the dark vision in the prologue of <u>Paradise</u> as a
reflection of both WM's own mind and of his troubled times, and upon
themes in <u>Sigurd</u> and <u>Poems by the Way</u>.

3   HUDSON, W.H. <u>Men, Books and Birds</u>. London: Eveleigh, Nash and
    Grayson, pp. 219-22.
        Asserts that some of WM's verse is "the most careless, even
sloppy, go as you please sort of verse ever written. He never tried
to recapture the magic of that first book of his."

4   HUNT, VIOLET. "Kelmscott to Kelmscott." <u>London Mercury</u> 11, no.
    6 (January):268-75.
        Recalls, rather dimly, seeing WM, DeMorgan, and others going
up the Thames on two river boats, and builds upon that recollection
to discuss "Topsy," some of his poetry, and some of the
personalities, especially Rossetti, from the Oxford and Red Lion
Square days. This lively and confusing account is reprinted, with a
few additional paragraphs, in 1968.17.

5   KNICKERBOCKER, WILLIAM. Creative Oxford: Its Influence on
    Victorian Literature. Syracuse, N.Y.: Syracuse University
    Press, pp. 162-68, passim.
        Discusses WM and Oxford humanism, recalling the immediate
effects of his Oxford lecture, "Art under Plutocracy," in 1883, when
Ruskin was in the chair.

6   MARILLIER, H.C. "The Merton Abbey Tapestries: WM's Great
    Revival." Landmark 7:155-58.
        Reviews significance of WM's revival of tapestry weaving at
Merton Abbey; here the best tapestry designs in 150 years were
produced. Describes many of the designs done by Burne-Jones and the
present location of the tapestries, and mentions others designed by
Byron Shaw, Bernard Partridge, and Mrs. Akers Douglas.

7   MASON, EUGENE. "The Medievalism of WM." In Considered Writers,
    Old and New. London: Methuen, pp. 97-119.
        General but graceful survey of WM's achievements, so diverse
yet powerful that the man seems to be "Gladstone and Tennyson and
Selfridge in a single person." Asserts that only one rubric can
cover all those interests and achievements: his "love of the Middle
Ages." Useful summaries of various medieval influences on WM's
writings, his decorative arts, and his politics follow.

8   NEWDIGATE, B.H. "Kelmscott Press." London Mercury 11, no. 64
    (February):418-19.
        Note on May Morris's description of the Walker lecture which
marks the beginnings of Kelmscott Press, and on Halliday Sparling's
recent book on the Press (1924.6): "the most valuable thing in his
book is Morris's own 'Note on Aims in Founding Kelmscott Press.'"

9   NEWDIGATE, B.H. "Was WM Wrong?" TLS, no. 1204 (12
    February):104.
        A response to a reviewer of Sparling's book (1924.6) who had
written that WM was wrong in his opinions about printing, wrong also
as a practitioner, for he had merely copied. Points out that WM had
on the contrary borrowed what was best; as his work with SPAB should
suggest he was against copying; as a practitioner of the book arts
the Kelmscott Press volumes speak for themselves, for their
"workmanship and beauty have never been surpassed."

10 SUGDEN, ALAN; EDMUNDSON, VICTOR, and LUDLAM, JOHN. "The Coming
    of WM." In A History of English Wallpaper, 1509-1914. London:
    Batsford, pp. 159-76.
       Biographical sketch provided so that wallpaper designs are
seen within the context of a "movement which brought modern domestic
ornamentation once more into living contact and kinship with pure
art." Wallpapers were one of the few articles which the Firm did
not produce; the sixty or more papers WM designed were manufactured
by Jeffrey and Co., who continued to produce Morris and Co.
wallpapers until the Firm closed. Discusses specific designs and
Morris and Co. influence on continental wallpapers.

11 YEATS, W.B. A Vision. London: T. Werner Laurie. Reprint.
    London: Macmillan, 1937, p. 111.
       Comments on Birdalone's loves and struggles in Water, saying
that she represents a "woman of Phase Three reflected in the
antithetical mind."

1926

1 CLAYTON, JOSEPH. The Rise and Decline of Socialism in Great
    Britain, 1884-1924. London: Faber and Guyer, pp. 17-22, passim.
       Discusses WM and his important role in the Socialist League
during the five years (1885-89) when "it was very much alive," when
it was "recognized in Europe as the genuine Marxist article and the
SDF dismissed as a moderate affair."

2 COBDEN-SANDERSON, T.J. The Journals of Thomas Cobden-Sanderson,
    1879-1922. London: Thavies Inn; New York: Macmillan, 2 vols.,
    passim.
       Cobden-Sanderson, WM's neighbor at Hammersmith, ran a bindery
before beginning Doves Press. Here are two references to WM from
these interesting and moody journals: "Though we have not done much
binding for Kelmscott Press, we have done a great deal of mending,
re-binding, and re-covering for the library of early-printed books
which Morris is collecting." The second was written in September
1896: "Morris is dying, slowly. It is an astonishing spectacle. He
sits speechless, waiting for the end to come."

3 CRICHTON-BROWN, JAMES. Victorian Jottings. London: Etchell and
    MacDonald, p. 252.
       Recalls that Walker, "the great Pauline," once said that "at
Oxford they used to call Morris 'Mad Morris' because whenever
anything was said that pleased him, he used to go and butt his head
against a wall."

4   GWYNN, STEPHEN. <u>The</u> <u>Experiences</u> <u>of</u> <u>a</u> <u>Literary</u> <u>Man</u>. New York:
    Henry Holt and Co., pp. 41-44.
         Recalls how Ruskin, in response to consternation caused among
    an Oxford audience by WM's lecture, "Art and Plutocracy," stood and
    "with a few courteous, well-chosen sentences made everybody feel
    that we were an assembly of gentleman." Of a WM lecture in Dublin,
    the author reports that WM had trouble with disputants but was
    congenial and informative at a party after the lecture, when he
    spoke of Yeats and of stained glass.

5   HUBBARD, ELBERT. "WM." In <u>Guide</u> <u>Book</u> <u>for</u> <u>Little</u> <u>Journeys</u> <u>to</u>
    <u>the</u> <u>Homes</u> <u>of</u> <u>the</u> <u>Great</u>. New York: W.H. Wise and Co., p. 32.
         A one-volume guide to the essays in the multivolume set of
    <u>Little</u> <u>Journeys</u> (1900.8). There WM appears with "British Poets."
    But in the present guide he is listed under "Business and Economics"
    and rests, uncomfortably, one supposes, between Philip D. Armour and
    Andrew Carnegie.

6   JACKSON, HOLBROOK. <u>WM</u>. London: Cape, 160 pp. Reprint.
    Westport, Conn.: Greenwood Press, 1971.
         Revision of 1908.6. Each of the ten chapters from the
    earlier edition are lengthened and four chapters added; these
    include sketches of WM as individual and as man of letters, an
    estimation of his final achievement, and a description of Kelmscott
    Press. Some negative comments on Kelmscott Press volumes are
    unusual, as are comparisons of WM to Whitman and claims about why WM
    would not appreciate post-1917 Russia.

7   LE GALLIENNE, RICHARD. <u>The</u> <u>Romantic</u> <u>90s</u>. Garden City, N.Y.:
    Doubleday, pp. 121-27.
         Recalls seeing WM at a lecture in the 1890s and visiting
    Kelmscott Manor a few years after WM's death.

8   LUBBOCK, PERCY, ed. <u>The</u> <u>Diary</u> <u>of</u> <u>Arthur</u> <u>Christopher</u> <u>Benson</u>.
    London: Longmans, pp. 96, 130, passim.
         These diary entries include graceful remarks on the
    excellence of Mackail (1899.10), upon the beauties of Kelmscott
    Manor, and upon WM's poetic debt to Keats. Reports also upon the WM
    manuscripts that Murray gave to the Fitzwilliam and that Henry James
    had once referred to WM as a "bloody, lusty, noisy grotesque."

9   MACKAIL, J.W.   "WM." In Studies of English Poets. London:
     Longmans, pp. 173-97.
          Reprint of 1910.7.

10   MARTIN, HUGH. "A Study of WM." Congregational Quarterly 4, no.
     2 (April):172-80.
          General biographical facts stress WM's "love and concern for
     the Home," its decorations and setting. Comments on Morris and Co.
     extend into a discussion of WM's philosophy of art and work, and
     comments on the socialist lectures conclude with thought that WM
     would surely be welcomed into heaven, even though he was "reticent"
     about Christianity. Reprinted: 1927.6.

11   NEEDHAM, H.A. Le developpement de l'esthetique sociologique en
     France et en Angleterre an XIXe siecle. Paris: Champion, pp.
     171.94.
          A chapter, "The Problem of Art and Industry (1850-1900)," has
     sections on England and on the influence of Ruskin and WM in both
     England and France. Includes a discussion of lectures in Hopes and
     a detailed survey of French scholarship and criticism; an extensive
     bibliography appears on pp. 289-311.

12   ORCUTT, WILLIAM DANA. In Quest of the Perfect Book:
     Reminiscences and Reflections of a Bookman. London: Murray;
     Boston: Little, Brown, pp. 259-68, passim.
          A survey of all the other work WM had undertaken in 1894 and
     1895 suggests why the Kelmscott Chaucer took a year and nine months
     to complete. Claims that this book is not meant to be read so much
     as to be "looked at," that the Doves Press Bible is a "relief after
     the riotous beauty of the Morris pages."

13   RALLI, AUGUSTUS JOHN. "The Earthly Paradise." North American
     Review 222:299-310.
          Asserts that Jason and the prologue and the first four tales
     of Paradise represent WM at his finest as a poet, since their
     Grecian themes incorporate eternal truths. Other Paradise tales are
     merely pathetic. Reprinted: 1927.8.

14   READ, HERBERT. "WM and the Modern Movement." In English
     Stained Glass. London and New York: G.P. Putnam's Sons.
     Reprint. Milwood, N.Y.: Kraus Reprint Co., 1973, pp. 221-26.
          Claims that WM, through Morris and Co. designs for stained
     glass, enabled the artistry of Burne-Jones to become widely known.
     Offers specific dates and subjects of windows Burne-Jones designed,
     discusses the implications of Morris and Co. not putting new windows
     in old churches, and points out that the principles of WM have not

been followed in the stained glass the Firm has done since his
death.

15 TEA, EVA. "WM e Boni." I libri del giorno 9 (October):514-16.
        Reprints and comments upon letters WM sent in 1892 to Giacomo
Boni regarding SPAB and the Campo Santo Pisano.

*16 ZACHRISSEN, WALDEMAN. WM. Goteborg, 40 pp.
        Cited in New York City Public Library catalogues.

1927

1 AUSLANDER, JOSEPH, and HILL, FRANK ERNEST. "Under Steam and
       Stone." In The Winged Horse: The Story of Poets and their
       Poetry. Garden City, N.Y.: Doubleday. Reprint. New York:
       Haskell House, 1969, pp. 365-88.
        Rossetti, Swinburne, and WM are characterized as writers "who
turned their backs on life and made a dream life to suit
themselves."

2 FRITZSCHE, GUSTAV. WM's Sozialismus und anarchistischer
       Kommunismus: Darstellung des Systems und Untersuchung den
       Quellen. Leipzig: Bernhard Tauchnitz, 132 pp. Reprint. New
       York: Johnson Reprint, 1966.
        Traces WM's growth from a social reformer to a socialist to,
finally, an anarchist socialist, discussing the influence of Ruskin,
Fourier, Marx, and Kropotkin. The second section has a schematic
outline of parts of Das Kapital placed beside passages from WM's
lectures. In the final section parallels are drawn between passages
from Kropotkin and Nowhere. Unfortunately, has no index. Originally
a 1925 University of Leipzig dissertation.

3 MAC MURTRIE, DOUGLAS. "Fitness to Purpose vs. Beauty in Book
       Design." Publisher's Weekly 111, no. 20 (14 May):1883-85.
        Since Kelmscott Press books "are not readable," they violate
the principle of "fitness to purpose," but WM deserves our homage
because at Kelmscott Press he established "new standards of
craftsmanship in composition, paper-making, presswork, and binding,"
and he thus set an example for many subsequent printers. Reprint.
New York: Privately Printed, 1933, 8 pp.

4   MAC MURTRIE, DOUGLAS. "A Typographical Messiah." In The Golden
     Book: The Story of Fine Books and Book-making--Past and Present.
     New York: Covici-Friede. 3d ed., 1934, pp. 276-90, passim.
          Discusses the founding of Kelmscott Press, from the slide
     lecture by Walker through descriptions of the fine paper and ink
     used, as well as its influence. Includes seven full-page
     illustrations. Reprinted: 1943.2.

5   MARILLIER, H.C. History of the Merton Abbey Tapestry Works
     Founded by WM. London: Constable, 65 pp.
          WM taught himself to weave tapestries, beginning in 1879 with
     "Cabbage and Vine," and then taught others, notably Henry Dearle who
     was destined to become chief designer and manager of Morris and Co.
     History of works at Merton Abbey set forth, along with details of
     various tapestries, the chief of which are the Grail tapestries done
     for Stanmore Hall (1978.65), and of various loom techniques and the
     few advances made by modern weavers. Points out that these tapestry
     works are "flourishing still. Their work is incomparably the best
     that is being produced in the world today; and its preservation as a
     link with the past and a continuation of one of the most ancient and
     most honorable crafts, might seem not unreasonably to be a matter of
     national significance." Includes a chronolgical list of all
     tapestries completed up to 1927 and twenty-eight plates.

6   MARTIN, HUGH. "WM, 1834-1896." In Christian Social Reformers
     of the Nineteenth Century. Edited by Hugh Martin. London:
     Student Christian Movement, pp. 163-81.
          Reprint of 1926.10.

7   PHELAN, ANNA AUGUSTA VON HELMHOLTZ. The Social Philosophy of
     WM. Durham, N.C.: Duke University Press, 207 pp. Reprint.
     Folcroft, Pa.: Folcroft Library Editions, 1974, 1976. Norwood,
     Pa.: Norwood Editions, 1977. Philadelphia: R. West, 1978.
          A four-part biography, the first citing the usual
     biographical details, drawn largely from Mackail (1899.10), with
     attempts to "emphasize only the influences and events which made WM
     a social thinker." Part 2 discusses nineteenth-century socialists
     like Owen and Fourier, and it also offers passages from Commonweal
     that demonstrate WM's objections to both "palliation" and anarchism.
     Part 3 comments upon the significance of WM's social ideals and
     offers extensive paraphrase and quotation from the socialist
     lectures and from Nowhere. Concludes with statement: "Give man
     intelligent work is Morris's answer to the social question of how to
     obtain a whole and worthy life." Revision of 1908.11.

8   RALLI, AUGUSTUS JOHN. "The Earthly Paradise." In Critiques.
     London: Longmans, pp. 19-33. Reprint. Freeport, N.Y.: Books
     for Libraries, 1966.
          Reprint of 1926.13.

9   "WM and Anti-Scrape." TLS, no. 1310 (10 March):149-50.
          Convinced that neo-Gothic revivalists had done more in fifty
     years to damage medieval buildings than all the previous centuries'
     ravages had accomplished, WM in 1877 established SPAB and became its
     first secretary. Discusses the particular restorations that moved
     WM to write the letter that brought the Society into being, quotes
     from it, from WM's later writings for SPAB. He remained active in
     the Society's work for the rest of his life, and the Society still
     exists, its philosophy still based on WM's precepts, its problems
     with arrogant architects and "planners" remarkably similar to those
     that moved WM to write the letter in 1877 that launched the Society.

10   Books Printed by WM at Kelmscott Press. Catalogue of an
     Exhibition at the Newberry Library. Chicago: Ludlow Co., 13 pp.
          Briefly describes every Kelmscott Press volume, and all of
     them were included in this exhibition.

                              1928

*1   ARSCOTT, CHRISTINE M. "A Study of Jason, Paradise and Sigurd,
     with Special Reference to WM's Treatment of his Sources."
     Dissertation, University of London.
          Cited in 1968.25.

2   CAINE, HALL. Recollections of Rossetti. London: Cassell and
     Co., 174-75, 200-201.
          Has some references to the Morrises, especially to Janey, not
     in 1909.4. Speaks of guilt of Rossetti, who "engaging himself to
     one woman in all honour and good faith had fallen in love with
     another, and then gone on to marry the first out of a mistaken sense
     of loyalty and a fear of giving pain." This led to suicide, to
     infidelity, to WM's wholehearted devotion to his work.

3   CLARK, KENNETH. The Gothic Revival: An Essay in the History of
     Taste. London: Constable. 2d ed., 1949. Reprint. New York:
     Harper and Row: 1962, pp. 141, 202, 218, 223.
          Credits WM with making Victorian drawing rooms less drab,
     suggesting also that his influence and that of the Arts and Crafts
     Movement on nineteenth-century art and architecture was significant.

4   GOULD, FREDERIC. <u>Hyndman: Prophet of Socialism</u> (1842-1921).
     London: Allen and Unwin, pp. 11-12, passim.
         Quotes Hyndman on the quarrel which led to WM leaving the SDF
as the saddest event in his career, and then offers the following,
supposedly from WM in the 1890s: "Hyndman was quite right, and I was
quite wrong!" Implies that WM mistook plans for intrigue and that
he was more interested in the spiritual than the pragmatic aspects
of socialism.

5   GRIERSON, HERBERT J.C. <u>Lyrical Poetry from Blake to Hardy</u>.
     London: Hogarth Press, pp. 107-11. New York: Harcourt, Brace,
     1929, as <u>Lyrical Poetry of the Nineteenth Century</u>.
         Discusses Rossetti, WM, and Swinburne as the most significant
of the Pre-Raphaelite poets, stressing WM's ability to render from
the Middle Ages the "passionate soul of great lovers and great
fighters and goodly builders and craftsmen." WM's best poems are
lyrical and the later narrative poems tend to monotony, but the
burden of all his poetry is the same: "delight in beauty, the beauty
of nature and of craftsmanship, things made with human hands, the
beauty of strength and courage, courage in the face of death which
awaits all men." Concludes that "few poets have written so
abundantly, unless it be Spencer, on so few notes, in so narrow a
range of moods."

6   KUSTER, ELISABET. <u>Mittelalter und Antike bei WM</u>. Berlin and
     Leipzig: Walter de Gruyter, 239 pp.
         Discusses ways that WM adds medieval features to classical
scenes and characters in <u>Jason</u> and in Homeric translations,
accounting for these amalgamations by asserting that WM had a
"monomania" for the sensuous details he found in medieval life and
decoration, a monomania that separates him from other
nineteenth-century poets, both British and German, who deal with
classical themes. Has three sections; the first surveys the
backgrounds of nineteenth-century medievalism, touching on the
contributions of writers like Pugin and Ruskin; the second presents
examples of changes that WM makes in the Homeric translations and in
<u>Jason</u>; the third offers some aesthetic speculation upon the effects
of WM's tendencies to bring medieval ideas to his classical poems.

7   LUCAS, E.V. <u>The Colvins and Their Friends</u>. New York:
     Scribners, pp. 35-36.
         Includes a description of WM written in 1870 by Rosalind
Howard (later Lady Carlisle); she found him shy but friendly, saying
"he talks so clearly and seems to think so clearly. He lacks
sympathy and humanity though."

*8   MAC MINN, NEY LANNES. "The Letters of WM to the Press,
      1868-1895." Dissertation, Northwestern University.
          Cited in 1968.25.

9   MEGROZ, RANDOLPHE. Rossetti: Painter, Poet of Heaven in Earth.
     London: Faber and Gwyer, 108-17, 241-45, passim.
          Describes the adventure of the Oxford Union murals and the
     Rossetti watercolors which WM bought, those which influenced the
     imagery he used in a few early poems. Has reasonable speculations
     about Janey and Rossetti: "It is not possible to read Mackail
     (1899.10) without getting the impression that Morris was as troubled
     about his marriage to Janey Burden as Rossetti a little later was to
     be about his own marriage to Lizzie Siddall."

10   MORRIS, MAY. "A WM Memorial Hall." TLS, no. 1369 (26
     April):313.
          Mentions her father's world-wide reputation "as the great
     poet who brought back to English literature the magic of Chaucer,"
     as the decorative artist and reforming socialist whose name is still
     widely known. Yet only at Kelmscott did he feel "at home," and so a
     memorial hall is to be raised there, and this letter is an appeal
     for funds.

*11   NETTLAU, MAX. Prologue to Noticias de Ninguna Parte. Buenos
      Aires: Editorial la Protesta, pp. 1-28.
          Introduction to Spanish edition of Nowhere. Cited in 1936.3.

12   ORCUTT, WILLIAM DANA. "WM: The Art of Printing Comes Back into
     its Own." In Master Makers of the Book: Being a Consecutive
     Story of the Book from a Century before the Invention of
     Printing through the Era of the Doves Press. Garden City, N.Y.:
     Doubleday, pp. 207-28.
          A biographical sketch precedes the fuller treatment given to
     the founding of Kelmscott Press. Has useful, detailed discussions
     about the three types, about the Kelmscott Chaucer and WM's
     justified anxiety over delays in its publication, and about the
     importance of Walker, without whom neither the Kelmscott nor the
     Doves presses would have been possible.

13   PERRY, MARSDEN. A Chronological List of the Books Printed at
     Kelmscott Press. Boston: Merrymount Press, 47 pp.
          H.C. Marillier brought together this impressive collection,
     which was acquired by J. Marsden Perry and includes a complete set
     of Kelmscott Press books, both those on vellum and on paper, the
     minor pieces of printing done at the Press, and the complete set of
     illustrations for Kelmscott Chaucer. The 243 items are described,

and an appendix includes a note WM wrote about the Augsburg Bible as well as a Quaritch letter about Burne-Jones and Chaucer.

14   ROGERS, P.   "WM's 'Summer Dawn.'"   TLS, no. 1377 (21 June):459.
     Suggests new puncuation for line two in "Summer Dawn," a semicolon after "me."

15   SCOTT, FRANK HOPE.   "The Poetry of WM."   Humberside 3:71-80.
     A rambling discussion of WM's poetry which attributes his success as a poet to his "feeling for nature." WM also had a "quick ear for sounds, combined with an exceptionally retentive memory for scenes."

16   TOMKINSON, G.S.   "The Kelmscott Press."   In A Select
     Bibliography of Modern Presses.   London: First Edition Club, pp. 104-31.
     Describes WM's aims at Kelmscott Press, the different typefaces, and all of the publications: each of the fifty-three books and the sixteen other items printed there, from invitations to scholarly certificates.

17   WAUGH, EVELYN.   Rossetti: His Life and Works.   London:
     Duckworth. 2d ed., 1931.   Reprint.   1975, pp. 182-90, passim.
     Has the usual details about Burne-Jones and WM working with Rossetti in London, but suggests that the "two years Morris studied under Rossetti with servile deference were by far the two least profitable years in his life." Goes into more detail about Rossetti's stint at Kelmscott Manor, his incompatability with the place ("a dark shadow across the sun-bathed water meadows"), and the paintings he finished there.   Sets forth the arguments surrounding the dissolution of Morris, Marshall, Faulkner Co. in ways sympathetic to Brown and Rossetti.

<u>1929</u>

1   PARRY, JOHN J.   "A Note on the Prosody of WM."   MLN 44, no. 5
    (May):306-9.
    Comments on the "unorthodox" nature of many of WM's rhymes, suggesting that certain of these peculiarities (especially those involving stress) occur commonly in Welsh, "the language of Morris's ancestors." If we scan some of WM's "bad" lines according to Welsh metrical practices, then "the lines take on a new beauty." That WM never learned Welsh apparently does not concern the author.

2   RANSOM, WILL. "Kelmscott Press." In Private Presses and Their
     Books. New York: R.R. Bowker, pp. 43-50, passim.
         Claims that there are three kinds of Kelmscott Press books:
     (1) the "jolly, friendly, humanistic, little volumes" (like the
     first six), (2) the rest of the list, and (3) Kelmscott Chaucer.
     Brief discussions of WM and Kelmscott Press in relation to other
     presses and printers: Walker, Cobden-Sanderson, Ricketts. Also has
     a complete list of Kelmscott Press publications.

3   WELBY, T. EARLE. The Victorian Romantics, 1850-1870. London:
     Gerald Howe. Reprint. Hamden, Conn.: Archon Books, 1966, pp.
     34-40, passim.
         Notes parallels between Rossetti and his work for Germ, and
     WM and his for the Oxford and Cambridge Magazine, for which he wrote
     eight stories, five poems, two articles, and a review. Judges the
     verse to be of higher quality than the stories and points out that
     Swinburne was influenced by the medieval themes in these pieces.

4   WINDISCH, ALBERT. "WM als Drucker." Gutenberg Jahrbuch
     4:238-48.
         Sketches in biographical backgrounds, going into some detail
     about ways that WM was influenced by German incunabula. Discusses
     the three Kelmscott Press typefaces and praises the Kelmscott
     Chaucer.

5   A Catalogue of an Exhibition of the Fifty-Three Books Printed by
     WM at Kelmscott Press, 1891-1898. A Loan Exhibition Arranged by
     Mrs. G.M. Millard at the Little Museum of La Miniature in
     Pasadena. Los Angeles: Young and McAllister, 16 pp.
         Includes short descriptions of the fifty-three titles from
     the Kelmscott Press included in the exhibit.

                                1930

1   BLONDAL, SIGFUS. "WM og Island." Arsrit hins islenzka
     Fraethafelags 11:65-84.
         In Icelandic. Examines associations, literary and personal,
     that WM had with Iceland, offering fresh details about, for
     instance, WM's interest in Icelandic textiles, some of which he
     brought back from his journeys to Iceland, and also about archaic
     diction in saga translations, both in WM and in Danish translations
     of the sagas. Comments upon the flattering reference to Icelanders
     in John Ball, discusses "Gudrun" and its source, Laxdaela Saga,
     pondering the effects of changes WM made. The Iceland Relief
     Committee, the appearance of Icelandic names in the prose romances
     and the affinities many Icelanders continue to feel for WM are also
     discussed.

2   BOTTOMLY, GORDON. Foreword to Two Poems by WM: "The Defence of
     Guenevere" and "King Arthur's Tomb." London: Fanfrolico Press,
     16 pp.
        Expresses confidence that WM's poetic reputation will again
rise, and then demonstrates why it should by offering new insights
into "Scenes from the Fall of Troy." Includes eight collographs of
drawings by Rossetti.

3   EDDISON, E.R. "Terminal Essay: On Some Principles of
     Translation." Egil's Saga. Cambridge: Cambridge University
     Press, pp. 229-42.
        Asserts that George Dasent and WM are the two best British
translators of Icelandic sagas, discusses their strengths and
weaknesses, pointing out that WM's "joy in words" leads him "into a
curiosity of archaism that has a sophisticated and literary effect
quite alien to the works he is translating."

4   HOARE, AGNES D.M. "The Works of WM and Yeats in Relation to
     Early Saga Literature." Dissertation, Cambridge University.
        Revised for publication: 1937.4.

5   HUNT, VIOLET. "Stunners." Artwork 6 (Summer):77-87.
        Calls WM "the patron of medieval stunners" because of his
sympathetic, if psychologically puzzling, portraits of women in
Defence poems. Discusses these heroines, especially Guenevere, in
subjective, rhapsodic ways, often making interesting links to
several of Rossetti's models--though not to Janey.

6   JOHNSTON, PAUL. "WM and Printing Style: The Whittingtons to
     WM." In Biblio-Typographica: A Survey of Contemporary Fine
     Printing Style. New York: Covici-Friede, pp. 3-8, 9-13, passim.
        Asserts that Kelmscott Press was an "expression of
romanticism" and that with it WM established no school or movement;
instead he inspired printers like Updike and Rogers, who built the
foundation for modern tendencies in fine book-making. And Francis
Meynell took the next important step by establishing the Nonesuch
Press. Concludes with high praise for Walker.

7   KNAPPERT, E.C. "WM, 1834-1896." Leven en werken (Amsterdam)
     15, pt. 2:442-61.
        In Dutch. Biographical sketch precedes a discussion of the
pertinence of what WM had to say about work, why it should and must
become a source of satisfaction, and even of joy.

8   LUCAS, F.L. "WM." In Eight Victorian Poets. Cambridge:
    Cambridge University Press, pp. 91-112.
        Compares WM to Dr. Johnson: thanks to a combination of
    intellectual force and downright animal spirits, "both men waged a
    lifelong war on cant and unreality." Mixes biographical detail with
    graceful generalizations about the ways that WM's medieval
    sensibilities emerge in Defence, Jason, and Paradise, whose tales
    "establish him as the greatest master of long narrative in modern
    English poetry." Celebrates Love Is Enough, which critics have "too
    much overlooked," says of Sigurd, "it has a unity of atmosphere not
    soon forgotten," and that WM's poetry will be "read and remembered
    as long as there exist words romantic enough to rebel against the
    prosaic materialism of modern civilization." Reprinted: 1940.12.

9   MUMBY, FRANK A. The Romance of Book-Selling. London: Cape.
    Reprint. Metuchen, N.J.: Scarecrow, 1967, pp. 333-34.
        Speaks of WM's decision to take on publication of Kelmscott
    Press books; the earlier volumes, from Plain to More's Utopia, were
    published by Reeves and Turner, the poems of Rossetti and Tennyson
    by other publishers. WM published all the rest, and he made a
    profit from the venture.

10 PARRINGTON, VERNON. Main Currents in American Thought. Vol. 3.
    New York: Harcourt, Brace, pp. 224-25.
        Contrasts WM's medievalism with that of Henry Adams, saying
    that the former "discovered the secret of that earlier civilization
    in the guild rather than the church," that it was a pity that Adams
    never met "the one Victorian he should most have delighted in--the
    nineteenth-century craftsman who found in his workshop the good life
    the historian dreamed of." Judges WM to have been an important
    influence on Howells's Through the Eye of the Needle.

11 WOODS, MARGARET L. "The Roots of the Eighties." In The
    Eighteen-eighties, Essays by Fellows of the Royal Society of
    Literature. Edited by Walter De La Mare. Cambridge: Cambridge
    University Press, pp. 4-6.
        Suggests that WM's facility in composing long verse
    narratives might be the source of their vagueness and their
    consequent neglect. Comments on Defence poems and on Nowhere,
    asserting that the latter's politics are impractical, that it is
    naive about human nature.

1931

1   BALL, A.H.R., ed. Introduction to <u>Selections</u> <u>from</u> <u>the</u> <u>Prose</u>
     <u>Works</u> <u>of</u> <u>WM</u>. Cambridge: Cambridge University Press, pp. xi-xl.
          Sketches in the usual biographical details, stressing the
     importance of Ruskin's influence. Concludes with useful comments
     upon WM's prose style.

2   BENSON, E.F. <u>As</u> <u>We</u> <u>Were</u>: <u>A</u> <u>Victorian</u> <u>Peep</u> <u>Show</u>. London:
     Longmans, pp. 204, 221, passim.
          WM is referred to as "the poet of the Pre-Raphaelite
     Brotherhood," and Wilde is applauded for lecturing on the Morris
     chair while on his American tour.

3   CHARTERIS, E.E. <u>The</u> <u>Life</u> <u>and</u> <u>Letters</u> <u>of</u> <u>Sir</u> <u>Edmund</u> <u>Gosse</u>. New
     York: Harper and Brothers, pp. 33, 36-39, 66.
          Gosse's excitement at meeting WM, "the greatest gun of all"
     here expressed in letters to his father; he also reports upon a
     discussion he had with WM about Iceland, and he brags that WM read
     him parts of <u>Icelandic</u> <u>Journals</u>.

4   COLE, G.D.H. "WM." In <u>Revaluations</u>: <u>Studies</u> <u>in</u> <u>Biography</u>.
     Edited by L. Abercrombie. Oxford: Oxford University Press, pp.
     131-54.
          Admits that as a youth, he was charmed by <u>Defence</u> poems, and
     that <u>Nowhere</u> "made me a Socialist, and I have never had cause to
     regret either the fact or the manner of my conversion." Contrasts
     the prose romances, where there is too much mere decoration, to the
     lectures and the socialist romances, where there is more
     "vitality." Comments upon WM's achievements in the decorative arts,
     concluding that these shall remain a lasting and significant
     influence.

5   CUFFE, LIONEL. "WM." <u>Architectural</u> <u>Review</u> 69, no. 414
     (May):151.
          Laments that contemporary artists have left applied design to
     "weary art students and commercial hacks," forgetting WM's ideas on
     craftmanship, the example he provided that "artist and manufacturer
     combined can produce good and lasting work." Includes two plates of
     Morris and Co. wallpapers: Bower and Powdered.

6   ELTON, GODFREY. "WM, 1883-1884." In England Arise: A Study of
     the Pioneer Days of the Labour Movement. London: Cape, pp.
     56-72, passim.
        A biographical sketch stresses how WM's artistic and
intellectual interests caused him to develop real insights into the
reasons socialism should replace capitalism; this, along with his
wide reputation as a poet, made him a very important recruit to the
socialist cause. His relationship with Hyndman is discussed, and so
is the famous lecture he gave at Oxford.

7   EVANS, JOAN. Pattern: A Study of Ornament in Western Europe.
     Oxford: Clarendon Press, 2:196-97, passim.
        Discusses the sources, both in medieval Herbals and in the
British countryside, of many of WM's floral patterns. Points out
that he loved the North, that therefore "the Italianism of the
Pre-Raphaelites did not influence him. So he was able to elide the
centuries of the Renaissance and to breathe life into medieval
craftmanship," and to use intuitively his materials, this "in an age
which generally endeavored merely to subdue material to industrial
use."

8   FARMER, ALBERT J. Le mouvement esthetique et decadent en
     Angleterre (1873-1900). Paris: Champion, pp. 19-21, passim.
        Suggests that Defence, Jason, and Paradise adumbrate
attitudes and themes associated with poets of the 1890s, with
"aesthetic" poetry and ideas of "art for art's sake."

9   HARRIS, FRANK. Bernard Shaw. New York: Simon and Schuster, pp.
     81, 120, passim.
        Refers to WM's influence on Shaw, calls WM the "one
unquestionably Great Man" among the early British socialists.

*10 MARILLIER, H.C. The Morris Movement: A Lecture. London:
     Chiswick Press.
        Cited in 1936.3.

11   RHYS, ERNEST. Everyman Remembers. London: J.M. Dent, pp.
     48-53, passim.
        Comments on WM's platform style, contrasting it to that of
Shaw. Remarks also upon WM as thespian, upon the fun of seeing his
"burly form" in "archiepiscopal robes and speaking with unction" in
The Tables Turned, or Nupkins Awakened, the only play he ever wrote.

12 ROBERTSON, W. GRAHAM. Time Was. London: Hamish Hamilton, pp.
    92-97, passim. New York: Harpers, as Life Was Worth Living.
        The writer was a good friend of Burne-Jones, and so he often
saw WM at the Grange; he mused about the "lofty" conversations that
must have transpired at those Sunday morning breakfasts, "until I
discovered that they usually read aloud to each other from a comic
paper." These memoirs include the famed anecdote about dragons and
brothers (the sharp retort WM had for Rossetti), and the oft-quoted
description of Maria Spartali as "Mrs. Morris for Beginners."

13 ROTHENSTEIN, WILLIAM. Men and Memories: Recollections of
    William Rothenstein. London: Faber and Faber. 2d ed., 1934, pp.
    287-88, passim.
        Recollections of May and Janey Morris, of anecdotes about WM
told by Shaw and York-Powell. Discusses similarities Rowley and
Webb shared with WM.

                              1932

1   BICKLEY, FRANCIS. The Pre-Raphaelite Comedy. London:
    Constable, pp. 245-48, passim.
        A biographical sketch, one that lingers over the Oxford
experiences, the period when both Burne-Jones and WM were under the
spell of Malory and Rossetti.

2   BLOOMFIELD, PAUL. "WM and Hammersmith." In Imaginary Worlds or
    The Evolution of Utopia. London: Hamish Hamilton, pp. 159-78.
        Avers that Nowhere is "the only Utopian book that can move
one to tears," and also that it is "different from the others in
that Morris was a lover and practitioner of art who could fancy no
ideal without art." Makes useful comparisons between Nowhere and
earlier utopias.

3   COLE, G.D.H. A Short History of the British Working Class
    Movement, 1789-1947. London: Allen and Unwin. Revised, 1948.
    Reprinted. 1951, 1952, 1960, pp. 234-36, passim.
        WM called a "powerful recruit, one who brought both money and
energy to the Socialist cause." Sketches in reasons for the
acrimony that led to the formation of the Socialist League;
characterizes the content and the caliber of the writing WM did for
Commonweal.

4   DAVIES, FRANK J.J. "WM's 'Sir Peter Harpdon's End.'" PQ 11,
    no. 3 (July):314-17.
        Glances at "raw material" in Froissart to comment upon ways
that WM "wove into his pattern" of violence and intrigue a few facts
about a Harpdon, or Harpendon, to create this "new story."

5   DOORN, WILLIAM VAN. Theory and Practice of English Narrative
    Verse Since 1833: An Inquiry. Amsterdam: N.V. De Arbeiderspers,
    pp. 62-81, passim.
        Examines WM's use of sources in Sigurd, attempting to account
for omissions and changes in terms of WM's aesthetic, pointing to
biblical references and echoes that tend to make of "Sigurd a
Christian hero," adding that he is also "Alfred the Great, William
the Silent, and Simon Bolivar in one." Includes brief comments on
prosody and diction in Sigurd.

6   EHMCKE, F.H. "Das Problem der Maschine: WM." Archiv fur
    Buchgewerbe und Gebrauchsgraphik 69:329-33.
        WM and his ideas about machines and alienated work are here
set against modern problems of unemployment, the changing status of
colonized lands, and the like, in ways that make him seem prescient
indeed. Contrasts Ruskin's hatred of machines to WM's hopes that
they could be utilized so as to free people for joyful labor.

7   ELIOT, T.S. Selected Essays, 1917-1932. New York: Harcourt,
    Brace, pp. 258-60.
        Compares several lines from WM's "The Nymph's Song to Hylas"
to lines also describing a garden in Marvell's "The Nymph and the
Fawn," observing that the "effect of Morris's charming poem depends
upon the mistiness of the feeling and the vagueness of the object;
the effect of Marvell's poem upon its bright, hard precision."

8   HENDERSON, ARCHIBALD. Bernard Shaw: Playboy and Prophet.
    London and New York: Appleton, pp. 193-96, 274-80, passim.
        Essentially the same remarks on WM that appeared in the
earlier biography (1911.5) are repeated here. Comments on ways that
Shaw, because of Kelmscott Press volumes, changed his attitudes
toward the design of his own books. Revised slightly, expanded in
1956.5.

9   HOSFORD, DOROTHY. Sons of the Volsungs: From "Sigurd" by WM.
    New York: Macmillan, 170 pp. Reprint. New York: Holt, 1949.
    London: Bodley Head, 1965.
        This prose "adaptation," evidently for juvenile readers,
retains WM's archaic syntax and much of the original vocabulary.
Concludes, however, with Sigurd and Brynhild living happily ever
after.

10 HUBBARD, ELBERT II. "The First Philistine." Roycrofter
    6:203-7.
        Recounts his father's 1895 visit to WM at Hammersmith, as set
forth in 1900.8, and his subsequent decision to emulate WM in all
ways, and to begin publishing The Philistine: A Periodical of
Protest.

11 HUNT, VIOLET. The Wife of Rossetti: Her Life and Death. New
    York: E.P. Dutton, 1932, pp. 170-76, 180-87, passim.
        Highly anecdotal account of Rossetti and all his associates
has some fresh details about WM just before and after his marriage,
but these details are often colored by her sensational approach and
purple prose.

12 LUCAS, E.V. Reading, Writing and Remembering: A Literary
    Record. New York and London: Harper and Brothers, pp. 95-96.
        When the laureateship became vacant in 1892, two Morrises
were considered for the seat: "Lewis (from Wales) and William (from
'Paradise')." Some verses the latter might have used in declining
the honor are offered: "Of queen and state I have no time to sing,
Good store of work is mine in Editing," and so forth.

13 MURRY, JOHN MIDDLETON. "The Greatness of WM." Adelphi 4, no. 5
    (August):774.
        Those who think WM was a "Utopian socialist" because he wrote
a Utopia are quite wrong; if they could only realize that he was the
English Marxist, this might "well serve by itself to be the
spiritual foundation of the new Socialism--the English Communism."

14 MURRY, JOHN MIDDLETON. "The Return to Fundamentals: Marx and
    WM." Adelphi 5, no. 1 (October):19-29; no. 2 (November):97-109.
        Argues that the British Left must become "resolutely Marxist"
and avoid any possibility, thus following WM's counsel of four
decades earlier, of getting enmeshed in parliamentary reform.
Points out that the ideas of Marx and WM, contrary to the beliefs of
many contemporary Marxists, were not opposed at all. WM discovered
that the joy--what Marx called "the intellectual potentiality--had
gone out of human labour." Quotes from an 1890 WM address to show
how prescient he was about the dangers of parliamentary mergers and

the growth of a welfare state. Urges, finally, all modern
socialists to read WM.

15 MURRY, JOHN MIDDLETON. "WM." In The Great Victorians. Edited
    by H.J. Massingham and H. Massingham, London: Nicolson and
    Watson, pp. 325-41.
        Biographical sketch precedes a fuller discussion of WM's
socialism, and ways that that aspect of his life has been so
"grievously misunderstood." Stresses that WM was a Marxist, a "far
more revolutionary socialist than has appeared in this country since
his death." Points out that WM realized it was impossible to
improve art without changing social conditions, and that events have
proved him right; art has grown "steadily more sterile" and the
politcal palliation WM warned against has led to trade unions and a
new layer of the bourgeois. Reprinted: 1934.48; 1938.6.

16 RUSSELL, FRANCES THERESA. Touring Utopia: The Realm of
    Constructive Humanism. New York: Dial Press, passim.
        Nowhere is set within a comprehensive survey of common themes
in scores of Utopias written between 1516 and 1932. Though WM is
ranked, finally, with Plato and More, at one point ideas about
education in Nowhere are linked to Henry Ford's famous assertion:
"History is bunk."

17 SHAW, GEORGE BERNARD. "WM." In Pen Portraits and Reviews.
    London: Constable, pp. 201-10.
        Reprinted from 1899.13.

1933

1   ACKERMAN, PHYLLIS. Tapestry, the Mirror of Civilization. New
    York and London: Oxford University Press, pp. 298-302.
        Argues that WM and his associates "not only attempted to
revive tapestry and clothe it in a new style, but undertook to
confront and combat the evils of the century," and that this
undertaking, this "infantile, romantic socialism," became the
"epitome of muddling." Even though Morris and Co. tapestries are
better than those produced in other countries, "the world would have
been no poorer if no one of them had ever been conceived."

2   BRINTON, CRANE. "The Prosperous Victorians: WM." In <u>English</u>
     <u>Political</u> <u>Thought</u> <u>in</u> <u>the</u> <u>Nineteenth</u> <u>Century</u>. London: Benn.
     Reprint. 1949. Revised. New York: Harper and Row, 1962, pp.
     252-66.
          Quoting judiciously from the socialist lectures and from
     <u>Nowhere</u>, Brinton reconstructs the main features of WM's political
     philosophy, belittling it slightly when he suggests that WM took a
     "Bohemian pleasure in defying mere convention," that he did not
     understand Marx's theory of value, that <u>Nowhere</u> was "even more than
     most Utopias the idyllic refuge of a disheartened man." But many of
     his other comments on <u>Nowhere</u>, on making Art an absolute, for
     instance, are useful, and his respect for WM's critique of
     capitalism is genuine.

3   CARROL, OWEN. "WM among the Reds." <u>Everyman</u> 4 (23
     September):79-80.
          Recalls seeing WM at a meeting of the International Club,
     near Shoreditch, in the 1890s and contrasts his reputation among the
     upper classes (an "amiable crank") and among the workers, comrades
     to whom he lectured about a future when "the slums and villas would
     be swept away." Reprints a letter in which WM declines an offer to
     make a play out of <u>John</u> <u>Ball</u>, saying that he had been interested in
     "the Socialist dialogue at the end rather than dealing with the
     literary and dramatic side of the story."

4   CHILD, HAROLD. "Some English Utopias." <u>Journal</u> <u>of</u> <u>the</u> <u>Royal</u>
     <u>Society</u> <u>of</u> <u>Literature</u>, n.s., 12, no. 2:31-60.
          Surveys the contents of several Utopias, <u>Looking</u> <u>Backward</u> and
     <u>Nowhere</u> among them, observing that "it is a joy to leave the Boston
     of the future and come to Morris's <u>Nowhere</u>."

5   COMPTON-RICKETT, ARTHUR. "The WM Circle." In <u>I</u> <u>Look</u> <u>Back:</u>
     <u>Memories</u> <u>of</u> <u>Fifty</u> <u>Years</u>. London: Herbert Jenkins, pp. 157-71.
          Opens with description of WM as hearty, pipe-smoking, "genial
     vagabond," but then proceeds to make valid points about ways his
     socialism followed logically from his love of art. Says that
     booksellers have told him that now WM is a "back number" and
     concludes, "so much the worse for today."

6   EINARSSON, STEFAN. "Eirikr Magnusson and His Saga
     Translations." <u>SS</u> 13:17-32.
          Using Magnusson letters now in National Library in Reykjavik,
     discusses his work before he met WM as well as their translations,
     commenting upon contemporary reactions to these collaborations.
     Suggests that the two men had similar personalities.

7   EINARSSON, STEFAN. "Samvinna vid WM" [Collaboration]. Saga
     Eiriks Magnussonar. Reykjavik: Isafold, pp. 93-113, passim.
          In Icelandic. A sketch of WM precedes a detailed discussion
of the 1871 journey to Iceland, each saga translation, and the
famine conditions in northern Iceland in 1882, which led to the
formation of the Iceland Relief Committee.

8   EVANS, B. IFOR. "WM." In English Poetry in the Later
     Nineteenth Century. London: Methuen. 2d ed., 1966, pp. 104-27,
     passim.
          A biographical sketch precedes opinionated judgments of both
WM's politics and his poetry. Rates the Defence poems very highly
and suggests that marital problems were responsible for the
slackening of his "poetic fibre" in the later poetry.

9   HORNER, FRANCIS. Time Remembered. London: Heinemann, pp.
     126-28, passim.
          The author's father, William Graham, was a rich Glasgow
merchant who collected Pre-Raphaelite paintings, and she therefore
became an acquaintance and friend of Burne-Jones. She recalls
seeing WM at Burne-Jones's studios, recounts some WM anecdotes.

10   HOUSMAN, LAWRENCE. "Pre-Rapaelitism in Art and Poetry."
     Transactions of the Royal Society of Literature, n.s., 12:1-29.
          Claims that Pre-Raphaelite qualities in poetry are best
represented in Defence. Originally a lecture to Royal Society in
1929.

11   LARG, DAVID. Trial by Virgins: Fragment of a Biography.
     London: Peter Davies, pp. 229-30, 257-73, passim.
          Asserts that WM, knowing that he could never paint as well as
Rossetti, had therefore "misery mixed with his adoration." Claims
also that WM had a "housewifely way of combining art and
usefulness," that the Oxford Union murals experience turned him into
a decorator, and that he was invariably made fun of. Always
provocative, but often misleading and even wrong.

*12 LITZENBERG, KARL. "Contributions of the Old Norse Language and
     Literature to the Style and Substance of the Writings of WM,
     1858-1876." Dissertation, University of Michigan.
          Cited in 1968.25.

13 LITZENBERG, KARL. "Social Philosophy of WM and the Doom of the
    Gods." University of Michigan Publications (Essays and Studies
    in English and Comparative Literature) 10:183-203.
        Attempts to prove that WM's "ideal for the future, in its
method of attainment, and in its result, is almost identical with
the Doom of the Gods, the 'Ragnarok,' of the Elder and Younger
Eddas." Reviews WM's early studies in Old Norse, and cites passages
from the poetry, the lectures, the letters that correspond to those
parts of the Eddas dealing with the Doom of the Gods.

14 LITZENBERG, KARL. "WM and Scandinavian Literature: A
    Bibliographical Essay." SS 13:93-105.
        Lists and describes over fifty works by WM connected with the
Scandinavian, these ranging from short poems to complete
translations of Icelandic sagas. Places these works within the
following categories: those with "Northern" material, like "Gertha's
Lovers," those translated from Danish, those adapted from Northern
sources, like "Pool," those translated from the Icelandic, all in
collaboration with Magnusson and including all of the great Family
sagas (except Njala) and most of the Eddic poetry, those adapted
from Old Icelandic, like "Gudrun" and Sigurd, and, finally, original
poems on Iceland or Icelandic literature.

15 MAC KENZIE, COMPTON. Literature in My Time. London: Rich and
    Cowan. Reprint. Freeport, N.Y: Books for Libraries Press,
    1967, pp. 97-98.
        Argues that WM was attracted to the medieval period because
he thought craftsmen had thrived then, and that his socialism had
"more in common with the distributionism advocated by G.K.
Chesterton than with the socialism we now associate with politics."

16 REES, RICHARD. "Marx, WM and Keir Hardie." Adelphi 7, no. 1
    (October):62-63.
        Both WM and Keir Hardie were "rare types," the former an
intellectual who understood the "historical movement as a whole" and
still went over to the proletariat, the latter a religious man, a
worker, who led the proletariat.

17 WINWAR, FRANCES. Poor Splendid Wings: The Rossettis and Their
    Circle. Boston: Little, Brown, pp. 89-92, 95-97, passim.
    London: Hurst and Blackett, 1934, as The Rossettis and Their
    Circle.
        Has exuberant, and misleading, narrative accounts of WM's
courtship of Janey and of Rossetti's influence on WM. Other details
and anecdotes often interesting, but based largely on Mackail
(1899.10).

1934

1   ARKELL, REGINALD. "Kelmscott: A Footnote to the WM Centenary."
    Bookman (London) 86 (April):56-57.
        Descriptions, evidently by a Kelmscott resident, of the
    surrounding area, the village, Kelmscott Manor.

2   ARNOT, R. PAGE. "WM versus the Morris Myth." Labour Monthly
    16, no. 3 (March):178-84.
        Warns a socialist audience that in WM's centenary year, both
    bourgeois and Labour party functionaries shall push their versions,
    their myths, of WM: a quirky Leonardo who experimented with protest
    or a gentle socialist. WM was actually a prescient, scientific
    socialist, and if he had lived ten years longer he would have seen
    "enacted in the year 1905 in Russia what he wrote of." It is thus
    "high time the Morris myth was destroyed." Revised, expanded into
    monograph: 1934.3.

3   ARNOT, R. PAGE. WM: A Vindication. London: Martin Lawrence, 32
    pp.
        Provides a biographical sketch that stresses at every point
    that WM was a "revolutionary socialist," one who has recently been
    subjected to an "orgy of canonization" by the liberal establishment
    who would thus remove the sting from the radical critique WM leveled
    at British society. Discusses both the "bourgeois myth" and the
    "Labour Party myth," suggesting reasons for their creation as ways
    of explaining WM's achievements. Four of the short chapters in this
    pamphlet Arnot used in his later book (1964.1).

4   BARCLAY, TOM. Memoirs and Medleys: The Autobiography of a
    Bottle Washer. Leicester: Edgar Backens, pp. 82-94.
        A product of a working men's college, an inveterate reader
    full of Gaelic fulminations, Barclay's anecdotes about the plight of
    the workers, about WM, Carpenter, Shaw, and the like, are colorful
    and interesting.

5   BENTLEY, WILDER. "The WM Influence." Publisher's Weekly 125,
    no. 19 (12 May):1782-83.
        Refers to 1934.11, suggesting that Bradley was unfair in
    down-playing WM's influence on American presses and in suggesting
    that Gothic type was always heavy and gloomy. He might have paid
    some attention to printers in California, where "some of us even
    believe that the Master of Hammersmith belongs to America's
    future."

6   BETTMANN, OTTO. "WM." Gebrauchsgraphik 11:50-57.
         Centenary essay celebrates, in general terms, WM's attempts
to direct his contemporaries out of "chaos of tastelessness" of the
modern world. An English translation accompanies the German text,
as do several illustrations of Kelmscott Press designs.

7   BLOOMFIELD, PAUL. "The Life and Work of WM." Journal of the
         Royal Society of Arts 82, no. 4270 (21 September):1103-16; no.
         4271 (28 September):1119-32.
         A biographical sketch with detailed discussions of Morris and
Co. and ways that Rossetti, Taylor, and Webb were important to the
Firm's success. Clients were attracted by Rossetti's reputation,
Taylor brought order to the Firm's books, and Webb--architect for
the rich--gained important commissions for Morris and Co.
Misleading about supposedly positive effects Iceland's society had
on WM's politics, but otherwise generally reliable on the nature and
significance of WM's socialism.

8   BLOOMFIELD, PAUL. Life and Work of WM. London: Arthur Barker,
         314 pp. Folcroft, Pa.: Folcroft Press, 1969. Folcroft, Pa.:
         Folcroft Library Editions, 1973. Norwood, Pa.: Norwood
         Editions, 1977. Philadelphia: R. West, 1978.
         Uses, often skillfully, the anecdotes and scholarship from
previous biographies, liberal quotations from WM's own works, to
provide a view of WM as "sage." Descriptions of Merton Abbey and of
WM's satiric play, The Tables Turned, or Nupkin's Awakened, are full
and fresh, and the rest is an adequate introduction, during the
centenary year, to WM's life and works.

9   BODKIN, MAUD. Archetypal Patterns in Poetry. London: Oxford
         University Press. New York: Vintage, pp. 11-18.
         Discusses the Paradise-Hades motif as illustrated in both
WM's poetry and in his life. The journeys to Iceland, his work at
socialist propaganda, "which probably shortened his life," are seen
as examples of WM pursuing shadows and desolation. Suggests that no
other poet has so "vividly conveyed the drama of the changing
year--the glory of the summer, with the shadow always imminent of
wintry death."

10   BOSWORTH, GEORGE F., ed. "Episode Ten: WM: Dreamer of Dreams."
         In The Book of the Walthamstow Pageant, 1934. London:
         Walthamstow Antiquarian Society, no. 30, pp. 45-53.
         Episode 10, in a pageant celebrating the high points of
Walthamstow's history, opens with a chorus singing, "One hundred
years ago, within sight of this spot, at Elm House, was born our
greatest man--WM." A chronicler reads from Paradise and John Ball,
and tableaux with scenes from Sigurd and the Grail Quest recall

Morris and Co. tapestries. A wreath is laid at the base of WM's
bust, the chorus concludes with more praise.

11   BRADLEY, WILL. "WM: A Review of His Influence on the Centenary
     of His Birth." Publisher's Weekly 125, no. 14 (7
     April):1373-76.
         Mentions several British presses (Vale, Eragny) and
magazines, like the Savoy and Yellow Book, which "might well have
been the natural outgrowth of seeds of individualism, as opposed to
commercialism, sown by WM at Kelmscott Press." Suggests that
influences upon American printing were slight, though Updike and
Rogers certainly learned from WM. Remarks upon a Grabhorn Press
souvenir (Kelmscott Chaucer pages) and WM centenary exhibitions at
Mills College and the Huntington Library.

12   BRINTON, ANNA [Cox]. A Pre-Raphaelite "Aeneid" of Virgil in the
     Collection of Mrs. Edward Laurence Doheny of Los Angeles. Los
     Angeles: Ward Ritchie Press, 40 pp.
         Describes the folio containing The Aeneid, which WM began to
copy onto vellum in 1875. Such work, and he completed hundreds of
pages of lettering and illumination between 1870 and 1875, is here
seen as a prelude to Kelmscott Press work, to problems of page
design and the like, that WM would confront fifteen years later.

13   BROOKS, VAN WYCK. Three Essays on America. New York: E.P.
     Dutton, pp. 105-7.
         Reprint of 1915.2.

14   BROOKS, VAN WYCK. Three Essays on America. New York: E.P.
     Dutton, pp. 175-78.
         Reprint of 1918.3.

15   BULLETT, GERALD. "WM: Poet and Craftsman." John O'London's
     Weekly, 10 March, 860, 862.
         Deplores the fact that Arts and Crafts Movement, and the
types associated with it, are often regarded with a derision that
tends to place WM in a bad light, and this detailed biographical
sketch is replete with high praise. Offers a spirited and sensible
defense of WM's diction in the prose romances.

16 CALTHROP, HERBERT. "Topsy-Turvey." Architects' Journal 79 (29
    March):455-58.
        Subjective and lively account of WM's achievements and
    influence: despite those who persist in believing "that his
    contribution to civilization was the
    arty-crafty-Cotswaldie-handie-wrottie world," his true descendents
    are Gropius, Le Corbusier, Aalto.

17 CARTER, JOHN, and POLLARD, GRAHAM. "WM." In An Enquiry into
    the Nature of Certain Nineteenth Century Pamphlets. London:
    Constable; New York: Scribners, pp. 205-12, passim.
        Two WM pamphlets, "Sir Galahad: A Christmas Mystery," and
    "The Two Sides of the River," were among some forty works suspected,
    in the early decades of this century, of being forgeries. This
    detailed study offers proof that the former was indeed a forgery,
    the other quite possibly so, and traces them back to Thomas J. Wise,
    a well-known bibliographer. Explains Forman's role in getting WM to
    sign one of the Galahad pamphlets and suggests that Forman was
    implicated in these literary frauds in other ways; this has since
    been proved true; see Collins (1972.3).

18 CARY, MELBERT W. "A Brief Account of the Wanderings of Albion
    Press no. 6551, Its Various Owners and the Work it has Done."
    In Some Thoughts on the Ornamented Manuscripts of the Middle
    Ages by WM. New York: Whooly Whale Press, pp. 13-20.
        History of perigrinations and owners of one of the presses
    used at Kelmscott Press is here appended to a WM essay on ornamental
    manuscripts.

19 CHEN, KARL. "A Study of the Sources and Influences upon WM's
    Defence." Dissertation, Yale University.
        Abstracted: DAI 30:1977-A.

20 COLE, G.D.H., ed. Introduction to WM: Stories in Prose, Stories
    in Verse, Shorter Poems, Lectures and Essays. New York: Random
    House; Bloomsbury: Nonesuch Press, pp. vii-xxiv. Reprinted.
    1942, 1946, 1948.
        Claims that WM's poetry has fallen out of fashion because of
    its "picture-making," because WM preferred sensuous softness rather
    than the "angularity" popular in the twentieth century. This
    Centenary Edition therefore includes more than twice as much prose
    as poetry, and several of the socialist lectures because in them WM
    seems "alive," and in them "he gives a clear and telling
    presentation of what he was trying to do." Since this still needed
    doing, the prose seemed more pertinent than most of the poetry, the
    best of which (like Sigurd) the editor did not wish to print only a
    piece of. Introduction has useful comments on the importance of
    Iceland to WM, on the development of his socialist thought, and on

works like Pilgrims, John Ball, and Nowhere. These all appear in
their entirety, as do tracts like "A Factory as it Might Be," which
had not been included in the Collected Works, and all of the
significant socialist lectures. Cole thus made WM's important prose
widely available for the first time.

21 CROW, GERALD. WM: Designer. Special Winter Number, edited by
    C.G. Holme. London: Studio; New York: Studio Publications, 120
    pp. Reprint. Folcroft, Pa.: Folcroft Library Editions, 1975.
    Norwood, Pa.: Norwood Editions, 1977.
        A special centenary issue of the Studio, reliable in its
detailed biographical sketch of WM's life and works, but
particularly valuable for its full-page illustrations and color
plates. Discusses WM's short-sightedness regarding machines and the
possibilities that design and execution can be separated. Has
useful comments on Nowhere and the advanced portrayals of women
therein. Concludes that WM's "life is a criticism of two aspects of
modern civilization which he hated, its tameness and its
specialization."

22 DENNISON, BAIRD. "Great Amateur." Architectural Review 75:133.
        General comments as to why WM's "stature is still
undetermined" were inspired by the recent biographies of Weekley
(1934.75) and Bloomfield (1934.8). Asserts that both WM and Ruskin
should have realized that classic rather than Gothic models and
inspiration would have been more fitting for English character and
taste.

23 DRINKWATER, JOHN. "The Literary Influence of WM." In Speeches
    in Commemoration of WM Delivered at a Town Meeting Held in the
    Bath's Hall, Walthamstow, 24 March 1934. London: Walthamstow
    Borough Council, pp. 3-8.
        Recalls that his own first literary achievement was a book on
WM (1912.3), work on which convinced him that WM was both a great
man and a great poet. He is now therefore unhappy that those poems
of "vigorous shining light" have been discarded by literary fashion,
that Sigurd was not included in the recently published Nonesuch
anthology (1934.20).

24 EHMCKE, F.H. "Was bedeutet WM fur unser Zeit?" Gutenberg
    Jahrbuch 9:261-70.
        Centenary article contrasts rural Germany of 1834 with its
urban counterpart of a century later to suggest that WM was
prescient regarding the dangers of civilization, that his theories
about art and work have great contemporary significance. Asserts,
however, that his greatest achievement was the founding of Kelmscott
Press.

25 EVANS, B. IFOR. "WM, His Influence and Reputation."
    Contemporary Review 145 (March):315-23.
        Laments that what WM strived for now seems very distant,
"equally removed from the proletarian despotism of Russia and the
dreary collective bargaining of English Trade Unionism," that few
read his poetry, and that his designs have given way to starker
tastes. Even WM the man is thought of as a Beerbohm caricature.
Asserts that "it will not do!" Offers graceful reminders of the
pertinence of what WM taught, both in the lectures and in Nowhere,
of the beauty of his poetry.

26 FINNBOGASSON, GUTHMUNDAR. "WM: Minningarorth: 24 May, 1934"
    [Memorial]. Skirnir 108:182-90.
        In Icelandic. Surveys extent of WM's writings and his other
achievements, suggesting that such talents invite comparisons to
Leonardo da Vinci. Stresses the importance of Red House to British
architecture and interior design, goes into some detail about Morris
and Co. and Kelmscott Press.

27 GOUDY, FREDERIC. "WM: His Influence on American Printing."
    Philobiblon 7, no. 4:185-91.
        Rehearses the story of Kelmscott Press beginnings, reviews
the received opinions about WM's influence, and concludes that in
England "his attempts to better printing received but little
encouragement," while in America his influence has been great--if
"largely indirect." He taught everyone about the effect of "unity"
in books; in printing, WM may be "the greatest figure since
Gutenberg."

28 GRAHAM, R.B. CUNNINGHAM. With the North-West Wind. Berkeley
    Heights, N.J.: Oriole Press, 14 pp.
        Reprinting of two obituary-tributes that originally appeared
in 1896; the first, perhaps the most eloquent reaction to WM's
death, got its title from the direction the wind blew on the stormy
October day he was buried. In the second, Carpenter recalls the
effects of a speech WM gave at the 1889 Socialist Congress, the
Second International, in Paris.

29 GREENWOOD, GEORGE. "WM: Artist, Poet, and Reformer." Millgate
    Monthly (Manchester) 29 (March):327-30.
        Celebrates memory of WM, who "helped to change the face of
social England." Recounts most of his achievements, but his
political significance is undercut by such generalizations as "he
was a Socialist of the heart rather than the head."

30 HARASZTI, ZOLTAN. "The Centenary of WM." More Books: Bulletin
    of the Boston Public Library 9, no. 5 (May):153-60.
        Reports on an exhibition of first editions of WM books and of
Kelmscott Press volumes arranged in the Treasure Room of the Boston
Public Library in honor of WM's centenary. Laments that WM's
"figure is still obscured by the haze of superficial prejudices,"
and attempts in the full descriptive notes on the exhibited items to
rectify this.

31 HEWITT, GRAILY. "The Illuminated Manuscripts of WM." In Three
    WM Centenary Papers. London: Shenval Press, pp. 1-12.
        Discusses the six books of the Aeneid WM copied out and gave
to Fairfax Murray, who at the beginning of the century commissioned
the author to finish the remaining six books. He did so and thus
gained special insights into WM's genius as a calligrapher and
illuminator. The Kelmscott Chaucer is called "an illumination,
denied its consummation: colour."

32 JACKSON, HOLBROOK. "The Typography of WM." In Three WM
    Centenary Papers. London: Shenval Press, pp. 15-21.
        Comments upon WM's pride in the desigh of Roots and suggests
that even though he became a printer of genius, he was too
interested in decoration; Kelmscott Press books are thus
"overdrest," and they deny the first rule of printing, the rule of
legibility. Asserts that they shall remain "typographical
curiousities" and "museum pieces." Originally a lecture given at
the Double Crown Club, London, 2 May 1934. Reprinted: 1934.33;
1939.5; 1951.8.

33 JACKSON, HOLBROOK. "The Typography of WM." American Book
    Collecter 5 (August-September):251-53.
        Reprint of 1934.32.

34 JACKSON, HOLBROOK. "WM and the Arts and Crafts Movement."
    Speeches in Commemoration of WM Delivered at a Town Meeting Held
    in the Bath's Hall, Walthamstow, 24 March 1934. London:
    Walthamstow Borough Council, pp. 9-15.
        Suggests that modern notions about industrial progress have
obliterated whatever influence WM and Arts and Crafts ideals might
have had on society generally, but that the "arts are all the better
for his reassertion of principles underlying association of form and
utility."

35 JACKSON, HOLBROOK. "WM and the Arts and Crafts." Book
    Collecters Quarterly 14 (April-June):1-10.
        Reprint of 1934.34.

36 JACKSON, HOLBROOK. WM and the Arts and Crafts Movement.
    Berkeley Heights, N.J.: Oriole Press, 17 pp. Reprint. Folcroft
    Pa.: Folcroft Library Editions, 1974. Norwood, Pa.: Norwood
    Editions, 1977.
        Reprint of 1934.34.

37 JOHNSON, A.F. "WM as Printer." Printing Review 3, no. 3
    (Spring):163-65.
        Even though "no printer since Bodoni has been so
    extravagantly lauded" as WM, his influence on twentieth-century
    printers, and especially on modern printing, is here minimized.
    Discusses WM's developing interests in typography, his experiments
    with various types, and the resulting black-page effect, using the
    Keats volume as an example.

38 JOHNSON, A.F. Type Designs: Their History and Development.
    London: Andre Deutsch. 3d ed., 1966, pp. 15, passim.
        Points out that "WM and his pupils did much to raise the
    level of printing," but that they had little influence on the types
    used by ordinairy printers. Comments upon the Basle roman type,
    which WM used for Wolfings and for Roots.

39 KENT, W. "WM: Freethinker and Utopian." Literary Guide and
    Rationalist Review, n.s., no. 454 (April):67-68.
        Quotations from Gissing, Middleton Murry, Shaw, and WM
    himself are woven into this hearty celebration of WM, the socialist
    reformer, a searcher after the Grail, who, if he had found it, would
    have used it "as a loving cup at some Mermaid tavern."

40 KOCH, RUDOLPH. "WM." Philobiblon 7, no. 4:172.
        Short memorial, in German, celebrates WM and his work at the
    Kelmscott Press.

41 KREEMERS, D.R. "WM: 1834-1934." Dietsche Warande en Belfort 34
    (October):641-64.
        In Dutch. Detailed survey of WM's life and achievements and
    influence, a survey that celebrates his multifaceted talent. Offers
    specific points regarding Ruskin's importance for WM and places WM
    next to John Dryden as translator and storyteller.

42 LASKI, H.J. "The Social Philosophy of WM." In Speeches in
    Commemoration of WM Delivered at a Town Meeting Held in the
    Bath's Hall, Walthamstow, 24 March 1934. London: Walthamstow
    Borough Council, pp. 16-23.
        Recalls WM's importance in the 1880s to the cause of
socialism, ways that his courage and commitment inspired others,
ways that his writings, epecially in Commonweal, continue to be
relevant.

43 MACKAIL, J.W. "WM." Journal of the Royal Institute of British
    Architects 41, no. 11 (14 April):557-67.
        When an Oxford undergraduate, WM aspired to be involved in
"the bettering of the world in so far as lies in me." This graceful
biographical sketch is built upon the premise that WM never flagged
in his attempt to change his world, both through imagination and
action, through his writings and his public achievements.

44 MEINER, ANNEMARIE. "WM: Zum 100. Geburtstag am 24 Marz 1934."
    Imprimatur: Ein Jahrbuch fur Bucherfreunde 5:118-27.
        Celebrates WM's achievements, his abiding influence,
especially upon the book arts, by lacing a typical biographical
sketch with high praise. WM'S interests in folk art, in the
Teutonic Middle Ages, and in German incunabula, strike responsive
chords in the author.

45 MORRIS, MAY. "A Talk on WM." Philobiblon 7, no. 4, 3 pp.
        Harkens back to 1862 when WM and a small group of loyal
friends, in that "holiday time" of the building and decorating of
Red House, laid the foundation for the Arts and Crafts Movement.
Suggests that the "strain" of socialist activities caused her father
to die "before his due time." This is an insert that has no
pagination.

46 MORRIS, MAY. "Reminiscences about My Father." Philobiblon 7,
    no. 4:169-72.
        Recalls that WM and Burne-Jones had entertained the idea of
fine book production for twenty-five years before the Kelmscott
Press venture. Stresses the importance of Walker throughout that
venture and offers examples of the great care and intelligence WM
put into the daily work of the Press. Appears in both English and
German.

47 MORRIS, MAY. "WM." TLS, no. 1685 (17 May):360.
        May Morris again would "try to arrest the growth of a
legend," this one based on Rossetti's oft-quoted aside, "Topsy never
gave a penny to a beggar," that seems to have gained real currency,
since a recent TLS article on the beauty of England (3 May 1934)
presents it as a fact. For the earlier attempt, see 1919.7.

48 MURRY, JOHN MIDDLETON. "WM." Adelphi 8, no. 3 (June):157-71.
        Reprint of 1932.15.

49 NASH, JOHN HENRY. WM: 1834-96, Craftsman, Romancer, Poet,
        Prophet. San Francisco: J.H. Nash, 4 pp.
        Finely printed pamphlet with woodcut of WM and a paragraph
from one of the lectures. Printed on the occasion of a 1934
exhibition at Mills College.

50 NEIL, ADAM. "WM, Pioneer of Fascism." Fascist Week, 30 March-5
        April, p.7
        Asserts that it is impossible to imagine WM in either "that
organized Cowardice, the Labour Party," or in a "Marxist strait
jacket. For he was a Man." Comments upon the cooperative forms of
social life and Nordic races depicted in the prose romances,
concluding that WM would have recognized in today's "Fascist
corporations the modern equivalents of the Guilds whose workings he
describes so lovingly."

51 NEWDIGATE, B.H. "WM." London Mercury 29, no. 174
        (April):545-46.
        WM'S "goodness" as a printer and his subsequent influence
depend not so much on details as on "the soundness of the principles
on which his work was built and on the congruity as well as the good
quality of all its constituent parts." Suggests that there is a
"happy union" between type and illustration in Kelmscott Press
books.

52 O'CONOR, BEATRICE. "Shaw and WM." New Stateman and Nation,
        n.s., 8, no. 194 (10 November):660.
        Uses Glasier (1921.3) to point out that WM was a
"Marxaphobe," and chides Shaw for declaring otherwise. A reply the
following week, on 17 November, p. 715, concisely defends Shaw: WM
was a socialist of real caliber who understood and used Marx. And
then O'Conor attempts a rebuttal on 24 November, p. 751.

53 O'CONOR, NORREYS JEPHSON. "WM." Landmark 16:127-30.
    A centenary celebration of WM's achievements which claims
that he was "a forerunner of twentieth-century poetry," a founder of
the "present-day profession of interior decoration," comparable to a
Leonardo. Includes a few off-hand comments on his socialism.

*54 OHTSKI, KENJI. List of New Contributions, Home and Foreign, to
    the WM Bibliography in His Centenary Year. Tokyo, 5 pp.
    Cited in 1965.7.

55 OLIVER, LORD. "WM, Born March 24, 1834." Spectator, no. 5517
    (23 March):440-41.
    Comments upon the continuing pertinence of WM's warnings
about capitalistic ravages of the environment, both natural and
man-made. Recalls a lecture he himself gave at Hammersmith and WM
agreeing with him about Zola's realism.

56 READ, HERBERT. "WM." In Art and Industry. London: Faber and
    Faber. Revised, 1944, 1953; New York: Horizon Press, 1953.
    Reprint. Bloomington: Indiana University Press, 1961, pp.
    29-35, 79.
    Suggests that the publication of Ruskin's Stones of Venice
"determined the rest of Morris's life," for he used its ideals about
art to shape his own beliefs on how art might enter, through
individual creation, the life of all. With such beliefs, WM was of
course opposed to the development of machinery, but--as passages
from "The Aims of Art" suggest--he would probably have modified his
position on machines had he lived on into the twentieth century.

57 REES, RICHARD. "WM." Adelphi 7, no. 5 (February):393-96.
    Introduces passages from a lecture WM gave in 1893 on
communism, saying that their pertinence four decades later, in their
warning to liberals of the dangers and futility of short-term
compromises, make them "the most fitting tribute on his
anniversary."

58 RICHARDS, GRANT. Author Hunting by an Old Literary Sportsman;
    Memories of Years Spent Mainly in Publishing, 1827-1925. London:
    H. Hamilton; New York: Coward-MacCann, pp. 30-32, 128.
    Comments, in some detail, about the appearance of Kelmscott
Press books, about blemishes that were later pointed out by
Massingham and Pennell.

59 ROEBUCK, GEORGE, ed. Some Appreciations of WM: 24 March 1934.
    London: Walthamstow Antiquarian Society, 36 pp.
         Twenty-nine luminaries wrote short "Appreciations" for this
    centenary pamphlet; they included prelates, politicians, and various
    literary figures. Chesterton here calls WM a "very great
    Distributist," Marillier "easily the first of the great Victorians,"
    Shaw, "extraordinairy." One of the most thoughtful is G.D.H.
    Cole's: WM was the "man who saw most clearly that the artist and the
    intellectual cannot make for themselves a decent society unless they
    make it for all men."

60 ROLLINS, CARL PURINGTON. "New WM Item." Saturday Review of
    Literature, 29 September, p.151.
         Discusses one of the presses WM used at Kelmscott Press,
    commenting upon 1934.18. Includes an attack upon Elbert Hubbard:
    that this charlatan could be regarded as an American WM "is so
    absurd and so grotesque that it is almost incredible."

61 ROLLINS, CARL PURINGTON. "The Ordeal of WM." In Addresses
    Delivered in Commemoration of the One Hundredth Anniversary of
    the Birth of WM. Stamford, Conn.: Overbrook Press, pp. 23-33.
    Reprinted as a Typophile Keepsake, n.d., 12 pp.
         An address in 1934 to Yale Library Associates, one that
    stresses how "healthy" were WM's activities and ideas and that
    insists his socialism was admirable because he was a poet rather
    than a cold economist. Concludes that Kelmscott Press was perhaps
    the most "effective activity of his life."

62 ROLLINS, CARL PURINGTON. "The Work of WM." Yale University
    Library Gazette 9, no. 3 (January):62-64.
         Reports upon a WM exhibit in the Rare Book Room at Yale; at
    its opening on 29 October, Tinker spoke on WM as poet (1934.69) and
    Rollins on WM and his world (1934.61). The exhibit included a
    complete set of Kelmscott Press volumes, bound in leather, loaned by
    Mrs. Elisha Ely Garrison.

63 ROLLINS, CARL PURINGTON. "WM." Saturday Review of Literature
    11, no. 9 (15 September):119.
         Comments on the special WM number of the Philobiblon and on
    publications by Ward Ritchie and the Grabhorn Press.

64 SHAND, JAMES. "The Typography of WM." In Three WM Centenary Papers. London: Shenval Press, pp. 25-32.
   Asserts that any printer, and he is one, must be especially thrilled by a Kelmscott Press book, the typographic consummation of author, decorator, and printer. Judges many other books printed at Oxford and Cambridge during the 1890s to be "shoddy" by comparison.

65 SHAW, ALBERT. "The Versatile WM." Golden Book Magazine 20, no. 116 (August):168-75.
   Memoir with biographical sketch followed by puzzling comments: if WM "were with us now he would have wise words to say to the un-employed about self-help." Perhaps such comments are meant to introduce "A King's Lesson" which is here reprinted.

66 SQUIRE, JOHN. "Editorial Notes: WM." London Mercury 29, no. 173 (March):385-88.
   Mentions "heterogeneous quality" of contributors to the Walthamstow Appreciations booklet (1934.59): "the one thing missing is a bishop," and comments briefly on the content of the speeches, concluding with thoughts on WM's socialism, which "might never have been heard of had he not had a private income," and on his abiding influence in the "world of Arts and Crafts where he created a revolution."

67 TEALL, EDWARD N. "Kelmscott Press Featured in Stone House-Organ." Inland Printer, February, pp. 38-39.
   Comments upon and reprints short introductory article on Kelmscott Press, along with four illustrations of the Chaucer, all of which had appeared in Stone's Impressions, a house-organ put out by Stone Printing of Roanoke, Virginia.

68 TILLOTSON, GEOFFREY. "WM and Machines." Fortnightly Review 141 (April):464-71.
   Though he "turned to the Dark Ages for enlightenment" and often railed against machines, WM became very upset when the trains were not on time. So he used machines and too often ignored the pleasures possible when working with them, the fine work, even the art, that machines can produce. Reminds us that we, however, owe a great deal to WM, "who applied himself to making agreeable the overlooked portions of daily life." Reprinted: 1942.5.

69 TINKER, C.B. "WM as Poet." In Addresses Delivered in
    Commemoration of the One Hundredth Anniversary of the Birth of
    WM. Stamford, Conn.: Overbrook Press, pp. 3-19.
        Contrasts WM's Defence poems, with their graphic and colorful
    descriptions of medieval life, to the "pallid romanticism" of
    Tennyson's Arthurian poems, offering high praise to "Haystack in the
    Floods." Asserts that WM's subsequent poetry reveals a "progressive
    impoverishment." Originally an address to the Yale Library
    Associates; reprinted: 1948.12.

70 WAGNER, CARL. "WM, 1834-1896." Archiv fur Buchgewerbe und
    Gebrauchgraphik 71:365-68.
        Celebrates WM's contribution to the book arts and traces his
    influence, via Jugendstil artists, to Germany. Sketches in history
    of Kelmscott Press, commenting on medieval models and drawing
    interesting parallels to WM's work with stained glass. Recalls a
    visit to Hammersmith in terms that suggest a pilgrimage.

71 WARD, SYDNEY. "The Great Trinity of Presses, 1891-1933." Paper
    and Print 7 (Autumn):244-48.
        Article intended as "humble tribute" to Kelmscott, Doves, and
    Ashendene presses. Quotes WM on his aims, on his attempts to use
    only the best materials. Concludes that Kelmscott Press books as
    "examples of typography have faults, but as decorative books they
    stand supreme."

72 WARD, SYDNEY. "WM and His Papermaker, Joseph Batchelor."
    Philobiblon 7, no. 4:177-80.
        Discusses letters WM wrote during 1890-91 to Batchelor,
    pointing out WM's attention to detail, his concern that only the
    finest paper be used at Kelmscott Press.

73 WARDROP, JAMES. "The WM Centenary Exhibition." Apollo 19, no.
    112 (April):206-9.
        Opens with general comments on WM's great influence in the
    twentieth century on the industrial arts, then ponders how ideas of
    beauty have changed in just four decades. Praises the exhibition
    for the display of WM's calligraphy, for it indicates his genius in
    the book arts long before Kelmscott Press. The exhibition is also a
    fine tribute to the long friendship between WM and Burne-Jones.

74 WARDROP, JAMES. "WM Centenary Exhibition." <u>Apollo</u> 19, no. 111
    (March):167.
        Has high praise for WM centenary exhibition at the Victoria
and Albert, recently opened by the Right Honorable Stanley Baldwin.

75 WEEKLEY, MONTAGUE. <u>WM</u>. Vol. 33 in Great Lives Series. London:
    Duckworth, 136 pp. Reprint. Folcroft, Pa.: Folcroft Library
    Editions, 1973. Norwood, Pa.: Norwood Editions, 1978.
        There is nothing remarkable nor objectionable in this short,
centenary biography, one that follows Mackail (1899.10) in most
respects, but frequently adds new insights, referring for instance
to Yeats's well-known judgment that WM was the "happiest" of poets
to make the following point: "Mr. Yeats disregards the tortured
emotion, the stark horror and strangled cries that surge up from the
early poems in <u>Defence</u>; add to them the obsession with death, a
thread wound through <u>Paradise</u>, or some of the ghostly visions in
<u>Sigurd</u>, and the other Morris is revealed."

76 WEST, GEOFFREY. "WM--Man Creative: An Estimate of His
    Significance Today." <u>Bookman</u> (London) 85 (March):472-74.
        Judges that neither WM's poetry nor prose is presently read
because it seems so outdated, and his decorative arts are easier to
admire in a museum "than to imagine as integral parts of our daily
lives at home." Claims that what WM said about art and society is,
however, still significant.

77 WHITAKER, CHARLES HARRIS. "WM, 1834-1896." <u>American Magazine
    of Art</u> 27, no. 80 (August):436-38.
        A graceful centenary appreciation, one that exults in WM's
"voyage to the far lands of the Middle Ages" so that he could write
of, and emulate, endeavors that "teach men honor and integrity, and
the respect for tools and materials." Includes, however, typical
assertions about WM's inability to understand economic forces
"pervading and enmeshing all work and all men."

78 WITCUTT, W.P. "WM: Distributist." <u>American Review</u> 2, no. 3
    (January):311-15.
        Argues that WM "was a Socialist only through a
misunderstanding." Since he believed in a "system of small
producers," he was obviously a Distributist.

79 YEATS, W.B. "Louis Lambert." London Mercury 30, no. 177
      (July):235.
         During lectures in America, Yeats was asked about his
favorite authors; he named four: Shakespeare, the Arabian Nights in
the latest English version, "then WM, who gave us all the great
stories, Homer and the sagas included, then Balzac." Reprinted:
1961.36.

80 ZABEL, MORTON. "Two Versions of the Nineteenth Century."
      Poetry 44 (August):270-76.
         Points out that WM's reputation as a writer, thirty-eight
years after his death, is slight indeed, compared to that of Hopkins
who wrote only one small book of poems, and to that of Butler who
wrote only one novel. Suggests that WM's lack of influence stems
from his having tried to do too much.

81 "Centenary of WM." Journal of the Royal Society of Arts 82, no.
      4239 (16 February):393-94.
         Uses occasion of the WM centenary exhibit at the Victoria and
Albert (1934.88) to point out that WM is "not merely rather
neglected by the present generation, but into the bargain
persistently misinterpreted." This has happened because WM "had
that sense of the past which our contemporaries are proud of
lacking."

82 "In Memoriam WM." Philobiblon 7, no. 4 (April):167-91.
         Special WM memorial issue includes essays by Sydney Ward
(1934.72), May Morris (1934.46), Frederic W. Goudy (1934.27), and
Rudolf Koch (1934.40). The last is an "inset" and thus without
pagination, as are a BBC "Talk on WM" by May Morris (1934.45) and
WM's "Note on the Founding of Kelmscott Press" and Cockerell's
"Short History of Kelmscott Press."

83 "The Beauty of England." TLS, no. 1683 (3 May):309-10.
         WM and SPAB are at the center of this essay, which argues
that Britain's natural and historical heritage must be more
conscientiously preserved. Cites preservation projects, some of
them controversial, that SPAB has undertaken in the twentieth
century.

84 "WM." TLS, no. 1677 (22 March):201-2.
     Comments upon WM's contemporary significance, noting that he
was remembered by many at centenary celebrations: "Pilgrims of hope
did look backward with gratitude to their early leader." Equates
Iceland with WM's youthful dreams and with his creation of utopias.

85 "WM Centenary." Art Digest 8, no. 13 (1 April):23.
     Comments on centenary exhibitions at the Huntington, at the
Met, and at the Victoria and Albert.

86 Brief of an Exhibition Displayed at the Houghton Library
     Commemorating the Centenary of the Birth of WM, March 24.
     Pasadena: R. Baughman, 7 pp.
     Catalogue-pamphlet describing some twenty items, eight of
them Kelmscott Press books, including a Kelmscott Chaucer, at a
small centenary exhibition at the Houghton.

87 A WM Bibliography, or the Catalogue of the Exhibition of
     Morrisiana Held by the Tokyo WM Society at Marazan Co. Catalogue
     of an Exhibition of Morrisiana 24 April-3 May 1934. Tokyo: WM
     Society, 44 pp.
     Catalogue of some 300 items, mainly books, acquired by the
University of Tokyo and a WM Society there; these include several
Kelmscott Press editions, one of which was a gift signed by
Chamberlain in 1929. Also exhibited were Japanese translations,
prints of Morris and Co. wall-papers, photographs of the Morris
family, a list of works by WM, and a calendar of events.

88 In Celebration of the Centenary of WM. Catalogue of an
     Exhibition, 9 February-8 April, 1934, at the Victoria and
     Albert. London: HMSO, 42 pp.
     In a brief introduction Mackail states that to revivify the
decorative arts, WM went "back to the Middle Ages, not with the idea
that the life of a past age could be reinstated, but in order that a
fresh start might be made from the point at which he held that it
had taken a wrong direction." Includes a descriptive sketch of
Morris and Co. and a list of all 352 items exhibited, these drawn
mainly from the decorative arts but including also some holograph
manuscripts. Has eleven plates.

<u>1935</u>

1   CRUSE, AMY. The <u>Victorians</u> <u>and</u> <u>their</u> <u>Reading</u>. Boston: Houghton
    Mifflin; Cambridge: Riverside Press, pp. 168-69, passim.
         Mentions several books and authors WM preferred, from Scott
    and Yonge through Dickens and Browning. WM also liked Thackeray,
    was lukewarm to Swinburne, and disliked <u>Anna</u> <u>Karenina</u>, because of
    its ending.

2   LETHABY, WILLIAM. <u>Philip</u> <u>Webb</u> <u>and</u> <u>His</u> <u>Work</u>. Oxford: Oxford
    University Press. Reprint. London: Raven Oak Press, 1979, pp.
    13-62, passim.
         Some might think that WM appears too often in this biography
    of Webb, but "the two men worked together so closely and influenced
    one another so much that they can hardly be separated." Their
    association is here surveyed beginning with the Oxford days,
    concluding with a description of the gravestone Webb designed for
    WM. Rich in anecdotes about the 1858 boat trip down the Seine, when
    the plans for Red House were first discussed, rich in details--many
    drawn from Taylor's letters to him--about Webb's important
    contributions to Morris and Co. and to the work of SPAB. Because
    Webb shared WM's love for the English land, for the "very earth" and
    the buildings upon it, he was a valued colleague in SPAB and in most
    of WM's endeavors.

3   LITZENBERG, KARL. "Allusions to the <u>Elder</u> <u>Edda</u> in the
    'Non-Norse' Poems of WM." <u>SS</u> 14:17-24.
         Several allusions to the <u>Elder</u> <u>Edda</u> in poems WM wrote before
    1869 are significant, for they indicate how much WM knew about Old
    Icelandic literature before he began working with Magnusson. Finds
    and briefly discusses eight such allusions.

4   LITZENBERG, KARL. "WM and the Burning of Njal." <u>SS</u> 14:40-41.
         Suggests that phrases like "Norse torches" in "Rapunzel" and
    "rooftree whereto the torch is set" in "The Proud King" reflect the
    famous burning-in at the center of <u>Njals</u> <u>Saga</u>, and that the
    increased accuracy of the second reference shows the "growth and
    development in Morris's knowledge and use of Norse materials," even
    before meeting Magnusson.

5   LITZENBERG, KARL. "WM and the <u>Heimskringla</u>. " <u>SS</u> 14:33-39.
         Discusses allusions in "The Wanderers" to Old Norse heroes
    and geography which indicate that WM had read Laing's 1844
    translation of the <u>Heimskringla</u>.

6 MASSE, H.J.L.J. <u>The Art Worker's Guild:</u> <u>1884-1934</u>. Oxford: Shakespeare Head Press, p. 48, passim.

WM, the sixth Master (for 1892) of the Art-Workers Guild, did not attend its meetings faithfully. In this careful history of fifty years of the Guild, we also learn that in 1893 WM could not get a resolution passed by the Guild protesting the removal of fourteenth-century statues from St. Mary's Church.

*7 MAURER, OSCAR. "<u>Paradise</u>, by WM." Dissertation, Yale University.

Cited in 1960.1.

8 MUNDAY, G.P. "WM and MacDonald." <u>Adelphi</u> 10, no. 1 (April):55-57.

Reports upon ceremonies at opening of WM Hall at Kelmscott. Ramsey MacDonald was an "unexpected visitor" and his diffidence suggested some dislocation between his old ideals, which he recalled because of the paeans to WM, and his own present political realities.

9 PECK, WALTER EDWIN. "The Master of Kelmscott." In <u>"Chants"</u> <u>by</u> <u>WM</u>. New York: New Horizon Press, pp. 5-8.

Introduction to WM's <u>Chants</u> includes a list of his major writings and achievements.

10 POORTENAAR, JAN. <u>The Art of the Book and its Illustration</u>. London: Harrap, pp. 24, 84-89, passim.

Sets forth history of Kelmscott Press, stressing that it was WM's reestablishment of sound priciples in book design and making that proved so influential on printers in Europe and America; several of the private presses so influenced are mentioned. Includes several fine illustrations.

11 WALTON, THOMAS. "A French Disciple of WM, Jean Lahor." <u>Revue</u> <u>de litterature comparee</u> 15, no. 3:524-35.

In his first article on WM, written in 1894, Lahor [Cazalis] argued that the work of WM and his contemporaries was a "menace to France's artistic superiority," but in his later work (1897.2) Lahor was important in spreading WM's fame in France. He remained a disciple of WM, founding a French version of SPAB and becoming an advocate of environmental preservation.

1936

1   CHESTERTON, GILBERT K.   "About WM."   In As I Was Saying.
    London: Methuen.   Reprint.   Freeport, N.Y.: Books for Libraries
    Press, 1966, pp. 127-32.
       Sardonically questions claims made during the centenary
    celebrations by many politicians and artists, suggesting that WM
    would scorn the "ugly proletarian art of the modern Bolshevists."

2   CUNCLIFFE, JOHN.   "WM (1834-1896)."   In Leaders of the Victorian
    Revolution.   New York: Appleton-Century-Crofts, pp. 248-52.
       A biographical sketch, some brief comments on the poetry, on
    the idyllic setting of Nowhere. Asserts that WM "had no grasp of
    economics" but that the improvements in the conditions of British
    workers "is in part owing to the arousing of the conscience of
    England by Morris and his master, Ruskin."

3   EHRSAM, THEODORE G.   "WM."   Bibliographies of Twelve Victorian
    Authors.   New York: H.W. Wilson, pp. 162-87.   Reprint.   New
    York: Octagon, 1968.
       Divided into three sections: (1) Chronological Outline, (2)
    Bibliographical Material, (3) Biographical and Critical Material.
    The last section has over 700 entries, all of which are included in
    the present book, with the exception of pre-1897 studies, reviews,
    and references to Masters' theses (forty-six, mainly American, are
    cited).   This section has enigmatic and erroneous entries.

4   ENSOR, R. C. K.   England: 1870-1914.   Oxford: Clarendon Press,
    pp. 155, passim.
       Remarks on WM's importance, especially in design, saying that
    "few men with a keener sense of craftsmanship, or greater natural
    gifts for giving effect to it, have ever lived."

5   GILL, ERIC.   The Necessity of Belief.   London: Faber and Faber,
    pp. 303-5.
       In Carlylean tones, insists that WM and the "Arts and Crafts
    Movement were necessarily failures.   You cannot have Gothic churches
    in the nineteenth century (except sham ones), or revive
    responsibility among factory workers who do not want it."   Suggests
    that WM's failure arose from the fact that he was "an unbeliever.
    He saw no being beyond doing; he saw no city of God behind an
    earthly paradise."

6   GITTLEMAN, DAVID. "The Vision of WM--A Briton's Way to
     Utopia." Unity 118 (19 October):66-73.
         A biographical sketch followed by a paraphrase and commentary
on Nowhere, some of it blurred by particularly American notions.
Suggests, for instance, that WM had a copy of the Declaration of
Independence before himself as he wrote, but the estimation of WM's
intentions and success in fulfilling them is generous, insightful,
and appreciative.

7   HUGHES, MAY. From Heavenly Spheres: A Book Written by
     Inspiration from WM, Poet, Socialist, and Idealist, Who Passed
     October 3rd. London: Rider and Co., 154 pp.
         Purports to be the words of WM, who speaks "from the other
side of the Veil called Death," about all manner of religious
doctrine. Why this lady-spiritualist chose WM to be her conduit for
these abstractions remains vague.

8   LITZENBERG, KARL. "WM and the Reviews: A Study in the Fame of a
     Poet." Review of English Studies 12, no. 48 (October):413-28.
         Examines scores of reviews, mainly of the poetry, published
during WM's lifetime in British and American periodicals, in an
attempt to answer three questions: When did WM attain literary fame?
What was the nature of this fame? How was it qualified? Finds that
with the publication of Paradise in 1870, WM "was welcomed into the
company of great narrative poets." Discusses various
qualifications, sometimes based on his socialism, that recur; notes
the shift of critical favor in this century away from the narrative
poems to Defence.

9   MORRIS, MAY, ed. WM: Artist, Writer, Socialist. Oxford:
     Blackwell, 2 vols., 1,334 pp. Reprint. New York: Russell and
     Russell, 1966.
         This supplement to the Collected Works is as valuable for the
introductions as for the previously unpublished material by WM. The
first volume has two sections, "The Art of WM" and "WM as a Writer,"
and the second volume is titled Morris as a Socialist. It opens
with Shaw's famous memoir (1936.12), and this is followed by
thirteen chapters which introduce eighteen lectures and articles,
and a section with a few personal letters. Concludes with seven
appendixes and an index. Fresh anecdotes and recollections (many
inspired by centenary celebrations just past) enliven these detailed
introductions and allow May Morris to encourage new perspectives on
WM's works, especially his socialist writings, and to change some
impressions encouraged by Mackail (1899.10), for instance, the harsh
one of Rossetti. Suggests that Love Is Enough provides insights
into her father's personal life, discusses his collaborations with
Magnusson on the translations from the Icelandic, and comments upon
the high reputation Morris and Co. enjoys, the increasing value of
all its works.

10 PEVSNER, NIKOLAUS. "WM, C.R. Ashbee und das zwanzigste
    Jahrhundert." Deutsche Vierteljahrschrift fur
    Literaturwissenschaft und Geistegeschichte 14:536-62.
        A biographical sketch emphasizes that WM, politically, became
the most significant artist of the nineteenth century because he
asked such questions as "What business have we with art at all
unless all can share it?" and because he launched Morris, Marshall,
Faulkner Co. in 1861, a date that future historians will use to mark
an epoch. Asserts that the only original thinker among WM's
followers was C.R. Ashbee, that his work with guild-schools and his
ideas about arts and crafts, have great potential importance for the
twentieth century. Translated: 1956.14.

11 PEVSNER, NIKOLAUS. Pioneers of the Modern Movement. London:
    Faber and Faber. New York: Museum of Modern Art, 1949 as
    Pioneers of Modern Design: From WM to Walter Gropius.
    Harmondworth: Pelican. 4th ed., 1975, pp. 21-25, 49-54, passim.
        Argues that in architecture and design WM is the "prophet of
the twentieth century." His insistence that art should belong to
all removed it from "aesthetics to the wider field of social
science." Says that "the revival of decorative honesty in Morris's
designs counts for more in the history of the Modern Movement than
his connection with bygone styles." Asserts that Ruskin, WM, and
his followers were out of phase, however, in their "hatred of the
machine and consequently the new steel and glass architecture." But
along with art nouveau and steel building design, the "Morris
Movement" must be regarded as one of the "three principal lines of
progress" leading into the Modern Movement.

12 SHAW, GEORGE BERNARD. "WM as I Knew Him." In WM: Artist,
    Writer, Socialist. Edited by May Morris. Oxford: Blackwell,
    2:10-42. Reprint. New York: Dodd, Mead and Co., 1936. London:
    WM Society, 1966.
        An insider's view of WM's activities and achievements,
especially during the 1880s, a view modified by four decades of
alert attention to the ways socialism had developed in England and
abroad, by Shaw's witty reversals of received opinion, and by his
sly characterizations of fellow socialists and adversaries like
Hyndman. Of WM's supposed problems with understanding Marxist
theory, Shaw asserts that the dialectic which made "Communist
thinking difficult and uncongenial, Morris put aside as the
intellectual trifling it actually is." Includes humorous anecdotes
about Janey, about his own "celestial betrothal" to May Morris,
about WM's intolerance for fools, and his support, intellectual and
financial, for the cause of revolution. Anticipates E.P. Thompson
(1955.15), when he praises WM's socialist writings as the "best
books in the Bible of socialism," suggesting that they called forth,
for the first time, all of WM's mental powers, that they have been
too long ignored by his biographers. Concludes that WM "towers

greater and greater above the horizon beneath which his best
advertized contemporaries have disappeared."

13 STRACHEY, JOHN. The Theory and Practice of Socialism. New
     York: Random House, pp. 314-17.
        Agrees with the general view of Nowhere as an ode to the
rural beauty of Britain, but points out also WM's insights into
political realities, especially in the chapter, "How the Change
Came." Suggests that WM was prescient about fascism in his
descriptions of the "Friends of Order," and that as the long
dialogue in John Ball makes obvious he understood Marx and
scientific socialism.

14 WEYGANDT, CORNELIUS. "WM." In The Time of Tennyson: English
     Victorian Poetry as it Affected America. New York and London: D.
     Appleton-Century, pp. 217-25, passim.
        Warns readers that they "must come to Morris a little removed
from the workaday world, if you are to come under his spell."
Judges "Haystack in the Floods" to be the best poem in WM's canon,
for there is "no typical Morrisean haze about the writing."

15 WILLIAMS, J.R. "Artist and Prophet: WM and His Life Work."
     Wheatsheaf 40 (October):155-56.
        A celebration of WM and his works, one inspired by the
publication of May Morris (1936.9). Claims that WM will be
remembered more for "giving a new direction to the decorative arts"
than for his poetry, even though "every boy should read Sigurd."
Wonders at WM taking up so fervently, at midlife, the socialist
banner: "one of the most startling revelations of altruism that has
ever been made."

16 "An Idle Dreamer at Work: WM's Way to Serenity." TLS, no. 1801
     (8 August):645.
        A graceful response to May Morris's two-volume supplement
(1936.9) to the Collected Works, one which rehearses the essential
unities in WM's life, which praises the Shaw memoir (1936.12) that
opens volume two.

17 "Eighty Years After." Architectural Review 79, no. 474
     (May):247-50.
        Reprints Times article on celebration of the recently
completed restoration, by Professor Tristram, of the Oxford Union
murals. Includes an 1857 description, by Coventry Patmore, of the
original undertaking, and a similar passage from Mackail (1899.10).

<u>1937</u>

1   BALDWIN, STANLEY. "WM: A Speech Delivered at the WM Centenary
    Exhibition, London, February 9, 1934." In <u>The</u> <u>Torch</u> <u>of</u> <u>Freedom:</u>
    <u>Speeches</u> <u>and</u> <u>Addresses</u>. London: Hodder and Stoughton, pp.
    180-85.
        Recalls visiting WM in 1896, claims that he was "probably the
    greatest craftsman of all time," that he provided the "leaven" that
    shall "hasten the day when the beautiful will thrive."

2   BUSH, DOUGLAS. "WM." In <u>Mythology</u> <u>and</u> <u>the</u> <u>Romantic</u> <u>Tradition</u>
    <u>in</u> <u>English</u> <u>Poetry</u>. Cambridge, Mass.: Harvard University Press.
    Reprint. New York: W.W. Norton, 1963, pp. 297-327.
        States that "if poets were to be discussed in proportion to
    the bulk of their mythological verse, this chapter would be the
    longest in the book. If written solely from the critical standpoint
    of the present, it would probably be the shortest." Judges that the
    frame of <u>Paradise</u> is "perfectly adapted to Morris's narrative
    conventions," that these poems and <u>Jason</u> have the "even uniformity
    of tapestry," that they are unlikely to hold any appeal for mature
    readers.

3   DAVIES, IDRIS. "WM." <u>Wales</u> 3, no. 1 (Summer):83.
        A sixteen-line poem addressed to WM, the "idle singer," who
    would not understand modern times, for "We honour dolts in racing
    cars/And dirty dogs and talkie stars."

4   HOARE, DOROTHY. <u>The</u> <u>Works</u> <u>of</u> <u>WM</u> <u>and</u> <u>Yeats</u> <u>in</u> <u>Relation</u> <u>to</u> <u>Early</u>
    <u>Saga</u> <u>Literature</u>. Cambridge: Cambridge University Press, 179 pp.
    Reprint. Folcroft, Pa.: Folcroft Press, 1970. New York:
    Russell and Russell, 1971. Norwood, Pa.: Norwood Editions,
    1975. Philadelphia: R. West, 1977.
        Surveys differences, which are considerable, between Irish
    and Icelandic sagas. Discusses WM's fascination with the Teutonic
    North, and the translations he did with Magnusson, finding fault
    with the latter: "from any point of view the translations are
    failures." A fuller discussion of the two poetic narratives,
    "Gudrun" and <u>Sigurd</u>, singles out the fundamental differences between
    them and their sources in the sagas, again finding fault with WM's
    renderings, which lack the vitality of the originals. Concludes
    that WM and Yeats used the old stories, necessarily changing them,
    because they distrusted and despised contemporary realities.
    Revision of 1930.4.

5   KIPLING, RUDYARD. Something of Myself. Garden City, N.Y.:
     Doubleday, Doran, pp. 16-17.
         Kipling enjoyed visits at the Grange, for his aunt, Georgie
Burne-Jones, was particularly kind. There he often saw WM who
rarely noticed children, but Kipling recalls an "amazing
exception." WM climbed onto "our big rocking-horse. There, slowly
surging back and forth while the poor beast creaked, he told us a
tale full of fascinating horrors," one that was probably Icelandic
because it involved cows' tails and dried fish.

6   LITZENBERG, KARL. "The Diction of WM: A Discussion of his
     Translations from the Old Norse." Arkiv for Nordisk Filologi
     53:327-63.
         This careful study finds that WM was not the "neologist
supreme" suggested by many previous commentators, that in fact most
of the "non-modern" words used in his Norse translations had been
used "by Chaucer, Malory, the ballad writers, and Lord Berners." In
these translations (his study did not include Heimskringla) only
eighteen actual neologisms occur. The vocabulary in these
translations is very like that in the late prose romances. Includes
several pages of tables, the data to support his generalizations,
and concludes with comments about other translators of Old Norse.

7   LOHMANN, OTTO. "Die Rahmenerzahlung von WM's Paradise." Archiv
     fur das Studium der neueren Sprachen und Literaturen 172:42-46.
         Speculates upon possible sources for the frame-story in
Paradise, sources that include Boccaccio's Decameron, the legend of
Bran, and "Mesate," an Italian tale that Salvuccio Salvucci wrote in
1591.

8   MORRIS, MAY. "Letter to Yeats, October, 1937." In Letters to
     Yeats. Edited by R.J. Finnerman et al. New York: Columbia
     University Press, p. 595.
         Writes that she is pleased to hear of Yeats's "re-reading of
Sigurd: it is not only the splendor of the poem that carries one on
and on, but the dexterity." She also cites T.E. Lawrence as a
"great lover of WM's works."

9   RIDDEHOUGH, GEOFFREY B. "WM's Translation of the Aeneid." JEGP
     36, no. 3:338-46.
         Points out and discusses many errors and inelegancies in WM's
renderings of Virgil, suggesting that WM's medieval diction and
motifs are interesting for what they tell us about his poetic
development, but that they only distort the classical tale.

10 ULLMANN, STEPHEN. "Synaesthetic Metaphors in WM: An Essay on
    the Decorative Arts of the Pre-Raphaelites." <u>Angol Filologai
    Tanulmanyok</u> [Studies in English philology] Budapest 2:143-51.
        Cites previous studies of synaesthesia, and asserts that a
    many-sided artist like WM should not have been so long ignored by
    such aestheticians, since "he was predestined to make full use of
    synaesthetic effects." Finds 302 synaesthetic images in WM's early
    prose and poetry, but these are not listed and no reason is given
    for excluding <u>Paradise</u> poems from the count. Concludes with a few
    examples, like "honied songs," and "the hot sun bit," which add
    "decorative effects" to WM's poetry.

11 YOUNG, GEORGE MALCOLM. "Topsy." In <u>Daylight and Champagne:
    Essays</u>. London: Cape, pp. 65-71.
        Compares his delight in reading <u>Paradise</u> to that felt when he
    reads Homer, and commends WM's socialist essays for their clarity,
    but he adds that neither WM nor "his master, Ruskin, really
    apprehended, or even faced, the problem of machinery." Concludes
    that WM's "socialism was the final synthesis of all his purposes:
    and without it his character would have been unfinished, his life
    incomplete."

<u>1938</u>

1   COLE, G.D.H. "WM and the Modern World." In <u>Persons and
    Periods: Studies</u>. London and New York: Macmillan. Reprint.
    Freeport, N.Y.: Books for Libraries Press, 1967, pp. 284-306.
        Though WM's influence lives on, much of his decorative work
    and most of his writings have gone out of fashion; the former seems
    too ornamental, the latter too romantic. But <u>Nowhere</u> is the only
    Utopia since More's that "deserves to be remembered as literature,"
    and his socialist writings are still relevant. "Where Morris went
    wrong was not in affirming the need for pleasure in labour, but in
    resting this pleasure on too narrow a basis," and in assuming that
    all work could yield the sorts of pleasure an artist receives.
    Praises WM's faith in fellowship and suggests that in Russia some of
    WM's ideals are bearing fruit.

2   COLE, G.D.H., and POSTGATE, RAYMOND. <u>The British Common People:
    1746-1946</u>. London: Methuen. New York: Knopf. Reprint.
    London: Methuen. New York: Barnes and Noble, 1961, pp. 421,
    passim.
        WM linked to Bradlaugh, Tom Mann, John Burns, and Keir
    Hardie, all men with "strong integrity of character, of greater
    nature than their immediate successors."

3   DAICHES, DAVID. Literature and Society. London: Sacker and
    Warburg. Reprint. New York: Haskell House, 1970, pp. 247-53,
    passim.
        Compares Ruskin to WM; though they both "approached economics
    through art," the latter was more realistic and tested theories with
    practical activities. Discusses WM's work with the Socialist
    League, commenting upon contending factions and problems with the
    radical left in England in the 1880s.

4   LITZENBERG, KARL. "Tyrfing into Excalibur? A Note on WM's
    Unfinished Poem, 'In Arthur's House.'" SS 15:81-83.
        Discusses an early, unpublished poem, "In Arthur's House," in
    which WM used the Norse sword, "Tyrfing," in a context appropriate
    to Excalibur. Speculates about his sources, since this poem was
    written at least four years before he met Magnusson.

5   MOSER, MAX. "WM." In Richard Wagner in der englischen
    Literatur des XIX. Jahrhunderts. Bern: A. Franck, pp. 32-37.
        Points out that both Wagner and WM hated the effects of
    nineteenth-century civilization and that both offered combat with
    their art, Wagner with opera and WM with an attempt to revive the
    arts and crafts. Offers short biographical sketches, mentioning
    parallel interests in Teutonic myth, in the Tannhauser legend.
    Quotes from WM's diatribes against Wagner.

6   MURRY, JOHN MIDDLETON. "WM: The Church Re-edified." In Heroes
    of Thought. New York; J. Messner, pp. 344-64.
        Argues that even though WM was rooted in the past, he was no
    antiquarian; he was a Marxist, was in fact "the one man in England
    really capable of understanding and completing Marx's revolutionary
    theory of history." Insists that WM went beyond Marx in realizing
    the role of art in creating revolutionary change.

7   ORMEROD, JAMES. The Poetry of WM. Derby: Harpur and Sons, 25
    pp. Reprint. Folcroft, Pa.: Folcroft Press, 1970. Folcroft,
    Pa.: Folcroft Library Editions, 1974. Norwood, Pa.: Norwood
    Editions, 1977.
        This attempt to "rescue WM's poetry from the temporary
    neglect into which it has seemingly fallen" consists of praiseful
    paraphrase of Defence, Jason, Paradise, and Sigurd.

8   REID, MARGARET J.C. The Arthurian Legend: Comparison of
     Treatments in Modern and Medieval Literature. London: Oliver and
     Boyd, pp. 95-101.
         Suggests that complexities of WM's Arthurian poems are due to
     his craftsman's eye for decorative effects as well as to a love of
     things medieval and romantic that thus "clouded his power of judging
     fairly." But interesting psychological effects are added.

9   ROSS, HARRY. "My Utopia and WM." In Utopias Old and New.
     London: Nicolson and Watson, pp. 216-32, passim.
         Though Nowhere is often thought of as a kind of rural escape,
     Ross asserts that it "displays to my mind a psychological insight
     into the realities of the problem of human relationships that exists
     in no other Utopia." Praises Hammond's description of the great
     change as both "fine reading and good economics," and concludes that
     "I would rather have written Nowhere than almost any other book in
     the English language."

10   WALL, BERNARD. "WM and Karl Marx." Dublin Review 202, nos.
     404-5 (January-June):39-47.
         Compares Marx and WM in terms of their temperments, with the
     latter getting the edge, since he had the "impulsive kindness" of an
     Englishman. Argues that WM desired the rebirth of medieval culture
     and that such a desire was incompatible with his hopes for
     communism.

11   WEITENKAMPF, FRANK. The Illustrated Book. Cambridge, Mass.:
     Harvard University Press, pp. 205-6, passim.
         Faults WM for at times letting decoration intrude on text,
     but concludes that "he clearly brought before us the importance of
     attending to the relation of the parts of the book to each other,
     leading to unity in design."

12   YEATS, W.B. "Four Years: 1887-1891." In The Autobiography of
     William Butler Yeats. New York: Macmillan. Reprint. 1965, pp.
     93-100.
         Reprint of 1921.7.

<u>1939</u>

1   FUCILLA, JOSEPH G. "Bibliographies of Twelve Victorian Authors:
    A Supplement." <u>MP</u> 37, no. 1 (August):92.
        Lists three articles on WM. All are included in the present
book.

2   GLENISTER, S.H. "WM: Artist-Craftsman." In <u>Stories</u> <u>of</u> <u>Great</u>
    <u>Craftsmen</u>. London: Clark, Irwin. Reprint. Freeport, N.Y.:
    Books for Libraries Press, 1970, pp. 193-213.
        Biographical sketch laced with dramatic dialogue, as when
young William tells his father that he wants to be a craftsman and
receives this response: "William! Only the poor work with their
hands." Concludes with high praise for Kelmscott Press volumes.

3   HICKS, GRANVILLE. "Socialism and WM." In <u>Figures</u> <u>of</u>
    <u>Transition</u>: <u>A</u> <u>Study</u> <u>of</u> <u>British</u> <u>Literature</u> <u>at</u> <u>the</u> <u>End</u> <u>of</u> <u>the</u>
    <u>Nineteenth</u> <u>Century</u>. New York: Macmillan, pp. 69-108, passim.
        Opens with a fresh approach: "Since Socialism was to become
more and more important in what we call modern literature, the first
author to adopt it as his political creed becomes in some sense a
modern. No label would on the surface of things, seem less
applicable to WM." This paradox is examined, interesting questions
are raised (why was WM the only one of his contemporary poets and
artists to grasp Marx so wholeheartedly?), which are woven into a
biographical sketch that isolates the Eastern Question Association
and SPAB as partial causes for WM's socialism. Discusses WM's
differences with the Fabians, pointing out that a "glance at Fabian
writers increases our respect for WM." Concludes that it is "good
that England's first socialist poet was a Great Man and a Marxist."

4   JACKSON, HOLBROOK. "The Nonage of Nineteenth Century
    Printing." In <u>The</u> <u>Printing</u> <u>of</u> <u>Books</u>. London: Grant Richards.
    Reprint. Freeport, N.Y.: Books for Libraries Press, 1970, pp.
    12-24.
        Reprint of 1924.3.

5   JACKSON, HOLBROOK. "The Typography of WM." <u>The</u> <u>Printing</u> <u>of</u>
    <u>Books</u>. London: Cassell. Reprint. Freeport, N.Y.: Books for
    Libraries Press, 1970, pp. 175-85.
        Reprint of 1934.32.

6   LEWIS, C.S. "WM." In Rehabilitations and Other Essays.
     Oxford: Oxford University Press, pp. 35-55.
         Argues that Wardour Street English is an inappropriate label
     for WM's prose, one based on "dogmatisms that will go down at a
     touch." Points out that WM's style is as classically simple as that
     of Dr. Johnson. Sees the prose romances as the "real crown of his
     work," for their pictures of "daily life, health [physical love is
     seen as a function of health], and preservation of the community"
     are neither socialist nor Christian; instead they are pictures of
     experience "ineluctably true." Reprinted: 1969.19.

7   **STOCK, A.G. "Yeats on Spenser,"** In In Excited Reverie: A
     Centenary Tribute to Yeats, 1865-1939. Edited by A.N. Jeffares
     and K.G.W. Cross. New York: Macmillan, pp. 93-97.
         Four poets were particularly influential upon Yeats and his
     lifelong meditations upon poetry; they were Spenser, Blake, Shelley,
     and WM. Yeats said WM had given him the incentive to ponder the
     social implications of poetry, that he deserved to receive the
     laureateship after Tennyson.

8   WALL, BERNARD. "Bequest from Miss May Morris." Bodleian
     Library Review 1 (April):57.
         Lists WM manuscripts, mainly on the decorative arts, that May
     Morris left to the Bodleian.

                                  1940

1   ALDRED, GUY A. "The Socialism of WM; WM and
     Anti-Parliamentarism." Pioneers of Anti-Parliamentarism.
     Glasgow: Bakunin Press, pp. 11-24.
         Mentions the fashion of appreciating WM the poet while
     ignoring WM the socialist, and the following biographical sketch is
     laced with socialist bromides about the bourgeois culture which
     shaped WM and which he reacted against. Asserts also that WM gave
     to socialism a "joy of being which Marx never brought to it," and
     that he remained, despite a renewed alliance with the SDF in 1894, a
     true Anti-Parliamentarian.

2   ANDERSON, KARL O.E. "Scandinavian Elements in the Works of
     WM." Dissertation, Harvard University, 1035 pp.
         This unpublished work surveys all of WM's associations with
     Norse mythology, Danish ballads, and Old Icelandic poetry and sagas.
     Particularly full and helpful on the translations WM and Magnusson
     did from the Icelandic.

3   BALCH, DAVID. <u>Elbert</u> <u>Hubbard:</u> <u>Genius</u> <u>of</u> <u>Roycroft</u>. New York:
     Frederick Stokes, pp. 134-39, passim.
        Hubbard supposedly visited WM in 1895, and "an epoch-making
idea was born--the idea of the Roycroft Shops in East Aurora--that
was to make the name of Elbert Hubbard known throughout the entire
English-speaking world." Similar exaggerated references about WM
occur frequently, since Balch accepts at face value everything
Hubbard reported about WM in both 1900.8 and 1907.5.

4   BAUM, PAUL F. <u>Rossetti's</u> <u>Letters</u> <u>to</u> <u>Fanny</u> <u>Cornforth</u>.
     Baltimore: Johns Hopkins Press, pp. 13-14, passim.
        Introductory material and notes have references to WM and to
the early years at Kelmscott Manor, where many of these letters were
written. Suggests contrasts between Janey and Fanny Cornforth.

5   BENDER, ALBERT M. <u>An</u> <u>Evening</u> <u>with</u> <u>WM's</u> <u>Albion</u> <u>Proof</u> <u>Press</u>. San
     Mateo, Calif.: Quercus Press, 2 pp.
        Judges it to be both pleasant and fitting that one of WM's
Albion presses has ended up in San Francisco, where many fine
presses, under the influence of Kelmscott Press, sprang up in the
early years of the twentieth century.

6   BROOKS, VAN WYCK. <u>New</u> <u>England:</u> <u>Indian</u> <u>Summer</u>. New York: E.P.
     Dutton, pp. 224, 230, 331, 392.
        Mentions Morris and Co. windows in Boston's Trinity Church,
asserting that their "color and splendor indicated forcibly the
break of the Boston mind with its Puritan past." Compares Howells's
Utopian novel, <u>A</u> <u>Traveler</u> <u>from</u> <u>Altruria</u>, to <u>Nowhere</u>.

7   CURTIN, FRANK DANIEL. "Aesthetics in English Social Reform:
     Ruskin and His Followers." In <u>Nineteenth</u> <u>Century</u> <u>Studies</u>.
     Edited by H. Davis, W.C. DeVane and R.C. Bald. Ithaca, N.Y.:
     Cornell University Press. Reprint. New York: Greenwood Press,
     1968, pp. 199-245.
        Repeats WM's praise of "The Nature of Gothic," insisting that
despite his acceptance of Marxian socialism, WM "retained in his
social ideals various aesthetic and humanistic principles which he
learned from Ruskin." Many of Ruskin's ideas were therefore
carried, via SPAB or the Arts and Crafts Movement, or within the
pages of <u>Nowhere</u>, forward into the twentieth century. Social
critics like Patrick Geddes, Lewis Mumford, and John A. Hobson
learned from WM, but they were also repeating Ruskin's vital ideas.

8   ESHLEMAN, LLOYD W. A Victorian Rebel: The Life of WM. New
     York: Scribners, 386 pp. Reprint. New York: Octagon Books,
     1971.
        A "personalized" biography with chapter headings like "A
Little Boy Questions His Small World," and with invented
conversations; a relative, for instance, exclaims: "to think of any
child of four learning to read these long, difficult novels."
Frequent attempts to be confidential create misconceptions, as when
he says that Rossetti engineered WM's marriage or that WM used as a
political model something called "The Icelandic Federation," which
of course never existed. More serious are the mistakes that occur
in the chapters on socialism, for here he relies heavily on Glasier
(1921.3), whom he calls WM's Boswell. This book's largest claim to
fame is the thundering judgments it has drawn from E.P. Thompson, in
1951.15, 1955.15, and in 1976.50, where he called this biography a
"nauseous and thoroughly dishonest book." Reappeared as 1949.4,
with Eshleman transformed into Lloyd Eric Grey.

9   FLOWER, ROBERT. "The WM Manuscripts." British Museum Quarterly
     14, no. 4:8-12.
        The WM manuscripts are in two series: the May Morris bequest
in forty volumes (Add. MSS 45298-337) and the WM Papers in
twenty-two volumes (Add. MSS 45338-41; 45407-11). These bequests
supplemented other WM material, and manuscripts, which the Museum
had already owned. All are here briefly described.

10   HARROLD, CHARLES F. "Recent Trends in Victorian Studies." SP
     37, no. 4 (October):684-85.
        Annotates a few articles on WM, most of them by Litzenberg.
All are included in the present book.

*11 JEDLICKA, AUGUSTE. "Naturauffassung und Naturschilderungen bei
     WM." Dissertation, University of Vienna.
            Cited in 1960.1.

12   LUCAS, F.L. "WM." In Ten Victorian Poets. Cambridge:
     Cambridge University Press. 3d ed., 1948. Reprint. London:
     Archon Books, 1966, pp. 139-60.
            Reprint of 1930.8.

13 MAURER, OSCAR. "WM and the Poetry of Escape." In <u>Nineteenth</u>
    <u>Century Studies</u>. Edited by H. Davis, W.C. DeVane, and R.C.
    Bald. Ithaca, N. Y.: Cornell University Press. Reprint. New
    York: Greenwood Press, 1968, pp. 247-76.
        Describes the critical reception of <u>Paradise</u>, pointing out
    that it was generally favorable and that a majority of readers
    appreciated the solace that pastoral brings or the pleasure of
    aesthetic contemplation. Concludes with a helpful list of all
    British and American reviews of both <u>Jason</u> and <u>Paradise</u>.

14 PEVSNER, NIKOLAUS. <u>Acadamies of Art, Past and Present</u>.
    Cambridge: Cambridge University Press, pp. 259-65, passim.
        Points out that Morris and Co. was important for bringing
    leading artists together in a cooperative venture for "designing and
    producing articles for everyday use," that WM was the first to
    perceive and write about the "organic inter-relation between
    material, working process, purpose and aesthetic," and therefore a
    revival of handicraft and industrial art took place. Asserts that
    the modern movement is more indebted to WM than to any other
    nineteenth-century artist.

15 ROBERTSON, JOHN CHARLES. "The Social Ideas of Plato and WM."
    In <u>Mixed Company</u>. London: J.M. Dent. Reprint. Freeport, N.Y.:
    Books for Libraries Press, 1970, pp. 56-79.
        Opines that as "charming" as <u>Nowhere</u> can be, it is inferior
    to <u>The Republic</u>, for Plato was interested in the "fundamental
    principles" that must support a commonwealth, in idealism of the
    highest order, but <u>Nowhere</u> seems to stress sensual, materialistic
    individualism. Still, the two works have much in common: doctrines
    involving cooperation and brotherly goodwill; virtuous activities
    that are their own reward and a concern for improving the
    environment.

<u>1941</u>

1   DAVIS, ARTHUR KYLE JR. "WM and the Eastern Question, with a
    Fugitive Political Poem by Morris." In <u>Humanistic Studies in</u>
    <u>Honor of John Calvin Metcalfe</u>. University of Virginia Studies,
    vol. 1. Charlottesville, Virginia: University of Virginia
    Press, pp. 28-47.
        Sketches in backgrounds of the Eastern Question Association
    and WM's involvement. Reprints and discusses his "Wake, London
    Lads," which is here called a "poetic key" to WM's transition from
    an "aristocratic aversion to politics" to a real "conversion to
    socialism."

2   DUPONT, VICTOR. "La pensee et les oeuvres utopiques de WM." In *l'utopie et le Roman Utopique dans la Litterature anglaise*. Paris: M. Didier, pp. 474-521.

     Discusses Nowhere against both its contemporary social context and also its similarities to novels like Jeffries's *After London* and Hudson's *A Crystal Age*. A biographical sketch is followed by a plot summary of Nowhere.

3   GRAY, NICOLETE. "WM, Eric Gill and Catholicism." *Architectural Review* 89, no. 532 (March):61-62.

     WM and Gill both blamed industrial capitalist society for the plight of the worker and the decline of art, and here passages illustrating their similar indictments are discussed; major differences arise from Gill's strong religious beliefs, his distrust of social reform, and his conviction that it was "foolishness to hope for the kingdom of God on earth."

*4   POLLACK, GRETE. "Bild und bildlicher Ausdruck in der Dichtungen von WM." Dissertation, University of Vienna.

     Cited in 1960.1.

5   RIDDEHOUGH, GEOFFREY B. "WM's Translation of the Odyssey." *JEGP* 40, no. 4:558-61.

     Comments upon the effects of WM's "curious hatred of the Latin element in the English language," an attitude that causes him to accentuate the primitive in the original text, to falsify his translation of Homer, much as he had of Virgil, though there is "much less of the medieval" in this than in his translation of the Latin epic, a translation this same critic discussed in 1937.9. Points out also that WM borrowed certain phrases and epithets from the Butcher and Lang translation of 1879.

6   WOODWARD, GWENDOLYN. "Kelmscott Chaucer." *TLS*, no. 2055 (21 June):299.

     Letter reports upon the signed copy of the Kelmscott Chaucer that WM presented to Skeat, a copy now in Cambridge.

1942

1   BROWN, E.K., ed. Introduction to *Victorian Poetry*. New York: Ronald Press, pp. 577-625.

     Brief introduction claims that the "poetic career of Morris is one of perpetual experiment," that Jason "remains one of the most beautiful and one of the best constructed poems in modern literature." Selection includes several Defence poems.

2   GAUNT, WILLIAM. "From King Arthur to Karl Marx." In The
     Pre-Raphaelite Tragedy. London: Cape. New York: Harcourt,
     Brace, pp. 184-95, passim. Reprinted as The Pre-Raphaelite
     Dream. London: Reprint Society, 1943.
         WM is placed within the Pre-Raphaelite umbra: as Woolner went
to Australia and Hunt to Palestine to achieve their quests, so WM
went to Iceland to achieve his. And WM's socialism is seen as
Pre-Raphaelite, because "it derived from that idea which lurked even
in the original Pre-Raphaelite discussions: that everyone should be
an artist." Kelmscott Chaucer called the "final Pre-Raphaelite
masterpiece." WM is here displayed as an uncompromising man of
action whose socialism grew out of his own experience with crafts
work and his love of the Middle Ages: "Karl Marx he ploughed through
with some dispirit."

3   PEARSON, HESKETH. Bernard Shaw: His Life and Personality.
     London: Collins, pp. 81-83, 92-101, passim.
         Includes many anecdotes about WM, some drawn from discussions
with Shaw, others from 1936.12. Mentioned are WM's dislike for
Aveling, his delight in Shaw's remarks on Nordau and in Wilde's
visits, and his response to the Trafalgar Square Riot. WM is here
reported to have coined the term "Shavian."

4   TILLOTSON, GEOFFREY. "WM, Word Spinner." In Essays in
     Criticism and Research. Cambridge: Cambridge University Press,
     pp. 141-43.
         Suggests that WM was not a great poet because he was too fine
a craftsman; poetry was too easy for him. Invites us to consider
Milton's dozen hard-won daily lines alongside the 700 WM is reported
to have completed in one day. WM wrote without a specific audience
in mind; therefore, the poetry, with the exception of Defence and
the socialist songs, is "bland."

5   TILLOTSON, GEOFFREY. "WM and Machines." In Essays in Criticism
     and Research. Cambridge: Cambridge University Press. Reprint.
     1967, pp. 144-52.
         Reprinted from 1934.68.

6   WOOD, H.G. "WM and Marx." New Statesman no. 612 (14
     November):321.
         Comments upon and quotes from Glasier (1921.3), attempting
then to make distinctions between the types of socialism espoused by
WM and by Hyndman.

1943

1   HONE, JOSEPH. Yeats: 1865-1939. New York: Macmillan, pp. 12,
    27-28, 66-69, passim.
        Includes several anecdotes about WM that Yeats recalled from
    the period he visited Hammersmith frequently; one about WM starting
    a French class for young socialists seems fresh. Reports also upon
    resemblances Yeats saw between WM and Gerhard Hauptman.

2   MAC MURTRIE, DOUGLAS. "The Revival of Craftsmanship." In The
    Book: the Story of Printing and Bookmaking. London and New
    York: Oxford University Press. 9th printing, 1967, pp. 451-61,
    passim.
        Reprint of 1927.4.

3   PEVSNER, NIKOLAUS. An Outline of English Architecture.
    Harmondsworth: Penguin. 7th ed., 1972, pp. 390-91, passim.
        WM'S work with Morris and Co., ideas in his lectures are seen
    as significant, for "by trying to revive the old faith in service,
    by indicting the contemporary architect's and artist's arrogant
    indifference to design for everyday needs, by discrediting any art
    created by individual genius for a small group of conoisseurs, and
    by forcing home with untiring zest the principle that art matters
    only if all can share it, he laid the foundation for the Modern
    Movement."

*4 SCHUPPANZIGH-FRANKENBACH, ALEXANDRA. "WM: Sigurd im Verhaltnis
    zu Richard Wagner's Ring." Dissertation, University of Graz.
        Cited in 1960.1.

5   TUNSTALL, EDWARD A., and KERR, ANTHONY. "The Painted Room at
    the Queen's College, Oxford." Burlington Magazine 82, no. 479
    (February):42-46.
        Describes paintings and designs, medieval figures and floral
    patterns, within a room at Queen's College, a room that WM and
    Burne-Jones might have stayed in during the long vacation of 1856,
    and they are thus presumed to have done these decorations. Includes
    six illustrations.

1944

1   COOLIDGE, JOHN. "WM and the Preservation of Historic
    Monuments." Journal of the American Society of Architectural
    Historians 4, no. 2 (April):34-36.
        Quotes from two lectures that WM read to SPAB, "Architecture
    and History" on 1 July 1884 and "Westminster Abbey" in June 1893,
    noting with approval how sternly WM castigates those with the
    arrogance to think they can restore or imitate what is by its very
    nature "inimitable."

*2 DEMUS, MARGARET. "Studien zu dem spaten Prosaromanzen von WM."
    Dissertation, University of Vienna.
        Cited in 1960.1.

*3 EVANS, M. "WM and Post-War Reconstruction." Journal of
    Southwest Essex Technical College 1 (Spring):215-43.
        Cited in personal correspondence.

4   FORD, GEORGE H. "WM and His Masters." In Keats and the
    Victorians: A Study of His Influence and Rise to Fame,
    1821-1895. New Haven: Yale University Press, pp. 49-63, passim.
        Asserts that "Keats and Chaucer were perhaps the only English
    poets who satisfied WM permanently and whole-heartedly." Yet no one
    has closely examined WM's poetry for Keatsian influences. Here a
    few "echoes" are noted, as are parallel pictorial scenes; there are
    many such in Jason and Paradise, and their use "contributed mightily
    to the Victorian revival of Keats."

5   MAXWELL, VIVIAN M. "Kelmscott Books at Colby." Colby Library
    Quarterly, 1st ser., no. 6 (March):95-104.
        A survey of Kelmscott Press titles in New England college and
    university libraries puts Colby, with twenty-one, second to
    Harvard's forty-seven. Six libraries have a Kelmscott Chaucer; the
    only Kelmscott Press publication not present in any of the libraries
    are the Froissart trial pages.

6   MORTON, A.L. "WM: Architect of the Future." Our Time 3, no. 7
    (February):8.
        Argues that Nowhere is "unique in that it is a Utopia based
    on scientific socialism," that WM's vision has been confirmed by the
    achievements of the Russian revolution.

7   MUMFORD, LEWIS. The Condition of Man. New York: Harcourt
     Brace, pp. 301, 307, 336, 382.
        Offers examples of WM's recoil from industrialism and its
effects, pointing out that he was no mere reactionary: "on the
contrary he remarked that the iron steamships that were a-building
in Glasgow were the cathedrals of the Industrial Age, and he exulted
not only in their craftsmanship but the working unison they brought
about." Concludes that Nowhere "now turns out to be closer to a
desirable reality" than many other socialist schemes.

8   NORDLUNDE, C.V. WM, en Biografi. Copenhagen: Nyt Nordisk
     Forlag, 71 pp.
        In Danish. Biographical sketch stresses WM's contributions
to the book arts, and the influence into the twentieth century of
Kelmscott Press. Includes fifteen pages of Kelmscott Press
illustrations, a list of the books published at the Press, and
capsule biographies of a few of WM's associates.

9   PHILLIPS, LAWRENCE. "WM." N and Q 186 (6 May):229.
        Asks if WM was correct in stating in Nowhere that the British
government had once sent smallpox-infected blankets to the Indians.

10 SHAW, GEORGE BERNARD. Everybody's Political What's What.
     London: Constable. New York: Dodd, Mead, pp. 16, 49, passim.
        Calls WM the "greatest of our English Communists," and also
comments on his attitudes toward education and music.

11 SHORT, CLARICE. "WM and Keats." PMLA 59, no. 2 (June):513-23.
        Points to shared backgrounds and interests of Keats and WM,
spending their boyhoods near Epping Forest, enthralled by the Middle
Ages and by Chaucer. Discusses several paired passages with similar
themes and images, concluding that WM must have memorized many poems
by Keats, since there are at least forty passages with striking
similarities.

12 STEVENS, EDWARD F. "The Kelmscott Influence in Maine." Colby
     Library Quarterly, 1st ser., no. 6 (March):92-95.
        Discusses Kelmscott Press influence on books from the Colby
College Press, and also on the publications of Thomas Mosher, whose
fine press miniatures include several WM titles.

13 WADIMAR. "WM." N and Q 186 (3 June):278.
     A reply to 1944.9: yes, small-poxed blankets were indeed
given, by Sir Jeffrey Amherst, to the Indians. So WM's allusion in
Nowhere is historically accurate.

1945

1   GRENNAN, MARGARET R. WM: Medievalist and Revolutionary. New
    York: King's Crown Press. Reprint. New York: Russell and
    Russell, 1970, 175 pp.
        Victorian attempts to "cure modern social ills by
resuscitating old ideals" are "brought to focus in WM, who used the
medieval more consistently than any other writer and whose social
philosophy may have present day implications." Examines the
"interrelations of Morris' medievalism and his socialism," claiming
that her emphasis is not biographical. But she offers specific
discussions of the major events and people in WM's life. The
opening chapters have useful summaries of works by Cobbett, Southey,
Carlyle, and Ruskin, and also of ways the Oxford years and his
Northern interests influenced WM's sense of the medieval past. Of
Iceland she notes that "it is one of the ironies of history that a
real lover of freedom found spiritual satisfaction in what was to
provide, seventy years after, the Goerings and Rosenbergs with a
theory of Iceland as the 'cradle of Germanic culture'--Nazi
variety." Argues that WM's approach to socialism via interests in
medieval narrative and especially in medieval crafts "saved him from
the doctrinairre," for he preached a fifteenth-century ideal of art
and work; he knew of medieval vices, but preferred them to modern
hypocricies. Includes fresh observations on WM's ideas about
medieval and nineteenth-century Catholicism and about medieval
guilds, "the leaven of freedom at work in a heirarchical world."
Claims that "hardly a lecture from 1883 until his death is without
its appeal to the Middle Ages," which he knew well since "research
in connection with the Firm's revival of earlier crafts resulted in
a very real acquaintance with labor history and he found many of his
own conclusions verified and his difficulties cleared away by
Marxian explanations." But she also says, following Glasier
(1921.3), "of the Marxian theory of value he understood little and
cared less." There are many fine summaries and conclusions: "Morris
once said that socialism was a religion. We can consider the
propaganda as his catechism; the lectures on art as the rubrics of a
new and unusual liturgy. But the prose romances are like a medieval
Book of the Hours, colored in green and gold and cinnebar, figured
with flowers, birds and beasts--a hymn of praise to the things he
loved in any time, past, present or future. To ignore them is to
know one half or less of the man who created the Vision of the
society of equals." Discusses WM's distrust of state socialism, of
parliamentary reform, and the ways that Distributionists and Guild
Socialists and others have claimed WM, but his Vision, "clothed in
the well-loved forms of the past," continues to defy easy
categorization.

2   MORTON, A.L.   "A Scale Model of the Future." In Language of
     Men. London: Corbett Press, pp. 58-61.
         Claims that Nowhere is unique because it is based on
"scientific socialism solidified and given life by the imagination
of a great poet," one who only discovered in his forties that he was
himself a socialist. Claims that WM's interests in individuals, in
higher social relationships in Nowhere, prefigure socialist
successes in the Soviet Union.

3   ORCUTT, WILLIAM DANA. "Glorious Inconsistencies of WM." In
     From My Library Walls: A Kaleidoscope of Memories. Toronto and
     New York: Longmans, pp. 124-27.
         Wonders how a great poet and designer could also be a
protesting socialist; concludes that, "as a matter of fact, WM never
fitted into the socialist picture at all." His conception of what
workers needed--Art and Beauty--did not square with their desires,
so he tried to reach them through fine books, but these proved too
costly. Does include, however, some useful comments on Kelmscott
Press volumes.

4   READ, HERBERT. "WM." In A Coat of Many Colours: Occasional
     Essays. London: George Routledge and Sons, pp. 76-79. Rev.
     ed., New York: Horizon Press, 1956.
         Comments on the importance of Ruskin as an influence on WM,
on the development of his Golden Rule: "Have nothing in your houses
that you do not know to be useful or believe to be beautiful,"
pondering why he used "or," thus creating a distinction "between a
knowledge of the useful and a belief in the beautiful." Does there
lurk under this division "a conception of art as decoration rather
than form?"

5   SEYMOUR, RALPH FLETCHER. Some Went This Way: A Forty Year
     Pilgrimage Among Artists, Bookmen and Printers. Chicago: R.F.
     Seymour, pp. 102-6, passim.
         Comments upon WM as a prophet of beauty, one who used books
to demonstrate his theories, but includes helpful and specific
remarks on Kelmscott Press influence in America.

6   TEMPLEMAN, WILLIAM D., ed. "WM." In Bibliographies of Studies
     in Victorian Literature for the Thirteen Years, 1932-44. Urbana:
     University of Illinois Press, 104-5, 257-58, passim.
         This reprinting of the annual bibliographies from MP has
dozens of citations to articles and books (and some reviews) on WM.
Except for the reviews, all are included in the present book.

1946

1   DEARMOND, ANNA JANNEY. "What is Pre-Raphaelitism in Poetry?"
     Delaware Notes, 19th ser.:67-88.
          Considers, after substantial commentary on the poetry of the
     Rossettis, the opinion put forward by Housman (1933.10) that because
     of a "Pre-Raphaelite spirit" the "Middle Ages have sprung to life"
     in Defence. Agrees that WM "seems to have captured all the various
     elements that make up the second phase of the movement," but
     suggests that that phase should be called "Medieval Revival of the
     Fifties" rather than "Pre-Raphaelite," which suggests a high
     seriousness that WM's poems lack.

2   LITZENBERG, KARL. "WM and the 'Literary' Tradition." Michigan
     Alumnus 53:48-55.
          Argues that WM's social philosophy was grounded in
     "Mythology, Medievalism, and perhaps in Monasticism--but not, let it
     be added, in Marx." The author thus sees parallels between ways
     that WM writes of revolution achieving a healthy society and
     depictions of "Ragnarok" in the Icelandic Eddas, between ideals of
     Fellowship and the medieval guild system, and he asserts that such
     parallels must be impractical, for they cannot "urge men to
     action." He also says that WM always castigated mechanization, and
     in several other places he likewise indicates that he has not read
     the socialist lectures with any degree of care.

3   MEYNELL, FRANCIS. English Printed Books. London: Collins, pp.
     31-33, passim.
          Includes a sketch of the founding of Kelmscott Press,
     assertions about Kelmscott Press volumes expressing essential
     qualities of WM: "fecund, devoted, impassioned about texture,
     integrated, public-spirited."

4   SCHILLING, BERNHARD N. "WM." In Human Dignity and the Great
     Victorians. New York: Columbia University Press. Reprint.
     Hamden, Conn.: Archon Books, 1972, pp. 175-203.
          Includes a biographical sketch, quotations from the socialist
     lectures, and a sympathetic discussion of Nowhere, but he argues
     that WM's socialism derives more from his literary predecessors than
     from Marx.

5   WEBER, CARL J. "Another Kelmscott 'Hand and Soul.'" Colby
     Library Quarterly, 1st ser., no. 15 (June):240-41.
         Reports on acquisition of two copies of Kelmscott Press
     edition of Rossetti's Hand and Soul, and brings up to date the
     census of Kelmscott Press books at New England colleges and
     universities, reported upon in 1944.12 and 1946.6.

6   WEBER, CARL J. "Books from Kelmscott Press." Colby Library
     Quarterly, 1st ser., no. 16 (October):249-56.
         Reports on up-coming (October 1946) exhibit of Kelmscott
     Press works at Colby. Reprints the census of Kelmscott Press
     volumes owned by New England colleges and universities "to let our
     Library Associates know which books are now at Colby and which are
     still missing." They had thirty-three, up twelve from the 1944
     total; see 1944.5 and 1950.13.

7   "The Utopia of WM." TLS, no. 2231 (5 October):478.
         Suggests that WM attempted to revive a Northern heritage in
     Britain, but he failed. Even though MacNiece and Auden went to
     Iceland between the wars (but not because of WM), Latin culture is
     still dominant in England. WM likewise failed in attempts to create
     socialists; even though many governments call themselves
     "socialist," what they practice is far from what WM preached.
     Slogans like "We have no need for the past" and an abiding concern
     with productivity do not remind us of WM's model in Nowhere, nor of
     points he makes in the socialist lectures.

                                1947

1   BRIGGS, MARTIN S. "John Ruskin and WM." In Men of Taste.
     London: Batsford; New York: Scribners, pp. 214-24.
         An essay that discusses the social and artistic concerns that
     Ruskin and WM shared.

2   DERRICK, FREDA. "A WM Pilgrimage: From Red House to
     Inglewood." Illustrated Carpenter and Builder, July-February,
     pp. 690-91, 746-47, passim.
         Records impressions of Red House (after eighty-six years and
     two near-misses by V-2 rockets, it is in splendid condition), of
     Kelmscott Manor gardens and furnishings, of Kelmscott cottages which
     May Morris, with the help of Webb's designs, restored. Pilgrimage
     continues to Oxford, and then to the homes of others influenced by
     WM, ending at Inglewood, which Gimson built in 1892. This detailed,
     illustrated article is spread over seventeen issues of the magazine.

3   DE CARLO, GIANCARLO. WM. Milan: Il Balcone, 91 pp.
      A survey of trends in nineteenth-century British architecture
and design precedes a discussion of Ruskin's influence on WM, and a
biographical sketch that stresses WM's importance as one of the
founders of the Modern Movement. Includes many illustrations.

*4   EKSTROM, WILLIAM F. "The Social Idealism of WM and of W.D.
      Howells: A Study in Four Utopian Novels." Dissertation,
      University of Illinois.
      Cited in Doctoral Dissertations Accepted by American
Universities, 14 (1946-47):82.

5   GLOAG, JOHN. "The Revival of the Crafts." The English
      Tradition in Design. New York and London: King Penguin, pp.
      24-28, passim.
      Speaks of WM's "country-gentleman's socialism," but also
makes useful comments about WM as both designer and craftsman, about
the importance and influence of Morris and Co. Includes four plates
with WM designs.

6   GODWIN, EDWARD, and GODWIN, STEPHANI. Warrior Bard: The Life of
      WM. London: Harrap, 176 pp. Reprint. Port Washington, N.Y.:
      Kennikat Press, 1970.
      Aims to turn WM's life "into a really vivid story," and the
invented dialogues and sentimental asides are often disconcerting,
misleading, or wrong: "Certainly had there been anything serious
between them [Rossetti and Janey], Morris, who adored Janey all his
life, and was no fool, would never have left them alone together
when he went to Iceland." Such a misreading of WM's motives is
unsettling.

7   HOUGH, GRAHAM. "WM." In The Last Romantics. London: Gerald
      Duckworth. Reprint. London: Methuen; New York: Barnes and
      Noble, 1961, pp. 83-133.
      Useful and detailed expositions of WM's contributions both to
the Gothic Revival and to English socialism precede a third section
on his poetry. Connections between Pugin, Ruskin, and WM are
clearly drawn, and Pugin's influence (via Ruskin who did not admit
it) on WM, especially on his practical ideas regarding ways design
and execution must be subordinated to materials, is set forth
convincingly. Discusses problems with WM's aesthetics, pointing out
how wrong he was in his insistence that art and luxury could not
coexist and in his refusal to accept fully the implications of
technology, either for the artisan or the social planner. Traces
WM's socialism to his "despair at the prospects of art under
capitalism," stressing that he was a Marxist and that he believed in
the necessity of class war. Though such warfare initiates the just
society of Nowhere, the tale is here discussed as merely another

version of the Golden Age: it "has really very little to do with
modern Socialism or the result of an economic revolution." It is
also suggested, though his other socialist writings are not
examined, that WM had no effect on the development of Socialist
thought. Compares his poetry to that of the earlier romantics,
discussing Paradise and the use of medieval motifs as attempts to
avoid reality and death; suggests that the Icelandic sagas provided
WM motifs which allowed him to adopt more stoic attitudes and to
write exceptional poetry, but that such romantic narratives hold
small appeal for modern readers.

8   JACKSON, HOLBROOK, ed. Introduction to WM: On Art and
     Socialism: Essays and Lectures. London: John Lehmann, pp. 4-23.
          Discusses the growth of WM's socialist commitment, his debt
to Ruskin and others, placing individual lectures within the context
of his active work for the Socialist League. Praises WM's work as a
craftsman, comparing him to the masters of the Italian Renaissance,
and conjectures about reasons WM's hopes for art have gone awry.
Anthology includes nineteen lectures and essays.

9   LITZENBERG, KARL. "The Victorians and the Vikings: A
     Bibliographical Essay in Anglo-Norse Literary Relations."
     University of Michigan Contributions in Modern Philology no. 3
     (April):1-27.
          Argues that a complete history of Anglo-Norse literary
relations needs doing and suggests lines it might follow by
outlining what has already been done and the nature and scope of the
materials that need covering. Surveys authors from Scott to
Bottomly, mentioning dozens of writers and giving special
consideration to WM. Defends the style of WM's translations,
pointing out that this poetic diction was "purposively and
systematically developed" and that it appears also in the late prose
romances. Comments on the influence Old Norse ideas, like the
"Ragnarok," (doom of the gods), had on WM's "social philosophy,"
which it is suggested was worked out in Sigurd.

10   MEYNELL, ESTHER. Portrait of WM. London: Chapman and Hall, 238
     pp.
          Promises that she shall explicate what is "strange and
unexplained about WM," but she falls into leafy metaphors and
assertions about what was "instinctive" in him instead. She also
makes large claims for the influence Rossetti exerted on WM.
Follows Mackail (1899.10), but offers new information on the
DeMorgans and provocative insights into Iceland's attractions: "a
late-discovered and half-terrified love." But she speaks
disparagingly of the "Gorgon head of Socialism," not only
distracting WM from proper pursuits but as the main cause for his
poor health and final illness.

11 MITCHELL, CHARLES. "WM at St. James Palace." Architectural
    Review 101, no. 601 (January):37-39.
        Using Office of Works papers, Morris and Co. records, WM
    correspondence, and the like, the author demonstrates how WM was
    able to bring about a "revolution in official decorative taste."
    The Firm won an extremely important commission for work at St. James
    Palace, doing the Armour and Tapestry rooms in 1866-67 and in
    1880-1882 still more extensive decorating, some of which, like
    curtains in the Blue Room and wall hangings in the Ante Room,
    remained in 1947, "just as WM installed them." Reprinted, in 1960,
    by the WM Society, as a keepsake of its visit to St. James Palace.

12 ROBSJOHN-GIBBINGS, TERENCE. Mona Lisa's Mustache: A Dissection
    of Modern Art. New York: Knopf, pp. 32-38.
        Misleading comments about Pre-Raphaelites and "poor, muddled,
    kind-hearted Topsy, who believed that he could bring back the Middle
    Ages," who "dabbled in socialism."

13 ROE, FREDERICK W., ed. "WM: Chronology and Introduction." In
    Victorian Prose. New York: Ronald Press, pp. 515-66.
        Short introduction continues the stereotype of WM "struggling
    desperately to find a clue to the labyrinth of Marxian economics."
    Includes selections from Hopes and Signs, "How I Became a
    Socialist," a bibliography, and notes.

                               1948

1   ALDEN, J.E. The Pre-Raphaelites in Oxford: A Descriptive
    Handbook. Oxford: Alden and Co., pp. 26-34, passim.
        General introduction to Pre-Raphaelites in Oxford followed by
    specific short descriptions of "what Oxford has to show of
    Pre-Raphaelite art, and where it may be seen." In the chapter, "The
    Decorative Arts," are useful discussions of WM and Burne-Jones
    collaborations on Christ Church windows, the Chaucer wardrobe, some
    tapestries, etc. Also has short chapters on Oxford Union murals and
    on Kelmscott Manor.

2   COLE, MARGARET. "The Fellowship of WM." Virginia Quarterly
    Review 24, no. 2 (Spring):260-77.
        Reprint of 1948.3.

3   COLE, MARGARET. "WM (1834-1896)." In Makers of the Labour
    Movement. London: Longmans, pp. 165-84.
        This biographical sketch has new insights into effects of
WM's work: "the man who could never own a Morris tapestry or a
Kelmscott book yet owed a debt to Morris every time he bought a
pleasant glass dish from Woolworth's or a six-penny Penguin." Sets
WM's entry into full-scale socialist work against background of the
depression of 1878-79, imperialist adventures abroad, and the
contributions of other agitators. Concludes that WM's importance to
socialism was "much greater than his achievements in it would
suggest," since his efforts impressed so many. Reprinted: 1948.2.

4   DUTTON, RALPH. The English Interior: 1500-1900. London:
    Batsford, pp. 177-79.
        Claims that Red House is "almost as important a landmark in
the development of English architecture as Inigo Jones' Queen
House," an inspiration for a series of architects from Norman Shaw
to Lutyens. Discusses its decorations and the consequent rise of
the Firm.

5   ELLMANN, RICHARD. Yeats: The Man and the Masks. New York:
    Macmillan, pp. 76, 101, passim.
        Touches on various influences WM exerted on Yeats, from the
latter's habit of wearing blue shirts to his descriptions of a
better society, quite like that in Nowhere, "where men plow and sow
and reap, not a place where there are great wheels turning and great
chimneys vomiting smoke."

6   GAUNT, WILLIAM, ed. Introduction to Selected Writings of WM.
    London: Falcoln Press, pp. 5-14.
        Portrays WM as a Pre-Raphaelite socialist, and there are thus
skewed estimations of, for example, his use of archaic language.
Even worse, Sigurd is called a translation and Beowulf a socialist
poem. The anthology includes selections from the early prose and
poetry and all of "A Factory as it Might Be."

7   GIEDION, SIGFRIED. Mechanization Takes Command. New York and
    Oxford: Oxford University Press. Reprint. 1971, pp. 482-84,
    passim.
        Asserts that the basic aim of the "Morris circle" was a
"revival of handicraft together with a return to the late Gothic."
But a few useful comments occur also regarding the "moral
orientation" of WM designs and craftswork, and the subsequent
influence of the Arts and Crafts Movement in America on
mission-style furniture and on the Craftsman.

8   GREEN, ROGER LANCELYN. "WM's First Poem." TLS, no. 2414 (8 May):261.
    Contrary to Mackail's assertion that WM burned his first poem, "The Willow and the Red Cliff" (a point borrowed, like so many others, by subsequent biographers), the poem does exist and was in fact published in volume 21 of the Collected Works. Discusses the effect it had on WM's contemporaries, Burne-Jones and Dixon especially.

9   JACKSON, HOLBROOK. "WM." In Dreamers of Dreams: The Rise and Fall of Nineteenth Century Idealism. London: Faber and Faber, pp. 137-67.
    An evocative rendering of the high points of WM's life, tracing the ways that his love for history, for the English countryside, and for art all led logically to his radical attempts to achieve socialism. Discusses Ruskin's influence: "WM, the craftsman-socialist is Ruskin's greatest work." Contrasts Ruskin's inability to put his ideas into practice (the road building scheme at Oxford) to the ease with which WM translated designs and dreams into artifacts and poems. Judges that the "best of WM as thinker and writer" is in John Ball. Concludes that WM "lives in these days of violence and transition as an example rather than an influence."

*10 LEHISTE, ILSE. "Uber die Ethik der nach altnordischen Quellen geschaffenen Werke von WM." Dissertation, University of Hamburg.
    Cited in 1960.1.

11 LINDSAY, JACK, ed. Introduction to Selected Poems by William Morris. London: Gray Walls Press, pp. 7-22.
    A concise biographical sketch that stresses WM's growing anger at industrial capitalism; it asserts that he was not a dreamy socialist: "he was by far the most practical and clearest-eyed of all the socialists of his epoch." Brief concluding comments on Defence, which "carried English romanticism to its climax," and on Pilgrims, in which WM "sought to found the poetry of the future." The selected poems include a dozen from Defence, another dozen from Poems by the Way, and pieces from the longer poems.

12 TINKER, C.B. "WM as Poet." Essays in Retrospect: Collected Articles and Addresses. London: Oxford; New Haven: Yale University Press. Reprint. Port Washington, N.Y.: Kennikat Press, 1969, pp. 62-74.
    Reprint of 1934.69.

<u>1949</u>

1   ADAMS-ACTON, MURRAY. "Vandalism in English Churches."
     <u>Connoisseur</u> 124, no. 514 (December):72-78.
         Compares WM to Viollet-le-Duc, the great French medieval
     scholar who unfortunately had a hand in the sorts of restoration
     that WM abhorred; he was "enraged at the destruction of ancient
     buildings and churches carried out under the specious pretext of
     restoration." In rhetoric that WM would have admired, the author
     comments on some restoration of British churches in the 1930s, on
     "Taussand-Disneyesque displays" that must be halted. Quotes from
     WM's letter to <u>Athenaeum</u>, the letter that launched SPAB.

2   ANGELI, HELEN ROSSETTI. "WM." In <u>Rossetti: His Friends and</u>
     <u>Enemies</u>. London: Hamish Hamilton, 110-19, passim.
         Speculates upon Rossetti's extremely strong influence on WM
     early on, saying that this perhaps led to the strong animosities
     later. Comments on Rossetti's inability to appreciate WM's
     boisterousness and his love of the North.

3   DOUGHTY, OSWALD. "The Idle Singer of an Empty Day." In
     <u>Rossetti: A Victorian Romantic</u>. London: Frederick Muller; New
     Haven: Yale University Press, pp. 458-68, passim. 2d ed., 1960.
         Discusses circumstances behind WM and Rossetti leasing
     Kelmscott Manor and ways that WM's unhappiness is reflected in the
     novel he had attempted to write (see 1982.15) and in various
     <u>Paradise</u> lyrics. WM'S decision to journey to Iceland so that his
     wife and Rossetti could sort things out at Kelmscott Manor suggests
     how advanced were his views on marriage; he was the "antithesis of
     Soames Forsythe." That Rossetti pushed Janey into marrying WM,
     though here called a "cynical story," is supported by Doughty's
     readings of the <u>House of Life</u> sonnets, by references to Rossetti's
     confession to Hall Caine (1928.2) of "the secret of his life's
     frustration, his passion for Janey." An early chapter, "The Jovial
     Campaign," casts new light on WM's role in the episode of the Oxford
     Union murals and his discipleship to Rossetti. There are minor
     additions in 1960.10.

4   GREY, LLOYD ERIC. <u>WM, Prophet of England's New Order</u>. London:
     Cassell, 400 pp.
         Reprint of 1940.8.

5   SHAW, GEORGE BERNARD.   "More About WM."   Sunday Observer, no.
    8266 (6 November):7.
        An essay inspired by Grey's biography (1949.4 and 1940.8),
    which chides him for implying that WM had a humorous attitude about
    his outbursts of temper, for they "were eclampsias and left him
    shaken as men are shaken after a fit. The worst sorrow of his life
    was when his daughter Jenny became a hopeless epileptic and he knew
    it was an inheritance from himself." Shaw also points out here that
    WM was not jealous of Rossetti, that the actual hero of Lady
    Burne-Jones's biography of her husband was WM, that Wolfings was
    WM's "first attempt to restore Don Quixote's destroyed library," and
    so in this short essay Shaw added several points to WM lore that
    have been picked up by subsequent biographers.

6   ZAPF, HERMANN.   WM, sein Leben und Werk in der Geschicte der
    Buch und Schriftkunst.   Monographien Kunstlerischen Schrift,
    vol. 11. Lubeck: Klaus Blankertz Verlag, 62 pp.
        Monograph intended to introduce WM to a German audience,
    especially as regards his achievements in the book arts. Since WM
    drew power and inspiration from the German past, from both its
    ancient Teutonic heroes and its fifteenth-century printers, the
    author claims that he belongs to Germany, pointing out also that he
    influenced many early twentieth-century German printers like Rudolph
    Koch; the more that contemporary Germans know about this remarkable
    man, the more likely it is that his influence shall again be felt.
    A full biographical sketch precedes sections on WM's political
    ideals, his calligraphy, and on Kelmscott Press, with half the
    thirty-three pages of text devoted to the Press. Includes many
    prints and illustrations.

                                1950

1   BERNERI, MARIE LOUISE.   "WM: Nowhere."   In Journey Through
    Utopia.   London: Routledge and Kegan Paul. Reprint. Freeport,
    N.Y.: Books For Libraries Press, 1969, pp. 255-81, passim.
        This study of over twenty utopian writers, from Plato to
    Huxley, celebrates Nowhere as one of the very few which is
    anti-authoritarian: it is "an oasis where we would like to stay, if
    not for ever, at least for a long time." Contrasts Nowhere to
    Looking Backward, pointing out that WM stresses that a new society
    will not evolve from the old or be handed over by a benevolent
    Napoleon; it will be won, as it is in Nowhere, by men and women who
    work together for revolution. Paraphrases and offers liberal
    quotations from Nowhere, ranked as among the very best of Western
    utopias.

2   CHURCHILL, C.R.   "WM and Society."   Adam: International Review
      195 (January-February):22-25.
            Uses Jackson's edition of WM's essays and lectures (1947.8)
      to comment upon WM's communism: "the obvious, common-sensical kind,
      only remarkable because he was led to it from the text of Ruskin."
      Faults WM for overlooking the large number of jobs within any
      society which must yield neither pleasure nor variety, while
      ignoring the advances science has wrought, since medieval times, in
      combatting disease: "I imagine that not even a part in the making of
      Salisbury Cathedral could quite console a workman for the death of a
      favorite child."

3   COCKERELL, S.C.   Introduction to The Life of WM, by J.W.
      Mackail. No. 521 in the World's Classics Series. London and
      New York: Oxford University Press, pp. 5-19.
            Since the author had known WM and many of those whom Mackail
      had consulted fifty years earlier, this introduction has a special
      poignance and authority. He attempts to set down his "lasting
      impressions" of WM, who was "utterly unlike anyone I have since
      encountered," and why this was so emerges from the anecdotes about
      Thursday evening meals on the Strand, visits to Kelmscott Manor, a
      shared vacation in France, and his work as secretary to the
      Kelmscott Press. Speculates on ways WM might have influenced what
      social progress had occurred since his death, and concludes with a
      note on Mackail, who died in 1945 at the age of 86.

4   COCKERELL, S.C.   "WM and Oscar Wilde."   TLS, no. 2505 (3
      February):73.
            Letter attempts to lay to rest the legend, popular among
      Wilde biographers, that Wilde visited WM on his deathbed. As WM's
      secretary, Cockerell was constantly with him, and he does not recall
      a Wilde visit; more significantly, Wilde was in prison during the
      months of WM's last illness.

5   ELLIS, HAVELOCK.   "WM."   In From Marlowe to Shaw. Edited by
      John Gawsworth. London: Williams and Norgate, pp. 213-20.
            Recalls the several times he saw WM, in Hyde Park and in
      various lecture halls, celebrating him here as a great craftsman and
      as one of the three great prophets (the other two are Carlyle and
      Ruskin) of the Victorian age. Concludes that today (these essays
      were all originally written in the 1930s) we travel "however slowly
      and painfully" along roads WM charted.

6   ESHER. "The Influence of WM." TLS, no. 2515 (14 April):229.
     In response to a TLS article, "Beaten Gold" (1950.15), which
suggested that WM's influence in the modern world was slight, the
chairman of SPAB writes, "that 'restoration' has almost universally
given way to repair is almost entirely due to the pioneering
influence of WM."

7   HEATH-STUBBS, JOHN. The Darkling Plain. London: Eyre and
     Spottiswoode, pp. 163-69.
     Asserts that WM was "less at home in Chaucer's complex and
sophisticated world than in that of the Icelandic sagas and the
oldest poetry of the North." Reprinted: 1974.11.

8   HENDERSON, PHILIP. The Letters of WM to his Family and
     Friends. London and New York: Longmans, 473 pp. Reprint. New
     York: AMS Press, 1978.
     A detailed, fifty-page biographical introduction precedes the
selected letters, which are arranged chronologically under five
headings that suggest WM's major activities during each period of
his life. Three appendixes include the prospectus of Morris,
Marshall, Faulkner Co., the "Working Men of England," and "Morris
before Mr. Saunders." An index of correspondents (sixty-six are
listed) and a full general index concludes this important edition of
scores of WM's letters.

9   JACKSON, HOLBROOK. "The Aesthetics of Printing."
     Gutenberg-Jahrbuch 25:395-96.
     WM, in lectures and by example, questioned all narrow
distinctions between crafts and arts, and at Kelmscott Press he
showed how to raise craft to perfection; using materials
intelligently, he made, as in the days of Gutenberg, printing again
an art. But, ironically, his success led to imitation, to the
opening of small presses, to ideas about fine printing and the "art
book," which served to provoke the old distinctions and thus to
"pervert his message."

10   KAUFMAN, EDGAR. "Furniture." Architectural Review 108, no. 644
     (August):127-29.
     Summarizes the various, and conflicting, descriptions of the
so-called "Morris chair," as well as claims about its inventor and
its significance. Points out that Morris and Co. did sell chairs,
ca. 1912, with adjustable backs, that they called them "Morris
chairs," even though they were not invented by WM and were not
particularly modern. Such chairs were made as early as the
sixteenth century. Has several illustrations.

11 MAURER, OSCAR. "Some Sources of WM's 'The Wanderers.'"
    University of Texas Studies in English 29:222-30.
        Although "The Wanderers," the prologue to Paradise, is in
outline and conception original to WM, he did draw details from Old
Norse literature, notably Laing's translation of Heimskringla and
Percy's translation of Mallet's Northern Antiquities. He also used
Mandeville and Froissart, and parallels are here set forth and
discussed.

12 SCHROEDER, FRANCIS DE N. "WM and the Arts and Crafts Revival."
    Interiors 110, no. 2 (September):122-27.
        One in a series of popularized essays on "Makers of
Tradition," this sketch of WM's life and influence on the decorative
arts is misleading and includes puzzling mistakes about, for
instance, the locations of Red House and Kelmscott Manor. And WM is
said to have received a "commission" to work on the murals at the
Oxford Union.

13 WEBER, CARL J. "Kelmscott Complete." Colby Library Quarterly,
    2d ser., no. 14 (May):238-40.
        Reports that Colby College acquired those volumes needed for
a complete set of Kelmscott Press editions; see 1946.5-6.

14 WOODCOCK, GEORGE, and AVAKUMOVIC, IVAN. The Anarchist Prince: A
    Biographical Study of Peter Kropotkin. London and New York:
    T.V. Boardman, pp. 128, 184, 205-6, passim.
        WM is often mentioned in those sections dealing with
Kropotkin's years in London. WM was one of the signers of a
petition to get Kropotkin released from a French prison; he helped
Kropotkin print his Freedom and protested with him against the
persecution of the Chicago anarchists. WM had a negative attitude
toward anarchism, but Kropotkin's ideas on mutual aid might have
satisfied him; they were, however, not elaborated until after his
death. Stresses that WM was never hostile to Kropotkin and that in
1893 he regarded him as "the only important socialist still among
the anti-parliamentarians." Kropotkin thought WM's influence had
kept the Labour Movement in England from "following the
authoritarian course which social democracy had taken elsewhere."

15 "Beaten Gold." TLS, no. 2513 (31 March):201.
        Asserts that many still agree with Ruskin: WM is "beaten
gold," and it is therefore all the more surprising that his
influence has not been greater in Britain, whether in design (the
Scandinavian "ease of touch" is lacking) or in politics, where too
much "ardour" is now devoted to the economic aspects of governmental
programs.

1951

1   ALLEN, LEWIS. "A Visit to Kelmscott Manor House, 1951." Book
    Club of California Quarterly Newsletter 17, no. 1:10-12.
       Describes Kelmscott, the village, the churchyard with its
    well-known gravestone, and the manor itself, with the Rossetti
    paintings "highlighting the scene."

2   ARNOT, R. PAGE. "Unpublished Letters of WM." Labour Monthly,
    pamphlet no. 6, 16 pp.
       Twenty-one letters survive that WM wrote to Dr. Glasse in
    Edinburgh between February 1886 and March 1895; the bulk of them,
    and these the most interesting, were written in 1887-89, and
    thirteen of these are here reprinted, along with full commentary on
    the personalities and issues, from anarchists to Commonweal
    subscriptions, which arose during these busy years of Socialist
    League work.

3   BALSTON, THOMAS. "The Kelmscott Types." In The Cambridge
    University Press Collection of Private Press Types. Cambridge:
    Cambridge University Press, pp. 1-20.
       Comments on WM's early interest in book arts, on the printing
    of Wolfings in 1899. Discusses that November evening when Walker
    gave the lecture "which has revolutionized the book-production of
    the Western world." Asserts that WM had a passion for Gothic
    decoration, suggesting that Updike was right when he said that WM's
    typographical achievements are more those of a decorator than a
    printer. Presents engrossing details about problems with Golden
    type, with attempts to retain Gothic characteristics in the Troy
    type, with modifications made in the Chaucer type.

4   BLAND, DAVID. The Illustration of Books. London: Faber and
    Faber. 3d ed., 1962, pp. 88-91, passim.
       Discusses WM's use of woodcuts; "he felt that type, which is
    printed in relief, should be accompanied by blocks which are cut in
    relief." He cut many of the blocks for his decorated borders and
    initials, and "marginal decoration was given a new lease on life in
    modern times," especially in countries like Germany and Holland,
    where WM's influence was strong.

5   BUCKLEY, JEROME. The Victorian Temper: A Study in Literary
    Culture. Cambridge, Mass.: Harvard University Press. Reprint.
    New York: Random House, pp. 141-42, 175-77, passim.
       Sees WM as "ablest disciple" of Ruskin, and "more than any
    other decorator, Morris helped clear the Victorian home of the ugly,
    the ornate, and the inorganic." In Defence, WM "sketched the drift
    of ghosts through a nightmare of passion, the movement of creatures
    helplessly predestined, reasonless, without conscience, wholly

untouched by ethical conflict." Suggests that such verse is more
ornamental than incisively poetic.

6   DOUGHTY, OSWALD. "Rossetti and Mrs. Morris." TLS, no. 2575 (8
     June):357.
          Previously unpublished letters from Rossetti to T.G. Hake are
     here quoted; they prove that Doughty was right in his biography of
     Rossetti (1949.3) about Janey being the subject of sonnets in the
     House of Life and about Rossetti's 1872 breakdown being "due to some
     obstacle to his continuing or resuming residence with Mrs. Morris at
     Kelmscott Manor."

7   HENDERSON, PHILIP. "Rossetti and Mrs. Morris." TLS, no. 2588
     (7 September):565.
          Quotes passage from a letter Mackail wrote on 12 May 1899
     about how difficult it was to employ "tact" when writing about "the
     stormy years of the Paradise time." From this and other fresh
     evidence, especially in 1949.3, Henderson concludes that "WM emerges
     as an even greater man than before, and that what at first might
     appear to be scandal resolves itself into tragedy and the stuff of
     poetry."

8   JACKSON, HOLBROOK. "The Typography of WM." In Books and
     Printing: A Treasury for Typophiles. Edited by Paul A. Bennett.
     Cleveland and New York: World Publishing Co., pp. 233-38.
          Reprint of 1934.32.

9   MC LEAN, RUARI. "The Beginning of the Revival." In Modern
     Book Design. British Council Arts in Britain Series. London:
     Longmans, pp. 8-14, passim.
          Discusses a nineteenth-century decline in printing standards,
     one checked by WM's work at Kelmscott Press. Recounts his early
     interests in the book arts, the importance of Walker's 1888 lecture,
     the experiments with typefaces. Concludes with reminder that a
     twentieth-century revival of printing was not based on WM's
     typography, but that Kelmscott Press did have a profound effect on
     the study of printing and the private press movement. Another
     example of "his direct influence on ordinary book design is afforded
     by the pages of all Bernard Shaw's plays." Sketches in Kelmscott
     Press influence on several twentieth-century presses. Translated:
     1957.9. Revised: 1958.8.

10   PEARSE, BRIAN.   "WM and Bulgaria."   <u>Central</u> <u>European</u> <u>Observer</u> 4,
     no. 14 (7 July):222-23.
          Recounts, from a Bulgarian point of view, WM's activities in
     the Eastern Question Association, insisting that he was able "to
     mobilize British opinion on the side of the Bulgarian National
     Revolt which began in 1876."   Quotes from letters WM wrote at the
     time and also from his "Wake, London Lads."

11   PEVSNER, NIKOLAUS.   <u>High</u> <u>Victorian</u> <u>Design:</u> <u>A</u> <u>Study</u> <u>of</u> <u>the</u>
     <u>Exhibits</u> <u>of</u> <u>1851</u>.   London: Architectural Press, 1951, pp. 31,
     115, passim.
          Points out that WM disliked the Crystal Palace because of its
     independence from any tradition and its confused standards of taste.
     Concludes that British taste improved generally because of WM's
     achievements at Morris and Co., and because in his essays he was the
     first to "see that design is not only an aesthetic problem, but also
     an integral part of a larger social problem."

12   POLLARD, ALFRED W.   "The Trained Printer and the Amateur."   In
     <u>Books</u> <u>and</u> <u>Printing:</u> <u>A</u> <u>Treasure</u> <u>for</u> <u>Typophiles</u>.   Edited by Paul
     A. Bennett.   Cleveland and New York: World Publishing Co., pp.
     182-90.
          A discussion of some early famed printers precedes comments
     on WM, who "must be classed as an amateur, and his press as a
     private press, because he printed to please himself."   Mentions
     other private presses started because of attempts to emulate WM,
     "one of the world's greatest craftsmen, and certainly if we consider
     his versatility, his sureness of touch and his imagination, the
     finest that the British Isles has ever produced."

13   PROUTING, NORMAN.   "WM and the Victorian Revival."   <u>Apollo</u> 54,
     nos. 317-18 (July-August):17-21, 51-56.
          Laments that "WM's work as an artist, particularly in the
     decorative sphere, still awaits rediscovery," and that the "Victoria
     and Albert opens his famous refreshment room no longer, and can show
     but one example of his furniture."   Some moderns apparently feel
     uncomfortable with mid-Victorian design, finding it "amusing," while
     ignoring the vulgarity that WM was reacting against.   Discusses
     Morris and Co. decorations at Swan House, Chelsea, carried out
     during 1877-81 and points out that Sandersons has available Morris
     and Co. designs, wonders if the time is not "ripe for a revival of
     Morris taste."

*14 STOKES, E.E. "WM and Bernard Shaw: A Socialist-Artistic
      Relationship." Dissertation, University of Texas.
         Cited in <u>Doctoral</u> <u>Dissertations</u> <u>Accepted</u> <u>by</u> <u>American</u>
      <u>Universities</u>, 18 (1950-51):229.

15 THOMPSON, E.P. "The Murder of WM." <u>Arena</u> 2, no. 7
      (April-May):9-28.
         Traces a few of the ways that WM's socialist activities have
      been cloaked over the years, with labels like "sentimental" or
      "aesthetic." Many commentators have seized upon WM's "good-humoured
      confession that he 'suffered agonies of the brain' when he read
      Marx," so that they could then treat the socialism as a kind of
      abberation. Glances at the conclusions of a few such critics as a
      prelude to a harsh and convincing critique of the Grey/Eshleman
      biography (1940.8/1949.4) and its favorable reception by bourgeois
      reviewers.

16 THOMPSON, E.P. "WM and the Moral Issues Today." <u>Arena</u> 2, no. 8
      (June-July):25-30.
         Originally a lecture at a conference on the "Americam Threat
      to British Culture," and therefore the discussion of WM's moral
      values is preceded by a diatribe against the spread of American
      values via Hollywood and the bombing of Korean peasants. Urges
      audience to look to their own British traditions and to what
      thinkers like WM represent.

17 THOMPSON, LAURENCE. <u>Robert</u> <u>Blatchford:</u> <u>Portrait</u> <u>of</u> <u>an</u>
      <u>Englishman</u>. London: Victor Gollancz, pp. 57-58, passim.
         The writings and example of WM were important influences upon
      Robert Blatchford, whose "socialism was WM's socialism" and whose
      romance, <u>The</u> <u>Sorcery</u> <u>Shop</u>, is here called "the dying voice of WM."

18 WILES, H.V. <u>WM</u> <u>of</u> <u>Walthamstow</u>. London: Walthamstow Press, 132
      pp.
         Written in connection with Festival of Britain activities,
      this booklet is more about Walthamstow than WM, but its genial
      patriotism and high regard for the rural Walthamstow that influenced
      him would have appealed to WM. The foreword by Clement Attlee, with
      its attempts to claim WM for the Labour party, would have affected
      him differently. Has interviews with several octogenerians who
      recalled WM and various associations he had enjoyed with
      Walthamstow.

<u>1952</u>

1   DENT, ALAN, ed. <u>Bernard Shaw and Mrs. Patrick Campbell: Their</u>
     <u>Correspondence</u>. New York: Knopf, pp. 89-90.
          In an amusing letter, Shaw recalls WM often at a loss for
     words when writing prose, but with verse WM "could sling rhymes
     without having to think about them."

2   HENDERSON, PHILIP. <u>WM</u>. London: Longmans, 43 pp.
          This monograph, a British Council biography, contains concise
     and reliable introductory discussions of WM's life and achievements.

3   MAKER, HAROLD J. "WM, Master Printer, and Kelmscott Press."
     <u>Hobbies: The Magazine for Collectors</u> 57, no. 9
     (November):131-34.
          Biographical sketch indicates how and why WM developed into
     the "savior of printing," and the rise of Kelmscott Press is then
     described. Goes into fresh and useful detail about WM's great skill
     in choosing fellow experts to work with him. "By no means was
     Kelmscott Press ever a one man team." Concludes with reasons why
     the poor legibility of Kelmscott Press books should not be a
     consideration in judging them.

4   MORTON, A.L. "The Dream of WM." In <u>The English Utopia</u>.
     London: Lawrence and Wishart, pp. 149-82, passim.
          Calls WM "the first great English Marxist" and also "the
     writer of the only book of its class which is worthy of a place
     besides <u>Utopia</u>." Discusses the assumptions behind <u>Looking Backward</u>
     and why WM disliked it so, quoting from his <u>Commonweal</u> review at
     length. Argues that WM was a thoroughgoing, knowledgable Marxist
     and that this is apparent in <u>Nowhere</u>, the "crown and climax" of all
     his work.

5   PEVSNER, NIKOLAUS. "Art Furniture of the Eighteen-Seventies."
     <u>Architectural Review</u> 111, no. 661 (January):43-50.
          Stresses that WM was not the first nor the earliest designer
     to rebel against Victorian tastes in furnishings; he was preceded by
     Pugin, Owen Jones, and others, many of whom were more optimistic
     about improving artistic taste than was WM, who remained pessimistic
     because he was convinced that art was rooted in social life. Points
     out that Taylor "discovered" the Sussex chair, which came to be
     well-known as the "Morris chair," in 1865, and that the Firm made
     many simple, rustic pieces, as well as ornate furniture.

6   RANSOM, WILL, ed. Introduction to <u>Kelmscott, Doves and
     Ashendene; The Private Press Credos</u>. Los Angeles: Typophiles,
     197 pp.
          In the mid-1890s Kelmscott Press types were copied, without
     permission, by the American Type Founders Co., and this fact as well
     as the Kelmscott Press volumes themselves, and WM's statements about
     printing, all influenced the rapid spread of private presses. This
     anthology reprints the principal statements of the owners of these
     presses, including "Printing" (1893), by WM and Walker, and two
     documents associated with Kelmscott Press: WM's "Note" and
     Cockerell's "Short History."

7   RICKETTS, CHARLES S. "WM and His Influence on the Arts and
     Crafts." Translated by Richard K. Kellenberger. <u>Colby Library
     Quarterly</u> 3, no. 5 (February):69-75.
          Translation of 1897.15.

8   "Kelmscott Chaucer." <u>Princeton University Library Chronicle</u> 13,
     no. 4 (Summer):215-16.
          Note on bequest to Princeton of a Kelmscott Chaucer, one of
     forty-eight bound in white pig-skin by Cobden-Sanderson at the Doves
     Press in 1903.

                                1953

1   DICKASON, DAVID. <u>The Daring Young Men: The Story of the
     American Pre-Raphaelites</u>. Bloomington: Indiana University
     Press, passim.
          Discusses the American magazine, <u>Craftsman</u>, an illustrated
     monthly whose fifteen-year existence (1901-16) corresponded to the
     heyday of crafts in America, the period of most intense interest in
     the Pre-Raphaelite principles and attitudes that motivated most of
     the artists discussed in this study.

2   MAC HUGH, ROGER, ed. <u>Yeats: Letters to Katherine Tynan</u>. New
     York: MacMullen Books, pp. 33, 34, passim.
          These letters have several interesting references to WM, for
     Yeats spent many Sunday evenings at Hammersmith. He saw WM act in
     his own socialist play ("he really acts very well"), and he heard
     him discourse on hero-worship, on English merchants as "the Jews of
     the North," and on his reasons for preferring Teutonic gods over the
     Greek ones. Yeats was delighted when WM praised his <u>Oisen</u>, curious
     as to what May Morris saw in Sparling.

3   MORTON, A.L. "Utopias Yesterday and Today." <u>Science</u> <u>and</u>
     <u>Society</u> 17, no. 3 (Summer):258-63.
        Makes theoretical points about Utopian fiction generally and
     about <u>Nowhere</u> specifically, warning that class issues must be
     considered or the real importance of works like <u>Nowhere</u> will be
     missed. Claims that <u>Nowhere</u> is the "most profound, the most
     powerful and the most moving" of all modern Utopias, largely because
     WM shows how a classless future society can emerge from present-day
     conflicts.

4   PEVSNER, NIKOLAUS. "Colonel Gillum and the Pre-Raphaelites."
     <u>Burlington</u> <u>Magazine</u> 95, no. 600 (March):78-81.
        References to WM within a discussion of William Gillum
     (1827-1910), who in 1861 gave Morris, Marshall, Faulkner Co. one of
     its first important commissions.

5   ROGERS, BRUCE. "Progress of Modern Printing in the United
     States." In <u>PI</u>: <u>A</u> <u>Hodge-Podge</u> <u>of</u> <u>the</u> <u>Letters,</u> <u>Papers,</u> <u>and</u>
     <u>Addresses</u> <u>Written</u> <u>during</u> <u>the</u> <u>Last</u> <u>Sixty</u> <u>Years</u> <u>by</u> <u>Bruce</u> <u>Rogers</u>.
     Cleveland and New York: World Publishing Co., pp. 16-30.
        Reprint of 1912.12.

6   RUBENSTEIN, ANNETTE. <u>The</u> <u>Great</u> <u>Tradition</u> <u>in</u> <u>English</u> <u>Literature</u>
     <u>from</u> <u>Shakespeare</u> <u>to</u> <u>Shaw</u>. New York: Citadel Press. Reprint.
     London and New York: Modern Reader Paperbacks, 1969, pp. 854-75.
        Discusses WM as Ruskin's disciple and then as the first
     British writer to understand how "socialism could free man to be
     himself." Finds it "somewhat surprising that most American readers,
     at least, associate Morris, somewhat vaguely, with the revival of a
     rather medieval form of long narrative poetry, the creation of the
     Morris chair, and the formation of a nostalgic sort of arts and
     crafts movement." She attempts to correct such perceptions by
     discussing WM's socialist ideas, his compassion for workingmen, his
     conviction that work should liberate rather than oppress, and his
     rhetorical skills in the socialist essays. Provides useful insights
     into <u>John</u> <u>Ball</u>, <u>Nowhere</u>, and WM's relationship to writers like Shaw
     and W.E.B. Du Bois.

*7   SOKKARI, S. EL Y. "The Prose Romances of WM." Dissertation,
     University of Manchester.
        Cited in 1968.25.

8   STOKES, E.E.   "Shaw and WM."   Shaw Bulletin 4 (Summer):16-19.
        Since WM "constituted for Shaw an important link with much of
what was best in high Victorianism and, for that matter, in the
Middle Ages as well," there is a real need for a full-fledged study
of WM's influence. Suggests some of the directions that study might
take. Concludes that the "friendship with Morris made a deeper and
more lasting impression upon Shaw than any other contact in his long
and complex life."

9   WELLAND, D.S.R.   "Pre-Raphaelite Medievalism." In The
        Pre-Raphaelites in Literature and Art. London: Harrap.
        Reprint. Freeport, N.Y.: Books for Libraries Press, 1969, pp.
        38-44, passim.
        Suggests that for the Pre-Raphaelites a "link between
painting and literature was maintained in their treatment of
medieval subjects," and that in WM's poetry and prose medieval
themes are enhanced by a sharp pictorial quality. Discusses the
Pre-Raphaelites and book illustration and other aspects of their
work and relevance. Anthologized are five poems from Defence,
selections from Jason, Paradise, and Plain, all of "Unknown Church,"
and part of "The Aims of Art."

10   "WM and His Associates." In Victorian and Edwardian Decorative
        Arts. Catalogue of an Exhibition, October 1952-January 1953, at
        the Victoria and Albert. London: HMSO, pp. 38-50.
        An important exhibition, one celebrating the centenary of the
Victoria and Albert Museum, put together by Peter Floud. His
precise scholarship is everywhere apparent, especially in this
section on WM, which describes eighty-four items, ranging from
furniture to wallpapers (book arts were excluded from the entire
exhibition). Includes an introduction by Peter Floud and short
biographies of WM, Burne-Jones, Webb, George Jack, and Kate
Faulkner.

1954

1   BLISS, CAREY S.   "The WM Press."   Huntington Library Quarterly
        17, no. 3 (May):n.p.
        Brief description of the Demy Folio Iron Albion Printing
Press used by WM at the Kelmscott Press and subsequently in
California for years; it had now been left to the Huntington. See
also Lilienthal (1961.21).

2   BOWLE, JOHN. Politics and Opinion in the Nineteenth Century.
    New York: Oxford University Press, pp. 426-33, passim.
       A biographical sketch showing how WM's concern for
    craftmanship led him to embrace socialism precedes a discussion of
    WM's influence on British socialism, here regarded as decisive.
    Contrasts the Fabians, with their "steady administrative zeal,
    command of detail, and belief in the capture of political power" to
    WM's impatient and visionary efforts to change society. Relies
    heavily on Glasier: 1921.3.

3   BRIGGS, ASA. Victorian People: A Reassessment of Persons and
    Themes, 1851-67. London: Oxford University Press. Reprint.
    Chicago: University of Chicago Press, 1955. New York: Harper
    and Row, 1963, p. 40.
       Contrasts WM's reaction to the Crystal Palace: "wonderfully
    ugly," to that of William Whitely, who dreamed of large retail
    stores with plate glass fronts.

4   COLE, G.D.H. Marxism and Anarchism: 1850-1890. Vol. 2. A
    History of Socialist Thought . London: Macmillan; New York: St.
    Martin's. Reprint. 1957, 1961, 1964, 1969, pp. 414-24, passim.
       Detailed discussions of personalities and issues that caused
    WM to leave the SDF and, six years later, the Socialist League:
    parliamentary compromise on the one hand and threats of violent
    action on the other. "He therefore became more and more isolated,
    though respected by almost everyone." General comments on WM's
    ideas about creative work and fellowship, and about the particlarly
    "friendly" nature of the society in Nowhere, are informed and
    helpful.

5   DAHL, CURTIS. "WM's 'The Chapel in Lyoness': An
    Interpretation." SP 51, no. 3 (July):482-91.
       Discusses both medieval tales in which Sir Ozana appears and
    which involve the Grail quest, tales which WM assumed his readers
    would know almost as well as he did. Asserts, then, that "in the
    light of Arthurian legend, 'The Chapel in Lyonesse' reveals a
    coherent and forceful spiritual drama." Later revisions, never
    published, support this reading of Ozana's achievement of spiritual
    salvation.

6   DUTTON, RALPH. The Victorian Home: Some Aspects of Nineteenth
    Century Taste and Manners. London: Batsford, pp. 95-99, passim.
       Links WM to Webb and the training they both received in
    Street's offices, where WM added a "useful architectural basis to
    his talent for design." Discusses the significance of Red House and
    its interior decoration in terms of the formation of Morris and Co.
    and the shaping of British tastes in design generally.

7   ELLMANN, RICHARD. The Identity of Yeats. Oxford: Oxford
     University Press. Reprint. New York: Galaxy, 1964, pp. 12-13,
     21-23, passim.
         Suggests that Yeats wanted his poetic heroes and heroines to
"look and act like figures in a Morris tapestry, static, statuesque,
and exalted." Says also that "shell and birds, which in Morris
would have been mere scenery, are in Yeats symbols." Quotes from a
letter to Sturge Moore where Yeats compares WM to Chaucer, Dante,
and Blake.

8   EVANS, JOAN. John Ruskin. New York: Oxford University Press,
     pp. 204, 229-30, passim.
         Points out that Ruskin's and WM's ideas about political
economy were inspired by their sense of beauty and that by 1880
Ruskin's "mantle had fallen upon the shoulders of WM, a man whom he
had never understood or greatly liked; a man in closer touch with
reality than himself, who linked a power of decorative creation and
poetic expression to a grasp of practical things."

9   FLOUD, PETER. "The Inconsistencies of WM." Listener 52, no.
     1337 (14 October):615-17.
         Originally a BBC Third Program talk, given on 14 October
1954; see the annotation for 1954.10.

10   FLOUD, PETER. "WM as an Artist: A New View." Listener 52, no.
     1336 (7 October):562-64.
         Originally a BBC Third Program talk, given on 19 September
1954. Points out that WM was actually not the revolutionary
designer tradition has presented to us. Combined with an equally
important talk given the following week and transformed into the
1956 Morris Memorial Lecture which was published in a shortened
version as "Dating Morris Patterns" (1959.4); a later article is
accompanied by illustrations in color: 1960.15.

11   LINDSAY, JACK. "The Paris Commune and English Literature."
     Marxist Quarterly 1, no. 3 (July):169-80.
         Comments upon the significant sections of Pilgrims, one of
the few British poems to deal with the Paris Commune of 1871.
Concludes that WM's "tremendous importance in British culture has
been denied, obscured, falsified in every way by the bourgeois. The
rediscovery of Morris and the understanding of his work and thought
are essential first steps in the fight for the true British
tradition in culture today; he is the direct link between our own
world and all that was rebellious and virtually based in the people
in the Romantic movement."

12 MAC LEOD, R.D. WM Without Mackail. Glasgow: W. and R. Holmes,
      1954, 23 pp.
        Claims that Mackail (1899.10) "contains a considerable amount
of special pleading," that therefore it should be useful to review
and recall what others less "cloistered and academic" had to say
about WM's personality and achievements. Discusses the first
reviews the official biography received and complains that certain
associates like Glasier were ignored, others like Scheu barely
mentioned; quotes from Shaw's shrewd estimation of difficulties
Mackail, as the son-in-law of the Burne-Joneses, had to contend
with. Strings together other responses from a wide variety of
writers, many concerning WM's lectures in Glasgow (Macleod was
evidently offended by remarks WM made about Glasgow artists).
Concludes that "WM's attack on life must have been conditioned by
the fact that he was born to money and could do what he wanted."
Reprinted as WM (As Seen By His Contemporaries) (1956.9).

13 MAURER, OSCAR. "WM's Treatment of Greek Legend in Paradise."
      University of Texas Studies in English 33:103-18.
        Though WM had studied the classics, he used the plot outlines
in John Lempriere's Classical Dictionary as a source for ten of the
twelve Greek tales in Paradise. Only "Cupid and Psyche" and "The
Death of Paris" have different sources. Parallels to Lempriere are
here set forth and discussed, and it is suggested that some
modifications WM made reflect his own personal sadness. There is a
"remarkable consistency of tone and treatment" throughout these
Greek tales, one brought on by the certainty that "quick-coming
death" shall swallow all beauty, a tone that makes these tales
neither classical nor medievalized (like the earlier "Scenes from
Troy"); these tales are "Morris's own."

14 PELLING, HENRY. The Origins of the Labour Party, 1880-1900.
      Oxford: Clarendon Press. 2d ed., 1965, pp. 23-32.
        Includes fresh details about the Socialist League, its
membership, the successes Faulkner had with the Oxford branch, and
the problems WM had with the Northern branches.

15 TVETERAS, EGIL. To Boktrykkere: Benjamin Franklin and WM [Two
      publishers]. Oslo: Aas and Wahls, 85 pp.
        In Norwegian. Has the usual biographical facts,
concentrating here on Kelmscott Press years. Compares use of
illustrations and typefaces, with Franklin receiving fuller and more
detailed treatment than WM.

16 WADE, ALLAN, ed. The Letters of W.B. Yeats. London: Rupert
Hart-Davis, pp. 41, 42, 758, passim.
    WM is mentioned over forty times in this collection of Yeats
letters written between 1887 and 1939; many of the references are
casual; others are more important, especially those dealing with the
growing friendship Yeats and his sister enjoyed with the Morrises in
the 1880s. Also includes Yeats's reactions to WM's verse (1954.20)
and his comments on the "astringent joy" he received from the prose
romances (1954.19). Contains a single late letter to Janey.

*17 WAHL, JOHN ROBERT. "Two Pre-Raphaelite Poets: Studies in the
Poetry and Poetic Theory of WM and Rossetti." Dissertation,
Oxford University.
    Cited in 1960.1.

18 WAHL, JOHN ROBERT. The Kelmscott Love Sonnets of Rossetti.
Capetown and Amsterdam: A. Balkema, passim.
    WM mentioned several times, as is Janey, the heroine and
recipient of many of the sonnets here introduced. The edition
includes over thirty poems, most of them sonnets, the introduction,
and helpful notes.

19 YEATS, W.B. "Letter to Florence Farr, July 1905." In The
Letters of W.B. Yeats. Edited by A. Wade. London: Rupert
Hart-Davis, p. 456.
    Says that monotony was something that "the ancients were more
alive to in all the arts than we are; Chaucer for instance follows
his noble 'Knight's Tale' with an unspeakable tale told by a drunken
miller. If Morris had done the like, everyone would have read his
Paradise forever."

20 YEATS, W.B. "Letter to Olivia Shakespear, October, 1933." In
The Letters of W.B. Yeats. Edited by A. Wade. London: Rupert
Hart-Davis, p. 816.
    Recalls "reading Morris's Sigurd to Anne and last night when
I came to the description of the birth of Sigurd and that wonderful
first nursing of the child, I could hardly read for my tears."

21 "A Death Song Comes to Life." Daily Worker, no. 7082 (29
June):2.
    An upcoming British Independence rally at Trafalgar Square is
used to remind readers of how Free Speech was won in the "famous
battle" of 1887. Recounts circumstances of Linnell's death, the
mass march at his funeral, and the singing of WM's "A Death Song,"
which is here reprinted. Promises, in conclusion, that it will be
sung at the upcoming rally: "At a time when the American government
pins its faith to mass murder with atomic weapons, and the British

government is slaughtering Africans in cold blood, Morris's song is more timely than ever."

22 Morris-Drucke und andere Meisterwerke englisher und
    amerikanischer Privatpressen. Catalogue of an Exhibition at
    Gutenburg Museum, Mainz, Germany. Mainz: Gutenburg Press, 32
    pp.
        Describes the 114 items exhibited; these were mainly books
influenced by WM and Kelmscott Press examples.

1955

1   ARNOT, R. PAGE. "Artist and Revolutionary." Daily Worker, no.
    7329 (20 June):2.
        Points out that in 1952 at a cultural conference held by the
Communist party of Great Britain, WM was termed the greatest
Englishman of the late nineteenth century, and a new biography
(1955.15) verifies that judgment. Claims that E.P. Thompson has
written the best book yet on WM and has "laid to rest lies about
him, has brought his teachings back before us all." Urges party
members to read the book.

2   ARNOT, R. PAGE. "WM, Communist." Marxist Quarterly 2, no. 4
    (October):237-45.
        Asserts that WM was neither the bourgeois poet-designer whose
socialism was an "unfortunate abberation," nor the Utopian socialist
dilettante who preached a better world but was "above the battle."
Most previous commentators placed him within one of these two
catagories; here it is carefully argued that WM was actually a
scientific socialist, a Marxist, whose work for the socialist cause,
especially as reflected in Commonweal, proves him to have been a
real pioneer in the development of European socialism. Recent
publications, especially E.P. Thompson (1955.15), are helping to
dispel the "Morris-myth."

3   AUSUBEL, HERMAN. The Late Victorians: A Short History. New
    York: Van Norstrand, pp. 31, 63-66, 147-51.
        Discusses problems that led WM to leave the SDF and set up
the Socialist League; calls Commonweal the "most literary Socialist
newspaper of the nineteenth century" and reprints "The Day Is
Coming."

4   BEERBOHM, MAX. "Hethway Speaking." <u>Listener</u>, 29 December, pp.
     1117-19.
          Reports upon the supposed recollections of one Sylvester
Hethway and the problems he once had trying to convince WM that he
did not want his rooms redecorated, and so some fun is made of
Morris and Co. furniture and of medieval murals.

5   CLAYDON, STELLA. "WM Believed in Britain's Future." <u>Daily</u>
     <u>Worker</u>, no. 7265 (20 January):2.
          Note paraphrases and praises <u>Nowhere</u>, concluding that "at the
heart of Morris's work is his love of the people and of England, and
his disgust at the way capitalism cripples people and disfigures
England."

6   GERBER, RICHARD. <u>Utopian Fantasy: A Study of Utopian Fiction</u>
     <u>Since the End of the 19th Century</u>. London: Routledge and Kegan
     Paul. Reprint. New York: McGraw-Hill, 1973, pp. 113-15,
     passim.
          Discusses <u>Nowhere</u> in light of Utopian traditions, motifs, and
stereotypes, asserting that it is the only well-known "dream
Utopia," and that its portrayal of science as unexplained magic is
unusual, quite unlike portrayals of scientific achievements in the
fictions of Wells.

7   GROOM, BERNHARD. "WM." In <u>The Diction of Poetry from Spencer</u>
     <u>to Bridges</u>. Toronto: University of Toronto Press. Reprint
     1960, 1966, pp. 252-65.
          Accuses WM of living in the past, and therefore a poem like
"Haystack in the Floods" must necessarily lack the "inner tension"
that a modern poem like Rossetti's "Jenny" has. Generalizes about
"true" epithets, discusses <u>Sigurd</u> as a "clearing-house for all the
Saxonisms of the century, true and false."

8   KEGEL, CHARLES. "WM's <u>John Ball</u>: A Study in Reactionary
     Liberalism." <u>Papers of the Michigan Academy of Science, Arts,</u>
     <u>and Letters</u> 40, pt. 4 (1954 Meeting):303-12.
          As sources for <u>John Ball</u>, WM used Froissart, whom he loved,
for colorful detail, etc., but he turned to contemporary historians
like Thorold Rogers for economic interpretations. This useful study
identifies specific sources and discusses the reasons WM chose to
highlight John Ball rather than Wat Tyler.

9   LEWIS, C.S. Surprised by Joy. New York: Harcourt Brace, pp.
    163-64, passim.
        Lewis recalls that, as a teenager, "my great author at this
time was WM," all of whose works he had evidently read, but he took
"little notice of the socialism."

10 PARROT, T.M., and MARTIN, R.B. "WM: 1834-1896." In A Companion
    to Victorian Literature. New York: Scribners, pp. 222-27,
    passim.
        Has basic bibliography, primary and secondary, and summarizes
the significant literary and biographical facts, and surmises that
WM was "perhaps the best storyteller in English verse since the time
of Chaucer."

11 QUIRK, RANDOLPH. "Dasent, WM, and Problems of Translation."
    Saga Book of the Viking Society 14:64-77.
        Examines the profound differences between these two
translators and finds that the most striking feature of a passage
from Dasent is "that there is little that is striking in it," but a
passage from WM is remarkable not just because of its archaic forms,
but because WM, through these forms, is trying to share with his
readers the "acute pleasure which the forms and arrangements of the
Icelandic have upon him." Reprinted: 1974.19.

12 SCHMIDT-KUNSEMULLER, FRIEDRICH ADOLF. WM und die neuere
    Buchkunst. Wiesbaden: Harrassowitz, 184 pp.
        An introductory chapter sketches in the growth of WM's
attitudes toward art and society, the art of the book, and the state
of English printing in the nineteenth century. A short history of
Kelmscott Press is followed by three detailed chapters on WM's
influence on the book arts in England, America, and Germany; the
chapter on the book arts in Germany is especially full, and should
itself be regarded as a necessary complement to 1977.38.

13 SCHMUTZLER, ROBERT. "The English Origins of Art Nouveau."
    Architectural Review 117, no. 698 (February):108-16.
        An examination of pattern designs beginning with those of
Owen Thomas in 1856 indicates a "latent Art Nouveau," even then, and
the stylized, flat, floral patterns, the trunks and tendrils in WM's
decorations carry on this influence, and these are present in
Beardsley, where they are "uncovered." Includes many illustrations.

14 SMITH, H. "The Economics of Socialism Reconsidered." <u>Economic</u>
    <u>Journal</u> <u>of</u> <u>the</u> <u>Royal</u> <u>Economic</u> <u>Society</u> 65 (June):411-21.
        A detailed exposition, pointing out why pure socialism
recedes beyond the horizon in both Britain and Russia, asserts that
WM had a better grasp of the economic realities of socialism than
most economists, and that WM was correct in "insisting that a
socialist society (as distinct from a liberalized capitalism or a
planned economy) must be permeated by a deeply rooted
conservatism." This is the socialist society WM described in his
lectures and created in <u>Nowhere</u>.

15 THOMPSON, E.P. <u>WM: Romantic to Revolutionary</u>. London: Lawrence
    and Wishart. Reprint. New York: Monthly Review Press, 1961,
    908 pp.
        Since Mackail (1899.10) is "likely to remain the standard
year-by-year narrative of the main events in Morris's life," this
book is meant to be a "study" rather than a biography; it uses
sources either not available to Mackail or ignored by him. Part 3,
"Practical Socialism," takes up over 400 pages, covering every
important event and touching upon every important figure active
during that decade; it amounts to a succinct and definitive history
of the Socialist League. Part 1 uses the "world of the Gradgrind"
as a trope, and discusses ways that Blake and Keats, Carlyle and
Ruskin, Rossetti and the Pre-Raphaelites, reacted against that stiff
and logical world, ways that WM built upon their critiques, and why,
especially in <u>Defence</u>, he should be seen as "the true inheritor of
the mantle of Keats." Part 2, "The Years of Conflict," brings WM
from happy Red House days and the establishment of the Firm and of
his poetic fame, with <u>Paradise</u>, up through the personal problems of
the early 1870s and the Icelandic experience, here given great
significance: "There can be few more striking examples in history of
the revolutionary power of culture than this renewal of courage and
of faith in humanity which was blown to WM across the waters of the
North Sea and eight hundred years of time." He was thus ready for
his vigorous work both with the Eastern Question Association, where
he learned of the "moral cowardice of professional politicians," and
with SPAB, where he attempted to stem the arrogance of progressive
architects and theologians. WM'S work in these societies is
presented in rich detail and in ways that clearly show him striding
toward that "River of Fire" that he crossed in 1882 when he became a
socialist, an event presented here as unique: "The transformation of
the eccentric artist and romantic literary man into the Socialist
agitator may be counted among the great conversions of the world."
Part 3 is fully detailed, with capsule biographies of all the
principal figures and with reasoned analyses of why WM left Hyndman
and the SDF in 1894 and the Socialist League and <u>Commonweal</u> six
years later. Stresses the importance of <u>Commonweal</u>; it records WM's
growth into an important socialist theorist. Argues that he did not
stop working for socialism after 1890. Part 4, "Necessity and
Desire," also debunks other received ideas about WM, tracing the
ways the literary and political establishment, following the lead of

writers like Glasier (1921.3), created a Morris wholly false to the
one who emerges from these pages: a revolutionary thinker who
tempered Marxist ideas about historical necessity, ideas he grasped
fully ("Morris was not a mere muddle-headed convert to Marxism"),
with his own ideas about the importance of human desire finding
outlets in joyful work, hence art, and in true fellowship.
Concludes that WM is "still in the van--beckoning us forward to the
measureless bounty of life. He is one of those men whom history
will never overtake." Four appendixes include the Manifesto of
Socialist League, previously unpublished correspondence, and a
discussion of Glasier's treatment of WM's Marxism (1921.3).
Revised: 1976.50.

16   "WM." In English Chintzes: Two Centuries of Changing Taste.
     Catalogue of 1955 Exhibition at the Victoria and Albert, and in
     the Style Centre, Manchester. London: Victoria and Albert, pp.
     43-45.
         An exhibition of English chintzes included twelve of the
forty-four chintz designs produced by WM; has short introduction and
notes.

1956

1   BROWN, T.J. "English Literary Autographs: WM, 1834-1896." Book
     Collector 5 (Summer):151.
         A response to an observation in Mackail (1899.10) that WM's
handwriting improved after 1870 when he took up calligraphy, noting
that even before then his hand had been "fine." The fair copy of
Sigurd, a specimen of which is here reproduced, "is perhaps the
handsomest literary autograph in the British Museum."

2   BUNGE, MARIO. "On WM's Socialism." Science and Society 20, no.
     2 (Spring):142-44.
         Contrary to what several recent Marxist writers have
maintained, Nowhere does not depict a socialist society, "but a sort
of stagnant medieval society without classes," and this is true
because, though WM was a courageous socialist, he was not a Marxist.
Maintains that he understood neither economic theory nor history; he
ignored the role that machines could play in human liberation and
the fact that the Middle Ages was a "time of exploitation, misery,
and endless uprisings, an epoch of wars, plagues and famines."

3   ERVINE, ST. JOHN. <u>Bernard</u> <u>Shaw:</u> <u>His</u> <u>Life,</u> <u>Work</u> <u>and</u> <u>Friends</u>.
     New York: William Morrow and Co., pp. 168-70, passim.
          Surveys the associations WM and Shaw had from 1883 onwards,
     and judges WM's death to be the "first great personal loss that Shaw
     felt." Suggests that WM's "communism belonged not to the age of
     Marx but to the ages of the Icelandic sagas."

4   FULLER, RONALD, ed. <u>WM</u>. Sheldonian English Series. Oxford:
     Oxford University Press, 190 pp.
          Anthology that attempts, "on a necessarily limited scale, to
     represent the development and variety" of WM's writings. Brief but
     helpful biographical and critical commentary links the selections,
     arranged chronologically.

5   HENDERSON, ARCHIBALD. "WM and Wells: Friend and Foe." In
     <u>George</u> <u>Bernard</u> <u>Shaw:</u> <u>Man</u> <u>of</u> <u>the</u> <u>Century</u>. New York:
     Appleton-Century Crofts, pp. 243-50, passim.
          Essentially the same anecdotes and quotations that appear in
     the earlier two versions of this biography (1911.5 and 1932.8), with
     some additions and with pointed contrasts made here between Wells
     and WM.

6   JAMIESON, PAUL F. "WM's 'The Nymph's Song to Hylas' ('A Garden
     by the Sea')." <u>Explicator</u> 14, no. 6 (March):36.
          The lyric, "The Nymph's Song to Hylas," fits its context
     well, for it "epitomises the <u>ubi</u> <u>sunt</u> undercurrent of <u>Jason</u>."
     (1956.16 has the same title.)

7   JONES, HOWARD MUMFORD. "The Pre-Raphaelites." In <u>The</u> <u>Victorian</u>
     <u>Poets:</u> <u>A</u> <u>Guide</u> <u>to</u> <u>Research</u>. Edited by F.E. Faverty. Cambridge,
     Mass.: Harvard University Press, pp. 191-95, passim.
          Reviews criticism and scholarship on the Pre-Raphaelites,
     commenting upon problems with definitions and influences and
     pointing out that, for some unknown reason, "groups of talented
     young men swirled and eddied around a central enigma named Rossetti,
     who took it as a matter of course that art is one of the primary
     functions of any intelligent human being." Suggests that recent
     attention paid to WM concerns the social reformer more than the poet
     or designer; discusses a few dozen studies of WM's writings, all of
     which are included in the present book.

8   KEGEL, CHARLES. "An Undergraduate Magazine, 1856 Style." Basic
    College Quarterly 2 (Winter):27-32.
        Finds that more than one half of the pieces published in the
    Oxford and Cambridge Magazine were by WM and William Fulford, and
    that all of its stories were strongly influenced by Tennysonian
    melancholia, perhaps to the same degree that modern undergraduate
    fiction is influenced by Hemingwayesque realism.

9   MAC LEOD, R.D. WM (As Seen By His Contemporaries). Glasgow: W.
    and R. Holmes, 23 pp. Reprint. Folcroft, Pa.: Folcroft Press,
    1969. Folcroft, Pa.: Folcroft Library Editions, 1974. Norwood,
    Pa.: Norwood Editions, 1977.
        Reprint, with new title, of 1954.12.

10 MADSEN, S.T. Sources of Art Nouveau. Translated by R.
    Christopherson. Oslo: H. Aschehoug. Reprint. New York: DeCapo
    Press, 1975, pp. 88-94, passim.
        Discusses Morris and Co. artifacts, WM's ideas, as
    significant influences on art nouveau. Offers striking parallels
    between WM and artists on both sides of the channel, and includes
    many illustrations.

11 MANSFIELD, BRUCE E. "The Socialism of WM." Historical Studies:
    Australia and New Zealand 7, no. 27 (November):271-90.
        Suggests that WM's socialism arose from his regard for
    popular art and medieval craftsmanship, as well as from his hatred
    of modern conditions which aborted such art and craftsmanship.
    Discusses the Socialist League, the nature of its internal
    conflicts, and the links between WM and Australian socialism. In
    1887 a Socialist League was established in Sydney, evidently by a
    member of the British Socialist League; its problems, its journal,
    and its eventual demise were strikingly similar to those of the
    parent organization.

12 MERRIAM, EVE. Emma Lazarus: Woman with a Torch. New York:
    Citadel Press, pp. 120-22, 144-45.
        Describes Emma Lazarus's visit to WM in 1883, lacing with
    socialist credos a conversation they supposedly had, repeating the
    falsehood that WM sold his library for the cause. Reports on WM's
    satisfaction with the article Lazarus wrote about him, which
    appeared in 1886.

13 MORTON, A.L., and TATE, GEORGE. The British Labour Movement:
    1770-1920. London: Lawrence and Wishart, pp. 166-75.
        Insists that WM's "understanding of historical materialism
was profound," citing both fictional narratives and socialist
lectures as proof. Comments upon the import of poems like "Wake,
London Lads" and of WM's many contributions to Commonweal, a
reflection of his energy and talent too often neglected by modern
commentators. Discusses WM's work with the Eastern Question
Association and the reasons he left the SDF.

14 PEVSNER, NIKOLAUS. "WM, C.R. Ashbee and the Twentieth
    Century." Translated by E. Heaton. Manchester Review 7
    (Summer):437-58.
        Pevsner added a foreword to this translation of 1936.10.

15 ROTHSTEIN, ANDREW. "The Great Pioneer." Labour Monthly 38, no.
    3 (March):133-39.
        Accuses the establishment, the media, of an "immense
confidence trick" played on the workers since 1915, for they were
constantly told to beware communism, which was seen as "un-British,"
and therefore British capitalism survived postwar and depression
crises. Arnot (1934.3) and E.P. Thompson (1955.15) have undercut
media lies, especially about WM and British socialism, and their
works should be more widely read.

16 RUTHERFORD, ANDREW. "WM's 'The Nymph's Song to Hylas' ('A
    Garden by the Sea')." Explicator 14, no. 6 (March):36.
        The lyric, "The Nymph's Song to Hylas," should not be read
for meaning: it "expresses a vague yearning, and no more." (1956.6
has the same title.)

17 TORR, DONA. "WM and Tom Mann, WM and Hyndman." In Tom Mann and
    His Times. London: Lawrence and Wishart, pp. 186-205.
        Ways that Tom Mann, who joined the SDF in 1885 and went on to
become a leader of the Union Movement, was influenced by WM are set
against an unusually rich and detailed exposition of political
protest and reform from the Peasants' Rebellion up through the
Reform Acts of the nineteenth century. Mann appreciated WM because
of his attitudes toward "scrappy, half-educated people like me," his
continuing distrust of parliamentry politics, and his trenchant
pronouncements on art and society ("twenty of his words can outweigh
200 of Hyndman's"). The author criticizes WM's "infantile leftism
in regard to working-class organization which ultimately led him
into the domestic seclusion of the Hammersmith Socialist Society."

18 WRIGHT, AUSTIN, ed. "WM." In Bibliographies of Studies in
    Victorian Literature for the Ten Years 1945-1954. Urbana:
    University of Illinois Press, passim.
        This reprinting of the annual bibliographies from MP, a
sequel to 1945.6, lists several studies of WM; with the exception of
the reviews, all are included in the present book.

                              1957

1   ARNOT, R. PAGE. Bernard Shaw and WM. London: WM Society, 26
    pp. Reprint. Folcroft, Pa.: Folcroft Editions, 1973. Norwood,
    Pa.: Norwood Editions, 1975. Norwood, Pa.: Telegraph Books,
    1980.
        Judges that it is fitting to consider together Shaw and WM
since "Shaw, much more than any other writer, treasured the words of
Morris and kept his memory green." Points out ways that WM
influenced Shaw's "social outlook," repeats several Shavian
anecdotes about WM (many drawn from 1936.12), and quotes from a
perceptive review WM wrote of Cashel Byron's Profession. Originally
a lecture to the Shaw society on the occasion of the Shaw centenary,
11 May 1956.

2   BOE, ALF. "Handicraft, Legend, and the Beauty of the Earth:
    WM." In From Gothic Revival to Functional Form: A Study in
    Victorian Theories of Design. Oslo Studies in English, no. 9.
    Oslo: Oslo University Press, pp. 104-27, passim.
        Even though WM in his lectures was more concerned with the
conditions under which art might thrive than with theory, it is
possible to reconstruct his theories about design from both the
lectures and also from the many artifacts he created. Uses an
embroidered wall-hanging (ca. 1880) as an example of WM design at
its best, offering a detailed discussion of its form and harmonies.
Comments on other WM designs, referring to accompanying
illustrations, and concluding that WM was important for carrying the
"most central ideas of Ruskin into life" and for setting an example
that has had an immense influence on modern design, on both policies
and practices.

3   DEWSNAP, TERENCE. "Symmetry in the Early Poetry of WM." N and
    Q 202 (March):132-33.
        Touches on "symmetry" of a few descriptions of characters and
settings in a few poems from Defence, suggesting that "we get only a
front view of his characters, fixed as they are in their settings."

4   DUPONT, VICTOR. Introduction to <u>Nouvelles</u> <u>de</u> <u>nulle</u> <u>part</u>.
     Editions Montaigne. Paris: Aubier, pp. 12-81.
        This full introduction to a French edition of <u>Nowhere</u>, with
facing-page translation, opens with WM's 1883 letter to Andreas
Scheu, and then the main events of WM's life are surveyed, the
achievements weighed, with his political career, and writings from
1883 onward, receiving the most attention. Includes a discussion of
Western Utopias from Plato through More to Bellamy.

5   FONTAINE VERWEY, E. DE LA. "De uitgaven van de Kelmscott Press
     in de Koninklijke Bibliotheek." <u>Het</u> <u>Boek</u> 32:247-49.
        In Dutch. The Royal Library in The Hague had received a
complete set of Kelmscott Press editions, and this report comments
upon the backgrounds of the press and its influence on Dutch
printers.

6   FRYE, NORTHROP. <u>Anatomy</u> <u>of</u> <u>Criticism:</u> <u>Four</u> <u>Essays</u>. Princeton,
     N.J.: Princeton University Press, pp. 305-6, passim.
        Includes brief but provocative comments on <u>Paradise</u> and why
it fits into the sixth "phase" of romance; also comments on the
"very obvious sexual mythopoeia" in the prose romances.

7   HOGGART, RICHARD. <u>The</u> <u>Uses</u> <u>of</u> <u>Literacy:</u> <u>Changing</u> <u>Patterns</u> <u>in</u>
     <u>English</u> <u>Mass</u> <u>Culture</u>. London: Chatto and Windus, pp. 200, 234,
     passim.
        Comments on WM looking forward to a time when the gap between
riches and poverty might be narrowed, with a resulting rise in
popular art. The gap has narrowed somewhat, but modern mass art,
unfortunately, hardly corresponds to WM's ideas of popular art.

8   HUTT, ALLEN. "WM, Marxism and Typography." <u>Labour</u> <u>Monthly</u> 39,
     no. 10 (October):467-78
        Asserts that WM's Kelmscott Press activities were a "true
culmination of his thought and action as a socialist, a
revolutionary Marxist socialist, a Communist," and furthermore, that
"few, if any, arts are more profoundly dialectical than the art of
printing."

9   MC LEAN, RUARI. "Hedendaagse boekkunst" [Modern book design].
     Translated by J. Kemp. <u>Folium</u> 5:3-10, 97-120.
        Translation, into Dutch, of 1951.9.

10   PEVSNER, NIKOLAUS.   "Architecture and WM."   RIBA Journal 64
     (Summer):1-6.
         An address, here reprinted along with polite comments from
     three respondents, given to the Royal Institute of British
     Architects, on 19 February 1957. Discusses ways that WM's love for
     architecture grew out of ideas about the Middle Ages, when a
     building was neccessarily a cooperative effort. Points out that at
     least two of the principles WM formulated for SPAB were new: leave
     weathered exteriors and accumulations of "furniture" alone; and that
     many of his ideas about architecture, town planning, ecology, and
     the like, were indeed prescient.

11   "WM by Daylight."   In British Printer. London: WM Society, 1 p.
         Recalls that Franklin wanted on his tombstone only "Benjamin
     Franklin, Printer," and asserts that the only other "personality of
     comparable scale" so fascinated by printing was WM whose example
     influenced Bruce Rogers, D.B. Updike, and Oliver Simon. This is a
     reprint, for WM Society members, of an editorial (not seen) which
     had commented on the "Typographical Adventure" exhibition (1957.12).

12   The Typographical Adventure of WM: An Exhibition Arranged by WM
     Society. Catalogue of an Exhibition 30 July-16 August 1957 at
     St. Bride Foundation Institute, London, and elsewhere: London:
     WM Society, 56 pp.
         Has a foreword by Cockerell and an introduction by R.C. H.
     Briggs which contains a capsule biography of Walker, the "spur" who
     released WM's latent interests in printing. The catalogue for this
     large exhibition is divided into four parts: (1) Morris before
     Walker, (2) transition, (3) the adventure, and (4) after Kelmscott.
     Though WM directed the Kelmscott Press for only five years, he had
     had three decades of experience as a designer, and that experience
     and the ways it blossomed at the Press are here set forth. Also
     charts the influence of Kelmscott Press into the twentieth century,
     with seventy-six items shown under part four. Exhibition had
     sixteen separate showings and traveled until March 1959.

                              1958

1   BLAND, DAVID. A History of Book Illustration: The Illustrated
     MS and the Printed Book. Los Angeles and Berkeley: University of
     California Press. 2d ed., 1969, pp. 273-75, passim.
         Discusses incunabula that WM admired, and sometimes
     purchased, books that inspired his own Kelmscott Press volumes.
     Since WM thought of illustrations more in terms of design than of
     storytelling, few of the Kelmscott Press books are notable for their
     illustrations, and the crowded pages have not appealed to all. But
     some American and European illustraters were influenced, and they
     are here mentioned.

2   CANNING, GEORGE R.. "WM: Man and Literary Artist."
     Dissertation, University of Wisconsin.
          Abstracted: DA 19:1753.

3   CLARKE, I.F. "The Nineteenth Century Utopia." Quarterly Review
     296, no. 615 (January):80-91.
          Nowhere is classed with Besant's Revolt of Man; both have a
     "curiously juvenile streak," and "schoolboy jokes and adolescent
     behaviour form the background for Nowhere." Its rejection of
     industrial society, its optimism about the future, mark a turning
     point in the course of nineteenth-century Utopias. Afterwards
     Utopias, like those by Wells, become more pessimistic.

4   FLOUD, PETER. Introduction to WM. Small Picture Books, no. 43.
     Victoria and Albert. London: HMSO, 1 p.
          Short introduction to WM designs at the Victoria and Albert
     Museum emphasizes "that Morris's own work was entirely limited to
     the field of flat design, and never ventured into the
     three-dimensional. Within this self-imposed limitation, however, he
     mastered no less than twelve different techniques." Ten of those
     are represented in the twenty-seven illustrations, with notes, in
     this booklet.

5   HENDERSON, PHILIP. "La Belle Iseult." Saturday Book 18:139-53.
          Draws parallels between King Arthur's love for his fellow
     knights and apparent disregard for Guenevere ("for queens I might
     have enough," Malory) and WM's "love for his friends and fellow
     crusaders which meant more to him, by and large, than his
     frustrating relationship with his picturesque but dumb wife."
     Comments upon biographical implications in certain verses from
     Paradise and certain sonnets from Rossetti's House of Life,
     suggesting then that WM's unhappy marriage accounts, in part, for
     the vast amount of work he completed, and for his unremitting labors
     for socialism.

6   HUNTER, DARD. My Life with Paper: An Autobiography. New York:
     Knopf, pp. 35-36, passim.
          Claims that a Kelmscott Press book in his father's library
     had a "pronounced influence," causing him to "read everything I
     could find relating to the life and work of WM." Contrasts his own
     attempts at bookmaking with those of WM, who "had the best talent of
     England at his command." Recounts May Morris's angry reaction (she
     was lecturing in Buffalo, in 1907) when he gave her an invitation to
     visit Elbert Hubbard at his Roycroft Shops a few miles away in East
     Aurora.

7   KEGEL, CHARLES. "WM and the Religion of Fellowship." <u>Western</u>
    <u>Humanities Review</u> 12, no. 3 (Summer):223-40.
        Discusses the "contribution toward WM's secularization" made
by his reading of Carlyle and Ruskin. WM grew to scorn "any
religious structure which disparaged our earthly existence and
turned men's minds instead toward a vague, abstract notion of an
afterlife. His desires for human fellowship were framed, however,
in religious terms.

8   MC LEAN, RUARI. "WM." In <u>Modern</u> <u>Book</u> <u>Design</u> <u>from</u> <u>WM</u> <u>to</u> <u>the</u>
    <u>Present</u> <u>Day</u>. London: Faber and Faber, pp. 7-12, 23-28, passim.
    Reprint. Fairlawn, N.J.: Essential Books, 1959.
        Revised, expanded version of 1951.9, with thirty-two
additional plates.

9   PATRICK, JOHN M. "WM and Froissart: 'Geoffrey Teste Noire' and
    'Haystack in the Floods.'" <u>N</u> <u>and</u> <u>Q</u> 203 (October):425-27.
        Points out, discusses briefly, several specific parallels
between Froissart's <u>Chronicles</u> and "Concerning Geffray Teste Noire"
and "Haystack in the Floods," parallels between characters and
motifs, even images like skeletons and wet hay.

10 RITCHIE, WARD. <u>WM</u> <u>and</u> <u>His</u> <u>"Praise</u> <u>of</u> <u>Wine"</u>. Los Angeles: Ward
    Ritchie Press, 11 pp.
        Reprints a sonnet that WM drafted, ca. 1868, on back of
"Praise of Wine" manuscript, and then offers a sympathetic sketch of
WM's life and activities during this period, wondering if the sonnet
reflects, as it seems to, WM's growing sorrow about Janey's
attraction for Rossetti.

11 ROBSON, W.W. "Pre-Raphaelite Poetry." In <u>The</u> <u>Pelican</u> <u>Guide</u> <u>to</u>
    <u>English</u> <u>Literature</u>. Edited by Boris Ford. Vol. 6. <u>From</u> <u>Dickens</u>
    <u>to</u> <u>Hardy</u>. Harmondsworth: Penguin, pp. 352-70.
        Discusses WM's poetry, especially <u>Defence</u>, in comparison to
that of Rossetti and Christina Rossetti. Praises title poem of
<u>Defence</u> for its "clear outlines and distinct colours," as well as
for the "thrill" the speaking voice gives. Such qualities are never
found in Tennyson's Arthurian poems, nor in WM's later poetry, which
is merely "charming." The more robust side of WM, so evident in
this early poetry, was later devoted to SPAB and to socialist work
and the like, not to the poetry. Reprinted: 1967.20, 1969.23.

12 ROLLINS, CARL.PURINGTON. "WM's Typographical Adventure."
    Printing and Graphic Arts 6:29-32.
        Notes the conjunction of the 1956 sale at Sothebys of
Cockerell's collection of Kelmscott Press items and the exhibition
"The Typographical Adventure of WM" (1957.12), suggesting that such
events will restore the prestige of the Press and of WM's
achievements in the book arts.

13 VERVLIET, D. "WM en de herleving van de laat-negentiende-eeuwse
    Antwerpse typografie" [WM and the inheritance of late
    nineteenth-century typography in Antwerp]. Antwerpen 1
    (April-May):42-48.
        In Dutch. Announces the arrival in Antwerp of the exhibit
"The Typographical Adventure of WM" (1957.12), and then discusses in
some detail the great influence WM and his Kelmscott Press volumes
had at the turn of the century on Van de Velde, Pol de Mont, and
other printers and presses, both European and American. A
biographical sketch of WM stresses his lifelong interest in the
book-arts.

14 WILLIAMS, RAYMOND. Culture and Society: 1780-1950. London:
    Chatto and Windus. New York: Columbia University Press.
    Reprint. New York: Harper and Row, 1966, pp. 148-58, passim.
        Places WM within the tradition of romantic radicalism,
commenting upon Pugin and Ruskin and pointing out how WM changed the
tradition by attaching radical value to the working class. Wishes
that more people would read the socialist lectures, where WM proves
himself to be a pivotal figure between nineteenth- and
twentieth-century modes of leftist politics.

15 WINTERICH, JOHN T., ed. Introduction to The Works of Geoffrey
    Chaucer: A Facsimile of the WM Kelmscott Chaucer, with the
    Original 87 Illustrations by Sir Edward Burne-Jones. New York
    and Cleveland: World Publishing Co., pp. i-xx.
        WM in his Kelmscott Press years "established a validity and
prestige that still make him the most powerful and pervasive
influence in book design in the English-speaking, English-reading
world." Offers details of Kelmscott Press innovations, these
followed by a glossary "based on Skeats' annotations, designed to
help the reader understand Chaucer's works in the original." Since
the page size has been "slightly reduced" in this facsimile, the
editor describes it "as the first Kelmscott Chaucer ever published
that is designed for reading."

16 Catalogue of the WM Collections. Walthamstow: WM Gallery, 53 pp.
     Describes the holdings of the Gallery which include the Brangwyn Gift (nineteenth-century art and sculpture) and the Mackmurdo Bequest (designs, furniture, and textiles made by the Centenary Guild) as well as the Morris Collection of cartoons and original designs, ceramics and stained glass, textiles and wallpapers, manuscripts and books, and "personal relics." Has useful biographical notes and an index of wallpaper and textile designs. Revised edition: 1969.29.

17 WM. Small Picture Books, no. 43. Victoria and Albert. London: HMSO, 32 pp.
     Has a short introduction by Peter Floud, twenty-seven plates, and three pages of technical notes. WM designs for stained glass, embroidery, wallpapers, and tapestries are among the illustrations.

1959

1 ARMITAGE, E. LIDDALL. Stained Glass: History, Technology, and Practice. Newton, Mass.: C.T. Branford, pp. 59, 63.
     A chapter on nineteenth-century stained glass surveys the achievements of WM and Morris and Co.; the Birmingham Cathedral windows judged to be the Firm's most successful, and the "St. George and the Dragon" window called an "example of domestic glass which Morris to some extent popularized."

2 CAFLISH, MAX. WM: Der Erneuren der Buchkunst. Bern: Monotype Corporation, 24 pp.
     Pamphlet written for Swiss viewers of the traveling exhibition, "The Typographical Adventure of WM" (1957.12). Includes a biographical sketch and a history of Kelmscott Press, with four pages illustrating the different typefaces.

3 ERSITES, T.H. "WM and the Kelmscott Press." American Book Collector 10:19-25.
     Presents full discussions of typefaces, paper, ink, watermarks, even about the first employees, at Kelmscott Press. Such details are supplemented by useful generalizations like the following: "what WM sought in books was analogous to what Rossetti and his circle sought in painting: a return to medievalism to the first principles upon which to develop a new and distinct kind of art."

4   FLOUD, PETER. "Dating WM Patterns." <u>Architectural Review</u> 126,
     no. 750 (July):14-20.
         Uses new evidence from records of design patents to place,
for the first time, WM's wallpaper and chintz designs in a precise
chronolgical order, reaching conclusions whose "validity can only be
judged visually," so the thirty-three illustrations that accompany
this significant article are not merely decorative. Omits three
early designs (Trellis, Daisy, and Pomegranete) and places the
remaining seventy-two within four clearly defined periods between
1872 and 1896. Designs underwent a real change in 1876, when what
was fluid and free became rigid; this change was caused by WM's new
interest in weaving and his study of woven fabrics at the South
Kensington. Juxtaposed illustrations show that "some of Morris's
patterns were much more directly inspired by historic examples than
has hitherto been supposed," namely, the rigid and repetitive
patterns just after 1876 and also diagonal patterns directly
influenced by a "magnificent Italian cut velvet" the Museum acquired
in 1883. A revised version of the Morris Memorial Lecture, given 3
October 1956 under the title "WM's Designs: Some Controversial
Points Reconsidered."

5   METZDORF, ROBERT F., ed. <u>The Tinker Library: A Bibliographical
     Catalogue of the Books Collected by Chauncey Brewster Tinker</u>.
     New Haven: Yale University Press, pp. 320-26.
         Describes WM materials (four manuscripts and forty-seven
printed works) which were in the library of Chauncey Brewster
Tinker. These included a complete run of the <u>Oxford and Cambridge
Magazine</u>, many separately published socialist lectures, and several
Kelmscott Press volumes.

6   PATRICK, JOHN M. "WM and Froissart Again: 'Sir Peter Harpdon's
     End.'" <u>N and Q</u> 204 (September):331-33.
         Points out, discusses briefly, several allusions and
descriptions of characters in "Sir Peter Harpdon's End" that WM
apparently borrowed from Froissart, which have the effect of
"exposing the grim nature of medieval warfare."

*7   SHVEDOR, U.I., ed. <u>Selections from WM</u>. Moscow: Moscow State
     Library Publishing.
         Cited in 1960 <u>WM Society Newsletter</u>. Introduction and notes
in Russian; English selections taken from Cole's Nonesuch edition
(1934.20).

8   STAVENOW, ELIZABET. "Vallfart till Red House" [Pilgrimage to
    Red House]. Arkitektur (Copenhagen) 12:261-64.
        In Danish. Describes visit to Red House, going into detail
about the grounds, the shape of the house, and the trappings within,
and then commenting upon the ways that some of Ruskin's ideas were
apparently incorporated into the designs. Quotes Muthesius
(1904.11) on the architectural significance of Red House; includes
several photographs.

9   WAHL, JOHN ROBERT. "The Mood of Energy and the Mood of
    Idleness: A Note on Paradise." English Studies in Africa 2, no.
    1 (March):90-97.
        Uses distinctions WM himself had made in in an 1886 lecture,
"The Aims of Art," to suggest that Paradise was written during a
"mood of idleness," and that is why many of the poems therein seem
vague and blurred. The poems in Defence, on the other hand, are
firm and precise, and so is Sigurd, because these were written
during a "mood of energy."

10 "The Typographical Adventure of WM." Book Design and Production
    2, no. 1:34-43.
        The exhibit "The Typographical Adventure of WM" (1957.12)
began in London and then went to several more British and
continental cities; this article compares the typography and design
on invitations and notices sent from museums in those various cities
to advertise the exhibit.

1960

1   ALTICK, RICHARD D., and MATTHEWS, WILLIAM R. Guide to Doctoral
    Dissertations in Victorian Literature: 1886-1958. Westport,
    Conn.: Greenwood Press, pp. 69-71.
        Lists thirty-two dissertations on WM, the majority of them in
English. All of them are included in the present book.

2   BALDWIN, A.W. The MacDonald Sisters. London: Peter Davies, pp.
    41, 51, 89-91, passim.
        Includes anecdotes about Red House excursions and parties,
many of them drawn from Georgie Burne-Jones's biography of her
husband (1904.3), and recounts also their sad reactions to WM's
death, Georgie judging that Kelmscott Manor was a "nightmare now.
It was Topsy who put life into it and kept it going--glorious
creature!"

3   BATSON, ERIC J. "A Visit to Red House." Regional (New York
     Shaw Society) 3, no. 2 (August):4-5.
         Recounts 1960 visit to Red House, claiming that it was a
"forerunner of much that was to come in the way of building homes
for decent people of good taste." Includes some impressionistic
descriptions and some generalizations about affinities between WM
and Shaw.

4   BELL, DANIEL. The End of Ideology. Glencoe, Ill.: Free Press,
     pp. 252, 255, 274.
         Contrasts WM's "humanistic socialism" to other
nineteenth-century varieties, notably that of Bellamy.

5   BELLAS, RALPH. "WM's Treatment of Sources in Paradise."
     Dissertation, University of Kansas.
         Abstracted: DA 22:857-58.

6   BRIGGS, R.C.H. Tributes to Peter Floud. London: WM Society, 8
     pp.
         Summarizes Floud's achievements, the importance of his work
at the Victoria and Albert, and the significance of his lectures and
articles on WM's designs, now open to reinterpretation because of
new light that Floud's research in the Patent Office has shed.

7   CAMMELL, CHARLES RICHARD. "WM: Kelmscott House, Upper Mall,
     Hammersmith." In The Name on the Wall. London: Arthur Barker,
     pp. 145-68.
         Biographical sketch accompanies descriptions of Thames-side
dwellings in Hammersmith with the focus on Kelmscott House; comments
also on others who had lived nearby (the poet, James Thompson) or in
the same house (the writer George MacDonald, whose name for the
house, "The Retreat," did not suit the active and vigorous WM).
Details of Kelmscott Press and of WM's socialist work shimmer behind
the reverential rhetoric used throughout. Neglects to mention the
shed beside the famous house, the shed in which the Sunday evening
socialist lectures were given.

8   COLE, G.D.H. WM as a Socialist. London: WM Society, 19 pp.
     Reprint. Folcroft, Pa.: Folcroft Library Editions, 1973.
     Norwood, Pa.: Norwood Editions, 1977.
         Recalls how Nowhere turned him into a socialist, and then
contrasts WM's vision of a future society to that of present-day
Marxists with their "high contempt for the small-scale producer" and
their tendencies "to subordinate everything else to the quest for
higher output." Some of WM's regard for beauty and decency of
conduct should be incorporated into modern socialist planning.
Concludes that the two socialists who influenced him the most were

Fourier and WM, and he touches on certain parallels between them.

9   DAICHES, DAVID. A Critical History of English Literature.
    London: Sacker and Warburg; New York: Ronald Press, pp. 982-86,
    passim.
        Discusses Nowhere and WM's lectures and essays within the
    context of his "intense practical enthusiasm for art which led him,
    as it had led Ruskin, to inquire into the function of art and the
    social conditions necessary for its healthy production." Relates
    WM's socialist activities to those of other socialists, pointing out
    that "his political ideas influenced a generation, notable among
    whom was Shaw." Discusses the uniqueness of imagery in Defence,
    which he prefers to the narrative verse. Concludes that for WM
    "craftsmanship, supreme in the Middle Ages, was the heritage and the
    gaurantee of free men everywhere; poetry was a craft like any other,
    and he was as prepared to weave words as he was to weave carpets."

10 DOUGHTY, OSWALD. "The Idle Singer of an Empty Day." In
    Rossetti: A Victorian Romantic. 2d ed., London: Oxford
    University Press, pp. 458-68, passim.
        Substantially the same as the first edition (1949.3), but the
    following new paragraph concludes this chapter: "Once only, so far
    as we know, did Morris break silence as to his opinion of Rossetti,
    and that was long after Gabriel's death. 'Sometimes,' he told a
    Glasgow professor, 'Rossetti was an angel; and sometimes he was a
    damned scoundrel.'" And an author's note reveals that the person
    alluded to in the first edition who could have spoken with authority
    on Rossetti and Janey, was Mackail.

11 DUNLAP, JOSEPH R. "The Typographical Shaw: George Bernard Shaw
    and the Revival of Printing." Bulletin of the New York Public
    Library 64, no. 10 (October):534-47.
        Surveys history of printing, of nineteenth-century practices,
    and of WM's influence, here called "explosive." It certainly
    touched Shaw, and this is apparent if one examines the printing in
    Shaw's books after 1897, when Grant Richards became Shaw's publisher
    and let him have a hand in type and page design.

12 DUSCHNES, PHILIP C. "On WM and the Kelmscott Press." In WM and
    the Kelmscott Press. A Catalogue of an Exhibition Held in the
    Brown University Library from 9 October-31 December, 1959.
    Providence, R.I.: Brown University Press, pp. 35-49.
        Calls Walker the "John the Baptist to WM's New Testament of
    Typography." Repeats the error that WM sold precious manuscripts
    and incunabula to support socialist causes, but other details about
    typefaces, paper production, and the like, are reliable. Includes
    interesting facts about the changing prices of Kelmscott Press
    books.

13 ENTWHISTLE, E.A. A Literary History of Wallpaper. London:
    Batsford, pp. 123-24, passim.
        Lists sixteen titles, with short annotations, of works that
refer to Morris and Co. wallpapers; all of them are included in the
present book.

14 FAULKNER, PETER. "Yeats and WM." Threshold 4:18-27.
        Quotes and discusses Yeats's changing attitudes to the
writings of WM, the essay thus offering a sense of Yeats as critic
and of WM's influence upon him. Yeats claimed that WM's prose set a
"standard of excellence," but that his poetry lacked "intensity."
Concludes that Yeats was "always to admire Morris, but the
admiration came to be focused more on the man and less on the poet,"
as Yeats discarded his early romantic assumptions about poetry.

15 FLOUD, PETER. "The Wallpaper Designs of WM." Penrose Annual
    54:41-45.
        Even though WM's wallpapers were responsible for his large
reputation as a designer, very little was known about them before
Floud's research in the Patent Office established that WM designed
forty-one wallpapers and five ceiling papers, and that he was not
responsible for others often attributed to him, which were in fact
designed by Dearle or others at Morris and Co., thirty-one of which
appeared after WM's death. Until 1930 Morris and Co. papers were
produced at Jeffrey and Co., and WM was obviously happy with their
work, since he never involved himself in production matters, as he
did with every other Morris and Co. product. Points out also that
WM papers were not revolutionary; several decorating firms in the
1850s, inspired by Pugin and Owen Jones, had moved away from bright,
naturalistic, floral designs and were actually more innovative than
WM in his early designs; his later designs, between 1876 and 1896,
were more formal but not so popular. Includes twenty illustrations,
four in color. Reprinted and included in "Tributes to Peter Floud,"
1960.6.

16 GIROUARD, MARK. "Red House, Bexley Heath, Kent." Country Life
    127, no. 3302 (16 June):1382-85.
        Detailed description of Red House, especially its central
rooms and their furnishings, keyed to nine photographs and the
original contract floor plans drawn by Webb in April 1859. Suggests
that the eagerness and vitality of WM and Webb, and of their fellow
planners and decorators, is still apparent in Red House one hundred
years after it was built.

17 GORDON, W.K. "A Critical Selected Edition of WM's Oxford and
    Cambridge Magazine." Dissertation, University of Pennsylvania.
    Abstracted: DA 21:3781-82.

18 JORDAN, R. FURNEAUX. The Medieval Vision of WM. London: WM
    Society, 31 pp.
        Argues that we must find among WM's "multiplicity of
    activities a single vision," and that that vision is medieval; the
    same links that bound WM to medieval institutions and values are the
    same ones that bound him to socialism. Suggests that all such links
    can be found in Ruskin's "The Nature of Gothic." Originally a
    lecture given in 1957.

19 KOCMANOVA, JESSIE. "Some Remarks on E.P. Thompson's Opinion of
    the Poetry of WM." Philologica Pragensia, 3, no. 3:168-78.
        While agreeing that E.P. Thompson (1955.15) is authoritative
    and valuable, that that book should make it difficult for those who
    would side-step WM's socialism, this article insists that its
    judgments about WM's literary output are weak and that it is
    "ahistorical to condemn Morris's choice of the form of Paradise as
    pure escapism." Argues that Paradise is an important "first stage"
    toward a synthesis for WM of longing and achievement, that within
    its cycle "Gudrun" signals a turn toward realism and a new
    responsibility to face squarely personal and social issues, not only
    in the political prose he was to write (which E.P. Thompson covers
    adequately), but also in his subsequent poetry and prose romances.

20 KOCMANOVA, JESSIE. "Two Uses of the Dream Form as a Means of
    Confronting the Present with the National Past: WM and Svatopluk
    Chech." Brno Studies in English, no. 2:113-48. (Vol. 68, Opera
    Universitatis Purkynianae Brunenis.)
        Compares John Ball and Svatopluk Chech's The New,
    Epoch-making Journey of Mr. Beetle Back to the Fifteenth Century
    (Prague, 1888). The contemporary setting within each fiction is the
    1880s, and each one has a dreamer awake in the medieval past, where
    his comments on that society reflect on problems within his own.
    Offers a biographical sketch of WM and a useful discussion of John
    Ball and why its exposition is effective both as narrative and as
    political polemic, finely tuned for Commonweal readers. The Czech
    satire is, on the other hand, an erratic mix of seriousness and
    iconoclastic humor.

21 LOWE, W.F. "Restoration of Morris Windows at the Victorian and Albert Museum." Museums Journal 60 (August):121-22.
     The windows in "The Green Dining Room" (now "The WM Room") at the Victoria and Albert were severely damaged during the blitz. This short article describes some of the problems faced when the six windows were restored.

22 MAC DONALD, JEAN. A Guide to Red House. London: WM Society, 1960, 8 pp.
     Presents history of Red House, its inception, its setting, and its significance as a "landmark in English domestic architecture," as a "starting point for a revolt against the mid-Victorian commercialism which was producing the cheap and ugly household articles shown at the 1851 exhibition." That revolt led ultimately to Morris and Co., to the rise of modern interior design, all via Red House. Its design, decorations, and furnishings are discussed in detail. Includes commentary on changes made over the years and the condition and location of certain pieces, and the like.

23 PERRINE, LAURENCE. "WM's Guenevere: An Interpretation." PQ 39, no. 2 (April):234-41.
     Reminds us of an essential point: "The Defence of Guenevere" was "written by a reader of Malory for readers of Malory," and therefore we must recognize that WM did indeed consider Guenevere guilty, but in her own defense of her actions (not WM's), she is made to seem sympathetic and "intensely alive." WM, unlike Tennyson, avoids didacticism, sees his task as "not to excuse or to blame, but to vivify." See 1963.6.

24 SEWTER, A.C. "D.G. Rossetti's Designs for Stained Glass." British Society of Master Glass-Painters Journal 13:419-24.
     Since H.C. Marillier's 1899 list of Rossetti's designs for windows is incomplete and full of errors, the author here attempts a complete list of the designs Rossetti made for Morris and Co. stained glass. Includes four full-page illustrations.

25 SEWTER, A.C. "WM's Designs for Stained Glass." Architectural Review 127, no. 757 (March):196-200.
     An examination of over 1,000 windows in 400 buildings all across England, and a close look at the Marillier records show that WM's designs for Morris and Co. stained glass went far beyond the mere background and foliage that Mackail (1899.10) suggested. He did 129 cartoons, many of them large figures, and background devices of astonishing variety, these showing the influence of his work with tapestries. He also learned to use yellow stain so as to render on glass the equivalent of embroidery or damask in costumes. The Archangels window at King's Walden, perhaps the single "greatest

success in modern stained glass," was designed in its entirety by WM, and it shows his skill with figures, backgrounds, and yellow stain. Includes lavish illustrations.

*26 SHRAGIN, B. "Nasledie WM" [The legacy of WM]. Dekorativnoe iskusstvo v SSSR, no. 5.
      In Russian. Translated: 1960.27.

27 SHRAGIN, B. "The Legacy of WM." Anglo-Soviet Journal 21 (Autumn):15-21.
      Castigates those bourgeois critics who have perpetrated ideas that WM was only an idealistic dreamer rather than a progressive socialist who had correctly understood the relationship between decorative arts and objective social conditions. Contrasts WM's attitudes on history to those of Ruskin, seen here as a nostalgic reporter, and underlines WM's debt to Marx. Concludes with a summary of "A Factory as it Might Be." Translated from 1960.26.

28 STEDMAN, JANE. "A Victorian in Iceland." Opera News 24, no. 16 (20 February):8-9, 23.
      WM had more exact knowledge of the Volsung tales than Wagner did, but he wanted to transmit the story, not transform it. Comments upon the translations and transformations, quotes WM on Wagner, and concludes that we may now doubt WM's judgment that Wagner was "anti-artistic."

*29 STINGLE, RICHARD. "WM." Association of Canadian Teachers of English Report, Spring, pp. 4-10.
      Cited in 1964.13.

30 WILSON, F.A.C. Yeats's Iconography. London: Gollancz, pp. 52-59, passim.
      Paraphrases Well, pointing out its archetypal patterns, arguing that Yeats valued the romance highly and that a full understanding of his At the Hawk's Well depends upon a knowledge of Yeats's attitude toward WM and his prose romances. Discusses Yeats's "difficult essay" (1903.9) on WM.

31 WRIGHT, FRANK LLOYD. "The Art and Craft of the Machine." In Writings and Buildings. Selected by E. Kaufman and J.B. Raeburn. New York: Horizon Press, pp. 55-74.
      Argues that "in the machine lies the only future of art and craft," despite what the disciples of Ruskin and WM say to the contrary. Though WM was wrong about the machine, failing to perceive that it could bring democracy to design, all artists must honor him: "He did the best in his time for art and will live in

history as the great socialist." A lecture given to the Chicago
Arts and Crafts Society on 6 March 1901 and printed in full for the
first time in this collection.

32 WM and the Kelmscott Press. A Catalogue of an Exhibition Held
    in the Brown University Library from 9 October-31 December,
    1959. Providence, R.I.: Brown University Press, 49 pp.
        Exhibited items here arranged under nine general categories
ranging from "The Universal Artist" to three separate ones on the
Kelmscott Chaucer, one of which is on Burne-Jones's illustrations.
Since many of these items were once owned by Cockerell, specific
insertions and memorabilia are of particular interest. Includes
sixteen plates and an address given by Philip C. Duschnes to the
Friends of the Library of Brown University on 7 December 1959
(1960.12).

                              1961

1   ARMYTAGE, W.H.G. Heavens Below: Utopian Experiments in England:
    1560-1960. London: Routledge and Kegan Paul, pp. 307-8, passim.
        Points out that WM focused the Ruskinian social vision so
that future reformers could make better use of it. Comments upon
John Ball and Nowhere, and compares WM to Sir Thomas Browne and his
concern with the destruction time brings.

2   BARLING, ELIZABETH. "Picnic Encore." Gazette of the John Lewis
    Partnership 43 (7 October):839.
        Describes a visit members of the Partnership undertook to
Standen, a house designed by Webb, one with a splendid Morris and
Co. interior.

3   BARLING, ELIZABETH. "Picnic Extraordinairy 1961." Gazette of
    the John Lewis Partnership 43 (24 June):484-86.
        Reports upon a visit fifty "partners" undertook to Red House,
where they all were duly impressed by the grounds and interiors. At
the picnic, they listened to readings from WM, who--as a
profit-sharing manufacturer--is here regarded as a sort of spiritual
father of the John Lewis Partnership.

4   BELL, MALCOLM. Sir Burne-Jones. London: G. Bell and Sons,
    passim.
        Among other brief remarks on the collaboration of WM and
Burne-Jones, he asserts that the friendship begun at Oxford "has had
an influence quite immeasurable upon the art of the last thirty
years."

5   BRIGGS, R.C.H.   "Editorial Note."   JWMS 1, no. 1 (Winter):3.
      Offers reasons, both financial and ideological, for the
appearance of the JWMS six years after the founding of the Society.

6   BRIGGS, R.C.H.   "Trafalgar Square, 13 November 1887."   JWMS 1,
      no. 1 (Winter):28-31.
      Reprints and comments upon forceful letters WM wrote
protesting the Tory government's 1887 decision to close Trafalgar
Square for public meetings.

7   BRIGGS, R.C.H.   A Handlist of the Public Addresses of WM to be
      Found in Generally Accessible Publications.   London: WM Society,
      16 pp.
      Includes a short history of WM's career as a public speaker
from his first address in December 1877 to the Trades Guild of
Learning "in a dismal hole near Oxford Street" through the peak
years of 1886-87, when he gave some sixty lectures a year. Listed
here are seventy-five lectures, the dates they were first given, the
audiences, and the places where they have been published.

8   BUSHELL, HUGH.   "In the Footsteps of WM."   Times Educational
      Supplement no. 2426 (17 November):681.
      A shorter version of 1961.9; includes a few photographs.

9   BUSHELL, HUGH.   "News from Iceland."   JWMS 1, no. 1
      (Winter):7-12.
      Comments on WM's two journeys to Iceland and on the
importance of the Icelandic Journals, suggesting that there are
revealing passages in them that answer, indirectly, the question,
"What Came We Forth to See?" Reports on the 1961 journey to Iceland
of four WM Society members who "set out in July in search of this
Northern spirit in Morris." Though they used Land Rovers instead of
ponies, the trek over all of WM's 1871 route and part of that for
1873 still had many hazards. Concludes with examples that suggest
WM is better-known in Iceland than in Britain. Reprinted. 1961.8.

10 COCKERELL, S.C.   "The President Writes."   JWMS 1, no. 1
      (Winter):1.
      Cockerell, the first president of WM Society, here recalls,
for the opening number of JWMS, the meals he shared with WM at
Gatti's in the Strand (his diaries show that he ate with him there
125 times) "as among the happiest and merriest in my long life."

11 DUNLAP, JOSEPH R. "Forsooth, Brothers." In Morris Lore, Arm
    and Torch Series, no. 4. San Francisco: M. Sanford, 4 pp.
        Biographical sketch lauding WM's achievements, inviting "all
who have felt his influence or would know more about WM" to join the
WM Society; membership dues were two dollars a year.

12 FAIRBANK, ALFRED. "WM and Calligraphy." JWMS 1, no. 1
    (Winter):5-6.
        Reprints a page of WM's calligraphy and comments on his
pioneering use of the italic hand.

13 FLOUD, PETER. "The Influence of WM." CIBA Review 1:21-23.
        In no field was WM's influence "more striking" than in
printed textiles. Discusses his association with Thomas Wardle with
whom he produced sixteen fabrics before removing to Merton Abbey
where his remaining twenty-eight chintz designs were printed. These
fabrics became immensely popular in England and America, and WM's
"liberating example" influenced Crane and MacMurdo.

14 GLOAG, JOHN. Victorian Comfort: A Social History of Design from
    1830 to 1900. London: Adam and Charles Black; Newton Abbot:
    David and Charles, pp. 52-53, passim.
        Morris and Co. products were sometimes esteemed by "happy
intellectuals," who adapted a hand-woven look and sought out
Cotswald cottages to live in, a type lampooned by Punch. But others
also purchased Morris and Co. furniture, much of it reasonably
priced, and so WM and his Firm made a significant contribution to
Victorian ideas of gracious living.

15 GRAHAM, HUGH. "Morris and Company." Spectator, no. 6930 (21
    April):559.
        Despite some misleading comments about wanting to return to
the Middle Ages and about having started the Arts and Crafts
Society, this article makes several valid points about WM and Morris
and Co., and about its significance to modern decorative arts.
Suggests reasons for Morris and Co.'s decline in the twentieth
century.

16 GRAY, DONALD J. "Arthur, Roland, Empedocles, Sigurd, and the
    Despair of Heroes in Victorian Poetry." Boston University
    Studies in English 5, no. 1 (Spring):1-17.
        Asserts that all four of these heroes "attempt to establish
in the error and anarchy and waste of their times a code which will
regenerate men and direct their actions toward good. Whatever their
personal triumphs, each fails to accomplish his purpose." Suggests
that this failure has to do with Victorian malaise, thus overlooking

fact that, in Sigurd's case at least, the failure is woven into the traditional narrative that WM followed.

17 HABERLY, LOYD. "By His Works." JWMS 1, no. 1 (Winter):19-20.
    Recalls a few anecdotes about WM, as designer, told him by Mrs. Gaskell and Catterson-Smith.

18 HILL, SHEILA. "A WM Revival?" Harrodian Gazette, January, pp. 20-21.
    A biographical sketch stresses WM's work in the decorative arts, its lasting influence; points out that WM wallpapers and chintzes are presently available in London, at Sandersons, and elsewhere.

19 JOHNSTON, GEORGE. "On Translation: II." Saga Book of the Viking Society. 15:394-402.
    Argues that modern English is not necessarily wrong for saga rhetoric, as long as the translation is "close." A free rendering into idiomatic modern English will miss certain pecularities, like shifting tenses, which are hallmarks of saga style.

*20 LAMB, AINSLIE. "WM--The Socialism of Culture." Radical (Melbourne, Australia), September, p. 7.
    Cited in 1964.13.

21 LILIENTHAL, THEODORE. A WM Press Goes West. Berkeley, Calif.: Tamalpais Press, 6 pp.
    Recounts how the smaller of the Kelmscott presses made its way from a London bookshop in the 1920s to California, where it now resides in the Huntington Library. Reprinted from Hoja Volante, a quarterly publication of the Zamorano Club in Los Angeles.

22 LINDSAY, JACK. WM: Writer. London: WM Society, 30 pp.
    A lecture delivered to WM Society 14 November 1958 which asserts that the increasing attention paid to WM as designer and as politician has obscured the fact that there are "elements of greatness in his writing, above all in his earlier poems, in Nowhere, in many of his later lectures or essays." Discusses these works in some detail, making fresh points regarding links between the Spasmodic poets of the 1840s and Defence, and the direct influence WM had on Yeats: "Without Morris it would be impossible to conceive Yeats' development into a great poet."

23 MAXWELL, IAN R. "On Translation: I." Saga Book of the Viking
    Society 15:383-93.
         Claims that the archaic language in WM's translations serves
    "to clog the vigour of the original," admitting that for some
    readers that language might provide a sense of Germanic style and
    even of ironic possibilities. Discusses several examples.

24 MEIER, PAUL. "WM: l'homme, l'ecrivain, le militant." In WM:
    "Nouvelles de nulle part". Paris: Editions Sociales, pp. 7-87.
         Full and detailed introduction takes up many of the issues to
    be explored more comprehensively in the two-volume study published a
    decade later (1972.19), issues which demonstrate how Nowhere is
    dependent in significant ways upon Marxist ideas and assumptions.

25 MORRIS, BARBARA. Introduction to Morris and Company,
    1861-1940. Catalogue of a Commemorative Centenary Exhibition,
    April 1961, at the Victoria and Albert. London: Arts Council,
    pp. 5-8.
         Offers precise information on the backgrounds of Morris and
    Co. and its achievements and influence.

26 MORRIS, BARBARA. "WM: A Twentieth Century View of His Woven
    Textiles." Handweaver and Craftsman 12 (Spring):6-11, 54-55.
         Though WM is heralded as responsible for the revival of
    handweaving, his views and practices differ widely from those now
    held: "the type of handwoven fabrics designed by Morris would almost
    certainly be excluded from any exhibition of handwoven fabrics
    today." Quotes from and comments upon WM's ideas about weaving in
    "The Lesser Arts of Life," and then discusses the designs and
    techniques of extant Morris and Co. fabrics. Because only nine of
    fifty designs attributed to WM were registered, this discussion is
    necessarily tentative, but it is fully detailed and includes
    comments upon the influence on WM of fabric designs at the South
    Kensington, the weaving conditions at Merton Abbey ("idyllic"), and
    the other firms who contracted Morris and Co. work. Concludes with
    lists of Morris and Co. fabrics held by the Metropolitan and Cooper
    Union museums in New York City.

27 MORRIS, BARBARA. "WM: His Designs for Carpets and Tapestries."
    Handweaver and Craftsman 12 (Fall):18-21, 36.
         Though WM had small regard for the machine-made carpets
    outside firms produced for Morris and Co., he took pains with their
    design, and "some of his most attractive patterns are found in this
    comparatively humble field." Of the dozen or more designs WM made
    for such carpets only a few examples survive; these are here
    discussed, as are WM's attitudes toward Persian carpets, which he
    admired immensely while arguing that they must not be imitated by
    modern, western designers. Describes WM's ideas about tapestries,

his own efforts to teach himself to weave them, and the splendid
Merton Abbey tapestries designed by himself and Burne-Jones.
Concludes that the "best of Merton Abbey tapestries can proudly take
their place beside the most splendid products of the medieval
looms."

28 PETERS, ROBERT L., ed. Victorians on Literature and Art. New
    York: Appleton-Century-Crofts, pp. 279-96.
       Includes two lectures: "Art and the People" and "At a Picture
Show." Both have been "slightly shortened," and both have a brief
introduction.

29 ROSENBERG, JOHN D. The Darkening Glass: A Portrait of Ruskin's
    Genius. New York: Columbia University Press, pp. 52-53, passim.
       Discusses ways that Ruskin's "The Nature of Gothic"
influenced WM. Points out that in Nowhere, WM "with documentary
horror depicts a bloody class-war," but once the revolution is over
the new society is a sort of pastoral Eden, one that is close to a
national British ideal through the nineteenth and twentieth
centuries.

30 SEWTER, A.C. "Notes on Morris and Company's Domestic Stained
    Glass." JWMS 1, no. 1 (Winter):22-28.
       Lists, under seven subject categories, the stained glass that
Morris and Co. made for private houses, giving present locations if
known, requesting information on the possible whereabouts of missing
pieces. The categories: (1) Viking subjects, including planets, (2)
figures of poets, (3) Chaucer's good women, (4) Chaucer's heroines
in roundels, (5) minstrel figures, (6) scenes from the Life of St.
George, (7) miscellaneous.

31 STOKES, E.E. "WM and Bernard Shaw." JWMS 1, no. 1
    (Winter):13-18.
       Argues that Shaw's "twelve-year friendship with WM was the
single most valuable contact in Shaw's long and varied life,"
offering evidence turned up in the Shaw Collection at the University
of Texas. Not only Shaw's attention "to handsomeness of the
published book," but also "to the aesthetic quality" of socialism,
he owed to WM. Divides their socialist relationship into active and
intellectual phases, with Bloody Sunday marking the division.
Offers some details of their common interests and goals, pointing
out that Shaw's essay (1936.12) is the best source for understanding
and estimating WM's continuing influence on Shaw and that his
founding in 1907 of the Fabian Arts Group was "intended as a
demonstration of the Morrisian principle that socialism and art
might be blended."

32 SWANNELL, J.N. "WM as an Interpreter of Old Norse." <u>Saga</u> <u>Book</u>
    <u>of</u> <u>the</u> <u>Viking</u> <u>Society</u> 15:365-82.
        Demonstrates why and how Old Norse was "an overwhelming
    influence" on WM, offering fresh insights into "Gudrun" and <u>Sigurd</u>,
    and into the translation practices of WM and Magnusson; concludes
    that the volumes in <u>The</u> <u>Saga</u> <u>Library</u> are a "fitting memorial to the
    twenty years of close collaboration between the two men."

33 SWANNELL, J.N. <u>WM</u> <u>and</u> <u>Old</u> <u>Norse</u> <u>Literature:</u> <u>A</u> <u>Lecture</u> <u>Given</u> <u>on</u>
    <u>18</u> <u>December</u> <u>1958</u>. London: WM Society, 21 pp.
        Recounts how his own love for Old Norse led him "to a wider
    appreciation of the greatness of Morris as a man and as a writer."
    Says that "Morris, more than any writer of his time, had identified
    himself with the spirit and the literature of the vikings."
    Demonstrates, then, how this is true by drawing on both casual
    comments from the letters, reviews, and lectures, and also on
    explications of Norse themes in the poetry, especially from "The
    Fostering of Aslaug" and from "Gudrun." Concludes with sensitive
    comments about his saga translations, which though they might be "a
    hindrance to the modern reader" were for WM a necessary preparation
    for "the strange and wonderful prose romances of his later years."

34 TAVERNE, DICK. "The WM Tradition." <u>Socialist</u> <u>Commentary</u>
    (October):26-27.
        Discusses an important tradition of socialist thought, one
    concerned with the quality of life rather than with mere economics,
    maintaining that WM was its most eloquent spokesman and that this
    tradition now deserves a central place in Leftist politics.

35 TSUZUKI, CHUSHICHI. <u>H.M.</u> <u>Hyndman</u> <u>and</u> <u>British</u> <u>Socialism</u>.
    Oxford: Oxford University Press, pp. 61-67, passim.
        Presents Hyndman's position on the issues that separated him
    and WM, discussing also those issues upon which they agreed, like
    the Jameson raid, which they both denounced. Comments upon the
    editorial and financial arrangements at the offices of <u>Justice</u>,
    contrasting that journal to <u>Commonweal</u>.

36 YEATS, W.B. "Louis Lambert." In <u>Essays</u> <u>and</u> <u>Introductions</u>. New
    York: Macmillan, p. 447.
        Reprint of 1934.79.

37 "Morris and Company." New Yorker (23 November):43-44.
     A note on Columbia University's exhibit which celebrated the
centenary of Morris and Co.; WM's many achievements impress even the
scribe for "The Talk of the Town."

38 "WM, Esquire." Interior Design 32, no. 2 (February):132-33.
     Noting that April 1961 marks the centenary of Morris and Co.,
the author reminds his readers that "with the founding of the
company, our contemporary profession had its virtual inauguration."
Touches upon circumstances of Morris and Co.'s opening, and mentions
modern American firms that carry Morris and Co. designs.

39 Designs for Beauty And Use: an Exhibition Commemorating the
     Founding of Morris and Co.: 1861-1940. Catalogue of an
     Exhibition during October-November at Columbia University. New
     York: WM Society and Columbia University, 8 pp.
     A short introduction plus a chronology of the Firm precedes
descriptions of the exhibited items which included original designs,
fabrics, Kelmscott Press books, and photographs.

40 Morris and Company, 1861-1940. Catalogue of a Commemorative
     Centenary Exhibition, April 1961, at the Victoria and Albert.
     London: Arts Council, 32 pp.
     Has short descriptions for the ninety-two exhibited items,
which appear under five chronological headings, from "Morris,
Marshall, Faulkner Co., 1861-1865" to "Morris and Co., 1896-1940:
The Successors." Includes a short introduction by Barbara Morris
(1961.25), three pages of biographical notes, a few plates.

1962

1 ASLIN, ELIZABETH. "Morris and Company." In Nineteenth Century
     English Furniture. London: Faber and Faber, pp. 55-59, passim.
     Even though "two of the most popular Victorian chairs bear
his name and so much furniture is attributed to him, it is almost
certain that WM never designed any furniture." Sketches in growth
of Morris and Co., commenting on the furniture Brown and Webb
designed, pointing out that furniture production was not significant
at Morris and Co. until 1890 when new cabinet-making premises were
acquired and when George Jack became the chief furniture designer.

2   BAYLEN, J.O. "Shaw and the Socialist League: Some Unpublished
     Letters." International Review of Social History 7, pt.
     3:426-40.
         Though Shaw never joined the Socialist League, he was an
effective speaker for their cause, and this article includes twenty
letters, and cards, which he wrote to the Socialist League
secretaries between 20 January 1885 and 26 October 1887; these are
usually to fix lecture dates, but other issues and figures, like
Gordon in Khartoum, Mrs. Besant, and a Shaw debate with Bradlaugh,
make them of more than passing interest.

3   BOWMAN, SYLVIA. Edward Bellamy Abroad: An American Prophet's
     Influence. New York: Twayne Publishers, pp. 90-94, passim.
         WM castigated Bellamy for assuming that a "new society could
be the result of evolution rather than revolution." Asserts that WM
misunderstood Bellamy's "moral and intellectual objectives" without
stating why, or what these were. Paraphrases sections of Nowhere.

4   BRIGGS, ASA, ed. Introduction to WM: Selected Writings and
     Designs. With a supplement by Graeme Shankland on WM, designer,
     illustrated by twenty-four plates. Harmondsorth and Baltimore:
     Penguin Books, pp. 13-26. Reprint. 1968, 1973, 1977, 1980.
         Short but detailed biographical sketch emphasizes WM's social
commitment and presents him as "one of the most searching critics of
British society in the nineteenth century." Includes a note on
basic sources and a chronological table of WM's life and chief
publications. The fifty-two selections in the anthology include
sixteen from the poetry, the remainder from lectures, letters,
articles from both Justice and Commonweal, and most of Nowhere
(chapters 19-32 are omitted). An insert on WM as designer has
twenty-four plates and an introduction by Graeme Shankland to the
more than 600 original designs created by WM within several
different crafts; see 1962.42.

5   BRIGGS, R.C.H. "I am, Sir, your Obedient Servant." JWMS 1, no.
     2 (Winter):18-26.
         Lists over one hundred letters, from 1883 to 1962, that
Cockerell sent "to the Press." Many of the themes are pertinent to
prevailing interests of WM, and sixteen deal directly with WM or the
Kelmscott Press.

6   BRIGGS, R.C.H.   "'She and He.'"   <u>JWMS</u> 1, no. 2 (Winter):15-17.
      Reprints drafts as well as fair copy made by Cockerell of a
poem, "She and He," written by WM in 1896. Includes brief
introduction.

7   BRIGGS, R.C.H.   <u>A</u> <u>Guide</u> <u>to</u> <u>Kelmscott</u> <u>House</u>. London: WM Society,
      20 pp.
      Describes Kelmscott House, built ca. 1780, and some of its
previous owners, including the inventor of the electric telegraph
and the novelist George Macdonald. Reprints letters WM sent to
Janey, who needed some convincing since she thought the house too
distant from London, but they moved in by October 1878. Concludes
with descriptions of Kelmscott House gleaned from the writings of
Shaw, Katherine Tynan, and May Morris.

8   BUENGER, SIEGFRIED. <u>Friedrich</u> <u>Engels</u> <u>und</u> <u>die</u> <u>britische</u>
      <u>sozialistische</u> <u>Bewegung,</u> <u>1881-1895</u>. Berlin: Rutten and Loenig,
      pp. 70-78, passim.
      Because Engels is the main focus of this fully detailed study
and because Germans figured in controversies that led to formation
of the Socialist League as well as to WM's departure from it five
years later, some new light is shed on WM's significance to British
socialism and on the ways that significance emerged in his
collaborations with Bax and in his writings for <u>Commonweal</u>.

9   CARTER, SEBASTIAN. "The Two Typographies." <u>Granta</u> 65
      (January):2-8.
      Discusses the "legend" (the famed slide-show) of the founding
of Kelmscott Press, pointing out that not all pre-Kelmscott printing
was bad, that WM's often is: Chaucer type is called "a rotund Gothic
of considerable massiveness and illegibility." Points out that
critics should distinguish between the stylistic and the ideological
influence of Kelmscott Press, mentioning several presses and
printers as examples.

10 CASSON, HUGH. <u>An</u> <u>Introduction</u> <u>to</u> <u>Victorian</u> <u>Architecture</u>. New
      York: Pellegrini and Cudehy, pp. 38-41.
      A biographical sketch precedes descriptions of Red House and
its significance for modern architecture: "to the Gothicists it
seemed as if Webb had dropped a brick at Bexley. But it was the
first of a cartload."

11 COCKERELL, S.C. "Notes on Warington Taylor and Philip Webb."
     JWMS 1, no. 2 (Winter):6-10.
        Sketches in connections both Webb and Taylor had with Morris,
Marshall, Faulkner Co., and Morris and Co., stressing that Taylor
"was not only a master of figures, but an expert in business
methods." Includes a biographical sketch of Taylor and his own
memories of Webb.

*12 ELEMER, NAGY. "The Studio of WM." Magyar Epitomuveszet,
     Spring, pp. 47-49.
        In Hungarian. Cited in 1964.13.

13 FAULKNER, PETER. WM and Yeats. Dublin: Dolmen Press, 31 pp.
        Points out that although the "final political and social
attitudes of Morris and Yeats are in the strongest contrast," with
the one "democratic and optimistic," the other "aristocratic and
pessimistic," there are still "intimate connections between the two
men." In this prize-winning essay (the Peter Floud Memorial
Competition for 1961), such connections are examined and three
aspects of WM's influence are considered: "as poet, as generous
personality, as social critic." Concludes that WM was not a major
influence as poet, that, in fact, "the process by which Yeats became
aware of the limitations of Morris's poetry was part of the critical
effort by which he himself became a great poet," using for instance
colloquial diction rather than conscious archaism. In WM's
personality, Yeats particularly admired his spontanaity and passion.
And in WM's "denunciation of commercialism with its attendant
avarice and shoddiness" Yeats found elements that gave "a ferocity
to his verse."

14 GLOAG, JOHN. "Ruskin to WM." In Victorian Taste: Some Social
     Aspects of Architecture and Design from 1820 to 1900. London:
     Adam and Charles Black, pp. 71-100, passim.
        A biographical sketch which lingers over the Oxford days of
"Brotherhood" and discusses Red House as a "progenitor of a new
school of architecture." Quotes from Nowhere, but undercuts and
downplays WM's socialism. Points to WM influence on Ragnar
Ostberg's Townhall in Stockholm.

15 GRIERSON, JANET. Isabella Gilmore, Sister to WM. London:
     S.P.C.K., pp. 1-4, 233-35, passim.
        WM gave her away when Isabella, his sister, was married in
1860, and after her husband, a naval officer, died in 1882 WM saw
her more frequently, commenting once, "I preach socialism; you
practice it." She trained to be a nurse, was ordained a deaconess,
and at her brother's urgings Webb designed a chapel for her.

16 GRYLLS, R. GLYNN [Mander, Rosalie]. "Wightwick Manor--a WM
    Period Piece." Connoisseur 149, no. 599 (January):3-11.
        Theodore Mander who built Wightwick Manor, near
Wolverhampton, in the late 1880s, was "aesthetically advanced enough
in his day to order his furnishings and wall-coverings from the Firm
of Morris and Co." The Manor was accepted by the National Trust in
1937, and the present occupants have maintained the Morris and Co.
decor, adding paintings, Swinburne's bed, and other period articles;
includes ten plates that help give an idea of the treasures within
the Manor.

17 GUTMAN, ROBERT W., ed.   Introduction to "Volsunga," Translated
    by WM. London and New York: Collier Books, pp. 13-79. Reprint.
    1967.
        Discusses both the Icelandic and German versions of the
Volsung legends and tales, and then carefully relates them to the
two greatest nineteenth-century redactions: Wagner's operatic cycle
and WM's Sigurd. Surveys WM's early interests in Old Norse, his
collaborations with Magnusson, his journeys to Iceland, and reasons
he thought the Volsung legend so wonderful, Wagner's treatment of it
so demeaning. Concludes with a discussion of Sigurd and of the
Morris-Magnusson translation, Volsunga.

18 HENDERSON, PHILIP. "Visiting Sir Sydney." JWMS 1, no. 2
    (Winter):12-14.
        Henderson visited Cockerell several times during 1948 and
1949, and here he reports upon his incisive and reverential memories
of WM and his works.

*19 KAGARLITSKY, YURI, trans.   Nowhere. Moscow: Moscow State Library
    Publishing.
        Cited in 1964.13.

20 LEMIRE, E.D. "The Unpublished Lectures of WM: A Critical
    Edition, Including an Introductory Survey and a Calendar and
    Bibliography." Dissertation, Wayne State University.
        Abstracted: DA 24:3325-A. Revised for publication: 1969.18.

21 LIEBERMAN, BEN. "The Liberty Bell on the Kelmscott Goudy
    Press." Black Art 1, no. 2 (Summer):41-49.
        Recounts history and perigrinations of an Albion press which
WM had purchased specifically for heavy work on Kelmscott Chaucer.
Later Ashbee acquired it, using it at his Essex House Press; in 1924
it was shipped to New York and used by Goudy at the Village Press,
then by several other printers before finding a home with the
Liebermans, who added atop it a bell: "So long as the private press
wears liberty as her crown, the people are free."

22 LISTER, RAYMOND. "WM: Universal Craftsman." In <u>Great</u>
    <u>Craftsmen</u>. London: G. Bell and Sons, pp. 157-73.
        Unremarkable sketch, one intended for juvenile readers, with
misleading generalities: marriage provided WM a "happy domestic
background, a circumstance always of the greatest importance to an
energetic and creative worker."

23 MAC BRIER, A.M. <u>Fabian Socialism and English Politics,</u>
    <u>1884-1918</u>. Cambridge: Cambridge University Press, pp. 8, 20-21,
    296-97.
        Comments favorably on WM's continuing efforts to warn
socialists away from the temptations of parliamentary reform,
pointing out that Glasier in this respect did not heed his master
and that a "great deal of nonsense has been written about Morris's
relation with Marxism solely on the basis of an anecdote in which he
confessed he was not an expert in Marxist economics."

24 MAYFIELD, JOHN S. "Unequivocal WM." <u>Courier</u> (Syracuse
    University Library) 2:16.
        Reprints and comments briefly upon a short letter, one with a
resounding "No," which WM wrote to Furnivall.

25 MORISON, STANLEY. "WM." In <u>On Type Design, Past and Present: A</u>
    <u>Brief Introduction</u>. London: Ernest Benn, pp. 67-69, passim.
        Sets Kelmscott Press types within a broad survey of five
hundred years of type design, suggesting that Kelmscott Press
altered press traditions in Germany more than in Britain or America.
Mentions several German printers and private presses.

26 MORRIS, BARBARA. "WM Embroideries." In <u>Victorian Embroidery</u>.
    London: Herbert Jenkins. Reprint. New York: Universe Books,
    1970, pp. 95-112, passim.
        WM completed embroideries, like the "If I Can" piece and the
"Illustrious Women" hangings for Red House, long before the Firm
advertised "embroideries of all kinds." Those early achievements as
well as the many later commissions done by Morris and Co. are here
discussed in detail, as is the influence that Morris and Co.
embroideries had in Britain and in America.

27 MUNBY, LIONEL L. "WM's Romances and the Society of the
    Future." <u>Zeitschrift fur Anglistik und Amerikanistik</u> 10:56-70.
        Originally a lecture for an East German audience, and since
WM's prose romances are "almost unattainable" there, considerable
quotation and paraphrase accompany interpretations that see the
romances as efforts "to understand the morality of Communist
society," as well as works that can illuminate WM's more

specifically socialist writings, with <u>Pilgrims</u>, for example, seen as
<u>Wolfings</u> in a contemporary setting.

28 PURKIS, JOHN. <u>The Icelandic Jaunt: A Study of the Expeditions</u>
    <u>Made by WM to Iceland in 1871 and 1873.</u> London: WM Society, 28
    pp. Reprint. Folcroft, Pa.: Folcroft Editions, 1973, 1977.
    Norwood, Pa.: Norwood Editions, 1978.
        Essay that sets forth reasons why "WM in Iceland is an
    attractive figure," one who because of his journeys there formed
    "his character thereafter on the model of its courageous and active
    heroes." Judges the <u>Icelandic Journals</u>, "our record of this
    transformation," to be one of WM's "great books," in style and
    rhetoric unlike much of his other prose. Contrasts the 1871 record
    with the 1873, which he claims has a "greater emotional detachment"
    and thus a "truer insight into the real Iceland" and into WM having
    "worked out a neurosis."

*29 SAMAAN, ANGELE BOTRAS. "A Poet's Vision of the Socialist
     Millennium: <u>Nowhere</u> and Its Critics." <u>Bulletin of the Faculty</u>
     <u>of Arts, Cairo University</u> 24, no. 2 (December).
         Cited in paper read by L. Sargent at 1984 MLA session on WM.

30 SEWTER, A.C. "Victorian Stained Glass." <u>Apollo</u> 76:760-65.
        WM'S talents and energies drew artists and designers like
    Burne-Jones and Webb into Morris and Co. projects, and they produced
    some of the finest stained glass made in England since the sixteenth
    century. Such achievements influenced many other artists working in
    stained glass, and several of them are here mentioned.

31 STAVENOW, ELISABET. "WM i nytt ljus" [WM in a new light].
    <u>Form</u> (Stockholm) 10:658-63.
        In Swedish. Reports upon the research of Peter Floud on WM's
    inconsistencies (1959.4). Includes a biographical sketch and
    several illustrations as well as comments upon WM's influence in
    Sweden.

32 TSCHAN, ANDRE. <u>WM [1834-1896]: poete, ecrivain, esthete,</u>
    <u>renovateur de l'art du livre, tribun politique et imprimeur</u>.
    Paris: Societe Anonyme Monotype, 36 pp.
        Opens with biographical sketch, which is followed by a full
    and specific discussion of all aspects of Kelmscott Press. Here the
    evidence was first presented that WM's Golden type was based on
    Jacques Le Rouge rather than on Jansen types. Concludes with a
    brief discussion of Kelmscott Press influence in Europe and America.

*33 WATKINSON, RAY. "WM, a Socialist Artist." Magyar
     Epitomuveszet, Spring, pp. 44-45.
         In Hungarian. Cited in 1964.13.

34 WEEVERS, THEODOOR. "On the Origins of an Accentual Verse Form
    Used by WM and Henriette Roland Holst." Neophilologus 46, no.
    3:210-26.
        Suggests influence WM had on Dutch poetess, Henriette Roland
    Holst, both in terms of socialist ideas and of her prosody, pointing
    out similarities between structures in her poems and those of WM,
    notably Pilgrims and Sigurd.

35 WINGLER, HANS M. Das Bauhaus. Cologne: Rasch. Translated by
    W. Jabs and B. Gilbert as The Bauhaus: Weimar, Dessau, Berlin,
    Chicago. Cambridge, Mass.: MIT Press, p. 19.
        Comments on the importance and wide influence, especially on
    ideas within the Bauhaus group about the environment, that an 1884
    WM lecture exerted in Germany, thanks to a translation done in 1901
    and then widely distributed.

36 YEATS, W.B. Introduction to Lady Gregory's Cuchulaine. In
    Explorations. New York: Macmillan, pp. 3-8.
        Reprint of 1902.16.

37 YEATS, W.B. "Literature and the Living Voice." In
    Explorations. New York: Macmillan, pp. 210-11.
        Reprint of 1906.21.

38 YEATS, W.B. "If I Were Four and Twenty." In Explorations. New
    York: Macmillan, pp. 265-67.
        Reprint of 1919.8.

39 "Art and Politics." TLS, no. 3150 (13 July):516.
        Comments upon the contents of the first issue of JWMS,
    finding it interesting that the only article which might be
    construed as political is by an American: Stokes (1961.31).

40 "A Recommendation from WM." JWMS 1, no. 2 (Winter):27-28.
        Reprints holograph copy of December 1892 letter that WM
    wrote, recommending Cockerell for the curatorship of Soane's Museum
    in Lincoln's Inn Fields. Includes explanatory note.

41 "Leonardo of Retailing." Gazette of the John Lewis Partnership
    44, no. 7 (17 March):158-60.
        Reprints the 1886 "A Day in Surrey" by Emma Lazarus as well
    as an 1884 letter WM sent to her, this because the John Lewis
    Partnership had recently become a corporate member of the WM
    Society. Concludes with comments upon parallels that the author
    perceives between WM at Merton Abbey and the John Lewis Partnership
    and its workers.

42 The Work of WM. Catalogue of an Exhibition arranged by WM
    Society. London: Times Bookshop, 75 pp.
        This important exhibition was arranged to mark the
    publication of WM: Selected Writings and Designs (1962.4) and, like
    the book, it "seeks to present Morris the whole man" and to
    demonstrate the unity of his work. Detailed descriptions of the
    seventy-six items exhibited, ranging from illuminated manuscripts
    and decorated books to tapestries and socialist lectures, are
    arranged under six general headings, and each of these is provided
    with a short introduction.

43 WM: 1834-1896. London: Arthur Sanderson and Sons, 11 pp.
        Points out the connections between the London firm of
    Sanderson and Sons and Morris and Co.; includes a biographical
    sketch and details on Morris and Co. prints and wallpapers, many of
    which are currently produced by Sandersons.

                              1963

1   BANHAM, RAYNER. "The Reputation of WM." New Statesman 65, no.
    1669 (8 March):350-51.
        Suggests that Floud's research on WM's designs (1959.4) is a
    cause for WM's sagging reputation, and then wonders why that
    reputation had been so huge in the first place. Finds that Nowhere
    does not hold up, psychologically or politically.

2   BENEVOLO, LEONARDO. "Architettura e socialismo." Cultura
    moderna 4, 62 (October):6-8.
        Though WM's attitudes to socialism have been known in Italy
    at least since 1922, when Nowhere was first translated into Italian,
    his ideas about architecture have only recently become available to
    Italian readers.

3   BRANDON-JONES, JOHN. "Philip Webb." In <u>Victorian</u>
    <u>Architecture</u>. Edited by Peter Farraday. London: Cape.
    Reprint. New York: J.B. Lippincott, 1964, pp. 249-65.
        Discusses WM's close association with Webb from 1856 when
they were both employed by the architect George Street. Judges Red
House to be less innovative than usually suggested, pointing out
ways it resembled a vicerage house Webb designed with Street.
Giving servants a garden view was more revolutionary than any of the
architectural features. Characterizes Webb as the "grey eminence"
of Morris and Co, commenting upon his continuing importance to the
Firm.

4   BRIGGS, ASA. <u>Victorian Cities</u>. London: Oxford University
    Press. New York: Harper and Row, 1970, pp. 75, 329, 379-80.
        Comments upon Trafalgar Square Riot against the background of
urban problems in London and elsewhere, and discusses the London
that appears in <u>Nowhere</u> as a medieval city.

5   BRIGGS, R.C.H. "Printers of Hammersmith Reach." <u>British</u>
    <u>Printer</u>, July, 2 pp. Reprinted for WM Society members.
        Remarks on several buildings along the Upper Mall in
Hammersmith, buildings that housed famous printers at the end of the
nineteenth century. These range from Cobden-Sanderson to WM, and
the nearby residences of others associated with the book arts are
mentioned in this short and informal sort of tour-guide.

6   CARSON, MOTHER ANGELA. "WM's Guenevere: A Further Note." <u>PQ</u>
    42, no. 1 (January):131-34.
        Responds to Perrine's discussion of Guenevere's guilt
(1960.23), suggesting that WM followed up on portrayals in Malory of
Guenevere, who could honestly plead innocent to specific charges
while remaining generally guilty of adultery.

7   DAVIS, FRANK. "Expedition to Walthamstow." <u>Illustrated London</u>
    <u>News</u> 243 (7 September):352.
        Surveys the sorts of items exhibited at the WM Gallery in
Walthamstow, from cup and saucer WM used at his Sunday breakfasts
with Burne-Jones, to fine paintings by Courbet and Pissaro left to
the Gallery by Brangwyn.

8   DUFTY, A.R. "WM and the Kelmscott Estate." Antiquaries Journal
     43, pt. 1:97-116.
        Discusses not just Kelmscott Manor but also the adjacent
cottages and fields and how it all became the property of the
Society of Antiquaries; the article is meant "to answer inquiries
and to provide a record" of how a judgment was found that May
Morris's bequest of the Kelmscott Estate to Oxford was invalid.
Includes May Morris's will, with a list of contents of every room in
the Manor.

9   FAULKNER, PETER. "WM and Yeats." JWMS 1, no. 3 (Summer):19-23.
        Warns not to overemphasize WM's influence on Yeats's poetry;
in the "sphere of social ideas, however, WM exacted a much stronger
influence." A shortened version of 1962.13.

10   GARDNER, DELBERT. "WM's Poetic Reputation in England,
     1858-1900." Dissertation, University of Rochester.
        Abstracted: DA 24:2030-31-A. Revised for publication:
1975.24.

11   GRIEVE, HAROLD W. "WM: Designer, Craftsman--Victorian." Arts
     and Architecture 80, no. 3 (March):26, 32.
        Written on the occassion of the Los Angeles County Museum
acquiring three rolls of WM fabrics, this short article comments
appreciatively on "revolutionary" changes WM wrought on British
attitudes toward design and on some modern designers. Includes nine
illustrations of WM chintzes.

12   GRYLLS, R. GLYNN [Mander, Rosalie]. "Rossetti's Models."
     Apollo, n.s., 78, no. 17 (July):18-22.
        Suggests that Janey was "bored" with WM; in "later life,
periods of misery did set in so that she became in truth the lady of
La Pia imprisoned by her husband" and not simply the model for this
famous painting, now at the University of Kansas. Includes several
plates.

13   HOLDEN-JONES, MARGARET. [Letter on Kelmscott Manor]. Christian
     Science Monitor 55, no. 300 (16 November):12.
        Letter mentions annual up-Thames journeys sponsored by WM
Society and the treasures to be seen at Kelmscott Manor, namely, the
great four-poster bed with its valence.

14 HUTT, ALLEN. "WM--The True and Complete Socialist." <u>Daily</u>
    <u>Worker</u>, no. 9739 (24 January):2.
        Inspired by Asa Briggs's edition (1962.4), this essay-review
comments upon the "unUtopian" pertinence of <u>Nowhere</u> and the
"absolute modernity of Morris the Marxist," illustrating his points
with quotations from the socialist lectures.

15 LEMIRE, E.D. "WM's Reply to Whistler." <u>JWMS</u> 1, no. 3
    (Summer):3-10.
        Argues that WM counters some of Whistler's elitist ideas
about art with his own "doctrine of popular art, a doctrine that
assumed the general distribution of the artistic instinct" and that
also insisted that technical mastery need not lead to "the tyranny
of technique." WM can therefore be regarded as the leader of the
"second wave" of the Pre-Raphaelites.

16 MC LEAN, RUARI. "The End of an Epoch." In <u>Victorian</u> <u>Book</u>
    <u>Design</u> <u>and</u> <u>Color</u> <u>Printing</u>. London: Faber and Faber, pp. 160-68,
    passim.
        Just as Kelmscott Press was a convenient beginning for his
previous study of book design (1958.8), it is "an equally convenient
terminal for the Victorian period. Kelmscott Press was in fact both
an end and a beginning. It was entirely inspired by the past, yet
it inspired the future." Points out that if Kelmscott Press had
never existed, a reformation of print design would have happened
anyway; WM did show, however, that an entire book could be beautiful
and that care must be taken with all its parts, from paper to ink;
from such care stems his wide influence.

17 MAURER, OSCAR. "WM and <u>Laxdaela</u> <u>Saga</u>." <u>Texas</u> <u>Studies</u> <u>in</u>
    <u>Literature</u> <u>and</u> <u>Language</u> 5, no. 3 (Autumn):422-37.
        Discusses the manner in which WM and Magnusson collaborated
and then paraphrases <u>Laxdaela</u> <u>Saga</u> in order to demonstrate how
judiciously WM excised and compressed incidents and reshaped
characters (none more drastically than the heroine) as he created
his version, "Gudrun," of this northern tragedy. Suggests that the
softening of Gudrun's character occurred because WM associated her
with Janey.

18 MEIER, PAUL. "L'utopie de WM--aboutissement ou etape." <u>JWMS</u> 1,
    no. 3 (Summer):10-13.
        Comments on <u>Nowhere</u>, raising questions about the nature of a
true socialist society.

19 MOODY, CATHERINE. "Let Us Get Clear of the Fog." JWMS 1, no. 3
    (Summer):14-19.
        General and optimistic appraisal of the effects of WM's
    achievement: "We can feel that much of the work of WM, and of the
    humanitarians of his time, has now borne fruit." All that is left
    to be done is "encouragement of craftsmanship on a national scale."

20 MORISON, STANLEY. Introduction to The Typographic Book:
    1450-1935. Edited by Kenneth Day. London: Ernest Benn.
    Chicago: University of Chicago Press, pp. 49-55, passim.
        Judges that WM's "perfect craftmanship and his whole-hearted
    attention to detail are his most enduring inspirations," and the
    presses influenced by Kelmscott Press are here mentioned. Even
    though the Kelmscott Chaucer is "the most lavishly decorated piece
    of typography of the whole post-medieval period, yet in comparison,
    with say, the mid-fourteenth-century Psalter, it is a plain book."
    Has 378 illustrations, including three from Kelmscott Press books.

21 NORDLUNDE, C.V. "Fra WM til den elementaere typografi." In
    Eftertryk Udsendt paa 75-Aars Dagen den 15 Juni 1963 af en Kreds
    af Venner [Special 75th birthday edition from a circle of
    friends]. Copenhagen: Arnold Busck, pp. 21-32.
        In Danish. Reports upon WM's early interests in the book
    arts and book design, and then discusses the founding of Kelmscott
    Press; when he had his own press the attention he paid to all
    details and to all materials was unusual, and the results account
    for his vast influence on subsequent book design.

22 READ, HERBERT. "The Politics of the Unpolitical." In To Hell
    with Culture, and Other Essays on Art and Society. New York:
    Schocken Books, pp. 38-48.
        Posits Sermon on the Mount as the "source of all the politics
    of the unpolitical" and among Christ's disciples Ruskin and
    Kropotkin, WM and Tolstoy, Gandhi and Eric Gill. Judges WM's
    lecture, "The Policy of Abstention," to be the "best statement of
    the case against parliamentary action ever made in English."

23 STOKES, E.E. "The WM Letters at Texas." JWMS 1, no. 3
    (Summer):23-30.
        Comments on Murray correspondence acquired by the University
    of Texas in 1961 and on letters he received between 1866 and 1917;
    there are forty-eight from WM, ten from Janey, and fifty-three from
    May Morris. Quotations indicate how important Murray was to the
    Morrises, especially to May when she was editing the Collected
    Works.

24   THOMAS, HELEN. "Melting the Shyness of WM." <u>Times</u>, no. 55,600 (16 January):10.

Recalls a visit she and four other girls, members of a literary club, paid to WM at Kelmscott House in 1895. After a moment of shyness on both sides, WM showed them several medieval manuscripts and spoke to them about the origins of lace-making. The author (later the wife of the poet, Edward Thomas) remembered WM's anger when one of the girls touched some gold ornamentation and how quickly it turned to anxious concern that they should see more of his treasures. Reprinted: 1978.56, 1979.48.

25   "WM, 1834-1896, Kelmscott Churchyard, Oxfordshire." <u>Monumental Journal</u> <u>and</u> <u>Commemorative</u> <u>Art</u> 30 (August):214-16.

Describes Kelmscott, the manor, the memorial cottages, and the gabled gravestone designed by Webb.

<u>1964</u>

1   ARNOT, R. PAGE. <u>WM: The Man and the Myth</u>. New York: Monthly Review Press; London: Lawrence and Wishart, 131 pp. Reprint. Westport, Conn.: Greenwood Press, 1976.

Points out that there were actually two myths: a Bourgeois myth that stressed WM the poet-craftsman, and a Menshevik myth that insisted that WM was a reformer and a gentle socialist. Both myths have been promoted by "anti-Marxist aesthetes" who overlooked WM's lectures and his <u>Commonweal</u> writings. In 1934 there was "an orgy of canonization" that had prompted Arnot to write <u>WM: A Vindication</u> (1934.3), and in this book he uses ideas from that pamphlet to introduce and provide background for forty-nine letters WM wrote to socialist colleagues, J.L. Mahon and John Glasse between 1884 and 1895. These letters (fourteen of them were previously published in the <u>Labour Monthly</u>, in 1951.2) suggest both WM's energy and influence, especially in Scotland, during his most active years of socialist work. Includes analyses of <u>Nowhere</u> and <u>John Ball</u>, pointing out the influence of <u>Das Kapital</u> on the latter.

2   BENNETT, PAUL A. "WM's Kelmscott Adventure Revealed in Grolier Club Exhibit." <u>Publisher's Weekly</u> 186, no. 19 (9 November):108-12.

Describes an exhibit of WM materials, drawn from the collection of John M. Crawford, shown at the Grolier Club. The exhibition featured editions of Kelmscott Chaucer in both vellum and paper, and eleven of the pencil drawings Burne-Jones made for Kelmscott Chaucer illustrations.

3   BLUNT, WILFRID. "WM, and Kelmscott Press." <u>Cockerell: Friend</u>
     <u>of Ruskin and WM and Director of the Fitzwilliam Museum,</u>
     <u>Cambridge</u>. London: Hamish Hamilton, pp. 46-66, passim.
         Traces Cockerell's associations with WM from the first
     meeting in 1886 through the long period when he remained the trusted
     advisor and friend to the remaining Morris women. Cites ways that
     he helped May Morris with the <u>Collected Works</u>, ways also that Morris
     materials found their way to the Fitzwilliam. Includes Henderson's
     account of visits to Cockerell in 1948-49.

4   BRANDON-JONES, JOHN. "Memories of WM in London: No. 7
     Hammersmith Terrace." <u>Country Life</u> 135 (14 May):1194-95.
         Describes the Hammersmith Terrace home where Walker lived
     from 1903 to 1933 and his daughter, Dorothy, until her death in
     1963. The Morris and Co. furniture, hangings, wallpaper, and the
     library with its fine editions make these Thames-side rooms unique,
     and their contents should therefore not be dispersed. Reprinted for
     WM Society members.

*5   BRIGGS, R.C.H., ed. Introduction to <u>The Morris Collection, Hand</u>
     <u>Painted by Sanderson</u>. London: Sanderson and Sons.
         Cited in Fredeman (1966.7): "Sixty wallpaper blocks in color
     by Morris of thirty-four separate patterns, with monochrome
     photographs of full designs for many of the blocks. Published in
     celebration of the centenary of Morris' wallpapers in 1963."

6   BRIGGS, R.C.H. "Letters to Janey." <u>JWMS</u> 1, no.4 (Summer):3-22.
         Detailed descriptions of 192 letters Rossetti sent to Janey
     between 6 March 1868 and 4 October 1882, letters not released for
     public scrutiny until 27 January 1964. Their tone is
     "affectionate," their "dominant theme is Rossetti's obsessive
     concern for Mrs. Morris's health." There are many references to
     WM's contemporaries, to WM himself, and a few of the latter show
     Rossetti's "old condescension for his erstwhile disciple." See
     1976.4.

7   BROMBERGER, FREDERICK S. "WM's Concept of an Ideal Human
     Society as Indicated in Public Lectures, 1877-1894; and in Three
     Prose Romances, 1886-1890." Dissertation, University of
     Southern California.
         Abstracted: DA 25:3550-51.

8   DUNLAP, JOSEPH R. "Morrisian and Shavian Typography: A Few
     Illustrations." Independent Shavian 3, no. 1 (Fall):6-7.
          Argues that Shaw's typographical practices were not
influenced by the typography in WM's Roots, presenting page portions
as illustrative proof. A sequel to "A Note on Shaw's 'Formula' and
Pre-Kelmscott Printing," Independent Shavian, 2, no. 2 (Winter,
1963):20. Dunlap there refuted a claim by Holbrook Jackson that
Shaw had borrowed a typographic "formula" from WM.

9   DUNLAP, JOSEPH R. William Caxton and WM: Comparisons and
     Contrasts. London: WM Society, 29 pp.
          States that this lecture might well be called "Gossip about
two extraordinairy printers." Demonstrates parallels between the
England of Caxton and of WM, between their careers as translators
and printers, between books published. "They were members of the
most enterprising class, and they took seriously the responsibility
of guiding the tastes of their fellows." Originally a lecture given
to WM Society April 1957.

10   ELLISON, RUTH C. "An Unpublished Poem by WM." English 15, no.
     87 (Autumn):100-102.
          A previously unpublished lyric by "Vilhjalmr Vandraethaskald"
(William, the troubled skald) shows the "outspoken and poignant
expression of regret" still felt by WM in 1873 when he returned to
Iceland for a second time, leaving Janey and Rossetti together,
again for a second time, at Kelmscott Manor. The fifty-six-line
lyric, its form and rhetoric modeled on Old Norse Eddic conventions,
is here reprinted, along with a concise introduction and full
explanatory notes.

11   ENGELBORG, EDWARD. The Vast Design: Patterns in Yeats's
     Aesthetic. Toronto: University of Toronto Press, pp. 191-4.
          Suggests that image of WM "with eyes of dreaming beast"
hovers over "The Statues," a poem Yeats wrote in 1938.

12   ENTWHISTLE, E.A. "WM and Later Designers." In Wallpapers of
     the Victorian Era. Essex, Leigh-on-Sea: F. Lewis, pp. 41-45.
          A biographical sketch precedes a useful discussion of
production techniques and problems; we learn why, for instance, WM
probably did chintzes before papers. Suggests the extent of WM's
influence on twentieth-century wallpaper design, and includes five
plates with WM designs.

13 FREDEMAN, WILLIAM E. "WM and His Circle: A Selective
Bibliography of Publications, 1960-1962." JWMS 1, no. 4
(Summer):23-33.
   Items in these bibliographical lists have short annotations,
and all those dealing directly with WM are included in the present
book.

14 GLOAG, JOHN. The Englishman's Chair: Origins, Design, and
Social History of Seat Furniture in England. London: Allen and
Unwin, pp. 285, passim.
   Discusses WM's influence on furniture design generally and on
chair design specifically. He "blessed and made popular the old
Wycombe rush-bottomed chair."

15 GRYLLS, R. GLYNN [Mander, Rosalie]. "The Reserved Rossetti
Letters." TLS, no. 3231 (30 January):96.
   Note on Rossetti letters to Janey that had been opened to
public scrutiny the previous Monday, 27 January 1964, and that
failed to lay to rest conjectures about their affair. Comments upon
the one passage, in an 1869 letter, which suggests they were lovers,
and conjectures about WM as a compliant King Arthur to Rossetti's
Lancelot. See 1964.6 and 1976.4.

16 GRYLLS, R. GLYNN [Mander, Rosalie]. Portrait of Rossetti.
London: Mac donald, pp. 60-69.
   The usual details about Burne-Jones and WM coming under the
influence of Rossetti during the days at Red Lion Square and during
the adventure of the Oxford Union murals are here puncuated by
unusual asides about WM; she wonders, for instance, if "the
smallness of the eyes in that fine head hinted at limitations." She
speaks about Rossetti and Janey as Lancelot and Guenevere, contrasts
Rossetti's love poetry to WM's, saying that it is no wonder she
preferred Rossetti's. Has a description, in appendix 1, of the just
released Janey and Rossetti correspondence: 1964.6 and 1976.4.

17 KOCMANOVA, JESSIE. The Poetic Maturing of WM from "Paradise" to
"Pilgrims". Brno Studies in English, vol. 5. Prague: Statni
Pedagogiake Nakladatelstri, 222 pp. Reprint. Folcroft, Pa.:
Folcroft, Library Editions. Norwood, Pa.: Norwood Editions,
1978.
   Now that WM, the "first great writer in England to become a
declared Marxist," has been rescued by writers like E.P. Thompson
from revisionist Labour leaders and thus shown to be a true
scientific socialist, it is time to reevaluate his poetry, to show
how it too, from Paradise onwards, helps us to perceive WM as a
realist coming to grips with history and art. Offers sensitive,
full readings of each of Paradise tales, arguing that they are
preludes to his later writings where he would assume a more open

socialist role. Asserts that the 1871 journey to Iceland turned WM
toward reality and that Love Is Enough must be read in that light,
that Sigurd portrays the fellowship of the kindred, and the like.
Includes useful commentary on shorter lyrics, both those on Iceland
and those with socialist themes, pointing out that the latter often
had a direct influence on agitators like Tom Mann, and that they
expressed the workers' own hopes and ideologies in ways that the
radical poems of a Shelley or Byron seldom do. Concludes that
before we can determine WM's correct position in the history of
English poetry, careful rereadings of his middle and later poetry
must be undertaken, readings of the sort often demonstrated in this
study.

18 LOCKHEAD, MARION. "Artists at Home." In The Victorian
    Household. London: John Murray, pp. 170-76.
        An attempt to "picture the Victorians at home," includes
brief discussions of WM's London homes and of Kelmscott Manor.

19 MADSEN, S.T. "WM and Munthe." JWMS 1, no. 4 (Summer):34-40.
        Although there is no reason to assume direct influence, the
Norwegian painter Gerhard Munthe (1849-1926) shared many of WM's
interests: in the Middle Ages, in wallpaper design, in the arts and
crafts generally.

20 SEWTER, A.C. "WM Windows at Dedworth." Architectural Review
    136, no. 814 (December):457-58.
        Describes in great detail a series of seven windows done by
Morris and Co. between 1863 and 1887 for Church of all Saints in
Dedworth. Since the church was to be razed, to save the windows was
imperative; all are of high quality, but perhaps the most
interesting is a Resurrection window designed by WM and never
repeated elsewhere. Includes black and white illustrations of all
the windows.

21 WAHL, JOHN ROBERT. No Idle Singer: "Gudrun" and "Sigurd".
    Amsterdam and Capetown: A.A. Balkema, 18 pp.
        Discusses and evaluates "Gudrun" and Sigurd, finding the
first full of "self-pity and frustration," which arose from WM's
reactions to the affair between Janey and Rossetti. The two
journeys to Iceland helped WM gain self-confidence and optimism, and
these traits are reflected in Sigurd, which is here regarded as the
"noblest monument in English literature to the heroic spirit of the
North." Includes a useful discussion of the revisions of Sigurd.
Originally an inaugural lecture at the University of Orange Free
State.

22 WILSON, ARNOLD. "More from Morris and Co." Apollo, n.s., 80, no. 29 (July):57-59.
A description of a painted cabinet, with DeMorgan tiles, designed by Webb for Morris and Co. indicates how rich and varied was the work of the Firm. Includes several illustrations.

1965

1 ARCHER, MICHAEL. "Pre-Raphaelite Painted Furniture." Country Life 137, no. 3552 (1 April):720-22.
Though WM himself evidently did not design furniture after the Red Lion Square days, he approved of designs done by Rossetti and Brown during the early years of the Firm. Several of the more famous pieces and types are here described, and Brown is judged the most important furniture designer of the group. Includes six monochrome illustrations.

2 CLAIR, COLIN. "WM and Kelmscott Press." In A History of Printing in Britain. London: Cassell, pp. 243-47.
Discusses the founding of Kelmscott Press, adding fresh details about the two extra presses added later and concluding that the volumes WM produced at the Press do not appeal to modern tastes for simplicity, but that all agree about their excellence of workmanship and material.

3 DELAURA, DAVID J. "An Unpublished Poem of WM." MP 62, no. 4 (May):340-41.
A holograph poem, in WM's hand, of "Lonely Love and Loveless Death" (the manuscript is now at the University of Texas) is here published for the first time and commented upon in terms of its thematic connections to other poems WM wrote in the late 1860s. Suggests that his anguish over Rossetti and Janey caused the "personal, even revealing intensity" of the poem and kept WM from publishing it.

4 DOUGHTY, OSWALD, and WAHL, JOHN, eds. Letters of Rossetti. Oxford: Clarendon Press, 4 vols., passim.
There are many references to "Topsy" in these letters, especially in those written between 1858 and 1872. A letter of 16 July 1869 includes the anecdote, widely used by WM biographers, about WM writing 700 lines of Paradise in one day. The letters are accompanied by full notes, but the absence of an index makes the volumes difficult to use.

5   DUNLAP, JOSEPH R.   "Morrisiana I."   Circum-spice 2 (15
      April):1-4.
          Describes a recent acquisition of the City College of New
York: trial pages for the Kelmscott Press volume of Froissart's
Chronicles, a volume that WM did not live to complete.   Includes a
full-sized reproduction of the lower half of one of the trial pages.

6   FLEISSNER, R.F.   "'Percute Hic': WM's Terrestial Paradise."   VP
      3, no. 2 (Summer):171-77.
          Maintains that the label "idle singer" has had the effect of
making WM a "neglected singer," especially as regards the poems in
Paradise. But readers who employ WM's own percute hic ("strike
here") are likely to find a coherent moral tradition beneath the
surface of myth and legend in the Paradise tales.   Concludes that WM
urges upon us not escape, but pursuit of a life full of "faith,
hope, and charity."

7   FREDEMAN, WILLIAM E.   "WM."   In Pre-Raphaeliteism: A
      Bibliocritical Study.   Cambridge, Mass.: Harvard University
      Press, pp. 67-69, 162-75, passim.
          An authoritative bibliography which attempts "to indicate the
extent of the material available rather than to make the compilation
meticulously definitive."   Has four parts and one hundred sections,
with part 1 describing major collections and important exhibitions,
part 2 the major figures (here 180 WM items, both primary and
secondary, are listed; all the secondary references are included in
the present book).   Part 3, "devoted to the movement as a whole,
provides a comprehensive survey of works relating directly to the
various activities of the Pre-Raphaelites in all three stages of the
movement."   Part 4 covers Pre-Raphaelite illustrations.   This is an
important and useful book, particularly valuable for its range of
coverage and for its detailed introductions.

8   FRYE, NORTHROP.   "Varieties of Literary Utopias."   Daedalus 94,
      no. 2 (Spring):323-47.
          Comments upon Nowhere are placed within a general discussion
of utopian writing from Plato to More and into the modern period.
Points out that WM "started not with the Marxist question, 'Who are
the workers?' But with the more deeply revolutionary question,
'What is Work?'" and that he posited an answer, "the expression of
what is creative in the worker," within a Utopia whose pastoralism
is its most striking feature, concluding that "we are indebted to
the most unreligious of the great English writers for one of the
most convincing pictures of the state of innocence."

9   HENLEY-READ, CHARLES. World Furniture: An Illustrated History.
     Edited by H. Hayward et al. New York: McGraw-Hill, pp. 207-29.
         Discusses the foundation of Morris and Co. and the quality of
the designers and artists who insured the reputation of its
furniture, which "was from the first soundly constructed in
conscious revolt against the shoddy products of commerce."

10 HOLLIS, CHRISTOPHER. The Oxford Union. London: Evans, pp.
     96-102.
         Descriptions of the personalities involved in the adventure
of the Oxford Union murals gain precision here because they are set
against the history of the Union itself, a building that "for all
its distinction has been a distressingly philistine place," except
for this one period when it became "the patron of the most vigorous
and artistic movement of the times."

11 HURLIMANN, MARTIN. "WM und die Anti-Viktorianen." Du Atlantis
     25 (September):640-57.
         Sets WM's protests against the age within the tradition of
the romantic and radical critique of Victorian capitalism, asserting
that WM's socialism was closer to that of Thomas More than that of
Marx. Comments also on the influence of Kelmscott Press.

12 IRWIN, JOHN. "A Gift From WM." Victoria and Albert Museum
     Bulletin 1, no. 1 (January):38-40.
         In 1869 WM gave to the South Kensington Museum (later the
Victoria and Albert) its "first outstanding work of Indian art--a
gift which apparently evoked neither gratitude nor recognition
during his lifetime." Describes this twelfth-century bronze figure
of Hanuman, the monkey god, and suggests that WM acquired it through
Wilfrid Healy, a friend in the service of the East India company.

13 JACKMAN, SYDNEY W. "The Artist and Intellectual as Socialist:
     WM." In The English Reform Tradition: 1790-1910. Englewood
     Cliffs, N.J.: Prentice-Hall, pp. 150-53.
         A short introduction plus selections from Chants make up one
chapter in this anthology of the writings of British reformers.

14 LAURENCE, DAN H., ed. Bernard Shaw's Collected Letters,
     1874-1897. London: Max Reinhardt, 2 vols., passim.
         Includes a few letters to WM, one in 1887 recalling how they
had all "skedaddled" away from the police during the Trafalgar
Square demonstrations, another from Venice in 1891 commenting on
architecture and unscrupulous guides. Many references to WM occur
in other letters; his intelligence, his artistic integrity, and his
inability to bargain for books or manuscripts he had decided he

wanted are mentioned. A letter to Archibald Henderson in 1905 is completely about WM.

15 LAWSON, ANDREW. "Maid for WM." Isis 2 (11 November):15-16.
        A short interview with Floss Gunner, a kitchen maid for the Morrises from 1891 to 1896. She worked, and sometimes "it did amount to slavery," for nine pounds a year, and "we had a day off now and again, but never a half-day and never on Sunday."

16 MAYFIELD, JOHN S. "WM Demurs." Courier (Syracuse University
        Library), 5:23-25.
        WM'S American publisher, Roberts Brothers of Boston, had asked him to write an introduction or preface for a second edition of Sigurd, in 1879. In a terse letter, here reprinted, WM declined, saying a preface would "flatten the whole thing."

17 MORRIS, BARBARA. "WM und Company." Du Atlantis 25
        (September):658-70.
        Describes Morris and Co. from its formation in 1861 and through the period of its reorganization in 1875 up until its closing in 1940, mentioning the key figures, the types of products made, and the sorts of influence exerted. Includes twelve pages of illustrations.

18 MUMFORD, LEWIS. "WM." In Atlantic Brief Lives: A Biographical
        Companion to the Arts. Edited by L. Kronenberger. Toronto and
        Boston: Little, Brown. Reprint. 1971, pp. 546-49.
        Capsule biography and brief bibliography followed by a fuller appreciation of the significance of WM's life and works, wherein WM is described as one "who produced nothing but forward-looking disciples," men like Lethaby who were "exponents of a humanized functionalism."

19 ROTZLER, WILLY. "Der englische Jugendstil und die Schule von
        Glasgow." Du Atlantis 25 (September):684-99.
        Discusses WM's influence on a generation of "Jugendstil" artists who flourished near the end of the nineteenth century. Mentions Macmurdo, Voysey, and Beardsley, comparing WM's decorative effects to those of Mackintosh and other artists of the Glasgow School. Includes fourteen illustrations, two in color.

20 TANNER, ROBIN. "WM and a Primary School." <u>Times</u> <u>Educational</u>
    <u>Supplement</u>, no. 2634 (12 November):1022-23.
        Reports upon a primary school in the village of Langford,
near Kelmscott Manor, and the activities students engaged in there,
activities like making dyes for their own hand-spun wool, then
spinning their own cloth. These students were learning by doing,
were transcending "what we are pleased to call their intelligence
quotients." Judges, correctly, that WM would have been pleased.

21 THOMAS, J.D. "The Soul of Man Under Socialism: An Essay in
    Context." <u>Rice University Studies</u> 51, no. 1 (Winter):83-95.
        Wilde's essay, "The Soul of Man under Socialism," is a
treatise on individualism, which in the nineteenth century was the
antonym of socialism, yet in another sense it can be regarded as
<u>Nowhere</u> in essay form, since there are many correspondences between
the two works. These are discussed, and other influences from
Kropotkin to Shaw are mentioned.

22 THOMPSON, E.P. <u>The Communism of WM</u>. London: WM Society, 19 pp.
        Reflects upon the reception given his biography of WM
(1955.15) and upon the assessment of WM's communism he had then
made; he now judges WM's moral critique of society to be as
significant as Marx's political critique; he also now thinks that
Marx might have been better able to recognize WM's stature than
Engels who thought WM sentimental and impractical. Argues that WM
was actually intensely practical and realistic--and prophetic, for
the "innate moral baseness" of capitalist society, which WM
perceived so clearly, demands more than parliamentary reform. Hopes
that present-day socialists will recognize how WM "transformed a
great tradition of liberal and humane criticism of society and how
he brought this into the common revolutionary stream." Reprints
letter WM sent to a Reverend Sharman, one with his ideas on raising
children. Originally a lecture given in 1959.

23 WICKERT, MAX ALBRECHT. "Form and Archetype in the Works of WM,
    1855-1870." Dissertation, Yale University.
        Abstracted: DA 27:489-90-A.

<u>1966</u>

1   BLACKWELL, BASIL. Introduction to <u>Morris as I Knew Him</u>, by
    Shaw. London: WM Society, pp. 7-9.
        Reveals that he must bear ultimate responsibility for Shaw's
famous memoir, for he had encouraged May Morris, back in 1934, to
publish the volumes for which Shaw wrote the piece. Recalls also
Miss Lobb's attitude toward the enterprise, her determination to
protect May Morris.

2   CREESE, WALTER L.   "WM and Howard--Boston and Chicago." In The
    Search for Environment: The Garden City, Before and After.
    London and New Haven: Yale University Press, pp. 144-57, passim.
        The ideas of Ebeneezer Howard and WM merge in the work of
Barry Parker and Raymond Unwin, the designers of the first Garden
City at Letchworth; their ideas and relationships to the city
depicted in Looking Backward and the villages in Nowhere are
discussed in detail, and the design of Pimpernell wallpaper is
compared to an urban pattern.

3   DAY, KENNETH, ed. Book Typography: 1815-1965, in Europe and the
    United States. Chicago: University of Chicago Press, passim.
        Discusses WM's pioneering influence on typography in Belgium,
Germany, the Netherlands, and the United States; and his influence
on printers like Van de Velde, de Bom, Rudolph Koch, de Vinne,
Updike, Rogers, Rollins, Hubbard, and Nash.

4   EVANS, J.N. "WM, 1834-1896." Great Figures in the Labour
    Movement. London and New York: Pergamon Press, pp. 23-33.
        A biographical sketch includes discussions of WM's work with
the Socialist League and on Commonweal. Other chapters are devoted
to figures like the Webbs, Attlee, and Bevan, and some basic
differences between their politics and those of WM are ignored.

5   FAULKNER, PETER. "WM and the Two Cultures." JWMS 2, no. 1
    (Spring):9-12.
        Reconstructs C.P. Snow's treatise on the Two Cultures as well
as F.R. Leavis's objections to Snow's sanguine hopes for technology,
and then suggests that WM's writings about art and technology offer
clear insights into the problem and also some practical solutions.

6   FREDEMAN, WILLIAM E.   "WM's Funeral." JWMS 2, no. 1
    (Spring):28-35.
        Compares the description of the funeral in Mackail (1899.10)
and in Cunninghame-Grahame to one recently found in a letter from
the painter Arthur Hughes to Alice Boyd of Penkill Castle. Reprints
the entire letter.

7   FREDEMAN, WILLIAM E. "WM and His Circle: A Selective
    Bibliography of Publications, 1963-65." JWMS 2, no. 1
    (Spring):13-26.
        Items in these bibliographical lists have short annotations,
and all those dealing directly with WM are included in the present
book.

8   GLOAG, JOHN. A <u>Social</u> <u>History</u> <u>of</u> <u>Furniture</u> <u>Design</u>. New York:
    Crown Publishers, pp. 47-48.
        Points out the ways that WM "aroused interest in simple,
    well-made furniture and the natural beauty of wood as a material,"
    and then traces his influence on furniture design up through modern
    Scandinavian.

9   GORDON, W.K. "Pre-Rapaelitism and <u>Oxford</u> <u>and</u> <u>Cambridge</u>
    <u>Magazine</u>." <u>Journal</u> <u>of</u> <u>Rutgers</u> <u>University</u> <u>Library</u> 29, no. 2
    (June):43-51.
        Rutgers has a rare complete run of all twelve issues of the
    <u>Oxford</u> <u>and</u> <u>Cambridge</u> <u>Magazine</u>, and here all sixty-nine contributions
    are surveyed and some of the authors discussed. "The first vague
    hint that the magazine would have to be taken seriously came with
    the February issue, in which Morris wrote 'The Churches of North
    France.'" Suggests also that WM's favorable review of Browning's
    <u>Men</u> <u>and</u> <u>Women</u> was remarkable.

10 HOLLOWAY, JOHN. <u>Widening</u> <u>Horizons</u> <u>in</u> <u>English</u> <u>Verse</u>. London:
    Routledge and Kegan Paul, pp. 27-29.
        Points out that in <u>Sigurd</u> there is a "softening of a harsh
    Norse reality." Compares WM's "Iceland First Seen" to Auden's
    "Journey to Iceland."

*11 JOHNSON, RUTH and JOHNSON, FOSTER. <u>Kelmscott</u> <u>Revisited</u>.
    Meriden, Conn.: Bayberry Hill Press, 32 pp.
        Cited in Yale University card catalogue.

*12 JONSSON, SNAEBJORN. "WM, 1834-1896: Minnzt sjotugustu artidar
    hans" [Seventieth anniversary memorial]. <u>Lesbok</u> <u>Morginblad</u> 35:10,13.
        Cited in MHRA bibliography for 1966.

13 KOCMANOVA, JESSIE. "The Aesthetic Purpose of WM in the Context
    of the Late Prose Romances." <u>Brno</u> <u>Studies</u> <u>in</u> <u>English</u>, no.
    6:75-146. (Vol. 109, Opera Universitatis Purkynianae
    Brunensis.)
        Though the work of Arnot (1934.3 and 1964.1) and E.P.
Thompson (1955.15), and of Floud (1959.4) has led to significant
revaluations of WM the political thinker and of WM the designer,
this has been at the expense of WM the man of letters. His
reputation as a poet has remained remarkably constant since Scott
(1912.14) noted a great decline after <u>Defence</u>. This article argues
that WM's poetry and his literary art continued to develop, and that
this growth can be seen in the "relationship between WM's aesthetic
and the philosophical position of scientific communism." This leads
to statements about the early poetry showing WM's "rudimentary
conception of the class struggle in the Middle Ages," but there also

occur here many useful and provocative insights into Jason,
Paradise, and the late prose romances, "the fairest flowering of his
mature Marxist thought."

14 LEWIS, JOHN. Typography: Basic Principles. London: Studio
    Books; New York: Reinhold. 2d ed., 1967. Reprinted. 1968, pp.
    9-13.
        Biographical sketch stresses Kelmscott Press, quoting from
    WM's "Aims," commenting in detail on the three typefaces,
    particularly upon the ways that WM modified Jenson's typeface in
    order to achieve "a close textured, rich, dark page." Concludes
    that WM's typographic designs do not amount to mere
    "mock-medievalism." He might, in fact, have "prepared the ground
    for Die Neue Typographie."

15 LEWIS, W.H., ed. Letters of C.S. Lewis. London: Geoffrey Blas;
    New York: Harcourt Brace, pp. 110, passim.
        Several references to the prose romances: "I wish he had
    written a hundred of them." Ponders what a "rum thing that Morris
    should have wanted so desperately to be like Chaucer and succeeded
    in being so exactly like Gower," and suggests that in WM's writings
    one finds "the final statement of good Paganism: a faithful account
    of what things are and always must be to the natural man."

16 MAC LEOD, ROBERT. "The Art of Moral Building: Some Late
    Victorian and Edwardian Architectural Ideas." Building 211, no.
    6449 (23 December):31-34.
        Discusses WM as inheritor of the ideas of Ruskin, and
    separates such ideas, and also those of Webb and Norman Shaw, from
    any sort of nostalgic medievalism; these men were historically
    learned, and there was a moral conviction behind all their creative
    work. Points out that, contrary to popular belief, Red House was
    not a great pioneering feat and that Webb later designed buildings
    that were much more innovative.

17 MORISON, STANLEY. Foreword to Morris as I Knew Him by Bernard
    Shaw. London: WM Society, pp. 5-6.
        Judges that Shaw's 14,000 word memoir (1936.12) is "the most
    intimate and observant biographical presentation of Morris that has
    proceeded from the pen of a contemporary observer," and he also
    reveals that Shaw had told him, in 1946, that he would not attempt
    to improve upon it.

18 NOCHLIN, LINDA. "WM: 1834-1896." In Realism and Tradition in
    Art: 1848-1900. Englewood Cliffs, N.J.: Prentice-Hall, pp.
    129-41.
        Short introduction stressing WM's distaste for the effects of
    modern civilization precedes the reprinting of "The Aims of Art,"
    one of a handful of documents representing England in this useful
    anthology.

19 PEVSNER, NIKOLAUS. Funfhundert Jahre Kunstlerausbildung: WM.
    Darmstadt: Bauhaus Archiv, 23 pp.
        A biographical survey points out how WM studied and
    understood the artistic techniques from the Middle Ages, turning
    them to good account in his lectures and essays, in his designs for
    Morris and Co., and in the volumes that he published at Kelmscott
    Press. Originally a lecture delivered 12 October 1962.

20 RAYMOND, MEREDITH. "The Arthurian Group in Defence." VP 4, no.
    3 (Summer):213-18.
        Reviews previous approaches to the four Arthurian poems that
    open Defence and then suggests that they can be regarded as a
    "spiritual drama--a unit with a certain observable structure." This
    structure is then set forth, a bifurcation of the four poems into
    two pairs, and many interesting links between images, themes, and
    characters are pointed out.

21 ROTHSTEIN, ANDREW. "WM at Clerkenwell." Times, 11 April.
    Reprinted for WM Society members, 1 p.
        Discusses the effects of WM's financial aid to the Patriotic
    Club, a workers' organization that in 1893 set up the Twentieth
    Century Press, the first socialist publishers in Britain.

22 SUMMERSON, JOHN. "Ruskin, WM, and the 'Anti-Scrape'
    Philosophy." In Historic Preservation Today: Essays Presented
    to the Seminar on Preservation and Restoration. Charlottesville:
    University Press of Virginia, pp. 23-32.
        Discusses the origins in Ruskin of the philosophy of
    preserving ancient buildings and ways that WM was influenced by
    Ruskin, sometimes toning down his enthusiasms. Points out that WM
    was not in favor of preserving all old buildings and that at times
    he was inconsistent and subjective.

23 TAYLOR, JOHN R. The Art Nouveau Book in Britain. London:
    Methuen, pp. 28, 32, passim.
        Though Crane said that art nouveau was an "antithesis to the
    Morris School of Decoration," both Crane and WM have often been
    associated with art nouveau book decorations; these associations are
    discussed and some facts regarding influence reviewed.

24 TROXELL, JANET CAMP. "The Paintings of WM." JWMS 2, no. 2
    (Spring):4-8.
        Attempts to correct oft-repeated errors about WM's extant
    paintings. Concludes that "Sir Tristram and the Dog" probably never
    existed; there remains only a pencil study for a "Tristram and
    Iseult," and finally there is the Tate Gallery's La Belle Iseult,
    which some still persist in calling Queen Guenevere.

25 WOODCOCK, GEORGE. The Crystal Spirit: A Study of George
    Orwell. Boston: Little, Brown; London: Cape. Reprint. New
    York: Minerva Press, 1968, pp. 83-84, passim.
        Points out that Orwell, like WM, disliked machines, "loved to
    make things with his own hands," and also that he "had a great
    nostalgia for a past which he tended to idealize." Orwell's
    idealized past was, however, located in the nineteenth rather than
    the fourteenth century.

26 [Note on the purchase of four WM letters]. Columbia Library
    Columns 15:52.
        A notice that Columbia had recently acquired four letters
    that WM wrote to the Reverend George Bainton in 1888; these letters
    were published anonymously by Thomas J. Wise in 1894.

27 "An Introduction from Ruskin." JWMS 2, no. 1 (Spring):2.
        Reproduces a letter in the John Rylands Library, Manchester,
    that Ruskin wrote to E.A. Bond, keeper of manuscripts at the British
    Museum, sometime during 1857, a letter introducing "my friend, WM,
    whose gift for illumination is I believe as great as any
    thirteenth-century draughtsman."

1967

1   AVIS, F.C. "The English Private Presses." In Edward Philip
    Prince: Type Punchcutter. London: Glenview Press, pp. 34-40,
    passim.
        WM, who of course got to know something about the craft of
    cutting type punches in steel, lauded the intelligence and skill of
    Edward Prince who cut all three sets of Kelmscott Press types. The
    total number of punches made, including trial letters, was
    approximately 250.

2   BRAUN, HELENE THOMAS. "Henry van de Velde et WM." Cahiers
    Henry van de Velde 81:21-27.
        Reviews WM's life and works, lingering over the journeys to
Iceland, the creation of wallpaper patterns, then pondering how such
matters are paralleled by the life and works of van de Velde, often
via direct influence, but sometimes not. Discusses WM and his
homes, and where they can still be viewed in London.

3   CREESE, WALTER L. The Legacy of Raymond Unwin: A Human Pattern
    for Planning. London and Cambridge, Mass.: MIT Press, pp.
    11-12, passim.
        Raymond Unwin (1863-1940) preached at Labour Churches, wrote
articles for Commonweal, was influenced by WM's ideas on the
importance of pleasure arising from work, on the importance of
simple and healthy housing for all. Both in an introduction and in
the collected essays that follow, there are references to WM and to
the specific ways he influenced Unwin.

4   D'AMICO, MASOLINO. "Oscar Wilde between Socialism and
    Aestheticism." English Miscellany 18:111-39.
        Discusses "points of contact" between Nowhere and Wilde's
"The Soul of Man under Socialism." They coincide in attitudes to
government, marriage, and criminal law; they do not agree in
attitudes toward work or the use of machines.

5   FLEETWOOD-HESKETH, PETER. "A Watchdog of Preservation: Ninety
    Years of SPAB." Country Life 146, no. 3654 (16 March):580-82.
        Recounts circumstances leading to the founding of SPAB,
assesses the value of its work over ninety years, and discusses its
present responsibilities, with 3,500 members, and its consideration
of 400 cases each year.

6   FRY, KENNETH. "The Victorian Decorative Impulse in the Poetry
    of WM." Dissertation, University of Missouri.
        Abstracted: DA 27:3452-53-A.

7   GAL, ISTVAN. "WM's Matyas-novellja" [Matthew tale]. Filolgiai
    Kozlony 16:488-92.
        In Hungarian. Introduction and notes accompany a portion of
A King's Lesson.

8   GOLDZAMT, EDMUND. WM et la genese sociale de l'architecture
     moderne. Wroclaw: Polskiej Akademii Nauk, 58 pp. Reprint.
     Dresden: Verlag der Kunst, 1976.
          States that WM was a "precursor of modern architecture in
Poland" largely because in his writings he stressed that design and
architecture should never be separated from social concerns, and
such ideas were eagerly grasped by Polish architects in the 1920s
and 1930s. A synopsis of this monograph, with the same title,
appeared in 1971.9.

9   HARRIS, S. DALE. "Evaluating WM." Quarterly Newsletter, Book
     Club of California 33, no. 1(Winter):3-10.
          Asserts that if WM's legacy is closely examined, "it has a
tendency to diminish in intrinsic value." Agrees with Swinburne
that WM's muse "drops her robes as she walks," and he also finds the
prose too little "individualized," with the same message (joy in
work equals art) repeated again and again. WM is therefore seen as
an influence only, one who fought against the evils of his age with
heart and instinct rather than reason.

10   HARRIS, S. DALE. WM: 1834-1896. San Francisco: Pacific
     Lithograph, 4 pp.
          An appreciation of WM's achievements, printed on the occasion
of the opening of a WM exhibit at Stanford University Library on 18
May 1967.

11   HENDERSON, PHILIP. WM: His Life, Work and Friends. London:
     Thames and Hudson; New York: McGraw-Hill. 2d ed., Harmondsworth:
     Penguin, 1973, 388 pp.
          An important biography, one which uses new material, such as
the Rossetti-Janey letters, and thus a necessary supplement to
Mackail (1899.10). Discusses ways Janey's affair led to WM's
decisions to travel to Iceland, and the like. Includes full
analyses of all of WM's literary works, stressing that they were not
escapist, since he was not a sentimental dreamer but a realist
trying to preserve the finest achievements of our European heritage.
Insists that modern attempts to nurture creativity within a
standardized environment stem from WM's struggles, from his clearly
articulated concerns for a host of problems dealing with art and
society. He was a central figure of his time, and his many
associations with important artists, poets, and politicians, his
involvement in many organizations and causes, are here displayed so
fully that it becomes apparent that WM is also a central figure for
our time. Uses a modern perspective; details are therefore framed
with such comments as "In the year in which WM was born, six
Dorsetshire farm labourers were sentenced to seven years'
transportation for forming a union." On Russia's attempts in the
1870s to move into the Balkans, the author observes, "she has now
achieved the same end in Eastern Europe." But careful scholarship

usually reigns, and hosts of new insights occur, for example, into
the workings of Morris and Co. and the delicate arrangements at
Kelmscott Manor with Rossetti and Janey, and concerning the
importance to WM of friends like Georgie Burne-Jones and Aglaia
Coronio, of colleagues like Webb, Taylor, Shaw, and Bax, and of
acquaintances like Wilde and Engels, all because of the author's
careful use of hundreds of letters, many not available to previous
biographers. Asserts that it is impossible to conclude a book on
WM, "since so many of the things he fought for are still our
problems today." This study underscores WM's importance in defining
these problems and suggesting solutions.

12 KOCMANOVA, JESSIE. "The Aesthetic Opinions of WM." Comparative
   Literature Studies 4, no. 4:409-24.
      Examines the development of WM's "social, collective and
non-individualistic conception of art," which received its initial
impulse from Ruskin's "The Nature of Gothic" and which was
influenced by Marx's ideas, causing his own to fall into a "logical
sequence" and then to flower into an aesthetic that is here gleaned
from several of the lectures from the eighties. This aesthetic, one
which insists that "art is the heritage of humanity and human
labour," is still valid. Compares WM to Henry Adams, an American
with similar medieval interests (with perhaps a deeper knowledge of
thirteenth-century France), whose aesthetic led him to despair
rather than optimism, this because it was based on a different
attitude toward history.

13 MAC ALINDON, T. "The Idea of Byzantium in WM and Yeats." MP
   64, no. 4 (May):307-19.
      WM often praised Byzantium in lectures, calling its art a
"new-born Gothic," its culture a harmony of East and West, of pagan
and Christian. Such ideas influenced Yeats's more elaborate notions
of Byzantine unities; Yeats does not admit the influence, and very
few commentators on WM realize how extensive his knowlege of
Byzantium was, that he was in fact a "seminal thinker" in the
history of art and not just a popularizer of Ruskinian notions, as
many critics have suggested.

14 MADSEN, S.T. Art Nouveau. Translated by R. Christopherson.
   New York: McGraw-Hill; London: George Weidenfeld and Nicolson,
   passim. Reprint. 1976.
      Within a general discussion of art nouveau, trends leading up
to it as well its broad manifestations across Europe, there are many
references to WM and to his influence upon a wide variety of artists
and designers from Jules Charet to Louis Comfort Tiffany.

15 MAKALASHINA, N.K. "Esteticheskiy poziciya Williama Morrissa,
    1880-1890"   [The aesthetic position of WM, 1880-1890]. Uchenye
    Zapiski 280:271-88.
        In Russian. Quoting extensively from the socialist lectures
and essays, discusses the pertinence of WM's ideas about art for the
people, about his prescience on the emergence of a true proletarian
art.

16 MAKALASHINA, N.K. "Stanovlenye socialno-politicheskih vzglyadov
    Williama Morrissa, 1880-1890"   [WM's social-political attitudes
    and vision]. Uchenye Zapiski 280:251-70.
        In Russian. Reports upon a 1952 conference of the British
Communist party in which WM's influence was discussed; here WM's
importance to the socialist movement is elaborated upon with
generous quotations from the lectures and from his letters.

17 MEIER, PAUL. "WM en Tchecoslovaquie." La pensee 131:127-29.
        Academics in Eastern bloc countries often know of WM, but
only in Czechoslovakia is there a body of significant critical work:
Professor Jessie Kocmanova at the University of Brno is responsible;
she has written several penetrating analyses of WM's writings, and
here some indication of their content is given.

18 PENNING-ROWSELL, EDMUND. "Kelmscott Manor Restored." Country
    Life 142, no. 3688 (9 November):1190-92.
        Kelmscott Manor passed from the control of Oxford University,
to whom May Morris had bequeathed it, to the Society of Antiquaries,
by a "series of coincidences, not all of them initially
propitious." These are described, as are the extensive renovations
undertaken by the Society. Includes five photographs.

19 RITCHIE, WARD. WM and Kelmscott Press. San Francisco: Pacific
    Lithograph, 3 pp.
        Brief comments on typefaces, on the beginnings of Kelmscott
Press, and on its influence on modern printing are included in this
pamphlet printed for the opening of a WM exhibit at the Stanford
University Library, 18 May 1967.

20 ROBSON, W.W. "Three Victorian Poets." In Critical Essays. New
    York: Barnes and Noble; London: Routledge and Kegan Paul, pp.
    200-221.
        Slightly revised text of 1958.11. Reprinted: 1969.23.

21 SCHORSKE, CARL. "The Quest for the Grail: Wagner and WM." In
    The Critical Spirit: Essays in Honor of Herbert Marcuse. Edited
    by K.H. Wolff and B. Moore, Jr. Boston: Beacon Press, pp.
    216-32.
        Both WM and Wagner "quested for the future in the relics of
the past," and those relics (Arthurian story and Norse legend) were
strikingly similar, but their quests went in opposing political
directions. If one compares, however, the activities and associates
at Bayreuth and at Hammersmith, it seems they both gathered around
themselves at the end a "brotherhood of redeemers." Concludes with
comments on Nowhere and its depiction of the sort of community the
young Wagner loved to dream about.

22 SEWTER, A.C., and TAYLOR, NICHOLAS. "WM in Hospital."
    Architectural Review 141, no. 841 (March):224-27.
        In 1873 Morris and Co. did a window for a hospital chapel at
Ventnor on the Isle of Wight; the designs were by Burne-Jones,
Brown, and WM, who was responsible for two of the lower panels:
Christ raising Jairus's daughter and Lazarus. This striking window
is now in danger of destruction since the hospital and chapel are no
longer in use.

23 SILVER, CAROLE. "No Idle Singer: A Study of the Poems and
    Romances of WM." Dissertation, Columbia University.
        Abstracted: DA 22:644-A.

24 SLACK, ROBERT C., ed. "WM." In Bibliographies of Studies in
    Victorian Literature for the Ten Years 1955-1964. Urbana,
    Chicago, and London: University of Illinois Press, passim.
        A reprinting of bibliographies from MP (1956-57) and VS, a
sequel to 1945.6 and 1956.18; lists many studies of WM; with the
exception of the reviews, all are included in the present book.

25 STALLMAN, ROBERT. "The Quest of WM." Dissertation, University
    of Oregon.
        Abstracted: DA 27:3064-65-A.

26 TEMKO, ALLAN. Foreword to WM: His Life, Work and Friends. by
    Philip Henderson. New York and London: McGraw-Hill, 4 pp.
        Points out that WM's prophecies of the evils capitalism would
inflict have come true with a vengeance in America, where the "evils
of insensate technological power" have intensified. Though most
have not heeded his warnings or his advice about our
responsibilities to the physical environment, a few architects and
humanists keep WM's ideas alive.

27 THOMAS, ALAN G. "Private Presses." In <u>Fine</u> <u>Books</u>. London:
    Weidenfeld and Nicolson, pp. 103-19.
        Insists that the "Private Press movement owed its inception
and most of its momentum to WM." Covers the beginnings of Kelmscott
Press, and has fresh details about the Kelmscott Chaucer, chosen as
a gift and "foundation stone" for a new library in Tokyo and by Shaw
as a "worthy gift for a great artist," one he presented to Rodin.
Discusses the influence Kelmscott Press had on several small
presses, mainly in England, concluding that the "best books of today
do not look in the least like Kelmscotts, but without Morris they
might never have been created at all." Includes several well-chosen
illustrations. Reprinted. 1975.53.

28 THOMPSON, PAUL. <u>Socialists,</u> <u>Liberals</u> <u>and</u> <u>Labour:</u> <u>The</u> <u>Struggle</u>
    <u>for</u> <u>London,</u> <u>1885-1914</u>. London: Routledge and Kegan Paul;
    Toronto: University of Toronto Press, pp. 113-14, passim.
        Discusses reasons WM left the Socialist League, offering
fresh details about other leftist groups and personalities, and
about the Hammersmith Socialist Society. Mentions some labor
leaders who read and wrote about WM after the turn of the century.

29 THOMPSON, PAUL. <u>The</u> <u>Work</u> <u>of</u> <u>WM</u>. London: Heineman; New York:
    Viking, 315 pp.
        Biography introduces WM's work and ideas, taking into account
recent research, like that of MacLean (1958.8) on books, Sewter
(1962.30) on stained glass, Morris (1962.26) on embroidery and
textiles, Aslin (1962.1) on furniture, Boe (1957.2) on design
theory, and Floud (1959.4) on pattern design. This work "has shown
that Morris was closer to the best designers of his own period and
less important in the evolution of the modern movement than had
previously been thought." An opening biographical sketch uses the
customary facts and anecdotes to provide background for the chapters
on WM's works, and it has fresh insights as well: "It was symbolic
of his settled state [in 1859-62] that with other patriotic friends
he joined the volunteer militia." This section also briefly
discusses an issue avoided in Mackail (1899.10), the affair between
Rossetti and Janey, and WM's consequent decision to journey to
Iceland, and the like. More important and useful are the subsequent
chapters with their detailed discussions of WM and his ideas about
architecture, home furnishings, textiles, stained glass, etc., ways
that his ideas departed from his applications and also from the
ideas and applications of other Victorian designers. Final chapters
on WM's political work, its context, its connections to Marxist
ideas, the relevance of <u>Nowhere</u>, are helpful. Includes a short
annotated bibliography and a gazeteer with museums, private homes,
and churches where many of the works discussed in the text can still
be seen, often in their original settings. Revised: 1977.37.

30 TOMPKINS, J.M.S. "The Earthly Paradise of WM." In The High
    Victorian Cultural Achievement. Report of the Second Victorian
    Society Conference. Oxford: Truexpress, pp. 47-53.
        Summarizes a paper which had considered new attitudes to the
    types of diction and narrative that "had not been stumbling blocks"
    to her generation's appreciation of Paradise. Comments also upon the
    figure of the "sad lover" in several of the poems as a reflection of
    WM.

*31 TSUCHITANI, SHIGERU. "On WM." Memoirs of the Faculty of
    Education, Niigata University 9, no. 1 (Spring):100-115.
        Cited in personal correspondence with J.R. Dunlap.

32 TSUZUKI, CHUSHICHI. The Life of Eleanor Marx, 1855-1898: A
    Socialist Tragedy. Oxford: Clarendon Press, pp. 118-23.
        Has some fresh details about WM's work with the Avelings (He
    went with them to Paris, for the Second International), about
    Engels's attitudes to Hyndman and WM, and about other Socialist
    League activities.

33 VON HENDY, ANDREW. "Histories and Flowers: The Organic Unity of
    WM's Late Art." Victorian Newsletter 32 (Fall):18-19.
        Points out interesting relationships between the floral
    designs WM created for Kelmscott Press borders and initials and the
    themes of the prose romances he wrote during the same period. The
    designs suggest the beauty and abundance of Nature, the "tale of the
    Earth," a theme celebrated in the romances.

34 WATKINSON, RAY. "WM and the Bauhaus." Labour Monthly 49, no. 7
    (July):310-11.
        Traces the movement of ideas regarding design schools from
    Hermann Muthesius to Walter Gropius who from 1919 to 1934 headed the
    Bauhaus, the "focal point of experiment toward design for the new
    world which technology makes possible." Stresses that Gropius, like
    WM, was extremely interested in human implications of architecture
    and design and that both thought in terms of "fellowship."

35 WATKINSON, RAY. WM as Designer. London: Studio Vista; New
    York: Reinhold, 174 pp. 2d ed., London: Studio Vista, 1979.
        Opens with a biographical sketch that sometimes challenges
    widely accepted views, as when Red House is called a landmark for WM
    more than for nineteenth-century architecture. But WM's lasting
    influence, whether through his own designs and theories or via the
    Arts and Crafts Movement, upon specific twentieth-century figures
    and movements is set forth with authority and precision. Includes
    helpful discussions of Morris and Co., its precursors, and WM's work
    with pattern designs and the book arts, as well as ninety

well-chosen plates, two dozen in color, that offer further proof of
the range and beauty of WM's achievement in design.

36   WEINTRAUB, STANLEY.   Beardsley: A Biography.   London: W.H.
       Allen; New York: Braziller, pp. 31, 33, passim.
       Has a fresh anecdote about Aymer Vallance urging Beardsley to
design a frontispiece for the Kelmscott Press Sidonia the Sorceress;
he did so, and WM disparaged the effort.   Later Beardsley frequently
attacked WM's decorative designs.

37   "More News from Nowhere."   TLS, no. 3394 (16 March):214.
       Uses publication of Paul Thompson's book (1967.29) to discuss
problems WM, in his multiplicity, poses for his biographers,
congratulating Thompson on his decision to write about WM primarily
as a designer; finds this book to be "the fairest, most rounded view
of Morris available," for it clears away old myths about Morris
hating machines and not understanding Marxism, and it also points
out that Red House and Kelmscott Press did not revolutionize
architecture and the book arts.

38   "WM."   TLS, no. 3430 (23 November):1108.
       Charts shifts in attitudes toward WM and his contemporary
significance, shifts influenced by Doughty's biography of Rossetti
(1949.3), by E.P. Thompson (1955.15), and by Floud's revaluation of
WM as designer (1959.4).   These new attitudes are apparent in the
two new books here discussed with general approval: Henderson's
biography (1967.11) and Watkinson's study of WM the designer
(1967.35).

                                   1968

1   ANTIPPAS, ANDY P.   "WM and the Murder of Art."   Tulane Studies
       in English 16:49-62.
       Argues that what connects WM the poet to WM the socialist is
his hatred of civilization and the ways that it had degraded, among
other things, art.   His love of the art of the past, "the
perpetuator of the race's finer sentiments," led him to develop
theories of the lesser arts, to go back to medieval models for
crafts' techniques, to found societies like SPAB.

2   ARMYTAGE, W.H.G.   "The Debate: WM's London, A.D. 2012."   In
    Yesterday's Tomorrows: A Historical Survey of Future Societies.
    London: Routledge and Kegan Paul; Toronto: University of Toronto
    Press, pp. 78-81.
        Claims that WM was "shocked" by Looking Backward and that it
    was "the restlessness of America that Morris saw as dangerous."
    Recalls that in Nowhere we learn that what was formerly the United
    States had become a great wasteland.   Paraphrases other parts of
    Nowhere, suggests that W.D. Howells was strongly influenced by WM.

3   BLENCH, J.W.   "WM's Sigurd: A Reappraisal."   Durham University
    Journal, n.s., 30, no. 1 (December):1-17.
        Mentions differing attitudes critics have had to Sigurd,
    which is "at present unjustly neglected."   A careful survey of the
    poem's structure, meter and diction follows.   Finds that WM omitted
    from his sources all "primitive and savage behaviour," adding "human
    touches" (these implying later socialist concerns), that the meter
    is appropriate for narrative and the expression of emotion, and that
    the diction adds to the "richness" and "psychological range" of the
    poem.   Concludes that Sigurd is indeed an important work, but that
    Wagner's version is still more "endlessly fascinating."

4   CHAMPNEY, FREEMAN.   Art and Glory: The Story of Elbert Hubbard.
    New York: Crown Publishers, pp. 3, 50, 58-60, passim.
        A bit more restrained than Hubbard himself or his earlier
    biographers; here we learn only that Hubbard "was a disciple, in his
    fashion, of WM," that the "visit to WM's establishment at
    Hammersmith and a meeting with the Old Man himself" was a major
    event in 1894, one that led Hubbard to set up the Roycroft Press.
    Refers to May Morris's scornful refusal, in 1907, to visit the
    Roycrofters, when she was lecturing only a few miles away, in
    Buffalo.   See 1958.6.

5   CHAPMAN, RAYMOND.   The Victorian Debate: English Literature and
    Society, 1832-1900.   London: Weidenfeld and Nicolson, pp. 248-55,
    passim.
        Biographical sketch stresses that a concern for beauty and
    for art led WM toward socialism, pointing out that he remained sane
    while some of his earlier Pre-Raphaelite associates drifted into a
    confusing aestheticism.   Discusses Nowhere, the ways that political
    facts "rub awkwardly against high-flown dreams."

6   DUFTY, A.R. "Kelmscott, WM's Holiday Home." Connoisseur 169,
      no. 682 (December):205-12.
          Surveys the history of Kelmscott Manor, from its construction
in 1570 through the period of the Morris tenure, up to its
restoration between 1964 and 1967, under the direction of its
present owners, the Society of Antiquaries. Describes the contents
of the Manor, rich in products from Morris and Co. and in paintings
and drawings by Rossetti. Includes fourteen plates.

7   DUNLAP, BARBARA. "Morrisians in Albion." News from Anywhere 10
      (November):1-7.
          Recounts visits to WM sites in London, Oxford, Cambridge,
Kelmscott, commenting that in the Walker house on Hammersmith
Terrace, "one can touch, taste and sense the kind of life Morris
himself lived and labored that others might know."

8   DUNLAP, BENJAMIN. "The Heavy Trouble, The Bewildering Care."
      Sewanee Review 76, no. 3 (July-September):512-15.
          An essay provoked by recent biographies of WM opens with
lament that "no one reads the poetry of WM today, despite the fact
that everyone agrees his influence is ubiquitous in almost
everything else." Calls WM a "Victorian George Plimpton," one who
in the estimation of his biographers has gone from "warrior bard to
hapless cuckold." The first appelation is part of the title of
1947.6, and the second--both misleading and unfair--is drawn from
discussions in Henderson (1967.11), based on the newly released
Rossetti letters.

9   FAULKNER, PETER. "WM Today." Humanist 83, no. 9
      (September):276-78.
          Since too many otherwise well-informed people tend to regard
WM as a "well-meaning blunderer, a romantic medievalist who thought
that man should abandon machinery and return to the simple life,"
the appearance of Morton's edition of Three Works by WM (1968.27)
and of biographies by Paul Thompson (1967.29) and Henderson
(1967.11) is here welcomed and used as the occasion to reconsider WM
and to insist that his work has messages that are still relevant.

10 FIELDING, UNA. "Memories of May Morris: 1928-1938." JWMS 2,
      no. 3 (Winter):2-5.
          Recalls several visits with May Morris, the author's
great-aunt, made between 1923, when the author left Australia, and
1938, when May Morris died. Reveals that she liked detective
stories, particularly those of Dorothy Sayers.

11 FRANKLIN, COLIN. "The Kelmscott Press: An Album from the
    Nineties." JWMS 2, no. 2 (Summer):14-18.
         Comments on both reviews and trade catalogues from the 1890s
    to judge the contemporary reputation of Kelmscott Press books,
    finding that only a few years after their publication they were
    termed "scarce" by booksellers, and that they were held in general
    high regard by reviewers also. Quotes 1890s prices for several
    Kelmscott Press editions.

12 FREDEMAN, WILLIAM E. "The Pre-Raphaelites." In The Victorian
    Poets: A Guide to Research. Edited by Frederic E. Faverty. 2d
    ed., Cambridge, Mass.: Harvard University Press, pp. 252-316.
         Asserts that "few of the more than twenty biographies of WM
    add substantially to the knowledge of his life and works" provided
    by Mackail (1899.10), Georgie Burne-Jones (1904.3), and May Morris
    (1910.9). An exception is E.P. Thompson (1955.15), which is here
    discussed; so are many articles published since the first edition of
    this Guide (1956.7). All of these are included in the present book.

13 GOODE, JOHN. "Gissing, WM and English Socialism." VS
    12:201-26.
         Gissing's novel, Demos, is at the center of this discussion
    of the relationship between art and history. The novel distorts
    socialism, and its Morrisean character, Westlake, is only a dreamy
    idealist, but its various distortions do square with contemporary
    views of socialism and with a "contemporary journalistic image" of
    WM. Points out that Nowhere, through its invention of a history of
    socialism, also contains distortions.

14 GOODWIN, K.L. "WM's 'New and Lighter Design.'" JWMS 2, no. 3
    (Winter):24-31.
         Most commentators on the Oxford Union designs (not the wall
    paintings) claim they were done by WM in 1857, refurbished by Morris
    and Co. in 1375, and brought to light through cleaning in 1936.
    Actually, the 1875 designs were completely new. The 1857 designs
    featured the sorts of animals that grace the margins of medieval
    manuscripts.

15 HASCALL, DUDLEY L. "Volsungasaga and Two Transformations."
    JWMS 2, no. 3 (Winter):18-23.
         Compares Volsunga and Sigurd to each other and to the Old
    Icelandic original. Discusses effects of archaisms and
    alliteration and of "small plot changes and other points more
    semantic than grammatical." Concludes that even though Sigurd is
    not "poetry of the first order," it succeeds in "presenting an
    Icelandic story to Englishmen in a familiar form."

16 HUNT, JOHN DIXON. The Pre-Raphaelite Imagination: 1848-1900.
       London: Routledge and Kegan Paul, pp. 39-47, passim.
          Discusses symbolist methods in "Hollow Land" and glances
    briefly at a few of the Defence poems (insisting here that
    Rossetti's influence was of extreme importance), lamenting the
    archaisms and obscurity of most of WM's poetry. Only Sigurd is
    regarded favorably: "a powerful Victorian myth." Draws parallels
    between Pre-Raphaelite Brotherhood of 1848 and Morris and Co., and
    remarks upon Kelmscott Press volumes.

17 HUNT, VIOLET. "Kelmscott to Kelmscott." JWMS 2, no. 3
       (Winter):6-16.
          Reprint of 1925.4 (not 1955, as the "Editor's Note" states);
    Lady Mander adds a few paragraphs from the original manuscript notes
    by Violet Hunt.

18 INSALL, DONALD W. "Kelmscott Manor and its Repair for the
       Society of Antiquaries." Monumentum, Spring, pp. 1-21.
          Traces history of the legal maneuvers that enabled the
    Society of Antiquaries to obtain Kelmscott Manor. Ways that SPAB
    ideals informed those who then renovated the manor are set forth in
    detail. Has a three-page synopsis in French.

19 IRVINE, A.L. "WM at Oxford and Dublin." JWMS 2, no. 2
       (Summer):3-5.
          Paraphrases Stephen Gwynn's anecdotes (1926.4) about WM
    lecturing in Oxford and Dublin.

20 JOHNSON, FRIDOLF. "WM." American Artist 32, no. 10
       (December):43-49.
          A biographical sketch precedes comments about WM's modern
    importance. Includes the oft-repeated but incorrect assertion that
    WM "sold bulk of his valuable collection of books to finance his
    crusade," and locates Merton Abbey on the Thames rather than the
    Wardle. Has many monochrome illustrations.

21 JOHNSON, THORVALDUR. "The WM-Magnusson Saga Translations." In
       Timarit Thjodraeknisfelags Islendinga. Edited by G. Jonsson.
       Winnipeg: Thjodraeknisfelagi Islendinga i Vesturheimi, pp.
       58-63.
          Stressing Magnusson's good fortune in meeting and then
    working with WM, this article comments upon translation habits, upon
    the sagas so expeditiously finished and published, and on a few
    problems brought on by archaic language. Recounts some of the
    events and sites visited on both Icelandic journeys.

22 LANG, CECIL Y., ed. "WM." In The Pre-Raphaelites and Their
    Circle. Boston: Houghton Miflin, pp. 161-291, passim.
         Has brief comments on WM as a Pre-Raphaelite figure, one who
    is "elusive. For Morris was not a normal man, he was a kind of
    superman. He did all things and did them well." Anthologized here
    are Defence poems, selections from Paradise and Poems by the Way.

23 LEMIRE, E.D. "A Note on WM's Western Outlet." News from
    Anywhere 10:14-15.
         Reports that there was an active WM Society in Chicago in the
    early years of this century, and that there was a Chicago department
    store with a "Morris Room." Reprints an advertisement for the
    fabrics and furniture sold there, at the Tobey Furniture Co.

24 MAC EACHEN, DOUGALD B. "Trial by Water in WM's 'Haystack in the
    Floods.'" VP 6, no. 1 (Spring):73-75.
         Glosses, with facts about judicial ordeals, Jehane's fearful
    exclamation (11. 49-56) that she will be immersed in the cold
    Seine, commenting that WM and many subsequent anthologists had
    gotten those facts wrong. See 1969.15.

25 MAC NAMEE, LAWRENCE F. "WM." In Dissertations in English and
    American Literature: Theses Accepted by American, British, and
    German Universities, 1865-1964. New York and London: Bowker, pp.
    169-70. Supplement one, 1969, pp. 169-70. Supplement two,
    1974, pp. 170-71.
         Lists twenty-eight dissertations on WM. The supplements list
    another twenty; all are included in the present book.

26 MENCH, MARTHA DUVALL. "The Argonautic Tradition in WM's Jason:
    A Study in Poetic Eclecticism." Dissertation, Yale University.
         Abstracted: DA 29:1212-A.

27 MORTON, A.L., ed. Introduction to Three Works by WM. London:
    Lawrence and Wishart; New York: International Publishers, pp.
    11-32.
         A biographical sketch, "Morris's Path to Socialism," is
    useful, but it makes too much of the 1871 journey to Iceland as a
    key event in WM's political development. Succinct introductions are
    provided for each of the three socialist narratives here
    anthologized; Pilgrims is judged a partial success, John Ball is
    said to employ a precise Marxist analysis of the history of class
    struggle, and Nowhere is acclaimed as unique, stirring, and at the
    same time, a scientific Utopia.

28 MUMFORD, LEWIS. "A Universal Man." New York Review of Books,
    23 May, pp. 8-15.
        Argues that WM "harbored three different personae which were
never, through any single work, so completely fused that he could
utilize to the full his magnificent native gifts." The three
(Craftsman, Writer, Political Agitator) are discussed in this review
article of books by Henderson (1967.11), Watkinson (1967.35), and
Paul Thompson (1967.29). Suggests also that WM's frustration about
his marriage caused his furious activity and his many achievements,
saying that there is "probably no better example of sublimation and
autotherapy on record." Adds that "the tragic flaw in his marital
relations limited his emotional development; more than anything
else, possibly, it kept the three personae from coming together for
their mutual support and enlargement." Reprinted: 1973.26; 1973.27.

29 PEVSNER, NIKOLAUS. "Triple WM." Architectural Review 144, no.
    860 (October):287-88.
        Essay inspired by Henderson's biography (1967.11), which is
called Mackail (1899.10) "brought up to date." Discusses the newly
released letters (1964.6) and what they suggest about the triangle
and about WM's patience and goodwill and whether or not he was
thereby driven to his work to find refuge.

30 PEVSNER, NIKOLAUS. The Sources of Modern Architecture and
    Design. London: Thames and Hudson, pp. 18-29, 33, passim.
        Argues that in the nineteenth century the "impetus in the
fields of aesthetic and social renewal came from England and centres
in the larger than life figure of WM." Comments on the "essential
originality" of WM's designs, with their "closeness and density of
nature observed." Sketches influence that WM had on Mackmurdo and
on art nouveau generally. States that many developments in
twentieth-century architecture, from garden cities to Bauhaus, arose
from WM's "faith in serving people's needs."

31 PHILIP, EJNAR. "WM og Alfred Lord Tennyson; Maud, et melodrama,
    Kelmscott Press." Bogvennen (Copenhagen) 2:74-77.
        In Danish. Has less to do with Tennyson than the title
suggests. Comments upon Kelmscott Press designs and how the
medieval atmosphere WM achieved could sometimes hinder legibility.
Discusses WM's influence on the Doves and Nonesuch presses.

32 PIPER, JOHN. Stained Glass: Art or Anti-Art. London: Studio
     Vista; New York: Reinhold, pp. 32-33.
          Discusses Morris and Co. success with stained glass, a result
of making windows "designed by the best contemporary artists Morris
could find" and of rarely accepting jobs for medieval churches,
thereby setting a "precedent, to act on and to quote."

33 PYE, DAVID. The Nature and Art of Workmanship. Cambridge:
     Cambridge University Press, pp. 66-70, passim.
          Offers fresh insights into Ruskin's "Nature of Gothic" and
its influence on WM. Asserts that their ideas were harmful; they
"diverted the attention of educated people from what was good in the
workmanship of their time, encouraged them to despise it, and so
hastened its eventual decline."

34 RUFF, WILLIAM. "Shaw on Wilde and WM: A Clarification." Shaw
     Review 11, no. 1 (January):32-33.
          It is not Shaw but Hesketh Pearson, in his biography of Shaw
(1942.3), who is responsible for the anecdote that WM, when he was
dying slowly, enjoyed a visit from Wilde more than anyone else.
The point seems worth making since Wilde had been in prison for
eighteen months when WM died.

35 SCHULZ, H.C. "English Literary Manuscripts in the Huntington
     Library." Huntington Library Quarterly 31, no. 3 (May):251-302.
          Includes a list of thirty-six items, many of them manuscript
fragments, by WM.

36 SEWTER, A.C. "A Check-List of Designs for Stained Glass by
     Brown." JWMS 2, no. 2 (Summer):19-29.
          Comments on the nature and extent of the stained glass
designs Brown executed, alone and with Burne-Jones, for Morris and
Co., and includes a checklist of designs, locations of cartoons, and
windows.

37 SMITH, JACK. "WM and His Theory of Art: Its Bases and Its
     Meaning." Southern Quarterly 7, no. 1 (October):59-71.
          A biographical sketch is followed by a discussion of the ways
which WM embraced and then went well beyond the basic Pre-Raphaelite
attitudes toward art, since WM pointed out clearly the effects art
might have on all individuals if only it could grow naturally out of
a healthy society.

38   STANGE, G. ROBERT. "The Victorian City and the Frightened
     Poets." VS 9, (Summer):627-40.
        WM is one of several poets whose attitudes toward London, as
reflected in their poetry, are here surveyed. Finds that he did not
attempt to confront the metropolis, preferring a "nameless city in a
distant sea."

39   STOKES, E.E. "WM to Louisa Baldwin: More Letters at Texas."
     JWMS 2, no. 2 (Summer):5-8.
        Summarizes the contents of twelve letters from WM to Louisa
Baldwin written between 1871 and 1875 and acquired by the University
of Texas in 1965. Six of the letters are as yet unpublished.

40   SUSSMAN, HERBERT. "The Production of Art in the Machine Age:
     WM." In Victorians and the Machine: The Literary Response to
     Technology. Cambridge: Harvard University Press, pp. 104-34,
     passim.
        Places WM's ideas about work and society against those of
Carlyle, which suggest power, and those of Ruskin, which suggest
worship, pointing out that WM secularized Ruskin and that his ideas
about work led directly to ideas about social revolution. Discusses
Nowhere as the culmination of Victorian primitivism and the ways
that WM's social vision contrasts with that of Wells. Suggests that
contracts won by the Firm often caused WM to forgo his ideal of the
designer-craftsman. Despite this Merton Abbey did manage to absorb
technology into a pastoral setting; it turned out products truthful
to their texture and function, and it did not rely on machinery to
lower prices.

41   SYPHER, WYLIE. Literature and Technology: The Alien Vision.
     New York: Random House. New York: Vintage, 1971, pp. 235-39,
     passim
        Discusses Art as defined by Ruskin and WM, and by their
twentieth-century disciples Lewis Mumford and Herbert Read, as
involving pleasure with labor; such a perception might be "the most
genuine refuge or resistance" to the encroachments of technological
sterility, for if Art "penetrates" technology it must necessarily
change it. Links WM's two-dimensional designs and rejection of fine
arts to Robbe-Grillet's rejection of concealed meanings, and
concludes that "in returning to the existential practice of design,
Morris laid a foundation for the Bauhaus."

42 TAYLOR, NICHOLAS, and SYMONDSON, ANTHONY. "Burges and WM at
Bingley: A Discovery." Architectural Review 144, no. 857
(July):35-38.
Oakwood, a Gothic villa near the Yorkshire town of Bingley,
has "some of the finest early stained glass by Morris and Co. that
has yet been discovered." Those windows, depicting St. George and
female figures, Chaucer and four of his heroines, are here
described, and other extant Morris and Co. windows in the region are
mentioned. Has several illustrations, the majority of them Burges's
designs for different rooms.

43 TREFMAN, SUNNY. "WM: The Modernization of Myth." Dissertation,
New York University.
Cited in American Doctoral Dissertations (1967-68):22.

44 WILKES, J.A. "Memories of Kelmscott House." JWMS 2, no. 2
(Summer):9-13.
Recollections of James Alfred Wilkes (1860-1938), member of
the Hammersmith Socialist Society, of lectures in the coach house
and at the foot of Hammersmith Bridge. Reprinted from 1917.6.

45 YEATS, JOHN BUTLER. "WM, Pencil Sketch." JWMS 2, no. 2
(Summer):2.
Reproduction of pencil sketch of WM made by John Butler
Yeats, father of Yeats.

46 YEATS, W.B. "The Happiest of Poets." In Essays and
Introductions. New York: Macmillan, pp. 53-64.
Reprint of 1903.9.

47 Daniel Berkeley Updike to WM. San Marino, Calif.: Huntington
Library, 4 pp.
Reprint of letter Updike wrote to WM in 1893 requesting
permission to purchase founts of Golden type. WM never replied.

1969

1 ARINSHTEIN, LEONID M. "A WM Letter: His Struggle Against a
Possible Anglo-Russian War." N and Q 214 (June):218-20.
Reprints and comments upon a letter WM wrote on 17 May 1877,
at an intense moment in the work of the Eastern Question
Association, to a correspondent in Russia. WM informs the
"colleague" that the Eastern Question Association has no available
funds. The unknown correspondent is probably Madame Olga Novikoff;
the letter is now in the Institute of Russian Literature in
Leningrad.

2   ASLIN, ELIZABETH. The Aesthetic Movement. London: Elek, pp.
     175-79, passim.
          Suggests that "the missionary aspect of the aesthetic
     movement can be traced to WM," as can specific designs and attitudes
     toward materials used; the influence of Morris and Co. upon the
     Aesthetic Movement and art nouveau is discussed in some detail.

3   BURROUGH, B.G. "Three Disciples of WM: 1, Ernest Gimson."
     Connoisseur 171, no. 690 (August):228-32; 172, no. 691
     (September):8-14.
          In 1884 WM met Ernest Gimson (1864-1919) and helped him find
     work with a London architect; the young man joined SPAB and exulted
     in WM's company; he later became a famous cabinet-maker, opening his
     own work-shops, and attempting to follow WM's ideas on crafts work.
     Includes twenty-six plates.

4   BURROUGH, B.G. "Three Disciples of WM: 2, Charles Robert
     Ashbee." Connoisseur 172, no. 692 (October):85-90; no. 694
     (December):262-66.
          Charles Robert Ashbee (1863-1942) went to Cambridge and then
     to work for Bodley, and thus became acquainted with Morris and Co.,
     with WM himself at a Hammersmith Sunday lecture. Ashbee launched
     the Guild of Handicrafts in 1888, and though he did not agree
     entirely with its credo, WM lectured at its school. Ashbee bought
     one of WM's presses and printed eighty-three books at his Essex
     House Press; these and some of Ashbee's other achievements
     discussed. Part 2 of this article deals with Ashbee's silverwork.

5   BURROUGH, B.G. "Three Disciples of WM: 3, W.R. Lethaby."
     Connoisseur 173, no. 695 (January):33-37.
          W.R. Lethaby (1857-1931) along with other assistants of
     Norman Shaw formed the St. Georges Art Society, which became the Art
     Workers Guild, and then, in turn, the Arts and Crafts Exhibition
     Society. Lethaby met WM in 1891, shared with him many interests,
     and was a dutiful and gifted pupil.

6   CECIL, DAVID. Visionary and Dreamer, Two Poetic Painters:
     Samuel Palmer and Burne-Jones. Princeton: Princeton University
     Press, pp. 2-5, passim.
          Discusses the friendship between WM and Burne-Jones, but
     includes unusual references to WM's "hooded eyes, as bright and
     inhuman as those of a bird," to his "inhuman strain" that would show
     itself later in his relationship to Burne-Jones. Suggests WM might
     have done "more for society by writing poetry, which he did well,
     than by addressing mobs, which he did badly. For Morris was not a
     success as a politician."

7   DUFTY, A.R. <u>Kelmscott:</u> <u>A</u> <u>Short</u> <u>Guide</u>. Dorking, Surrey: Adlard
    and Son, 12 pp.
        Offers history of the manor from 1570, when the main section
was built, through its additions, made in 1670, improvements WM made
after he leased it in 1871, and developments after it was purchased
by Janey in 1913, left to Oxford in 1938 by May Morris, and finally
turned over to the Society of Antiquaries in 1962. Also describes
tapestries, paintings, and furnishings in every room of the Manor.

8   DUFTY, A.R. <u>Kelmscott:</u> <u>An</u> <u>Illustrated</u> <u>Guide</u>. London: Society
    of Antiquaries. Reprint. 1977, 35 pp.
        A detailed, room-by-room description of Kelmscott Manor;
every tapestry, painting, wallpaper, and book is mentioned, the
history of most of them set forth. Includes twenty-eight
illustrations, four of them in color, and all are keyed to the text.
Concludes with an "Envoi" recording the names of "those who
accomplished the rehabilitation of Kelmscott Manor between 1964 and
1967" and appreciation for the "altruism" of the Society of
Antiquaries who footed the bill.

9   FRANKLIN, COLIN. "Kelmscott Press and WM." In <u>The</u> <u>Private</u>
    <u>Presses</u>. London: Studio Vista; Chester Springs, Pa.: Dufour,
    pp. 35-44, passi
        Contrary to received opinion, Kelmscott Press was not a
pioneer, "was not the greatest influence, but was quite without a
peer. It was a paradox." Even though WM admired some modern
publishers, getting along well, for instance, with Chiswick, he went
back to fifteenth-century books for models, ideas about paper, ink,
print, everything. To go back to such models for tapestries or
stained glass made sense, but for books it "must have looked
impossibly difficult or arrogant." But he succeeded, and the proof,
the wonderful unmatched set of volumes, and many of the reasons for
that success, like his good luck with illustraters, are here set
forth with clarity and authority. Includes a discussion of
Kelmscott Press ephemera, such as notices and menus for the annual
dinners. Later chapters on other private presses, from the elegant
Ashendene to the hucksterish Roycrofters, often comment on Kelmscott
Press, weighing degrees of indebtedness. Concludes with a "Select
Bibliography of Private Presses with Some Recent Auction Room
Prices," compiled by David Lincoln, and with some sensible and witty
advice on collecting.

*10 GOODWIN, K.L. "The Relationships Between the Narrative Poetry
     of WM, His Art and Craft-Work, and His Aesthetic Theories."
     Dissertation, Oxford University.
          Cited in Index to Theses Accepted for Higher Degrees in the
     Universities of Great Britain, 20 (1969-70):19..

 11 GORDON, JAN B. "WM's Destiny of Art." Journal of Aesthetics
     and Art Criticism 27, no. 3 (Spring):271-79.
          Reviews WM's ideas as to why nineteenth-century civilization
     had made discordant the internal **rhythms of nature and art and had**
     also removed man from the natural world and hence the possibilities
     of again creating and enjoying a healthy art. Further discussion of
     the "mythology of WM's aesthetic" draws eclectically from his
     lectures and from a wide array of late nineteenth-century writers.

 12 GRIGSON, GEOFFREY, ed. Introduction to A Choice of WM's Verse.
     London: Faber and Faber, pp. 9-19.
          Discusses the power of the imagery in several of the poems
     from Defence and refers to the "tortured confessional poems of the
     late sixties," and even worse, to Janey as "wife of matchless
     stupidity." Most of the poems here anthologized are from Defence,
     but selections from Paradise and Sigurd are also included, and so
     are a few of the socialist poems.

 13 HAUGEN, EINAR. "On Translating from the Scandinavian." In Old
     Norse Literature and Mythology: A Symposium. Edited by Edgar
     Palome. London and Austin: University of Texas Press, pp. 3-18.
          Discusses WM's preferences for archaic Germanic diction
     within the context of a general critique of "journalese," a personal
     antagonism for French loan words, which "colored his view of the
     style of the sagas, distorting it into something grotesque and
     wonderful."

 14 HAWKINS, MARK F. "The Late Prose Romances of WM: A Biographical
     Interpretation." Dissertation, University of California at
     Berkeley.
          Abstracted: DA 30:4451-A.

 15 HOLLOW, JOHN. "WM's 'Haystack in the Floods.'" VP 7, no. 4
     (Winter):353-55.
          Responds to MacEacham's article (1968.24), noting that even
     though WM may have been wrong about medieval judicial ordeals,
     Jehane's plight, like that of Isabella in Measure for Measure,
     exploits a theme about divine judgment present in WM's other early
     writings, a theme that reflects his "growing agnosticism."

16 HOSMON, ROBERT STAHR. "The <u>Germ</u> (1850) and <u>Oxford</u> <u>and</u> <u>Cambridge</u>
    <u>Magazine</u> (1856)." <u>Victorian</u> <u>Periodicals</u> <u>Newsletter</u> 4
    (April):36-47.
        Attempts to identify correct authors for every contribution
    to the four issues of the <u>Germ</u>, the twelve issues of the <u>Oxford</u> <u>and</u>
    <u>Cambridge</u> <u>Magazine</u>; some previous attributions revised.

17 JONES, HOWARD MUMFORD. "Imperial Elegies." <u>VP</u> 7, no. 4
    (Winter):281-83.
        "The Tune of Windsor Towers by WM" was one of five parodies
    read by the author at a celebration of the 150th birthday of Queen
    Victoria.

18 LEMIRE, E.D., ed. <u>The</u> <u>Unpublished</u> <u>Lectures</u> <u>of</u> <u>WM</u>. Detroit:
    Wayne State University Press, 331 pp.
        Between 1877 and 1896, WM prepared and delivered scores of
    speeches and lectures; many have not survived, others were never
    published, and there was confusion about original titles, dates, and
    locations. This edition corrects that situation. Includes ten
    lectures, nine of them previously unpublished, as well as two very
    important appendixes: "A Calendar of WM's Platform Career" and "A
    Bibliographical Checklist of Morris's Speeches and Lectures." The
    former lists only those occasions which were public, but there are
    more than 600 in the calendar; the second contains 197 "speeches and
    lectures for which there are known titles, subjects, or texts," with
    references to all extant manuscript and printed texts. Revision of
    1962.20.

19 LEWIS, C.S. "WM." In <u>Selected</u> <u>Literary</u> <u>Essays</u>. Edited by W.H.
    Hooper. Cambridge: Cambridge University Press, pp. 219-31.
        Reprint of 1939.6.

20 LONG, LITTLETON. "WM and Timekeeping." <u>Victorian</u> <u>Newsletter</u> 35
    (Spring):25-28.
        Reviews medieval attitudes toward time and promptness, which
    were quite casual, and then accuses WM of an anachronism in
    "Haystack in the Floods," when he has Godmar give Jehane one hour to
    decide; the image of minutes creeping "round to the twelve again" is
    not medieval. But there are appropriate images of tolling bells and
    the like in <u>Paradise</u>, and in <u>Nowhere</u>, we have, appropriately, a
    "clock-free future."

21 MAURER, OSCAR. "WM and the Gesta Romanarum." In <u>Studies</u> <u>in</u> <u>the</u>
    <u>Language,</u> <u>Literature,</u> <u>and</u> <u>Culture</u> <u>of</u> <u>the</u> <u>Middle</u> <u>Ages</u> <u>and</u> <u>Later</u>.
    Edited by E.B. Atwood and A.A. Hill. Austin: University of
    Texas, pp. 369-81.
        Discusses the three <u>Paradise</u> tales derived from <u>Gesta</u>
<u>Romanarum</u>; they are "The Man Born to be King," "The Proud King," and
"The Writing on the Image," pointing out how and suggesting why WM
made changes in his immediate sources. Concludes that these Latin
"didactic apologues are reworked by WM's craftmanship, subdued by
his melancholy and paganism," into tales much more dreamlike than
the originals.

22 MORRIS, JAMES, ed. Introduction to <u>Icelandic</u> <u>Journals</u>, by WM.
    Fontwell, Sussex: Centaur, pp. 15-22.
        Discusses abiding British interests in Iceland as well as
WM's "passionate involvement with the mystique of the North."
Remarks upon the substance and spirit of these <u>Icelandic</u> <u>Journals</u>
(this is a facsimile reprinting of volume 9 of the <u>Collected</u> <u>Works</u>),
concluding that "nobody writing in English has better captured the
astonishing chill beauty of Iceland."

23 ROBSON, W.W. "Three Victorian Poets." In <u>British</u> <u>Victorian</u>
    <u>Literature:</u> <u>Recent</u> <u>Revaluations</u>. Edited by S.K. Kumar. New
    York: New York University Press, pp. 172-91.
        Reprint of 1967.20.

24 SILVER, CAROLE. "'The Defence of Guenevere': A Further
    Interpretation." <u>SEL</u> 9, no. 4 (Autumn):695-702.
        Agrees in general with Perrine (1960.23) and Carson (1963.6)
interpretations of the poem, but goes on to explore other ironies
and ambiguities, especially with regard to ways Guenevere "hints at
her crime, half-confessing through double-meaning statements,
slipping, through the imagery she uses, into temporarily admitting
adultery." The use of Gawaine as accuser is seen as purposeful,
since in Malory (but in an earlier tale in the cycle) he is an
adulterer also; thus further ironies occur. Concludes that
Guenevere's defense is a powerful testament not to her innocence but
to her love and her rhetorical skill, and also, finally, to
"Morris's profound psychological grasp of illicit romantic
passion."

25 STALLMAN, ROBERT. "'Rapunzel' Unravelled." VP 7, no. 2
(Autumn):221-32.
Argues that five scenes in the poem have a dramatic structure
that suggests a "rite of passage" from the "bondage of childhood to
the freedom of adult love." Looks closely at diction, image, and
symbol in each scene, offering both Freudian interpretations and
eclectic comparisons to Malory, Poe, Dostoevski, and De La Motte
Fouque. See 1973.33 and 1974.23.

26 TALBOT, NORMAN. "Women and Goddesses in the Romances of WM."
Southern Review (Adelaide) 3, no. 4:339-57.
Discusses the late prose romances, suggesting that
sophisticated themes lurk beneath their nonrealistic surfaces.
Offers a close reading of Well, one that employs Jungian
terminology, concluding that WM often praises heroines who resemble
archetypes of love and blessing. Includes a useful appendix that
lists occurrences of witch-captive motif in the prose romances as
well as in Paradise narratives.

27 VON LAUE, T.H. The Global City. New York: J.B. Lippincott, pp.
158-59.
Quotes passage that includes WM's statement of his abiding
"hatred of civilization," using this as a key example of urban
critiques in the nineteenth century.

28 WEINTRAUB, STANLEY, ed. "WM and Others." In Shaw: An
Autobiography. New York: Weybright and Yalley, 2 vols., passim.
Includes many references to WM, most of them lifted from an
obituary article and from the famous memoir: 1936.12. But many
fresh anecdotes, drawn mainly from Shaw's correspondence, also
appear here, among them the mistake concerning Wilde's supposed
visits to WM on his deathbed.

29 Catalogue of the WM Collection. Walthamstow: WM Gallery, 76 pp.
Revised edition of 1958.16. Its increased length is due to
an indefinite loan of textiles and cartoons from the Barking Museum.

1970

1 ALBRECHT, WILLIAM T.. "WM's Well: An Exploration and a Study."
Dissertation, University of Pennsylvania.
Abstracted: DAI 31:5347-A.

2   ALTHOLZ, JOSEF L. "WM." In Victorian England: 1837-1901.
     Cambridge: Cambridge University Press, pp. 73, passim.
        Many references to WM appear under different categories, such
as "History of the Fine Arts." All of them are included in the
present book.

3   ANDERSON, J.R.L. The Upper Thames. London: Eyre and
     Spotiswode, pp. 234-35.
        Describes Kelmscott Manor, its setting on the Thames, its
history and owners, notably WM and his family.

4   BLOOM, HAROLD. Yeats. New York: Oxford University Press, pp.
     294-96, passim.
        Argues that Yeats's "relation to Morris is a very complex
one" and that WM's influence on At the Hawk's Well is "crucial." In
the abundance of the prose romances, Yeats "recognized what he and
Morris lacked, the luck of the true quester," and in this play Yeats
"displaces this recognition into another realm, not Morris's
florabundant world, but the daimonic wastes of the Sidhe," where the
hero achieves self-recognition.

5   CALDER, GRACE, ed. Introduction to The Story of Kormak, Son of
     Ogmund, by WM and Magnusson. London: WM Society, pp. 1-46.
        Full and helpful introduction to this translation, printed
here for the first time, from a hand-lettered manuscript that WM
made in 1871, the year his marital problems increased and thus of
his first journey to Iceland. So Kormaks Saga, whose themes involve
tragic love, is here discussed as a "key to a chapter of Morris's
life that was all-important to his literary career and crucial to
his personal history." Discusses methods WM and Magnusson used in
translating thirteenth-century Icelandic prose and poetry into
quasi-modern English, listing the sagas published, commenting upon
critical reactions, and recalling that there were few scholarly
works available in 1871 to aid them over the rough places,
especially with the many skaldic verses in this saga. Includes
notes by Alfred Fairbanks on WM's calligraphy (1970.11) and by
Hallberg Hallmundsson on skaldic verse (1970.17), as well as twelve
plates that display WM's calligraphy.

6   CHANDLER, ALICE. "Art and Society: Ruskin and WM." In A Dream
     of Order: The Medieval Ideal in Nineteenth-Century English
     Literature. Lincoln: University of Nebraska Press, pp. 184-230,
     passim.
        WM is the last British author treated in this survey of
nineteenth-century medievalism, and links to predecessors like
Scott, Carlyle, and Ruskin are elucidated. Commentary on WM's
interest in things medieval, from boyhood onward, is woven into
discussions of Morris and Co, where WM's experiences as a happy and

productive artisan influenced his ideas about both medieval and
modern society. Marx and historians like Thorold Rogers also shaped
WM's attitudes toward the Middle Ages, and their influence in <u>John
Ball</u> is more apparent than in <u>Nowhere</u>, which is here seen as mere
myth.

7   CHAPMAN, RAYMOND. <u>Faith</u> <u>and</u> <u>Revolt</u>: <u>Studies</u> <u>in</u> <u>the</u> <u>Literary</u>
     <u>Influence</u> <u>of</u> <u>the</u> <u>Oxford</u> <u>Movement</u>. London: Weidenfeld and
     Nicolson, pp. 232-43, passim.
        The "Brotherhood" that WM and Burne-Jones contemplated during
the Oxford years is here made to seem much more seriously religious
than in other studies, and WM is said to "have been one of the most
devout members of the Brotherhood." It is also pointed out that
Burne-Jones and WM "conceived a great regard for the theological
writings of Robert Wilberforce."

8   CHAPPLE, J.A.V. <u>Documentary</u> <u>and</u> <u>Imaginative</u> <u>Literature</u>:
     <u>1880-1920</u>. London: Blandford; New York: Barnes and Noble, pp.
     106-14, passim.
        Comments upon <u>Nowhere</u> and <u>Looking</u> <u>Backward</u>, pointing out that
WM "is looking backward," that the sorts of celebrations of modern
organization or engineering that occur in Bellamy or Wells are of
course not present in WM's writings. But suggests that <u>Nowhere</u> has
"perhaps in the long run more important qualities," that its
descriptions and structure "embodied potential history in order to
inspire the men and women who might have made it actual."

9   DUNLAP, BARBARA. "Reviewers Reviewed." <u>News</u> <u>from</u> <u>Anywhere</u>
     12:12-22.
        Comments upon the reviews received by the three major books
published in 1967 on WM, books by Thompson (1967.29), Watkinson
(1967.35), and Henderson (1967.11), finding tendencies to simplify
and misrepresent. Also accuses reviewers of ignoring authorial
expertise or bias.

10   EGBERT, DONALD D. "The Continuing Influence of WM." In <u>Social</u>
     <u>Radicalism</u> <u>and</u> <u>the</u> <u>Arts</u>, <u>Western</u> <u>Europe</u>: <u>A</u> <u>Cultural</u> <u>History</u> <u>from</u>
     <u>the</u> <u>French</u> <u>Revolution</u> <u>to</u> <u>1968</u>. New York: Knopf, pp. 472-91,
     passim.
        Surveys all the artisans and movements, in England and
abroad, influenced by WM's theories on the elemental connections
between society and art. Subsections of the preceding chapter cover
WM and socialist colleagues from the Avelings through Wilde, and
there are capsule descriptions of WM and the Fabians, the Arts and
Crafts Movement, the Pre-Raphaelites, and the like.

11 FAIRBANK, ALFRED. "A Note on the Manuscript Work of WM." In
    The Story of Kormak, Son of Ogmund, by WM and Magnusson. Edited
    by Grace Calder. London: WM Society, pp. 53-69.
        Between 1870 and 1875 WM completed over 1,500 pages of
    calligraphy, experimenting with different scripts, employing
    elaborate illumination techniques, and demonstrating almost
    astounding expertise, especially when we consider that this was all
    done in his spare time and described as mere "pleasure work."
    Discusses the manuscripts and WM's methods in great detail;
    concludes with an "Annotated List of Manuscript Work," describing
    the eighteen books, many partially done, as well as the trial pages
    and fragments, giving their present locations.

12 FAULKNER, PETER. "Senghor and WM: Socialists." JWMS 2, no. 4
    (Summer):2-7.
        Finds interesting parallels between WM and Leopold Sedar
    Senghor, twentieth-century Senegalese poet and statesman, who--like
    WM--was strongly influenced by both Marx and a firm sense of the
    importance of traditional lore. Senghor's ideas about brotherhood,
    love, art, and culture, and about an all-embracing Negritude, gave
    his politics the kind of moral base that WM's ideas might have
    provided for European Marxists if his socialist lectures had
    received the attention due them.

13 FRANKLIN, COLIN. "On the Binding of Kelmscott Press Books."
    JWMS 2, no. 4 (Summer):28-30.
        About the only aspect of Kelmscott Press operations WM did
    not attend to was the bindings, perhaps because he did not regard
    them as permanent, assuming that owners might later choose bindings
    that would fit their private collections. But few modern collectors
    have done so, and the vellum exteriors of Kelmscott Press volumes
    crack and stain, looking worse and worse as they age. When the
    volumes are properly, that is, tightly, bound other problems have
    arisen: decorations on the inner margins have, for instance,
    disappeared.

14 FREDEMAN, WILLIAM E. "Prelude to the Last Decade: Rossetti in
    the Summer of 1872." Bulletin of the John Rylands Library 53,
    nos. 1-2 (Autumn-Spring):75-121, 272-328.
        There are several references to WM within this detailed
    study, based largely on unpublished correspondence, of Rossetti and
    the great concern his sickness caused his brother and a few friends
    during the summer of 1872, a sickness they felt had been caused, in
    part, by his affair with Janey. WM is referred to condescendingly
    in the letters as "a most amiable husband." He evidently retained a
    calm equanimity, even offering in June 1872 to sit with the ailing
    Rossetti.

*15 GENT, MARGARET. "Theme and Symbol in the Poetry of WM."
     Dissertation, University of Leeds.
         Cited in Index to Theses Accepted for Higher Degrees in the
     Universities of Great Britain, 20 (1969-70):18.

16 GENT, MARGARET. "The Drowned Phoenician Sailor: T.S. Eliot and
     WM." N and Q 215 (February):50-51.
         Considers specific similarities between Eliot's Phlebas in
     The Waste Land and "The Nymph's Song to Hylas" in Jason, a poem we
     know Eliot had recently read because he comments upon it in his
     essay on Marvell (1932.7).

17 HALLMUNDSSON, HALLBERG. "A Note on Drottkvaett." In The Story
     of Kormak, Son of Ogmund, by WM and Magnusson. Edited by Grace
     Calder. London: WM Society, pp. 47-51.
         A detailed introduction to the intricate prosody of Icelandic
     court poetry, one that deepens our appreciation of WM's patience and
     skill in translating the many skaldic verses that appear in Kormak's
     Saga.

18 HARVIE, CHRISTOPHER; MARTIN, GRAHAM; and SCHARF, AARON.   "WM."
     Industrialization and Culture, 1830-1914. London: Macmillan,
     Open University Press, pp. 322-28, passim.
         A collection of readings to be used with Open University
     courses on changes industrialization brought to British society, and
     since two of the eight units deal with industry and art, WM is
     mentioned many times. Extracts from several of his lectures and
     from Nowhere, are reprinted along with concise introductions and
     notes.

19 HILTON, TIMOTHY. "A Palace of Art." In The Pre-Raphaelites.
     London: Thames and Hudson, pp. 161-73, passim.
         Stresses importance of Rossetti and of Oxford influences on
     WM's early achievement, and suggests that Janey "determined the
     alignment of her husband's artistic interests," because their
     marriage was "totally removed from the upper-middle-class Victorian
     milieu in which Morris had been brought up." Asserts that WM had a
     "totally static sense of history" and that his "classic" production
     is wallpaper, which his poetry unfortunately resembles.

20 HOLLOW, JOHN. "Singer of an Empty Day: WM and the Desire for
    Immortality." Dissertation, University of Rochester.
        Abstracted: DAI 30:3461-A.

21 HULSE, JAMES W. "WM: Pilgrim of Hope." In Revolutionists in
    London: A Study of Five Unorthodox Socialists. Oxford:
    Clarendon Press, pp. 77-110, passim.
        Argues that this relatively short study, an "experiment in
    synthesis," should make these five reformers easier to understand
    because continual comparisons will be made. Thus the chapter on WM,
    full of useful detail, often refers to points made in chapters on
    Stepniak, Kropotkin, Shaw, and Bernstein. Argues that WM was more
    of an eclectic liberal than a true Marxist, despite the findings of
    scholars like E.P. Thompson: 1955.15.

22 HUTCHINGS, F.G.B. The Impact of WM. Saskatchewan: Copp Clark
    Publishing, 22 pp.
        Sketches in general biographical backgrounds, and then
    stresses WM's influence on twentieth-century printing. Touches on
    WM's influence on the Golden Cockerell Press and on Bruce Rogers.
    This lecture accompanied an exhibition in Saskatchewan on modern
    printing.

23 KOCMANOVA, JESSIE. "The Living Language of WM." Brno Studies
    in English no. 9:17-34. (Vol. 166, Opera Universitatis
    Purkynianae Brunensis.)
        Attempts to describe and categorize five different prose
    styles that WM used, from the utilitarian through the artistic which
    adorned the late romances, whose style equaled the "culmination of
    all the levels of his prose writing throughout his life." The
    "stylistic characteristics" she approves of, however, occur
    everywhere and are never rigorously defined; labels like "forceful,"
    and "concrete," and "rhythmic" are rarely pinned to actual diction
    and syntax.

24 LEWIS, JOHN. The Anatomy of Printing. New York: Watson-Guptil,
    pp. 185-86, 203-4, passim.
        A biographical sketch, one that stresses the influence of
    Ruskin, precedes an introduction to Kelmscott Press and a discussion
    of its influence on other presses.

25 LOUGY, ROBERT. "WM's Nowhere: The Novel as Psychology of Art."
     English Literature in Transition (1880-1920) 13, no. 1:1-8.
         Discusses reasons WM disliked Bellamy's Looking Backward,
pointing out that the society he created as a response, Nowhere, is
impractical. But if it is read as about Art, then it succeeds; it
has a structure that can be linked to Freudian "periods of
ideation," to three categories here labeled "intense desire,"
"return to childhood," and "wish fulfillment." Such ideas and
formulations are often provocative, and confusing.

26 MAAS, H.; DUNCAN, J.L.; and GOOD, W.C., eds. The Letters of
     Aubrey Beardsley. Cranberry, N.J.: Associated University Press,
     pp. 44, passim.
         Beardsley registers his admiration for Paradise, but also
boasts that his own work is fresher than WM's, which is a "mere
imitation of the old stuff."

27 MAC DONALD, STUART. "WM, Crane and Applied Art." In The
     History and Philosophy of Art Education. New York: American
     Elsevier Publishing, pp. 312-14, passim.
         Summarizes evidence WM gave before the Royal Commission on
Technical Education, evidence that suggests he was unaware of the
latest educational theories. He, like Ruskin, was cool toward the
idea of government art schools, but he himself became the first
president, in 1890, of the Birmingham School of Art, and his
writings proved to be influential for other educational innovaters,
like the Germans who developed the Bauhaus.

28 MIDDLEBRO', TOM. "Brief Thoughts on Nowhere." JWMS 2, no. 4
     (Summer):8-12.
         Makes interesting and useful distinctions between arcadias
and utopias, putting Nowhere in the former category, since it is
rural, socially unstructured, and creative, while utopias are urban,
heirarchical, and uniform--containing those features WM hated in
Looking Backward. Speaks also of arcadian elements in
twentieth-century dystopias.

*29 MORRIS, HENRY. A Visit to Hayle Mill. North Hills, Pa., pp.
     22-45.
         According to Peterson's Bibliography of the Kelmscott Press
(Oxford, 1984), p. xix, this includes WM's correspondence with his
papermaker, Joseph Batchelor.

30 MUMFORD, LEWIS. <u>The</u> <u>Myth</u> <u>of</u> <u>the</u> <u>Machine:</u> <u>The</u> <u>Pentagon</u> <u>of</u>
   <u>Power</u>. New York: Harcourt Brace, pp. 135, 144, passim.
        Celebrates WM as one who briefly rescued craftsmen and
tool-users from the flood of mechanization that has now engulfed us,
and says that WM's mastery of handicrafts contains a lesson that has
"still to be soberly appraised and applied to contemporary
society--a society now debilitated by lack of engrossing manual
work, and its increasing resistance to work of any kind." Of
<u>Nowhere</u>, he asserts that it implied "good news, for it indicated a
return to the human center: the liquidation of the power complex and
the institutional fixations which cripple and abort human
development."

31 REDMOND, JAMES, ed. Introduction to <u>Nowhere</u>. London: Routledge
   and Kegan Paul, pp. xi-xlii. Reprint. 1972, 1973, 1974, 1976,
   1977, 1979, 1981.
        Detailed and helpful introduction is divided into four parts:
(1) "Life of WM," (2) "Myths, Legends, and Utopian Dreams," (3)
"Nineteenth Century Medievalism: A Dream of Ultimate Rest," and (4)
"Man is the Measure." WM'S early life, and the inculcation of rural
and medieval ideals, are discussed as significant for theme and
setting in both <u>Paradise</u> and <u>Nowhere</u>, for the latter also involves
nostalgic escape; it should not be judged as though it were a
Victorian novel. Points out correspondences <u>Nowhere</u> shares with the
<u>Germania</u> of Tacitus, with the theories of Rousseau and Marx, and
with More's <u>Utopia</u>. Touches on nineteenth-century influences,
especially Ruskin's ideas about nature and beauty, and discusses the
ways that <u>Nowhere</u> differs from other nineteenth- and
twentieth-century Utopias, concluding that WM created a society
where man would be the measure, where "simplicity, directness, and
sensuous delight" would outweigh all other, merely political,
factors.

32 SAMBROOK, JAMES. "The Rossettis and other Contemporary Poets."
   In <u>The</u> <u>Victorians</u>. History of Literature in the English
   Language, edited by A. Pollard, vol. 6. London: Barrie and
   Jenkins, pp. 349-52, passim.
        Discusses a few <u>Defence</u> poems, suggesting that they reveal
"the sensibility of the designer rather than, say, the moralist."
Offers short evaluations of <u>Paradise</u>, <u>Sigurd</u>, and the prose
romances, characterizing them as "somniferous." Asserts that in
<u>Nowhere</u> WM portrays a "Rosseau-Godwinesque-anarchist-pastoral-arts
and crafts-ideal society."

33 SEEBER, HANS ULRICH. "Zuruck <u>Nowhere</u> nach Arcadien: Die
    utopische Idylle." In <u>Wandlungen</u> <u>der</u> <u>Form</u> <u>in</u> <u>der</u> <u>literarischen</u>
    <u>Utopie</u>, <u>Studien</u> <u>zur</u> <u>Entfaltung</u> <u>des</u> <u>utopischen</u> <u>Romans</u> <u>in</u> <u>England</u>.
    Goppingen: Goppingen Academic Studies, no. 13, pp. 112-34.
        Characteristics that <u>Nowhere</u> shares with other
    nineteenth-century "Arcadian Utopias" are discussed, and then
    <u>Nowhere</u> is analyzed in some detail, with categories like "Die
    Lehrgesprache" controlling the analysis. Typical vocabulary and
    characterization also discussed.

34 SLYTHE, R. MARGARET. <u>The</u> <u>Art</u> <u>of</u> <u>Illustration</u>: <u>1750-1900</u>.
    London: Library Association, pp. 14, 35-36.
        Comments on the Kelmscott Chaucer, calling WM the "greatest
    figure of the transition period between original nineteenth-century
    and modern illustration."

35 SONSTROEM, DAVID. <u>Rossetti</u> <u>and</u> <u>the</u> <u>Fair</u> <u>Lady</u>. Middletown,
    Conn.: Wesleyan University Press, pp. 71-80, passim.
        Sketches in Red Lion Square days when it "was blue summer
    from Christmas to Christmas," discussing ways that WM and
    Burne-Jones drew Rossetti into their medieval dreamworlds,
    introducing him to Malory. Discusses the biographical overtones in
    paintings like <u>La</u> <u>Pia</u> and in sonnets from the <u>House</u> <u>of</u> <u>Life</u>
    sequence, making use of Doughty's imaginative deductions (1949.3).

36 STENNING, H.J. "1906 and All That." <u>JWMS</u> 2, no. 4
    (Summer):31-33.
        The SDF and the Socialist League, in the doldrums when WM
    died, suffered real setbacks three years later, with the outbreak of
    the Boer War. In 1906, however, there was a resurgence of the SDF,
    and the author recalls meetings and speakers like Hyndman and Shaw.

37 TALBOT, NORMAN C. "The Girl's Journey and the Lad's Quest: A
    Study in the Romances of WM." In <u>Australasian</u> <u>Languages</u> <u>and</u>
    <u>Literature</u> <u>Association</u>; <u>Proceedings</u> <u>and</u> <u>Papers</u> <u>of</u> <u>the</u> <u>Twelfth</u>
    <u>Congress</u>. Edited by A.P. Treweek. Sydney: AULLA, pp.
    233-34.
        Synopsis of paper read at 1969 Australasian Conference on two
    of WM's prose romances, which "were described in terms of the
    secular Grail-quest, the Jungian pilgrimage to the self," and labels
    such as "archetype," "anima," "emanation," "virgin-bride," "terrible
    mother," and the like, were used throughout the discussion of <u>Well</u>
    and <u>Water</u>.

38   TOMPKINS, J.M.S.   "The Work of WM: A Cord of Triple Strand."
     Dalhousie Review 50, no. 1 (Spring):97-111.
         Suggests that it is impossible "for any one critic or
     biographer to write with authority on all the aspects of Morris's
     life and genius," that this will probably remain true. Attempts to
     show how WM's romantic poetry and prose contain aspects, or
     "strands," of his socialism and of design theory.

39   WATKINSON, RAY.   "Burne-Jones, WM, and Rossetti."   In
     Pre-Raphaelite Art and Design. London: Studio Vista; Greenwich,
     Conn.: New York Graphic Society, pp. 162-72, passim.
         Points out that WM's influence on nineteenth-century design
     has often been exaggerated; certain innovations would have occurred
     even if WM had never lived. But Morris and Co. gave a "peculiar
     character" to British design; the reasons for the success of the
     Firm, the importance of artists like Rossetti in breaking down
     conventions, are discussed. Asserts that both WM's designs and his
     lectures made him the "greatest figure in the design world in the
     last quarter of the nineteenth century."

40   WICK, PETER A.   Introduction to The Turn of a Century:
     1885-1910. Art Nouveau and Jugendstil Books. Catalogue of an
     Exhibition at Harvard.   Cambridge: Houghton Library, passim.
         WM described as the "platform from which modern book design
     started," and his Kelmscott Press achievements are often referred to
     in the introduction and in subsequent descriptions of the many books
     from England and the Continent that were included in this exhibit.
     Reports that WM considered legal action against Beardsley, so
     offensive did he find his illustrations for Malory.

41   WODZICKE, HELEN.   "The Emery Walker Photographs at St. Brides."
     JWMS 2, no. 4 (Summer):13-27.
         Discusses the photographic negatives made by Walker, their
     dispersal, and the collection at St. Brides Printing Library, where
     there are several of WM and his family, and also of photographs and
     paintings that Rossetti had made of Janey. Eight prints and a
     checklist of the negatives held by St. Brides accompany the article.

                                1971

1   BERRY, RALPH.   "Defence."   VP 9, no. 3 (Autumn):277-86.
         Points out that twenty of the thirty poems in Defence end in
     death and "defeat, coupled usually with sexual frustration," and
     then suggests that WM adopted a medieval "mode" so that he could
     express his deepest preoccupations: fears of death and personal
     inadequacies.

2   CASTLE, BARBARA. "The Vision Splendid." New Statesman 82, no.
     2115 (1 October):450-51.
       Reading Water fifty years after she had first heard it read
aloud, she finds that the tale still has real power. Comments upon
the sensual descriptions of the earth and the female body, and
concludes that this is "strong meat for most of us these days,
caught as we are between kitchen sink drama and women's magazines."

3   CAVE, RODERICK. "Printing as One of the Fine Arts: WM and
     Kelmscott Press." In The Private Press. London: Faber and
     Faber; New York: Watson-Guptil, pp. 133-42, passim.
       Offering a few new details, like the fact that Kelmscott
Press in seven years had a "turn-over" of 50,000 pounds, and
suggesting that the volumes issued from the Press were works of art
and a "revolutionary manifesto for better printing," but not books,
this is a lively and informed introduction to Kelmscott Press and
its influence and significance. Includes contemporary critiques
from Crane and Thorsten Veblen.

4   CHIANESE, ROBERT L., ed. Peaceable Kingdoms: An Anthology of
     Utopian Writings. New York: Harcourt Brace, pp. 4-8, 86-193.
       Brief biographical introduction precedes a "very slightly
abridged" Nowhere. Actually whole chapters are, without explanation
or annotation, omitted.

5   COLE, MARGARET. The Life of G.D.H. Cole. London: Macmillan,
     pp. 33-35, passim.
       Of her husband's conversion to socialism, she says, "he seems
to have skipped almost straight from Toryism to Socialism, and for
this there was one cause and one only--WM." Cole read Defence
before Nowhere and appreciated the latter out of "ethical-aesthetic"
rather than economic convictions; his regard for WM was abiding.

6   DUNLAP, JOSEPH R. The Book that Never Was. New York: Oriole
     Press, 86 pp.
       Contents of this detailed study are suggested by its
subtitle: "The Argument: How WM and Burne-Jones Attempted to Make of
Paradise a book with 'Lots of Pictures'; How They Fared in this
Endeavor; and How Their Dream, though it Evaded Them, Has Yet
Outlived Them." One reason that they failed was their "collision
with mid-century typography," and this is demonstrated here by
illustrations that bring together the woodcuts WM made from
Burne-Jones drawings and the pallid type available from publishers
like Chiswick. Also discussed are trial pages that survive from a
planned illustrated edition of Love Is Enough, and these demonstrate
the same incongruities between design and type. Such problems were
not solved until WM designed his own type faces with the founding of
Kelmscott Press. Includes two appendixes: (1) accounts by George

263

Wardle of engraving the blocks for "Cupid and Psyche," and (2) WM's
list of illustrations for "Cupid and Psyche."

7   EGGERS, JOHN P. "Rival Visions: WM." In King Arthur's
    Laureate: A Study of Tennyson's "Idylls of the King." New York:
    New York University Press, pp. 119-31.
        Discusses "Hollow Land" and the Arthurian poems in Defence,
    saying of the title poem that WM, in contrast to both Malory and
    Tennyson, saves the queen, judging her to be a "reproach to the
    meagerness of the pedestrian moral climate in which she is forced to
    live."

8   FASS, BARBARA. "WM and the Tannhauser Legend: A Gloss on the
    Paradise Motif." Victorian Newsletter 40 (Fall):22-26.
        Suggests that Paradise is not "escapist so much as it is
    about escape," and that therefore the Tannhauser legend
    appropriately comes last ("The Hill of Venus," the second poem for
    February, is the twenty-fourth in the cycle). The hero's decision
    to leave Venus parallels WM's desire to leave aestheticism behind to
    enter the world of action and joyful work.

9   GOLDZAMT, EDMUND. "WM et la genese sociale de l'architecture
    moderne." L'architecture d'aujourd'hui 43, no. 155
    (April):84-87.
        A synopsis of 1967.8.

10 GOODE, JOHN. "WM and the Dream of Revolution." In Literature
    and Politics in the Nineteenth Century. Edited by John Lucas.
    London: Methuen, pp. 221-80.
        Argues against the prevailing habit of considering WM's
    "creative writing" apart from his socialist works, offering
    interesting readings of works like Sigurd and Wolfings that reveal
    socialist ideologies, readings that use neo-Marxist categories drawn
    from modern critics like Lukacs. Contrasts WM to nineteenth-century
    realists like Gissing and James, concluding that WM "creates a
    revolutionary literature because he discovers forms which dramatize
    the tension of the revolutionary mind. And I do not know any other
    writer in English who does that."

11 GOODWIN, K.L. "Morris and Company's Adelaide Patron." Art and
    Australia 8, no. 4 (March):342-45.
        No city in the world, with the possible exception of London,
    has as much Morris and Co. stained glass as Adelaide, Australia.
    These windows, in eight different buildings, can be attributed to
    the activities and donations of a wealthy collecter, George Brookman
    (1850-1927), who introduced Morris and Co. windows, and later even
    some tapestries, to Adelaide. Describes the window, designed by

Dearle, for the Australian Stock Exchange. Includes color
illustrations.

12 HOENNIGHAUSEN, LOTHER. Praraphaeliten und Fin de Siecle.
    Munich: Wilhelm Fink, 185-88, passim.
        Comments upon the colors, the "Farbstruktur," in several
    poems from Defence, particularly in "Golden Wings," and discusses
    the use of garden settings in these poems.

13 HOLLOW, JOHN. "WM and the Judgment of God." PMLA 86, no. 3
    (May):446-51.
        A major theme in some of WM's early writings is that if God
    does exist "He must mean for men to ignore Him." The hero of "Pool"
    learns this, as do the medieval knights in "Hollow Land" and in "The
    Judgment of God." In "The Defence of Guenevere," the heroine does
    not "deny adultery, she denies Gauwaine's claim to know God's
    judgment of her." The business of choosing blue over red is
    logical, since mortals, lacking the judgment of God, are bound to
    opt for beauty, for heaven's color. In the next poem, "King
    Arthur's Tomb," Guenevere does admit her sin, but against Arthur,
    not against God, for of that higher culpability she cannot judge.
    WM insists that "no man had the power to sing of heaven or hell, of
    God's judgments."

14 LE BOURGEOIS, JOHN. "The Youth of WM, 1934-76: An
    Interpretation." Dissertation, Tulane University.
        Abstracted: DAI 32:2035-A.

15 LE BOURGEOIS, JOHN. "A Rossetti-WM Letter." N and Q 216
    (July):255.
        Reprints, and comments upon, a letter Rossetti sent to WM in
    1874, at the time of the dissolution of Morris, Marshall, Faulkner
    Co. It indicates that Rossetti had done more designs than Mackail
    (1899.10) had reported, that he hoped to continue working with the
    reorganized company, and that he was at this late date still on
    fairly friendly terms with WM.

16 LIBERMAN, MICHAEL. "WM's Nowhere: A Critical and Annotated
    Edition." Dissertation, University of Nebraska.
        Abstracted: DAI 32:3956-A.

17 LUX, SIMONETTA. "Ruskin e WM." In Art, societa e technica.
    Rome and Assisi: B. Carucci, pp. 11-17, passim.
        Biographical sketch includes comments about WM's debt to
Ruskin's indictment of industrialism.

18 MEIER, PAUL. "An Unpublished Lecture of WM: 'How Shall We Live
    Then?'" International Review of Social History 16, pt. 2:1-24.
        Has high praise for Lemire's work on WM's lectures (1969.18),
especially the calendar and the checklist; the former reports that
WM gave a lecture, "How Shall We Live Then?," five times in 1889-90,
and the checklist informs us that "no text remains." But the
original was preserved in the archives of the International
Institute of Social History in Amsterdam, and it is here reprinted,
along with introductory comments that speculate about how the
manuscript might have arrived in Amsterdam and that show how WM
attempted to mold the content and tone of the lecture to appeal to
its initial audience, a group of Fabians. He wanted to reach them,
to heal wounds caused by recent accusations, but he was still
"fighting uncompromisingly against reformist ideology." The lecture
also demonstrates WM's understanding of the two stages of the
revolution, of the need for machines in the new socialist society;
it is very important for understanding WM's "ideological
evolution."

19 MEIER, PAUL. "Friedrich Engels and WM." La pensee 156:68-80.
        Though none of WM's early biographers even mention Engels,
though Engels in a few letters refers in a disparaging fashion to WM
as a "sentimental socialist," there is still compelling evidence
that the two men saw each other often and that WM was strongly
influenced by Engels's writings and also by conversations with him.
This evidence resides in passages from WM's lectures that provide
striking parallels to theories of both Marx and Engels not published
until long after their deaths. Reprints a letter, written in 1885,
in which WM invites Engels to contribute an article to Commonweal.

20 MEIER, PAUL. "La pensee utopique de WM." Raison presente 21
    (January-March):87-94.
        Summary of the 1971 Sorbonne thesis that won "mention tres
honorable" and was to become the two-volume study of WM and his
contributions to utopian literature and socialist theory (1972.19).

21 MELVIN, ANDREW. WM: Wallpapers and Designs. London: Academy
     Editions, 55 pp.
         An introductory sketch stresses that WM was a paradox.
     Includes fifty-two reproductions of WM designs. Introduction
     reprinted: 1973.7.

22 MORTON, JOCELYN. Three Generations in a Family Textile Firm.
     London: Routledge and Kegan Paul, pp. 97-117.
         In a history of a Glasgow textile firm over three
     generations, WM is mentioned as an important influence, via both his
     precepts and practices, upon James Morton, head of the firm in its
     second generation. A lecture (1901.15) shows him in full agreement
     with both Ruskin and WM about using nature as a source and about the
     need to learn from, quarry from, past designers. But James Morton
     used machines whenever he could; the resulting textiles were
     cheaper, and better. Suggests that WM, in practice if not in
     precept, had come to realize how important machines were to the
     production of textiles. James Morton's two greatest heroes were WM
     and Abraham Lincoln.

23 MUIR, PERCY. Victorian Illustrated Books. New York: Praeger,
     pp. 188-90, passim.
         A survey of illustrated books includes some irreverent
     remarks about WM's work at Kelmscott Press: "some day, perhaps,
     someone will write a treatise about his work in general from a
     standpoint this side of idolatry." Calls WM the "great
     anti-technologist."

24 NAYLOR, GILLIAN. "Theory into Practice: WM." In The Arts and
     Crafts Movement: A Study of its Sources, Ideals and Influence on
     Design Theory. London: Studio Vista, pp. 96-112, passim.
         Discusses the origins of the Arts and Crafts Movement and its
     abiding concern to see design problems within social contexts. Has
     101 plates and a selective bibliography. The chapter on WM argues
     that he "did most to establish England's reputation as a nation of
     dedicated designers." Has useful information on Ashbee's importance
     in spreading Arts and Crafts ideas to America and the Continent.
     Discusses recent trends in Scandinavian design as fulfilling some
     Arts and Crafts ideals.

25 NELSON, JAMES G. The Early Nineties: A View from Bodley Head.
     Cambridge, Mass.: Harvard University Press, pp. 37, 41, passim.
         Between 1887 and 1894 the Bodley Head, a small bookshop and
     publishing firm, published over 100 books; some of them were
     influenced by WM's example, and many of them proved more beautiful
     and more readable than Kelmscott Press volumes.

26 NOCHLIN, LINDA. Realism. Harmondsworth: Penguin, pp. 217-18,
    passim.
        Speaks of WM's vision as "remarkably prophetic of the demands
of today's revolutionaries for a return to natural life, handicraft
modes of production, the small face-to-face group or commune as the
social unit," and of WM's attitudes toward vernacular architecture
as "strikingly analagous to an important new direction in
architectural thinking of the present day."

27 OBERG, CHARLOTTE. "The Pagan Prophet: Unity of Vision in the
    Narrative Poetry of WM." Dissertation, University of Virginia.
        Abstracted: DAI 31:4786-A. Revised for publication: 1978.42.

28 SURTEES, VIRGINIA. The Paintings and Drawings of Rossetti: A
    Catalogue Raisonne. Oxford: Clarendon Press, 2 vols., passim.
        WM was the model for figures within sixteen Rossetti drawings
or designs, and he was the original owner of several Rossetti works.
There are thus dozens of references to WM, to Morris and Co., to
WM's literary works, and of course to Janey, within the detailed
notes that make up the second volume of this inclusive catalogue.

29 THOMPSON, LAURENCE. The Enthusiasts: A Biography of John and
    Katherine Bruce Glasier. London: Victor Gollancz, pp. 35-38,
    41-49, passim.
        Describes Glasier's reactions to lectures WM gave in Glasgow,
as well as Katherine Glasier's first lecture at Hammersmith.
Discusses E.P. Thompson's objections (1955.15) to Glasier's woolly
account of WM's socialism, but since that book (1921.3) was written
under the influence of morphia, it should be considered
"impressionist."

30 "Kelmscott on Thames." Country Life 149, no. 3857 (13
    May):1151.
        Describes Kelmscott House, recently bequeathed by Helena
Stephenson to WM Society.

31 Sanderson WM Exhibition. Catalogue of a 4 June-1 July 1971
    Exhibition; London: Sandersons, 8 pp.
        A catalogue-pamphlet describing several wallpapers and
fabrics from Morris and Co., these arranged as a display of
decorated rooms in a modern flat.

<u>1972</u>

1   BARNARD, JULIAN. "WM, DeMorgan and the Craft Tradition." In
     <u>Victorian</u> <u>Ceramic</u> <u>Tiles</u>. London: Studio Vista, pp. 117-23,
     passim.
          WM was interested in decorative tiles at Red House and the
     Firm produced them from the outset, but he was never directly
     involved. His other designs influenced Victorian tile-makers.
     Discusses DeMorgan's associations with the Firm and Burne-Jones's
     designs, namely, for the "Beauty and the Beast" panel.

2   CALHOUN, CATHERINE B. "The Pastoral Aesthetic of WM: A Reading
     of <u>Paradise</u>." Dissertation, University of North Carolina.
          Abstracted: DAI 33:1137-A. Revised for publication: 1975.11.

3   COLLINS, JOHN. "Harry Buxton Forman and WM: A Preliminary
     Inquiry." <u>Book</u> <u>Collector</u> 21, no. 4 (Winter):503-23.
          Certain discrepancies between notes Forman took on three WM
     pamphlets and his published accounts inspired the careful and
     exhaustive research behind this article, research that demonstrates
     how Forman improved these handouts (cheaply printed copies of WM
     speeches) by adding printed wrappers and by indicating then in his
     descriptions of WM's books (1897.9) that these were separately
     published. Some were sold and some titles turned up in Scott's
     bibliography (1897.16), but Cockerell's suspicions about these
     "special copies" finally curbed Forman, who had also gotten WM to
     inscribe one of the Thomas Wise forgeries (1934.17).

4   ELLISON, RUTH C. "'The Undying Glory of Dreams': WM and 'The
     Northland of Old.'" In <u>Victorian</u> <u>Poetry</u>. Edited by M. Bradbury
     and D. Palmer. London: E. Arnold, pp. 138-75.
          Assays <u>Defence</u> poems, their diction and intended audience,
     before turning to a "new and important factor in Morris's artistic
     development," his interest in Iceland and its ancient literature.
     Argues that WM understood the sagas, and even if he did not
     re-create their "elegant terseness" in his writings based on them,
     their themes influenced him personally. Discusses WM's reworking of
     sagas in both "Gudrun," and <u>Sigurd</u>, showing how he altered
     characters and emphases in the former, achieving finally an
     unfortunate "combination of hysteria and sentimentality." But in
     the latter, "Sigurd becomes the symbol, to Morris, of hope in a dark
     age," and the poem is "a work one can fairly call great."

5   GENT, MARGARET. "'To Flinch from Modern Varnish': The Appeal of
     the Past to the Victorian Imagination." In <u>Victorian</u> <u>Poetry</u>.
     Edited by M. Bradbury and D. Palmer. London: E. Arnold, pp.
     10-35.
         Cites works by Dickens, Browning, and some Victorian painters
who "set up a dialogue between the present and the past," before
moving on to WM whom she sees as the "chief example" of one who used
historical settings in ways much more complex than those suggested
in a few oft-quoted lines from <u>Paradise</u>. <u>Paradise</u> is, in fact, a
"massive piece of self-destructive irony, which more than any other
work is the key to Morris's elusive character." Suggests also that
"the whole of <u>Paradise</u> is a deliberate underachievement in order to
point the moral that art is a poor substitute for life." There are
also some comments on <u>Defence</u> poems, on--for instance--"Haystack in
the Floods," as a "Pre-Raphaelite painting rendered into words."

6   GERMANN, GEORG. <u>Gothic</u> <u>Revival</u> <u>in</u> <u>Europe</u> <u>and</u> <u>Britain</u>: <u>Sources,</u>
     <u>Influences</u> <u>and</u> <u>Ideas.</u> Translated by G. Onn. London: Lund
     Humphries; Cambridge: M.I.T.Press, pp. 170-71, 178.
         Points out how WM's ideas about functional design influenced
Herman Muthesius (1861-1927), and how he carried these ideas back to
Germany, to Gropius, and thence into the ideology behind the
Bauhaus.

7   GLASSIE, HENRY. <u>Folklore</u> <u>and</u> <u>Folklife</u>: <u>An</u> <u>Introduction</u>.
     Chicago: University of Chicago Press, pp. 254-56, 278.
         A chapter on folk art opens with a discussion of WM's
abhorrence of the "waste of labour and life" that occurs in modern
civilization. Points out that WM's search for an alternative
involved an "organic aesthetic that he ascribed to the medieval
craftsman."

8   HAIGHT, GORDON S., ed. "Incentive in a Communist Society." In
     <u>The</u> <u>Portable</u> <u>Victorian</u> <u>Reader</u>. New York: Viking. Reprint.
     1973, 1975. Harmondsworth: Penguin, 1976. Reprint. 1977,
     1981, pp. 300-306.
         Under the title "Incentive in a Communist Society," appear
these few pages from chapter fifteen in <u>Nowhere</u>, the only selection
from WM in this anthology.

9   HOUGHTON, WALTER E., et al. "<u>Oxford</u> <u>and</u> <u>Cambridge</u> <u>Magazine</u>,
     1856." <u>Wellesley</u> <u>Index</u> <u>to</u> <u>Victorian</u> <u>Periodicals,</u> <u>1824-1900</u>.
     Toronto: University of Toronto Press, 2:723-31.
         Short introduction touches upon the noble aspirations of "The
Brotherhood," whose enthusiasm, along with WM's cash, launched and
maintained for a year the <u>Oxford</u> <u>and</u> <u>Cambridge</u> <u>Magazine</u>, a
periodical for which there exist four different lists of
attributions, and these do not agree. But "of the seventy

contributions to its pages, there are eighteen short stories (eight
by Morris), seventeen poems (five by Morris) and thirty-five
essays."

10 HUGHES, MICHAEL, ed. The Letters of Lewis Mumford and Frederic
     J. Osborn. New York: Praeger, 401, 404-5, passim.
          Osborn ranks WM with Ruskin and Raymond Unwin, saying that he
     was "a deep sympathizer with deprived humanity who wanted everybody
     to have the fullest possible life in every way including his own
     special cultural pleasures."

11 JONES, E. WILLIS. "WM." In Heritage of the Graphic Arts.
     Edited by C.B. Grannis. New York and London: R.R. Bowker, pp.
     19-28.
          A biographical sketch stresses WM's rebellion against the
     mediocrities and unfairness engendered by capitalism, as well as his
     lifelong interests in the book arts. Discusses Kelmscott Press
     achievements and its wide influence. Includes illustrations of
     typefaces and of two decorated pages.

12 JUTZI, ALAN. "Intramuralia: WM Letters." Huntington Library
     Quarterly 36, no. 1 (November):85.
          Note on acquisition of twenty-one letters WM wrote between
     1892 and 1895 to the artist Charles Marsh Gere.

13 KORNWOLF, JAMES. M.H. Bailie Scott and the Arts and Crafts
     Movement. Baltimore: Johns Hopkins Press, pp. 11-14, 26-34,
     passim.
          Discusses ways that the theories of Ruskin and WM were
     embodied in the buildings Bailie Scott designed and decorated. Red
     House seen as a "vehicle for testing new, loftier objectives in
     architecture and design," and thus a significant model for later
     architects. The Arts and Crafts Movement, by putting man at the
     center and denouncing greedy industry, was also a positive influence
     on architectural design.

14 LOURIE, MARGARET A.. "WM's Defence. An Introduction with
     Historical and Critical Commentary." Dissertation, University
     of Chicago.
          Revised for publication: 1981.34.

15 MAC CARTHY, FIONA. <u>All Things Bright and Beautiful: Design in
    Britain, 1830 to Today</u>. London: Allen and Unwin; Toronto:
    University of Toronto Press, pp. 34-41, passim.
        Discusses the painted furniture of Red Lion Square days as
    "all quite dilettante, a high-flown kind of hobby," but it led to "a
    tradition of designers in small workshops, establishing a cult of
    straightforwardness and soundness, truth to materials, attention to
    detail, that British industrial design, as we now know it," was
    directly influenced by. That influence is traced in a discussion of
    the development of the Design Council, one that corresponds to
    Carrington's (1976.8). Comments upon the products of Morris and
    Co., suggesting why they became a "powerful fashion among the
    cultured people," touching upon WM's ability to embrace the ideals
    of Ruskin, to work with Webb on SPAB and to write about the lesser
    arts, and yet "to make friends with, and take work from, the people
    he opposed, the advocates of commerce." Discusses WM's influence on
    a wide variety of designers, from Mackmurdo to Gimson and Lethaby,
    on the formation of committees and guilds across the British Isles,
    and across the channel ("The Arts and Crafts, as usual, were more
    honored on the Continent than they were in Britain"). Has many
    illustrations. Revised, with all WM commentary essentially the
    same: 1979.30.

16 MAC GANN, JEROME J. "The Beauty of the Medusa." <u>Studies in
    Romanticism</u> 11, no. 1 (Winter):3-25.
        Contrasts WM's use of the Medusa figure to Shelley's and
    Swinburne's, where it is "thrilling" or inspires fear and horror,
    but in WM's "Doom of King Acrisius" Medusa is turned into a
    "sentimental figure." We do not fear her; we fear her predicament,
    and Perseus "kills her out of a wonderful love," thus causing us to
    revalue the meanings of life and death.

17 MAKALASHINA, N.K. "Istoricheskaya povest Morrisa <u>Son pro Dzhone
    Bolla</u>." [WM's historical tale, John Ball]. <u>Uchenye Zapiski</u>
    30:138-57.
        In Russian. Paraphrases <u>John Ball</u>, quoting from it
    liberally, praising WM for his correct historical perspective and
    for his defense of the people against the forces of reaction.

18 MEIER, PAUL. "A propos de WM et de deux manuscrits inconnus."
    <u>Etudes anglaises</u> 25, no. 2 (April-June):308-18.
        Though <u>Nowhere</u> is often spoken of as a mere romantic utopia,
    a careful reading reveals that it is actually a scientific Utopia,
    one that offers unusually precise details concerning the two stages
    of the revolution, details of the type set forth by Marx in his
    essay on the Gotha Program, which had, however, not yet been
    published when WM wrote <u>Nowhere</u>. Suggests that WM learned such
    matters from Engels, offering as proof two letters, from WM to
    Engels, that reveal the closeness of their association.

*19 MEIER, PAUL. La pensee utopique de WM. 2 vols. Paris: Editions
     sociales.
          Translated: 1978.37.

20 PATTERSON, KENT. "A Terrible Beauty; Medusa in Three Victorian
     Poets." Tennesee Studies in Literature 17:111-20.
          Glances at the differing ways Rossetti, WM, and Swinburne
     interpreted and changed Ovid's original image of Medusa, asserting
     that WM's interests in popular art caused him to bring Medusa down
     to the level of the common reader; she becomes, therefore, a
     sentimentalized "abandoned female," and this is "perhaps the most
     important symbol of economic desperation conceived by early
     reform-minded novelists." This last point is not linked to the poem
     in question, "The Doom of King Acrisius."

21 PEVSNER, NIKOLAUS. "WM." In Some Architectural Writers of the
     Nineteenth Century. Oxford: Clarendon Press, pp. 269-89.
          Concludes a comprehensive survey of important
     nineteenth-century architectural writers with this chapter on WM
     because his "concentration on practical work of a kind directed to
     the future distinguishes him from all others recorded in this
     book." He is therefore here discussed both as a pioneer for
     twentieth-century innovations, a direct influence on designers and
     architects like van de Velde and Behrens (through his published
     lectures), and as the thinker who consummated critiques couched
     within the Gothic revival.

22 PRESTON, JEAN F. "Intramuralia." Huntington Library Quarterly
     36, no. 1 (November):85.
          Reports upon an acquisition of letters Cockerell received
     from WM and others.

23 STEVENSON, LIONEL. "WM." In The Pre-Raphaelite Poets. Chapel
     Hill: University of North Carolina Press, pp.123-83, passim.
          Includes substantial and useful close readings of several of
     the poems from Defence, as well as misleading remarks about, for
     example, the degree to which WM was "enslaved" by Rossetti or
     indebted to Sir Thomas More: Nowhere is "closely modeled on More's
     Utopia." Also claims that John Ball is presented through the
     persona of Chaucer.

24 TAMES, RICHARD. WM: An Illustrated Life. Aylesbury, Bucks.:
    Shire Publications, 48 pp.
        Brief survey of WM's achievements; the numerous photographs
    and illustrations are the best aspect of this guide.

25 THOMPSON, SUSAN OTIS. "The Arts and Crafts Book." In The Arts
    and Crafts Movement in America: 1876-1916. Catalogue of an
    Exhibit organized by the Princeton Art Museum and the Art
    Institute of Chicago. Edited by R.J. Clark. Princeton:
    Princeton University Press, pp. 93-116.
        Demonstrates that Kelmscott Press was a major catalyst for
    Arts and Crafts bookmaking in America, especially because of the
    emphasis on craftsmanship and handmade materials. There are many
    references to WM in the descriptions that accompany the thirty-three
    plates.

26 THOMPSON, SUSAN OTIS. "Kelmscott Influence on American Book
    Design." Dissertation, Columbia University.
        Revised for publication: 1977.38.

27 TOMASSON, RICHARD F. "Iceland on the Brain." American
    Scandinavian Review 60 (Winter):380-91.
        Surveys travelers' accounts of journeys to Iceland and finds
    WM's observations "rather boring," because he rarely goes into any
    detail about contemporary Icelanders.

                              1973

1   ALTICK, RICHARD D.. Victorian People and Ideas: A Companion for
    the Modern Reader of Victorian Literature. New York: W.W.
    Norton, pp. 103-5, passim.
        Includes general remarks on WM's importance, pointing out
    that he "popularized the idea of art as an accompaniment to daily
    life."

2   ARBLASTER, ANTHONY. "WM: Art and Revolution." In People for
    the People; Radical Ideas and Personalities in British History.
    Edited by David Rubenstein. London: Ithaca Press; New York:
    Humanities Press, 1974, pp. 130-38.
        It is ironic and unfortunate that present-day workers know
    little or nothing about WM since he predicted so clearly, as early
    as 1893, their plight within a welfare state. WM was also prescient
    about the ravages industrial capitalism would continue to wreak on
    man-made and natural environments. WM still has much to teach, and
    his essays should become more available; this might occur if notions
    that he was merely an artsy-craftsy dreamer could be discarded.

3   BLUMENTHAL, JOSEPH. "The Great Printers and Their Books: WM."
     In <u>Art of the Printed Book</u>. New York: Pierpont Morgan Library,
     pp. 34-37
        Intoductory description of Kelmscott Press that stresses
mainly the Kelmscott Chaucer and the three types; mentions WM's
influence (because of his "passionate craftsmanship," not his
typographic design) on printers as diverse as Jan van Krimpen and
Bruce Rogers. Among the scores of fine plates are two of Kelmscott
Press volumes.

4   BRANTLINGER, PATRICK. "A Reading of WM's <u>Defence</u>." <u>Victorian
     Newsletter</u> 44 (Fall):18-24.
        Suggests that the <u>Defence</u> poems do have "thematic material
bearing on the problems of modern life," that they stress the
"significance generally of artificial beauty in an inimical world,"
and that they are best viewed as pairs that heighten "the contrast
between harsh fact and lovely fantasy, between life and art."
Discusses "Sir Peter Harpdon's End" and "Rapunzel" as such a pair,
concluding that the "structure of the whole volume is
dialectical--although it is a dialectic that results in no
synthesis," for no synthesis can occur in an age that does not
perceive beauty.

5   CARPENTER, L.P. <u>G.D.H. Cole: An Intellectual Biography</u>.
     Cambridge: Cambridge University Press, pp. 8-11, passim.
        Stresses the importance of WM's influence on Cole, as much by
means of his "egalitarian, energetic, and libertarian spirit" as by
his writings. Cole's many activities and achievements accounted for
by fact that "he had decided at the outset to follow his master
Morris in doing everything well, rather than one thing superbly."

6   CARTER, LIN. "From Uruk to Utterbol: WM and the First Fantasy
     Novels." In <u>Imaginary Worlds: The Art of Fantasy</u>. New York:
     Ballantyne, pp. 13-26.
        Suggests that the epic of Gilgamesh was the first heroic
fantasy, that Malory and Milton worked in the same tradition, and
that the "modern history of the fantasy novel begins with the
pioneering Victorian romances of WM." A brief biographical sketch
of WM is equally misleading.

7   CLARK, FIONA. <u>WM: Wallpapers and Chintzes</u>. London: Academy
     Editions; New York: St. Martin's Press, 95 pp. 2d ed., 1974.
        Descriptions and commentary accompany illustrations of
forty-nine wallpapers, four ceiling papers, and thirty-seven
chintzes. Also has information on public institutions with
significant collections of WM papers and chintzes, on homes where
the original Morris and Co. interiors are still intact, and on the
availability today of Morris and Co. designs. The short

introduction, by Andrew Melvin, appeared originally in 1971.21.

8   DUNLAP, BENJAMIN. "Bear Me Witness in Love: WM's Love Is
      Enough." VIJ 2:3-21.
          Love Is Enough reflects the "anfractuous confusion" of WM's
     personal life, an "emotional labyrinth of evasion and betrayal"
     during the several months of 1872 when the writing of the poem, like
     the Iceland trips before and after, served as a means to understand
     and relieve his anxieties and pain. Discusses the themes and
     structures of this "sort of masque," its sources in The Mabinogian,
     in Paradise, and elsewhere; brings in pertinent biographical matter,
     such as WM's friendship with Aglaia Coronio, his chief confidante
     during these years, one to whom the poem is perhaps addressed, who
     is evidently associated with its heroine, Azalais. The latter is
     "one of the sisterhood of Habundia and Birdalone," linked to a
     sensuous love of the Earth, the only love that is truly enough.

9   DUNLAP, JOSEPH R. Preface to The Introductions to the
      "Collected Works" of WM. New York: Oriole Editions, pp. 5-8.
          Since May Morris was "her father's helper and companion"
     through a wide range of his many activities, "she was in a unique
     position to observe, record, and discuss the events of her father's
     life," and thus a uniquely qualified editor of his works. "Morris
     was very fortunate in his friends and associates, in his
     biographers, and in having a daughter whose ability to describe him
     clearly matched her sympathy as to his aims in life." And we are
     fortunate to have these introductions available in this new format,
     for "they constitute in their own right a single work by May
     Morris."

10   FAULKNER, PETER, ed. Introduction to WM: Early Romances in
      Prose and Verse. London: J.M. Dent and Sons, pp. vii-xx.
          Finds connections between the somber atmosphere and anxiety
     in the early prose tales and the prevailing situations in the
     Defence poems that justify a decision to treat all these writings as
     "romance." Speculates upon ways themes therein merge with WM's own
     life. Includes all the Defence poems, seven Oxford and Cambridge
     Magazine tales, and brief notes.

11   FAULKNER, PETER, ed. WM: The Critical Heritage. London:
      Routledge and Kegan Paul, 465 pp.
          Reprints a few contemporary reactions to WM's design work and
     over eighty reviews of his publications, from Defence to Flood.
     Includes two additional sections: "Comments by Contemporary Men of
     Letters" and "Southern American Views of WM." The former has
     appreciations by the likes of Ruskin, Tennyson, Rossetti, and
     Hopkins; the latter by Lanier and Haine. Includes obituaries by
     Kropotkin and Crane and a review of Well by Wells that has colorful

characterizations of the Hammersmith Sunday evenings. Has concise
introductions to various sections and a useful account of
nineteenth-century reviewing practices and the patterns of response
to WM's writings.

12 FISHER, VIVIAN. "The Search for Reality through Dreams: A Study
    of the Works of WM from 1856-1872." Dissertation, Emory
    University.
       Abstracted: DAI 34:767-A.

13 FRANKLIN, COLIN. "Walker and WM." In Walker: Some Light on His
    Theories of Printing and on His Relationship with WM and
    Cobden-Sanderson. Cambridge, pp. 26-31, passim.
       Letters that Walker received from WM plus an autobiographical
    brief that Walker wrote for his lawyers contain new information
    about the last decade of WM's life and the importance of Walker as
    both friend and teacher.

14 GABRIELI, ISELIN MARIA. "WM e l'antichita nordica." Rendiconti
    delli Istituto Lombardo 107, no. 1:259-306.
       A comprehensive survey of the effects of WM's lifelong
    interest in the Teutonic North opens with a discussion of other
    nineteenth-century editions, translations, poems based on the
    Icelandic, and works of the sort WM could have read at Oxford that
    would have suggested themes for the tales he wrote then. Offers
    detailed comments on WM's collaboration with Magnusson along with
    close readings of their translations, both of the poetry and prose;
    discusses the 1871 voyage to Iceland and how it shaped imagery in a
    few of the later lyric poems; has useful analyses of both Sigurd and
    "Gudrun," with concluding comments upon the ways WM's romantic
    tendencies clash with saga realism.

*15 GOOCH, VELMA L. "WM: Toward Unity in Art and Life."
     Dissertation, University of Manchester.
        Cited in Index to Theses Accepted for Higher Degrees in the
     Universities of Great Britain, 28 (1972-73):7.

16 HARDWICK, MICHAEL. A Literary Atlas and Gazeteer of the British
    Isles. Newton Abbot: David and Charles, pp. 35, 41, 60, 73,
    182.
       Locates on detailed maps and briefly discusses the importance
    for WM of sites at Merton, Kent, Walthamstow, Kelmscott and London.
    But Kelmscott House and Hammersmith are omitted.

17 HARRISON, MARTIN, and WALTERS, BILL. Burne-Jones. New York and
    London: Barrie and Jenkins, pp. 9-10, passim.
        Discusses friendship of Burne-Jones and WM from Oxford on,
dwelling upon the former's designs for Morris and Co. and for the
Kelmscott Chaucer. Includes many illustrations and a list of
stained glass windows designed by Burne-Jones.

18 JOHNSON, FRIDOLF, ed. WM: Ornamentation and Illustration for
    the Kelmscott Chaucer. New York: Dover Books, 126 pp.
        Short introduction avers that "the name of WM, it may be,
will stand second in rank to that of Gutenburg." Reproduced here
are one hundred pages from the Kelmscott Chaucer, including all of
the woodcut illustrations from Burne-Jones's drawings and all of
WM's large borders and decorated initials.

19 LAMBOURNE, LIONEL. "The Arts and Crafts Movement, an
    Introduction." In The Arts and Crafts Movement: Artists,
    Craftsmen, and Designers: 1890-1940. Catalogue of an Exhibition
    at the Fine Art Society in 1973. London: Fine Art Society, pp.
    4-9.
        Downplays WM's influence on the Arts and Crafts Movement,
pointing out why he was not optimistic about its aspirations for
improving social conditions.

20 LEVINE, GEORGE. "From 'Know-Not-Where' to Nowhere: The City in
    Carlyle, Ruskin, and WM." In The Victorian City: Images and
    Realities. Edited by H.J. Dyos and Michael Wolff. London and
    Boston: Routledge and Kegan Paul, pp. 495-516.
        Carlyle, Ruskin, and WM shared a revulsion for the Victorian
city, "necessarily for them the major symptom of the diseases of
modern life," a source of incidents and images to contrast to the
older, the rural, the natural. Points out how WM used Ruskin's
critique of nineteenth-century civilization, stripping it of its
mysticism, shaping it for a "direct battle with capitalism."
Concludes that "there is no city in Morris's imagination, nor in the
best imaginations of the great prose writers of Victorian England."

21 LE BOURGEOIS, JOHN. "WM to George Bernard Shaw." Durham
    University Journal, n.s., 34, no. 2 (March):205-11.
        While Shaw's admiration for WM has long been on record,
"Morris's attitude and appreciation of Shaw has been largely a
matter of conjecture." The extant letters, now in the Shaw Papers
at the British Museum, dispell some of that vagueness. All thirteen
are here reprinted; the most interesting record WM's reactions to
Beardsley's illustrations and WM's conviction that the 1896 voyage
to Norway had been useless.

*22 MADLENER, ALAN FRED. "Primitivism and Related Ideas in the
     Literary Works of WM." Dissertation, University of California
     at Berkeley.
        Cited in American Doctoral Dissertations (1972-73):311.

23 MAGEE, DAVID. Infinite Riches: The Adventures of a Rare Book
    Dealer. New York: Paul S. Eriksson, pp. 209-13.
       Describes contents of some archives of Morris and Co., among
    them a small book of minutes, which he purchased and then sold to
    Sanford Berger in Berkeley, California.

24 MATHEWS, RICHARD. "The Fantasy of Secular Redemption."
    Dissertation, University of Virginia.
       Abstracted: DAI 34:4211-A.

25 MORTON, A.L., ed. Introduction to Political Writings of WM.
    London: Lawrence and Wishart; Berlin: Seven Seas Publishers; New
    York: International Publishers, pp. 9-30.
       Argues that for WM socialism was a logical outcome of his
    early practical interests, that his socialist writings are vigorous
    and true because he was not a political theorist. Offers a useful
    biographical sketch, one that is however wrong about the types of
    influence Iceland exerted on WM's politics. Stresses the importance
    of the Eastern Question Association and outlines his work for the
    socialist cause. Selections for the anthology are intended to give
    a broad view of WM's political writings, and they include eight
    lectures, five articles, and two letters he wrote to Jenny. Each
    selection has a short bibliographical introduction.

26 MUMFORD, LEWIS. "Polytechnic Creativity: Lewis Mumford and the
    Snow Queen." RIBA Journal 80 (October 1973):481-86.
       Reprint of 1968.28.

27 MUMFORD, LEWIS. "WM: Polytechnic Creativity." In
    Interpretations and Forecasts, 1922-1972. New York: Harcourt
    Brace. London: Seckert and Warburg, pp. 209-17.
       Reprint of 1968.28.

28 OIJI, TAKERO. "Chusei e no Dokei to Kakumei e no Yume: WM no
    John Ball" [Longing for the Middle Ages and a dream of
    revolution]. Eigo Seinen [Rising generation] 119, no. 8 (1
    November):8-9.
       In Japanese. Ponders effects of WM's descriptions of rural
    fourteenth-century life, suggesting that John Ball offers us a
    firmer sense of WM's psychology than does Nowhere, pointing out that

his dream of revolution is tied to a longing for the values of the
Middle Ages.

*29   ONO, JIRO. Uiriamu Morisu. [WM] Tokyo: Chuo Koronsha, 215 pp.
        In Japanese. Cited in 1974 MLA bibliography.

30   PARSSINEN, T.M. "Bellamy, WM and the Image of the Industrial
       City in Victorian Social Criticism." Midwest Quarterly 14, no.
       3 (Spring):257-66.
         Comments upon the great popularity of Looking Backward and
upon WM's "revulsion" as expressed in his Commonweal review.
Paraphrases both works and demonstrates why they are "radically
different, the one taming the city, the other eliminating it."

31   PIERSON, STANLEY. "WM: The Marxist as Utopian." In Marxism and
       the Origins of British Socialism: The Struggle for a New
       Consciousness. Ithaca and London: Cornell University Press, pp.
       75-89, passim.
         Surveys correspondences between Ruskin and WM on judging
social development by the vitality of art; says that for WM work
properly understood would equal art, and this accounts for WM's
disdain both for Calvinists, who equate work with punishment, and
for aesthetes, who place art above the reach of the common man.
Ways that such ideas squared with those of the early Marx are
discussed. Traces causes for the breakup of the Socialist League,
and WM's many attempts to mediate between Reformists and Anarchists
are placed against full discussions of the Fabian Society, Ethical
Socialism, Labour Churches, and the development of the Labour party.
Though Engels and other Marxists accused WM of "aesthetic
reductionism," the fusion he "effected between the Romantic vision
and Marxism opened up new avenues for British Socialist
development." Links WM to twentieth-century Marxist intellectuals
like Lukacs and Silone.

32   REDMOND, JAMES. "WM and Shaw: Two Faces of Victorian
       Socialism." In The Victorians and Social Protest: A Symposium.
       Edited by J. Butt and I.F. Clark. Newton Abbot, Devon: David
       and Charles; Hamden, Conn.: Archon, pp. 156-76.
         Though tradition, and even recent scholarly opinion (Stokes,
1961.31), has it that the politics of WM and Shaw were very similar,
this article argues that "the ideal Socialism of Morris and the
ideal Socialism of Shaw define the extreme positions between which
lies the whole Socialist spectrum." Equates Shaw with Plato and an
ideal state based on repression of desire, WM with Blake and an
ideal involving sensual freedom.

33 REED, MICHAEL D. "WM's 'Rapunzel' as an Oedipal Fantasy."
    American Imago 30, no. 3 (Fall):313-22.
        Response to Stallman's mythic interpretation of "Rapunzel"
    (1969.25) finds sexual imagery in strange places and turns the witch
    into a father figure in order to argue that "the poem is at heart a
    positive Oedipal fantasy."

34 SEMBACH, KLAUS-JURGEN. "WM Heute." In Praraffaeliten.
    Catalogue for 23 November 1973-24 February 1974 Baden-Baden
    Exhibition. Stuttgart: Dr. Cantz'sche, pp. 301-5.
        Opens with high praise for WM, his unique role in history,
    for he followed his master, Ruskin, and then cleared a path from the
    cathedral to the marketplace. Suggests that WM's reputation and
    influence have declined since the turn of the century. Following
    this introduction are two sections that describe WM items--drawings
    and Kelmscott Press editions--which were in the exhibition. In
    "Burne-Jones and Perseus Saga," an earlier section of the catalogue,
    WM is frequently mentioned.

35 SIMPSON, J.M. "Eyrbyggja Saga and Nineteenth Century
    Scholarship." In Proceedings of the First International Saga
    Conference, 1971. London: Viking Society, pp. 369-76.
        Compares Morris-Magnusson translations to other
    nineteenth-century renditions of Eyrbyggja Saga and quotes Robert
    Louis Stevenson's humorous remarks on WM's excessive use of
    "whereas" in the saga translations.

36 SOLOMON, MAYNARD, ed. Marxism and Art: Essays Classic and
    Contemporary. New York: Knopf. Reprint. New York: Vintage,
    1974. Brighton, Sussex: Harvester Press, 1979. Detroit: Wayne
    State University Press, 1979, pp. 79-83.
        Discusses the several selections from the socialist lectures
    here anthologized, as well as WM's significance as a socialist: he
    was "extraordinarily acute (more so than any Marxist up to the
    1920s) in ferreting out and following the outlines and applications
    of the Marxist theories of alienated labor and revolutionary
    humanism--it took an artist and a humanist to rediscover them."

37 STAINES, DAVID. "WM's Treatment of His Medieval Sources in
    Defence." SP 70, no. 4 (October):439-64.
        Reviews meager and unfavorable reactions to Defence poems and
    argues that consideration of the medieval sources can help us
    "perceive the nature of poetic creation as Morris himself understood
    and practiced it in 1858." Finds influence of Malory in the first
    four poems "evident in the personal names, basic structure of
    incidents, and in the general atmosphere of the medieval world."
    Echoes from Froissart are even less tangible. Concludes that WM
    used medieval tales to create a world more intense than that

depicted by their authors and that the poetry he wrote after <u>Defence</u>
never attained the same levels of poetic creativity.

38 STANFORD, DEREK, ed. <u>Pre-Raphaelite Writing: An Anthology</u>.
    Totowa, N.J.: Rowman and Littlefield; London: J.M. Dent and
    Sons, passim.
        Discusses WM's connections with Rossetti, his paintings and
. poems. Anthology has selections from the <u>Oxford</u> and <u>Cambridge</u>
<u>Magazine</u>, from <u>Defence</u>, and from <u>Water</u>.

39 STATHAM, H.H. "WM's 'Wonderful Versatility of Talents.'" In
    <u>WM: The Critical Heritage</u>. Edited by Peter Faulkner. London:
    Routledge and Kegan Paul, pp. 431-50.
        Reprint of 1897.18.

40 THOMPSON, LAURENCE. "Gentlemen of the Socialist Press." In
    <u>People for the People; Radical Ideas and Personalities in
    British History</u>. Edited by David Rubenstein. London: Ithaca
    Press; New York: Humanities Press, 1974, pp. 170-78.
        Discusses <u>Commonweal</u>, suggesting that it was as unique to
socialist journalism as WM was to British socialism. Speaks of
<u>Commonweal</u>'s influence on Blatchford's <u>Clarion</u>, and on the <u>Labour
Leader</u>, especially when it was edited by Glasier.

41 THOMPSON, SUSAN OTIS. "A Golden Age in American Printing."
    <u>Columbia Library Columns</u> 22, no. 2 (February):22-33.
        Though it was fashionable to look down on American books of
the 1890s as largely imitations, we now have a clearer picture and
realize that printers like Updike were themselves important
innovaters, that WM and the Kelmscott Press encouraged many to open
small presses, but that his influence did not extend into every
aspect of the making of books.

42 TRILLING, LIONEL. "Aggression and Utopia: A Note on WM's
    <u>Nowhere</u>." <u>Psychoanalytic Quarterly</u> 42, no. 2 (April):214-25.
        Comments upon <u>Nowhere</u>'s "certitude that aggression can be
rooted out of human nature," upon the book's apparent repudiation of
the Western ideal of pursuing goals "with unremitting energy, with
ceaseless devotion in the face of defeat and frustration." Because
WM equated genius (or the cruel demands of the superego) with "the
ruthless ethos of capitalist competition, there are no geniuses in
<u>Nowhere</u>." Because many voices in contemporary America are similarly
raised against ambition and genius, "against the presuppositions of
the humanistic tradition" itself, Trilling now reads <u>Nowhere</u> with a
"degree of anxiety" not present when he had first read it a
generation earlier. Reprinted: 1974.27.

43 VALENTINE, K.B. "A Patterned Imagination: WM's Use of Pattern
    in Decorative Design and the Last Prose Romances."
    Dissertation, University of Utah.
        Abstracted: DAI 35:1777-A.

44 WATERS, WILLIAM. An Illustrated Life of Sir Burne-Jones,
    1833-1898. Lifelines Series, no. 9. London: Shire
    Publications, pp. 7-9, passim.
        Stresses the depth and extent of Rossetti's influence on both
    WM and Burne-Jones, pointing to parallels in ways that WM's poetry
    and Burne-Jones's paintings, especially in the 1860s, developed.
    Comments also on Morris and Co. influence on the themes of
    Burne-Jones's paintings.

45 WATTS, THEODORE. "Review of Water." WM: The Critical
    Heritage. Edited by Peter Faulkner. London: Routledge and
    Kegan Paul, pp. 418-26.
        Reprint of 1897.23.

46 WILLIAMS, RAYMOND. The Country and the City. London: Chatto
    and Windus. Reprint. St. Albans: Paladin, 1975, pp. 326-28,
    passim.
        Sees in Nowhere "a combination of what is essentially
    restoration, turning back history and drawing on medieval and rural
    patterns, and what was to express itself, formally, as town
    planning, the creation of urban order and control." Contrasts WM's
    vision, his sense that a new London could grow from socialist
    activities, to the more negative visions of James Thomson and Wells.

47 "Review of Flood." In WM: The Critical Heritage. Edited by
    Peter Faulkner. London: Routledge and Kegan Paul, pp. 427-31.
        Reprint of 1897.30.

                              1974

1   ADEY, LIONEL. "The Light of Holiness: Some Comments on WM by
    C.S. Lewis." JWMS 3, no. 1 (Spring):10-22.
        Has gleaned from the letters of C.S. Lewis all references to
    WM with whom he had much in common: they shared an "ecological
    conservatism and hatred of industry," they had similar family
    backgrounds and personal traits and tastes. But their attitudes
    toward the working classes and their hopes for the future were
    dissimilar. Lewis thought WM "the most essentially pagan of all the
    poets," but thought also that a "light of holiness" shone throughout
    Love Is Enough.

2   CHRISTIAN, JOHN. The Pre-Raphaelites in Oxford. Oxford:
    Ashmolean Museum, pp. 24-44.
        Surveys the numerous connections WM had with Oxford from 1853
through 1883, when his lecture on art and democracy scandalized many
of the fellows at University College.

3   CLAYRE, ALASDAIR. "WM and His English Predecessors." In Work
    and Play: Ideas and Experience of Work and Leisure. London:
    Weidenfeld and Nicolson, pp. 63-78.
        Argues that WM's socialism was homegrown, owing much more to
Ruskin than to Marx and any continental traditions. His attitudes
toward work and art, and toward the importance of human happiness,
are therefore unique and furnished real contributions to both
British and continental socialist thought.

4   COX, DAVID. "Edmund New's 'Diary of a Visit to Kelmscott Manor
    House.'" JWMS 3, no. 1 (Spring):2-7.
        Edmund New, who did the illustrations for Mackail (1899.10),
visited Kelmscott Manor in October 1895 and recorded his impressions
over four days, and those are here reprinted. His comments on the
household routines, the daily walks, writing, whist, and talks with
WM, are interesting. So is the biographical material on New and his
achievements.

5   DE CAMP, L. SPRAGUE. "Jack of All Arts." In Fantastic
    Stories. Flushing, N.Y.: Ultimate Publishing Co., pp. 37-49.
        Asserts that in the late prose romances WM "combined the
antiquarian romanticism of Scott and his imitaters with the
supernaturalism of Walpole," and he thereby created what de Camp
followers like to call "heroic fantasy, moribund since the death of
medieval romance." A biographical sketch precedes brief discussions
of the plots of the late prose romances. Reprinted: 1976.12.

6   DREYFUS, JOHN. "New Light on the Design of Types for the
    Kelmscott and Doves Presses." Library, 5th ser., 29, no. 1
    (March):36-41.
        Study of new documents has led to this fuller account of the
great pains WM took in designing the Golden type, and of the
important role of Walker in preparing type designs for both
Kelmscott Press and Doves Press

7   DUFTY, A.R. Introduction to The Story of Cupid and Psyche.
     London and Cambridge: Clover Hill, 2 vols., 164 pp.
     Volume 1 includes full commentary upon the planned
illustrated edition of Paradise, how it was well begun with dozens
of drawings by Burne-Jones for "The Story of Cupid and Psyche" and
why it was not completed. From the drawings, forty-five woodcuts
were made, perhaps as many as forty by WM himself; these
illustrations and engravings, their relationship to the text, and
the text itself and its sources are all discussed in great detail,
as are reasons the project failed and how it was, in this present
edition, finally resumed and completed. In the second volume, the
illustrations appear "for the first time in their proper context,"
with the poem, here set in Troy type, newly cast from the original
matrices. Also printed were 100 box-shaped folios containing sets
of proofs of forty-seven drawings and forty-four engravings.

8   DUNLAP, JOSEPH R. "Iceland: 1931 and 1871." News from Anywhere
     15 (Fall):30-32.
     Summarizes and comments upon diary notes and memories of Miss
Mary Pierce, an American girl who accompanied May Morris, Miss Lobb,
and Miss Margaret Pierce on their 1931 journey to Iceland, a trek
that covered some of the same trails WM had traversed in 1871.

9   FREDEMAN, WILLIAM E. "The Pre-Raphaelites." In Guide to the
     Year's Work in Victorian Poetry. Edited by R.C. Tobias. VP 12
     (Spring):77-99.
     Reports on a plethora of studies that have appeared on the
Pre-Raphaelites since his own bibliocritical study (1965.7) was
published. The section on WM includes several books, both reprints
and editions, as well as twenty articles and essays, all with
useful, specific annotation. Supplements earlier bibliographical
essays by Fredeman (1968.12) and by Jones (1956.7). All those works
referring to WM are included in the present book.

10   GRIGSON, GEOFFREY. "WM." In The Contrary View: Glimpses of
     Fudge and Gold. London: Macmillan. Totowa, N.J.: Rowan and
     Littlefield, pp. 77-97.
     A gathering of four short essay-reviews inspired by books
published on WM in 1967 and by Auden's translation of the Elder Edda
in 1969. Comments upon WM's shifting reputation as poet, offering
insights into "Shameful Death." Praises the landscape descriptions
in Paradise and in Icelandic Journals, where WM becomes "almost like
a Cezanne of the North." Compares Auden's fascination with the
North to WM's.

11 HEATH-STUBBES, JOHN. "Pre-Raphaelitism and the Aesthetic
    Withdrawal." In Pre-Raphaelitism: A Collection of Critical
    Essays. Edited by James Sambrook. Chicago: University of
    Chicago Press, pp. 148-78.
        Reprinted from 1950.7.

12 HORNUNG, CLARENCE P., ed. Will Bradley: His Graphic Art. New
    York: Dover, pp. 5-6.
        Some of Will Bradley's autobiographical notes suggest how
significant WM's influence was on a young American printer in the
1890s.

13 KELLER, DONALD. "WM: Dreams and the End of Dreams." Eildon
    Tree 1:4-7.
        Laments that so few fantasy fans seem to appreciate WM's
prose romances, since they marked the beginning of the modern
fantasy novel.

14 LE BOURGEOIS, JOHN. "The Financial Crisis of WM." Durham
    University Journal, n.s., 35, no. 2 (March):202-205.
        Taylor's letters to Webb reveal that WM's financial situation
in 1869 was far from stable; portions of these letters, now at the
Victoria and Albert, are quoted, and then it is suggested that the
letters caused WM to be more careful with expenditures. By 1875 he
had reorganized the Firm, and it was bringing in a good living.
Equates the stability of the Firm with the stability of WM's
marriage.

15 LE BOURGEOIS, JOHN. "WM at St. James Palace: A Sequel." JWMS
    3, no. 1 (Spring):7-9.
        Suggests that the fledgling Morris, Marshall, Faulkner Co.
landed the important contract to redecorate the Armour and Tapestry
Room at St. James Palace because Rossetti met and impressed William
Cowper, then the first commissioner of public works.

16 MOZLEY, ELIZABETH. "Thomas James Cobden-Sanderson: A Study
    Based on His Journals." Courier 2:21-37.
        Ways that WM influenced Cobden-Sanderson's ideas about
handicrafts, and the book arts generally, are discussed within this
survey based on the journals Cobden-Sanderson began keeping in 1879;
see 1926.2.

17 POLLARD, ALFRED W. Fine Books. London: Methuen; New York:
    Cooper Square Publishers, pp. 304-8, passim.
        Discusses WM as an authority on incunabula and as a designer
    whose ideas about margins were absolutely correct, whose floral
    decorations equaled those of the medieval Italian masters. "No
    other printer since printing began has ever produced such a series
    of books as the fifty-three which passed from Kelmscott Press."

18 PURTILL, RICHARD. Lord of the Elves and Eldils: Fantasy and
    Philosophy in C.S. Lewis and J.R.R. Tolkien. Grand Rapids,
    Mich.: Zondervan Books, pp. 204-6.
        Quotes C.S. Lewis (1939.6) on WM's language, pointing out
    that that description also neatly embraces Tolkien's "generalizing
    style." Differences between WM and Tolkien, like the sexuality in
    the former, are briefly discussed.

19 QUIRK, RANDOLPH. "Dasent, WM, and Aspects of Translation." In
    The Linguist and the English Language. London: Edward Arnold,
    pp. 97-109.
        Reprinted, with slight revisions, from 1955.11.

20 RANDLE, JOHN. "WM and Cobden-Sanderson." JWMS 3, no. 1
    (Spring):22-26.
        Offers extracts from Cobden-Sanderson's journals that have to
    do with the Morrises from 1883, when Janey suggested he take up
    bookbinding, to 1896 and his reflections upon WM's death; see
    1926.2.

21 REGINA, FRANCESCO LA. "WM e 'Anti-Restoration Movement.'"
    Restauro 3, nos. 13-14 (May-August):77-149.
        A comprehensive article that begins with a survey of
    nineteenth-century critiques of industrial capitalism and the rise
    of socialism in Britain. A sketch of WM's life and major
    achievements then precedes a full discussion of his founding of
    SPAB. Includes quotations from the socialist lectures and from
    periodical articles that argued against restoration of ancient
    buildings, from St. Mark's in Venice to rural village churches.

22 ROCCHI, GUISEPPE. "John Ruskin e le origini della moderna
    teoria del restauro." Restauro 3, nos. 13-14
    (May-August):13-73.
        Commentary on WM within a general discussion of Ruskin's
    theories of restoration and his ideas about the dialectic between
    buildings and society. Red House is here described as a sort of
    minor-league, neo-Gothic Fonthill, and there are other such
    provocative comparisons in this eclectic article.

23 SADOFF, DIANE. "Imaginative Transformation in WM's
      'Rapunzel.'" VP 12, no. 3 (Summer):153-64.
       Responds to Stallman's archetypal reading of the poem
(1969.25), arguing that the poem actually "functions primarily to
explore the Romantic dialectic of consciousness and imagination."
The poem is not a "Victorian tale of maturity," as Stallman
suggested, but instead a romantic version of fairy-tale
transformation.

24 SCHOFIELD, JOHN. "Defence and Contemporary Critics." JWMS 3,
      no. 1 (Spring):27-30.
       To counter an assertion in Mackail (1899.10), one then picked
up on (as always) by subsequent biographers, that Defence was
ignored by its first critics, the writer discusses five of the six
extant contemporary reviews and finds only one, from the Spectator,
to be "short and dismissive." The others are full and favorable.

25 SEWTER, A.C. The Stained Glass of WM and His Circle. New
      Haven: Yale University Press. Vol. 1, 377 pp. Vol. 2, 1975, 335
      pp.
       Points out that stained glass is an excellent avenue toward
understanding changing Victorian aesthetics since both past masters
and materials were reinterpreted, and never more profitably than by
WM whose firm created some of "the most important stained glass of
the last 300 years." Summarizes early nineteenth-century work, and
then discusses Burne-Jones's achievements with stained glass. Even
before joining Morris and Co., he "had advanced English stained
glass from imitative medievalism to modern creative art, far ahead
of anything being produced elsewhere." Discusses other designers of
stained glass for the firm, namely Webb, WM himself, and Dearle,
concluding with a chapter on the Morris Firm after 1898. Has
sixteen color plates and 665 reproductions of cartoons and windows.
The second volume "aims at presenting a complete list and
description of all the stained-glass windows made by the Firm from
its foundation in 1861 to its closure in 1940, and also of windows
designed by Morris's associates in the few years prior to the
establishment of Morris's firm." This exhaustive list is
supplemented by six appendixes that summarize and arrange the
material chronologically and geographically. Concludes with indexes
that include names of owners, donors and persons commemorated,
subjects, and finally a general index.

26 SMITH, R.S. "A Reviewer Reviewed." JWMS 3, no. 1
    (Spring):30-31.
       Clarifies Floud's reassessment (1959.4) of WM (which had been
    misunderstood by a recent critic), stressing that a "profound
    respect for Morris underlay his reappraisal." He states that WM
    used older tapestries to learn techniques, not to slavishly copy,
    that he did not use "sweated labor" and middlemen, and that he did
    indeed practice the crafts that he preached.

27 TRILLING, LIONEL. "Aggression and Utopia: A Note on WM's
    Nowhere." News from Anywhere 15 (Fall):3-14.
       Reprint of 1973.42.

28 TYZACK, CHARLES R.P. "'King Arthur's Tomb': The Versions of
    Rossetti and WM Compared." Trivium 8:127-32.
       Parses the iconography, visual and verbal, of the Rossetti
    and WM versions of "King Arthur's Tomb." Concludes that "Rossetti
    and Morris find the Lancelot-Guenevere story an appropriate image
    for their feelings of sexual guilt and, in Morris's case,
    inadequacy."

29 ZWERDLING, ALEX. Orwell and the Left. New Haven and London:
    Yale University Press, pp. 17, 18, 34-35.
       Suggests several parallels between Orwell and WM, pointing
    out that Orwell, for instance, "would certainly have agreed with
    Morris's final rejection of bourgeoise socialism."

30 "Biography: WM." Italix 4, no. 2 (Winter):8-19.
       A biographical sketch with a few detailed comments on
    Kelmscott Press books, to which are appended six illustrations
    (poorly reproduced) of WM's calligraphy. Joseph R. Dunlap has
    written notes for the reproductions, and this "WM Number" also has a
    drawing of WM by Joseph Papin.

31 "The WM Collection at Syracuse University." Courier (Syracuse
    University Library) 2:3-20.
       A list of WM materials, both primary and secondary, in the
    Rare Book Department of the George Arents Research Library at
    Syracuse University. Includes several illustrations and
    biographical sketches of the major donors to this significant WM
    collection.

32   Pre-Raphaelite Graphics and Woodcuts by Burne-Jones and WM.
      Catalogue of an Exhibition of Pre-Raphaelite Graphics Held 18
      March-5 1974 at Hartnoll and Eyre. London: Robert Stockwell, 83
      pp.
         Includes introduction and eighty-three reproductions of
woodcuts for the projected edition of Paradise; thirty-five are by
WM and Burne-Jones.

1975

1   ADBURGHAM, ALISON. Liberty's: A Biography of a Shop. London:
      Allen and Unwin, pp. 25, 50, passim.
         Liberty's textiles compared to those of Morris and Co.; both
had textile works on the River Wandle; Liberty's was up-stream: "We
sent our dirty water down to Morris."

2   ALLEN, ELIZABETH, E. "The Prose Romances of WM." Dissertation,
      Tulane University.
         Abstracted: DAI 36:2211-A.

3   ARNASON, MAGNUS, trans. WM's "Dagbaekur ur Islands Ferthum,
      1871-1873" [WM's Icelandic Journals]. Reykjavik: Mal og
      Minning, 269 pp.
         This translation of Icelandic Journals indicates both the
strong interests modern Icelanders have in travelers' accounts of
their homeland, and in WM, better known in Iceland than one might
expect. Includes the introduction to 1969.22 and explanatory notes
for Icelandic readers.

4   BALCH, DENNIS R. "Guenevere's Fidelity to Arthur in 'The
      Defence of Guenevere' and 'King Arthur's Tomb.'" VP 13, nos.
      3-4 (Autumn-Winter):61-70.
         Discusses "Defence of Guenevere" and "King Arthur's Tomb" as
complementary and as an "homogeneous poetic construct," suggesting
that Guenevere's motives and character are more complex than
previous critics have recognized, that "she is far more faithful to
Arthur than any critic has yet suggested." A close reading of the
second poem reveals a "linkage" between Arthur and Christ, one that
makes Guenevere's earlier choice of the blue cloth seem correct:
"The spirit of Christian asceticism appears triumphant amid the
ruins of earthly happiness."

5   BASKIN, SCOTT, and BRACEWELL, CATHERINE, eds. The WM Essay
     Book. Stanford: Stanford Art Gallery, 116 pp.
         Nine essays by Stanford undergraduates, published on the
occasion of a WM exhibit (1975.58), originally written for a WM
colloquium. The essays, with fresh insights and revaluations of
WM's political relevance, include all of the following: "The Legacy
of WM" by J.W.M. Osborne; "The Making of a Socialist: Mill, Fourier,
and WM" by W.S. Bennett; "The Politicization of the Artist" by S.
Greene, "Morris as a Man of Action" by S.D. Baskin; "WM as Political
Activist: An Evaluation" by R.M. Kesner; "WM and Nowhere: A Study in
Art and Society" by R. Jasso; "WM and the Evolution of Architecture"
by B. Dawson; "WM and Raymond Unwin: The Origin of the Garden City
Movement" by G. Miller; and "Echoes from Froissart in WM's Defence"
by C. Bracewell.

6   BLACK, JUDITH BOOHER. "A Critical Look at WM's Guenevere."
     Dissertation, University of Miami.
         Abstracted: DAI 36:2836-A.

7   BLERSCH, STUART. "WM's Sigurd, Book I, An Edition with Variant
     Readings and Annotations." Dissertation, University of Ohio.
         Abstracted: 36:7430-A.

8   BONO, BARBARA. "The Prose Fictions of WM: A study in the
     Literary Aesthetic of a Victorian Social Reformer." VP 13, nos.
     3-4 (Autumn-Winter):43-59.
         Asserts that there are "radicalizing tendencies" in the prose
romances, pointing out and discussing scenes of "communal life in
its pristine form," in both Wolfings and Roots. Speaks of Water and
Well as "masterworks" in an "allegorical mode," as portraits of
ideal societies, and of John Ball and Nowhere as dream visions, the
former utilizing "the dialectical argument of Morris' lectures," the
latter depicting the "right relation of man, nature, and society."

9   BRANTLINGER, PATRICK. "Nowhere: WM's Socialist Anti-Novel." VS
     19, no. 1 (September):35-49.
         Suggests that in Nowhere WM is consciously "hostile to
virtually every aspect of the 'great tradition' of Victorian
fiction." His philosophical position on modern civilization argued
that it could not nurture art, and he disliked nineteenth-century
novels that depended on conflict for both plot and character
development. In Nowhere there are no such conflicts and hence such
"dreary introspective nonsense," as Ellen calls it, can be dismissed
out of hand; in Nowhere art takes on purely mythic, childlike
shapes; in Nowhere freedom from anger and anxiety turn life itself
into art: "It is Morris's great strength to be able to imagine the
forms which art and freedom might take in a world without
aggression."

10 BRIDGEMAN, HARRIET, and DRURY, ELIZABETH, eds. The Encyclopedia
    of Victoriana. New York: Macmillan, pp. 21, 23, 41-43, passim.
        This lavishly illustrated reference book, "intended to be
    read as the story of the decorative arts in Britain and the United
    States between 1837 and 1901," has many references to WM, and
    detailed essays on topics like "furniture," "textiles," and
    "wallpaper" stress the importance of Morris and Co.; also useful are
    the short biographies of key figures and the selective
    bibliographies.

11 CALHOUN, BLUE. The Pastoral Vision of WM. Athens: University
    of Georgia Press, 263 pp.
        Argues that Paradise, regarded as a nineteenth-century
    pastoral inspired by a particlar dialectic of idleness and energy
    (as defined in "The Lesser Arts") can help us "see the beginning of
    a pattern in Morris's writing." The first chapter discusses WM's
    life in terms of "symbols of country and city," and the responses of
    other Victorian writers to Industrialization are summarized.
    Subsequent chapters present certain poems from Defence as quests,
    within the ethos of heroic action. Paradise poems, on the other
    hand, are set within a pastoral tradition, and the narrator's
    "ironic disengagement from the energetic aesthetic of heroism" is
    stressed. These poems are discussed in terms (borrowing from both
    Frye and Jung) of their seasonal patterns of image and theme. A
    final chapter discusses the Paradise narrator as the "most complex
    creation in the poem," and here there occur useful close readings of
    the lyrics for each month, as well as comments on the narrators in
    John Ball and Nowhere. Concludes that Paradise is "unique," and that
    its descriptions of a "higher, simpler civilization" would influence
    everything else that WM wrote. Revision of 1972.2.

12 CARMASSI, GUIDO. "The Expanding Vision: Changes in Emphasis in
    WM's Late Prose Romances." Dissertation, University of Notre
    Dame.
        Abstracted: DAI 36:5312-A.

13 DAY, MICHAEL, and GARSTANG, KATE. "Socialist Theories and Sir
    Raymond Unwin." Town and Country Planning 43, nos. 7-8
    (July-August):346-49.
        Comments upon the key influence WM had upon Raymond Unwin who
    learned about discontent and its causes when he wrote for Commonweal
    in the 1880s, when he read WM on the "decency of surroundings." How
    he utilized many of these ideas in his own schemes and projects, as
    at Letchworth and Hampstead Gardens Suburb, is briefly discussed.

14 DUNLAP, JOSEPH R. "The Road to Kelmscott: WM and the Book Arts
    Before the Founding of Kelmscott Press." Dissertation, Columbia
    University.
        Abstracted: DAI 37:11-A.

15 DUNLAP, JOSEPH R. "WM and the Book Arts Before Kelmscott
    Press." VP 13, nos. 3-4 (Autumn-Winter):141-57.
        A thorough discussion of WM's interests in manuscripts and
    early printed books, his own experiments with manuscript
    illumination in the 1850s, the elaborate plans for the aborted
    Paradise folio in the 1860s, and the more than 1,500 pages of
    calligraphy he completed in the 1870s. Plates, several in color,
    are included.

16 FAULKNER, PETER. WM and Eric Gill. London: WM Society, 29 pp.
        Discusses essential similarities between WM and Gill,
    pointing out how their social criticism grew out of their interest
    in crafts, isolating similar passages in WM lectures and Gill essays
    that criticize the industrial conditions that deprive workers of any
    responsibility for their work and thus of any interest or pleasure
    in it. As craftsmen, both men recognized the significance for art
    and society of finding joy in work, and both thought the medieval
    worker better off than the modern one. Some areas of disagreement
    are also discussed, with the suggestion that many arose because Gill
    misunderstood WM's socialism and thus WM's skepticism about the
    possibilities of reform through Parliament, or through the Arts and
    Crafts Movement. Concludes that WM "was both humbler and more
    robust than Gill. That the two men moved in opposite directions in
    their attitudes to Parliament suggests this; Morris the idealist
    made himself accept political realities in a way Gill refused to do.
    Had he lived through the difficult years of this century, perhaps
    Morris might have been able to bring to the whole Labour Movement
    his splendid sense of the potential richness of life, and fought
    from within it against the tendencies to bureacracy and narrowness
    of vision which were to alienate men like D.H. Lawrence and Gill."

17 FITZGERALD, PENELOPE. "The Kelmscott Chaucer and the Parting of
    Friends." In Burne-Jones: A Biography. London: Michael Joseph,
    pp. 251-69, passim.
        The effects upon Burne-Jones of WM's last illness and death
    are here set forth against the larger context of London's social and
    artistic milieu. Draws upon diaries and letters not used by Georgie
    Burne-Jones in 1904.3, and so there are fresh glimpses of the
    significant relationships WM had with the Burne-Joneses, from the
    earlier one with Georgie to the final collaboration on the Kelmscott
    Chaucer with Burne-Jones.

18 FLAHERTY, CAROLYN. "The Late Victorian Art Movement."
    Old-House Journal 3, no. 4 (April):1, 9-11.
        Discusses WM as "one of the first and most influential of the
missionaries of good taste," one whose work with dyes, his
achievements in flat design, prepared the way for the Aesthetic
Movement. Such useful commentary cheapened by an aspersion that WM
was also "one of the most famous cuckolds."

19 FRAYNE, J.P., and JOHNSON, C., eds. The Uncollected Prose of
    Yeats. New York: Columbia University Press, pp. 125, 293,
    passim.
        In this collection of reviews and other miscellaneous prose,
written between 1897 and 1939, WM is mentioned fifteen times,
usually in casual references, as when in a BBC program Yeats recalls
effects of hearing WM read from Sigurd. He also maintains that in
America "the words of Ruskin and Morris have found hearers who have
listened better because of Thoreau and Emerson."

20 FREDEMAN, WILLIAM E., and LINDSAY, JACK, eds. "D.G. Rossetti's
    'The Death of Topsy'" VP 13, nos. 3, 4 (Fall-Winter):177-79.
        Introduces and prints a previously unpublished five-scene
satirical playlet, "The Death of Topsy, a Drama of the Future in One
Unspeakable Act," that Rossetti wrote in 1878 and sent to Janey, who
would certainly have "hidden it from her husband, and which was in
any case libelous about the Wardles." WM is depicted as loud,
scratching, profane; he is poisoned by the Wardles in the third
scene, and Morris and Co. becomes "Wardle and Co."

21 FREDEMAN, WILLIAM E. "WM: 'What May He Not Yet Do?'" VP 13,
    nos. 3-4 (Fall-Winter):xix-xxx.
        Question in the title was posed by Rossetti in 1869; Fredeman
uses it here, to introduce a special issue on WM, to point out why
Rossetti could never have guessed just how much remained for WM to
achieve, how varied his work would be in the next twenty-five years.
Reviews significant critical reactions to this work, especially to
the poetry. Concludes with comments on WM's attitudes toward art
and some sensible generalizations about Nowhere.

22 FRYBERGER, BETSY G. "Morris and Company." In Morris and
    Company. Catalogue of 4 March-4 May 1975 Exhibition at Stanford
    Art Gallery. Stanford Art Book, no. 15. Stanford: Stanford
    University Press, pp. 18-25.
        Discusses the prospectus of the Firm, pointing out that it
was not as revolutionary as often suggested; other firms were also
interested in improving design, but for various reasons WM's had a
more widespread and enduring influence. Sketches in dates,
locations, and contributions of artists, and of the bookkeeper,
Taylor, bringing the history of Morris and Co. down into the

twentieth century when the Dearles were in charge. Their papers
were the basis for this exhibition.

23 FUSSELL, PAUL. The Great War and Modern Memory. New York and
    London: Oxford University Press, pp. 21, 135-37.
       States that there was "hardly a literate man who fought
    between 1914 and 1918" who had not read Well, and that scenes from
    the "Woods Debatable" and "Perilous," the poison pool and dry tree,
    were used by veterans to recall and communicate their experiences on
    battlefields in World War I.

24 GARDNER, DELBERT. An Idle Singer and His Audience: A Study of
    WM's Poetic Reputation in England, 1858-1900. The Hague: Mouton,
    135 pp.
       A complete and useful survey of contemporary reviews of WM's
    poetry, including the late prose romances, which leads to
    conclusions about his changing reputation as a poet. Suggests that
    these changes are due to a growing "aestheticism" which would
    account, for instance, for favorable reactions to Defence in the
    1890s as opposed to the "brickbats hurled" at it in the 1850s, when
    reviewers were looking for "truth." Comments upon reasons Paradise
    won for WM an international reputation. Finds that WM's socialist
    poems were often ignored or neglected and that "the total effect of
    Morris's socialism on his poetic reputation was negative." Revision
    of 1963.10.

25 GERE, CHARLOTTE, and SKIPWITH, PEYTON. "The WM Movement."
    Connoisseur 201, no. 807 (May):32-39.
       Speculates upon how the founding of a Firm could possibly
    lead to a Movement. Points out that Webb, after designing and
    building a rich man's home, would of course point him toward Morris
    and Co. for interior decoration. Characterizes differences in the
    Firm's work after George Jack became chief designer in 1890.
    Includes twenty-four plates, thirteen in color, each with a detailed
    description.

26 GLASSIE, HENRY. All Silver and No Brass. London and
    Bloomington: Indiana University Press, pp. 53-56, passim.
       Compares WM to Yeats; what the latter attempted to discover
    in the Irish folk, a "reflection of a more unified age," WM found in
    medieval churches, tapestries, and poetry. WM'S attitudes toward
    folk art, the work of the people, also discussed.

27 GOODWIN, K.L. "An Unpublished Tale from Paradise." VP 13, nos.
    3-4 (Autumn-Winter):91-102.
        Some tales intended for Paradise but then set aside as WM's
plans changed were later published by May Morris, except for "The
Story of Dorothea," which remains unpublished, perhaps because May
Morris thought it too bawdy or sadistic. Parallels between the tale
and Burne-Jones's watercolor, "St. Theophilus and the Angel," are
discussed, and the tale is partially paraphrased and explicated.
"The literary quality of the work justifies the removal of the
suppression it has suffered."

28 GOODWIN, K.L. "Unpublished Lyrics of WM." Yearbook of English
    Studies 5:190-206.
        While eleven lectures have been added to the published canon,
to May Morris's editions, only three poems have been added in the
intervening four decades. These include a sonnet (discussed in
1958.10), "O Fair Gold Goddess," and "Lovely Love and Loveless
Death." These are here discussed, and two others, "Guileful Love"
and "A Summer Night," which appeared before only in the calligraphic
A Book of Verse, are also discussed and here reprinted. Concludes
with a list of unpublished poems and fragments among the materials
May Morris left to the British Museum, and conjectures about Georgie
Burne-Jones being the subject for many of these lyrics.

29 HARRIS, RICHARD L. "WM, Magnusson, and Iceland: A Survey of
    Correspondence." VP 13, nos. 3-4 (Autumn-Winter):119-30.
        As teacher, fellow-translator, guide on the 1871 journey, and
helper on the Iceland Relief Committee, Magnusson was WM's "key" to
Iceland, to its literature, and to an understanding of its
nineteenth-century people. Using previously unpublished letters,
this article contains new references to the translations, their
publication, and their reviews, as well as new evidence of the time
and energy WM spent on the Iceland Relief Committee. Concludes with
comments on Jon Jonsson, guide for the 1873 journey, who is here
seen as a "centralized symbol of Morris' interests in Iceland."

30 INGLE, STEPHEN. "Socialist Man: WM and Bernard Shaw." In The
    Concept of Socialism. Edited by Bhikhu Parekh. London: Croom,
    Helm; New York: Holmes and Meier, pp. 72-94.
        Asserts that WM was a fundamental egalitarian and Shaw an
heirarchical one, that Nowhere demonstrates WM's beliefs in both the
instinctive creativity of man and in the "Norse passion for
equality," while Shaw's works carry his conviction that man is not
by nature anything and can thus be molded, changed, improved.
Concludes that their respective heroes "are none other than Morris
and Shaw themselves living the kind of life they feel bourgeois
society prevented them from leading."

31   JOHNSON, WENDELL STACY. Sex and Marriage in Victorian Poetry.
     London and Ithaca: Cornell University Press, pp. 17, 90, 243.
         Points out that WM's descriptions of marriage involve
     "sacrament only in the sense that the whole immanent physical world
     is sacred."

32   KOCMANOVA, JESSIE. "'Landscape and Sentiment': WM's First
     Attempt in Longer Prose Fiction." VP 13, nos. 3-4
     (Autumn-Winter):103-17.
         In 1873, when WM complained that he was losing "invention,"
     even "imagination and enthusiasm," he was perhaps referring to
     problems he had had with his only attempt at realistic prose
     fiction, his "abortive novel." Argues that this unpublished
     narrative, since it is "closely bound up with Morris's development
     as a prose writer," deserves careful attention. A full discussion
     follows of setting (upper Thames countryside), of characters (a few
     modeled on Dickens and fairy-tale types), of plot (crucial problems
     he had here caused him to abandon the project, but he "used and
     carried to a higher power in his later prose romances many of the
     motifs and techniques adumbrated in this fragment"). It has
     recently been published: 1982.15.

33   LAURENCE, DAN H. "Shaw, Books, and Libraries." Publications of
     the Bibliographical Society of America 69, no. 4
     (October-December):465-79.
         Discusses what WM taught Shaw about book design, citing the
     appearance of type, the width of margins, and the like, in Plays
     Pleasant and Unpleasant.

34   LE BOURGEOIS, JOHN. "WM, Rossetti, and Warington Taylor." N
     and Q 220 (March):113-15.
         Reprints and comments upon letters Taylor sent to Webb,
     appealing for help with marital problems, help that he apparently
     felt WM would not give and that Rossetti finally did. Conjectures
     therefore that Taylor's problems might have been like WM's: both men
     were more interested in their work than their wives, and a sensitive
     Rossetti was able to intervene.

35   LIFE, ALLAN R. "Illustration and WM's Ideal Book." VP 13, nos.
     3-4 (Autumn-Winter):131-40.
         Points out that WM's comments on the book arts often have a
     strongly authoritarian and ethical tone; a printer, for instance, is
     condemned for his "licentious spacing." In his insistence that
     illustration be subordinate to text and its decoration, WM's
     influence on twentieth-century book illustration was nil, or
     counterproductive.

36   LINDSAY, JACK. <u>WM: His Life and Work</u>. London: Constable, 432
     pp. Reprint. New York: Taplinger Publishing Co., 1979.
        Stresses throughout the importance of WM's childhood, "how
much his whole hope for the future, for a happy and brotherly world,
is linked to his childhood memories." Such memories are turned to
good use in images repeated in his works, providing flower, leaf,
and bird within his designs, to cite a few examples. Stresses also
the childhood bond WM enjoyed with his sister, Emma, and how this
bond was broken when she married the Reverend Joseph Oldham in 1850.
Later the roles of Emma and Oldham were "more powerfully taken over
by Janey and Rossetti, while he himself vainly loved the wife of his
own best friend, Burne-Jones." Such personal problems, it is then
suggested, got submerged in a larger pattern: "he had to find the
childhood dream inside history and then struggle to refashion
history so that it led to that dream in a fully socialized form."
Explains for the first time what happened in the Marlborough College
Riots, involving some fireworks damage, some stone throwing, some
students being expelled. But Lindsay states that WM "had taken
part, albeit passively in an actual revolt, had seen in action for
the first time, however imperfectly, the privilege of fellowship."
Lindsay often follows closely, without attribution, both Mackail
(1899.10) and Henderson (1967.11), but new points are made; he
claims, for instance, that "Guenevere is the most rounded and
convincing image of the queen in all literature, an Emma-image
raised to a new level." He is equally bold on WM and Georgie,
finding in the poetry suggestions of "a summer night when he and
Georgie embraced." Lindsay is perhaps most provocative on WM and
socialism, insisting that Engels undervalued him, that Marx
influenced <u>John Ball</u>, that <u>Pilgrims</u> is the "most important poem of
contemporary narrative in England during the nineteenth century."
It "antedates the work of Gorky and other pioneers of socialist
realism." In <u>Nowhere</u>, Lindsay discusses the prophetic portrayal of
the fascist tendencies of the middle class, and the portraits of
what a world without commodity production might be like. Sees Ellen
in <u>Nowhere</u> as "the anti-Janey, who had many of the elements of
Georgie." Concludes that WM was "the only artist of the nineteenth
century who reached Marxism by the inner logic of the positions from
which he began," that he was "the first Marxist who grasped in its
fullness the nature of revolutionary change--indeed apart from
Lenin, almost the only one who never lost or diluted his sense of
the vital unity of the political, economic, aesthetic and moral
factors."

37   MORRIS, BARBARA. "WM and the South Kensington Museum." <u>VP</u> 13,
     nos. 3-4 (Autumn-Winter):159-75.
        Sketches the history of the South Kensington Museum (now the
Victoria and Albert), and discusses WM's thirty-five year
association with its collections, which he once said he had used "as
much as any man living." The Museum also used him: as advisor and
referee, donor and designer. Many of his textile designs,
especially those he executed after 1876, as Floud has pointed out

(1959.4), have prototypes in the Museum, and some of its other treasures, like the "Three Fates," are mentioned in his lectures. The Museum bought Morris and Co. stained glass as early as 1864, and its Green Dining Room has remained both a tribute to Morris and Co. designing genius and a durable, beautiful public room. Reports also on trips to Paris WM made for the Museum and on specific advice he tendered about whether Persian carpets or Icelandic textiles should be purchased.

38 MULOKOZI, M.M. "Two Utopias: A Comparative Examination of WM's
    Nowhere and Shaaban Robert's Siku ya Watenzi wote" [The day of
    all doers]. Umma 5:134-58.
        Contrasts Nowhere to Siku ya Watenzi wote, a Swahili novel
written in 1960 by the "Poet Laureate of East Africa," Shaaban
Robert (1909-62). Departs from paraphrases of and commentary upon
both works (he prefers Nowhere with its scientific socialism to the
Swahili novel with its religious solutions) to discuss contemporary
social and political problems in Africa, and the ways that European
colonialism created them. Praises WM for his analyses of links
between capitalism and colonialism, his warnings that parliamentary
politics would lead to the welfare state and to governmental sorts
of irresponsibilities that have occurred in our century.

39 NICOLL, JOHN. Dante Gabriel Rossetti. New York: Macmillan, pp.
    105, 113-19.
        Discusses WM's close association with Rossetti during the
period of the Oxford Union paintings, particularly their common
interests in Arthurian themes. Goes on to suggest that "The Blue
Closet" and "The Tune of the Seven Towers" are among WM's weaker
poems.

40 NUTTGENS, PATRICK. "A Full Life and an Honest Place." In
    Spirit of the Age. London: BBC, pp. 189-213.
        Claims that Red House is of great importance for modern
architecture "because of the furnishings and organization of its
interior, the ideology that lay behind it, and the personality of
the man for whom it was built." Includes a biographical sketch and
comments on the twentieth-century designers influenced by WM and by
the Arts and Crafts Movement. Originally the seventh of eight BBC
programs on architecture and society.

41 REED, JOHN R. <u>Victorian</u> <u>Conventions</u>. Columbus: Ohio University
    Press, pp. 431-33, passim.
        Contrasts "hopeful memory of the future" in <u>Nowhere</u> with the
    "memory of cosmic sorrow" in <u>The</u> <u>Time</u> <u>Machine</u>.

42 ROBINSON, DUNCAN. <u>A</u> <u>Companion</u> <u>Guide</u> <u>to</u> <u>the</u> <u>Kelmscott</u> <u>Chaucer</u>.
    London: Basilisk Press, 146 pp.
        A one-volume guide, with useful and precise information,
    particularly about Burne-Jones's illustrations, to accompany a folio
    facsimile, published at this same time, of the Kelmscott Chaucer.
    Covers the interest in Chaucer shared by the two friends, their
    earlier collaborations, and details about Kelmscott Press and the
    production of the Kelmscott Chaucer. Revised: 1982.30.

43 SADOFF, DIANE. "Erotic Murders: Structural and Rhetorical Irony
    in WM's Froissart Poems." <u>VP</u> 13, nos. 3-4
    (Autumn-Winter):11-26.
        Claims that <u>Defence</u> poems are not merely confusing or trite
    shards of bright nostalgia but actually "an effort to discover the
    dialectic of circumstantial irony and the human struggle for
    transcendence." Closely examines the rhetorical and "motivational
    relationships between death and sexuality in "Haystack in the
    Floods," "Concerning Geffray Teste Noire," and "Sir Peter Harpdon's
    End," commenting upon recent criticism (1958.9 and 1959.6) of these
    most Froissartian of <u>Defence</u> poems; their "violence and death
    displace and destroy frail human desires for sexual and
    interpersonal fulfillment." Points out that the medieval setting
    somehow "personalizes courage for the industrialized and
    depersonalized nineteenth century."

44 SCHMIDT-KUNSEMULLER, FRIEDRICH ADOLF, ed. <u>The</u> <u>Decorative</u> <u>Arts</u>
    <u>and</u> <u>The</u> <u>Aims</u> <u>of</u> <u>Art,</u> <u>by</u> <u>WM</u>. Osnabruck: Otto Zeller, pp. i-ix.
        General biographical introduction to the two lectures, an
    introduction that stresses WM's "praktischer Sozialismus."

45 SILVER, CAROLE. "The Earthly Paradise: Lost." <u>VP</u> 13, nos. 3-4
    (Autumn-Winter):27-42.
        Though <u>Paradise</u> made WM's contemporary reputation, in the
    twentieth century the poem has usually been censured or ignored,
    partly because of changing tastes but also because of a "lack of
    awareness of the poem's purpose, theme and structure, and equally
    important, of its central role in its creator's life and thought."
    This careful study clarifies WM's purpose, demonstrating his great
    skill in using various sources, showing how structure and imagery in
    specific tales and across the whole poem support pessimistic themes
    concerning the transcience of love and the vanity of human wishes,
    themes that reflect WM's marital problems during the period he wrote
    the poem.

46 SPATT, HARTLEY S. "WM: The Language of History and Myth."
    Dissertation, Johns Hopkins University.
        Abstracted: DAI 36:4518-19-A.

47 SPATT, HARTLEY S. "WM and the Uses of the Past." VP 13, nos.
    3-4 (Autumn-Winter):1-9.
        Many nineteenth-century thinkers were interested in history,
    in "the sources of the present," none more so than WM who recognized
    the "special gift of the past" as its proximity to the beautiful,
    the mythic, the eternal. Uses "Unknown Church" to discuss ways that
    WM attempts "to transform the new data of history," making it
    somehow live again within the minds of readers who learn that the
    "past exists within the present as a form of beauty whose
    archaeological content is irrelevant." Equally provocative
    formulations are made regarding Guenevere's use of historical icons
    to reject the "legalistic past of historic actions," of personalized
    icons to get Lancelot, and modern readers, to accept a "false
    memory." Concludes that WM was the "first great historicist,"
    brilliant in showing us characters who "perform individual acts of
    aesthetic recreation in order to avoid the tyranny of time."

48 SPENCER, ISOBEL. Walter Crane. New York: Macmillan; London:
    Studio Vista, pp. 8, 12, 100-103, 142-49, passim.
        Discusses ways and why WM was such an inspiration to Crane,
    pointing out that he was not so hopeful as Crane that mere arts and
    crafts could be a help to the workers and that Crane's lectures in
    Germany and America spread WM's ideas about art and socialism.
    Includes dozens of illustrations, along with commentary on many of
    those Crane did for Justice, Commonweal, and Kelmscott Press
    volumes.

49 STALLMAN, ROBERT. "The Lover's Progress: An Investigation of
    WM's 'The Defence of Guenevere' and 'King Arthur's Tomb.'" SEL
    15, no. 4 (Autumn):657-70.
        Recent interpretations of the Arthurian poems in Defence tend
    to overlook WM's "debt to Browning and the dramatic monologue,"
    ignoring the narrator, seen here as one of Lancelot's men, and thus
    a spy, and one who reports upon Guenevere's skillful defense with a
    good degree of sympathy. Comments about the way that Guenevere
    performs for this male audience are fresh and provocative: her
    monologue is "a victory for youth and springtime over the morality
    of age and empire." The second poem, "King Arthur's Tomb," should
    be read as a companion piece, "the completion of the lover's
    progress in the seasonal cycle," the apotheosis of Guenevere who is
    now able to lay her case before Christ and argue convincingly for
    herself and also for Lancelot.

50 STANSKY, PETER. Introduction to Morris and Company. Catalogue
    of 4 March-4 May 1975 Exhibition at Stanford Art Gallery.
    Stanford Art Book 15. Stanford: Stanford University Press, pp.
    9-11.
        Celebrates WM as a "force in the Victorian age, yes; but also
    an innovator, an influence, a precursor of the Modern in art and
    politics." Mentions those who started the 1861 Firm and the ways
    that their aims in design contrasted with those who staged
    exhibitions a decade earlier at the Crystal Palace. Concludes with
    thoughts on the aptness of a WM exhibit for a modern audience
    interested in the environment, since WM's ideal was "to achieve a
    world whose environment would be determined by beauty and necessity,
    harmoniously joined."

51 STEINER, GEORGE. After Babel: Aspects of Language and
    Translation. New York and London: Oxford University Press, pp.
    342-43.
        Quotes from WM's translation of the Odyssey, characterizing
    its style as "part Norse saga, part Tennyson, and part archaelogy."

52 STRODE, ELIZABETH. "The Crisis of Paradise: WM and Keats." VP
    13, nos. 3-4 (Autumn-Winter):71-81.
        Asserts that the introductory verses to "September" in
    Paradise are autobiographical, and therefore "The Death of Paris"
    must be also, that in fact the poem indicates the death of WM, the
    Pre-Raphaelite. Points out parallels between that poem and "Sleep
    and Poetry" by Keats, discussing themes that reappear throughout the
    history of British poetry.

53 THOMAS, ALAN G. "Private Press Books." Great Books and Book
    Collectors. London: Weidenfeld and Nicolson, pp. 214-21.
        Reprint of 1967.27, with a few additional illustrations.

54 VALENTINE, K.B. "Motifs from Nature in the Design Work and
    Prose Romances of WM, 1876-1896." VP 13, nos. 3-4
    (Autumn-Winter):83-89.
        Draws upon several examples of natural imagery in the late
    romances and upon the decorative designs WM completed in the last
    twenty years of his life to demonstrate his "delight in bristling
    nature," to discuss ways that images of flowers, animals, and water
    are used in the literary and visual works. WM was "guided by the
    belief that man could be infinitely more happy if only he learned to
    imitate nature's creativity."

55 WOLFE, WILLARD. From Radicalism to Socialism: Men and Ideas in
    the Foundation of Fabian Socialist Doctrines, 1881-1889. New
    Haven: Yale University Press, pp. 131-34, passim.
        WM is here placed within a useful exposition of the rise of
    Fabianism, and his associations with other socialists, namely Shaw,
    are discussed in some detail. Points out that Shaw and other
    socialist leaders learned from WM's lectures and that WM's
    insistence that "fellowship is life and lack of fellowship is death"
    became a powerful force for British socialists at the end of the
    nineteenth century.

56 An Exhibition of Books, Manuscripts, and Artifacts Associated
    with WM. Catalogue of an Exhibition 1 October-1 December 1975
    at the Botetourt Museum, College of William and Mary. Swem
    Library: Williamsburg, Virginia, 11 pp.
        Biographical sketch plus short descriptions of thirty-seven
    exhibited items, most of them Kelmscott Press volumes.

57 From Kelmscott Press: An Exhibition of Books. Catalogue of an
    Exhibition held 18 January-3 August 1975 at the Lowe Art Museum.
    Coral Gables, Fl., 19 pp.
        Includes short introduction, a list of all Kelmscott Press
    volumes, photographs of nine of the twenty books that were
    exhibited.

58 Morris and Company. Catalogue of 4 March-4 May 1975 Exhibition
    at the Stanford Art Gallery. Stanford Art Book, no. 15.
    Stanford: Stanford University Press, 75 pp.
        This exhibition, an attempt to survey the work of Morris and
    Co. and to assess WM's importance as a designer, consisted of 169
    items (most of them from the collection of Sanford and Helen Berger)
    arranged under two general headings: "Catalogue of Morris and Co."
    and "WM and his Work." There are short introductions to six
    subsections, from "Stained Glass" to "Embroideries," under the
    first, and chronological subdivisions, eight of them, from "Early
    Years" to "WM Today" within the second. Each of the 169 items
    displayed has here a full and specific description, and the
    catalogue includes chronology and full bibliography (pp. 69-75) by
    David W. Donaldson, as well as an introduction by Peter Stansky
    (1975.50) and an essay on Morris and Co. by Betsy G. Fryberger
    (1975.22).

59 Burne-Jones: The Paintings, Graphics and Decorative Work.
    Catalogue of Exhibitions in 1975-76 in London, Southampton and
    Birmingham. London: Arts Council, pp. 16-18, passim.
        Has detailed introductions to the various sections of the
    exhibition, the most comprehensive ever of the work of Burne-Jones,
    and there are several references to WM's influence and to
    Burne-Jones's designs for Morris and Co. within the introductions
    and the descriptions of the 387 items exhibited.

                                1976

1   BAYLEN, J.O. "WM and the Victorians' 'Best Hundred Books.'"
    VIJ 5:61-67.
        Many eminent Victorians responded to a request from the Pall
    Mall Gazette for a list of their one hundred "best books," and among
    them was WM, whose list as well as an explanatory letter are here
    reproduced. In the letter, he comments upon books read "for a
    definite purpose," such as works of "philosophy, economics, and
    modern or critical history," which he omitted from his list; the
    notes on this list about "Bibles" (national epics) and "sham" Latin
    classics, and about why he found Milton repelling, are as
    interesting as the list itself, which includes much medieval poetry
    and prose, Blake as well as Byron, Defoe as well as Dickens.

2   BOOS, FLORENCE. The Poetry of Dante G. Rossetti: A Critical
    Reading and Source Study. The Hague: Mouton, pp, 122-31,
    passim.
        Compares Rossetti's and WM's early portrayals of
    "Pre-Raphaelite women" and argues that WM's women are more unhappy,
    more intense, and more sharply drawn.

3   BRIGGS, R.C.H. "Editorial." JWMS 3, no. 2 (Summer):3.
        Informs readers of new production techniques to be used for
    the journal.

4   BRYSON, JOHN, and TROXELL, JANET CAMP, eds. Rossetti and Janey:
    Their Correspondence. Oxford: Oxford University Press, pp. 1,
    4, passim.
        The 114 letters from Rossetti to Janey, which "first became
    available for consultation" in 1964, contain many references to WM
    and his activities between 1868 and 1881, references not always
    flattering. The thirty-seven letters from Janey to Rossetti also
    contain pertinent references to WM. Edition includes an
    introduction, full notes, an index, three appendixes with additional
    Janey letters, and over fifty photographs and illustrations.

5   BUICK, ADAM. "WM's Incomplete Communism: A Critique of Paul
     Meier's Thesis." JWMS 3, no. 2 (Summer):16-32.
          Reviews statements by Marx, Engels, and even Lenin, to argue
against points made by Meier (1972.19) regarding WM's apparent
familiarity with these statements, with the idea that a period of
state socialism would necessarily precede the perfect communism of
Nowhere. Concludes with the hope that "in the course of this essay,
I have managed to clear Morris of Meier's contention that he would
have been a supporter of the Russian government and system."

6   BURY, SHIRLEY. "Rossetti and His Jewelry." Burlington Magazine
     118, no. 875 (February):94-102.
          Detailed report on Kelmscott Manor jewelry, especially those
pieces that appeared in Rossetti paintings and drawings and which,
like their wedding ring, have intimate associations with WM and
Janey. May Morris's will, her instructions to Miss Lobb, regarding
what items should be left to museums and under what conditions,
indicate her fiercely protective attitude toward her father's
memory.

7   CALHOUN, BLUE. "'The Little Land of Romance': Pastoral
     Perspective in the Late Prose Romances of WM." In Studies in
     the Late Romances of WM: Papers Presented at the Annual Meeting
     of the MLA, December, 1975. Edited by Carole Silver and Joseph
     R. Dunlap. New York: WM Society, pp. 55-76.
          Discusses the typical landscapes of the late prose romances,
which often suggest Oxfordshire dales, sometimes Northern scenes,
and which usually include a garden, or "naturally secluded spot,"
essential to the completion of the hero's quest. But this spot can
also be dangerous, especially if it is contrived or within a city,
for in the romances cities are full of "corruption, greed, and
turbulence."

8   CARRINGTON, NOEL. Industrial Design in Britain. London: Allen
     and Unwin, pp. 17-25, 52-63, passim.
          Discusses Modern Industrial Design Movement from its
inception in 1915, commenting upon its seven founders, men like
Lethaby, Morton, and Curwen, important designers who were influenced
by WM.

9   CRAWFORD, JOHN M., JR. "Memories of Collecting." In WM and The
     Art of the Book. Edited by Paul Needham. New York: Oxford
     University Press, pp. 13-18.
          This introductory essay recalls the joys of collecting
Kelmscott Press volumes, of exhibiting them, and of learning about
WM and his works.

10 CROMEY-HAWKE, N. "WM and Victorian Painted Furniture."
    Connoisseur 191, no. 767 (January):32-43.
      The heavily decorated "medieval" furniture which the Firm
displayed at the 1862 International Exhibition surprised viewers,
and for many it seemed a new departure in the decorative arts.
Whether it actually was, WM's role, and the importance of Red House
and its decorated furniture are points examined here against the
background of the Gothic Revival, Burges's earlier work, and the
influence of Street, who employed both Webb and WM. Includes
several monochrome illustrations.

11 DENINGTON, FRANCES B. "The Complete Book: An Investigation of
    the Development of WM's Aesthetic Theory and Literary
    Practice." Dissertation, McMasters University.
      Abstracted: DAI 37:2194-A.

12 DE CAMP, L. SPRAGUE. "Jack of all Arts." In Literary Swordsmen
    and Sorcerers: The Makers of Heroic Fantasy. Sauk City, Wis.:
    Arkham, pp. 31-47.
      Reprinted from 1974.5.

13 DREYFUS, JOHN. "WM: Typographer." In WM and the Art of the
    Book. Edited by Paul Needham. New York: Oxford University
    Press, pp. 71-94.
      Though WM became a typographer late in life, he gained
expertise rapidly because his earlier practical work in design and
manufacture provided a sound basis for his Kelmscott Press
achievements. Offers useful details about Walker, who was WM's
friend before the famed slide lecture and who worked so closely with
him later at the Press; he was "a partner in all but name."
Describes the design and development of the three typefaces,
experiments with papers and inks, and, finally, the extent of
Kelmscott Press influence on foreign presses and twentieth-century
typographical innovation.

14 DUNLAP, JOSEPH R. "From Westminster to Hammersmith via
    Chiswick: A Typographic Link between William Caxton and WM." In
    Caxton: An American Contribution to the Quincentenary
    Celebration. Edited by Susan Otis Thompson. New York:
    Typophiles, pp. 3-12.
      While certain connections between Caxton and WM are
wellknown, such as the names for the typefaces ("Golden" and "Troy")
taken from the titles of books printed by both of them, another
link, one that is pre-Kelmscott Press, has not been fully discussed.
WM used a type copied from Caxton for an 1890 edition, published by
the Chiswick Press, of his own translation of Gunnlaugs Saga. That
typeface, how the Chiswick Press happened to have it, and the ways

that WM used it in this edition (apprentice work for Kelmscott
Press) are here discussed in detail.

15 DUNLAP, JOSEPH R. "WM: Calligrapher." In WM and the Art of the
    Book. Edited by Paul Needham. New York: Oxford University
    Press, pp. 48-70.
        An exhaustive survey with full descriptions of all of the
calligraphy WM completed between 1856--when he was encouraged by
Rossetti to prepare a few stanzas for the Brownings--and 1890 when
he made a catalogue of his library in a "somewhat uneven Italic."
The amount of calligraphy and illuminated work that he turned out
between 1869 and 1875 was "astonishing," because during that period
he was also running a business, and suffering marital problems;
these problems spurred him to complete his illuminated manuscripts,
which were prepared for Georgie Burne-Jones. Has interesting
details on effects of leafy decorations intertwining with text and
on ways that calligraphic experiences flowered, finally, at
Kelmscott Press.

16 DUNLAP, JOSEPH R. On the Heritage of WM: Some Considerations,
    Typographic and Otherwise. New York: Typophiles, 26 pp.
        Discusses WM's early interests in book desigh, and its
achievements during the years of Kelmscott Press, and its subsequent
influence on printing and fine presses. Suggests that WM's
achievements in typography and printing were directly related to his
overall aims for the arts and crafts.

17 ELZEA, ROWLAND, and ELZEA, BETTY. The Pre-Raphaelite Era:
    1848-1914. Catalogue of an Exhibition 12 April-6 June 1976 at
    the Delaware Art Museum (An Exhibition in Celebration of the
    Nation's Bi-Centennial). Wilmington: Wilmington Society of Fine
    Arts, pp. 88-97, passim.
        The catalogue's fourth section, "The Second Generation,"
includes introductions to WM and to Morris and Co., and in the
exhibit itself there were several items ranging from Sussex chairs
to Kelmscott Press books; each item is carefully described.

18 FLEMING, JOHN. WM and Medievalism. London: WM Centre, 3 pp.
        One paragraph "Prefatory Comment," followed by a ten-item
bibliography, each with a one sentence annotation.

19 FRYE, NORTHROP. The Secular Scripture: A Study of the Structure
    of Romance. Cambridge, Mass.: Harvard University Press, pp.
    177-79, passim.
        Judges WM to be the most interesting writer in the romance
    tradition, one reason being his "encyclopedic approach to romance,
    his ambition to collect every major story in literature and retell
    it or translate it." Discusses Paradise narrators' attempts to
    avoid death by telling tales, and reasons for WM's positive
    attitudes toward medieval artisans and poets.

20 GHIBAUDI, SILVIA ROTA. "Utopia e propaganda: Il caso WM."
    Pensiero Politico 9, nos. 2-3:519-30.
        Opens with a theoretical discussion of the possible
    relationships between Utopian literature and propaganda,
    conjecturing then on the possibilities of such literature
    influencing motives and actions in the real world. Discusses
    Nowhere and selected biographical facts against that background,
    citing Marx, Engels, and Marcuse to support theoretical points.

21 GREYSMITH, BRENDA. Wallpaper. New York: Macmillan, pp. 136-40,
    passim.
        Discusses several WM designs for wallpapers, beginning with
    "Trellis." Concludes that Morris and Co. wallpapers remained
    "caviar for an elite, well beyond the means of the general public."

22 HARRIS, RICHARD L. "WM and Jon Jonsson, the Saddlesmith of
    Hlitharendakot." Musk-Ox 18:58-62.
        Object is "to understand Jon Jonsson and the fascination he
    held" for WM, who met him in 1871 and hired him for his guide in
    1873. Suggests that Jon "had something of the heroic in him," not
    only because of his size and appearance, but also because he knew
    and loved the sagas and the "old lore."

23 HOLLOW, JOHN. "Deliberate Happiness in the Late Prose Romances
    of WM." In Studies in the Late Romances of WM: Papers Presented
    at the Annual Meeting of the MLA, December 1975. Edited by
    Carole Silver and Joseph R. Dunlap. New York: WM Society, pp.
    79-94.
        Opens with a comment from Yeats concerning WM and his
    interest in earthly paradises, glossing it by looking at the
    situations in several of the late romances where heroes who "lose
    themselves in the future of their tribes" can thereby "possess the
    future through anticipation," thus exemplifying a religion of
    humanity. Concludes that WM, like Keats, might contemplate earthly
    paradises, but realized that "human life, even with its changes, is
    preferable to that cold pastoral."

24 HOSKINS, ROBERT. "Image and Motif in 'Haystack in the
    Floods.'" JWMS 3, no. 2 (Summer):4-7.
       Discusses "hand images" which are said to unify the poem and
    a betrayal motif which "adds richness and complexity," perhaps
    because it is here linked to Christ's ordeal in the Garden.

25 KAPP, YVONNE. Eleanor Marx: The Crowded Years. Vol. 2. New
    York: Pantheon; London: Lawrence and Wishart, pp. 240-45,
    passim.
       Asserts that WM was the "noblest and most gifted of Eleanor
    Marx's English associates," offering new insights into problems WM
    had with Hyndman, Aveling, and Engels. Includes descriptions of
    Trafalgar Square Riot, of Linnell's funeral, the procession 120,000
    strong, and the singing of WM's "Death Song" at the grave.

26 KELVIN, NORMAN. "The Erotic in Nowhere and Well." In Studies
    in the Late Romances of WM: Papers Presented at the Annual
    Meeting of the MLA, December, 1975. Edited by Carole Silver and
    Joseph R. Dunlap. New York: WM Society, pp. 97-114.
       Examines differing treatments of the erotic in Nowhere and in
    Well, written just afterwards but without the restraints apparent in
    Nowhere, where the society manages the erotic "by condoning
    infidelity and eliminating the material causes of jealousy," and
    where WM in the interests of narrative and thematic consistency must
    manage Guest's strong attraction for Ellen. In Well, on the other
    hand, the erotic "is the shaping force of society itself," and women
    are seen not only as friends and partners of men, but also as
    slaves; descriptions of fair captives in chains involve "erotic
    power fantasies" and raise questions "as to whether Morris is fully
    aware of the effects he achieves."

27 KIRCHHOFF, FREDERICK. Introduction to Studies in the Late
    Romances of WM: Papers Presented at the Annual Meeting of the
    MLA, December, 1975. Edited by Carole Silver and Joseph R.
    Dunlap. New York: WM Society, pp. 11-30.
       Asserts that "the prose romances of WM's final decade remain
    the least understood body of major Victorian fiction," partly
    because even serious scholars brush by or ignore them, even though
    they can yield insights into WM's social concerns and psychic
    states; as this collection of papers suggests, these romances can be
    seen as the "most deadly serious of Morris's literary
    undertakings." An approach that closely considers the role of women
    is then presented, beginning with the observation that Ellen is an
    emotional center in Nowhere, awakening the "narrator to the sharp
    awareness of his erotic unfulfillment," adding that heroines in
    later tales engage in complex dialectics with both nature and with
    the heroes' quests for spiritual growth.

28 LANGE, THOMAS V. "WM and Kelmscott Press." In The Illustrator
    and the Book in England from 1790 to 1914. Edited by Gordon N.
    Ray. Catalogue of Exhibition during March-April, 1976, at the
    Pierpont Morgan Library. New York: Pierpont Morgan, pp. 158-59.
        Biographical sketch followed by a description of the three
    Kelmscott Press volumes, and their illustrators, included in the
    exhibition: Nowhere, and Charles Gere; the Kelmscott Chaucer and
    Burne-Jones; and Spenser's Shepherdes Calendar and A.J. Gaskin, this
    last regarded as "perhaps the most successful" of the illustrated
    Kelmscott Press volumes.

29 LEE, L.; SEDDEN, G.; and STEPHENS, F., eds. Stained Glass. New
    York: Crown Publishers, pp. 151-53, passim.
        Places WM and Morris and Co. within a general history of
    stained glass from its beginnings into the twentieth century,
    stating that the "WM workshop heads any list of nineteenth-century
    glaziers," and that "WM and Burne-Jones had an inspired
    partnership." Short history of Morris and Co. supplemented with
    several color plates.

30 LE BOURGEOIS, JOHN. "WM and the Marxist Myth." Durham
    University Journal, n.s., 38, no. 1 (December):76-82.
        Argues that in the twenty years since E.P. Thompson (1955.15)
    "avenged the socialist spirit of WM," all subsequent critics have
    seemingly come to believe that WM was a full-fledged Marxist.
    Glances at a few contemporary comments on WM and his socialist work
    and then concludes that he was not a leading Marxist, that,
    moreover, "possibly the time has come for a serious re-assessment of
    Morris's socialism and, incidentally, a re-evaluation of J. Bruce
    Glasier's much maligned memoirs" (1921.3). It is imperative that
    one read E.P. Thompson's prompt and convincing reply (1977.36).

31 LLOYD, TREVOR. "WM vs. Hyndman: Commonweal and Justice."
    Victorian Periodicals Newsletter 9, no. 4 (December):119-28.
        Suggests that WM and Hyndman "provide much of the reason for
    studying Commonweal and Justice," so closely are their personalities
    linked to the journals and to the Socialist League and the SDF.
    Discusses the organizations and their journals. Commonweal tended
    to have more information, more interpretation (especially of foreign
    affairs), and better writing, but it never earned any money (WM was
    covering a loss of 500 pounds a year), and it consequently folded
    long before Justice. Other reasons for its demise are discussed.

32 MAC DONALD, J. ALEX. "The Revision of <u>Nowhere</u>." JWMS 3, no. 2
    (Summer):8-15.
        Studies changes WM made between publication of <u>Nowhere</u> in
    <u>Commonweal</u> (11 January-10 October 1890) and its first authorized
    publication in book form, in March 1891. More than half the
    revisions occur in the chapter, "How the Change Came," where WM
    added, for instance, a "Federation" of combined workers; such
    additions suggest a softening of purist attitudes about unions.

33 MANIERI ELIA, MARIO. <u>WM e l'ideologia dell'architettura</u>
    <u>moderna</u>. Rome and Bari: Laterza, 243 pp.
        Includes a biographical sketch and a discussion of WM's
    attitude toward the Neo-Gothic revival, which is contrasted to his
    high regard for medieval art and architecture; WM's influence on
    modern architecture is discussed, with new insights provided when
    cultural critics like Walter Benjamin are evoked. Has over fifty
    illustrations and, in an appendix, several chapters of <u>Nowhere</u>
    translated into Italian.

34 MASHEK, JOSEPH. "The Carpet Paradigm: Critical Prolegomena to a
    Theory of Flatness." <u>Arts</u> <u>Magazine</u> 51, no. 1
    (September):82-109.
        WM mentioned several times; his lectures on design are quoted
    in this theoretical study of perspective, plane surfaces, and ways
    that certain designs should merge with certain materials
    traditionally used, ways that WM grew to understand in his work with
    carpets and tapestries.

35 MATHEWS, RICHARD. <u>An</u> <u>Introductory</u> <u>Guide</u> <u>to</u> <u>the</u> <u>Utopian</u> <u>and</u>
    <u>Fantasy</u> <u>Writings</u> <u>of</u> <u>WM</u>. London: WM Centre, 17 pp.
        Discusses themes and structures of WM's prose romances,
    listing current editions and critical studies and suggesting that
    these tales are the "real crown" of WM's work. Finds many points
    where the romances have twentieth-century relevance (<u>Water</u> deals
    with women's liberation), and argues that they are precursors of the
    fantasy novel.

36 MATHEWS, RICHARD. Afterword to "<u>Golden</u> <u>Wings</u>" <u>and</u> <u>Other</u> <u>Stories</u>
    <u>by</u> <u>WM</u>. Van Nuys, Calif.: Newcastle Publishing, pp. 165-69.
        Remarks appended to this reprinting of one third of the
    Everyman edition (1907.10) of WM's romances assert that these early
    tales (they first appeared in the <u>Oxford</u> <u>and</u> <u>Cambridge</u> <u>Magazine</u>) are
    both "archetypal" and "revolutionary fiction," and also that the
    later prose romances "are in many ways the crowning achievement of
    WM's career."

37 MATHEWS, RICHARD. <u>Three</u> <u>Views</u> <u>of</u> <u>Kelmscott</u> <u>House</u>. London: WM
    Centre, 6 pp.
        Introduces the three views of Kelmscott House here reprinted:
(1) WM's positive description in an 1878 letter to Janey, urging
that they buy this place by the Thames with the fine garden, (2) May
Morris's description from volume 13 of the <u>Collected</u> <u>Works</u> that
stresses the river vistas and WM's work-room and the drawing room
above, and (3) Shaw's comments on why carpets on the wall and not
the floor imply an "artistic taste of extraordinairy integrity."
Concludes with the hope that Kelmscott House's reputation as a place
for creative fellowship shall grow and prosper now that it has also
become the WM Centre.

38 NEEDHAM, PAUL, ed. <u>WM</u> <u>and</u> <u>the</u> <u>Art</u> <u>of</u> <u>the</u> <u>Book</u>. London: Oxford
    University Press; New York: Pierpont Morgan Library, 254 pp.
        Catalogue of a major exhibition in 1976 at the Pierpont
Morgan Library, "repository of the largest and most valuable single
block of volumes from the Morris library." The items exhibited were
arranged under three headings: (1) "The Library of WM," (2)
"Calligraphy," (3) "Printing and Book Design." Full descriptions of
these items are preceded by prefaces by Ryskamp (1976.45) and
Crawford (1976.9), and essays by Dreyfuss (1976.13), Dunlap
(1976.15), and Needham (1976.39), who also wrote the detailed
descriptions and the introductions to each of the three sections.
Includes 114 plates.

39 NEEDHAM, PAUL. "WM: Book Collector." In <u>WM</u> <u>and</u> <u>The</u> <u>Art</u> <u>of</u> <u>the</u>
    <u>Book</u>. Edited by Paul Needham. New York: Oxford University
    Press, pp. 21-47
        Asserts that WM's tastes in book design were influenced by
his own "adventures in collecting," and thus a study of his library
(of "higher quality than [that of] any other major English literary
figure") is both pertinent and overdue. Charts purchases made from
the late 1860s over the next dozen years: thirteen incunabula, a
working library of dozens of Icelandic editions, and other
sixteenth- and seventeenth-century English books. After 1888, WM's
collecting of manuscripts and incunabula increased dramatically;
only Kelmscott Press--a corollary concern--claimed more of his
attention, and WM quickly became an authority on early printed books
and illuminated manuscripts. Corrects the widely held notion that
WM sold most of his important collection to further socialist
causes. The collection was intact at WM's death, but was later
split up and Morgan acquired only part of it.

40 OBERG, CHARLOTTE. "Motif and Theme in the Late Prose Romances
    of WM." In <u>Studies</u> <u>in</u> <u>the</u> <u>Late</u> <u>Romances</u> <u>of</u> <u>WM:</u> <u>Papers</u> <u>Presented</u>
    <u>at</u> <u>the</u> <u>Annual</u> <u>Meeting</u> <u>of</u> <u>the</u> <u>MLA,</u> <u>December,</u> <u>1975</u>. Edited by
    Carole Silver and Joseph R. Dunlap. New York: WM Society, pp.
    33-52.
        Argues that the prose romances WM wrote after <u>Nowhere</u> are
    more than mere entertainments and that they express human needs to
    escape isolation and tyranny, to achieve sexual and social equality,
    to become happy pagans and to realize, as did WM, "a deep love of
    the earth and life on it, and a passion for the history of the past
    of mankind."

41 PARRINDER, PATRICK. "<u>Nowhere</u>, <u>The</u> <u>Time</u> <u>Machine</u>, and the
    Break-up of Classical Realism." <u>Science</u> <u>Fiction</u> <u>Studies</u> 3, pt.
    3 (November):265-74.
        Discusses ways that both Bellamy and Dickens influenced WM's
    treatment of theme and character in <u>Nowhere</u>, commenting upon echoes
    from Dickens that helped to create a "mood of second childhood,"
    which allowed WM to move beyond realism and into utopian fiction.
    Wells's <u>Time</u> <u>Machine</u> offers a harsh critique of those innocent
    aspects of <u>Nowhere</u>, and is itself a "product of the warring poles of
    realism and utopianism."

42 RABKIN, ERIC S. <u>The</u> <u>Fantastic</u> <u>in</u> <u>Literature</u>. Princeton:
    Princeton University Press, pp. 18-19, passim.
        Asserts that WM, "only after the Queen herself, is perhaps
    the best exemplar of the age of Victorianism." Comments on modes of
    time in <u>Wood</u> and on <u>Nowhere</u> as a "non-science-fiction utopia based
    on reversal."

43 RENTON, J.D. <u>The</u> <u>Oxford</u> <u>Union</u> <u>Murals</u>. Oxford: Oxford
    University Press, 18 pp.
        Description of the Arthurian murals at the Oxford Union
    includes biographical sketches of each of the artists involved in
    the "adventure" that began during the long vacation of 1857.
    Concludes with an account of subsequent attempts to restore the
    murals.

44 ROBINSON, DAVID. "The Thematic Ambibuity of WM's 'King Arthur's
    Tomb.'" <u>Concerning</u> <u>Poetry</u> 9, no. 1 (Spring):41-44.
        Suggests that Guenevere in "King Arthur's Tomb" directs her
    defiance at Lancelot rather than at her accusers as she had in the
    preceding poem and that any ambiguities are "purposeful," for WM
    thereby extends to readers the conflicting emotions of the
    characters.

45 RYSKAMP, CHARLES. Preface to William Morris and the Art of the
    Book. Edited by Paul Needham. New York: Oxford University
    Press, pp. 9-12.
        Sets this catalogue within the context of several other
    studies and exhibitions that the Morgan Library, "the museum of the
    book," has sponsored in recent years, offering details of John M.
    Crawford's donations of WM materials to the Library.

46 SILVER, CAROLE, and DUNLAP, JOSEPH R., eds. Studies in the Late
    Prose Romances of WM: Papers Presented at the Annual Meeting of
    the MLA, December 1975. New York: WM Society, 139 pp.
        Includes a publisher's note, a chronology of the late
    romances, an introduction, Kirchhoff (1976.27), and five papers, all
    annotated herein: Calhoun (1976.7), Hollow (1976.23), Kelvin
    (1976.26), Oberg (1976.40), and Silver (1976.47.).

47 SILVER, CAROLE. "Myth and Ritual in the Last Romances of WM."
    In Studies in the Late Romances of WM: Papers Presented at the
    Annual Meeting of the MLA, December 1975. Edited by Carole
    Silver and Joseph R. Dunlap. New York: WM Society, pp. 117-39.
        WM grew up at a time when archaeologists and linguists were
    debating new ideas in folklore and myth, and he knew their work
    well; from it "he derived three important concepts which shape the
    prose romances he wrote between 1888 and 1896: the myth of
    barbarianism, the myth of the hero, and the myth of the fertile
    earth-mother." Finds sources for these concepts in the scholarly
    books WM read, and then examines their use in the romances, noting,
    for example, that the stage of upper barbarianism postulated by
    Morgan and then Engels is the basis for the tribes depicted in
    Wolfings and Roots, that Muller on solar myth influenced
    descriptions of heroes like Golden Walter, and that Fraser's
    formulations upon fertility goddesses helped WM shape heroines like
    the Lady of Abundance, Birdalone, and Habundia. Concludes with the
    following on WM's role: "a mortal becomes a maker and giver of myth
    and thereby is made immortal."

48 STRAUSS, SYLVIA. "Women in Utopia." South Atlantic Quarterly
    75, no. 1 (Winter):115-31.
        Compares Nowhere to Looking Backward and Wells's A Modern
    Utopia, discussing differences like WM's refusal to depict
    industrialism as positive in any sense. All three Utopias have a
    patriarchal bias, portraying societies that women had no part in
    creating and where their roles are still defined by males.

49 THOMPSON, E.P. "Romanticism, Moralism and Utopianism: The Case
    of WM." New Left Review 99 (September-October):83-111.
        Equals postscript to second edition of his biography
(1976.50), with a few pages omitted: 763-68 and 780-81. Has an
afternote that refers to an earlier argument in which WM is
mentioned: 1980.3.

50 THOMPSON, E.P. WM: Romantic to Revolutionary. 2d ed., New
    York: Pantheon, 825 pp. London: Merlin Press, 1977.
        This revised edition of 1955.15 omits many passages
containing what the author characterizes in a foreword as
"moralistic comments and pat political sentiments," and as "callow
fat." Many readers are apt to miss these tendentious and incisive
asides; also omitted are discussions of Blake and Shelley and early
activities of the Socialist League, of more than half of part 4, and
two of the original appendixes, which contained correspondence now
"sufficiently cited in the revised text." In a sixty-five-page
postscript, the author asserts that "twenty-one years harvest of
critical writing on Morris's poetry and prose is disappointing," but
he remarks favorably on work by Stanley Pierson (1973.31), Paul
Meier (1972.19), Miguel Abensour (forthcoming), and John Goode
(1971.10), finding real significance in Abensour's discussion of
ways that WM's Utopianism "liberates desire to an uninterrupted
interrogation of our values," going on to suggest that WM's writings
could provide an antidote to twentieth-century Marxist gradgrinds
concerned only with economic growth. Judges Goode's analysis of
John Ball to be "by far the best appreciation (and vindication) of
any of Morris's Socialist works of art." Concludes that "we still
have to make up our minds about WM," but that his importance,
whether as "our greatest diagnostician of alienation" or as a
theorist whose communism, independently derived from the romantic
tradition, is moralistic and compellingly different, should not be
denied.

51 TOD, IAN. "WM: Father of the Modern Movement." Forum 24, no.
    6:1-37.
        In Dutch, with English translation. A detailed biographical
sketch that incorporates new findings about WM's marriage, his
pattern designs, and the scientific nature of his socialism.
Attempts also to dispel some of the inaccuracies associated with
Pevsner's inspired and widely accepted notions of WM as the founder
of the modern movement (1936.11). Descries tendencies of some art
critics to ignore WM's socialism, which "truncates and emasculates
his thought." Admits the importance of Ruskin's influence, but
points out that in WM "we find clear concepts of revolution, class,
class struggles and the structure and dynamics of capitalism not
found in Ruskin." He also contrasts their attitudes toward the
Paris Commune and the burning of the Louvre; Ruskin was horrified,
WM accepted it as part of the "self-liberation of the proletariat."
Concludes with reasons why members of today's establishment (in art

and architectural circles) are willing to embrace WM; they thus
legitimize their own cooptation with capitalism, their own
willingness to put profit before social advancement.

52 TOWNSHEND, EMILY. "WM and the Communist Ideal." In Writers and
    Rebels: From the Fabian Biographical Series. Edited by Michael
    Katanka. London and Tonbridge: Charles Knight, pp. 192-220.
        Reprint of 1912.16.

53 VALENTINE, K.B. "The Woodpecker Tapestry." JWMS 3, no. 2
    (Summer):2, 7.
        Points out that the Woodpecker tapestry's "original referent"
is the Circe and Picus story from Ovid. Includes an illustration of
the tapestry.

54 WEINER, MARTIN J. "The Myth of WM." Albion 8, no. 1
    (Spring):67-82.
        Because of Arnot (1934.3) and E.P. Thompson (1955.15), we
have all learned to revalue WM, to "see the revolutionary within the
medievalist, the communist within the craftsman." That older myth
of WM, the country craftsman, has been set aside, but that myth did
serve an important cultural and political purpose for four decades.
As urban blight spread, as industrialism's products grew shoddier
and more expensive, WM's appeal grew, and this was aided by the
appearance of the Collected Works, beginning in 1910, which inspired
generalizations about the honesty and integrity, the essential
Britishness of rural crafts, etc., which sometimes got WM's name and
reputation linked, albeit in facile ways, to the pastoralism of
Georgian poets like Rupert Brooke and to the rural novels of Thomas
Hardy. This myth of WM corresponded neatly with the persistent
themes of English cultural life.

55 WILLIAMSON, AUDREY. "WM: Craft and Saga." In Artists and
    Writers in Revolt: The Pre-Raphaelites. London: David and
    Charles, pp. 85-102, passim.
        Biographical sketch has details about WM's associations with
Burne-Jones at Oxford, the influence of Rossetti, and the beginning
of the Firm. States that in socialism, WM "found something that
satisfied both the practical and visionary sides of his mind."
Speaks of the different ways that WM and Ruskin created a "socialist
legacy" and of the ways WM used More's Utopia in Nowhere.

56 YOKOYAMA, TADASHI. "Trip to 'Epoch-Making' Red House." Global
    Architecture: Houses 1:14-17.
        In Japanese. Recounts a visit of a Japanese contingent to
    Red House, their reactions to its architecture, decorations, and
    furniture. Includes several photographs, three of them in splendid
    color.

57 "Documents in the History of Science Fiction: A Review and a
    Foreword by WM." Science Fiction Studies 3, pt. 3
    (November):287-91.
        Reprints with slight emendations WM's review of Looking
    Backward from the 22 June 1889 Commonweal and his foreword to the
    1893 Kelmscott Press edition of More's Utopia, "two articles which
    should be known to all students of Utopian fiction."

58 In Fine Print: WM as Book Designer. Catalogue of an Exhibition
    Held at the William Morris Gallery. London: Libraries and Arts
    Department of the London Borough of Waltham Forest, 77 pp.
        Has four sections: "Early Projects," "Projects for Printed
    Books in the 1870s," "WM and Printing in the 1880s," and "Kelmscott
    Press." Each section has a useful and detailed introduction;
    concludes with biographical notes, a select bibliography, and
    explanatory notes. Reflects the variety and richness of the
    holdings at the Walthamstow Gallery, many of whose items were
    purchased from the Mackail and Cockerell collections in 1954 and
    1956.

                              1977

*1 BACON, A.K. "WM's Attitude toward Industrialism: A Study of the
    Lectures, Journalism, and Letters." Dissertation, University of
    Bangor, Wales.
        Cited in personal correspondence with P. Faulkner.

2   BAISSUS, J.M. "The Expedition of the Ark." JWMS 3, no. 3
    (Spring):2-11.
        Reproduces "Description of an expedition by boat from
    Kelmscott House Upper Mall Hammersmith to Kelmscott Manor Lechlade
    Oxfordshire with critical notes." The description, with full and
    often jocular details, was written by WM and covers events of 10-16
    August 1870 during a journey made memorable by DeMorgan's puns and
    WM's cooking.

3   BALCH, DENNIS R.   "Isolation and Community: The Theme and Form
     of WM's Poetry and Prose." Dissertation, University of Arizona.
     Abstracted: DAI 38:1402-A.

4   BLEDSOE, AUDREY SHAW.   "The Seasons of Camelot: WM's Arthurian
     Poems." South Atlantic Bulletin 42:114-22.
          Arranges WM's four Arthurian poems onto a Fryeian wheel,
     assigning "The Defence of Guenevere" to Summer, "King Arthur's Tomb"
     to Autumn, "Sir Galahad" to Winter, and "The Chapel in Lyoness" to
     Spring. Reasons for WM's departures from Malory are trimmed to fit
     within a discussion of seasonal images and movements of characters
     from physical to spiritual love: "all love unites finally in the
     love of Christ" is offered as a summary of the four poems.

5   BRANTLINGER, PATRICK.   The Spirit of Reform in British
     Literature and Politics, 1832-1867. Cambridge, Mass.: Harvard
     University Press, pp. 132-33, passim.
          Comments on WM and Nowhere set against a backdrop of various
     attempts to improve society through literature, attempts that WM
     questioned, since he believed, following Ruskin, that an improved
     society must precede the creation of great art. Invites us to
     consider the logic of Ellen's attack, in Nowhere, on the Victorian
     novel, and to contrast Tennyson's ideas about progress with those of
     WM, especially as exemplified in the Idylls and in Nowhere.

6   CLAYRE, ALASDAIR, ed.   Nature and Industrialization. London:
     Oxford University Press, pp. 381-82, 407.
          Selections from "Useful Work vs. Useless Toil" in an
     anthology that includes diverse writers, from Defoe to D.H.
     Lawrence, and their comments upon a threatened nature.

*7   COMANZO, CHRISTIAN.   "Geographie et imaginaire dans Paradise."
     Confluents 1:13-22.
          Cited in 1980 MLA bibliography.

8   CORNFORTH, JOHN.   "Where WM's Ideals Live On." Country Life
     161, no. 4160 (24 March):710-12.
          Celebrates the centenary of SPAB, stressing that the "P"
     stands for "Protection," not "Preservation," that such a distinction
     is important, for not all buildings can, or should, be preserved at
     all costs. Discusses some of the Society's recent work, mentioning
     its technical pamphlets and the sorts of problems that inflation,
     amenity societies, and the like, pose for the Society in the future.

9   DENTON, RAMONA. "WM and Rapunzel; or, What Was She Doing in
    Rouen?" N and Q 222 (October):416-17.
        Wonders why Rapunzel, in an impassioned prayer, mentions
Rouen, since she has supposedly never been out of the tower.
Suggests that WM, while working at the German source, recalled
another imprisoned maid, Joan of Arc in Rouen: "An association of
Rapunzel with Joan would explain Morris's characterization of
Rapunzel as Christian martyr."

10 DUNLAP, JOSEPH R. "One Spot Beloved Over All." Kipling Journal
    44, no. 201 (March):10-15.
        Examines parallels between WM and Rudyard Kipling
descriptions of the English countryside and their attitudes toward
it and their homes, Kelmscott Manor and Bateman's in Sussex. Both
loved places where the past was still alive, where "the tides of
history had rolled in and out."

11 EBBATSOM, J.R. "Visions of Wild England: WM and Richard
    Jefferies." JWMS 3, no. 3 (Spring):12-29.
        Reviews the recent critical interest in the eight prose
romances (the two socialist narratives are included) WM wrote in the
last decade of his life, asking "what impetus lay behind Morris's
turning to the romance form?" As a means of escape has become a
common answer, but a key source has been overlooked by all critics:
Richard Jefferies's After London (1885), a book WM often praised,
one whose theme is suggested in the oft-quoted comment WM made about
civilization being "doomed to destruction" and "barbarism once more
flooding the world." This convincing study includes a paraphrase of
After London, a sketch of Jefferies's life and works, and a
discussion of motifs and themes, like the quest over water, that WM
seems to have borrowed from Jefferies.

12 FRANK, ELLEN. "The Domestication of Nature: Five Houses in the
    Lake District." Nature and the Victorian Imagination. Edited
    by U.C. Knoepflmacher and G.B. Tennyson. Berkeley: University
    of California Press, pp. 68-92.
        Discusses the arts and crafts interiors of Blackwell, a
country house built by Bailie Scott in 1898, commenting upon their
debt to WM whose ideas of ornament, of wall decoration "bringing
nature indoors," are apparent in these sumptuous interiors.
Includes illustrations of three Morris and Co. wallpapers.

13 FRANKLIN, COLIN. The Triple Crown: Kelmscott, Doves and
    Ashendene. Dallas, Tex.: Southern Methodist University's
    Bridwell Library, 19 pp.
        Remarks upon the excellences shared by the three great
British presses, and upon Southern Methodist's good fortune in
having obtained a Doves Press Bible, an Ashendene Press Dante, and
the Kelmscott Chaucer. Includes some slightly more specific
comments on WM and typefaces he used.

14 GALYON, AUBREY, E. "WM: the Past as Standard." PQ 56, no. 2
    (Spring):245-49.
        One of five papers on "Arthur in Britain and America: Camelot
Revisited," a forum at the 1975 MLA sessions. Comments upon the
Arthurian poems in Defence, paraphrasing their content and the
earlier critical views of Hollow (1971.13).

15 GIROUARD, MARK. Sweetness and Light: The Queen Anne Movement,
    1860-1900. Oxford: Clarendon Press, pp. 13-18, passim.
        Suggests that Morris and Co. was very influential in moving
designers away from heavy Gothic styles toward a lighter mode,
toward what is here called a "Queen Anne" style. Morris and Co.
discussed and Taylor seen as important catalyst for change.

16 HAZEN, JAMES. "WM's 'Haystack in the Floods': The Fate of
    Vision." Pre-Raphaelite Review 1, no. 1 (November):49-56.
        Comments on previous criticism of "Haystack in the Floods,"
attempting then a fuller interpretation by considering the "highly
charged symbols" of the title, the ways that hay and water recur in
the poem and become linked to Jehane, who is both a visionary and a
sensuous, earthly woman. She reminds us of both Jeanne d'Arc and
Janey.

17 HOLZMAN, MICHAEL HOWARD. "On Attempting to Understand
    Nowhere." Dissertation, University of California at San Diego.
        Abstracted: DAI 37:580-A.

18 KIRCHHOFF, FREDERICK. "Love Is Enough: A Crisis in WM's Poetic
    Development." VP 15, no. 4 (Winter):297-306.
        Asserts that it is wrongheaded to argue, as many critics have
done, that art led WM to socialism when his art (his poetry in this
instance) is only vaguely understood. Suggests that "the pattern of
Morris's literary career is a dialectic," that Love Is Enough
reflects his personal difficulties as well as his 1871 trip to
Iceland where he had learned to face squarely life's tragedies.
Therefore the hero of the poem fails in his quest yet gains
"fulfillment of his vision" and power over his own fate. Various
problems with the poem, with the allegorical character, Love, for

instance, are fully discussed, and the poem is seen as an important
advance in WM's literary development and also as a means of working
out personal problems. Pharamond's alienation suggests Sigurd's
tragic doom, WM's own heroic self-awareness.

19 KIRCHHOFF, FREDERICK. "WM's 'Childe Roland': The Deformed Not
    Quite Transformed." Pre-Raphaelite Review 1, no. 1
    (November):95-105.
        Avers that WM's Oxford and Cambridge Magazine review of
Browning's Men and Women reveals his "attempt to ally himself
publicly with Rossetti and the other Pre-Raphaelites" and prefigures
his own treatment of literary characters in his early fiction, and
in Defence. Suggests that WM's misreading of Browning's "Childe
Harold to the Dark Tower Came," has parallels in "Unknown Church"
and in "Hollow Land," and that WM in fact gave this latter tale an
ending he thought the Browning poem should have had.

20 LANDOW, GEORGE. "WM to Swinburne: A Link in the
    Correspondence." N and Q 222 (October):415-16.
        Reprints exchange of letters that began in 1882 when
Swinburne asked WM "where Mallory gives the name of the Queen of
Orkney." WM's reply (now in the archives at Brown University) had
the information, but he said it was "Jenny's discovery." Reprinted:
1979.27.

*21 LEMIRE, E.D. "WM and Hardy on Ancient Buildings." In
    Australasian Victorian Studies Association. Wellington
    Conference Papers. Wellington, pp. 10-18.
        Cited in 1978 MLA bibliography.

22 LE BOURGEOIS, JOHN. "The Love and Marriage of WM: A New
    Interpretation." South Carolina Review 9, no. 2 (April):43-55.
        Argues that WM's boyhood love for his sister, Emma, was never
outgrown: "it was the re-surfacing of his feeling for her in the
mid-1860s which helped to wreck his marriage to Janey." Imaginative
readings of early poems, a Webb letter, and "Frank's Sealed Letter"
tend to support his points, but they have since been muted by newly
published evidence that Janey was in fact Rossetti's mistress
(1976.4 and 1981.19). Originally a lecture given in 1972.

23 LE BOURGEOIS, JOHN. "WM and Burne-Jones." N and Q 222
     (January-February):30-32.
          Suggests that "ego and money" caused strains in the
     friendship of WM and Burne-Jones in the late 1860s and early 1870s,
     using notes that both Burne-Jones and WM put into the Firm's account
     book as proof. Burne-Jones was unhappy with some of the fees he
     received for stained-glass designs, and WM disapproved of
     Burne-Jones's affair with Maria Zambaco.

24 LIPSEY, ROGER. "Coomaraswamy and WM: The Filiation." In
     Coomaraswamy: His Life and Work. Princeton: Princeton
     University Press, pp. 258-64.
          Coomaraswamy was nineteen years old and living in London when
     WM died; though there is no evidence that they ever met,
     Coomaraswamy seemed to have "absorbed nearly the whole range of
     Morris's concerns as his own." He worked at the Essex House Press,
     he met Magnusson, and together they translated "Voluspa," the
     greatest of the Eddic poems; and when he returned to Ceylon, he
     founded a society to protect ancient buildings. Throughout his life
     his conviction that art can thrive only in a healthy society never
     wavered. So close are the parallels that WM is here called the
     "father" of Coomaraswamy, who was also--it seems pertinent to add--a
     devoted fisherman.

25 LOURIE, MARGARET A. "The Embodiment of Dreams: WM's 'Blue
     Closet' Group." VP 15, no. 3 (Autumn):193-206.
          From the beginning critics have agreed that Pre-Raphaelite
     poetry is "dream-like," but post-Freudian critics have not followed
     that lead; this is an attempt to do so, to use Freudian notions to
     gloss "The Blue Closet" and six related poems from Defence. In such
     poems, WM "can journey down into the pre-logical and primarily
     image-making regions of the psyche." Some readers might agree that
     nuance, indirection, and vague folk- and fairy-tale "sources"
     somehow "increase the universality" of these poems, where "visual
     certitude replaces thought." Others will be puzzled and will
     welcome the more precise discussions of how WM's poem complements
     Rossetti's watercolor of the same title, and of ways that Yeats in
     his early poetry resembled WM in his.

26 MAC KENZIE, NORMAN, and MAC KENZIE, JEAN. The Fabians. New
     York: Simon and Schuster, pp. 83-86, passim.
          Discusses WM's relationships with certain of the Fabians,
     asserting that Shaw was the only one he got along with, since both
     hoped to destroy the capitalist order, and both expressed their
     hopes in art and literature. Comments upon Shaw's relations with
     May Morris, suggesting that his captivation and then his abandonment
     of her made it impossible for her, later, to love her husband.

27 MATHEWS, RICHARD. Introduction to <u>Child</u> <u>Christopher</u> <u>and</u>
    <u>Goldilind</u> <u>the</u> <u>Fair</u> by <u>WM</u>. North Hollywood, Calif.: Newcastle
    Publishing, pp. 11-16.
        Discusses WM's interests in medieval tales and his attempts
    to translate and retell them to suggest to readers something of
    their social and linguistic "roots." Points out ways that WM here
    changed his source, <u>Havelok</u> <u>the</u> <u>Dane</u>, so as to strengthen various
    unities--of theme and character, of natural images becoming
    psychological symbols, of archaic diction and page decoration--and
    thus to create a tale that is a "fusion of politics, morality, art
    and individual life which challenges our imagination and elevates
    our aspirations." The text of the tale itself is a facsimile
    reprinting of Thomas Mosher's edition of 1900, which was a
    reprinting of the 1895 Kelmscott Press edition.

28 MIGEON, JACQUES. "Red House and Ruskin." <u>JWMS</u> 3, no. 3
    (Spring):30-32.
        Suggests that Ruskin's <u>Lectures</u> <u>on</u> <u>Architecture</u> <u>and</u> <u>Painting</u>
    influenced Webb's designs for Red House, and convincing
    correspondences between the plans--now on file at the Victoria and
    Albert--and passages from the Ruskin lectures are presented: pointed
    arches, steep roofs, bow-windows, and the like. Concludes that Red
    House remains a "perfect illustration of Ruskin's precepts."

29 MURRAY, ISOBEL. "<u>Pilgrims</u>: Aspects of the Poetry of WM and
    Chesterton." <u>Chesterton</u> <u>Review</u> 4:7-36.
        Compares <u>Pilgrims</u> to Chesterton's "The Ballad of the White
    Horse" and Tennyson's "Maud," suggesting that such poems, because of
    ways their themes are conveyed, deserve careful critical readings.
    Both <u>Pilgrims</u> and the Chesterton poem express a "positive faith" in
    battle and death without lodging such faith in traditional heroes.
    Also argues that WM, in <u>Pilgrims</u>, borrowed and developed narrative
    techniques used in "Maud."

30 NIXON, PATRICIA D. "Ruskin and WM: Prophets of the Modern
    Ecology Movement." <u>VIJ</u> 3:37-43.
        Modern ecological concerns, a love of earth, air, water, were
    adumbrated by Ruskin and WM. Reich's book, <u>The</u> <u>Greening</u> <u>of</u> <u>America</u>,
    indicates that he is a disciple of both Ruskin and WM.

*31 ROTA GHIBAUDI, SILVIA. "Utopia e propaganda: Il caso WM." In
    <u>Studi</u> <u>sull'</u> <u>utopia</u>. Edited by Luigi Firpo. Florence: Olschki,
    pp. 344-60.
        Cited in 1978 MLA bibliography.

32 SHAW, GEORGE BERNARD. Flyleaves. Edited by Dan Laurence and
    Daniel Leary. Austin, Tex.: W. Thomas Taylor, p. 27.
        Shaw, writing in 1949, recalls WM's animosity to Beardsley,
whom he saw as a threat to Burne-Jones.

33 SOSSAMAN, STEPHEN. "WM's Sigurd and the Pre-Raphaelite Visual
    Aesthetic." Pre-Raphaelite Review 1, no. 2 (May):81-90.
        Suggests that Sigurd "derives much of its power from
exploiting the visual devices" of Pre-Raphaelite painters,
commenting upon several passages where colors are used
emblematically and details create tapestrylike set pieces.

34 SPATT, HARTLEY S. "Morrissaga: Sigurd." ELH 44:355-75.
        Discusses the reasons Sigurd, though WM's greatest poem, is
still a failure, one rooted in his attempts to impose upon the
Germanic tales and myths a "system of social rituals by which
Victorian men live and swear," thereby creating what is here seen as
a new myth, one "dedicated to the heroism of self-determination."
Since cognitive attempts to achieve narrative unities must cause
"myth to crumble," WM's Sigurd is a failure, albeit a grand one.
Reprinted, with opening paragraphs excised, in 1978.49.

35 SURTEES, VIRGINIA. "Portrait Head of Jane Morris by Dante
    Gabriel Rossetti." Bulletin of Philadelphia Museum of Art 73,
    no. 317 (June):12-17.
        Sketches in circumstances of Rossetti and WM meeting Janey at
Oxford, the marriage, her posing for Rossetti, and the like.
Comments then upon the "striking resemblance" between the chalk
drawing of her Rossetti completed in 1865 (now owned by the
Philadelphia Museum) and photographs that he took the same year.
Includes four monochrome plates.

36 THOMPSON, E.P. "A Wasp in September: WM, Glasier, and
    Marxism." Durham University Journal, n.s., 38, no. 2
    (June):225-30.
        A detailed and effective response that answers point by point
the objections that Le Bourgeois had raised (1976.30) about E.P.
Thompson's claims that Glasier was an unreliable witness concerning
WM's Marxism (1955.15). Uses the work of scholars like Meier
(1972.19) to again present the case that WM must be considered an
extremely important and original socialist thinker.

37 THOMPSON, PAUL. The Work of WM. 2d ed., London: Quartet Books, 317 pp.

Revised edition of 1967.29, with subsequent scholarship noted and added commentary about WM's "remarkable anticipation of the problems of socialism within a consumer society" and his significance as a prophet of alienation and as a writer who had entertained such radical notions as deschooling society even before the likes of Ivan Illich were born.

38 THOMPSON, SUSAN OTIS. American Book Design and WM. New York: R.R. Bowker, 258 pp.

Examines the impact of Kelmscott Press on American printing in the 1890s; it was dramatic because American printers had long been concerned with high quantities and low costs, and books that used fine material and careful decoration started a revolution, one that inspired and made famous all of the following: Updike, Rogers, Goudy, Bradley, Cleland, Dwiggins, Ransom, Nash, and Rollins. The presses such men established, both commercial and private, are discussed, and individual books are classified according to criteria that distinguish an arts and crafts style (here carefully defined for the first time) from an aesthetic. "The two styles represented not only the dichotomies of the Middle Ages versus the Renaissance but also individuality, decoration, exuberance, imagination, the Romantic, versus standardization, utilitarianism, restraint, rationalism, the Classical." Points out that previous claims for and definitions of an "art Nouveau Book" tend to be vague and misleading; the label should refer to ornament which might be applied to either book style. Includes over one hundred illustrations, an extensive bibliography, and an appendix: "Morris' Statements on Book Design." Revision of 1972.26.

39 WILLIAMS, RAYMOND. Marxism and Literature. Oxford: Oxford University Press, p. 161.

Discusses nineteenth-century attitudes toward craftsmen and modes of production, pointing out that concern over artistic and social meaning of work "was eventually consciously articulated and generally applied by WM."

40 WILSON, JOHN R. "WM's Love Is Enough: A Parabolic Morality." Pre-Raphaelite Review 1, no. 1 (November):16-26.

Asserts that critics have for too long ignored Love Is Enough and that if the poem is approached "parabolically," it yields insights into WM's genius at interpreting sophisticated themes. Analyzes the poem's speeches and the portrayal of Pharamond, concluding that in the poem, WM "testifies to the sufficiency of love."

41 YEO, STEPHEN. "A New Life: The Religion of Socialism in
Britain, 1883-1896." History Workshop 4:5-56.
    In the 1885 Manifesto of the Socialist League, WM argued the
need for a "single-hearted devotion to the religion of socialism."
This article discussess such rhetoric, probing newspapers,
autobiographies, and literary texts for examples. Comments upon its
use in Pilgrims, Nowhere, and the socialist lectures.

1978

1 ALINOVI, FRANCESCA. "New York: Ora l'arte dev'essere
decorative." Bolaffiarta 9 (April):16-19.
    Recent work of decorative designers in New York City
suggests, especially in their "neo-floral" patterns, the influence
of WM; as they turn away from geometrical abstractions and toward
designs based on nature they become "neo-morrisiano." Includes
several illustrations.

2 ANSCOMBE, ISABELLE, and GERE, CHARLOTTE. "WM and His Circle."
In Arts and Crafts in Britain and America. London: Academy
Editions; New York: Rizzoli, pp. 64-69, passim.
    Discusses Arts and Crafts Movement and its origins and its
spread to America, stressing the importance of Crane and Ashbee.
Includes succinct yet detailed biographies of other key figures;
there are also dozens of illustrations, a useful chronology, and a
bibliography.

3 BACON, A.K. "Some Additions to E.D. Lemire's Calendar and
Bibliography of WM's Speaking Career." N and Q, n.s., 25, no. 4
(August):324-26.
    Provides the following additions to the calendar of WM's
lectures, in Lemire (1969.18): (1) on 18 August 1899 a lecture on
machinery, (2) on 26 February 1894 a lecture which was apparently a
variant of "Art and Socialism," (3) a lecture on 4 June 1886 is
recorded in SPAB papers, and (4) the notes for a 3 October 1886
lecture are in the Victoria and Albert.

4 BALCH, DENNIS R. "'Gudrun,' Sigurd, and Wolfings: Three
Chapters in a Tale of the Individual and the Tribe." In The
After-Summer Seed: Reconsiderations of WM's "Sigurd". Edited by
J. Hollow. New York and London: WM Society, pp. 89-118.
    Argues that these three works with patterns that are,
respectively, linear, wavelike, and circular, demonstrate a
progression from "isolation and disrupted community" toward a
"vision of social stability." This shows that Morris's "literary
work does in fact confront rather than avoid the transitional
malaise and social dissolution of the nineteenth century."

5   BARGAINNIER, EARL F. "Pater, WM, and 'Aesthetic Poetry.'"
     Pre-Raphaelite Review 1, no. 2 (May):27-39.
        Recounts history of Pater's 1868 review of WM's early poetry,
a review that became "Aesthetic Poetry" in the 1889 Appreciations
and was omitted from its second edition; its final section then
became the "Conclusion" of The Renaissance, and from a second
edition of this was again omitted. This review-chapter, perhaps
because of Pater's own ambivalence toward it, has been neglected by
critics, and this is unfortunate, for it is significant as an
example of Pater's early criticism, of his "metaphorical method,"
and of his sympathy with the anti-establishment views of the
Pre-Raphaelites generally. Argues that Pater's interpretation of
WM's medievalism is important for understanding both Pater's
aesthetics and the unique qualities of certain poems in Defence.

6   BENTLY, D.M.R. "WM's 'The Wind.'" Trivium 13:31-37.
        Opens with interesting point that the "Olaf, king and saint"
mentioned in the final stanza of "The Wind" might well refer to Olaf
II of Norway, slain in a famous battle in 1016, but this point is
not brought into relation with the thesis of the article, that the
poem is a "satirical treatment of sexual denial and neurotic
fixation."

7   BERRY, RALPH. "The Symbolism of WM." JWMS 3, no. 4
     (Winter):20-34.
        Offers a general overview of WM's writings, with some
references to Red House and Kelmscott Manor, and to his socialist
work; suggests that WM's "vision focuses constantly upon a Paradise
Lost, and Regained."

8   BLERSCH, STUART. "The Craft of Revision: WM and Sigurd." In
     The After-Summer Seed: Reconsiderations of WM's "Sigurd".
     Edited by J. Hollow. New York and London: WM Society, pp.
     13-35.
        Contrary to the "popular notion" that WM never, or rarely,
revised a line of poetry, there is evidence that "he did take the
time to make the small corrections of a craftsman." Examines and
comments upon the fairly extensive revisions that continue right up
through the Kelmscott Press edition of Sigurd.

9   BORZELLO, FRANCES. "An Unnoted Speech by WM." N and Q, n.s.,
     25, no. 4 (August):314-16.
        Reprints, and comments upon, a summary of a WM speech found
in the 12 April 1884 East London Observer, an address he gave at the
opening of the Whitechapel Art Exhibition that year. References in
the speech to class warfare remind us that WM had started reading
Marx the previous year.

10 BRADLEY, IAN. WM and His World. London: Thames and Hudson; New
     York: Scribners, 127 pp.
         Despite limitations set by length and intended general
audience, has useful summaries of Oxford years, of Rossetti's affair
with Janey, of WM's socialist activities (though he implies that WM
was merely a sentimental socialist), and of WM's importance to the
twentieth century in terms of environmental preservation, both urban
and rural. Has 145 illustrations.

11 BROOK, MICHAEL. "A Swedish-American Translator of WM." JWMS 3,
     no. 4 (Winter):8-13.
         Several chapters of Nowhere were translated by Axel Lundberg
(1852-1940), a Swedish socialist who emigrated to America in 1888
and became an ardent admirer of Bellamy. The chapters were
published in Gnistan, a Minneapolis paper, in 1891.

12 BUCKLEY, CATHERINE. "WM and His Critics." JWMS 3, no. 4
     (Winter):14-19.
         Comments upon several hostile and ignorant critiques of WM's
socialism leveled at him in the 1880s; such attacks only made him
more firm in his convictions.

13 BUSH, DONALD J. "Thorstein Veblen's Economic Aesthetic."
     Leonardo 11, no. 4 (Autumn):281-85.
         Reviews issues and themes raised in Veblen's Theory of the
Leisure Class, pointing out how consistently he rejected the
ornamental for the functional. When Veblen traveled to England, he
was attracted to WM and of course to his socialism, if not to his
decorated books.

14 COLEMAN, CHRISTINE. "WM Lived Here." Homes and Gardens 59, no.
     8 (February):34-39.
         Ten color photographs are as important as the text which
outlines events of Red House years and describes the house as it
appeared in 1978, as restored and maintained by the Edward
Hollanbys.

15 DAWLEY, ALAN. "E.P. Thompson and the Peculiarities of the
     Americans." Radical History Review 19 (Winter):9-31.
         Points out E.P. Thompson's debt to WM, "who gave him the will
to argue with the Free World philistines," and then remarks on the
significant effects of WM having discovered Marxism: "The result was
a double transformation--romanticism re-entered the field of
political debate, and revolutionary socialism acquired a moral and
aesthetic vocabulary."

16 DUNNE, JOHN S. The Reasons of the Heart: A Journey into
    Solitude and Back Again into the Human Circle. New York:
    Macmillan; London: Collier, pp. 109-10.
        Ralph and Ursula, scenes and images from Well (like the water
    of the well), are here woven into a theological disquisition on
    salvation.

17 EIDELBERG, MARTIN. "British Floral Designs and Continental Art
    Nouveau." Connoisseur 197, no. 792 (February):116-24.
        Though it has become "almost obligatory to include at least
    one WM design in any study of Art Nouveau," it is often wrong to do
    so, for only the designs he did between 1872 and 1876 are pertinent;
    they have a "curvilinear idiom which leads to Art Nouveau style,"
    and something like the Tulip chintz forms a possible link between
    Owen Jones and Van de Velde. "Thus the seeds of Morris's ideas of
    some twenty years earlier finally took root, albeit on the other
    side of the Channel."

18 ELLOWAY, W.A.W. "Conference Exhibition." In WM: Aspects of the
    Man and His Work: Proceedings of the Conference on WM Held at
    Loughborough University of Technology. Loughborough:
    Loughborough Victorian Studies Group, pp. 106-16.
        Focuses on WM's furniture designs, specifically on the
    so-called Morris chair, which "in its formal simplicity and
    functional efficiency comes close to what Plato might have meant by
    the Form of a chair." Comments on WM and the influence he exerted
    on Loughborough College, and concludes with catalogue notes to the
    seventy-three items exhibited at the conference, forty of which were
    chairs.

19 FAULKNER, PETER. "WM's Poetry: From 'Guenevere' to Sigurd." In
    WM: Aspects of the Man and his Work: Proceedings of the
    Conference on WM Held at Loughborough University of Technology.
    Loughborough: Loughborough Victorian Studies Group, pp. 28-49.
        Points out that "the most obvious fact about WM's poetry,
    which puts him in partial contrast with most of his contemporaries
    as well as with subsequent poets, is that it is very often based on
    pre-existing stories." Discusses several poems in relation to their
    sources. Judges Defence poems, with their "martial drama" and
    "disturbing fancies" as never equaled in the later poetry. Feels
    "respect if not admiration" for Sigurd which "succeeds at least in
    giving the English reader some idea of the Great Story of the
    North." Concludes that WM's emphasis on story rather than poetic
    form, though it keeps him out of the ranks of the greatest poets,
    allowed him to achieve and transmit a "truly impressive sense of the
    timeless significance of courage and loyalty in a world of strife
    and chaos."

20 FISHER, B.F. "WM's 'What all men long for and what none shall
    have': Restorations and Reconsiderations." Library Chronicle
    43, no. 1 (Spring):47-54.
        In the Troxell Collection at Princeton is an autograph
manuscript of the lyric, "What all men long for and what none shall
have." It is here reprinted, and differences between it and the
text as published in 1936.9 are here discussed. Suggests that May
Morris had changed the original to disguise the "intensity" of her
father's feelings about his wife and Rossetti, but differences
between the two texts seem slight.

21 FONTANA, ERNEST. "Memory and Character in WM's 'The Judgment of
    God.'" Pre-Raphaelite Review 1, no. 2 (May):104-9.
        Ponders the puzzling chronology, brought on by shifts in verb
tense and diction, of "The Judgment of God," considering its
monologue point by point, arguing that "Roger's relationship with
Ellayne is at the center of the poem." She is dead and it is to her
judgment, not God's, that the narrator directs his appeal.

22 HARAP, LOUIS. "Profit and Illth: From Carlyle to Ruskin to
    WM." Monthly Review 30, no. 7 (December):50-61.
        Traces connections between Carlyle and Ruskin regarding their
critiques of capitalism, their isolation of the profit motive as a
basic defect; Ruskin began to suggest remedies, and WM completed the
process by advocating a radical solution: revolution. Quotes WM on
the tremendous waste caused by the pursuit of profits, the "illth"
thus created.

23 HASTY, MARA. "How the Isle of Ransom Reflects an Actual
    Icelandic Setting." Mythlore 5, no. 2 (February):24.
        Points out "areas of resemblance" Iceland shares with Plain,
such as climate, physical setting, and certain social arrangements.

24 HOLLOW, JOHN, ed. The After-Summer Seed: Reconsiderations of
    WM's "Sigurd". New York and London: WM Society, 149 pp.
        Collection of five articles on Sigurd, all based on papers
read at the 1976 MLA, all annotated herein: Balch (1978.4), Blersch
(1978.8), Meredith (1978.39), Spatt (1978.49), and Ugolnik
(1978.59). The editor contributed an introduction (1978.25), and
the text is graced by two illustrations done by Burne-Jones for the
Kelmscott Press edition of Sigurd.

25 HOLLOW, JOHN. "An Introduction: Sinfiotli." In The
    After-Summer Seed: Reconsiderations of WM's "Sigurd". Edited by
    J. Hollow. New York and London: WM Society, pp. 3-12.
        Considers the implications of Sinfiotli's cold determination,
    of Signy's implacable will, and of the fated ends of the other
    characters, to conclude that Sigurd is similar to other Victorian
    narratives; it is a tale of the "sea of time which sweeps over
    all."

26 HONNEF, KARL. Dichterische Illusion und gesellschaftliche
    Wirklichkeit: Zur asthetischen Struktur und historischen
    Funktion der Vers- und Prosaromanzen im werk von WM. Munich:
    Wilhelm Fink, 167 pp.
        A biographical sketch precedes thorough and thoughtful
    discussions of the early poetry, the socialist narratives, and the
    prose romances, using Freudian categories and assumptions about
    dreams to analyze the poetry, Marxist theories to discuss Nowhere
    and John Ball, and archetypal myth-criticism to reveal new layers of
    meaning in the prose romances. Concludes that it was no accident
    that WM chose to write romances; in them he could achieve
    coherencies that link the individual to Dream, the historical to
    Utopia, the natural to Myth; he could sublimate personal and social
    problems, working them out through textual strategies natural to the
    romance genre.

27 JOHNSON, PETER. "Art Nouveau." Art and Antiques Weekly, 18
    November, pp. 24-26.
        WM discussed as one of several figures significant for the
    development of art nouveau, concluding that WM's "vision enabled
    succeeding generations of artists, craftsmen, designers, and
    architects to seek new values and question accepted principles."

28 JOPPIEN, RUDIGR. "Ein Fliesenfeld von WM und William
    DeMorgan." Museen der Stadt Koln 10:1662-63.
        Describes a recent acquisition, a panel of sixty-six tiles
    designed by WM and DeMorgan, installed in Membland Hall by Morris
    and Co. in 1880.

29 LAING, DAVE. "Romanticism and Marxism." In The Marxist Theory
    of Art. Sussex: Harvester Press; Atlantic Highlands, N.J.:
    Humanities Press, pp. 123-25.
        Comments upon the debate set forth by Anderson (1980.3) as to
    the nature of a British Marxist tradition, and then states that the
    "first English Marxist of any stature" was WM and that he made
    contributions to a Marxist aesthetic by redefining the concept of
    art and by creating a new Utopianism. Nevertheless, WM's work
    "remains that of an isolated pioneer within British Marxism and
    Marxist aesthetics."

30 LEWIS, PETER, ed. <u>WM: Aspects of the Man and his Work:</u>
    <u>Proceedings of the Conference on WM Held at Loughborough</u>
    <u>University of Technology</u>. Loughborough: Loughborough Victorian
    Studies Group, 119 pp.
        Includes preface, introductory note, and five papers, all
    annotated herein: Elloway (1978.18), Faulkner (1978.19), Lindsay
    (1978.31), Strode (1978.55), and Watkinson (1978.62).

31 LINDSAY, JACK. "WM." In <u>WM; Aspects of the Man and His Work:</u>
    <u>Proceedings of the Conference on WM Held at Loughborough</u>
    <u>University of Technology</u>. Loughborough: Loughborough Victorian
    Studies Group, pp. 3-27.
        Offers a broad survey of WM's life and works, arguing for a
    "pervasive unity" in all WM's activities, a unity stemming from the
    "fact that in a deep sense Morris never outgrew his childhood."
    Sees his sources of inspiration in "the Garden of enjoyment and the
    Forest of freedom," in dreams of both childhood and of medieval
    coherencies and virtues, and a correspondent hatred of modern
    civilization. Asserts that WM grasped the essential philosophy of
    Marx and then added to it his own convictions of Garden and Forest,
    that WM was "the only thinker or artist of the nineteenth century
    who reached Marxism by the inner logic of the positions from which
    he began."

32 LOWCOCK, M. "Waterford Windows by WM and His Friends."
    <u>Hertfordshire Countryside Illustrated</u>, September, pp. 34-35.
        Note on upcoming festival at the parish church in Waterford;
    "the glory of the church lies in the stained glass windows by the
    famous firm of Morris and Co." Includes illustrations of five of
    them, one of which is WM's "St. Michael the Archangel."

33 MATHEWS, RICHARD. "WM, Mosher, and the Konglomerati Press." <u>Ex</u>
    <u>Libris</u> 2, no. 1 (Summer):1-3.
        Points out that the American printers and designers discussed
    in 1977.38 and influenced by WM were themselves influential on the
    Konglomerati Press of Florida. Two of them, Goudy and Mosher, were
    of particular importance; their achievements and their links to both
    the Kelmscott and Konglomerati presses are here outlined.

34 MATHEWS, RICHARD. "Goudy 'Thirty': An American Type of
    Distinction." <u>Konglomerati</u> 5, no. 2:3.
        WM shared with other printers the problem of making black
    letter styles readable; Goudy, an American printer, found the
    solution. Examples follow.

35 MATHEWS, RICHARD. Introduction to Wolfings, by WM. North
    Hollywood, Calif.: Newcastle Publishing, pp. 5-10.
         Points out that its first readers were puzzled by this tale,
    a "fiction which had both a futuristic and an antiquated sound."
    Mentions WM's other writings, thus providing a backdrop for a brief
    but useful discussion of thematic issues in Wolfings: of urban
    values as opposed to rural, of the individual opposed to the tribe,
    of Thiodolf who in dying for his people becomes a "type of pagan
    Christ figure."

36 MATHEWS, RICHARD. Worlds Beyond the World: The Fantastic Vision
    of WM. San Bernardino, Calif.: Borgo Press, 64 pp.
         Introduces all of WM's prose romances, from those seven tales
    written early on at Oxford, through John Ball and Nowhere (here
    grouped with Wolfings and Roots under the rubric, "The Dream of a
    Better World"), concluding with the final long romances WM wrote at
    the end of his life, those which nourish claims that WM is the
    "Father of heroic fantasy," a forerunner of Tolkien. Offering both
    paraphrase and analyses, often Jungian and Freudian, but always
    lucid and refreshingly eclectic in choice of analogues and examples,
    drawing upon both Shakespeare and the Nixon tapes, this study makes
    good its claim that WM's prose romances deserve further critical
    attention.

37 MEIER, PAUL. WM: The Marxist Dreamer. Translated by Frank
    Gubb. Hassocks, Sussex: Harvester Press; Atlantic Highlands,
    N.J.: Humanities Press, 2 vols., 740 pp.
         Pursues the vindication begun by Arnot (1934.3), who
    contributed a preface to this English edition, and documented by
    E.P. Thompson (1955.15): WM was a revolutionary socialist with new
    ideas and not the sentimental socialist created by Glasier (1921.3)
    and many others. Suggests that Marx's "Critique of the Gotha
    Program" is the source for descriptions of the two stages of the
    revolution in Nowhere, and that WM heard of such matters in
    conversations with Bax and Engels, with whom he was on better terms
    than tradition has it. This exhaustive survey of every possible
    source for Nowhere is valuable despite its attempts to claim for
    Marx and Engels what WM could as easily have gleaned from Ruskin and
    the romantic critique of capitalism and from his own experiences and
    reading. Has appendixes that include WM's notes for an 1885
    lecture, three letters WM sent to socialist colleagues, and a letter
    from Aveling to Laura LaFargue. Part 3, the most comprehensive
    analysis of Nowhere ever attempted, is often fascinating because of
    links Meier finds to the early works of Marx; the summaries in part
    2 of other authors WM had probably used is valuable, with references
    to WM's Commonweal writings and his lectures woven neatly in.
    Translation of 1972.19.

38 MENICHELLI, ALFREDO. "Utopia e desiderio in Nowhere: Forma
    dell' utopia." Studi Inglesi 5:165-88.
       Discusses Nowhere as part of a general British tradition that
    here includes More and Swift; theoretical points in his conclusion
    are derived, in large part, from recent work by Goode (1971.10) and
    E.P. Thompson (1976.50).

39 MEREDITH, EMILY. "Iceland and WM: In Search of the Whole." In
    The After-Summer Seed: Reconsiderations of WM's "Sigurd".
    Edited by J. Hollow. New York and London: WM Society, pp.
    69-87.
       Argues that Iceland's "literature, the land and its language
    offered the continuity and integration for which Morris hungered,
    symbolizing a kind of graphic and geographic immortality." In
    Sigurd, WM achieved an "ideal blending and balancing of disparate
    elements into an integrated whole."

40 MORRIS, BARBARA. Victorian Table Glass and Ornament. London:
    Barrie and Jenkins, pp. 166-69, passim.
       WM did not himself design glassware, but his lectures
    influenced attitudes about such design; as proof, points in "The
    Lesser Arts of Life" are discussed, linked to the work of artisans
    at Morris and Co. and elsewhere.

41 NUGENT, CONN. "Good Work, Good Rest: Some Ideas from WM."
    Co-Evolution Quarterly 18 (Summer):88-93.
       Parts of "Useful Work vs. Useless Toil" are here paraphrased
    and at times nearly disfigured by contemporary California rhetoric:
    "the most rewarding exertion of all is taking care of yourself,
    sometimes in concert with others, often alone," but this is in the
    main a sympathetic and useful introduction to WM's socialist
    aesthetic.

42 OBERG, CHARLOTTE. WM: A Pagan Prophet. Charlottesville:
    University Press of Virginia, 189 pp.
       Introduction includes a useful discussion of the paradoxes
    that are strung through WM's life and work, a review of significant
    criticism, and a convincing argument that a "serious reappraisal of
    WM's work is needed." She here begins that task with fresh
    considerations of the poetry and prose fiction. Three sections
    follow, with full discussions of the unity of Paradise, the "epic
    impulse," and "romantic visions and visionary romance," discussions
    that make new connections and achieve new insights while forsaking
    considerations of chronology and the personal and social pressures
    that caused WM to attempt new genres and themes. A final section
    discusses WM's significance as a "Pagan Prophet," as an important
    literary artist. Revision of 1971.27.

43 PARRY, LINDA. "The Stanmore Hall Tapestries." In Art at
    Auction. London: Sotheby Parke Bernet, pp. 418-22.
        W.K. D'Arcy commissioned Morris and Co. in 1890 to create a
set of tapestries for his dining room at Stanmore Hall, Middlesex.
Grail episodes from Malory were chosen, and six narrative scenes
were designed by Burne-Jones, the foregrounds by Dearle. They were
completed at Merton Abbey on three upright looms, each with three
weavers, during 1894-95. These tapestries represent "one of the
most interesting decorative schemes of the nineteenth century."

44 PEARSON, MARGERY. WM, 1834-1896: Aspects of His Life and Work.
    Catalogue of an Exhibition June-July 1978 at the University of
    Toronto. Toronto: University of Toronto Press, 13 pp.
        Biographical sketch accompanies short descriptions of
sixty-five items, mainly books, exhibited in the Thomas Fisher Rare
Book Library at the University of Toronto.

45 PENNING-ROSWELL, EDMUND. "The Remodeling of WM." TLS, no. 3984
    (11 August):913-14.
        Review-essay inspired by the translation of Meier (1978.37),
the second edition of E.P. Thompson (1976.50), and books by Oberg
(1978.42) and Bradley (1978.10). Comments upon WM's changing
reputation during the twentieth century and ways that a few writers
like E.P. Thompson have made our generation aware of the relevance
of WM's life and writings.

46 PETTIS, RUTH. The Goudy Presence at Konglomerati Press.
    Gulfport, Fl.: Konglomerati Press, 16 pp.
        Refers to Goudy's Village Press venture as one of the first
twentieth-century exemplars of Kelmscott Press ideals; Florida's
Konglomerati Press, established in 1971, follows in that same
tradition.

47 QUAIL, JOHN. The Slow-Burning Fuse: The Lost History of the
    British Anarchists. London: Granada, pp. 27-45, passim.
        Discusses personalities and conditions that led to the
formation of the Socialist League and a few years later to WM's
departure from it because he opposed anarchist tactics. Quotes
Engels on WM (an "emotional socialist") and points out the ways that
WM was radically different from other middle-class socialists.

48 SCHUSTER, VERA. "The Pre-Raphaelites in Oxford." Oxford Art
    Journal 1:7-13.
        Discusses the effect Oxford, with its decorated, medieval
houses and always the sound of bells, had on WM and Burne-Jones as
undergraduates. It was also at Oxford where they discovered
medieval manuscripts, Chaucer and Malory, and their first
Pre-Raphaelite painting, Millais's Return to the Ark. Discusses the
Union murals, going into detail about the bays used, WM's
decorations of the ceilings (he redecorated them in 1875, and in
1935 a complete restoration was attempted by Mobley). Mentions also
the Morris and Co. stained glass and tapestries at Oxford.

49 SPATT, HARTLEY S. "Morrissaga: Sigurd." In The After-Summer
    Seed: Reconsiderations of WM's "Sigurd". Edited by J. Hollow.
    New York and London: WM Society, pp. 119-48.
        Reprint of 1977.34.

50 SPAULDING, FRANCIS. Magnificent Dreams: Burne-Jones and the
    Late Victorians. New York: E.P. Dutton, pp. 33, 42.
        Brief remarks on Burne-Jones's friendship with WM and ways
that Paradise influenced the subject matter of Burne-Jones's
paintings.

51 SPENCER, CHARLES. "Il primo designer moderno." Bolaffiarte 9
    (April):9-13.
        Surveys reasons WM has been called the father of modern
design, stressing Red House and the beginnings of the Firm.

52 STAINES, DAVID. "Swinburne's Arthurian Poetry and its Medieval
    Sources." Studia Neophilologica 50, no. 1:53-70.
        Argues that Swinburne turned to Arthurian themes because of
Defence, that its intense and graphic descriptions influenced
portraits in "Queen Yseult" more than any medieval tales had.

53 STAM, DEIRDRE C. "Burne-Jones and the Kelmscott Golden
    Legend." Newberry Library Bulletin 6, no. 9 (August):339-49.
        Describes a "resplendent drawing" Burne-Jones made for
Kelmscott Press Golden Legend, as well as other illustrations he
executed for Kelmscott Press volumes; mentions other related
materials now at the Newberry Library.

54 STRODE, ELIZABETH. "A Matter of Art: WM's Propaganda Style,
    1883-1896." Prose Studies: 1800-1900 1, no. 2 (February):41-47.
        Discusses the stylistic and rhetorical qualities of some of
the socialist prose WM wrote between 1883, when he joined the SDF,
and 1896. Mackail suggested that this prose was mere journalism,
and many subsequent critics have ignored it. Argues that WM's
socialist prose is informed and inspired, and thus it deserves more
attention.

55 STRODE, ELIZABETH. "Beginnings and Endings: WM's Late Prose
    Romances." In WM: Aspects of the Man and His Work: Proceedings
    of the Conference on WM Held at Loughborough University of
    Technology. Loughborough: Loughborough Victorian Studies Group,
    pp. 50-73.
        Points to differences between the early and late prose
romances: the former inspire a "slight unease," while the latter
"convey the philosophy of life Morris developed," where one receives
the idea that by now he is "satisfied if not unscarred." Compares
themes in the late romances to ideas drawn from Tacitus, the works
of Engels, and the socialist lectures.

56 THOMAS, HELEN. "WM." In Time and Again: Memoirs and Letters.
    Edited by M. Thomas. Manchester: Carcenet, pp. 47-50.
        Reprinted from 1963.24. Reprinted: 1979.48.

57 TOD, IAN, and WHEELER, MICHAEL. "WM and Reasonable Strife." In
    Utopia. London: Orbis Publishing; New York: Harmony Books, pp.
    109-17, passim.
        A biographical sketch precedes a discussion of Utopian
writings and experiments in the nineteenth century and of Nowhere as
a specific reaction to Looking Backward.

58 TYSON, NANCY JANE. "Art and Society in the Late Prose
    Narratives of WM." Pre-Raphaelite Review 1, no. 2 (May):1-11.
        Though the late prose romances are not as overtly political
as John Ball or Nowhere, they still express WM's socialist vision.
Discusses passages from Well, as well as descriptions of Birdalone's
embroidery and Ralph's comments on cities, as representative of WM's
basic social ideals. Correctly links the rediscovery of these
romances to the recent surge of interest in fantasy literature.

59 UGOLNIK, ANTHONY. "The Victorian Skald: Old Icelandic and the
    Evolution of WM's Sigurd." In The After-Summer Seed:
    Reconsiderations of WM's "Sigurd". Edited by J. Hollow. New
    York and London: WM Society, pp. 37-67.
        To combat his own ornateness, as exemplified in Paradise, WM
    "drank deeply of Old Icelandic and the sagas." His Sigurd
    represents "the final fruit of his sustained poetic effort and the
    initiation of the political activity which occupied his later
    years." Has useful analyses of the ways that WM, in Volsunga
    translation, "made a new language for himself out of the Germanic
    elements of his present- day speech," how such linguistic and
    stylistic changes appeared six years later in Sigurd, a poem that
    offered "a mythic model for the English nation," but his English
    audience "was not disposed to hear." Suggests that the Icelandic
    journeys helped WM escape "from the lush Southern influence of
    Rossetti." They thus signal a new independence for WM.

60 WAGGONER, DIANA. The Hills of Faraway: A Guide to Fantasy. New
    York: Atheneum, pp. 36-38, 245-47.
        Presents plot outlines and short evaluations of "Hollow Land"
    and of the last six prose romances WM wrote, claiming that these
    works are the first heroic fantasies and that their hallmark is a
    quasi-medieval setting.

61 WARD, COLIN. "Will the Real WM Please Stand Up?" Vole, no.
    6:21-26.
        Essay that wonders at, but ultimately celebrates, the many
    achievements of WM; his continuing pertinence to modern times is
    suggested by new editions of E.P. Thompson (1955.15 and 1976.50) and
    Paul Thompson (1967.29 and 1977.37); these books are briefly
    discussed. Concludes with clever surmises about WM's probable
    reactions to working conditions in British and Polish shipyards and
    in the Red Star Tractor Factory in Budapest.

62 WATKINSON, RAY. "WM the Designer: Art, Work and Social Order."
    In WM: Aspects of the Man and His Work: Proceedings of the
    Conference on WM Held at Loughborough University of Technology.
    Loughborough: Loughborough Victorian Studies Group, pp. 74-105.
        Argues that WM was not just a designer, a maker, but also "a
    theorist of design whose theory is also, inescapably, social," but
    because he had no use for theory as such, it has to be searched out
    in his life and work, and it is "essentially a theory of the
    wholeness of life," one embodying fellowship. Detailed comments
    follow (these originally accompanied slides shown at the conference,
    and not reproduced here), about the work of the Firm and problems WM
    had with Brown and Rossetti. Discusses also the influence Kelmscott
    Press had on other small presses.

63 WHIPPLE, DAVID. "Textile Designs and Books by WM." Bulletin of
    the Cleveland Museum of Art 65 (September):247-57.
        Biographical sketch precedes a description of Morris and Co.
    printed fabrics, textile samples, and Kelmscott Press volumes (a
    complete set) at the Museum of Art in Cleveland.

64 WILLIAMS, RAYMOND. "Utopia and Science Fiction." Science
    Fiction Studies 5, pt. 3 (November):203-14.
        Mentions Engels's distinction between "Utopian" and
    "scientific" socialism, arguing then that Nowhere is, though a
    Utopia, scientific in its socialism because of the "crucial
    insertion of the transition to Utopia," the chapters which show the
    new society being fought for. Comments also on E.P. Thompson's
    ideas (1976.50) about Nowhere involving the "education of desire."
    Reprinted: 1979.50; 1980.50.

65 "A Champion for WM." Architect's Journal 168 (9 August):239.
        Note wonders if anyone wants to buy Stanmore Hall and thereby
    help preserve its "sumptuous WM interiors." The house, empty since
    1973, was decaying rapidly.

66 "A Very Fine and Rare Work of Art." JWMS 3, no. 4 (Winter):2-3,
    34.
        Reprints letter WM wrote in 1882 expressing his opinion upon
    the value of a Persian carpet; his confident expertise is apparent.

67 "The Pursuit of Beauty." TLS, n.s., 107, no. 196 (June):446-51.
        Comments upon American interests in the Pre-Raphaelites,
    referring to the friendship between Burne-Jones and Charles Eliot
    Norton, to WM articles in the Fogg Museum, and to Kelmscott Press
    influence on a Harvard magazine, the Knight Errant, published during
    the 1890s.

1979

1 BOOS, FLORENCE. "Medievalism in Alfred Tennyson and WM." VIJ
   7:19-24.
        Medieval motifs were important to both Tennyson and WM,
   enabling them, for instance, "to dramatize their political beliefs,
   discuss sexuality with more directness than Victorian norms would
   otherwise allow." Critics should, however, move beyond facile
   comparisons of the Arthurian poems and note how their uses of
   medieval motifs evolved over the years. Contrasts poems Tennyson
   wrote in 1842 to poems from Defence; their "emphasis on political
   chicanery, sexual frustration, and military defeat" offer "an
   alternative reading of the Arthurian cycle." Compares the Idylls to
   tales in Paradise, claiming that they are responses to "Victorian

agnosticism," that in both women are "stylized," but that WM does
not "moralize or degrade them as well." Has brief comments on WM's
use of the Scandinavian Middle Ages in "Gudrun" and Sigurd, the
British in John Ball and Nowhere. Wonders if at times "Morris
consciously designed his poetry to express tempermental distance
from Tennyson."

2   BOOS, FLORENCE. "Old Controversies, New Texts: Two Recent Books
    on Pre-Raphaeliteism." MP 77, no. 2 (November):172-81.
        Counters Bryson's claim (1976.4) that Rossetti's attitude
toward WM was one of "good-humored mockery," for in these letters
Rossetti consistently and unfairly railed at WM. Comments also on
Janey's letters to Rossetti and to Cockerell, the latter showing a
softening of her attitudes toward Kelmscott Manor and her husband's
varied achievements. Concludes that these letters show that
"Rossetti seems to have been genuinely considerate of Morris's near
invalid wife, Morris stoically endured her preference for another,
and Janey felt malice toward neither and some affection for both."

3   BOOS, FLORENCE. "The Medieval Tales of WM's Paradise." Studies
    in Medievalism 1, no. 1 (Spring):45-52.
        Laments that a "series of critical trivializations and
historical ironies" have tended to remove Paradise from serious
consideration by modern readers; they take at face value the main
narrator's self-depiction: "an idle singer of an empty day."
Reviews the structure of Paradise, suggesting that the twenty-four
tales fall into "five thematic patterns." Discusses two of the
medieval tales in some detail, showing how WM changed his sources
for "Ogier the Dane" and "The Fostering of Aslaug" to emphasize
themes of sexual experience and romantic love" and to create
narrative poems of "considerable subtlety," among the "most
attractive unread Victorian poetry."

4   CALLEN, ANTHEA. Angel in the Studio: Women in the Arts and
    Crafts Movement, 1870-1914. London: Architectural Press, pp.
    100-103, 114-15, passim. New York: Pantheon, as Women Artists
    of the Arts and Crafts Movement, 1870-1914.
        The seeds of the Arts and Crafts Movement were present in
Morris and Co., and the ways that women--mainly family members--were
involved in its work, usually its embroidery and the like,
reinforced a sexual division of labor "which was to be largely
repeated throughout Arts and Crafts Movement as a whole." Discusses
the effects of both the WM and Rossetti marriages, the
"paternalistic overtones" of such "raising" of working-class women.
Despite the fact that WM and other leaders retained older
assumptions about women and work, the Arts and Crafts Movement did,
finally, aid women's emancipation. Dozens of interesting
photographs accompany the detailed exposition in this monograph.

5   CROOK, J.M. "Two Pieces of Painted Furniture by William
     Burges." In Morris and Company. Catalogue of an Exhibition at
     the Fine Arts Society, 24 April-18 May. London: Fine Arts
     Society, pp. 12-16
          Traces differences between Burges's furniture and that
     designed by Morris and Co., concluding that Burges drifted away from
     Morris because he was "fundamentally apolitical."

6   CURRIE, ROBERT. "Had WM Gone Soft in the Head?" Essays in
     Criticism 29, no. 4 (October):341-56.
          The title, borrowed from E.P. Thompson (1955.15), suggests
     the stance assumed by scholars who can not square the WM of John
     Ball and the socialist essays with the author of the late prose
     romances. Argues that these tales should not be brushed aside,
     since they "develop Morris's chief social and psychological
     preoccupations, and are thus central to his work." Insists that one
     such preoccupation was with his manhood, and that is why he went to
     Iceland; he "returned smelling so strongly of raw fish and Norse
     sagas that the fastidious Rossetti fled." Similar comments about
     ways that WM's "pressing personal anxieties" emerge in the late
     romances are set forth with confidence and apparent seriousness.

7   DRESCHER, THOMAS. "A Critical Companion to WM's Defence."
     Dissertation, York University, Ontario.
          Abstracted: DAI 40:2661-62-A.

8   DUFFY, FRANCIS. "A Vision of the Factory in an Ideal Society."
     Financial Times, no. 27,782 (5 February):9.
          Comments upon attempts to brighten the workplace in Sweden
     and Holland, where a "concern with human factors" has overridden
     demands for increased productivity. In Britain, however, factories
     remain unpleasant, ugly, and unproductive, and it therefore seems
     unfortunate that WM's "A Factory as it Might Be" is known to so few.

9   ELLISON, RUTH C. "Hallaeri og Hneykslimal" [Famine and
     controversy]. Andvari, n.s., 21:62-79.
          Reviews the controversy surrounding money that WM helped to
     raise for the Iceland Relief Committee, as well as the actual
     conditions in the North of Iceland; based upon evidence she presents
     from contemporary diaries and the like, she concludes that
     conditions were indeed severe and that relief was needed.

10 FONTANA, ERNEST. "WM's Guenevere and Dante's Francesca:
    Allusion as Revision." English Miscellany 28-29:283-92.
        Dante's lovers in the second circle are blown about in
unending winds, and the wind is mentioned five times in "The Defence
of Guenevere." This "establishes the poem's situational and
thematic relationship to the Paolo and Francesca episode" in Dante.
The author seems surprised that this "ironic" allusion had not been
noted before.

11 GALLASCH, LINDA. The Use of Compounds and Archaic Diction in
    the Works of WM. European University Studies, vol. 60. Bern,
    Frankfurt, and Las Vegas: Peter Lang, 179 pp.
        A systematic examination of WM's diction which attempts to
identify and classify all archaic forms and all compounds,
particularly in the late prose romances. A chapter on WM's
attitudes toward nineteenth-century English as a literary medium
draws together quotations from many of his works; he obviously "had
an intense dislike for the language of his own day," and thus
borrowed archaic forms from Chaucer and Malory; the diction from his
Icelandic translations appears in the late prose romances. Tables,
lists, and a word-index should make this book useful for anyone
interested in the development of WM's literary style.

12 GERE, CHARLOTTE. "Morris and Company 1861-1939." In Morris and
    Company. Catalogue of an Exhibition at the Fine Arts Society,
    24 April-18 May. London: Fine Arts Society, pp. 5-12.
        Considers why "the influence of Morris and Company seems to
be out of all proportion to the small number of different objects
they produced or to the originality of their designs in all products
except for the textiles and wallpapers." Points out that because
"Morris was hopelessly undercapitalized and could never afford the
necessary machines," the furniture and tapestries were often very
expensive, and therefore well-known. Mentions famed designs and
designers and discusses the important commissions "which employed
all the varied talents of Morris and his associates."

13 GOOCH, BRYAN, and THATCHER, DAVID. "WM: 1834-1896." In Musical
    Settings of Early and Mid-Victorian Literature: A Catalogue. New
    York and London: Garland, pp. 400-408.
        Lists seventy-five citations to songs, most of them from the
late nineteenth and early twentieth century, whose lyrics are
derived from or inspired by WM poems. The majority are from
Defence; "Summer Dawn" has been set to music five times, "In Prison"
and "Rapunzel" four times each; Paradise and Love Is Enough inspired
several songs, and so of course did the socialist chants and
passages from Pilgrims.

14 HELMER, JOHN. "The Prettiness of Utopia." <u>JWMS</u> 4, no. 1
    (Winter):4-19.
        Discusses the frequency in <u>Nowhere</u> of use of adjectives like
    "pretty," "handsome," "dainty," and the like, suggesting that WM
    meant them to imply older meanings and values and to provide an
    "analytic mode of perception," one that might somehow be tied to
    Marxism and the value of objects.

15 HENDERSON, PHILIP. "The Death of Topsy." <u>JWMS</u> 4, no. 1
    (Winter):28-31.
        Reports on a recent acquisition of the British Library, a
    play that Rossetti wrote in 1878, "The Death of Topsy." Judges that
    it "would seem to demonstrate several things about Rossetti:
    bitterness about Morris' recent high-handed reorganization of the
    Firm under his sole control, resentment of Morris as an obstacle
    between himself and Janey, and a possibly subconscious wish for his
    death." This five-scene playlet was recently published for the
    first time (1975.20).

16 HUMPHREYS, ARTHUR LEE [A. Pendenys]. <u>A Letter to WM</u>. Toronto:
    Aliquando Press, 18 pp.
        This fine press miniature reprints a sardonic letter which
    opens, "Dear William, I presume that the Kelmscott books are
    published for your amusement, because I have inquired extensively
    and find they do not amuse anyone else." It appeared originally in
    1895 in <u>The Books of Today and the Books of Tomorrow</u>, but since its
    opinions are evidently shared by some modern printers (the edition
    was limited to 100 copies), it is included here.

17 IBACH, MARILYN. "Two Bloomsbury Tours." <u>Pre-Raphaelite Review</u>
    2, no. 2 (May):83-92.
        A guide to the homes and haunts of Pre-Raphaelites who lived
    in and near Bloomsbury includes a map with forty-three sites marked;
    descriptions of these contain information about WM and Red Lion
    Square.

18 IBACH, MARILYN. <u>A Guide to Morris and Company Stained Glass in</u>
    <u>Great Britain</u>. London: WM Society, 134 pp.
        Intended for those who wish to see Morris and Co. stained
    glass, as described in A.C. Sewter (1974.25). Includes new county
    names and specific locations in England, Wales, Scotland, the
    Channel Islands, and Northern Ireland; 160 of the 600 locations
    described were visited; all are charted on forty pages of maps.
    Ibach has completed a similar guide to Morris and Co. stained glass
    in North America, an 18 pp. pamphlet published by the WM Society in
    1983.

19 INGLE, STEPHEN. Socialist Thought in Imaginative Literature.
    London: Macmillan; Totowa, N.J.: Rowman and Littlefield, pp.
    82-87, passim.
        Discusses Nowhere along with several other twentieth-century
British works with political themes. Suggests that WM and Orwell
are moralists, and that Wells and Shaw are scientists. Asserts that
WM was naive in abolishing from Nowhere both technological expertise
and spiritual questioning; the inhabitants there remind one of
Wells' Eloi or the happy folk of Brave New World.

20 JANSEN, REAMY. "Afterword to the Commune of Paris Pamphlet."
    Phoenix 7, nos. 1-2 (Spring):252-58.
        Discusses an 1886 Socialist League pamphlet, A Short Account
of the Commune of Paris (which is here reprinted), as "the fourth in
a general educational and propaganda series" entitled "The Socialist
Platform." Places it in relation to WM's other work with the
Socialist League and contrasts its ideology to that of the SDF.
Stresses the importance of the Commune to Commonweal, in whose pages
it was discussed over thirty times within the two year period,
1885-86, and to WM himself, who mentioned it often in his lectures
and gave four speeches on it.

21 JOHNSON, LESLEY. "Arnold's Contemporaries: WM." In The
    Cultural Critics: From Matthew Arnold to Raymond Williams.
    London: Routledge and Kegan Paul, pp. 60-67, passim.
        Although WM was as disturbed by nineteenth-century
materialism as the other intellectuals discussed in this study, he
"displayed no particular interest in elaborating notions of the
specialness of artists or intellectuals," of their role, or indeed
their abilities, in enlightening the masses about art and culture.
Art had to be for all, had to grow naturally from daily life, and WM
worked to improve that daily life.

22 KANATANI, NOBUO. "Nowhere ni okeru WM no gorishugi hihan" [A
    new theory of human life: WM's criticism of rationalism in
    Nowhere]. SEL (Tokyo) 56:49-64.
        In Japanese. Discusses Nowhere in terms of developing
socialist ideologies in the nineteenth century and as a reaction to
Bellamy's Looking Backward.

23 KIRCHHOFF, FREDERICK. "Travel as Anti-Autobiography in WM's
    Icelandic Journals." In Approaches to Victorian Autobiography.
    Edited by G. Landow. Athens: Ohio University Press, pp.
    292-310.
        Maintains that Icelandic Journals "show Morris attempting to
present deep personal experience in an impersonal 'objective'
mode." the trips were responses to "multiple crises" in his life,

and the journals "an attempt to perceive an order in them."
Compares WM's confrontation with Nature to Wordsworth's.

24 KIRCHHOFF, FREDERICK. WM. Twayne's English Author's Series.
    Boston: Twayne; London: G. Prior, 182 pp.
        Too many short studies of WM attempt to cover all his
    achievements; this one is wisely limited to his literary development
    and thus contains many useful close readings and new insights.
    Opens with a biographical sketch that stresses WM's bohemian
    rebellion against the values of his family; to them WM's marriage to
    "the uneducated daughter of an Oxford stableman must have seemed the
    final humiliation." They did not attend the wedding; other
    biographers have not noted this small fact; it here is neatly woven
    together with other facts about WM's privileged youth and unhappy
    marriage into a psychological fabric against which themes in the
    poetry and prose romances are discussed. Stresses the significance,
    for understanding WM's development as a poet, of his review of
    Browning's Men and Women in the Oxford and Cambridge Magazine, and
    of the prose tales published there for understanding his personal
    development; roles he projected for himself, like the hopeless
    lover, will turn up in the later narratives. A psychological
    approach yields insights into Defence poems, the prologue (and its
    revisions) to Paradise, Jason, several of the narratives in
    Paradise, and the Icelandic Journals, which are linked to Love Is
    Enough, here given a fresh interpretation as "the first of Morris'
    imaginative works to reflect his experience of Iceland," and also to
    mark a new, affirmative phase in his writing. In Sigurd, Regin is
    regarded as a projection of WM, and his own personal concerns are
    also noted in the late prose romances, where terms like "erotic
    fulfillment" are often employed. But WM's social concerns are not
    ignored; an important chapter, "'How We Might Live': Morris as a
    Socialist," discusses the socialist lectures, John Ball, Wolfings,
    Roots, and Nowhere, with sympathetic intelligence. The final
    chapter deals with the late prose romances, where WM is seen
    "constructing--and testing--a set of psychological paradigms with
    which to come to terms with the motivations (and inadequacies)
    underlying his life's work."

25 KNIGHT, ISABEL. "Alienation, Eros and Work: The Good News from
    Nowhere." Alternative Futures 2:3-27.
        If, as Freud said, we repress Eros to achieve civilization,
    then if that civilization is bad, perhaps we should release Eros.
    WM seemed to have recognized this in Nowhere, which is here
    discussed as a place where individual pleasure can flow out into
    loving care for nature and for other people; the story is seen as
    the "imaginative counterpart" of the theories of Marcuse.

26 LANDOW, GEORGE. "And the World Became Strange: Realms of
    Literary Fantasy." In Fantastic Illustration and Design in
    Britain, 1850-1930. Catalogue of an Exhibition at the Museum of
    Art, Rhode Island School of Design. Bulletin of the Rhode
    Island School of Design Museum Notes 65, no. 5 (April):39-41.
       Suggests that the world WM creates in Water is one of
    "spiritualized eroticism," pointing out that Birdalone is an
    entirely new type of female character; such heroic and sensual young
    women had not appeared in other Pre-Raphaelite writings, nor in the
    earlier tales, as in Paradise, written by WM himself.

27 LANDOW, GEORGE. "WM and Swinburne." JWMS 4, no. 1
    (Winter):2-3.
       Reprint of 1977.20.

28 LATHAM, DAVID. "Gothic Architectonics: WM's 'Tune of Seven
    Towers.'" Pre-Raphaelite Review 2, no. 2 (May):49-58.
       WM'S comments about how easy it was for him to write poetry
    have deflected some critics from a careful examination of how
    intricate his poetic structures can be; many of these intricacies
    are here found in "The Tune of Seven Towers," which is presented as
    an elaborate dramatic monologue with parallels to those of Browning.

29 LATHAM, DAVID. "WM's Misunderstood Revision of 'Guenevere.'" N
    and Q, n.s., 26, no. 4 (August):322.
       Argues, on the basis of rhyme scheme, that the opening stanza
    of "The Defence of Guenevere" was indeed "not meant to follow the
    ninth stanza of the rejected proof sheet," and that therefore Paul
    Thompson's statement (1967.29) about the "pure luck" of the poem's
    dramatic opening should be disregarded.

30 MAC CARTHY, FIONA. A History of British Design, 1830-1970.
    London and Boston: Allen and Unwin, pp. 21-25, passim.
       Revised edition, with WM commentary essentially the same, of
    1972.15. Less glossy, with fewer plates.

31 MANN, NANCY D. "Eros and Community in the Fiction of WM."
    Nineteenth Century Fiction 34, no. 3 (December):302-25.
       Early and late prose romances display similarities in style,
    setting, themes of personal love and group loyalties. In the early
    romances, Eros is "transcendent and essentially private," and in the
    late romances Eros is "redefined as a marriage of natural passion
    and social commitment." Early personal disappointments, a loss of
    both fellowship and love, and then the journeys to Iceland and
    increasing involvement in social causes are discussed as influences
    that changed WM's attitudes toward love and community.

32 MANUEL, FRANK E., and MANUEL, FRITZIE P. "WM from Nowhere." In
    Utopian Thought in the Western World. Cambridge, Mass.: Belknap
    Press, pp. 768-72, passim.
        Discusses the influences of More and Bellamy upon WM's
    Nowhere, claiming that WM employs a "simplistic utopian psychology"
    and that he assumes incorrectly that everyone has a natural "desire
    to express oneself in work."

33 MARSHALL, RODERICK. WM and His Earthly Paradises. Tisbury,
    Wiltshire: Compton Press. Reprint. Totawa, N.J.: Barnes and
    Noble, 1980, 332 pp. New York: Braziller, 1981.
        The writer lived at Kelmscott Manor, and he thus sensed what
    the old house and the area had meant to WM; unhappy with
    "self-styled critics who seldom find anything but faded tapestry and
    marzipan in the poetry and romances," he reread everything,
    searching "between the lines of poetry and prose for the seeds of
    biography." Asserts that WM provides a fine example of "the
    struggle of man to integrate his personality and so to achieve the
    mandalic experience." There are many audacious attempts to find
    biographical data in the poems: evidence of the courtship of Jane
    Burden in Defence, of Janey's growing attraction for Rossetti in
    Paradise. Sees Jason as "farewell to Red House," the saga
    translations "as a means of neutralizing murderous fantasies about
    Rossetti and Jane," the heroines in the romances as representations
    of Georgie Burne-Jones, whom he suggests WM loved, asserting that
    when he died "his hand was in Georgiana's." Follows Glasier in
    suggesting that WM did not understand Marx (1921.3), blames "wind,
    rain, cold, irregular diet and apathetic or hectoring audiences,"
    that is to say, his socialist work, with shortening WM's life.
    There are, however, throughout the book fresh insights into the
    beauties of Kelmscott Manor, the many ways that it provided solace
    and inspiration to WM.

34 MEREDITH, EMILY. "Iceland as Metaphor for Integration in the
    Works of WM." Dissertation, University of Rhode Island.
    Abstracted: DAI 42:4045-A.

35 MICKELSSON, ULLA. "Virgil's Aeneid: The Culminating Achievement
    of WM's Illumination Work." Libri: International Library Review
    29, no. 3 (October):260-70.
        Describes why the "great folio manuscript of Virgil's Aeneid
    takes the first place among Morris's illuminated manuscripts."
    During 1874-75, WM wrote out the manuscript almost to the end of
    book 6; he also did some of the illuminating, some "great floriated
    marginal initials," and he engaged Burne-Jones to do many of the
    large illuminations (twenty-nine pencil drawings were completed).
    But only a few of these were added to the manuscript, and WM never
    returned to the copying or elaborate initials and border
    decorations. He sold the manuscript to C.F. Murray who later

employed Graily Hewitt to copy out the remaining six books.
Differences between his hand and that of WM are described, as are
many of the illuminations. Includes four monochrome plates. The
manuscript is now in the Doheny Memorial Library in Camarillo,
California.

36 MURPHY, BRIAN. "Nowhere." In Survey of Science Fiction
    Literature. Englewood Cliffs, N.J.: Salem Press, pp. 1516-20.
        Describes Nowhere as "futuristic Utopian novel," paraphrasing
it fairly accurately and concluding that it has "what all other
Utopias lack: one could imagine living there happily with freedom,
dignity, honesty, and beauty."

37 MUTHESIUS, HERMANN. "WM: The Development through Him and beside
    Him." In The English House. Translated by Janet Seligmann,
    edited by Denis Sharp. London: Lund Humphries; New York:
    Rizzoli, pp. 158-63, 168-74, passim.
        Translation, slightly condensed, of 1904.11.

38 NASLAS, MICHAEL. "The Concept of the Town in the Writings of
    WM." Architectural Association Quarterly 11, no. 3:21-31.
        Points out that the "argument that Morris was an impractical
idealist is a myth which was used to neutralize Morris during his
lifetime, and it has remained the dominant argument up to the
present day, distorting his actions and views." A clear and
detailed view of WM's ideas about cities (which he always scorned)
emerges from this careful survey of WM's essays and lectures (many
presented at SPAB meetings), and descriptions in Nowhere. Quotes
from "Art and Democracy," here judged to be one of WM's "most
brilliant and illuminating public speeches," one with messages about
the quality of life which are still pertinent.

*39 ONO, JIRO. Decorative Arts: WM and His Surroundings. Tokyo:
    Seido-sha, 339 pp.
        Cited in David and Sheila Latham's "WM: An Annotated
Bibliography." JWMS 5, no. 3 (Summer, 1983):36.

40 PIERSON, STANLEY. British Socialism: The Journey from Fantasy
    to Politics. Cambridge, Mass.: Harvard University Press, pp.
    29-30, 245-47, passim.
        The journey from vision and commitment to mere politics was
made by most British socialists, even though WM ("the most famous of
the British converts to socialism") continually warned them to avoid
politics, for fear they would lose sight of "ultimate aims."
Discusses the influence WM had, partly through example, mainly
through his writings (especially in Commonweal) on men like Shaw,

Glasier, Carpenter, and Blatchford, and in the twentieth century on
Herbert Read and G.D.H. Cole.

41 POST, JONATHAN. "Guenevere's Critical Performance." VP 17, no.
    4 (Winter):317-27.
        Reviews criticism of "The Defence of Guenevere" which has
usually debated degrees of her guilt or duplicity, ways and
wherefores that WM departed from his sources. A closer look at the
poem itself, especially at Guenevere's amazing verbal felicity
(romance heroines, as Tennyson recognized, are supposed to be
reticent), as she works out a rationale, a defense, for her actions,
suggests WM's high artistry. He has created a heroine who
beautifully handles narrative and image to get herself, and others,
"to believe that she is establishing a pact with God."

42 PRICKETT, STEPHEN. Victorian Fantasy. London and Bloomington:
    Indiana University Press, pp. 95-97, passim.
        Paraphrases "Pool" and suggests that the tale is unusual
because of hints of "unnamed vice and sexual unwholesomeness."

43 ROSEMONT, FRANKLIN. "Free Play and No Limits: An Introduction
    to Bellamy's Utopia." Cultural Correspondence 10:6-16.
        In this full discussion of Looking Backward, the effects of
WM's "peculiar blindness to Bellamy" are surveyed, and it becomes
apparent that there are more parallels between the two utopian
fictions than contrasts.

44 RUBY, DONA L. "The Late Prose Romances of WM." Dissertation,
    University of Illinois.
        Abstracted: DAI 40:2701-702-A.

45 SOUTH, JOAN. The WM Shopping Guide. London: WM Society, 39 pp.
        Guide to shops and institutions in Britain where Morris and
Co. goods, or imitations of them, can be purchased and where WM
films, prints, books are available.

46 SPENCER, CHARLES. "WM by Design." Art and Antiques Weekly, 17
    February, pp. 24-26.
        Compares WM to Diaghilev; both discussed as "figure-heads of
energy and influence." Red House, the establishment of the Firm,
WM's "schizophrenic dilemma" in making expensive artifacts and
embracing socialist ideals, are all mentioned.

47 SUVIN, DARKO. Metamorphoses of Science Fiction. On the Poetics
    and History of a Literary Genre. London and New Haven: Yale
    University Press, pp. 177-94, passim.
        Analyzes Nowhere, bringing other WM writings to bear in a
discussion of ways Nowhere does not fit Utopian categories but does
"bequeath" certain elements to science fiction. Asserts that the
"absence of sociopolitical organization in Nowhere is a gap that
cannot be argued away and denies it the status of a Utopia," but it
is the "finest specimen of Earthly Paradise story in modern
literature." Contrasts it to Looking Backward, compares it to
Twain's Connecticut Yankee in King Arthur's Court.

48 THOMAS, HELEN. A Visit to WM. Andoversford: Whittington, 12
    pp.
        Reprinted from 1963.24.

49 TITLEBAUM, RICHARD. "The Creation of Kelmscott Chaucer."
    Harvard Library Bulletin 27, no. 4 (October):471-88.
        Discusses Kelmscott Chaucer as a natural outgrowth of WM's
medieval interests and also as a culmination of the Gothic revival,
recalling that Burne-Jones had called the folio a "pocket
cathedral." Discusses typefaces, the illustrations (which
Burne-Jones often did not fit to the themes of certain tales), and
the general design of the book which was WM's responsibility and his
"supreme achievement."

50 WILLIAMS, RAYMOND. "Utopia and Science Fiction." In Science
    Fiction: A Critical Guide. Edited by Patrick Parrinder. London
    and New York: Longmans, pp. 52-6
        Reprint of 1978.64.

51 WILLIAMS, RAYMOND. Politics and Letters: Interviews with The
    New Left Review. London: New Left Books. Reprint. London:
    Verso, 1981, pp. 102, 104, passim.
        Agrees with interviewer that WM should have received more
prominence in 1958.14, since he represents the "classic moment of
the transvaluation" of the critique of industrialism. WM was also
unique in that he brought together socialist theory and the needs of
the working class.

52 WILSON, HARRISON, and HOEVELER, DIANE. "WM." In English Prose
    and Criticism in the Nineteenth Century: A Guide to Information
    Services. Detroit: Gale Research Co., pp. 205-15.
        Divided into six sections; the first, "Principal Prose
Works," lists only eight, and the fifth, "Critical Studies,"
includes only fifty-four articles and books whose short annotations
are sometimes misleading. All of the titles are included in the
present book.

53 WOLFSHOHL, CLARENCE. "WM's Wood: The Victorian World vs. the
    Mythic Eternities." Mythlore 6, no. 3 (Summer):29-32.
        Paraphrases Wood, labeling its hero, Walter, a "classic
Everyman." Speaks also of Walter's "entry into a sexual wilderness
paradise," where he encounters the Mistress Experience and the
Maiden Innocence, and of what happens then, what it all signifies.

54 WRIGHT. A.W. G.D.H. Cole and Socialist Democracy. Oxford:
    Clarendon Press, passim.
        Discusses the considerable influence WM's writings,
especially Nowhere, had on Cole, who often said that "It was Morris
who made me a socialist." It is suggested here that Cole "rescued"
WM; if he was the "grand diagnostician of alienation" as described
by E.P. Thompson (1955.15), then Cole carried forward that
diagnosis, notably in his advocacy of guild socialism.

55 "Morris, William: English Poet, Artist, Manufacturer,
    Socialist." In Guide to Literary Manuscripts in the Huntington
    Library. San Marino, Calif.: Huntington Library, pp. 331-33.
        Lists the WM materials in the archives of the Huntington
Library, where there are over seventy letters and documents and
forty-six holographs of his poetry and prose.

56 WM: 1834-1896, Personlichkeit und Werk. Catalogue of an
    Exhibition 23 May-12 August 1979 at the Bellerive Museum.
    Zurich: Kunstgewerbemuseum, 76 pp.
        Introduction includes biographical facts and selections from
WM's letter to Scheu and from scholars like Lewis F. Day and
Nikolaus Pevsner. Has thirteen plates and short descriptions of the
ninety items exhibited.

57 Morris and Company. Catalogue of an Exhibition at the Fine Arts
    Society, 24 April-18 May. London: Fine Arts Society, 56 pp.
        Introductory essays by Gere (1979.12) and Crook (1979.5)
    precede descriptions of exhibited items which are arranged under
    categories like "furniture" and "metal work" and "paintings and
    drawings." Includes forty-eight photographs and six color plates.

                                1980

1   ABSE, JOAN. John Ruskin: The Passionate Moralist. London:
    Quartet Books, pp. 305-6, passim.
        Discusses WM's famed estimation of "The Nature of Gothic,"
    judging that he was "mistaken only in limiting its significance to
    his own time." Calls WM Ruskin's greatest disciple and comments on
    the possible influence WM's lecture, "Art Under a Plutocracy," might
    have had on Ruskin, especially upon his 1884 lecture, "The Storm
    Cloud of the Nineteenth Century."

2   ADAM, STEPHEN. Decorative Stained Glass. London: Academy; New
    York: Rizzoli, pp. 2, 4, 5, 12.
        Points out that Morris and Co., with so many leading artists
    engaged in window designs, "put England in a leading position in the
    stained glass world for some thirty years." Includes color
    reproductions of four Morris and Co. windows, three from Burne-Jones
    designs, one by WM.

3   ANDERSON, PERRY. "Utopias." In Arguments within English
    Marxism. London: New Left Books, 157-75, passim.
        An important critique and reappraisal of E.P. Thompson's
    study of WM (1955.15) and of the postscript to its second edition
    (1976.50), one which raises questions about his handling of both
    Paul Meier and Miguel Abensour, and also his reading of Nowhere.
    Makes original points about the historical conditions that informed
    WM's Utopianism: since WM was not only born with the "highest gifts"
    of an artist but also "may have been among the 250 richest men in
    England," he was entirely "exempt from the deforming pressures of
    scarcity" and thus bound to envision a unique form for a perfect
    society. His Nowhere "generally involves a consistent repression of
    the history of capitalism," and thus a rejection of "technology,
    science, schools, novels, history, travel, feminism." Nowhere has
    affinities with Adorno's Minima Moralia and Marcuse's Eros and
    Civilization, books that also suggest a "calculated rejection of the
    Promethean motifs in Marx." Registers astonishment that E.P.
    Thompson did not deal more fully with WM as an important socialist
    strategist, for "what we witness in Morris's political writings is
    the first frontal engagement with reformism in the history of
    Marxism," and WM's prescience with regard to socialist developments
    in Britain, even in Chile, is remarkable (an analysis of "How the
    Change Came" in Nowhere is offered as proof). Suggests that E.P.

Thompson too often ignored WM the strategist in favor of WM the moralist.

4   ASLET, CLIVE, and BINNEY, MARCUS. "Where WM does not Rule."
     Country Life 167, no. 4314 (13 March):759.
          Wonders how WM might have reacted to a scheme to modernize a
seventeenth-century, timber-framed building, presently "The Hoop and
Grapes" in Aldgate High Street.

5   BAISSUS, J.M. "Victorian Semiotics: WM's Tapestries and
     Printing as Experiments in Multiple Communication." Cahiers
     Victoriens and Edouardiens 11 (April):19-43.
          Offers semiotic decodings of several of WM's works, starting
with the membership card he designed for the Hammersmith Socialist
Society, regarded here as a "poetic object." Messages are unraveled
from the following tapestries: the Woodpecker (1885), Pomona (1885),
Flora (1885), the Forest (1887) and the Orchard (1890); these are
discussed in terms of dialogues set up with the semantic messages in
the texts on each tapestry. The embroidered canopy on WM's
Kelmscott Manor bed is interpreted through similar "systems"--these
borrowed from R. Barthes; the entire bed is thus seen as a text, "a
mysterious meeting place where life, death, pleasure and suffering
are fused together." Concludes with equally provocative comments on
Kelmscott Press books where the text itself is said to carry only a
"fraction" of the message. Includes ten plates, all of which are
referred to within the exposition.

6   BAISSUS, J.M. WM: Poete. 3 vols., Paris: Librarie Honore
     Champion, 1,643 pp.
          Points out that even May Morris, in her two-volume supplement
(1936.9) to the Collected Works made few claims for WM as poet, but
his fame during the nineteenth century rested on his poetry; he was
considered for the Laureateship, and he himself admitted to being a
"poet," and "pretty well known," in the famed episode with the
magistrate. This ambitious study attempts to reclaim WM's identity
as a poet, to prove that he is as significant as Rossetti, that his
poetry can yield new insights into all his various achievements, and
that it deserves and demands our careful scrutiny. Using modern
critics like Jakobsen, de Saussure, Levi-Strauss, and Propp, careful
attention is given to a wide range of WM's poems and to their
phonological, syntactic, and narrative structures. The lyric poems
written after Paradise, and then after Sigurd, poems often ignored
by critics, who usually move directly from Defence to the longer
narratives, are here given very close readings. So too are prose
romances like Wolfings, whose "speech acts" are discussed. Includes
graphs, tables, appendixes that reprint short poems from three
different periods of WM's life, and a forty-page bibliography.

7   BOOS, FLORENCE. "Dislocation of Personal Identity in Narratives
    of WM." JPRS 1, no. 1:1-13.
        Compares ways that WM used narrative strategies in the early
    prose tale, "A Dream," and within the frame of Paradise and one of
    its tales, "Ogier the Dane," attempting thus to illustrate WM's
    poetic development up to 1870. Discusses the narrative strategies
    under thirteen specific categories, ranging from "Use of multiple
    narrators" to "Ideal union with the beloved in death."

8   BRADY, DARLENE, and SERBAN, WILLIAM. Stained Glass: A Guide to
    Information. Detroit: Gale Research Co., passim.
        Has thirty-five references, most of them with helpful
    annotations, to studies of Morris and Co. stained glass, all of
    which are included in the present book.

9   BREWER, ELIZABETH. "WM and the 'Kingsley Movement.'" JWMS 4,
    no. 2 (Summer):4-17.
        In 1883 WM said he read the novels of Charles Kingsley while
    at Oxford thirty years before, getting "into my head therefrom some
    socio-political ideas." Surveys the major themes of novels like The
    Saint's Tragedy, Yeast, Alton Locke, and Hypatia, and many parallels
    to prevailing ideas and arguments in WM's socialist lectures are set
    forth and carefully discussed.

10 BULLA, GUIDO, trans. Un sogno di John Ball. Cosenza: Edizione
    Lerici, 144 pp.
        Introduction includes a biographical sketch and a review of
    the fourteenth-century conditions that spawned the Peasants'
    Rebellion; an appendix has the chapters from Froissart, also
    translated into Italian, that cover the Rebellion.

11 BULLA, GUIDO. WM fra arte e rivoluzione. Cassino: Editrice
    Garigliano, 356 pp.
        This biography provides a chronological sketch of WM's life
    and works up through 1883, in part 1, and then moves into much
    fuller treatment of the socialist years and of WM's work with the
    Free Speech Movement and as the editor of Commonweal. The third and
    final part touches upon all of WM's writings during the 1880s and
    1890s, with full commentary on WM's negative reactions to Bellamy
    and a useful discussion of Nowhere. Includes detailed notes and a
    selective bibliography.

12 COHN, JAN. "WM and the Paris Prefecture." JWMS 4, no. 2
    (Summer):20-23.
        The co-founder of the French Communist party, Paul Lafargue,
    had a large police file, and in it were references to a "William
    Morice" (also "Maurice" and "Morrin"), all of whom were actually WM,
    made somewhat sinister by the misspellings and by the paranoia of
    the Parisian police.

13 COMINO, MARY. Gimson and the Barnsleys: "Wonderful Furniture of
    a Commonplace Kind." London: Evans Brothers; New York: Van
    Nostrand, pp. 20-28, passim.
        WM met Ernest Gimson in 1884 and helped him get employment in
    the offices of J.D. Sedding; Gimson joined SPAB in 1889, became a
    lifelong friend of Cockerell, built cottages for May Morris and
    designed the Hall at Kelmscott, and most importantly tried to remain
    faithful to the design ideals of WM throughout his long
    collaboration with the Barnsleys as a builder of fine furniture.

14 DAVEY, PETER. "The Prophet." In Architecture of the Arts and
    Crafts Movement. London: Architectural Press; New York:
    Rizzoli, pp. 21-29, passim.
        Though WM left Street's offices, thus never becoming an
    architect, he had firm ideas about the importance of architecture;
    these were shaped by Ruskin, and WM in turn influenced a whole
    generation of architects, any one of whom could have written a
    manifesto using only lines gleaned from WM's lectures. Points out
    that WM's vision of the town as it could be was as influential as
    his ideas about architecture, because that vision was used by garden
    city planners.

15 DUNLAP, JOSEPH R. "The Infernal Triangle" Independent Shavian
    18:35.
        Note accompanying photograph of Shaw, Walker, May Morris, and
    Sparling, one which might be titled, "Two Geniuses, the Lady and the
    Other," comments upon the diverse and talented figures surrounding
    WM at Kelmscott Press and also upon the attraction between Shaw and
    May Morris.

16 ERZGRABER, WILLI. Utopie und Anti-Utopie in der englischen
    Literatur. Munich: Wilhelm Fink, pp. 59-95, passim.
        In this university text on British Utopian fiction, one of
    the "Litteraturstudium" series, Nowhere is seen as part of a
    tradition beginning with More's Utopia and ending with Orwell's
    1984. A biographical sketch precedes an analytical discussion of
    Nowhere. Problems of the narrator, the frame, and the function of
    dreams and natural imagery and dialogue, are all succinctly set
    forth, as are basic questions regarding private property, the law,

the ethos of the community, etc. Discusses in some detail WM's
explanations of the three phases of the revolution.

17 FAULKNER, PETER. Against the Age: An Introduction to WM.
    London: Allen and Unwin, 204 pp.
        This trenchant introduction to WM, his times, his work, and
his continuing significance stresses throughout why WM, in his
poetry and prose, in his design work, in his lectures on behalf of
social change, remained "against the age," and also why his
achievements and example remain relevant: "As long as our industrial
society continues to perplex with such problems as pollution,
delinquency, commercial acquisitiveness and violence, so long will
we stand in need of Morris's vision of a society of equals in which
every man and woman finds proper fulfillment." Includes fresh and
useful commentary upon Defence poems, upon Jason and Nowhere, and
upon works often ignored, like the classical translations and Love
Is Enough; employs to good effect contemporary responses and
critical reviews.

18 FOWLES, JOHN. Introduction to After London, by Richard
    Jeffries. London: Oxford University Press, pp. viii-ix.
        Reflects upon WM's reaction to After London: "absurd hopes
curled around my heart as I read it." Asserts that three books,
Erewhon, After London, and Nowhere, "stand in a class of their own
as witnesses, through fantasy, to the central terror of their age:
the spectre of determinism."

19 FREEMAN, RONALD E., ed. "WM." In Bibliographies of Studies in
    Victorian Literature for the Ten Years 1965-1974. Urbana,
    Chicago, and London: University of Illinois Press, passim.
        A reprinting of the annual bibliographies from VS, a sequel
to 1945.6, 1956.18, and 1967.24, lists dozens of studies of WM; with
the exception of the reviews, all are included in the present book.

20 GRIBBEN, ALAN. Mark Twain's Library: A Reconstruction. Boston:
    G.K. Hall, pp. 486-87.
        Paradise and "Pygmalion and the Image" were in Mark Twain's
library and he evidently had purchased Sigurd. Furthermore, Howells
said that Mark Twain had "fiercely reveled" in certain lines from
"Shameful Death," lines dealing with revenge.

21 HARBISON, ROBERT. <u>Deliberate</u> <u>Regression</u>. New York: Knopf, pp.
     102-8, passim.
        Eclectic history of romantic individualism has insights into
significance of Red House design, of "slumbrous leaves" in the flat
designs corresponding to the "multipication of faceless densities"
in the prose romances. The Woodpecker Tapestry suggests a
"self-constraint remote from naturalism."

22 HARRISON, MARTIN. "The Secular Reaction: WM, Burne-Jones, and
     their Followers." In <u>Victorian</u> <u>Stained</u> <u>Glass</u>. London: Barrie
     and Jenkins, pp. 39-50, passim.
        Because books like Pevsner's <u>Buildings</u> <u>of</u> <u>England</u> singled out
Morris and Co. glass for praise, other Victorian stained glass has
not been properly assessed. This survey indicates where further
work needs doing, stressing those artists and firms that attempted
innovations. Attempts, also, "to make clear that Morris, and more
especially Burne-Jones, began consciously to reject the Gothic
revival, and in doing so founded an original nineteenth-century
manner," one that led to changes in color and design, if not in
technique. Discusses Rossetti, Burne-Jones, Webb, and WM designs
and collaborations with architects like Bodley, as well as WM's
refusal to deal with restorationists. Quotes from a letter to
George Howard regarding problems with borax, and includes an
appendix with a gazeteer of Victorian stained-glass studios, and a
list of several Morris and Co. windows that "have come to light"
since the publication of Sewter's study (1974.25).

23 HESKETT, JOHN. <u>Industrial</u> <u>Design</u>. London: Thames and Hudson;
     New York: Oxford University Press, pp. 85-87.
        Notes the wide influence of WM's ideas upon craft workshops
and upon the ideals and works of designers like Henry van de Velde
in Brussels at the turn of the century.

24 JANN, ROSEMARY. "Democratic Myths in Victorian Medievalism."
     <u>Browning</u> <u>Institute</u> <u>Studies</u> 8:129-49.
        Points out that descriptions of the dominant tradition of
Victorian medievalism, that of the nostalgic, aristocratic Tory,
have unfortunately overshadowed two other important traditions: the
Whig's which saw its own progressive policies in the events that led
to the Magna Carta, and the like; and the Socialist's which had
enlisted WM as a banner carrier, "among the ranks," as he himself
put it, "of those who are pledged to the forward movement of modern
life," and seek basic, radical changes in society, sometimes using
medieval examples as models and as inspiration.

25 KIRCHHOFF, FREDERICK. "The Aesthetic Discipline of Paradise."
    VP 18, no. 3 (Autumn):229-40.
        Examines changes WM made in Paradise prologue after 1865,
changes which suggest a "major clarification of his aims and
identity as a poet." Since "the wanderers were no longer merely
adventurers; they were now also poets," their quests became
interwoven with narrative and aesthetic problems that both they and
their creator had to face. By rejecting certain assumptions of the
romance poets regarding art and reality, and the dialectic between a
teller and his tale, WM was able to forge a new aesthetic.

26 KIRCHHOFF, FREDERICK. "WM's 'Land East of the Sun and West of
    the Moon.'" Pre-Raphaelite Review 3, no. 2 (May):14-24.
        Discusses complexities of observer-poet-protagonist sequence
of narration in the poem, concluding that WM's "texts anticipate
precisely those critical approaches that question the autonomy of
the text: psychological analysis and reader-response criticism."

27 LAMBOURNE, LIONEL. "The Earthly Paradox of WM." In Utopian
    Craftsmen: The Arts and Crafts Movement from the Cotswalds to
    Chicago. London: Astragal Books; Salt Lake City: Peregrine
    Smith, pp. 17-34, passim.
        Discusses the influence of Ruskin and WM upon the Arts and
Crafts Movement and upon the achievements of dozens of craftsmen.
Surveys the lives of some of these craftsmen, from Gimson to
Dolmetsch, and, in America, from Hubbard and Tiffany to Bradley and
Wright. The many illustrations and photographs are perhaps more
valuable than the sometimes skimpy surveys.

28 LONGFORD, ELIZABETH. A Pilgrimage of Passion: The Life of
    Wilfrid Scawen Blunt. London: Weidenfeld and Nicolson; New York:
    Knopf, pp. 278-79, passim.
        Repeats Blunt's impresssions of WM as a "hard-working
cheerful Welshman." Stresses WM's influence on Blunt's attitudes
toward both politics and religion--supposedly deflating them. But
the focus here is on Blunt's affair with Janey, and therefore
comments about WM are held up for us to enhance that perspective;
this does yield some fresh insights. Concludes with the puzzling
assertion that if "Blunt was anyone's disciple, he was WM's."

29 LYNN, CATHERINE. Wallpapers in America: From the Seventeenth
    Century to World War One. New York: W.W. Norton, pp. 382-84,
    passim.
        Discusses the importance of the Centennial Exhibition in
Philadelphia in 1876, the ways it served to publicize Morris and Co.
products, making WM "the most powerful and appealing spokesman for
the English Arts and Crafts Movement." Several WM designs are
discussed in detail.

30 MAC CORMICK, JUDITH KAY. "Biography and the Pattern of
    Regeneration in the Late Romances of WM." Dissertation, Kansas
    State University.
        Abstracted: DAI 41:2124-A.

31 MANGUEL, ALBERTO, and GUADALUPI, GIANNI. The Dictionary of
    Imaginary Places. New York: Macmillan, passim.
        Place-name dictionary includes short descriptions of a few
    places from Paradise, like "Forest Island," and a dozen places from
    five of the prose romances. Why only these places were chosen from
    the hundreds possible in WM's poetry and prose is nowhere explained
    (nor is Nowhere described, though there is an essay on "Utopia").

32 MANNING, ELFRIDA. "A Visit to May Morris, 1925." JWMS 4, no. 2
    (Summer):18-19.
        Reprints diary notes made in 1925 when the author and her
    parents (her father was the sculptor, Sir Hamo Thornycraft) visited
    Kelmscott Manor. These notes include descriptions of embroideries
    by May Morris.

33 MELADA, IVAN. "WM's Entry into Public Life." Studies in the
    Humanities 8, no. 1 (June):38-40.
        Reviews backgrounds of the Eastern Question and the British
    government's real reasons for planning to intervene, reasons that WM
    neatly exposed in an 1876 letter to the Daily News. Quotes from
    this and also from "To the Working Men of England," published the
    following May, commenting on WM's skillful and impassioned rhetoric.
    Concludes that the controversy not only gave to the English language
    "jingoism," but to the British left a great political activist: WM.

34 MOERAN, BRIAN. "Yanagi, WM, and Popular Art." Ceramic Review
    66:25-26.
        Compares the theories of Yanagi (founder in the 1920s of the
    Japanese Folkcraft Movement) to those of WM, pointing out that other
    parallels (preaching the beauty of the functional, the return to
    natural and communal production) suggest that "the whole idea of a
    popular art will only originate in highly urbanized and centralized
    societies."

35 MOORE, JOHN DAVID. "The Vision of the Feminine in WM's Water."
    Pre-Raphaelite Review 3, no. 2 (May):58-65.
        Argues that WM's portrayal of Birdalone in Water "testifies
    to his fascination with the feminine side of the human psyche" and
    also to his positive attitude toward women generally, which was in
    contradistinction to that of contemporaries like Rossetti and
    Swinburne, who often "paid homage to the fatal woman."

36 PAGE, MARIAN. "WM, 1834-1896." Furniture Designed by
    Architects. London: Architectural Press; New York: Whitney
    Library of Design, pp. 54-61, passim.
        Describes Red House decorations and Morris and Co.
achievements, but stresses that it was WM's "ideas that inspired the
Arts and Crafts theme that was inherited by many architects who
might never have designed furniture for their buildings if it had
not been for his example." They discarded his medievalism, but
embraced the idea of "good citizen's furniture, solid and well-made
and workmanlike." Includes illustrations.

37 POSTON, LAWRENCE. "Three Versions of Victorian Pastoral."
    Genre 13, no. 3 (Fall):305-35.
        Comments upon the use of pastoral traditions in Alexander
Smith's Dreamthorp, Nowhere, and Gissing's The Private Papers of
Henry Ryecroft. Finds similarities in the three works: in their
blending of author-narrator, in their use of "Nature" to underline a
message, and in their use of a Virgilian tradition that employs the
pastoral as both an escape from the urban and a "projection of the
imagination."

38 ROBINSON, DUNCAN, and WILDMAN, STEPHEN. Morris and Company in
    Cambridge. Catalogue of an Exhibition at the Fitzwilliam.
    Cambridge: Cambridge University Press, 113 pp.
        Suggests that works in this exhibition can help one
understand both the growth of Morris and Co. and of Cambridge, if
seen in the context of the Gothic Revival. The catalogue has
sections on the Pre-Raphaelites, on work Morris and Co. did in
Cambridge (through contracts awarded by G.F. Bodley), on Morris and
Co. artifacts now in the Fitzwilliam, and on Kelmscott Press books.
These books and the other artifacts ended up at the Fitzwilliam
because Cockerell, the one-time secretary of Kelmscott Press and
friend of the Morrises, became its curator. Many photographs and
illustrations are keyed to full introductions and detailed
descriptions of the 181 items exhibited.

39 SAMUEL, RAPHAEL. "British Marxist Historians, 1880-1980." New
    Left Review 120:21-96.
        A section on "Marxist Medievalism" discusses Socialism, Its
Growth and Outcome, pointing out that the book has three chapters on
the Middle Ages and four paragraphs on the Puritan revolution; and
it, like John Ball, first appeared serially in Commonweal and helped
to popularize ideas about the Middle Ages as a mecca for workers and
artisans. Discusses the historical writings of E.P. Thompson and,
briefly, his work on WM.

40 SHARRATT, BERNARD. "Nowhere: Detail and Desire." In Reading
    the Victorian Novel: Detail into Form. Edited by Ian Gregor.
    London: Vision; New York: Barnes and Noble, pp. 288-305.
         Since Nowhere "seems to straddle and implicitly challenge our
    current critical categories" (it is neither realistic fiction nor
    socialist tract), and since it has within it pejorative comments on
    nineteenth-century novels, as well as straightforward socialist
    propaganda, it must be read as WM's attempt to "undermine and
    modify" certain fictional conventions, using them to underline his
    social and political points. Such an attempt reminds us of his
    mastery of the conventions of other arts and crafts. That Guest and
    Ellen do not get together at the end disappoints readers used to
    naive romances, but it might encourage them to think of changing
    their own society. Concludes by linking WM to Brecht who also, but
    more successfully, created a "political propagandist art, aware of
    its own devices, its own artifiality, and which took as its material
    not only the political dilemmas of its day but also the popular and
    dominant forms of art, precisely to undermine them."

41 SHAW, W. DAVID. "Browning and Pre-Raphaelite Medievalism."
    Browning Institute Studies 8:73-83
         Compares Browning's techniques to those used by WM in "The
    Chapel in Lyoness," where details that contradict each other are
    here seen as part of a dramatic plan, where each stanza is like a
    frame in "a slow-motion movie."

42 SHIPPEY, TOM. Introduction to "Wood" by WM. Oxford: Oxford
    University Press, pp. v-xix.
         Asserts that "WM's last decade has long been a disappointment
    to his biographers," partly because they do not know what to make of
    the dreamy prose romances he wrote during those years. Suggests
    that "he wanted to reproduce for others the sensations that saga and
    romance had aroused in him," that these tales are like Burne-Jones
    paintings, sharply focused and full of minute detail, but "set in a
    narrative blank." Their ahistorical ambiguities are part of their
    charm.

43 STRONG, ROY. "WM, 1834-1896." In A Book of Verse by WM.
    London: Scolar Press, 1 p. Reprinted. 1981.
         Mentions the importance of Georgie Burne-Jones to WM,
    especially during the period in the late 1860s when he wrote and
    copied out these poems for her. A second introduction, Whalley
    (1980.48), has more information about the original text for this
    fine facsimile edition, which also includes three black and white
    photographs and a sample of WM's handwriting.

44 SUSSMAN, HERBERT. "The Pre-Raphaelites and the Mood of the
    Cloister." Browning Institute Studies 8:45-55.
        Compares WM's poems, "King Arthur's Tomb" and "The Blue
Closet," to Rossetti's watercolors with the same titles, pointing
out how distant both are from Malory, especially in ways they
portray distraught females; such images of the cloister suggest the
"repression and consequent distortion of Eros in nineteenth-century
society."

45 THOMPSON, F.P. Tapestry: Mirror of History. New York: Crown
    Publishers, pp. 154-62, passim.
        WM visited French and British tapestry works before setting
up a loom near his bed and teaching himself how to weave, and he
made scathing remarks about those other works, especially about
Gobelin's workshop in France. Such criticism encouraged debate
which, along with WM's reputation, caused his ideas about tapestries
to spread. Discusses such ideas, like his insistence on a high-warp
loom and frontal lighting, as well as several of the tapestries from
among the more than sixty sets of hangings or panels completed at
Merton Abbey between 1881 and 1927.

46 TIMO, HELEN. "A Church without God: WM's 'A Night in a
    Cathedral.'" JWMS 4, no. 2 (Summer):24-31.
        Although neither Mackail (1899.10) nor May Morris attribute
the Oxford and Cambridge Magazine tale, "A Night in a Cathedral," to
WM, there are several compelling correspondences between the
frightened narrator and the youthful WM, who had just visited French
cathedrals and also undergone a loss of religious faith.

47 WEEKS, JOHN, ed. "'The Two Partings' by WM." In The Dream
    Weavers: Tales of Fantasy by the Pre-Raphaelites. Santa Barbara,
    Calif.: Woodbridge Press, pp. 7-12, 69-78.
        WM'S "The Two Partings," written in 1856, is included in this
anthology of Pre-Raphaelite fiction, and is said to exhibit
"presciently and therefore poignantly his sexual fatalism."

48 WHALLEY, JOYCE IRENE. "WM: A Book of Verse 1870." In A Book of
    Verse by WM. London: Scolar Press, 3 pp. Reprinted. 1981.
        Discusses WM's interests in manuscript illumination and his
methods of work for this "painted book," for which he composed all
but two of the verses, and which he gave to Georgie Burne-Jones in
1870. The original of this beautifully produced facsimile was
purchased by the Victoria and Albert in 1952 at the sale of the
library of Mrs. Mackail, Georgie Burne-Jones's daughter.

49 WILDING, MICHAEL. "Nowhere." In Political Fictions. London:
    Routledge and Kegan Paul, pp. 48-90.
        Discusses relationships between narrative structures and the
    content and political significance of Nowhere in ways that are
    provocative: there is no "conclusion" to Nowhere because a future
    society will be "open", and in ways that are useful: Nowhere has
    none of the trappings of the bourgeois world, hence none from its
    fiction (wills, law-suits, a hero rising in the world). This is
    because WM's "aesthetics are not separated from his social
    vision--so in essence he is one of the first sociologists of
    literature." Judges, however, that WM's nineteenth-century habits
    of thought seem apparent in associations of sadness and sexuality.

50 WILLIAMS, RAYMOND. "Utopia and Science Fiction." In Problems
    in Materialism and Culture: Selected Essays. London: New Left
    Books, pp. 196-212.
        Reprint of 1978.64.

51 A Collector's Choice: The John J. Walsdorf Collection of WM in
    Private Press and Limited Editions. Catalogue of the Exhibition
    held at George Washington University, 26 November 1979-15
    February 1980. Washington, D. C.: George Washington University
    Press, 62 pp.
        Short descriptions of each of the 118 items exhibited, which
    ranged from WM letters and small press publications to Kelmscott
    Press editions. Blackwell recalls, in an introduction, instances of
    May Morris's devotion to her father.

52 WM in Private Press and Limited Edition. Catalogue of an
    Exhibition of the John J. Walsdorf Collection at the General
    Library of the University of Missouri-Kansas City, 14
    September-9 October. Kansas City: University of Missouri, 70
    pp.
        Has descriptions of 132 items ranging from autograph letters
    and Kelmscott Press editions to WM titles published at small presses
    in America and Britain. This is a slightly longer version of an
    earlier Walsdorf exhibition catalogue: 1980.51.

1981

1   ACHESON, JOSEPH. "'An Artist of Reputation': Rossetti and
    Kelmscott." In WM and Kelmscott. London: Design Council, pp.
    25-40.
        Summarizes Rossetti's early influence on WM and his
    contributions to Morris and Co. The importance to Rossetti of Janey
    as subject and inspiration for both his poems and paintings, from
    1871 to 1874, is treated here in some detail, and so is the period
    of "Rossetti's decline." Includes several illustrations and full notes.

2   BAKER, LARRY. "The Socialism of WM." In <u>WM</u> <u>and</u> <u>Kelmscott</u>.
     London: Design Council, pp. 93-95.
         Compares entries on WM in 1910 and 1978 editions of the
<u>Encyclopedia</u> <u>Britannica</u> to discuss changing attitudes toward his
efforts to achieve a socialist revolution. Suggests that <u>Nowhere</u> is
the "least utopian of all idylls of that name," touching upon
examples of political theory demonstrated therein.

3   BAKER, PATRICIA L. "WM and His Interest in the Orient." In <u>WM</u>
     <u>and</u> <u>Kelmscott</u>. London: Design Council, pp. 67-70.
         WM'S interests in Near Eastern decorative techniques and
designs were shared by others, like Frederic Leighton. Such
interests were reflected in an 1862 exhibit of Persian wares at the
South Kensington, whose holdings in Near Eastern art were extensive.
WM became an examiner there in 1876 and "revelled" in their Islamic
textiles; he was an acknowledged expert on them, and their flat
patterns and rich geometrical order influenced all his design work.

4   BARKER, THOMAS T. "The Shadow on the Tapestry: Irony in WM's
     <u>Paradise</u>." JPRS 2, no. 1:111-26.
         Surveys the major critical responses to <u>Paradise</u>, which is
usually labeled "escapist." Suggests that WM has, however,
"alienated the reader from escapist attitudes" by revealing how they
always lead to death. Discusses Rolf as the "primary proto-reader,"
and compares the poem to Spenser's <u>Fairie</u> <u>Queen</u>.

5   BATTISCOMBE, GEORGIANA. <u>Christina</u> <u>Rossetti</u>: <u>A</u> <u>Divided</u> <u>Life</u>.
     New York: Holt, Rinehart and Winston, pp. 84, 110. Passim.
         Includes some fresh anecdotes about WM: Rossetti borrowed the
phrase "prudent crocodile" from one of his sister's poems to apply
it to WM. We learn also that WM was not impressed witn Christina
Rossetti's wallpaper designs and that Christina had a high regard
for Janey.

6   BENNETT, JAMES R. "Plot Repetition: Theme and Variation in
     Narrative Macro Episodes." <u>Papers</u> <u>on</u> <u>Language</u> <u>and</u> <u>Literature</u>
     17, no. 4 (Fall):416-17.
         Embedded within a theoretical essay on plot structure in
various novels occurs commentary on <u>Water</u>, here called a "tour de
force of binary macro-episodic structure," which is defined as a
dual "geographical and psychical quest by the heroine."

7   BENSUSAN, GEOFFREY. "Twenty Years of the Journal." JWMS 4, no.
    4 (Winter):23-26.
        Lists all articles that have appeared in JWMS in the fifteen
issues published between 1961 and 1981. The compiler wonders if the
articles in those issues are "paying sufficient attention to social
consequences; more particularly in relation to the inadequacies, not
to say disasters, of our designed environment."

8   BOOS, FLORENCE, ed. WM's Socialist Diary. Iowa City: Windhover
    Press; London: WM Society, 46 pp.
        Though long excerpts appeared in Mackail (1899.10) and in
E.P. Thompson (1955.15), the diary WM kept concerning his socialist
work from January to April 1887 had never been published in its
entirety. This handsome, limited edition remedies that; it includes
a helpful short preface that sets WM's intense work for the
socialist cause during these few months within the larger context of
his political activities and writings. Reprinted, with full
introduction and extensive notes: 1982.7.

9   BORIS, EILEEN. "Art and Labor: John Ruskin, WM, and the
    Craftsman Ideal in America, 1876-1915." Dissertation, Brown
    University.
        Abstracted: DAI 43:488-A.

10 BOSOMWORTH, DOROTHY D. "Traditional Furniture and Personal
    Items from Kelmscott Manor." In WM and Kelmscott. London:
    Design Council, pp. 83-85.
        Discusses the difficulties in selecting items to exhibit from
the amalgam of furniture in Kelmscott Manor; all that the
furnishings have in common is their eclecticism and a richness in
design and texture. A few items, like WM's great bed, were present
when he lived there, but most were added later, and they reflect
both the tastes of May Morris and various recent efforts to include
Morris and Co. items. Final effect of the Manor's furnishings is
said to be "peaceful."

11 BRANDON-JONES, JOHN. "The Importance of Philip Webb." In WM
    and Kelmscott. London: Design Council, pp. 87-92.
        Traces Webb's involvement with WM from the designs for Red
House to those for the Kelmscott churchyard gravestone under which
all the Morrises now rest. Webb's grasp of practical matters was
important for the success of Morris and Co. as well as for SPAB.
Discusses many of his designs; includes letters that Janey wrote to
Webb about Kelmscott Manor improvements.

12 BRIGGS, ASA. "The Appeal of WM." In WM and Kelmscott. London:
    Design Council, pp. 17-23.
        For WM, "socialism came as a personal fulfillment as well as
    a conversion," and his ardent commitment to it and against the cant
    and complacency of his time help account for the contemporary
    relevance of his work. Comments upon WM's debt to thinkers like
    Ruskin and Marx, but suggests that he had more concern than either
    of them for the environments people must live within, hence his
    greater appeal today.

13 CLARK, DAVID. "Yeats' Dragons: The Sources of 'Michael Robartes
    and the Dancer' and 'Her Triumph' as Shown in the Manuscripts."
    Malahat Review 57 (January):35-88.
        Argues that the source for Yeats's imagery of dragon rings
    and sea birds in "Her Triumph" is within lines from WM's "The Doom
    of King Acrisius."

14 CROOK, J. MORDAUNT. William Burges and the High Victorian
    Dream. Chicago: University of Chicago Press, pp. 27-34, passim.
        Since Burges had responded to many of the same pressures and
    thinkers, like Pugin and Ruskin, who influenced WM, many useful
    parallels are drawn within discussions of the Neo-Gothic, of church
    restoration, of the use of medieval patterns for furniture
    decoration, and the like.

15 DUFTY, A.R. "Kelmscott" In WM and Kelmscott. London: Design
    Council, pp. 11-15.
        Describes Kelmscott Manor and the history of its occupancy
    from 1571 to 1896, when WM--its most famous tenant--died. May
    Morris left the house and some of its effects to Oxford University
    from which the Society of Antiquaries obtained it; in the 1960s the
    Society carried out much-needed restorations; these and some of the
    household furnishings are here described. Uses passages from
    Nowhere to suggest WM's love for this country house, once again
    solid and firm, still tranquil, "still hung with old tapestry."

16 DURANT, STUART. "WM and Victorian Decorative Art." In WM and
    Kelmscott. London: Design Council, pp. 63-66.
        Places WM's work within a tradition of Victorian designers
    who had attempted to "revitalize decorative art," drawing examples
    from Pugin, Owen Jones, and Ruskin and pointing out that they all
    advised designers to follow both nature and tradition, just as did
    WM in his lectures.

17 FAIRCLOUGH, OLIVER, and LEARY, EMMALINE. Textiles by WM and
    Morris and Company, 1861-1940. Catalogue of 13 March-3 May
    Exhibition at Birmingham. London: Thames and Hudson, 120 pp.
        "An introduction to, and a concise summary of, the textiles
    designed by WM and others for Morris and Co. between 1861 and 1940.
    This study arose from, and records, the largest exhibition on the
    subject yet organized." Judges 1875-81 to be the most important
    years in the Firm's history, for it was then that WM designed the
    profitable chintzes, which in effect subsidized the very expensive
    hand-made tapestries and carpets. Discusses the work of J.H.
    Dearle, rarely--especially after WM's death--more "than a pastiche
    of his master's," the work of H.C. Marillier, and the prestigious
    commissions done for the thrones used at the 1911 coronation.
    Subsequent work, until the Firm's closing in May 1940, "went down a
    creative blind alley." WM's work with embroideries, and his use of
    natural forms and colors, also discussed in some detail.

18 FAULKNER, PETER. "W.S. Blunt's First Visit to Kelmscott
    Manor." N and Q, n.s., 28, no. 5 (October):422-24.
        Material within the W.S. Blunt papers only recently made
    available indicates that he first visited Kelmscott Manor in 1888,
    when WM was not there, and not in 1889 as stated in his diaries:
    1919.1. The misrepresentation "seems to be to suggest the strength
    of the impression made upon him by WM, and to play down his
    relationship with Janey."

19 FAULKNER, PETER. Wilfrid Scawen Blunt and the Morrises.
    London: WM Society, 45 pp.
        A lecture-presentation (Pamela Faulkner read from the Janey
    selections at the original lecture) based on selections from the 145
    letters Janey sent to Blunt and on corresponding passages from his
    notebooks. These papers, recently made public, show that Janey had
    an affair with Blunt, but they also offer new insights into the
    character and personality of Janey, her relationship to her
    daughters (often difficult and strained) and to her husband.
    Suggests that WM had known about the earlier affair with Rossetti,
    and probably about this one also. But, apparently unperturbed, he
    always forged ahead with the work at hand.

20 FLEMING, MARGARET. "Where Janey Used to Live." JWMS 4, no. 4
    (Winter):2-17.
        Janey's refusal to allow an illustration of her Oxford home
    to appear in Mackail (1899.10) inspired the exhaustive research
    behind this article, which through descriptions of their domiciles
    and occupations suggests the poverty of the Burdens and, perhaps,
    reasons for Janey's attitude. Uses letters and diary entries
    written by those who were part of that Oxford menage in the 1850s to
    speculate, finally, that Janey probably "did marry Morris with
    reluctance and under pressure from her family."

21 GERLAGH, WIM. "Kunst en maatschappij: WM en de beginjaren van
    het Nederlandse socialisme" [WM and the beginnings of Dutch
    socialism]. Intermediair 17 (10 July):19-27.
        In Dutch. Points out that WM influenced Dutch socialists
    like Henri Polak and other Dutch artists and reformers (especially
    after the translation of Nowhere in 1894), and since his ideas about
    work, the environment, social inequality, etc., seem so pertinent
    today, he should be better known in Holland. The author sketches in
    the British cultural context that shaped WM's ideas, pointing to
    parallels in nineteenth-century Holland and mentioning the most
    important events and achievements in WM's career.

22 GIROUARD, MARK. The Return to Camelot: Chivalry and the English
    Gentleman. London and New Haven: Yale University Press, 188-93,
    passim.
        Early chapters in this study, with descriptions of the
    popularity of the Waverly novels, of The Broad Stone of Honour and
    The Heir of Redclyffe, cover the very works that WM read as a youth.
    Contrasts the "intensity of emotion" in Defence to the concern with
    morality in Tennyson's Idylls, and speculates upon real-life love
    triangles mirroring those WM found in Arthurian romance.

23 GRIBBLE, BARBARA. "To Grow to be a Hero: The Influence of
    Thomas Carlyle upon the Late Prose Romances of WM."
    Dissertation, University of Tennessee.
        Abstracted: DAI 42:4832-33-A.

24 HERALD, JACQUELINE. "On Designing Textiles With Birds." In WM
    and Kelmscott. London: Design Council, pp. 117-23.
        Even though WM could speak and write about birds with great
    ease, he had some difficulty portraying them in textiles. Discusses
    his studies of real birds, and his experiments with ancient dyes.
    Uses notebooks that WM kept when he was an examiner at the South
    Kensington Museum.

25 HERALD, JACQUELINE. "Textiles at Kelmscott, an Introduction."
    In WM and Kelmscott. London: Design Council, pp. 104-6.
        Though Kelmscott Manor textiles represent a very broad range
    of designs and techniques, for this particular exhibition only two
    aspects of WM's achievement with fabric design were chosen: his use
    of reds and blues, and of bird patterns. This choice was made
    because another recent exhibition was devoted entirely to WM
    textiles: 1981.17.

26 JANSEN, REAMY. "Introduction and Notes to 'Honesty is the Best
    Policy' by WM." Kairos 1, no. 1:86-105.
        The sketch, "Honesty is the Best Policy," that WM wrote for
    Commonweal in November 1887 is here reprinted, along with
    introduction and notes. The lighthearted, satirical dialogue
    between a poet and a capitalist takes place against a backdrop of
    strikes and Bloody Sunday rioting.

27 JUSSIM, ESTELLE. Slave to Beauty: The Eccentric Life and
    Controversial Career of F. Holland Day, Photographer, Publisher,
    Aesthete. Boston: Godine, pp. 53-56, 61-64.
        F. Holland Day, an American version of Oscar Wilde, was
    invited by WM, or so it says here, to come in with him on the
    Kelmscott Press venture; Day declined, but returned to Boston with
    WM's "craftsmanly ideals." In 1892, he began the Knight Errant, a
    magazine influenced by WM's ideas and designs.

28 KHOURI, NADIA. "The Clockwork and Eros: Models of Utopia in
    Edward Bellamy and WM." CLA Journal 24, no. 3 (March):376-99.
        Contrasts Looking Backward's "clockwork" society to Nowhere's
    "pastoral zero-growth" society and, despite "polyvalent" rhetoric,
    makes fresh points about Nowhere: the haymaking scene shows "an
    essential Utopian activity opposed to the compulsive drudgery of
    Victorian economy" and it is also a "parable for the carpe diem
    philosophy: seize the opportunity, not of profit but of life."

29 KIRKHAM, PAT. "WM's Early Furniture." JWMS 4, no. 3
    (Spring):25-28.
        Henry Price, furniture maker, recorded in his diary his
    recollections of a "gentleman who in after years became a noted
    socialist" and who ordered "some very old fashioned Furniture in the
    Mideavel style." This must certainly be the famed "intensely
    medieval" furniture for the Red Lion Square rooms, and this
    description of style and prices is unique.

30 LAGO, MARY, ed. Burne-Jones Talking: His Conversations,
    1895-1898, Preserved by His Studio Assistant Thomas Rooke.
    Columbia: University of Missouri Press; London: John Murray, pp.
    81-83, passim.
        Burne-Jones's studio assistant recorded conversations he
    overheard or participated in during this three-year period, and of
    course there are many references to WM, particularly during 1896
    when concerns about his deteriorating health combined with fears
    that the Kelmscott Chaucer would not be completed in time for him to
    see it. Since Georgie Burne-Jones used these notebooks in preparing
    the biography of her husband (1904.3), many of the anecdotes about
    WM first appeared there, and this edition allows one to appraise the
    ways Georgie Burne-Jones used Rooke's notes, what material she

omitted, etc. It is therefore unfortunate that Lago here edited
only one third of the notes, but among them are Burne-Jones's wry
comments, for instance, on WM's passions for Iceland and for
medieval manuscripts, here published for the first time. There are
also numerous references to WM in the introductory material and in
the notes.

31 LASDEN, SUSAN. Victorians at Home. New York: Viking, pp.
      119-21, passim.
        Describes the interior of the Burne-Jones home, the Grange,
as reflecting the "various phases in the development of the Firm's
taste." Morris and Co. linked to Charles Eastlake and his
medieval-style furniture.

32 LEARS, T.J. JACKSON. No Place of Grace: Antimodernism and the
      Transformation of American Culture, 1880-1920. New York:
      Pantheon Books, pp. 62-65, passim.
        Useful survey of ways that WM extended and changed Ruskin's
critique of capitalism precedes a detailed discussion of the extent
and nature of WM's influence in America, generally on Arts and
Crafts ideology, specifically on many writers and socialist
intellectuals. Mentioned briefly are O.L. Triggs who founded the
Industrial Arts League in 1899 and the Chicago WM Society in 1903,
Elbert Hubbard of Roycrofters fame, Mumford, Goodman, and Schumacer,
who are characterized as "WM's true heirs," those who have warned
against "galloping technological growth and gluttonous consumption
of resources," against "rationalizing elites who remain obsessed
with efficient productivity at the expense of satisfying labor and
humane community."

33 LEARY, EMMELINE. "The Red House Figure Embroideries." Apollo
      113, no. 230 (April):255-58.
        Uses unpublished notes Janey prepared for Mackail (1899.10)
to discuss Red House embroideries, from the Daisy pattern that both
Janey and WM worked into a piece of indigo-dyed blue serge to the
figure and tree tapestry planned for the dining room; seven of
twelve panels were completed, but only three are extant; these,
their present location, available cartoon designs, and the like, are
discussed in specific detail. Concludes that "it is a matter of
particular regret that these embroideries, which constitute a unique
facet of WM's contribution to textile design, remained unfinished."

34 LOURIE, MARGARET A., ed. <u>WM: Defence</u>. New York and London:
    Garland, 277 pp.
        Has a critical and an editorial introduction; the latter
    includes descriptions of the six significant texts of <u>Defence</u> with
    summaries of their major differences, texts which range from the few
    poems which survive in manuscript and those first printed in <u>Oxford
    and Cambridge Magazine</u> to the 1858 first edition, the 1875 reprint,
    the Kelmscott Press edition, and the edition May Morris prepared for
    the <u>Collected Works</u> in 1910, the one used for most modern
    reprintings. Lourie's text follows the first edition, incorporating
    changes WM made for the 1892 Kelmscott Press edition. The critical
    introduction (pp. 1-30) has three sections; the first, on WM and
    medievalism, includes the usual details about his medieval boyhood,
    the influences of Scott, Ruskin, Rossetti, and the Oxford ambience
    and brotherhood. The second, the nineteenth-century poetic
    heritage, comments upon the influence of Browning, and also of Keats
    and Tennyson. In the final section, on the legacy of <u>Defence</u>,
    Lourie makes strong claims about the book's importance for modern
    poetry: WM "exalted sight and unrefined emotion above rhetoric and
    refined sentiment and turned the poetic tide of the nineteenth
    century toward the twentieth." There are full and useful
    explanatory notes for each of the thirty poems, and an appendix that
    includes changes May Morris made in a few poems for the 1910
    edition; among them is what May Morris insisted was the original
    opening to the title poem, one discarded by her father. Others have
    maintained that the poem's abrupt opening was caused by the printer
    losing the first page of manuscript. Revision of 1972.14.

35 LUCIE-SMITH, EDWARD. <u>The Story of Craft: The Craftsman's Role
    in Society</u>. Ithaca: Cornell University Press; Oxford: Phaidon,
    pp. 209-16, passim.
        Discusses the influence that the Arts and Crafts ideals had
    on men like Ashbee, who helped spread WM's ideas to America, notably
    to Chicago which he visited twice; there was a Morris society in
    Chicago just after the turn of the century, and Marshall Field
    imported Morris and Co. products.

36 MAC CARTHY, FIONA. <u>The Simple Life: C.R. Ashbee in the
    Cotswalds</u>. London: Lund Humphries, pp. 90-91, passim.
        Asserts that "no one but Ashbee had attempted to develop the
    ideas of WM on so many fronts and in so ambitious a manner," and
    this history of Ashbee's plans and projects demonstrates this fact
    again and again.

37 MAC COLGAN, DENISE. "Naturalism in the Wallpaper Designs of
    WM." Arts Magazine 56, no. 1 (September):142-49.
        Argues that WM's floral designs are more progressive and
    innovative than Floud (1959.4) had suggested, pointing out that
    Ruskin's ideas about truth to nature bear fruit in WM's floral
    designs, which also in their attention to detail and their use of
    bright, unshadowed color indicate Pre-Raphaelite influence. Methods
    of production--the use of pear-wood blocks sloshed in paint and
    squeezed out on paper by hand--help create the "robust vitality"
    apparent in the patterns.

38 MENDELSON, MICHAEL TODD. "The Modernization of Prose Romance:
    The Radical Form of WM and George MacDonald." Dissertation,
    Washington State University.
        Abstracted: DAI 42:4460-A.

39 MORISON, STANLEY. "Memorandum on a Proposal to Revise the
    Typography of the Times." In Selected Essays in the History of
    Letter-Forms in manuscript and Print. Edited by D. MacKitterick.
    Cambridge: Cambridge University Press, pp. 306-8, passim.
        Comments on typefaces used at Kelmscott Press occur within an
    essay on letter-forms, typefaces, and the design and layout of the
    Times, whose text is set today in the same design as that seen in
    1880; WM's anachronistic experiments with typography had no
    influence on professional printing, and for that "we should all give
    thanks." Reprinted from privately printed circular done in 1930.

40 MORRIS, BARBARA. Introduction to Textiles by WM and Morris and
    Company, 1861-1940. Catalogue of 13 March-3 May Exhibition at
    Birmingham. London: Thames and Hudson, pp. 9-11.
        Points out that WM is "rightly regarded as one of the
    greatest textile designers of all time." His knowledge of the
    textiles of past ages and his ability to use motifs drawn from
    nature, like the acanthus, were unsurpassed. Distinguishes between
    types of designs in WM's woven fabrics as opposed to those in
    printed fabrics and wallpapers, thus undercutting some of Floud's
    points (1959.4) on WM's development. Mentions a few of the
    designers, such as Voysey and Butterfield, who were influenced by
    WM.

41 NAYLOR, GILLIAN. "'No Drawing Room Sort of Man.'" In WM and
    Kelmscott. London: Design Council, pp. 57-60.
        Uses a cynical note by Taylor regarding the social value of
    the Firm's work to discuss WM's own fears, as expressed once to
    Georgie Burne-Jones, that his work might add up finally to
    "make-believe." Comments also upon WM's growing conviction that
    attempts at social reform based on art must fail.

42 O'CONNER, DERYN. "Red and Blue." In <u>WM</u> <u>and</u> <u>Kelmscott</u>. London:
    Design Council, pp. 107-15.
        Suggests that for WM red and blue represented "richness,
generosity and honesty." Discusses the arduous processes he
mastered to utilize the "Great Dyes" (madder for red, indigo for
blue), adapting them to different fabrics and continually
experimenting, using modern methods as well as ancient ones. But he
preferred the latter, and he continued to stress the necessary--and
therefore artistic--connections between this difficult craft of
dyeing and traditional designs.

43 OLSEN, NINA DAHLMANN. "WM og den danske bogkunst."
    <u>Bogtrykkerbladet</u> 11:282-84.
        In Danish. Many modern Danish book designers were influenced
by Kelmscott Press books, and several of them are here mentioned,
from Hendriksen to Nordlunde. Includes illustrations, examples of
typefaces and page designs modeled on those of WM.

44 PAYNE, EDWARD. "Memories of Morris and Co." <u>JWMS</u> 4, no. 3
    (Spring):3-6.
        Describes the layout of buildings at Merton Abbey and their
interiors, in the 1920s, and recalls that the manager, Mr. Dearle,
was a "peppery" man. Speaks also of compromises and shoddy
workmanship on Morris and Co. stained glass in the 1920s and 1930s.

45 PEARSON, NICHOLAS. "Art, Socialism and the Division of
    Labour." <u>JWMS</u> 4, no. 3 (Spring):7-25
        Since WM's ideas about art and society are often
misinterpreted in books about art nouveau and the Bauhaus, for
example, the author proposes "to examine the intellectual coherence
of WM's analysis of art, capitalism and the division of labour as
expressed in lectures, letters, and articles from 1878 on." This
ambitious task is here fulfilled; the proper passages are set forth
and discussed with good sense and style: "Socialism was not, for
Morris, a matter of a more palatable sharing out of the national
cake; it was a matter, rather, of who controlled the making of that
cake."

46 PETERSON, WILLIAM S. "WM and the Damned Chemists: The Search
    for an Ideal Ink at Kelmscott Press." <u>Printing</u> <u>History</u> 3, no.
    2:4-11.
        Recounts various difficulties WM and his fellow workers at
Kelmscott Press had to face, partly because of WM's insistence on
quality materials. Includes diary entries by Cockerell, his account
of WM's attempts to find a good black ink, and some compromises he
had to make with technology.

47 RICHTER, DONALD C. <u>Riotous</u> <u>Victorians</u>. Athens: Ohio University
    Press, pp. 95, 144, passim.
        WM'S work for the Free Speech Movement, his difficulties at
the Dodd Street jail, and his actions at the Trafalgar Square Riot
are all discussed against a broad context of nineteenth century
political protest; new perspectives are thus gained.

48 RUDDICK, WILLIAM. "Byron and England." In <u>Byron's</u> <u>Political</u>
    <u>and</u> <u>Cultural</u> <u>Influence</u> <u>in</u> <u>Nineteenth</u> <u>Century</u> <u>Europe</u>: <u>A</u>
    <u>Symposium</u>. Edited by P.G. Trueblood. London: Macmillan, pp.
    40-41, 46.
        Compares Byron's "The Isles of Greece" to WM's <u>Nowhere</u>:
"common to both visions is the impassioned delight of foreseeing a
society in which a past ideal of beauty and liberty shall be
restored." Suggests that WM received Byronic ideals from the
writings of Ruskin and then passed them on to Shaw.

49 SHUTTLEWORTH, MARTIN. "Dear William." In <u>WM</u> <u>and</u> <u>Kelmscott</u>.
    London: Design Council, pp. 41-56.
        A rambling introductory essay, cast in the form of a personal
letter written to WM, that does manage to touch upon WM's early
life, events at Oxford, and the "tragedy of your private life."

50 SILVER, CAROLE. "Eden and Apocalypse: WM's Marxist Vision in
    the 1880s." <u>University</u> <u>of</u> <u>Hartford</u> <u>Studies</u> <u>in</u> <u>Literature</u> 13,
    no. 1 (Spring):62-77.
        Unlike Ruskin, WM welcomed the apparent apocalypse facing
England in the 1880s, and in the prose tales from this period he was
able to integrate "biblical, medieval, and Icelandic materials to
create a Marxist religion with its own individualized vision of eden
and apocalypse." States that the earthly Edens that WM created
early on showed people engaging "joyfully in labor, for work is both
prayer and pleasure," but after his conversion to socialism, the
romances demonstrate WM's "creation of a Marxist book of
revelation." <u>Pilgrims</u> becomes a paradigm for the prose romances,
<u>Wolfings</u> a tale that "brilliantly fuses the traditions of 'Ragnarok'
and Revelation." In <u>Nowhere</u>, he "turned his attention to the world
after apocalypse," creating a "document essentially medieval in its
spirit but utopian and Marxist in its doctrine."

51 SNOWDEN, HELEN. "'Good Citizens' Furniture.'" In <u>WM</u> <u>and</u>
    <u>Kelmscott</u>. London: Design Council, pp. 73-81.
        Considers the records Taylor kept, and the ways they reveal
the daily work of Morris and Co., pointing out that the Firm used
modern techniques for making and marketing furniture, utilizing
"skill specialization and the division of labor." WM was a
synthesizer rather than an innovator, one who in furniture brought
elegant and sturdy simplicity back into style.

52 SPEAR, JEFFREY L. "Political Questing: Ruskin, WM, and
    Romance." In New Approaches to Ruskin: Thirteen Essays.
    London: Routledge and Kegan Paul, pp. 175-93.
        Finds useful parallels between the experiences of Ruskin and
    WM; the "lost paradise of childhood" forced each of them to seek
    social change. Nowhere is said to have a vision that WM "shared
    with Ruskin: the extension of family into communal values." Points
    out also that in the garden England has become in Nowhere, the
    unalienated labor extends even to the building of roads.

53 STERNER, GABRIELE. "WM." In Jugendstil Art Deco: Malerei und
    Grafik. Munich: Heyne, pp. 42-52.
        Calls WM one of the most significant of Victorians; his
    "many-sidedness" here sketched in; his contributions to modern
    design and to the book arts are set forth against a discussion of
    the Pre-Raphaelite Brotherhood and the rise of Art Nouveau in
    Germany.

54 STOPPANI, LEONARD. "WM, Kelmscott and Farnham." In WM and
    Kelmscott. London: Design Council, pp. 7-8.
        Since Kelmscott Manor is too small to show properly all its
    treasures in a suitable exhibition, it was decided to hold an
    extensive 1981 exhibition at nearby West Surry College of Art and
    Design. Introduces planners and contributors to the present
    book-catalogue.

55 SYER, GEOFFREY. "WM and the Blunts." JWMS 4, no. 4
    (Winter):18-22.
        Recounts the similar backgrounds and radical beliefs of WM
    and Blunt, adding details of their friendship.

56 TILLING, P.M. "WM's Translation of Beowulf: Studies in His
    Vocabulary." In Studies in English Language and Early
    Literature in Honour of Paul Christopherson. Edited by P.M.
    Tilling. Ulster: New University, 163-75.
        Discusses the vocabulary in the WM-A.J. Wyatt translation of
    Beowulf, pointing out similarities to the diction in the Icelandic
    translations, attributing them to WM's eagerness to preserve the
    sound and shape of the original forms, even if obscurity is the
    result, and it often is: "gooms," for example, from O.E. "guma," is
    used instead of "men." The glossary, with only seventy-eight items,
    could be much longer.

57 TOLKIEN, J.R.R. The Letters of J.R.R. Tolkien. Edited by
    Humphrey Carpenter. London: George Allen and Unwin; Boston:
    Houghton Mifflin, pp. 7, 303.
        Concerning the images he used in the Dead Marshes episode in
the Ring trilogy, Tolkien admitted that they did "owe something to
Northern France after the Battle of the Marne. They owe more to WM
and his Huns and Romans, as in Wolfings and Roots."

58 WAINWRIGHT, CLIVE. "The Architect and the Decorative Arts." In
    Architect-Designers: Pugin to Mackintosh. London: The Fine Art
    Society, pp. 4-6.
        Quotes from WM's "The Lesser Arts of Life" to underline the
important links that many perceived between architecture and the
decorative arts.

*59 WANDEL, REINHOLD. Sozial Kritik und regressive Ideale in den
    politisch engagierten Schriften von WM. Frankfurt and Bonn:
    Lang, 277 pp.
        Cited in David and Sheila Latham's "WM: An Annotated
Bibliography." JWMS 5, no.3 (Summer, 1983):39.

60 WATKINSON, RAY. "Kelmscott Press: A Cornerstone of Modern
    Typography." In WM and Kelmscott. London: Design Council, pp.
    97-103.
        Despite an early and continuing love for the book arts, most
of WM's volumes of poetry and prose "were published in a dress at
best ordinairy, and sometimes downright bad." But at Kelmscott
Press he was in full control, able to combine new ideas about
typography with older ones about decoration, and thus produce books
that were indeed a "pleasure to look upon," and therefore a
significant influence upon both private presses and commercial
printing well into the twentieth century. Several illustrations
accompany a detailed exposition.

61 WEINER, MARTIN J. English Culture and the Decline of the
    Industrial Spirit, 1850-1980. Cambridge: Cambridge University
    Press, pp. 67-70, passim.
        Points out specific influences SPAB has had upon
preservationist groups from both ends of the political spectrum, and
upon legislation designed to protect not just buildings but other
artifacts which reflect uniquely British popular culture. WM
praised as a great intellectual, a prophet of "utopian realism," a
continuing influence on political thought.

62 WOOD, CHRISTOPHER. "The Palace of Art." In The
    Pre-Raphaelites. New York: Viking, pp. 109-12, passim.
        Biographical sketches of Burne-Jones and WM point out ways
    their interests in the Middle Ages flourished at Oxford and on their
    vacation tours of northern France. Suggests that WM's most
    significant contribution to Pre-Raphaelitism was that he got great
    artists involved in design and the decorative arts.

63 WYRICK, DEBORAH BAKER. "The Hieros Gamos in WM's 'Rapunzel.'"
    VP 19, no. 4 (Winter):367-80.
        Relates quest pattern in "Rapunzel" to what apparently
    transpires in alchemy, here called a "loose codification of rich
    mythical imagery originating in the collective unconscious."
    Therefore one can use such images to comment on WM's diction and
    characterization in "Rapunzel" and also in the opening poems of
    Defence, and one then perceives how "Rapunzel" allows male and
    female figures "to come to terms with their psycho-sexual
    identities," and then "to leave the incarcerating tower together and
    enact the triumpant unification of masculine and feminine" in a
    "heiros gamos," a sacred marriage.

64 "WM: 1834-1896." In Architect-Designers: Pugin to Mackintosh.
    Catalogue of an Exhibition at the Fine Art Society, 5-29 May.
    London: Fine Art Society, pp. 30-31.
        Has biographical sketch, a survey of the work of the Firm,
    and three plates demonstrating their designs in tile, glass, and
    tapestry. Further references to WM and to Morris and Co. occur
    among the other twenty-nine biographical sketches included herein.

65 WM and Kelmscott. Catalogue of an Exhibition Held at West
    Surrey College of Art, Farnham, in November, 1981. London:
    Design Council, 190 pp.
        A detailed description of each of the items exhibited--the
    paintings, prints, drawings, textiles, ceramics, furniture, books,
    and personal items--as well as a chronology and brief bibliography,
    precedes the sixteen articles on WM's various links to Kelmscott
    Manor, all of which are annotated herein: Acheson (1981.1), L.
    Baker (1981.2), P. Baker (1981.3), Bosomworth (1981.10),
    Brandon-Jones (1981.11), Briggs (1981.12), Dufty (1981.15), Durant
    (1981.16), Herald (1981.24 and 1981.25), Naylor (1981.41), O'Conner
    (1981.42), Shuttleworth (1981.49), Snowden (1981.51), Stoppani
    (1981.54), and Watkinson (1981.60).

<u>1982</u>

1   AHO, GARY L. "Following in the Footsteps of WM." <u>Iceland</u>
    <u>Review</u> 21 (Winter):93-99.
         Afoot and on horseback, the author covered several miles of
    the same track that WM and his party used in 1871 between Reykholt
    and Thingvellir. In this area of Iceland little has changed in the
    past century, so WM's entries in the <u>Icelandic Journals</u> are still
    current and when read on location offer new insights into WM's
    attitudes toward this ultimate island.

2   AHO, GARY L. "WM and Iceland." <u>Kairos</u> 1, no. 2:103-33.
         Argues that critics have overemphasized the importance of
    Iceland to WM's political development. Points out ways that WM's
    saga translations, with their fifteenth-century English forms,
    distort both the ethos and structure of the Icelandic sagas and the
    society they reflect. Suggests that <u>Icelandic Journals</u> contain
    insights into the sagas WM received from visiting saga sites and
    that they also have clues to WM's changing attitudes to Iceland, its
    people, and its literature.

3   BACON, A.K. "The History of Industrialism: WM's Debt to Marx."
    <u>JWMS</u> 5, no. 1 (Summer):2-8.
         His reading notes prove that WM read sections in <u>Das Kapital</u>
    dealing with the history of industrialism quite carefully, and
    parallel passages demonstrate their similarity of thought about the
    harmful effects of machines. But Marx remained more sanguine about
    the nineteenth-century factory ultimately freeing workers than WM
    did.

4   BAISSUS, J.M. "WM and the <u>Oxford and Cambridge Magazine</u>." <u>JWMS</u>
    5, no. 2 (Winter):2-13.
         Argues, pointing to precise points of correspondence, that
    two tales and one article in the <u>Oxford and Cambridge Magazine</u> not
    previously attributed to WM must have been written by him; the tales
    are "A Night in a Cathedral" and "The Two Partings," the article,
    "Ruskin and the Quarterly."

5   BAKER, LESLEY A. "The Earthly Paradise of WM and Burne-Jones."
    <u>JWMS</u> 5, no. 1 (Summer):25-30.
         Looks for correspondences between WM's poems and
    Burne-Jones's paintings under three headings: "Nature," "Beauty,"
    and "Transcience." A few such correspondences are found and then
    discussed.

6   BLAU, EVE. <u>Ruskinian</u> <u>Gothic:</u> <u>The</u> <u>Architecture</u> <u>of</u> <u>Deare</u> <u>and</u>
    <u>Woodward,</u> <u>1845-1861</u>. Princeton: Princeton University Press, pp.
    87-92, passim.
        Describes the Oxford Union Building, the purposes of the
    Hall, and its unusual design features before presenting a detailed
    discussion of the Arthurian murals, which "have been assigned a
    somewhat inglorious place in the history of painting, but their
    significance for the history of architecture has not been fully
    appreciated." This was one of the first times when mural paintings
    and neo-Gothic architecture were combined.

7   BOOS, FLORENCE, ed. "WM's Socialist Diary." <u>History</u> <u>Workshop</u>
    <u>Journal</u> 13, no. 1 (Spring):1-75.
        Reprinted from 1981.8, but accompanied here with a full
    introduction and with extensive annotation; there are 156 notes to
    the text, several of them amounting to short essays, and fifty-six
    capsule biographies of people referred to in the diaries, from
    luminaries like Shaw to obscure functionaries in Glasgow. An
    extremely useful and detailed exposition of not only WM's diaries
    but of British politics in the 1880s.

8   BRITAIN, IAN. "Three Fabian Essayists and WM." In <u>Fabianism</u>
    <u>and</u> <u>Culture:</u> <u>A</u> <u>Study</u> <u>in</u> <u>British</u> <u>Socialism</u> <u>and</u> <u>the</u> <u>Arts</u>.
    Cambridge: Cambridge University Press, pp. 71-95, passim.
        Traces "clear lines of sympathy" between points WM made in
    lectures and essays and the ideas of many Fabians; often WM must
    either have shaped or crystallized ideas about ecology, about the
    rebirth of art, and the like, for several Fabian essayists, who are
    also indebted to WM for the "nurturing of their youthful socialist
    instincts." This detailed study shows that WM's influence on the
    Fabians was much greater than previously recognized.

9   DANSON, LAWRENCE. "Max Beerbohm and the Mirror of the Past."
    <u>Princeton</u> <u>University</u> <u>Library</u> <u>Chronicle</u> 43, no. 2
    (Winter):77-153.
        Describes a Beerbohm manuscript of 100 unbound leaves, now in
    the Taylor Collection at Princeton, a manuscript that WM, Rossetti,
    others in on Oxford Union murals adventure all appear in, sometimes
    speaking in cleverly satiric dialogues about art and tradition.

10 DEAL, KENNETH. "Acts of Completion: The Search for Vocation in
    WM's Early Prose Romances." In <u>The</u> <u>Golden</u> <u>Chain:</u> <u>Essays</u> <u>on</u> <u>WM</u>
    <u>and</u> <u>Pre-Rapaelitism</u>. Edited by Carole Silver. New York and
    London: WM Society, pp. 53-74.
        Argues that the <u>Oxford</u> <u>and</u> <u>Cambridge</u> <u>Magazine</u> tales are
    "initiation fables," not so much for their heroes as for WM, "who
    attempts to discover himself vicariously in relation to work, women,
    his capacity for commitment, and an emerging awareness of personal

values." The tales are seen as "psychical biography," and this leads to some interesting interpretations of the clouded motives of their heroes.

11 DELLHEIM, CHARLES. The Face of the Past: The Preservation of the Medieval Inheritance in Victorian England. Cambridge: Cambridge University Press, pp. 85-87, passim.
       Discusses the significance of SPAB, its similarities to other such societies, and the number of well-known men whom WM managed to recruit to its cause, men like Leslie Stephen and Thomas Hardy. Quotes from WM's initial letter to the Athenaeum, commenting on why he thought ancient buildings to be "sacred."

12 DUBROY, MICHAEL. "Revolution and the Late Prose Romances of WM." Dissertation, University of Western Ontario.
       Abstracted: DAI 43:1539-A.

13 EVANS, TIMOTHY. "WM and the Study of Material Culture." Folk-Lore Forum 15, no. 1:69-86.
       Points out that many of WM's essays and lectures, especially those dealing with traditional crafts and the so-called lesser arts, should be better known to folklorists. To this end he includes a list of twenty-six WM titles, each with a useful and detailed annotation.

14 FITZGERALD, PENELOPE, ed. "The Novel on Blue Paper by WM." Dickens Studies Annual: Essays on Victorian Fiction 10:143-220.
       Reprint of 1982.15, with some slight changes in the introductory material, with the addition of thirty-four footnotes. Includes six facsimile pages of WM's holograph manuscript of fifty-three pages.

15 FITZGERALD, PENELOPE, ed. The Novel on Blue Paper by WM. London and West Nyack, N.J.: Journeyman Press, 94 pp.
       An unfinished and untitled novel that WM began and discarded in 1872 is here published for the first time, along with a useful introduction that recalls the personal problems WM had in the early 1870s and suggests that these problems are reflected in the plot of the novel, which was perhaps laid aside (at the urging of Georgie Burne-Jones?) because its characters and situations revealed too much about WM and Rossetti being in love with the same woman. Reprinted. 1982.14.

16 FRYE, NORTHROP. "The Meeting of Past and Future in WM."
    Studies in Romanticism 21, no. 3 (Fall):303-18.
         Asserts that "there is no one in English literature who
    raises more fascinating and complex questions connected with the
    relation of art to society than WM" and reviews the nature of these
    questions, of suggestions that a romantic socialist must be
    schizoid, etc. Concludes that WM "seems to be collecting the swords
    and spears of traditional heroism, of chivalry and romance and
    warfare and magic and mystery, so that they can be beaten into the
    plowshares and pruning hooks of a new world where man has made his
    peace with himself and with nature." Contrasts Looking Backward and
    Nowhere, pointing out that most modern socialist movements favor a
    Bellamy model, with economic centralization and mass production and
    urban centers, rather than the simple rural fraternity of Nowhere.

17 HARRISON, ANTONY H. "Cataclysm and Pre-Raphaelite Tragedy: WM's
    "Haystack in the Floods.'" South Atlantic Review 47, no. 4
    (November):43-51.
         A close reading of "Haystack in the Floods" suggests that it
    be defined as "a sibling genre of dramatic tragedy," a poem typical
    of others in the volume and of Pre-Raphaelite poetry generally.

18 HOLZMAN, MICHAEL. "Propaganda, Passion and Literary Art in WM's
    Pilgrims." Texas Studies in Literature and Language 24, no. 4
    (Winter):372-93.
         Discusses Pilgrims and its social context, pointing out the
    country-city contrasts which are crucial to the plot of the poem,
    and which are also indicative of WM's own deep feelings. Comments
    upon the features and articles that appeared in Commonweal alongside
    the serialized episodes of the poem, and upon thematic associations
    between them.

19 HORTON, MARGARET. "A Visit to May Morris." JWMS 5, no. 2
    (Winter):14-19.
         Recalls a 1925 interview she had with May Morris and the
    vicar at Kelmscott for the position of village school-mistress; the
    simple interiors at Kelmscott Manor and the kindness of May Morris
    remain strong in her memory.

20 KEANE, ROBERT. "Rossetti and WM: 'This Ever-Diverse Pair.'" In
    The Golden Chain: Essays on WM and Pre-Rapaelitism. Edited by
    Carole Silver. New York and London: WM Society, pp. 115-48.
         Discusses the fruitful reciprocal relationship early on
    between Rossetti and WM and ways that, for instance, WM got Rossetti
    interested in Malory. Demonstrates how certain Defence poems are
    linked to Rossetti watercolors on the same themes; specific
    comparisons of verbal and visual iconography are often fascinating.

21 KIRCHHOFF, FREDERICK. "Heroic Disintegration: WM's Medievalism
    and the Disappearance of Self." In The Golden Chain: Essays on
    WM and Pre-Rapaelitism. Edited by Carole Silver. New York and
    London: WM Society, pp. 75-95.
        Comments upon the striking differences between the tales WM
    wrote in the 1850s and the longer, more leisurely narratives he
    began writing ten years later, suggesting that the violence and sex
    ("favorite modes of adolescent self-expression") in the earlier
    tales are attempts by WM to overcome "inhibitions both psychosexual
    and poetic." Medieval settings allowed WM to express deep
    insecurities about his own sexual identity and the like that would
    appear as mere self-pity in contemporary settings. In this light
    discusses "Unknown Church" and "Hollow Land," mentioning the
    appearance of similar themes in others of the early romances and in
    a few of the poems from Defence. In these early works, "unrepressed
    desire" shattered both the ego and narrative control; in the later
    tales, there is control, but also a flat quality that marks a "dead
    end, both for Morris and for English poetry."

22 LATHAM, DAVID. "A Variorum Edition of the Omitted Prologue and
    Tales of WM's Paradise." Dissertation, University of York,
    Ontario.
        Abstracted: DAI 43:1554-A.

23 LOCK, TERESA. "The WM Family Remembered." JWMS 5, no. 2
    (Summer):9-15.
        There are still Oxfordshire residents alive who remember the
    Morrises: a Cotswald stonemason who was ten when WM died, a
    schoolmaster who recalls visits in 1914 from Janey, and a maid who
    began working for May Morris in 1922 and whose recollections of the
    interior of Kelmscott Manor and of May Morris's habits make up the
    bulk of this article.

24 MAC CARTHY, FIONA. British Design Since 1880: A Visual
    History. London: Lund, Humphries, pp. 55, passim.
        In this useful and lavishly illustrated survey WM and Morris
    and Co. are often mentioned, for in the design world of the 1880s WM
    was a "household word, as potent as Laura Ashley in the 1970s." He
    was, moreover, very influential in teaching others to be "true to
    the integrity of the material they work with."

25 MATHEWS, RICHARD. "WM's Roots: History into Metaphor." Cahiers
    Victoriens and Edouardiens 16:69-76.
       Suggests that a modern concern with "roots" parallels WM's
    perception a century ago of "the deadening rootlessness threatening
    the basic human dignity of the hard-pressed working class in
    England." He therefore created stories of tribal societies where
    individuals have dignity and a sense of place within their social
    group, stories whose characters and situations, as well as the
    language used to describe them, can help readers see what has been
    lost and "how things might be otherwise."

26 MYERS, RICHARD, and MYERS, HILARY. "Morris and Company Ceramic
    Tiles." Journal of the Tiles and Architectural Ceramics Society
    1:17-22.
       Tiles were among the earliest products of Morris, Marshall,
    Faulkner and Co., but they were fired at such low heat, that their
    colors have deteriorated and many have disappeared with the
    fireplaces, etc., that they graced. Discusses tile designers,
    painters, and all the most important surviving designs and patterns
    from single tiles to the "superb east wall at Findon Church in
    Sussex, the most important extant example of Morris tiling." The
    authors hope to gather still more information in order to complete a
    "fuller account of this least-published aspect of Morris's
    decorative work." This was originally a lecture presented at a "WM
    and Kelmscott" symposium on 22 November 1981.

27 NASLAS, MICHAEL. "Medievalism: A Major Part of WM's Artistic
    Theory." JWMS 5, no. 1 (Summer):16-24.
       Observes how WM's medievalism merged with ideas about
    architecture and design to become a "complex view of aesthetics
    related to social and political action." Offers paraphrases of
    pertinent sections of several lectures; stresses that WM was against
    mere revival and that he attempted to use his rich view of the past
    to plan an improved future.

28 OMAN, CHARLES C., and HAMILTON, JEAN. "WM." In Wallpaper: An
    International History and Illustrated Survey from the Victoria
    and Albert Museum. New York: Henry Abrams, 369-82, passim.
       Reprints with minor changes the introduction Oman wrote for
    the 1929 Victoria and Albert wallpaper catalogue, an historical
    survey from 1481 up to the nineteenth century; Hamilton's essay
    takes over from there, placing WM's wallpaper designs within a
    well-defined British tradition. Includes sixty-three black and
    white illustrations of the Morris and Co. papers at the Victoria and
    Albert, in two pattern books and separate portions, and also
    twenty-seven patterns being reproduced by Sandersons, ca. 1955.

29   PETERSON, WILLIAM S., ed.   Introduction to <u>The Ideal Book:</u>
     <u>Essays and Lectures on the Arts of the Book</u>, by WM.   Berkeley:
     University of California Press, pp. xi-xxxix.
        Discusses several influences on WM and his attitudes toward
the book-arts, including Ruskin's "The Nature of Gothic" and an 1877
exhibition on Caxton.   The former, with its arguments that medieval
artifacts implied a healthy social order, was a continuing
inspiration to WM, and Peterson suggests that the Kelmscott Press
can usefully be regarded as the "final phase of the Victorian Gothic
Revival."   The celebrations of Caxton led to a plethora of
experiments with old-style printing and quaint decorations, all of
which offended WM's sensibilities and provoked him to turn to
medieval models and to attempt to make his own finely decorated,
well-printed books.   Discusses his earlier ventures into the
book-arts, and then the major aspects of this last venture,
stressing Walker's importance and pointing out that it went far
beyond the famed slide-lecture of 1888: "it may never be possible to
do full justice to Walker's contribution."   An essay, "Printing"
(here anthologized), is marked by Walker's technical expertise and
WM's brilliant polemics against bad Victorian printing.   Discusses
ways that WM's theories are "rooted directly in the practice of
fifteenth-century printers," pointing to examples from accompanying
full-page illustrations.   Comments on the daily work at the Press,
on ways that WM wedded theories to practice, finally on the
influence his work had on modern private presses, and on book
publishing generally.   WM'S "search for the ideal book in the Middle
Ages helped to make possible the well-designed, machine-made book of
the twentieth century."   The edition includes "Some Thoughts on the
Ornamented Manuscripts of the Middle Ages," "Some Notes on the
Illuminated Books of the Middle Ages," "The Early Illustrations of
Gothic Books," "On the Artistic Qualities of the Woodcut Books of
Ulm and Augsburg in the Fifteenth Century," "Printing," "The Ideal
Book," and "A Note by WM on His Aims in Founding the Kelmscott
Press."   Two appendixes contain Cockerell's "Short History and
Description of the Kelmscott Press" and four interviews with WM,
originally published between 1891 and 1895.   They have fresh details
and provide a sense of the estimation his contemporaries had for WM,
the poet-printer.   Has full notes and many illustrations and
photographs.

30   ROBINSON, DUNCAN.   <u>WM, Burne-Jones and Kelmscott Chaucer</u>.
     London: Gordon Fraser, 116 pp.
        Provides biographical sketches and commentary upon the works
of WM and Burne-Jones, so as to emphasize why completion of the
Kelmscott Chaucer was the "supreme achievement of that final
partnership."   Pays particular attention to the eighty-seven
illustrations for woodcuts that Burne-Jones drew, clarifying the
roles of Catterson-Smith and Hooper in translating illustrations to
blocks, going into production problems, with the ink, for example,
which Burne-Jones for a time feared might keep WM, growing ever
weaker through 1896, from ever seeing the completed book.   But the

first two copies, leather-bound and lovely, were ready in good time, delivered into the hands of WM and Burne-Jones on 30 June 1896. Revised edition, with fuller details, of 1975.42.

31 SADOFF, DIANE. "The Poetics of Repetition and Defence." In The
     Golden Chain: Essays on WM and Pre-Rapaelitism. Edited by
     Carole Silver. New York and London: WM Society, pp. 97-113.
        Uses statements about past and present, about repeated
     "flowerings," drawn from essays by Kierkegaard and Pater, to
     elucidate the ways WM repeats medieval themes and conventions,
     especially in certain Defence poems, where we are invited to
     "recognize the pattern of eroticism and death as the outcome of
     primal, Oedipal repression." Comments also upon the "uncanny"
     repetition of the motif of triangular love, again building upon
     Freudian notions, in WM's writings.

32 SILVER, CAROLE, ed. The Golden Chain: Essays on WM and
     Pre-Rapaelitism. New York and London: WM Society, 153 pp.
        Collection of five papers on WM and Pre-Rapaelitism; the
     following four were first read at the 1977 MLA: Deal (1982.10),
     Keane (1982.20), Kirchhoff (1982.21), and Sadoff (1982.31).
     Silver's introduction (1982.34) and essay (1982.33) were added
     later.

33 SILVER, CAROLE. "Dreamers of Dreams: Toward a Definition of
     Literary Pre-Rapaelitism." In The Golden Chain: Essays on WM
     and Pre-Rapaelitism. Edited by Carole Silver. New York and
     London: WM Society, pp. 5-51
        Discusses the importance of dreams to Victorians generally
     and to specific Pre-Raphaelites, notably Rossetti, whose use of
     dreams and dream theory in paintings, tales, and poems is here set
     forth in compelling and useful detail. Discusses ways the
     "influence of Rossetti's dream vocabulary shines over the pages of
     Oxford and Cambridge Magazine," commenting upon each of WM's
     contributions and upon several of the confusing poems in Defence,
     "marked by a disjointed structure which is that of dream logic."
     Throughout this essay, specific points bolster its thesis: "Rossetti
     was the progenitor and Morris and Swinburne the shapers and
     transmitters of a literary tradition which, though never fully
     defined, has been called 'literary Pre-Raphaelitism.' It is a
     movement to which dream is central, a movement that utilizes
     accounts of actual dreams, dream language, dream symbol, and, most
     significantly, a movement with the characteristics of dream
     itself."

34 SILVER, CAROLE. Introduction to The Golden Chain: Essays on WM
    and Pre-Rapaelitism. Edited by Carole Silver. New York and
    London: WM Society, pp. 1-3.
       Approaches developed by the new critics in the 1950s began a
    "resuscitation of Morris' literary reputation," one that was
    continued into the 1960s by new interests in science fiction and
    fantasy literature and in the 1970s by the increased attention given
    to all Pre-Raphaelite painting and writing. Hence this volume, the
    first collection of critical essays on WM "to be devoted entirely to
    his works of the 1850s."

35 SILVER, CAROLE. The Romance of WM. Athens: Ohio University
    Press, 233 pp.
       Starts from the assumption that WM "perceived the self and
    the world with the eyes of a latter-day romantic. Through the genre
    of romance, he strove to create them both anew." The author is
    unrelenting in her pursuit of romance motifs and conventions that
    she imaginatively applies to WM's quest into the past, to his use of
    dreams, to the patterns that recur in narratives, designs, essays,
    and to his holistic vision of a better world, one that will cycle
    into a prelapsarian socialist future. Discussion of his literary
    works proceeds chronologically, with useful insights occurring in
    every chapter. Of the Oxford and Cambridge Magazine romances, it is
    suggested that WM was perfecting a "body of techniques" that would
    shape his later narratives; of Defence poems, the "nervousness and
    ambivalence of Morris's sexual desire is reflected in the agonized
    sensuousness of the poetry." Explications of the thematic
    structures of Paradise break new ground, as do her discussions of
    works often ignored, like Love Is Enough and the personal lyrics
    written during the early 1870s. Suggests that the 1873 entries in
    Icelandic Journals contrast strongly with those for 1871, for WM has
    forged a "new personal ethic," and he will thus now be open to
    broad, social concerns. Points out the use of saga conventions in
    Wolfings, and why Nowhere is unique: "it is probably the only
    autobiographical Marxist Utopian romance in literary history."
    Argues that in the late prose romances WM "proceeds to show the
    human race how it can make a Nowhere into Somewhere." Includes full
    notes and bibliography as well as an appendix containing the lyric,
    "Lonely Love and Loveless Death."

36 THESING, WILLIAM B. "Noel and WM: From Observation to
    Revolution." In The London Muse: Victorian Poetic Responses to
    the City. Athens: University of Georgia Press, pp. 107-34.
       Using categories and insights drawn from Lukacs, this study
    analyzes Pilgrims and contrasts it to Rodem Noel's "The Red Flag."
    The latter only describes, but in the former a participant in the
    action narrates, and we thus get a strong sense, perhaps for the
    first time, of how it felt to be down and out in London.

37 WATERS, CHRIS. "WM and the Socialism of Robert Blatchford."
    JWMS 5, no. 2 (Winter):20-31.
        Blatchford, the "most popular socialist of the 1890s" was
    converted to socialism by WM and thus embraced his brand of
    socialism (a wedding of Ruskin's romantic critiques and Marxism).
    He then, through his newspaper, the Clarion, and his book, Merrie
    England, popularized and spread WM's ideas, but he "ultimately
    sentimentalized and trivialized them."

*38 YAMAMOTO, SHOZO. WM no koto [Some thoughts on WM]. Tokyo:
    Sagami shabo, 246 pp.
        Cited in 1981 MLA bibliography.

39 Kandinsky in Munich: 1896-1914. Catalogue of a 1982 Exhibition
    at the Guggenheim. New York: Guggenheim Foundation, pp. 14-15.
        Discusses and compares the attempts both WM and Wagner made
    to find in medieval literature answers to nineteenth-century
    problems and suggests that their radiating influences merged,
    briefly, in Munich in the twentieth century.

Author Index

Abbott, Leonard, 1898.1; 1899.1
Abse, Joan, 1980.1
Acheson, Joseph, 1981.1
Ackerman, Phyllis, 1923.1; 1933.1
Adam, Stephen, 1980.2
Adams-Acton, Murray, 1949.1
Adburgham, Alison, 1975.1
Adey, Lionel, 1974.1
Agresti, Antonio, 1907.1
Aho, Gary L., 1982.1-2
Albrecht, William T., 1970.1
Alden, J.E., 1948.1
Aldred, Guy A., 1916.1; 1940.1
Alinovi, Francesca, 1978.1
Allen, Elizabeth, E., 1975.2
Allen, Lewis, 1951.1
Allingham, William, 1907.2
Altholz, Josef L., 1970.2
Altick, R., 1973.1
Altick, R., and Matthews, W.,
    1960.1
Anderson, J.R.L., 1970.3
Anderson, Karl O.E., 1940.2
Anderson, Perry, 1980.3
Angeli, Helen Rossetti, 1949.2
Anscombe, I., and Gere, C.,
    1978.2
Antippas, Andy P., 1968.1
Apgar, Genevieve, 1922.1
Arblaster, Anthony, 1973.2
Archer, Michael, 1965.1
Arinshtein, Leonid M., 1969.1
Arkell, Reginald, 1934.1
Armitage, E. Liddall, 1959.1
Armytage, W.H.G., 1961.1; 1968.2
Arnason, Magnus, 1975.3
Arnot, R. Page, 1934.2-3; 1951.2;
    1955.1-2; 1957.1; 1964.1
Aronstein, Philip, 1900.1
Arscott, Christine M., 1928.1

Ashbee, Charles, 1901.1; 1908.1;
    1909.1; 1910.1
Aslet, C., and Binney, M., 1980.4
Aslin, Elizabeth, 1962.1; 1969.2
Atkins, William, 1917.1
Auslander, J., and Hill, F.,
    1927.1
Ausubel, Herman, 1955.3
Avakumovic, I., and Woodcock, G.,
    1950.14
Avis, F.C., 1967.1

Bacon, A.K., 1977.1; 1978.3;
    1982.3
Baissus, J.M., 1977.2; 1980.5-6;
    1982.4
Baker, Larry, 1981.2
Baker, Lesley A., 1982.5
Baker, Patricia L., 1981.3
Balch, David, 1940.3
Balch, Dennis R., 1975.4; 1977.3;
    1978.4
Baldwin, A.W., 1960.2
Baldwin, Stanley, 1937.1
Ball, A.H.R., 1931.1
Balmforth, Ramsden, 1900.2
Balston, Thomas, 1951.3
Banham, Rayner, 1963.1
Barclay, Tom, 1934.4
Bargainnier, Earl F., 1978.5
Barker, Thomas T., 1981.4
Barling, Elizabeth, 1961.2-3
Barnard, Julian, 1972.1
Bart, Carol S., 1914.1
Bartels, Heinrich, 1906.1
Barton, J.E., 1911.1
Baschiere, Karl, 1923.2
Baskin, S., and Bracewell, C.,
    1975.5
Bate, Percy, 1899.2

Crane, Walter, 1897.6-7; 1899.3;
    1905.2; 1907.4; 1911.4
Crawford, John M., Jr., 1976.9
Crawford, Nelson, 1923.5
Creese, Walter L., 1966.2; 1967.3
Crichton-Brown, James, 1926.3
Cromey-Hawke, N., 1976.10
Crook, J.M., 1979.5; 1981.14
Crow, Gerald, 1934.21
Crowdy, Wallace L., 1901.8
Cruse, Amy, 1935.1
Cuffe, Lionel, 1931.5
Cuncliffe, John, 1936.2
Currie, Robert, 1979.6
Curtin, Frank Daniel, 1940.7

D'Amico, Masolino, 1967.4
Dahl, Curtis, 1954.5
Daiches, David, 1938.3; 1960.9
Danson, Lawrence, 1982.9
Davey, Peter, 1980.14
Davies, Frank J.J., 1932.4
Davies, Idris, 1937.3
Davis, Arthur Kyle, Jr., 1941.1
Davis, Frank, 1963.7
Dawley, Alan, 1978.15
Dawson, William J., 1906.8
Day, Kenneth, 1966.3
Day, Lewis Forman, 1899.4;
    1900.5; 1903.3; 1905.3
Day, M., and Garstang, K.,
    1975.13
Deal, Kenneth, 1982.10
Dearmond, Anna Janney, 1946.1
De Bom, Emmanuel, 1910.4
De Camp, L. Sprague, 1974.5;
    1976.12
De Carlo, Giancarlo, 1947.3
Delaura, David J., 1965.3
De Lisle, Fortunee, 1904.5
Dellheim, Charles, 1982.11
Demus, Margaret, 1944.2
Denington, Frances B., 1976.11
Dennison, Baird, 1934.22
Dent, Alan, 1952.1
Denton, Ramona, 1977.9
Derrick, Freda, 1947.2
De Selincourt, Ernest, 1915.4
De Vinne, Theodore Low, 1897.8;
    1899.5; 1900.6-7; 1902.5
Dewsnap, Terence, 1957.3

Dickason, David, 1953.1
Dickinson, Thomas, 1906.9
Dixon, W. Macneile, 1912.2
Dobree, B., and Batho, E., 1922.2
Dodds, T.L., 1909.5
Doorn, William Van, 1932.5
Doughty, O., 1949.3; 1951.6;
    1960.10
Doughty, O., and Wahl, J., 1965.4
Douglas, James, 1906.10
Drescher, Thomas, 1979.7
Dreyfus, John, 1974.6; 1976.13
Drinkwater, John, 1912.3; 1917.2;
    1923.6; 1934.23
Drury, E., and Bridgeman, H.,
    1975.10
Dubroy, Michael, 1982.12
Duffy, Francis, 1979.8
Dufty, A.R., 1963.8; 1968.6;
    1969.7-8; 1974.7; 1981.15
Duncan, J.; Good, W.; and Maas,
    H., 1970.26
Dunlap, Barbara, 1968.7; 1970.9
Dunlap, Benjamin, 1968.8; 1973.8
Dunlap, J.R., 1960.11; 1961.11;
    1964.8-9; 1965.5; 1971.6;
    1973.9; 1974.8; 1975.14-15;
    1976.14-16; 1977.10; 1980.15
Dunlap, J.R., and Silver, C.,
    1976.46
Dunn, Henry T., 1904.6
Dunne, John S., 1978.16
Dupont, Victor, 1941.2; 1957.4
Durant, Stuart, 1981.16
Durrant, William Scott, 1908.5
Duryea, Minga Pope, 1923.7
Duschnes, Philip C., 1960.12
Dutton, Ralph, 1948.4; 1954.6
Dyce, Alan, 1914.3

Ebbatsom, J.R., 1977.11
Eddison, E.R., 1930.3
Edgar, Madalen, 1906.11
Edmundson, J.; Ludlam, J.; and
    Sugden, A., 1925.10
Egbert, Donald D., 1970.10
Eggers, John P., 1971.7
Ehmcke, F.H., 1932.6; 1934.24
Ehrsam, Theodore G., 1936.3
Eidelberg, Martin, 1978.17
Einarsson, Stefan, 1933.6-7

Gere, C., and Skipworth, P.,
    1975.25
Gerlagh, Wim, 1981.21
Germann, Georg, 1972.6
Ghibaudi, Silvia Rota, 1976.20
Giedion, Sigfried, 1948.7
Gilder, J.L., 1899.6
Gill, Eric, 1936.5
Girouard, Mark, 1960.16; 1977.15;
    1981.22
Gittleman, David, 1936.6
Glasier, J. Bruce, 1919.4-5;
    1920.5; 1921.3
Glassie, Henry, 1972.7; 1975.26
Glenister, S.H., 1939.2
Gloag, John, 1947.5; 1961.14;
    1962.14; 1964.14; 1966.8
Glover, W.J., 1913.7
Godwin, E., and Godwin, S.,
    1947.6
Golding, Louis, 1922.6
Goldzamt, Edmund, 1967.8; 1971.9
Gooch, B., and Thatcher, D.,
    1979.13
Gooch, Velma L., 1973.15
Good, W.; Maas, H.; and Duncan,
    J., 1970.26
Goode, John, 1968.13; 1971.10
Goodwin, K.L., 1968.14; 1969.10;
    1971.11; 1975.27-28
Gordon, Jan B., 1969.11
Gordon, W.K., 1960.17; 1966.9
Gosse, Edmund, 1917.3
Goudy, Frederic, 1934.27
Gould, Frederic, 1928.4
Graham, Hugh, 1961.15
Graham, R.B. Cunningham, 1934.28
Grautoff, Otto, 1902.7
Gray, Donald J., 1961.16
Gray, Nicolete, 1941.3
Green, A. Romney, 1912.4
Green, Roger Lancelyn, 1948.8
Greenwood, George, 1934.29
Grennan, Margaret R., 1945.1
Greville, Francis Evelyn,
    Countess of Warwick, 1912.5
Grey, Lloyd Eric, 1949.4
Greysmith, Brenda, 1976.21
Gribble, Barbara, 1981.23
Gribben, Alan, 1980.20
Grierson, Herbert J.C., 1928.5

Grierson, Janet, 1962.15
Grieve, Harold W., 1963.11
Grigson, Geoffrey, 1969.12;
    1974.10
Groom, Bernhard, 1955.7
Grylls, R. Glynn (Rosalie
    Manders), 1962.16; 1963.12;
    1964.15-16
Guadalupi, G., and Manguel, A.,
    1980.31
Gutman, Robert W., 1962.17
Guyot, Edouard, 1909.6; 1913.8
Gwynne, Stephen, 1898.8; 1926.4

Haberly, Loyd, 1961.17
Haight, Gordon S., 1972.8
Hake, Thomas, 1902.8
Hallmundsson, Hallberg, 1970.17
Hamilton, J., and Oman, C.,
    1982.28
Hamilton, Mary Alice, 1921.4
Hannigan, D.F., 1897.11
Harap, Louis, 1978.22
Haraszti, Zoltan, 1934.30
Harbison, Robert, 1980.21
Hardwick, Michael, 1973.16
Harris, Frank, 1931.9
Harris, Richard L., 1975.29;
    1976.22
Harris, S. Dale, 1967.9-10
Harrison, Antony H., 1982.17
Harrison, M., 1980.22
Harrison, M., and Walters, B.,
    1973.17
Harrold, Charles F., 1940.10
Harvie, C.; Martin, G.; and
    Scharp, A., 1970.18
Hascall, Dudley L., 1968.15
Hasty, Mara, 1978.23
Haugen, Einar, 1969.13
Hawkins, Mark F., 1969.14
Hazen, James, 1977.16
Healy, Chris, 1904.7
Hearn, Lafcadio, 1916.4; 1922.7
Heath-Stubbes, John, 1950.7;
    1974.11
Helmer, John, 1979.14
Henderson, Archibald, 1911.5;
    1932.8; 1956.5
Henderson, Philip, 1950.8;
    1951.7; 1952.2; 1958.5;
    1962.18; 1967.11; 1979.15

Subject Index

Categories in this subject index reflect the ways that information within entries was entered into computer files; some repetition occurs, but the categories and subheadings suggest the broad range of WM's work and the many diverse reactions to it over the eighty-five years covered by this Reference Guide. The categories are so few that the index should pose no problems. Entries concerning WM's achievements in design and the book arts appear within ORGANIZATIONS AND MOVEMENTS under Kelmscott Press and Morris and Co. Following WRITINGS are four short sections listing books with bibliographical and biographical information, catalogues of important exhibitions, varied guides, and dissertations.

WM AND . . .

Adams, Henry, 1930.10; 1967.12
Adorno, Theodor, 1980.3
anarchism, 1908.7; 1909.11;
    1913.1; 1927.2
Ashley, Laura, 1982.24
Attlee, Clement, 1951.18; 1966.4
Auden, 1966.10; 1974.10
Baldwin, Stanley, 1937.1
British Communist Party, 1967.16
Brooke, Rupert, 1976.54
Browne, Sir Thomas, 1961.1
Darwin, 1914.3; 1924.6
Diaghilev, 1979.46
Distributists, 1934.78
Dostoievski, 1935.1; 1969.25
Dryden, 1934.41
DuBois, W.E.B., 1953.6
education, 1907.4; 1911.4;
    1957.7; 1965.20; 1970.27;
    1977.37
environment, 1973.2; 1975.50;
    1978.10
evolution, 1922.6, 12
favorite books, 1935.1; 1976.1
Flood, Peter, 1960.6; 1962.31;
    1963.1; 1974.26; 1981.37, 40
Ford, Henry, 1918.3

Franklin, Benjamin, 1954.15;
    1957.11
funeral, 1899.10; 1934.28; 1966.6
Gandhi, 1923.8
Hardy, 1976.54
Hauptman, Gerhard, 1943.1
Hopkins, 1934.80
Howells, 1947.4
industry, 1902.14; 1920.3;
    1934.56; 1936.2; 1976.8;
    1981.61
Johnson, Samuel, 1899.10, 18;
    1930.8; 1939.6
Keats, 1904.14; 1976.23
Lahor, Jean, 1935.11
the laureateship, 1899.10;
    1932.12
Lenin, 1975.36
Lukacs, 1971.10; 1973.31; 1982.36
MacDonald, Ramsey, 1935.8
machines, 1932.6; 1934.56, 68;
    1937.11; 1948.7; 1960.31
mandalic experience, 1979.33
Marcuse, 1976.20; 1980.3
Meier, Paul, 1976.5, 50; 1977.36
medievalism, 1901.2; 1902.1;
    1906.2; 1907.7; 1912.2;
    1920.6; 1924.4, 10; 1925.7;
    1928.6; 1933.12-14; 1945.1;

CONTEMPORARIES

1976.13-14, 38, 58; 1980.15;
  1982.29
-and autobiographical brief,
  1973.13
-and photographic negatives,
  1970.41
Wardle, 1899.10; 1911.10; 1927.5;
  1961.13; 1975.20
Watts, 1900.4
Watts-Dunton, 1897.32; 1902.8;
  1906.10; 1909.10; 1916.7
-and Aylwin, 1902.8
-and reviews of WM's poetry,
  1906.10
Webb, 1899.10; 1904.11; 1931.13;
  1934.7; 1935.2; 1936.9;
  1947.2; 1953.10; 1954.6;
  1956.10; 1957.2; 1960.16;
  1961.2; 1962.1, 10-11;
  1963.25; 1964.22; 1965.9;
  1966.16; 1967.29; 1972.13,
  15, 21; 1974.25; 1975.25;
  1976.10; 1977.22, 28;
  1979.12; 1980.14, 36;
  1981.11, 58; 1982.26
-and letter to WM, 1977.22
-and Ruskin, 1977.28
-and SPAB, 1981.11
-and WM's gravestone, 1963.25
Wells, 1922.9; 1968.40; 1973.46;
  1976.41
Whistler, 1908.10; 1912.10;
  1963.15
Wilberforce, Robert, 1970.7
Wilde, 1906.9; 1921.8; 1925.1;
  1931.2; 1942.3; 1950.4;
  1951.5; 1965.21; 1968.34;
  1969.28; 1972.23
-and American lectures, 1931.2
-and socialism, 1965.21
-and visits to WM, 1950.4;
  1968.34; 1969.28
Wise, Thomas, 1934.17; 1966.26;
  1972.3
Yeats, 1902.16; 1903.9; 1906.21;
  1919.8; 1921.7; 1925.11;
  1934.79; 1943.1; 1947.7;
  1948.5; 1953.2; 1954.16,
  19-20; 1962.13; 1963.9;
  1975.19, 26

-and "The Happiest of Poets,"
  1903.9
-and letters, 1953.2; 1954.16,
  19-20
-and Sigurd, 1954.20
-and Well, 1925.11
-and WM as an actor, 1953.2
York-Powell, Frederick, 1906.12
Zambaco, Maria, 1977.23

INFLUENCED BY WM

Aalto, Aino, 1934.16
Ashbee, 1901.1; 1908.1; 1909.1;
  1936.10-11; 1969.4; 1971.24;
  1976.8; 1978.2; 1981.35-36
Behrens, Peter, 1972.21
Blatchford, Robert, 1951.17;
  1955.15; 1973.40; 1979.40;
  1982.37
Cole, 1931.4; 1934.20; 1960.8;
  1971.5; 1973.5; 1979.40, 54
-and the Nonesuch edition,
  1934.20
Coomaraswamy, 1977.24
Curwen, 1976.8
Day, F. Holland, 1981.27
Eliot, T.S., 1970.16
Geddes, 1923.13
Gimson, Ernest, 1969.3; 1972.15;
  1980.13, 27
Goodman, Paul, 1981.32
Greenaway, Kate, 1923.19
Gropius, 1934.16; 1936.11;
  1967.34
Holst, H.R., 1962.34
Howells, 1930.10
Hubbard, Elbert, 1899.7; 1900.8;
  1907.5; 1926.5; 1932.10;
  1934.60; 1940.3; 1958.6;
  1968.4; 1969.9; 1977.38;
  1978.2; 1980.27; 1981.32
Koch, Rudolph, 1934.40; 1949.6;
  1955.12
Le Corbusier, 1934.16
Lethaby, 1901.12; 1969.5;
  1972.15; 1976.8
Lewis, C.S., 1939.6; 1955.9;
  1966.15; 1974.1, 18
Mackmurdo, 1968.30; 1972.15;
  1976.58

INFLUENCES ON WM

-handlist of lectures, 1961.7
-an unnoted 1884 lecture, 1978.9
Sonnets, 1914.7, 10; 1958.10
"The Story of Dorothea," 1975.27
Style, diction, prosody, 1899.10;
    1910.9-10; 1911.16; 1912.13;
    1913.12; 1917.4; 1920.12;
    1925.2; 1929.1; 1931.1;
    1937.6, 10; 1939.6; 1955.7;
    1961.22; 1970.23, 38; 1978.7,
    54; 1979.11; 1982.2
-and archaic diction, 1899.10;
    1910.9; 1937.6; 1979.11
-and ballad tone, 1911.6
-and symbolism, 1978.7
-and synasthetic metaphors,
    1937.10
-and Welsh prosody, 1929.1
The Tables Turned, or Nupkins
    Awakened, 1910.9; 1931.11;
    1934.8; 1953.2
"To the Working Men of England,"
    1950.8; 1980.33
Translations
-Aeneid, 1899.4, 10; 1937.9
-Beowulf, 1981.56
-Odyssey, 1899.10; 1910.2;
    1928.6; 1941.5; 1975.51;
    1980.17
-from the Icelandic, 1899.10;
    1901.16; 1913.12; 1918.5;
    1923.10-11; 1930.1, 3-4;
    1933.6-7, 12-14; 1937.4, 6;
    1940.2; 1947.9; 1955.11;
    1961.19, 23, 32-33; 1963.17;
    1968.21; 1969.13; 1970.5, 17;
    1972.4; 1973.14, 35; 1979.59;
    1982.1-2
--Eddic poetry, 1913.12;
    1933.12-14; 1935.3
--Family sagas, 1899.10; 1910.9;
    1914.10; 1935.4-5; 1970.5;
    1973.35
--Skaldic verse, 1970.17
Unpublished poem, by Vilhjalmr
    Vandraethaskald, 1964.10
Volsunga, 1901.6; 1913.12;
    1922.14; 1923.11; 1930.4;
    1932.5; 1960.28; 1962.17;
    1968.15; 1978.24, 59
-and ideas on staging, 1922.14

"Wake, London Lads," 1901.4;
    1941.1; 1954.11; 1956.13
Water, 1897.23, 25; 1903.9;
    1904.15; 1925.11; 1945.1;
    1966.13; 1970.37; 1971.2;
    1975.8; 1978.16, 36, 58;
    1979.26; 1980.35; 1981.6
-and allegory, 1975.8
-and the feminine psyche, 1980.35
-and Yeats, 1925.11
Well, 1914.12; 1945.1; 1969.26;
    1970.37; 1975.8, 23, 54;
    1976.26; 1978.16, 58
-and allegory, 1975.8
-and the erotic, 1976.26
-and World War One, 1975.23
"What All Men Long For, and What
    None Shall Have," 1978.20
"The Willow and the Red Cliff,"
    1948.8
Wolfings, 1939.6; 1945.1;
    1962.27; 1966.13; 1971.10;
    1975.8; 1978.4, 26, 35-36,
    55; 1979.24; 1980.6;
    1981.50; 1982.25, 35
-and "Gudrun" and Sigurd, 1978.4
-and Pilgrims, 1962.27
-and Ragnarok, 1981.50
-and socialist ideology, 1971.10
-and speech acts within, 1980.6
Wood, 1973.6; 1976.42; 1978.36;
    1979.53; 1980.42
-and ahistorical ambiguity,
    1980.42
-and mythic eternities, 1979.53

BIBLIOGRAPHIES

Altholz, 1970.2
Altick and Matthews, 1960.1
Batho and Dobree, 1922.2
Bensusan, 1981.7
Brady and Serban, 1980.8
Briggs, 1961.7
Cary, 1901.6
Ehrsam, 1936.3
Entwhistle, 1960.13
Evans, 1982.13
Flower, 1940.9
Forman, 1897.9

Subject Index

Fredeman, 1964.13; 1965.7;
    1966.7; 1968.12; 1974.9
Freeman, 1980.19
Fucilla, 1939.1
Gooch and Thatcher, 1979.13
Goodwin, 1975.28
Gribben, 1980.20
Harrold, 1940.10
Hosmon, 1969.16
Houghton, 1972.9
Jones, 1956.7
Litzenberg, 1933.14; 1947.9
MacNamee, 1968.25
Manguel and Guadalupi, 1980.31
Maurer, 1940.13
Maxwell, 1944.5
Metzdorf, 1959.5
Murphy, 1979.36
Parrot and Martin, 1955.10
Pollard, 1906.17; 1921.5
Scott, 1897.16
Slack, 1967.24
Templeman, 1945.6
Tomkinson, 1928.16
Vaughan, 1914.9
Waggoner, 1978.60
Wilson and Hoeveler, 1979.52
Wright, 1956.18

Henderson, 1952.2; 1967.11
Hubbard, 1907.5
Jackson, 1908.6; 1926.6
Kirchhoff, 1979.24
Leatham, 1900.10
Lindsay, 1975.36
Mackail, 1899.10
Manieri Elia, 1976.33
Marshall, 1979.33
Meier, 1972.19; 1978.37
Meynell, 1947.10
Nordlunde, 1944.8
Noyes, 1908.9
Ono, 1973.29
Phelan, 1927.7
Silver, 1982.33
Spargo, 1906.19
Sparling, 1924.6
Tames, 1972.24
Thompson, E.P., 1955.15; 1976.50
Thompson, Paul, 1967.29; 1977.37
Townshend, 1912.16
Triggs, 1900.16
Vallance, 1897.21-22
Watkinson, 1967.35
Weekley, 1934.75
Wiles, 1951.18
Zachrisen, 1926.16
Zapf, 1949.6

BIOGRAPHIES

Arnot, 1964.1
Birkedal, 1908.3
Bloomfield, 1934.8
Bradley, 1978.10
Bulla, 1980.11
Byron, 1912.1
Cary, 1902.2
Clutton-Brock, 1914.2
Colebrook, 1897.5
Compton-Rickett, 1913.3
Crow, 1934.21
De Carlo, 1947.3
Drinkwater, 1912.3
Eshleman, 1940.8
Faulkner, 1980.17
Glasier, 1921.3
Godwin and Godwin, 1947.6
Grennan, 1945.1
Greville, 1912.5
Grey, 1949.4

CATALOGUES AND GUIDES

Arts and Crafts Exhibition
    Society, 1899.3
Arts and Crafts Movement, 1973.19
Arts and Crafts Movement in
    America, 1972.25
Books, Manuscripts, and Artifacts
    of WM (College of William and
    Mary), 1975.56
Burne-Jones, Paintings, Graphics,
    Decorative Work, 1975.59
Companion Guide to Kelmscott
    Chaucer, 1975.42; 1982.30
Dictionary of Imaginary Places,
    1980.31
English Chintzes, 1955.16
Exhibition of Morrisiana (Tokyo),
    1934.87
From Kelmscott Press (Florida),
    1975.57

DISSERTATIONS